THE QUIET VOICES

JUDAIC STUDIES SERIES

Leon J. Weinberger

GENERAL EDITOR

The Quiet Voices

Southern Rabbis and Black Civil Rights,

1880s to 1990s

Edited by

Mark K. Bauman

and Berkley Kalin

THE UNIVERSITY OF ALABAMA PRESS
TUSCALOOSA AND LONDON

Library of Congress Cataloging-in-Publication Date

The quiet voices : southern rabbis and black civil rights, 1880s to
1990s / edited by Mark K. Bauman and Berkley Kalin.
p.   cm.   —   (Judaic studies series)
Includes bibliographical references and index.
ISBN 0-8173-0892-X (cloth : alk. paper)
1. Rabbis—Southern States—Political activity.   2. Afro-
Americans—Cvil rights—Southern States.   3. Afro-Americans—
Relations with Jews.   4. Civil rights—Religious aspects—Judaism.
5. Judaism and social problems.   6. Southern States—Race relations.
7. Civil rights workers—Southern States—Biography.   8. Southern
States—Ethnic relationt.   I. Bauman, Mark K., 1946-   .
II. Kalin, Berkley, 1936-   .   III. Series: Judaic studies series
(Unnumbered)
BM750.Q85   1998
323.1′196073′0088296—dc2   97-19187
                                                              CIP
                                                               r97

British Library Cataloguing-in-Publication Data available

To our children with love and respect—
Joel and Peter Bauman
Adam Kalin, Beth Halbach, Heidi Saharovici
and grandchildren Steven and Brooke Saharovici

Contents

Contents

Preface

In October 1992 several papers on southern rabbis and black civil rights were presented at the Southern Jewish Historical Society convention in Montgomery, Alabama. My colleague Berkley Kalin explained the Memphis experience of Rabbis Ettelson and Fineshriber, and Patricia LaPointe brought the discussion of that city into the heyday of the civil rights era with her work on James Wax. As so often happens, discussion continued in the hallways. Henry Green was researching Rabbi Leon Kronish of Miami, and Lee Shai Weissbach was knowledgeable about rabbis in the small towns of Kentucky. A UCLA graduate student, Marc Dollinger, gave a paper, based on his dissertation in progress, analyzing the experiences of Jews with the civil rights movement in the North and South. I compared my research on Atlanta's rabbis with Kalin's findings. Excitement mounted as those of us conversing realized that rabbinical participation in the civil rights movement in the South had begun earlier and had been far more widespread than the historiography indicated. Kalin and I agreed on a collaborative effort to introduce a more extensive body of research, and Malcolm MacDonald of the University of Alabama Press, who also attended the conference, encouraged the project.

One week after the Montgomery conference, I attended a session of the Southern Historical Association in Atlanta, where Raymond Mohl and Murray Friedman gave presentations on black-Jewish relations. Both speakers stressed the positive participation of Jews during the civil rights era. Pointed commentary was supplied by John Bracey, Jr., who questioned, among other things, the degree of involvement and motivation of Jews vis-à-vis the civil rights movement. The animated discussions I encountered at this session reinforced my resolve to gather under one cover as much of this important scholarship as I could.

Yet another opportunity presented itself during the weekend of 31 March 1995. I gave the keynote address at a conference that Kalin had organized at the University of Memphis, and many of the scholars whose work appears in this volume presented their findings.

Among the first detailed case studies of both well-known and hitherto little-known individuals, *The Quiet Voices* testifies to a far more widespread activism on the part of southern rabbis in the modern civil rights movement than has been acknowledged. These rabbis were motivated largely by their beliefs in prophetic Judaism, their consciousness of Jewish historical experiences with persecution, their understanding of their own rabbinic roles, and their exposure to discrimination. Most were mainstream reformers; few derived their inspiration from Marxist or other "radical" impulses. In fact many remained silent or delayed expressing their views because they believed participation jeopardized individual and group survival in the South.

The greatest contribution made by the authors in this volume may be the variety of conditions and responses that they uncover. Presenting southern rabbis as part of a much broader social and historical context underscores not only the magnitude of Jewish involvement in the civil rights movement but also the need for further research into the history of black-Jewish relations, particularly in the South.

Finally, we wish to acknowledge the assistance of the fine staff at the University of Alabama Press and the generous support given by the American Jewish Archives and the Southern Jewish Historical Society. Also, we greatly appreciate the helpful comments provided by Abraham Peck, Wayne Flynt, and Leon Weinberger, and we thank the following for allowing us to use portions of materials previously published:

The University of Alabama Press, *Rabbi Max Heller: Reformer, Zionist, Southerner, 1860–1929*, by Bobbie Malone (1997); and *Birmingham's Rabbi: Morris Newfield and Alabama, 1895–1940*, by Mark Cowett (1986);

The West Tennessee Historical Society Papers, "Rabbi William H. Fineshriber: The Memphis Years," by Berkley Kalin (1971, vol. 25);

The University of Arkansas Press, *A Corner of the Tapestry: A History of the Jewish Experience in Arkansas, 1820s–1990s*, by Carolyn Gray LeMaster (1994);

The *Fort Worth Star-Telegram*, materials on Rabbi Sidney Wolf; and

Mercer University Press, *One Voice: Rabbi Jacob M. Rothschild and the Troubled South*, by Janice Rothschild Blumberg (1985).

Mark K. Bauman

THE QUIET VOICES

Introduction

MARK K. BAUMAN

The study of black-Jewish relations has evolved into a hotbed of contro-versy among historians. Virtually every aspect of the historiography is open to revision and debate as a result of the paucity of scholarly groundwork and the implications for heated contemporary discussion.[1] As is frequently the case, the profession is far from immune to social biases and the problems of presentism because scholars' race, religion, politics, and other background elements often influence their interpre-tation.

In the broadest sense, one school of thought perceives of Jews as tending to treat African Americans more humanely than do other white groups. Likewise, African Americans are perceived as viewing Jews as a class separate from, and more moderate than, the majority of white so-ciety. The other position sees little difference between the ways Jewish and African Americans interact and the ways other ethnic groups in the United States and African Americans behave toward each other.

Actually, both camps accept the existence of gray areas and differ primarily in emphasis. For example, both recognize that some Jews took active roles in the modern civil rights movement. Disagreement revolves around whether these Jews were disproportionately represented and mo-tivated by a prophetic mission or whether they were few, secularized, and motivated by self-interest. Was there a real "coalition," or was the coalition "mythical"? Both camps also agree that Jews participated in slavery but disagree over whether the involvement was of primary or secondary importance.

Evidence is available to support the interpretations of both camps, yet when measuring the interaction between Jews and blacks relative to their relationships with other groups in society, one finds that the positive factors outweigh the negatives. Thus an analysis emphasizing the many variables and variations of this "ambiguous friendship" may come closest to any accurate summation.[2]

The subject of southern rabbis and their role in black civil rights is complex and can be examined on many levels. On the macro level the topic raises questions regarding issues as general as intergroup relations[3] and the roles of ethnic leaders.[4] The next, more specialized, level concerns African American and Jewish relations nationally throughout American history and particularly during this century. On the third level the subject is region specific, targeting black-Jewish relations in the South. This introductory chapter highlights some of the issues under discussion and presents tentative hypotheses based on the essays in the anthology.

The Catalyst?
The Lynching of Leo Frank and the Atlanta Experience

Southern Jewry and its rabbinic leaders have been criticized for succumbing to a silence wrought by fear, complying with regional mores, and placing a desire to be accepted above moral obligation. Steven Hertzberg describes what he believes to be the beginning of the fear: "The [Leo Frank] case was a watershed in the history of Jewish-black relations." When the Jewish factory manager accused of the murder of Mary Phagan was lynched in 1915 American Jews realized that they, too, could be subjected to the same persecutions as African Americans. Northern Jews responded by supporting black causes and by pointing out analogies between the conditions of African Americans in the southern United States and the conditions of Jews in Europe. The use of such analogies, Hertzberg reports, reflected what black leaders had been doing for a generation. He contends that Atlanta Jews reacted far differently. They turned to "caution, circumspection, and conformity in matters of race relations" for decades.[5]

Hertzberg's contentions concerning Atlanta Jewish reactions require some revision. Parallels were frequently drawn between Jews and blacks in Atlanta. Dr. M. Ashby Jones, a prominent Atlanta Baptist minister, addressing a rally protesting a Polish pogrom in 1919, compared the murders of the Jews to the lynching of blacks in Georgia. More comparisons were made with the rise of Adolf Hitler. The *Southern Israelite,* a regional newspaper published in Atlanta, referred to Jim Crow railways in the South in a 1936 editorial, " 'Ghetto Cars' Established for

Protection in Poland." The following January, the newspaper recounted W. E. B. Du Bois's speech before the Hollywood (California) Anti-Nazi League's Inter-Racial Commission concerning conditions in Europe. The editorial indicated, "[Du Bois's] appearance . . . is a new step in the fight against racial and religious persecution [and] points to the indisputable truth that minorities must defend each other if intolerance is to be vanquished."[6]

Coming to Atlanta in 1895 to fill the pulpit of the Hebrew Benevolent Congregation ("The Temple") after obtaining ordination from Hebrew Union College, David Marx, a New Orleans native, became the spokesperson for Atlanta Jewry. In the wake of the Atlanta race riot of 1906, Marx served on the civic league created to investigate the outrage and encourage interracial harmony. The rabbi traveled to New York to perform the burial ceremony for Leo Frank, one of his congregants. Although the Frank incident had a major impact on him, Marx continued to speak before African American churches and organizations. He worked for years as a member of the Commission on Interracial Cooperation and helped found its successor, the Southern Regional Council. The *Southern Israelite* paraphrased Marx's speech to a temple forum in 1937: "The test of any race or man is the measure of fairness with which the man or race regarded as inferior is treated. . . . The inferiority we attribute to other fellow men may only be a disguise to hide the fact of our own inferiority." Marx also expressed concern with the way the state's social service agencies responded to black needs. In this he was joined by Rhoda Kaufman, perhaps the state's foremost social worker. During the mid-1920s Kaufman worked closely with Thomas J. Woofter of the Interracial Commission and John Hope, president of Morehouse College, to obtain money from the Commonwealth and Rosenwald Funds. In 1930 Kaufman met with an employment worker of the Urban League to put her in touch with a white principal concerning the creation of an opportunity school.[7]

Kaufman was not alone. Edward Kahn, executive director of the major Jewish social service organizations of Atlanta, became a member of the Urban League within two years of his arrival in the city in 1928. In his annual reports during the mid-1940s Kahn regularly noted a "small group" of Atlanta Jews committed to "interracial work which aims at the promotion of better understanding and the development of good race relations based on principles of equity, justice and fair play." Josephine Joel Heyman, one of this group, had joined the Association of Southern Women for the Prevention of Lynching in 1930. Rebecca Mathis Gershon, Heyman's close friend and associate in these activities, served on the Atlanta Urban League Board and the Atlanta Council for a Permanent Fair Employment Practices Committee. Another, Armand May, co-chair of the council, appeared on Senator Theodore Bilbo's list of "off brand Americans."[8]

By the mid-1930s some national Jewish organizations supported antilynching laws, thereby winning the endorsement of the *Southern Israelite*. Joseph Jacobs, a labor lawyer and southern Jew, spoke before the Atlanta Jewish Education Alliance in 1940 on "Labor and Its Fight Against Racial Hatred." In 1946 the Atlanta Jewish Community Council, led by Kahn, passed a resolution praising the actions of law enforcement officials in quickly apprehending the murderers of four blacks in Monroe, Georgia. The resolution stated, "We believe the time has come for all good citizens of Georgia to recognize any violation of the sacredness of human life by mob action as a real threat and danger to rights and privileges of every citizen." A Jewish Atlantan was one of two women to initiate HOPE, Inc., a grassroots organization established in 1958 to keep the public schools open against the forces of massive resistance.[9]

Although Ed Kahn lamented the paucity of Jewish activists, some Atlanta Jews had clearly advocated black civil rights early and often. Their positions on race did not jeopardize their roles as spokespeople and core leaders of the Jewish community. No one in a similar position in the Jewish community appeared openly in support of segregation and intolerance.[10]

The Literature

The avalanche of current symposia, books, and even traveling exhibits concerned with southern Jews and the modern civil rights movement was foreshadowed during the 1960s as disagreements between the groups mounted.[11] Much of the literature discusses the role of the Reform rabbinate and their often reluctant congregants. A dissertation and article by Allen Krause provide the departure points.[12] Krause indicated that a Jewish population of two hundred thousand represented about seven-tenths of 1 percent of the total in the "many Souths." He found "vocal and active desegregationists," mostly newcomers to the region, and about an equal number of "vocal, card-carrying Jewish segregationists," mostly from old-time southern families. "The vast majority of southern Jews—some 75 percent of them—are in the middle; somewhat ambivalent about the whole issue, but tending toward thoughts sympathetic to the Negro." This major group remained silent out of fear.

Krause constructed a polarity between "Deep South 'closed communities' " and " 'less closed' societies." Congregations in most small communities knew that their rabbis stood for positive change. Such rabbis typically avoided controversy and limited their quiet activism to their areas. Their minds were willing, but they stated their social criticism with care and hesitated to act. After noting a few outspoken individuals such as Ira E. Sanders of Little Rock, Krause mentioned only one rabbi who identified openly with the segregationist camp. Nonetheless, he concluded that there was insufficient evidence to indicate "that most or even many rabbis in these very difficult communities played a significant part in abetting or hastening implementation" of the 1954 *Brown* school desegregation decision.[13]

In the more open southern communities Krause found numerous sermons in support of the *Brown* decision and of other issues concerning black civil rights. In fact, he found that a "large majority" of the rabbis had dealt with the subject, many "several times a year." Krause cited integrated services, social action committees and meetings (those by Rabbi Randall M. Falk of Nashville, in particular), and participation in ministerial associations (Rabbi Marvin M. Reznikoff of Baton Rouge was noted) as effective tools. Yet moral support was the norm provided by most rabbis.

Rabbi Krause identified the nature of the general and Jewish communities (the percentage of "new" and "old" Jews, the sources of income of the congregation members, percentage of the population) and the character of the individual rabbis. The Reform rabbinate, according to Krause, "played . . . a respectable, if not overly important role."[14]

Krause concluded with a call for greater involvement. From a moral perspective and for the reputation of the religion, one can clearly support Krause's wish. Yet an underlying question remains: Had the rabbis been more forceful and outspoken, would their efforts have contributed substantially to success? They represented a minority who worked under the threat of expulsion from the region. Whatever the degree of their individual effectiveness, the rabbis represented a positive force. If they had been joined by an equal percentage of southern mainstream religious spokespeople, the likelihood of making a major impact would have increased exponentially.[15]

Although perhaps the most comprehensive and far-reaching, Krause's studies were not alone. Many of the best articles were collected in Leonard Dinnerstein and Mary Dale Palsson's anthology, *Jews in the South*.[16] In this anthology, Leonard Reissman, positing a demarcated and unique Jewish community, found that segregationists demanded that individuals make a clear choice on the issue of desegregation in New Orleans after the *Brown* decision. Thus, because most New Orleans Jews did not join the ranks of ardent segregationists, they were viewed by the extremists as "integrationist and therefore an enemy. The Jews' sense of morality, of justice, and of equality tends to push them in the direction of integration even though this is not always their wish." The result was a dramatic rise in anti-Semitism.[17]

Joshua A. Fishman averred in his pseudonymous "Southern City" (Montgomery), Alabama, that a number of second-level, but still prominent, Jewish businessmen joined the White Citizens Council and acted defensively within the Jewish community. "A handful of women—white and Negro, Christian and Jew"—met as the Fellowship of the Concerned to help implement peaceful and gradual integration only to be hounded out of existence.

Fishman identified a variety of different perceptions in a small interview sample. Local Jews attempted to remain invisible because they believed that they would be persecuted as liberal integrationists. They still tended to hold moderate to liberal views, and "very few" were outspoken segregationists. Fearful of reaction, they did not want national Jewish organizations to advocate integration.[18] Blacks perceived the Jews as moderates who would succumb to fear and desert them in time of need. Non-Jewish whites tended to discount anti-Semitism.

During his stay in "Southern City," Fishman heard stories about two Jews, one a university professor who helped organize steel workers, the other a rabbi who gave sermons on liberal causes. The professor had been beaten into submission, the rabbi forced out of the pulpit. Fishman described the men as "symbols" of justice and of the possible consequences for those who remained.[19] It is difficult to measure influence, but Fishman's dual notion of symbolic exemplar of righteousness and suffering servant speaks to the possible role that the rabbis played where they did call for equal justice.

In the wake of a series of temple bombings in the late 1950s, Albert Vorspan attempted to describe "The Dilemma of the Southern Jew." He indicated that southern Jews were subject to multiple pressures. Depending on community goodwill and desiring to maintain "their carefully nurtured and still-fragile acceptance," they frequently also catered to a black clientele. Most supported black civil rights but feared taking a stand because they did not want to be perceived as different by other white southerners. As a result, "the Southern Jew is divided against himself, haunted by guilt." Vorspan concluded that this "inner conflict" led to these Jews "baiting their rabbis and national Jewish organizations."

Vorspan found little correlation between rabbinic support of civil rights and the bombing of synagogues. Often the temples of outspoken integrationists were not bombed, while the pulpits of silence were. Thus the bombings appeared to result more from "the climate of defiance of law" than from unpopular Jewish actions. Yet the violence had the unintended consequence of shattering "illusions" for many Jews. "One of these [illusions] was that they could find refuge in silent neutrality." Southern Jews were gradually recognizing that their fate was "linked" with that of African Americans even as African Americans were becoming disillusioned with the absence of southern Jewish assistance.[20]

Like Vorspan, Murray Friedman pointed to conflicts that resulted in a sense of guilt. Virginia Jews, he indicated, felt "caught in the middle." In an era of declining national anti-Semitism, they fervently believed that a stand in favor of black civil rights would lead to a dramatic rise in local anti-Semitism. They weighed the possible lack of significance of their potential efforts with the likely negative results and declined to act. They felt guilt for being "disloyal" to majority ideals and guilt for their resultant silence. Moreover, although many also did business with the black lower class and believed in the principle of black rights, Friedman reported, they did not want their children's schools integrated with that same population.[21]

The most recent study of a southern rabbi and civil rights, Melissa Faye Greene's *The Temple Bombing*, places greater emphasis on the prevalence of anti-Semitism than these earlier works.[22] Greene, tracing religious bigotry back to the 1930s, shows how those who bombed Atlanta's Temple in 1958 were motivated as much by anti-Semitism as by Rabbi Jacob Rothschild's outspoken stance in favor of integration and black rights. Greene's analysis may help explain Vorspan's disjunction.

A few studies undertaken in the late 1950s and early 1960s were based on surveys and polls. The following statement by Abraham D. Lavender characterizes their ambivalent findings: "The Jew in the South is a person in the middle—marginal, more liberal than the Southern Gentile but less liberal than the Northern Jew."[23] Lewis M. Killian stressed southern Jewish acceptance of community mores: "In terms of attitudes toward the black American and his problems, the Jewish or Catholic liberal has been a deviant member of his group as much as any other southern white liberal." Nonetheless, "some Jews and Catholics may find it easier to reconcile new patterns of race relations with those of other members of their religious groups and may therefore welcome the change."[24] Benjamin O. Ringer discovered that in 1959 blacks in the Deep South viewed Jews as more racist than their non-Jewish neighbors. But Ringer determined that the perception did not reflect reality. Jewish support for desegregation, he wrote, was "more widely underestimated than was the case with other groups." Still, wrote Ringer, "it is highly probable that they were much more divided and unsure than their cousins in other parts." Thus they pursued a "strategy of silence."[25]

Finding clear distinctions between people in different types of communities, Alfred O. Hero, Jr., described southern Jews as comparatively cosmopolitan and more moderate or liberal in their views than other southerners but less than northern Jews. They expressed uneasiness with integration although they thought of it as inevitable. Their "private attitudes" toward black rights were "considerably more equalitarian" then their public pronouncements. Those surveyed "were more than twice as likely as the Southern Protestant white average in surveys to feel that desegregation is both inevitable and, in general, desirable in the long run, and only about one third as inclined as the latter to believe that Negroes are constitutionally inferior." Southern Jews represented "a disproportionately large fraction of the desegregationist white-liberal minority." Hero also found that "[the] most conservative Jews were those least associated with the religion."[26]

Leonard Dinnerstein, perhaps the foremost historian writing on these issues, drew on many of the foregoing works in *Uneasy at Home*. Dinnerstein wrote, "In the South it is rare for a Jew to support publicly controversial issues. The best example of this is the position taken by most Southern Jews on civil rights and integration. While many privately believe the Negro should have equal rights, few come out and say so." He quoted one of the exceptions, Charles Mantinband, who in turn paraphrased Georgia author Lillian Smith, concerning "a conspiracy of silence."[27]

Dinnerstein found that the 1954 *Brown* decision clearly divided southern and northern Jews. Northern Jews openly espoused the cause of African Americans; their southern fellows decried the agitation and pleaded with them to stay away. Southern Jews were aware that, in times of crisis, they served as convenient scapegoats. Dinnerstein recognized variations and correlated Jewish activism with the degree of cosmopolitanism and liberalism of local communities. The rabbis, contended Dinnerstein, "[more] often than not . . . reflected the views of their congregations . . . [and] were cautious, shunned the limelight, and followed a moderate approach to desegregation. . . . Perhaps six to ten rabbis in the South worked diligently to promote the cause of civil rights. Two or three had the support of a significant number of their congregants. Others worked quietly, behind-the-scenes; and even though some Jews in their community knew of their activities their discretion allowed these individuals to continue with their work." Dinnerstein named Jacob Rothschild, Perry Nussbaum, and Charles Mantinband among the outspoken few and identified only Emmet Frank as a native southerner, albeit one from cosmopolitan New Orleans.[28]

Dinnerstein updated his arguments in *Antisemitism in America:* "Although most Jews opposed segregation, they were afraid to take a public stand that differed with the dominant regional values and sentiments of their communities. Such reluctance was based on sound fears since poll data for the 1950s and 1960s showed the South to be the most antisemitic region in the country." In a far more pragmatic assessment of the conditions than he had hitherto espoused, Dinnerstein reflected that southern Jews were viewed as aliens who recognized boundaries that had to be maintained to ward off overt discrimination.[29]

Only one study drew overwhelmingly positive conclusions. Robert St. John claimed, "Throughout the region rabbis mounted their pulpits and spoke out, fearlessly."[30] Besides those rabbis already mentioned, St. John noted the activities of Rabbi William B. Silverman of Nashville, who advocated compliance with the *Brown* decision and organized a biracial community relations council. The city's Jewish Community Center was bombed and Silverman's life was threatened. Marvin M. Reznikoff of Baton Rouge's Liberal Synagogue, another advocate of human rights, served on several local and state human relations councils. Robert I. Kahn of Houston gave numerous sermons stressing social justice. At his behest his Congregation Emanu-El adopted "a call to conscience," which described appropriate treatment of African Americans in terms of congregants' employment practices and suggested responses to businesses that discriminated. The congregation conducted open meetings on equal employment and provided space for the first Head Start project. To these rabbis St. John added Ariel Goldburg of Temple Ahabah in Richmond and Harold Hahn of Temple Beth-El in Charlotte among others from an Anti-Defamation League list of noteworthy southern rabbis who contributed to the struggle for black civil rights.[31]

In evaluating all of the arguments one must calculate the actual number of rabbis in the South, taking into consideration their relative isolation and factoring into the equation the ratio of participants to the total present. I attempted to identify the rabbis serving southern communities during 1954 or as close as possible to that year of the pivotal *Brown* decision. In 1955 the number of Reform rabbis in the twelve-state region approximated 118. Of those identified, five held emeritus status, four were unaffiliated, and ten likely served as assistant rabbis. These nineteen individuals occupied marginal leadership roles. Thus historians are actually dealing with only about one hundred Reform rabbis at a given time, many of whom held their pulpits for decades.[32]

Yet the number of Reform rabbis may have surpassed the Conservative and Orthodox total. In 1954 just forty-nine Conservative rabbis were listed in the South by the Rabbinical Assembly of America. Of these, eight were military chaplains. Two states, Kentucky and Mississippi, boasted only one Conservative rabbi each, and Arkansas had none. When chaplains are excluded, four other states—Alabama, North Carolina, South Carolina, and Tennessee—had three each.[33]

The *Rabbinic Registry* for 1954, issued by the Rabbinical Council of America, listed thirty-nine Orthodox rabbis in the South, two of whom were listed without congregational affiliation and one of whom served as a Hebrew Academy principal. According to this source, five states—Alabama, Arkansas, Kentucky, North Carolina, and Mississippi—claimed a total of three Orthodox rabbis. None are recorded in Florida outside of Miami and Miami Beach.[34] Given these statistics, one possible reason the number involved in civil rights may have been limited was that so few were actually present.

Little has been written concerning Orthodox and Conservative rabbis in the South. Only one published biography fills this void.[35] European-born, but educated in the United States, Lithuania, and Palestine, Rabbi Harry H. Epstein moved his Atlanta Congregation Ahavath Achim from modern Orthodoxy to Conservatism beginning in 1928. Epstein's primary mission during the 1920s and 1930s was to maintain a balance between tradition and change from the first to second generation. He was deeply taken with the plight of European Jewry and Zionism. These commitments were dramatically highlighted after 1933 with the rise of Hitler. His concerns were with the very survival of his group in a spiritual, ethnic, and finally the actual physical sense. For any leader of any ethnic group these would be valid priorities.

Nonetheless, Epstein did get involved with the issue of black civil rights. In 1948, under the auspices of the National Conference of Christians and Jews, Epstein spoke before separate, segregated high school student bodies concerning the need for understanding and unity to overcome prejudice. That same year he supported the stand of the Democratic party in its nominating convention and platform. Although many southerners supported Strom Thurmond and his Dixiecrats, Epstein hailed Hubert Humphrey and integration.

During the 1950s and 1960s the rabbi supported equal rights and opportunities because he believed all people deserved just treatment. After the *Brown* decision of 1954, Epstein supported integration of public schools, not only because integration had become the law but because he believed such support to be the correct ethical position as well. The rabbi also denigrated those who advocated the use of parochial schools and religious arguments in defiance of the court mandate. Linking the Jewish principle of justice with the popular desire for rights, by 1963 Epstein maintained that Israel "cannot accept apartheid" with its South African trade partner. He likened the Selma-to-Montgomery march led by Martin Luther King, Jr., to the Gemini space flights—illustrating people's failures and achievements. He believed that President Lyndon Johnson's "War on Poverty" represented Judaism's most cherished teachings.

Epstein had learned a valuable lesson from the Holocaust: to remain silent in the face of persecution constituted moral failure. Thus in 1966 when Democratic incumbent Charles Weltner chose not to run for re-election to Congress rather than support even tacitly the outspoken racism of fellow Democrat Lester Maddox, Epstein praised Weltner's stand against a "symbol of hate." When inner cities exploded with rage during the summers of the mid-1960s, Epstein stressed the complexity of the situation. Although people should not approve of destruction, they had to recognize its sources in the "struggle" for "dignity . . . opportunity . . . equality." The roots of the insurrections lay in continuing inadequacies in education, employment, and housing. Higher taxes and open housing were essential sacrifices for universal freedom. As black anti-Semitism rose in prominence, the rabbi lamented how easily Jews fit the role of scapegoat even for another oppressed minority. Yet Jews could not back down from their commitment to racial reform even when confronted with intergroup animosity. Epstein led his congregation in celebrating the annual memorial of the death of the Reverend Dr. Martin Luther King, Jr. Mayor Maynard Jackson appointed Rabbi Epstein to fill the seat of Rabbi Jacob Rothschild on Atlanta's Community Relations Committee following the latter's death. Epstein did not march and was clearly a peripheral figure. Nonetheless, he had not remained silent.

Nor was he alone. In May 1963, Conservative Judaism's Rabbinical Assembly met in New York. After a discussion of responsibility with reference to the Holocaust and a subsequent call to A. D. King, nineteen rabbis left the convention to demonstrate their support for black rights in Birmingham, Alabama, as representatives of the entire body. They were not welcomed by the local Jewish community, and the incident has been cited repeatedly to demonstrate the negative attitude of southern Jewry toward civil rights and toward northern Jewish liberals active in the South.

Two of those who flew from New York, Arie Becker and Moshe Cahana, held southern pulpits. Much of Becker's immediate family had perished in the Holocaust. Ordained in Poland, the young rabbi had fought with the Free Polish forces and in Israel's war for independence. Arriving in America in 1952 he served a Miami congregation before his election as spiritual leader of Memphis's Beth Sholom in 1959. Becker and his colleagues stayed at the Gaston Motel and spoke before various groups in area churches. On his return to Memphis many members of his congregation protested his actions although others came to his defense. He received threats and his home was stoned. Yet many Christian clergy praised his efforts and thus assuaged the fears and protests of his congregants. Becker was a member of the ministerial association. He joined with Rabbi James Wax, meeting with the mayor of Memphis in an attempt to settle the sanitation workers' strike that preceded the assassination of Martin Luther King, Jr. Becker occupied his pulpit until his death two decades hence. Rabbi Cahana, too, was subjected to bomb threats and Klan intimidation, but Cahana was more outspoken than Becker. Serving Congregation Brith Sholom in Bellaire, Texas, he advocated equal rights and justice at his own congregation and at local churches and political gatherings.[36]

Some tentative hypotheses can be drawn from this small sampling and from examples included in this anthology. Although usually removed from the centers of activism, some Conservative and Orthodox rabbis can be counted among those who took principled stands and bore the brunt of criticism. Representing a far more immediate immigrant/ ethnic experience, their point of departure was the European (particularly the Holocaust) perspective rather than the more Americanized Social Gospel of Reform's Pittsburgh Platform of 1885. Still the prophetic message served as a common denominator for all.

This Anthology[37]

Few book-length works have been published studying the roles of rabbis in the South.[38] Books and articles typically describe the activities of Charles Mantinband, Perry Nussbaum, and Jacob Rothschild in a few pages or paragraphs and then recognize others such as Emmet Frank with one or two sentences. Although several authors point out substantial differences characterizing local communities and the backgrounds of their Jewish populations, few either analyze the civil rights activities of rabbis over time or place these activities in the context of the rabbis' positions on other issues. The essays in this volume begin to address some of these shortcomings.

The first part of the book traces southern rabbinical involvement in black civil rights back to the late nineteenth century. The essays in this section show that Jews in the South advocated rights for African Americans long before the 1940s. Rabbis Max Heller, Morris Newfield, and William Fineshriber were influenced by their educations at Hebrew Union College under the inspiration of Isaac Mayer Wise, the institution builder of Reform Judaism in America.[39] Imbibing the strong sentiments of the Pittsburgh Platform, their empathy for justice for African Americans reflected in part their involvement with issues such as social work and prison reform.

Bobbie S. Malone relates Heller's changing awareness and support for African American rights to his unusual position as a Reform rabbi favoring Zionism and the East European Jewish immigrants. A heightened sense of ethnicity led him to a position Horace Kallen later defined as cultural pluralism. Ironically, Heller, whose mentor was abolitionist Bernhard Felsenthal, succeeded Rabbi James K. Gutheim, a champion of the Confederate cause.

With Mark Cowett's revisit to Morris Newfield, a range of views and actions begins to emerge. Newfield's personality was far less dynamic and his actions more circumspect than Heller's. He picked and chose his causes with extreme caution. Newfield's father-in-law, according to Cowett, was more outspoken in his advocacy of black rights than the rabbi. Perhaps this prominent individual could assume that role more openly because he did not represent the Jewish community in the same capacity.

Berkley Kalin's article on William H. Fineshriber of Memphis describes an early example of rabbinic leadership in the issuance of a ministerial association statement denouncing lynching and an environment in which the local political machine and power structure, acting partly at the instigation of a rabbi, effectively opposed the Ku Klux Klan.

The second part of the book, which focuses on the height of the civil rights period, opens with Marc Dollinger's comparative analysis of northern and southern Jews.[40] Dollinger argues that southern Jews were highly acculturated to regional racial mores and that their northern counterparts, largely self-interested, were not much more forthcoming with assistance in the black struggle for equal rights, especially when integration influenced them directly. Dollinger was granted access to the primary materials gathered by Allen Krause but, writing a generation later, draws different conclusions.

Following Dollinger's analysis, this section introduces a series of case studies, a number of which are the first detailed histories of lesser-known rabbis in small southern communities. Carolyn Gray LeMaster examines Arkansas Jewry to illustrate continuity from Rabbis Frisch and Teitelbaum during the early twentieth century through the 1930s to Sanders and then Palnick into the civil rights heyday and beyond.

Hollace Ava Weiner investigates the Jewish community of Corpus Christi, Texas, where the presence of a Latino population complicated race relations. Rabbi Sidney Wolf worked quietly and gradually to educate his congregants and the community, using his love for music to break down barriers and relieve tensions. Karl Preuss treats a second Texas rabbi, David Jacobson, in the triracial city of San Antonio. In this peripheral community spiritual leaders worked together, usually quietly, to foster integration. Lacking drama, Jacobson's and Wolf's participation and stories may seem insignificant, yet they illustrate the possibilities not realized in the more famous locations where confrontation reigned. One wonders how many communities shared similar experiences.

Patricia LaPointe illustrates the transition in Memphis from Rabbis Fineshriber and Ettelson to James Wax. In Wax's case a strike, King's assassination, and leadership of key committees brought him to the fore. LaPointe notes the irony of a rabbi sharing center stage with a Jewish-born mayor (in opposition) and a Jewish attorney in a battle over the rights of black sanitation workers.

Terry Barr's study of Milton Grafman of Birmingham parallels the story of Wax. Birmingham, like Memphis, attempted to overcome political difficulties through municipal reform. The reformers in both cities hoped this strategy would facilitate positive changes in race relations. Yet the political transformation took place too close to the unfolding drama of the civil rights movement. Both Grafman and Wax drew on examples of gradual, quiet, local, and peaceful change for the better in terms of black rights. Yet they also witnessed prominent Jews on the other side of the issue. Both used symbolic acts, such as rejecting speaking opportunities at Mississippi universities, to emphasize their views. Nonetheless, whereas Wax assumed a position of leadership that intensified under pressure, Grafman's role was far more equivocal. Joining with the ministerial association, he counseled obedience to Supreme Court dictates in opposition to Governor George Wallace. Grafman walked a very thin legalistic line when demonstrators led by King escalated confrontation. Grafman, like his predecessor, Morris Newfield, chose to be highly selective in his activism. Perhaps the power of the Klan and the violence in the Birmingham environment (in contrast to the early and relatively easy destruction of the Klan in Memphis) coupled with differences in the personalities of the individuals begins to explain the divergent stands taken by the two men and, by extension, others.

Leonard Rogoff describes the Durham Jewish community as relatively new, small, overwhelmingly East European in origin, and, after

1958, interactive with the Jewish intelligentsia of the local universities. He discovers the virtually unique leadership role of Hillel rabbis and a broad spectrum of reactions within a small college town. The "modern Orthodox" Israel Mowshowitz's role is reminiscent of Harry Epstein in Atlanta. Furthermore, the black community was highly organized and included a substantial middle class. Durham is the only location studied thus far where a coalition can be traced in which African Americans were at times in a better financial position than their Jewish neighbors and assisted local Jews in need. Thus the picture Rogoff draws, even with its blemishes, comes closest to a real coalition of relatively equal partners. The community itself was also more moderate, almost a miniature Atlanta. These factors account in part for the dramatic contrast between the actions of Mayors "Mutt" Evans of Durham and Henry Loeb of Memphis. On the other hand, even in a relatively benign environment congregational leaders often remained silent. Finally, Rogoff continues his study into the decades after the 1960s to illustrate a strengthened, more mature, yet still limited alliance.

Clive Webb details Rabbi Charles Mantinband's experiences. A native southerner, Mantinband led efforts in the small town of Hattiesburg, Mississippi. Webb criticizes Mantinband's rabbinic colleagues and congregants for rejecting the rabbi's activism but also documents their general support for black rights. In Hattiesburg, too, however, that support was often dramatically silenced by fear.

Concluding this section, Gary Phillip Zola chronicles the tribulations of Mantinband's Jackson, Mississippi, colleague, Perry Nussbaum. He, like James Wax, had Rabbi Isserman as a role model. Yet Nussbaum's journey into the thicket of civil rights agitation was plodding. The bombing of Atlanta's Hebrew Benevolent Congregation served as a pivotal event for Nussbaum as it did for others.

The three memoirs in the concluding part of the book reinforce conclusions drawn in earlier chapters by documenting the emotional extremes experienced by the participants. Janice Rothschild Blumberg has edited selections from, and supplemented, her biography of her late husband, Jacob Rothschild of Atlanta. Rothschild benefitted from relatively moderate Jewish and general communities but still felt the direct and violent effects of the hysteria. Especially poignant are his frustration and disillusionment with rabbinic colleagues, the general community, and the militant black expressions of continued frustration in the late 1960s.[41] Rabbis such as Rothschild, Nussbaum, and Mantinband were clearly torn between competing constituencies, each demanding allegiance to its own agenda.

In their ways, all of the rabbis in this section, with their accolades and reticence, held marginal status. Malcolm Stern forwarded the final revision of his memoir on 4 January 1994, the day before his untimely death. In describing his experiences in Norfolk, Virginia, he presents a picture of a rabbi who strove pragmatically for integration and civil rights. His activities illustrated the failure of communication between the national Jewish organizations and local community leaders even when the latter were working effectively and earnestly. Rabbi and historian Myron Berman's autobiographical essay of his years in Richmond, Virginia, beginning in 1965 offers an example of a Conservative rabbi coming late to the southern arena. His candid comments show a man drawn into a mediating position. Like Stern, he was pulled in different directions and had to balance justice, tactics, and emotions. The well-meaning community's actions were hopelessly inadequate and out of touch with the frustrations they were intended to assuage.

The final article, by father and son Howard and Micah Greenstein, serves as an afterword. Drawing on over fifty responses to a three-question survey sent to Reform rabbis throughout the South, the Greensteins shed light on the very different conditions that exist in southern Jewish communities today. The picture they limn is of ethnic groups with independent priorities only occasionally meeting on common ground.

Several themes emerging from this volume beg for further investigation. Although the authors concur with the historiography that most southern Jews remained silent as a result of fear and insecurity, they have also identified many rabbinic and lay activists. These individuals—few in most locations and often women involved in providing Jewish social services—nurtured a counteracting climate of conscience in their communities.

In the early phase a number of the rabbis were born in Europe but trained in American seminaries. Coming to America for freedom and opportunity, they brought a cosmopolitan perspective. A number of these, as well as the American-born rabbis, either remained in one southern congregation for decades or served several southern pulpits. Many involved in civil rights struggles during the 1950s arrived during the 1920s and 1930s. Few were forced out or left the area. Although pressure was applied, most congregations did not act on threats of firing. Moreover, it was not unusual for one activist to succeed another, thereby creating a pattern of reform and a base of action.

The struggle for racial justice was frequently enmeshed with labor union activity and municipal reform. This connection reinforces the point that the fight for black rights belongs in the broader context of social reform and that rabbinic participation flowed naturally out of deep-rooted concerns for social justice. Furthermore, several articles and some of the rabbis themselves point to long-term participation in community affairs as providing entrée into what were perceived as the more radical civil rights efforts. Even if from outside the South, they "paid their dues" as local leaders, thereby gaining legitimacy in the estimation of their communities.

To stand up, the rabbis required self-confidence, moral fervor, and determination. The activists often had role models such as Isaac M. Wise and Stephen S. Wise or rabbis from their youth who supported the independence of the clergy and a free pulpit. Possibly Abraham Joshua Heschel, a nationally recognized figure who marched with Martin Luther King, Jr., provided such a model for Conservative rabbis.[42]

The rabbis frequently participated in local ministerial associations that were drawn into the civil rights fray. Representatives of a tiny minority, the rabbis were often thrust into leadership positions in these groups. Their acceptance reflected not only southern respect for religion generally but also the leadership qualities of the individual rabbis themselves. From another perspective, there were usually only one or two rabbis in these associations. They may have gained prominence in that they were viewed as representing their entire denomination.

Behind the scenes, efforts were gradually being made on the local level to support opportunities and rights for African Americans. Coupled with continued national pressure, numerous efforts to open the schools and offer alternatives while schools were closed achieved positive results. It is impossible to gauge if, or how quickly, substantial progress would have occurred as a result of the gradualist approach, but rabbis in the South who recommended this method did have examples of at least limited success. It is instructive that even as courageous an individual as Charles Mantinband contended that the most effective tool would be gradual education and that Jacob Rothschild also worked behind the scenes particularly through the Christian clergy. The successes of King's civil rights efforts are evident in hindsight, however, and it is unlikely that the movement would have achieved nearly as much had the course of gradualism been followed. Yet this was not nearly as clear to those struggling with tactical issues in 1954 or 1956.

In almost all cases, the rabbis participated in civil rights activities over many years. They lived by what they preached and fought for publicly, befriending and working closely with particular African American individuals and treating all with respect. As they broke with southern mores, their commitment was more than abstract. All drew from a sense of social justice embedded in their interpretation of basic Judaism, although many times pivotal events brought the rabbis forward. The historical background—the Jewish immigrant experience, earlier instances of persecution of European Jewry, World War II (some had been chaplains), and the Holocaust—offered major points of reference.

When reading these essays, one is struck both by their variety and the complexity of the experiences and communities these rabbis encountered. The roles of southern rabbis in the struggle for equal rights are clearly far more subtle than has been previously recognized. Many "quiet voices" spoke, more of whom deserve to be heard through future research.

I

GENESIS

Genesis traces southern rabbinic involvement with black civil rights backward. By doing so it implicitly asks questions concerning the similarities and differences of two communities. The three rabbis represented in these pages acted during a period of heightened racism when civil rights were clearly in retreat. Nevertheless, their varied actions in some ways paralleled those of the rabbis who served during the contrasting heyday of the civil rights movement.

Max Heller, Morris Newfield, and William Fineshriber received educations at Hebrew Union College, an institution that promoted a strong social justice message. The backgrounds of the three rabbis, the influences of role models, direct association with racism in America, consciousness of European events, prior extended participation in other reform activities, and the position of the clergy in the South coupled with factors in the local environment contributed to the decisions the rabbis made. Politics, relations with clergymen of other religions, and organizational structures also played significant parts in the unfolding dramas.

Rabbi Max Heller, Zionism, and the "Negro Question": New Orleans, 1891–1911

BOBBIE S. MALONE

Born in Europe and educated in Cincinnati, Max Heller served in a pulpit previously held by a rabbi who epitomized loyalty to the Confederacy. Bobbie Malone's carefully nuanced study shows how and why Heller's ideas gradually diverged from those of his predecessor. Heller epitomized in many ways the marginal man: a Classical Reform Jew and a Zionist; rabbi of an assimilationist congregation and an advocate of cultural pluralism; an outsider and a member of the upper strata; a proponent of the ideas of W. E. B. Du Bois and Booker T. Washington; a man of thought and of action. His various identities as a Jew influenced his attitude toward African Americans and, conversely, were influenced by them to the extent that it is almost impossible to separate the evolution of the two. Heller's is the story of a man struggling with definitions of race and their impact on people's lives.

New Orleanian George Washington Cable was by far the most outspoken and best known of the small band of white southerners who dissented from the increasingly hostile racial climate of the late-nineteenth-century South. Like his other racial nonconformist contemporaries in the region, Cable was a well-established, Protestant native son. Although his outstanding reputation as a writer and his status as a former Confederate soldier guaranteed him some social security, these qualities did not afford him total protection. In 1885, after the hostile reaction to *The Freedman's Case in Equity* and *The Silent South*, Cable abandoned both his home and the lonely fight for racial equality.[1]

No one who remained in New Orleans picked up that fallen banner. But one New Orleanian who was neither Protestant nor a native son did attempt to stem the tide of racial extremism. Rabbi Max Heller, however, did not even arrive in the city until two years after Cable's departure. Cautiously speaking out over a decade later, Heller did not challenge directly the southern solution to race relations, but he did question the wisdom of the white supremacist oppression that had imposed a deafening silence on the region. Analyzing critical aspects of Heller's career at this crucial juncture tells as much about his ability to negotiate and survive as a well-respected local leader as it reveals the distinct limits of racial dissent in the South. Heller's circumspect and carefully articulated divergent views glow like embers in the ashes of racial liberalism, sparks waiting to be rekindled half a century later.[2]

In the spring of 1887 Heller, a young American-educated rabbi from Prague, accepted the position as spiritual leader of Temple Sinai, New Orleans's only Reform Jewish congregation. The largest and most prominent synagogue in what was then the South's largest city, Temple Sinai counted among its members many of the city's wealthiest and most prominent Jewish citizens. These citizens included several leading silk-stocking reformers and philanthropists, the Jewish "best men"[3] of New Orleans who easily accommodated to the mores of their Gentile peers. Although Heller was only twenty-seven years old when he arrived in the city, his social intelligence was keen, and he readily understood the pervasive effects of that assimilation on the congregants he served.

New Orleans was not that different in temperament from the Prague of his youth. Both cities were mercantile centers where Jewish citizens experienced a high degree of acculturation and often gained social prominence. The majority of Temple Sinai's members were at the upper end of the scale, socially and economically similar to the German-speaking Jews of Prague. Even their mercantile proclivities were similar, in that both cities' Jewish populations concentrated in some form of agriculturally related industry or manufacturing or sales. Because the business-oriented Jews of Prague and New Orleans sought an inconspicuous form of Judaism that would not impair their potential for upward mobility, progressive or Reform Judaism rooted successfully in each place.[4]

With his alluring synthesis of European charm and American training, Heller, handsomely erect in bearing and fastidious in dress, held sway in Temple Sinai's "richly carpeted" Moresque interior, one deemed to be "as fine as that of any church . . . in the South." Moreover, his eloquent English and obvious intellectual prowess contributed to an altogether urbane image, just the kind of religious leader the circumstances demanded. Later, he ironically noted that "whether the fashionable Jew likes it or not, his intelligence, his social standing, is measured among gentiles largely by the rabbi's scholarship and refinement."[5]

Early on Heller proved to be an outspoken and capable reformer, taking a prominent role in acceptable causes for civic betterment such as the fight against the notorious Louisiana lottery. Toward the end of the 1890s, however, as the state moved to disfranchise its African American voters and to segregate legally all public facilities, Heller carefully and gradually began publicly to champion the rights of African Americans. Unlike most southern liberals, Heller viewed the "Negro Question" as one aspect of an emerging global problem that turned on the issue of "how the widely divergent races of the world are to cooperate peacefully in mutual and united unfolding."[6]

Like his simultaneous evolution as a Zionist, his growth as a southern racial liberal was slow and measured, conversely gaining momentum as popular racial tolerance diminished between 1889 and 1915 and reached an ebb by the eve of America's entrance into World War I, a slough that continued through the following decade.[7] As Heller's racial liberalism gradually came to the fore, so too did his Zionist sympathies. These mutually reinforcing positions functioned as a release or outer manifestation of an inner passion for social justice for beleaguered populations—East European Jews and American blacks. They also, however, kept him at odds with the dominant cultures—southern and Reform Jewish—in which he lived. America's Reform Jewish population, mostly German in background, believed that the ideal of achieving a return to Zion and the ultimate reestablishment of a Jewish homeland in Palestine was antithetical to their cherished identity as Americans. The epidemic of southern racial extremism, on the other hand, with its insistence that the place of the Negro be at the bottom of American society, made white supremacy the litmus test of regional loyalty and extinguished nearly all discussion of liberal or moderate alternatives to militant racialism.[8] Heller's breach of southern silence was virtually unique in linking the Negrophobia of the South with the anti-Semitism of western Europe. The solutions he proposed—for his European brethren seeking a haven elsewhere and for African Americans seeking justice in Heller's adopted home—help illuminate the dimensions of a problem that still confronts and baffles the modern world.

Haltingly, as Heller surveyed the rising tide of racism here and abroad, he moved away from the optimistically assimilationist outlook of conventional or "Classical" Reform Judaism. In its place he substituted the concept of race as a major dynamic in human and, therefore, in regional and national relationships. Like Theodor Herzl, founder of modern political Zionism, on the one hand, and W. E. B. Du Bois, African

American intellectual leader, on the other, Heller attempted to invert the negative imperatives of racial thinking to arrive at a concept of political and cultural peoplehood that had the potential to reinvigorate both Jews and blacks.

As a German-speaking immigrant from Prague, Heller had experienced firsthand the conflicts of cultural reorientation during his education at Hebrew Union College in Cincinnati, where he concurrently mastered English and acquired bachelor and master's degrees of letters at the University of Cincinnati. Following his ordination in 1884, he served for two years as assistant rabbi to Bernhard Felsenthal in Chicago. German-born Felsenthal had become one of the dominant leaders of American Reform Judaism and an early advocate of social justice. When seeking a pulpit in the years before the Civil War, Felsenthal had turned down a position in Mobile because of his strong antislavery stand. He founded the first Reform congregation in Chicago and later played a primary role in shaping his assistant's conception of an activist and independent pulpit rabbi.[9]

Heller's first pulpit of his own was in Houston, but he was there only a few months before he received a call from New Orleans. Temple Sinai, then seventeen years old, was one of the South's leading Reform Jewish congregations. In late 1886 its beloved founding rabbi, James K. Gutheim, died, leaving the vacancy Heller was elected to fill. Also German-born, Gutheim had served as the acknowledged head of the entire New Orleans Jewish community and as an outstanding civic leader. Like Felsenthal, he was a man of principle, although on the issue of slavery, the two had been at opposite extremes. When Union troops occupied the city during the Civil War, Gutheim, Heller later wrote, "expatriated himself from home and friends rather than to soil his lips with an oath [loyalty to the Union] which his heart could not endorse." Gutheim, in ostentatiously demonstrating his southernness, earned the praise of his city and established a model that his well-assimilated congregation sought in his follower.[10]

In espousing a universalism that posited social justice and cultural assimilation as mutually reinforcing elements, Heller, at this point in his career, reflected the proclivities of late-nineteenth-century Reform Judaism. He acted on those inclinations during his early years in New Orleans by marrying into an elite southern Jewish family in 1889 and working closely the next year with upper-class Protestant clergy who opposed the Louisiana lottery.[11]

While fighting the lottery, Heller had his confidence in the outcome of Jewish assimilation shaken by several incidents of vigilante action, or "whitecapping," against north Louisiana Jewish merchants for not employing Gentiles. Responding to the wave of disorder, Heller had struck a moderate pose and argued that "antisemite" had been used by the daily papers "with . . . utter misunderstanding" of the significance of the name. He differentiated between the "Jew-hatred" of Germany based on "racial theories" and the "lawless rowdyism" in north Louisiana, and his optimism about the Jews' place in Louisiana remained strong in spite of the incidents. The virulent anti-Semitism in Russia and in eastern Europe, which since the 1880s had been driving Jews to immigrate to America, bore little in common with the isolated outbreaks of vigilante violence in his home state. In the columns of the *Jewish Chronicle*, a southern Jewish newspaper for which Heller sometimes wrote, he argued that those in "Northern Jewish circles" exaggerated the anti-Semitic content of the Delhi and Lake Providence, Louisiana, disturbances. "How little these troubles mean as regards the general feeling in Louisiana towards the Jews ought to be patent even to outsiders." Heller carefully clipped and pasted in his scrapbook articles from various newspapers documenting anti-Semitic atrocities in Russia that were going on at the same time that the whitecapping took place in northern Louisiana. The contrast undoubtedly contributed to Heller's perspective on the events. He emphasized the distinction between events in Louisiana and in eastern Europe when he cited the leadership positions that Jewish men had filled in the public life of the state. He praised the "perfect harmony prevailing between Jew and Gentile" evident in the forcefulness of the "unanimous, unreserved and repeated" condemnations of the outbreaks by the press, including even the *Morning Star* and *Catholic Messenger,* which spoke "in no uncertain voice of the 'Unchristian Spirit' manifested."[12]

Nevertheless, Heller also realized that America's golden door might not remain perpetually open. Refugees from European anti-Semitism were fueling American nativism, which had been steadily climbing during the past two decades as southern and eastern Europeans poured into the country. Earlier arriving German Jews, who had already successfully assimilated, did not want hordes of their more traditional coreligionists to jeopardize the gains the older group had achieved. These German Jews therefore hastily organized agencies to encourage the new arrivals to seek opportunities outside of northeastern port cities where they arrived and remained in tight and easily identifiable neighborhoods. Heller himself played an active role in the effort in New Orleans.[13] The fear was not irrational. By 1891 Congress had considered anti-immigration legislation, and Heller published numerous articles condemning attempts to bar entry to those fleeing persecution. The memories of his own immigrant experience and family hardships remained fresh, fueling his empathy with, and advocacy on behalf of, the new arrivals.

In the mid-1890s, Heller, still ambivalent on issues of cultural assertion or assimilation, vacillated on positions involving both blacks and Jews. In an editorial in the New Orleans *Jewish Ledger,* for example, he "slipped" by writing that he thought it desirable that "all children without distinction of creed, rank or color might mingle and associate in public schools." Two weeks later, he backed away from the "mischievous implications of our statement, as far as the qualification 'color' is concerned."[14] When Captain Alfred Dreyfus, an officer in the French army, was accused of espionage, anti-Semitism raged, and the case exploded into a cause célèbre. Heller was certain that Dreyfus's innocence would be recognized, but he was beginning to believe that the experience of the nineteenth century had taught a lesson that "national and racial prejudice undermines not only a nation's moral health, but endangers its very political existence."[15]

The Dreyfus affair had triggered Theodor Herzl's espousal of Jewish nationalism. The intense anti-Semitism of the French had shocked Herzl, at the time a sophisticated Viennese journalist in Paris. He had been a thoroughly assimilated Jew, but the Dreyfus affair, coupled with rising anti-Semitism in Vienna, forced him to question the cultural and political foundations of European liberalism. As he confronted his own assimilationist aspirations, he decided that the "Jewish Question" no longer represented merely a "symptom of European social malaise" but could be transformed into the raison d'être behind the creation of a Jewish state.[16]

Although Heller expressed sympathy for Herzl's cause, he felt that the scheme was inherently impractical and incompatible with the universalism espoused by the American Reform movement. He also remained reluctant to dissent immediately from the predominant anti-Zionist position of American Reform Jews, who feared the quest for a Jewish homeland might open them to the same charges of dual loyalties that had been leveled at American Catholics. By the end of the decade, however, he was prepared to take more controversial stands. For one, he had become disenchanted with the crass materialism and fawning assimilationism of his upwardly mobile, status-seeking congregants whom he often castigated in his sermons.[17]

Paradoxically, disenchantment with his congregants' attitudes and with the repressive atmosphere in post-Populist Louisiana was as instrumental as his identification with the suffering of European Jews in pushing Heller toward Zionism. After defrauding Louisiana Populists in the elections of 1892 and 1896, the state's dominant Bourbon faction set about to change the voting rules to forestall future challenges to the Democratic establishment by any possible class-based coalition of voters who might overcome racial antipathies to gain political power.[18] Cruel irony cast its mark over different aspects of the 1898 Disfranchisement Convention. In the first place, the delegates chose the nephew of Louisiana's most illustrious Jewish politician, the former U.S. senator and Confederate cabinet official, Judah P. Benjamin, to preside over the proceedings. In his acceptance speech, Ernest B. Kruttschnitt remarked that in the very hall where "thirty-two years ago, the negro first entered upon the unequal contest for supremacy," the convention, through its "organic law," would right "the relations between the races upon an everlasting foundation." Second, the proceedings coincided with Emile Zola's famous trial in Paris in connection with his support of Dreyfus. Kruttschnitt sent two invitations to Heller to appear at the convention in order to "open the proceedings with prayer," and, after the second invitation, Heller, like other prominent local ministers, complied.[19]

Although no record remains of Heller's explicit reaction to the wave of segregationist and disfranchisement activity that swept across Louisiana and other southern states after 1900, his response may be inferred from the content of sermons he delivered immediately prior to the 1898 constitutional convention. The *Times-Democrat* penned the headline, "The Dreyfus Case, Which Zola Is Mixed Up In, Treated by the Rabbi—Narrow Racial Prejudice Deprecated," for one of Heller's February 1898 sermons, "Modern Intolerance." In this sermon text he linked the Dreyfus affair to the local constitutional deliberations and expressed his bitter disappointment with the failure of "the brazen machinery of our finely contrived social organization" meant "to redeem mankind." He chided himself for his initial naive faith in the process of assimilation. In a century that had witnessed much "emancipating thought," including universal suffrage, freedom of the press, and the "deliverance of serfs and slaves," he had hoped that "the night-owl's shriek of intolerance would be heard no more." Heller asked his congregants, "Shall not . . . equality breed justice? Shall not republics be free from the taint of race hatred?" Sadly, Heller realized, "widening opportunities have only embittered the clash. . . . Even political enfranchisement . . . constitute[s] no safeguard whatever against those volcanic outbursts of blind injustice which vent the stored-up poison of decades." However veiled and hesitant, Heller's comments represented at least a tentative probing of the hegemonic white supremacist position.[20] Along with the Dreyfus trial, events that February in New Orleans allowed Heller to link eastern European attacks on Jewish rights with the contemporary southern assault on African American liberties. Slowly and tentatively, he began to ponder some of the larger lessons suggested by the political demise of European Jews and southern blacks.

One of the lessons concerned the centrality of racial theorizing at the turn of the century. Contemporary European anti-Semitism seemed to grow in tandem with American Negrophobia because both systems of prejudice drew upon the same European racial theories. The noxious doctrines attracted supporters on both sides of the Atlantic who were threatened by the changes posed by inclusion of those recently granted citizenship. Unhappily, Heller had come to recognize that, despite emancipation, European Jews were still considered "a plague-spot on the body politic," much as Cable had earlier argued against the accepted southern perception that "the man of color must always remain an alien."[21] In the United States, academic sociologists such as University of Chicago professor William I. Thomas affirmed a "scientific" basis of segregationist thought, viewing "race-prejudice" as too comprehensive and pervasive to disappear completely. Thomas explained that "race-prejudice" was part of a more comprehensive "instinct of hate" that had originated in the "tribal stage of society, when solidarity in feeling and action were essential to the preservation of the group." Given its ancient history in human relations, race-prejudice, "or some analogue of it," would probably never disappear completely. As a psychological phenomenon, prejudice could "neither be reasoned with nor legislated about very effectively, because it is connected with the affective, rather than the cognitive, process."[22]

Such voices intensified as segregationist legislation proliferated in the 1890s, and they were echoed in the rise of racial anti-Semitism in Germany. Intellectual leaders such as Felsenthal, Du Bois, and Heller had to leap the philosophical and psychological hurdle of squaring their universalistic humanism with the evermore scientifically respectable racialism that the era's great minds employed as a Social Darwinist explanation for the successes and failures of the world's national and racial groups. Like Du Bois, Heller was unwilling to abandon the concept of race, and Heller's turn to Zionism grew partly out of his quest for an intellectual and political alternative to the reactionary impulses of a race-conscious world.

At the same time, Heller championed a policy of self-help similar to that of Booker T. Washington, who admired Jews for their hard work and willingness to help their coreligionists. In 1894 Washington had argued that African Americans should follow the example of a Jewish peddler ("with all he owned in a cheap and much-worn satchel") who had stopped overnight in a hamlet near Tuskegee, Alabama, and then decided to stay. Four years later, after much hard work, he was earning $50,000 annually. Washington believed that "the colored man's present great opportunity in the South is in the matter of business" and that once he succeeded there he could then find "relief along other lines."[23] His reasoning can best be appreciated as a desperate strategy for securing at least an economic stake in a society that seemed bent on excluding blacks from social and political recognition. Heller's embrace of Zionism resulted initially from a similar, desperate attempt to deal with the inevitability of racial prejudice: Jews still in Europe had to help themselves by working to build a state of their own in Palestine because Europeans would never accept Jews as equals. But his initial proto-Zionist outlook also closely paralleled Du Bois's increasingly self-conscious emphasis on the distinct cultural heritage of African Americans. For southern blacks and for Russian Jews in America, however, Heller embraced Washington's self-help philosophy as a means of building the social and economic power of each group.

Like his mentor, Felsenthal, Heller constantly sought to refine and clarify his philosophical and religious ideas in the face of changing contemporary realities. Like Felsenthal and Du Bois, Heller saw himself as both the intellectual heir of the Enlightenment and the witness to his people's recent emancipation. These leaders painfully perceived the discrepancy between the powerful legacy of liberal thought and the increasingly persistent grip of racism.[24] Heller had arrived in New Orleans about the time that Cable departed, but as a Jew, he viewed the South through different eyes. Unlike liberal Gentiles, Heller drew an analogy between the narrowing of civil liberties in eastern Europe and the growing violence against Jews, the hardening of the caste system, and the lynching of blacks in the American South. Although the parallels must have been evident from the beginning, he did not explore them until the first years of the twentieth century.[25] In 1900 Heller turned forty, and now a mature rabbi, well-respected if not loved by his congregants, he was ready to become his own person. After nearly two decades as an American citizen and a decade and a half as a southerner, he very likely felt secure enough to speak from his heart. Then, too, the changes in the larger political arena of racial politics probably pushed him, reluctantly, to take a more forceful stand on issues that concerned him deeply and challenged his sense of manhood. Having integrated these diverse impulses, Heller was eagerly poised for the battles awaiting him.[26]

Although he left no record of his reaction to the terrible New Orleans race riot in 1900,[27] the next year Heller became a passionate and outspoken Zionist[28] and began increasingly to voice oblique criticism of the

South's racial caste system. For example, in his sermon on the eve of Yom Kippur, the solemn Jewish Day of Atonement, he began by telling his congregants that they had "not done their duty towards our brothers in Russia." In the middle of his speech he switched back to "our own Southland where we are so fond of declaiming about the white man's burden, of priding ourselves upon the condescending friendliness with which we treat the negro." He then asked in words that echoed Southern Methodist Bishop Atticus Haygood's *Our Brother in Black,* "If the negro is our weaker brother, where, indeed, is our active sympathy, our energetic aid that shall lift him, and with him the entire South, to higher levels of efficiency?" Haygood's views appealed to Heller as early as 1889, when his restless spiritual and intellectual quest for social justice had prompted him to correspond with George Washington Cable's Open Letter Club—a forum for discussing the "great moral, political and industrial revolution" then raging in the South. Heller's brief note commented favorably on Haygood's essay on southern race relations that Cable had reprinted and distributed to the club members.[29]

Heller had used the "weaker brother" imagery earlier in 1901, when a New York periodical, the *Jewish Daily News,* asked "some of the leading thinkers in Jewry" to respond to the question, "What should be done to bring about a greater community of interest between the Russian (Orthodox) and German (Reform) elements in American Jewry?" Describing the German Jew as "the elder brother so far as entrance upon modern civilization is concerned," Heller characterized the Reform Jew as feeling "bound by the closest ties with his Russian brother." He perceived that the German Jew's treatment of the Russian mirrored the way "he himself is treated by the Gentile," except that the German Jewish outlook involved "more liberality of pocket and less appreciation of intellect" than was true of Christians. Heller reserved special contempt for the Reform Jewish "alms beadle," a quintessential hypocrite, who exuded "kindly sentiments" in public, while privately scorning the "unfortunate Shlemihls" seeking aid. The prototypical almoner, Heller complained, reveals his duplicity as he metes out "starvation-doles" and then "prides himself in the annual report on his economy."[30] Heller had even less patience with those German Jews who visited a Russian synagogue on Yom Kippur just as they might go to a "negro baptizing," in both cases "only mocking blindly at their own shameful ignorance." To Russian Jews here, and later to southern blacks, he delivered a similar message: that each must learn to set aside the opinions of those hostile to them. Each Russian Jew or African American needed to redeem his "manliness of self-respect" by "standing by his colors as a man," by "know[ing] his own history," and by "uphold[ing] his own conventions, religious or otherwise."[31]

In the early spring of 1900, Edgar Gardner Murphy of Montgomery, Alabama, an Episcopalian minister, reformer, and racial moderate, organized a conference to be held May 8–10 in Montgomery under the auspices of the Southern Society for the Promotion of the Study of Race Conditions and Problems in the South. Heller received an invitation to the meeting, although no record exists of his attendance.[32] He may even have become a member of the society. Murphy and Heller may have had no direct contact, but the two held many views in common, especially their advocacy, as southern Progressives, of education as a key to solving social problems. Where they differed slightly was in their attitude toward white supremacy as an underlying tenet of racial separatism.[33]

Murphy had opposed disenfranchisement but accepted white supremacy "in the present stage of the development of the South" as affording the conditions "upon which the progress of the Negro is itself dependent." In a modification of Murphy's racial paternalism, Heller stressed his hope that "the benevolence of separation will appear in our efforts to lift the younger brother as speedily as possible to our own level."[34] He emphasized that "to recognize the backwardness of races must be also to acknowledge that they [eventually] may rise and become our equals." Although Murphy argued that white supremacy must be maintained "until the Negro had acquired sufficient education and property to vote constructively," in 1904 Heller dodged open criticism of either disenfranchisement or segregation. Instead he warned that "much rankling bitterness and sad confusion" would occur before the reconciliation of "humanity with discrimination" and called on the leaders of both races to exhibit "the utmost forbearance and mutual good will" to stem "the tide over the dangers of the transition."[35] In *The Present South*, which appeared that year, Murphy devoted a chapter to "The South and the Negro" in which he classified the "Negro Question" as a regional problem that grew more complex when "to the characteristics of the individual are added the characteristics which distinguish and differentiate the group—social, national, or racial—with which he is associated. When this group is brought into contact with another . . . or . . . other[s], the elements of complexity increased." Heller, on the other hand, realized that the "Negro Question" had still larger implications for an international situation in which increasing racism led directly to imperialism. As the U.S. crusade to aid beleaguered Cubans evolved into the Spanish-American War, Heller observed that the "white man's burden" had recently translated itself into the domestic use and export of Anglo-Saxon supremacy, which threatened any progress nonwhites could hope to make. Although he accepted the prevailing ideas of his time that all races were not inherently equal, Heller looked forward to a distant future when "all [racial] barriers may be safely superseded."[36]

Like Murphy and other southern moderates and liberals, Heller deplored lynching. In a memorial sermon delivered after the assassination of President McKinley, Heller decried many of the ills he had witnessed during the last decade, including "the drunken mob that kindles a pyre around a chained negro." Such "open anarchy" was, in truth, "the despair of legal process" and "an avowal of political incapacity which shames a whole people."[37] The argument struck a responsive chord in a fellow New Orleanian, who praised the sermon's "inspiring tone of respect for and obedience to law and condemnation of lawlessness" and identified himself as "a member of the Negro race—a race persecuted and oppressed by lawlessness and *anarchy*."[38] This letter was the first of several Heller received in which the writer chose to disclose his racial identity as a person of color. It seems evident that southern blacks were actively reaching out to sympathetic allies in the white community, even as the legal walls between the two groups were erected.

Although the white supremacist onslaught had effectively stifled racial dissent within the region, southern apologists continued to worry about national opinion. Theodore Roosevelt's reelection in 1904 generated fears that the president might dismantle the newly erected system of segregation. The *New Orleans Times-Democrat* called Roosevelt's dinner with Booker T. Washington at the White House three years earlier a "deliberate insult to every white man in the South." When a second editorial snorted at the idea of a "negro scholar" and "a negro gentleman,"[39] Heller could not sit by silently. He penned a response to the *Times-Democrat*, reminding the paper of its larger public obligations. Because its editorial opinion was "very apt to be accepted universally as a good criterion of prevailing Southern thought," the rabbi pointed out, the paper should not "confuse the matter of social equality with the question of social mingling." He saw no reason why "esteem" must be withheld from the Negro scholar nor "respect" from the Negro gentleman. "The difference in color between races can not obliterate the intellectual and moral differences that may obtain between two individuals, irrespective of race," Heller added. "Why we should regard scholarship or gentlemanliness in the negro as something that does not or can not make him the superior of any white man altogether passes my poor understanding." When challenged on two separate occasions in the

Times-Democrat, Heller, now more sure of himself and his ideas, refused to back down. He even let the editors know that he agreed with literary critics who thought that Booker T. Washington's autobiography made "a very valuable contribution."[40]

Rabbi Heller's admiration of Booker T. Washington was undoubtedly strengthened by the knowledge that Washington was a great admirer of Jews and that Washington numbered Tuskegee Jews among his major white supporters in Alabama. Not surprisingly, Washington believed that Jews were a people to be emulated. "The Jew," he wrote, once "in about the same position that the Negro is to-day" had achieved "complete recognition . . . because he has entwined himself about America in a business or industrial sense." He also saw Jews as people who had known suffering and had confronted it by clinging together, with "a certain amount of unity, pride, and love of race; and, as the years go on, they will be more and more influential in this country—a country where they were once despised." Jews had succeeded "largely because the Jewish race has had faith in itself."[41]

Respect for Washington also led Heller to challenge the conservative views of the New Orleans Jewish community. Assimilationist logic probably helped sweeten the bitter racism prevalent in the general community, making it palatable to some of the city's German Jews, as expressed in an unsigned editorial, "An Impudent Nigger," in the *Jewish Ledger.* Less than a year after the *Times-Democrat* scorned the idea of a "negro gentleman," the *Ledger* berated the Tuskegee educator for comparing contemporary black tribulations to the erstwhile persecutions of the Jews, whose social solidarity and success in business, Washington believed, were worthy of black emulation. In an unsigned editorial, the *Ledger* blasted the black leader for suggesting the comparison and then quoted the racist novelist Thomas Dixon. "To compare the Jew, who occupies the highest pinnacle of human superiority and intellectual attainment," wrote Dixon, "with the Negro, who forms the mud at its base, is something which only a Negro with more than the usual vanity and impudence of his race could attempt."[42]

A year and a half later, Heller delivered a sermon scolding those who forsook Judaism's best ethical traditions. In "How to Meet Prejudice," delivered in February 1907, Heller challenged his congregants to "pluck out from our own hearts whatever racial, national or religious prejudice may dwell there." He urged them to go further, "to champion . . . the cause of the oppressed and downtrodden of all races and climes," as he reminded them that "unreasoning racial antipathies" were particularly "ridiculous and absurd in the Jew, who must believe that all men are equally fashioned in God's own image." "The Jew," he concluded, "ought, of all men, to have the widest horizon." The next year on Yom Kippur Eve, Heller graphically argued that Judaism stressed equality before God, that because all mankind had been created in His image, all "the whites [sic] and the colored races descended from one pair of parents." Frances Joseph-Gaudet, founder and president of the Colored Industrial Home and School in New Orleans, wrote Heller that the sermon "was like a drink from the water of life, refreshing and encouraging . . . to the Soul who hungers for righteousness." Although he identified himself as a "colored Methodist," Gaudet averred that "none of your hearers could have enjoyed the sermon more."[43]

Although Heller often seemed to be a man completely dominated by the social and political currents that swirled around him, sometimes he exhibited a surprisingly detached and prophetic perspective. For the centenary of Abraham Lincoln's birth, Heller devoted a column to reconsidering the former president's reputation, admitting that the first decade of the twentieth century was still too close to the traumas of Civil War and Reconstruction to permit a "thorough and unbiased review of that controversial period." Not only were many Civil War veterans still alive, but the Reconstruction era in the South had not "quite reached its end." Especially during the past few years, "the question of the negro's place and rights" had "become more acute than ever." Although Americans everywhere allegedly realized that "the giant size" of the wartime president "towers above the quarrel of the sections," Heller predicted that it might not be until the centenary of Lincoln's death that "he will be canonized," taking "his abiding niche in the hall of American heroism and sainthood."[44]

The following Eve of Atonement, the religious service that traditionally draws the larger Jewish attendance, Heller again addressed the question of "the equality of all souls before God," claiming even more forthrightly than before that equality was axiomatic for both the "rich and the poor, the learned and the ignorant . . . white and black" and that recognizing this lay "at the foundation of all our duties to our fellow men," a religious conviction that he thought the Jews were first to teach. "Why," he exclaimed, "today there are people, right around us, who are too stupid or too inhuman to understand that the negro has a soul, with the same rights as our own, to all of God's truth and beauty." He believed that the Jew functioned as "God's appointed preacher of spiritual democracy." Because the Jew was "the oldest and most unflinching victim of persecution," it was his obligation to "frown down every inhuman barrier that separates races, ranks, and creeds."[45]

In December 1909, just three months later, Heller's outspokenness drew bitter criticism from both Jews and non-Jews in the community. As the lead editorial writer for the *American Israelite*, he had chosen a mid-December issue to discuss the Christmas "confusions" that the holiday season delivers to American Jews. He enjoyed the "prevailing atmosphere of geniality" offered by the festivities but felt torn as a Jew. He noted wryly that the "most enthusiastic patrons" and generous contributors to the *Times-Democrat* Christmas Doll and Toy Fund were Jews, "for whom the whole combination of childhood made happy . . . , of generosity from rich child to ragamuffin, has an irresistible fascination." As if he had not committed travesty enough in questioning or poking fun at Jewish participation, he went on to impugn the fund itself for donating the gifts to white children only, making its success "a great fuss . . . over very little real substance." "The really nasty and revolting part," he wrote, "is the drawing of the color line; either the colored child is not poor enough, the colored parent not mean enough, or the Christmas spirit not broad enough to obliterate that line; social distinctions must be upheld against the poor pickaninny; else white civilization would totter upon its throne."[46]

Obviously, the article was not written for a local New Orleans audience. But the *American Israelite* had subscribers in New Orleans, and Heller certainly had enemies. One of them must have clipped the article and sent it to the *Times-Democrat*, which not only published it in its entirety but reprimanded Heller editorially. The editorialist argued that the existence of "race bitterness," even among tots, had precipitated drawing the color line. "Forced to choose, so to speak, between the elimination of the white children or the elimination of the black," "naturally" preference had been given to the elimination of the black. "Dr. Heller is, we believe, the first white Orleanian to raise his voice in protest." The editors suggested that if Heller felt so strongly that the "children of the negro race should be provided for," he should organize a fund and conduct "an annual distribution for their benefit."[47]

Heller tried to explain away his criticism of Jewish confusion as "good-natured raillery." On the deeper question of racial discrimination, however, he minced no words in denouncing the "disdain and derision [with which] your paper has . . . , both editorially and in other columns, treated the colored race." Often tempted "to come forward in defense of a broader social toleration," he realized that his criticism would lead only to "much futile spilling of ink." After pointing out the absurdity of proposing that a rabbi should "supervise a consistent carrying out of the Christmas teaching," he concluded that "each religion [should] attend to its lessons, always under the guidance of a humanity which beats responsive to human hearts, be the color of the skin whatever it may."[48]

A prominent local Jewish attorney and old Heller foe from other battles jumped into the fray, assuring the *Times-Democrat* and its readers that Heller's opinion "in no degree represents the attitude of the Jewish people of our community."[49] That same day the Heller challenge prompted an editorial that encapsulated the paper's southern philosophy: "The *Times-Democrat* believes in white civilization and white supremacy, in the preservation of the integrity of the white race, in government by the white people, in the separation and the segregation of the races." "What has this paper done to the negroes," the editorialist wondered, "to cause Dr. Heller so much sorrow that he has with difficulty been unable to curb his desire to interfere?" A few days later the *Times-Democrat* charged that "the rabbi's attack" was a strike against "the entire South." Functioning as "the mouthpiece of public opinion," the daily had advocated only southern racial policy, "so declared again and again." Unfortunately, "the learned rabbi had been most successful in stirring up religious and racial bitterness" without winning the sympathy or support "of the community, of his coreligionists, nor, we believe, of his congregation."[50]

Articulate members of the black community recognized the rabbi's outspokenness and welcomed his commitment to their struggle. Valcour [?] Chapman, a black New Orleanian and Methodist Episcopal pastor, thanked Heller for his "manly stand" and hastened to mention that "no Negroes' letters would have been published as yours—and if they were, he would run the risk of being lynched."[51] By the time Heller faced an African American audience for the first time at the Central Congregational Church in the spring of 1911, he was probably already a fairly familiar figure. His talk, "Manliness versus Prejudice," concerned breaking the "habit of indiscriminate prejudgment," which he found "everywhere to be on the increase." The central question to confront, he argued, was "How shall we stand unswayed in the storm; how shall we hold our ground like men against whatever threatens to unsettle our self-respect and drag us down altogether?"

Warming to the subject, Heller told the large audience that the problems of race conflict had "become active" only during the last few decades. The kind of prejudice that concerned him was that of the "civilized man who aspires to fair dealing" while indulging the "immoral habit of judging the individual by the mass." Speaking several years after the notorious Kishinev pogrom in Russia, Heller argued that injustice must be countered by arousing "a sense of solidarity by which each individual accepts responsibility for all the others." Consistent with his cultural Zionism, he also emphasized that "in the education of every race room must be made for teaching its noble traditions, for fostering its historic pride." The black child therefore should be taught "all the negro has done for this country," from the role Crispus Attucks played as a leader in the Boston Massacre to "how invaluable negro labor has been to the development of the South," and especially the strides the race had made since emancipation. "Instead of being crushed under injuries," he added, "manhood learns its loftiest lessons under the burdens of experience." Heller therefore urged blacks to work "against every misrepresentation of caricature and gossip." Still affirming the eventual triumph of righteousness, he concluded, "you have a right, and a duty, to confront the injustice of prejudice with the legitimate prepossessions of a strengthened loyalty."[52]

Two dailies covered the event. The *Daily Picayune*'s caption ran "Rabbi Heller Analyzes Race Prejudice in a Special Sermon to Negroes," and the *Times-Democrat* piqued the interest of readers with the more sensational "Rabbi Would Stir Ambition in Negro."[53] "The church was packed with negroes," reported the *Times-Democrat*, "and the remarks of Rabbi Heller evidently made a strong impression upon them." Heller's appearance at Central Congregational Church practically coincided with the inception of a new movement, the interracial National Association for the Advancement of Colored People. Moreover, the occasion of his address prompted a response from W. E. B. Du Bois, the editor of the recently established NAACP journal, *Crisis*. In one of the journal's opening issues, Du Bois prefaced a lengthy quotation from Heller's talk, noting that the New Orleans rabbi had "defined race prejudice in a striking way." The American Missionary Association also published Heller's discourse in the association's journal, observing by way of introduction that many of the "Hebrew people" recently had shown sympathy toward the Negro. Because the Jews were "a people which has had many and long and hard lessons in the history of caste and prejudice," they "can speak with emphasis."[54]

In Heller's initial address to a black audience at Central Congregational Church, he had stressed that, in seeking to live meaningfully in a racially unjust world, the skillful survivor will "seek his brothers everywhere, especially among the persecuted and downtrodden."[55] His own quest for self-purpose and fulfillment carried Heller from the ranks of elite reformers to the more precarious role of self-appointed spokesperson for blacks and Jews who lived beyond the fringes of acceptable opinion. Following his own advice, he stood "unswayed" as he strived to resolve the inherent tensions between the Zionist separatism he pursued on behalf of those fleeing eastern European ghettos and the measure of racial justice he sought for his African American neighbors at home. His forty years of successful leadership as Temple Sinai's rabbi fostered a legacy to the New Orleans Jewish community. Three decades after his death, a new generation of New Orleans Jewish leaders, most of whom were Temple Sinai congregants, became prominent activists in building an interracial alliance in New Orleans. Until the 1960s Max Heller's keen sense of the larger mission of Reform Judaism—an allegiance to social justice here and in Israel—remained largely unvindicated. His outspokenness, then, is more than another "forgotten voice" that interrupted the silence of the period. He calls across the century, still begging to be heard.

Morris Newfield, Alabama, and Blacks, 1895–1940

MARK COWETT

*Like Heller an immigrant, social activist, and rabbi with a degree from He-
brew Union College, Morris Newfield was nonetheless far more circumspect
in his actions. Birmingham was a city that limited Social Gospel advocates
who wished to remain within the community. Yet questions arise: What if
Heller and Newfield had switched locations? Might the differences in their
temperaments and personalities have resulted in divergent responses?*

Morris Newfield was rabbi at Temple Emanu-El in Birmingham, Alabama, from 1895–1940, and in his tenure he played a variety of roles,
including serving as chief Jewish spokesman in the larger Birmingham
and Alabama communities. His authority lay in the power bestowed
upon him by Jews as their spokesperson and by Gentiles who perceived
him similarly. These factors are important as we consider this particular
rabbi's actions and attitudes toward blacks. As was the case with many
rabbis, Newfield's relationship with blacks was a complex one because of
the anomalous position of Jews in the South of his time.

I

Morris Newfield's background as a Hungarian and an early Reform
rabbinical student with Isaac Mayer Wise at Hebrew Union College in
Cincinnati significantly informed the roles he would play as a rabbi in
Birmingham. Born in Homanna, Hungary, in 1869, Newfield was a
member of a minority population that faced widening opportunities in
the latter half of the nineteenth century. The dominant Magyars needed

Jewish assistance in developing an industrial state in Hungary. Jews were allowed to operate in almost every branch of industry and trade. They could study for the "free professions" such as medicine, law, and journalism. Hungarian Jews, too, experienced a split between the Orthodox and more liberal sects. The "Neologs" broke off from the Orthodox and established a liberal seminary in Budapest in 1868.[1]

Mor Neufeld, as he was known in Hungary, was torn between his father's desire that he attend the Neolog institution and become a rabbi like himself and his own ambition to attend medical school. Young Newfield spent five years at the seminary from 1884–1889 but left, unbeknownst to his father, to attend the Royal Gymnasium in Budapest with the hope of moving on to the Medical College at the University of Budapest.[2]

Young Newfield's situation was finally resolved in 1891 when he vowed to his dying father that he would become a rabbi. That same year he came to the United States to attend Hebrew Union College and the University of Cincinnati simultaneously. At these two institutions he received training as a Reform rabbi as well as instruction in Social Gospel theology. This latter theology, emphasizing man's responsibilities to others in society, was a leading concern of the day. Listening to teachers such as Rev. Washington Gladden, Newfield understood that his role was to emphasize social concerns at the expense of individual soul saving. But he also understood from Wise that a rabbi needed to influence people both within and beyond the Jewish community. In Birmingham, Alabama, where he journeyed in 1895 to accept his one and only pulpit, Newfield's experience as a member of an able but minority subculture and his desire to foment excellent interfaith relationships would be vital.[3]

Newfield also became one of Alabama's leading social workers. In 1909 he helped establish the Associated Charities in Birmingham to dispense relief, ranging from milk stations and day care to cash for needy citizens. He also helped develop private agencies such as the Red Cross, Birmingham's primary relief dispenser in the 1920s and 1930s. The rabbi also helped found the Community Chest in 1925 and served as liaison between the professional social work community and business elites who advised chest boards and funded their programs.[4] But the rabbi's role as a social worker increased most dramatically in child-care matters. Here he moved beyond helping to develop relief resources: he assisted trained workers in improving child labor laws and in establishing ameliorative institutions such as the juvenile court in Birmingham in 1911 and the state department of child welfare in 1919 to carry out the dictates of those laws. Also in 1911, because of efforts by Newfield and others, the proceedings of the National Child Labor Committee—featuring Jane Addams, Florence Kelley, Felix Adler, and Theodore Roosevelt—were held in Birmingham. Two years later Newfield and two fellow clergymen—George Eaves and Newfield's best friend, Henry M. Edmonds—revived the Alabama Sociological Congress to provide a forum for discussion of important issues. Finally, in the 1920s he served as a member of the Alabama Conference on Social Work.[5]

II

During the first decades of the twentieth century, the Birmingham Jewish community was not large, numbering 3,500 or no more than 3 percent of the general population. It was composed of German Jews who had come after 1870, the year of the city's founding, and eastern European Jews who began filtering in between 1881 and 1905. German Jews maintained a dominant position in Birmingham's Jewish community and became an integral part of the community at large.

In the period up through World War II, Birmingham's German Jews became members and officials of many of the city's civic, commercial, and fraternal organizations. Siegfried and Burghardt Steiner, Samuel Marx, Moses V. Joseph, Jacob Burger, Simon Klotz, A. B. Loveman, and Ben and Bert Jacobs were some of the early successful businessmen. Newfield's future father-in-law, Samuel Ullman, as well as Jacob Burger and Burghardt Steiner, worked diligently as members of the board of education to raise standards. It is fair to say that their contributions to the community far outweighed their small numbers.[6]

The significance of Temple Emanu-El's Jews was even more profound. Many Birmingham Jews were related to Jews of other southern as well as northern cities, and this network of people, sharing close social and economic interests, kept up with each other. Birmingham was hardly a cultural outpost. Its wealthy Jews participated in national Jewish affairs. They were respected for their financial and professional acumen, and the efforts of their leaders, such as Newfield, complemented the work of others throughout the country.[7] Still, even though its German Jewish members assimilated easily and even became economic, educational, and political leaders, Jews never forgot their minority status as non-Christians in a region that valued its Christian characteristics.[8]

With his experience in Hungary and his rabbinical training, Newfield understood implicitly how to lead a small but enterprising minority, and that was to tread a narrow path between adhering to revered

Jewish traditions and accepting the cultural dictates of the majority sub-culture, in this case, Fundamentalist Christians. Newfield preached a Classical Reform Judaism, in keeping with the Pittsburgh Platform of 1885 and other lessons he had learned from Isaac Mayer Wise. It satis-fied his congregants, mostly enterprising businessmen and profession-als, who hoped to gain access to the wider avenues of social, political, and cultural power in Birmingham and simultaneously hold onto some Jewish traditions.[9]

As an "ambassador to the Gentiles," Newfield was also able to bridge many of the theological chasms that lay between his people and the wider Christian community. As a spokesman on religious matters, he often communicated Jewish responses on social issues of the day. He consequently acquired a certain respect and prestige among Birming-ham Christians because of his leadership status. Two roles demonstrate his stature. As a member of the Quid Pro Quo Club, he joined with Birmingham businessmen and social leaders to discuss the intellectual and social issues of their day. As an activist for interreligious unity and harmony, he traveled Alabama with Henry M. Edmonds of the High-land Avenue Presbyterian Church and Monsignor Eugene L. Sands, preaching toleration and brotherhood in opposition to the Klan.[10]

Newfield's oratorical style varied because he was aware of his great responsibilities and the diversity of his many followers. He could be out-spoken, even blunt, when he believed that explanations and actions should be straightforward and direct, circumspect and accommodating when he believed a more subtle strategy would effect greater influence. He knew that his success as well as Jewish group survival depended on the efforts of a leader who knew how to tread tactfully. His relationship with his congregation is instructive in this regard. At times he aligned himself with the interests of fairly conservative businessmen and pro-fessionals. At other times he moved boldly beyond these groups to a high moral ground because of his innate feeling for social justice and his con-cern for those who needed help. In short, Newfield was a careful but principled man whose varied responses took into account divergent in-terests and constituencies.

Against these roles as a Jewish leader in Birmingham and Alabama, Newfield's activities vis-à-vis blacks must be viewed. As I tried to dem-onstrate a decade ago in my book, *Birmingham's Rabbi: Morris Newfield and Alabama, 1895–1940,* his advocacy was limited by the era and by competing concerns. Rather than an apologist argument, this interpre-tation attempts to view Newfield's work in the light of his many, and often conflicting, tasks.[11]

III

Birmingham was a "New South" city that, in the wake of the Civil War, practiced racial policies similar to other cities throughout the South. Alabama legally instituted segregation after 1901, and whites and blacks lived in largely different worlds after that point. Blacks accounted for 39 percent of the city's total population in 1920, and whites continued to enforce segregated living patterns. Black neighborhoods were often situated in the city's vacant spaces along creek beds, railroad lines, or alleys—areas of undeveloped land bypassed by industry and white homeowners—and they lacked street lights, paved streets, sewers, and other city services. In short, Birmingham's residential patterns reflected the southern caste system, with zoning laws designed "to keep Negroes in certain districts."[12]

Economic conditions in post–World War I Birmingham augured an even more uncertain future for both blacks and whites. The bottom fell out of the cotton market in Alabama when prices slid from almost forty-two cents per pound in the New Orleans market in April 1920 to less than two cents per pound in December of that same year. This drop affected Birmingham's economy in various ways. First, it angered white southern farmers, who, as George Tindall explains, lost their first opportunity since the Civil War "to accumulate capital and break the chain of debt to merchants and cotton factors." Second, it forced black sharecroppers and tenant farmers off the land and into southern and northern cities because whites could no longer afford to parcel out their lands. Third, it caused unemployment in the cottonseed industry, one of the city's most important businesses.[13]

The pig iron and steel industry did not fare much better primarily because the U.S. Steel Corporation (centered in Pittsburgh), which had acquired the Tennessee Coal, Iron, and Railway Company, ensured that its southern subsidiary did not expand at the expense of its northern plants. It did so by forcing Birmingham's plants to charge higher prices than its northern ones, thus nullifying Birmingham's natural advantages. Consequently, the lot of Birmingham's industrial workers, most of whom were rural and black, "was none too good." Only long hours and low wages allowed southern industries to compete with the North. The largely black coal miners (blacks made up three fourths of the 27,000-man work force) also faced terrible conditions. Most of them lived in poorly constructed homes in company towns, bought overpriced food in company stores, and received low wages for long hours. Moreover, they could not secure adequate union representation, because of the machinations of the coal operators and politicos under the influence of their corporate patrons. At the end of the decade, disaster struck as capital investments in the business slowdown ceased. Pig iron and steel piled up, mills and mines closed, and furnaces ceased operations. A total of 123,000 men lost their jobs in Birmingham.[14]

IV

Morris Newfield was an advocate of social justice who believed that all men should be treated fairly and equally. He cannot be said to have supported black rights in every situation, but neither did he operate from a sense of white privilege or superiority that suggested blacks should be the last to share in the crumbs of the economic pie. His position was not a simple one. At times it placed him squarely at odds with his Birmingham business cohorts who were not advocates of equality, with Birmingham whites who were members of the Klan and opponents of blacks and Jews in the 1920s, and with his own congregants who were not interested in changing the status quo or fighting the social mores of their day. But, at other times, there is no indication that he went far beyond the thoughts and deeds of some of his more conservative congregants. Nevertheless, Morris Newfield recognized the need to distinguish between those black issues that he could confront publicly and those that required him to be more circumspect.

As stated in Virginia Hamilton's *Alabama: A Bicentennial History*, Birmingham's business community lacked a sense of noblesse oblige. This lack kept Birmingham a "great workshop town" rather than allowing it to develop into a cosmopolitan metropolis. Its populace remained sparsely educated, economically insecure, and racially divided. The great iron and steel manufacturing firms led by TCI, Republic Steel, Sloss-Sheffield Steel and Iron Company, Woodward Iron Company, and the Ingalls Iron Works not only located outside the city limits and taxing authority, in areas such as Ensley and Fairfield, but also failed to maintain capital investments during the 1920s, and, as stated before, thousands of people in Jefferson County lost their jobs. There is also no record of any enlightened leadership on their part on racial issues.[15]

During and after World War I, another group of whites, those disaffected by Birmingham's economic decline, as well as the failure of World War I to "make the world safe for democracy," revived the Ku Klux Klan and organized the Robert E. Lee Klan Number 1 in Birmingham. Blacks, Jews, and Catholics were attacked and abused between 1916 and the mid-1930s for reasons mentioned above as well as for more personal ones; for example, the city's health officer, J. M.

Dowling, a Catholic, was flogged because he demanded that various dairy farmers clean up their barns. Klan power was substantial. By 1926 the Klan claimed 18,000 members in Birmingham and 15,000 of the city's 32,000 registered voters. Most local, county, and state office holders recognized that Klan support was necessary to win elections. For example, Hugo Black, later a Supreme Court justice, courted Klan support in his successful run for the Senate in 1927. The Birmingham Pastor's Union, composed primarily of Fundamentalist Christian ministers, refused publicly to take a stand against this dominant force despite protestations of ministers such as Edmonds and Newfield.[16]

There is little indication that Newfield's congregants at Temple Emanu-El were strong supporters of black rights either. Although (or perhaps because) they were members of a minority group, too, some of these Jews believed blacks to be inferior. Nevertheless, it is not clear whether they shared racist attitudes with the dominant white subculture in Alabama or simply belittled blacks because they were businessmen and the blacks were primarily laborers. One example manifests this thought. Milton Fies, as a member of Emanu-El, a leading engineer, and vice-president of the DeBardeleben Coal Company and later of the Alabama Power Company, accentuated paternalistic "company welfare" schemes instead of tolerating union activities as a "reward for the Negro coal miners' contribution to non-union Alabama."[17]

Indirectly, Newfield supported the cause of African Americans by electing to promote interfaith programs to combat Klan activities in Alabama. In the mid-1920s Newfield joined with Eugene L. Sands and Henry M. Edmonds to develop a program of interfaith forums to educate citizens of Birmingham and of Alabama about religious brotherhood. These interfaith colloquia were an outgrowth of the early cooperative efforts of Temple Emanu-El's Jews and their Christian neighbors in Birmingham, including ministers such as Edmonds, Middleton Barnwell, A. J. Dickinson of the First Baptist Church, and E. C. McEvoy of the Methodist Episcopal Church, South.[18] As early as 1920 Newfield penned an article in the *Birmingham Age-Herald* in which he underscored his belief that religious institutions "have ever been social centers, places that make for brotherhood. They are the great hope of democracy, whose aim is to break down barriers of caste, class, and conditions." Beginning in the late 1920s Newfield, Sands, and Edmonds went on "barnstorming tours of the state to show that religions could get together."[19]

Immediately following the election of 1928 when Catholic Al Smith lost the presidential election to the Protestant Herbert Hoover, the three clergymen led a colloquium at Mary Beard's Tea Room on Twentieth

Street in Birmingham, feeling that they had to contend with nativist opinions expressed by Fundamentalist preachers and the Klan. As a consequence of this meeting the Birmingham chapter of the National Conference of Christians and Jews was founded to develop a common ground between people of different faiths.[20] No record exists of African American participation in any of these activities, but the argument can be made that efforts by Newfield and others to combat the Klan helped the cause of all embattled minorities. A case can be made for the thought that Klan influence declined after 1927 in Birmingham because many citizens, tiring of the fear and violence that Klan activities engendered there, developed a greater confidence in the city's future than the Klan could muster.

This cosmopolitan stance on Newfield's part was a necessarily shrewd position. The rabbi understood that he, as a Jew and one of the targets of the Klan, could not publicly attack the Klan as his friend Henry M. Edmonds had done. Rather he could attack the psychological fears stemming from this period of transition by reaffirming his faith in a common humanity. In a number of instances, however, he was a stronger and more public advocate of African American rights. One such instance involved Ed Jackson, a black janitor at Temple Emanu-El. Jackson had been accused of murder, and because some of the rabbi's congregants feared negative publicity, they asked Newfield to fire Jackson before he had been tried. Newfield refused to do so and continued to employ Jackson after he had been acquitted.[21]

The rabbi also developed a friendship with Booker T. Washington of the Tuskegee Institute. Not only was Newfield invited to speak at Tuskegee and dine at Washington's home, he also visited as a personal emissary of Julius Rosenwald, the noted Chicago Jewish philanthropist who donated millions of dollars to various African American causes, including the institute.[22] Evidence also suggests that as he grew increasingly comfortable in his tenure at Emanu-El, Newfield began to support publicly the rights of African American coal miners against efforts of mine owners in Birmingham in the 1920s. This was a distinct change from earlier and perhaps less courageous stands. In 1914 he rejected the cause of labor organizers, arguing that "those who agitate and arouse enmity between the classes do not serve the interest of humanity. What is needed is a better understanding . . . of each other's work."[23] But the greed of coal operators between 1917 and 1920 changed the rabbi's mind. Because of the shortage of coal during and after World War I, miners in Alabama were threatened with reprisals if they joined the United Mine Workers, which sought to organize workers at this time. Although the union never received official recognition, the coal miners participated in the national coal strike of November 1919. Violence erupted. Although it stopped when the miners agreed to submit their complaints to arbitration, Governor Thomas Kilby ruled in favor of the mine operators, and most of the striking miners lost their jobs. Convinced that businessmen had tried to take advantage of the miners to obtain larger profits, Newfield wrote sermons on behalf of the largely black miners. Conceding that some of his former ideas had been antiquated, he reasoned that "we do not claim that all Jews have been friendly to those demands for social justice . . . [but] we cannot tread old paths."[24]

On other occasions, however, he refused to stand openly with African Americans. He declined to defend the cause of the Scottsboro Boys even though other rabbis in Alabama did so. And evidence suggests that he was bowing to well-placed political pressure not to do so. In 1933, when the Scottsboro Boys were incarcerated in Birmingham, Morris Newfield, as president of the Central Conference of American Rabbis (CCAR), was asked to investigate the dismissal of his friend Rabbi Benjamin Goldstein of Temple Beth Or in Montgomery. Goldstein had complained that he had been fired because of his public support of both the Scottsboro Boys and black sharecroppers in Alabama.[25]

Rabbi Newfield spoke with Benjamin Goldstein and a few members of the board of Temple Beth Or and concluded that "dissatisfaction and friction have existed . . . almost since the first month of Goldstein's occupancy of that pulpit. . . . His radical ideas in matters of religion did not suit the vast majority. . . . The racial issue alone was not the cause of friction." But Simon Wampold, former president of Temple Beth Or and supporter of the dismissed rabbi, concluded that Newfield had not conducted a full and impartial investigation of the facts and complained: "I made a strenuous effort to see [Newfield] but was unable to do so. . . . These men [the leaders of the opposition] are trying to excuse the real situation by injecting the religious point of view." Wampold was convinced that Newfield and many Montgomery Jews did not want to help Goldstein because of his support for the Scottsboro Boys. He did not suggest why this was so, however.[26]

The Birmingham clergyman refused to serve on a special commission established by the CCAR to investigate the situation further. On 21 July 1933 Newfield wrote to Samuel Goldenson, his friend and president of the CCAR: "Have had some unpleasant correspondence with Rabbi Benjamin Goldstein. He charges me with the endeavor of inducing his former congregation and friends to shift the cause of his disagreement to religious grounds. . . . I am inclined to believe it would be unwise for me to act on the Special Committee. . . . After all my judgment is formed. I have formed it honestly on the basis of a thorough investigation. . . . I hope you see my point of view." In the absence of other evidence, we can only speculate about the factors that informed Newfield's point of view: perhaps Newfield was being totally candid and was simply not interested in supporting Goldstein's case against the board of the latter's congregation. His motives, however, may have been more mixed. He may have chosen to support the board because its president, Ernest Mayer, was a friend, or he may have feared the repercussions involved in supporting Goldstein, an outspoken advocate of black rights. Or the rabbi may not have wanted to jeopardize his standing among white Protestants by taking an equally outspoken position on behalf of the Scottsboro Boys.[27]

Newfield's connection with the Scottsboro Boys was not finished. Three years later he was asked to become a member of the Independent Scottsboro Committee, which was formed in June 1936 ostensibly to obtain justice for the nine black youths. The story is more complicated, however: although the committee was not convinced of the boys' innocence, it had come together to attempt to convince the boys to hire an Alabama lawyer, Roderick Beddow, instead of Samuel Lebowitz, a New York Jewish lawyer whom they did not believe could win in Alabama because he was employed by the International Labor Defense, a Marxist organization. On the committee were Newfield (the sole Jew) and some of his closest friends and professional associates, including Harry M. Ayres, publisher of the *Anniston Star,* Henry M. Edmonds, Guy E. Snavely of Birmingham-Southern College, and Beddow, at that time the leading criminal lawyer in Alabama. The efforts of the committee came to very little because their interests conflicted with others who were involved in the affair.[28]

In choosing to act cautiously when confronted by racial tensions unleashed by the Scottsboro trials, Rabbi Newfield might be contrasted with a young member of his congregation, Joseph Gelders, who taught physics at the University of Alabama. Gelders, reputed to have been a member of the Communist party, was an outspoken advocate of racial equality and union activities. For his beliefs he was brutally beaten by the Klan in the mid-1930s. He also fell out of favor with leading Jews of Birmingham as well as with the white Protestant power structure because of his political sympathies. Unfortunately, there is no record of Newfield's own feelings about Gelders's conduct. Nevertheless, comparing their stances is instructive: Gelders simply did not have the responsibilities of leadership that Newfield exercised among Birmingham Jews and, consequently, could be much less circumspect in some of his political activities.[29]

V

It has been ten years since *Birmingham's Rabbi* was published, thirty years since Birmingham experienced the traumas, tribulations, and ultimate successes of the civil rights movement led by Dr. Martin Luther King, Jr., and more than fifty years since Rabbi Newfield himself died. Of course, there is an implicit danger in writing such a piece on a Jewish clergyman and his relationships with, and attitudes toward, blacks in the South. If one labels him a product of his times and extols his limited deeds and virtues, one risks being called an "apologist." If, on the other hand, one takes what may be perceived as the more politically correct approach, criticizing the less expansive nature of those deeds and virtues, one risks oversimplifying the complexities of time and place in which this rabbi lived and labored.

This piece does neither, proposing rather that an objective evaluation of Newfield's work must fall somewhere in between these two extremes. Very simply, he supported black rights not when it was convenient for him to do so as a white man, but when it did not conflict with what he perceived his role as a leader of Birmingham Jews to necessitate. Through interfaith workshops he stood up to the Klan when it accentuated reaction and racism in the 1920s and 1930s. In doing so Newfield drew attention to the needs of every minority group threatened by its force. But, more important, he stood up to his own congregation and some of its less bold leaders as well as the white power structure of Birmingham when he challenged attitudes toward black miners in the period after the First World War. This was a fearless stance.

Newfield's record is mixed. In championing cosmopolitan ideals in a largely evangelical Protestant area and espousing largely accommodationist goals for Jews, he did not speak out on behalf of the Scottsboro Boys nor help a former friend, Benjamin Goldstein, in a time of need. Perhaps he had lost faith in the latter's sense of judgment, or maybe he felt he had different positions to protect. Still, Newfield's record needs not apology but understanding. As a Jewish leader in an area that demanded a strong sense of fealty in social matters, he made choices, sometimes ones that appear inconsistent, to protect himself, his flock, and the black community in Birmingham and in Alabama.

A Plea for Tolerance: Fineshriber in Memphis

BERKLEY KALIN

William Fineshriber, unlike other rabbis presented in this anthology, mixed the social justice message of Classical Reform with socialist inclinations. He pressed for action with the support of key elements of the Memphis power structure. Fineshriber's story again raises the question of the intertwining of events and movements. Although a dramatic lynching served as a catalyst, the rabbi's advocacy of black civil rights was linked inexorably with his concern for the rights of women and others who faced discrimination.

At the beginning of the twentieth century, Memphis "presented a strange paradox—a city modern in physical aspect but rural in background, rural in prejudice, and rural in habit," according to historian Gerald Capers.[1] The yellow fever epidemics of 1873, 1878, and 1879 had decimated the city's population. Besides the losses due to death, many of its prominent and cosmopolitan citizens, including many German Jews, fled to St. Louis and other northern urban centers never to return. Between 1879 and 1890 the city went "bankrupt," surrendering its charter and becoming a mere taxing district. From the hinterlands of Tennessee, Arkansas, and Mississippi came the new Memphians, steeped in country mores, evangelical fundamentalism, and distrust for outsiders.[2]

Memphis gained renown as the "murder capital of the nation" as the homicide rate exceeded all other American cities with more than twenty-five thousand people.[3] Violence fueled by devotion to the "lost cause," racism, and vestiges of the southern "code of honor" was commonplace.[4]

The Progressive Era brought new blood into Memphis politics and opened the door to reform. The young Edward Hull Crump, who later became *the* boss of Tennessee politics, represented progressivism with his passion for order and efficiency. Improved schools, parks ("City Beautiful" movement), roads (the parkway system), water quality (artesian wells), police and fire protection, and a good sewage disposal system helped transform the city.[5] As was true elsewhere, Progressive reform excluded blacks, although Crump manipulated the black vote for his purposes. Despite the influx of new industries courted by the business aristocracy, and perhaps as a lure to it, a plantation mentality prevailed, firmly rooted in the traditional faith in male paternalism and white supremacy.[6]

Local Protestant clerical influence extended far beyond the spiritual realm. H. L. Mencken dubbed Memphis the "buckle of the bible belt." Nonetheless, as Faulkner illustrated in *The Reivers* and other works, Memphis, with a well-deserved reputation for night life on Beale Street, served as the whorehouse town to the surrounding country people. A vibrant confluence of country, blues, and gospel music lured black composers, musicians, and singers and nurtured an artistic expression that contradicted the staid standards of the establishment. Layers of hypocrisy surrounded the gentlemen of country manners who frequented the brothels but objected to the vulgarity of touring Broadway productions.[7]

Into this strange admixture arrived a smallish scholar with wire-rimmed glasses. From 1911 to 1924 William H. Fineshriber served Congregation Children of Israel and the Memphis community, voicing his views on numerous social and economic questions.[8] His strong voice, universal message, and penetrating mind attracted large audiences from a variety of religious backgrounds. Babette Becker, his secretary throughout his Memphis rabbinate, accounts (in purplish hues) for his adulation: "[He] was a Hellene in the pulpit, a priest of light and life; and if he denuded Judaism of what might tend to be rigidity, hauteur and dogmatism, he gave to it a radiance that curiously or unconsciously the congregation felt and found good."[9]

Fineshriber's ecumenical appeal caught the attention of the broader community very early in his Memphis career. Just two months after his installation, for instance, Reverend John W. Rowlett, minister of the Unitarian Church, wrote:

An address that I heard since I have been in Memphis on Henry Ward Beecher, by Rabbi Fineshriber, was in perfect accord with your plea for a "United Church of God" [referring to an editorial in the *Commercial Appeal*]. The matter of his address was good, the diction superb, and the manner of delivery well-nigh perfect; but that which impressed me most was the comprehensiveness of the spirit of the speaker. Without saying so, he stood before his audience as a member of the race, a citizen of the world, representing a universal church and speaking in behalf of a universal religion. Such utterances . . . indicate great progress in religion, make one feel the fatherhood of God and the brotherhood of man are great truths, and that we may yet have a true catholic church, including every worthy human being who is seeking to live righteously and to help his fellowmen, no matter what intellectual shape his faith may assume.[10]

When a journalist asked Fineshriber his great ambition in life, he replied briefly, "to help somehow to make a reality of the 'Brotherhood of Man.' "[11] Throughout his long career he worked unceasingly to attain this goal. Memphis sermons titled "Jesus of Nazareth" and "The Crucifixion" express his great respect for Christianity.[12] More concretely, his interest in promoting greater understanding among youth manifested itself in one of the first interdenominational scout troops of the South.[13]

William H. Fineshriber was born in St. Louis, Missouri, on 21 February 1878. The family moved to Evansville, Illinois, when "Billy" was six. He had a voracious appetite for reading and became Evansville's unofficial assistant librarian at the age of twelve. His father, a reform rabbi, died at the age of thirty-seven, but even before his father's death, young William had decided to follow in his footsteps. At the age of thirteen he went on alone to Cincinnati, Ohio, where he continued his education at Hughes High School and enrolled at the Hebrew Union College for the eight-year course. After graduating from high school, he enrolled at the University of Cincinnati, where he majored in liberal arts, taking courses in Greek, mathematics, English history, psychology, philosophy, and biology. In 1900, having completed the required four years at the University of Cincinnati and the required eight years at Hebrew Union College, he was awarded his B.A. degree and was ordained a rabbi.[14]

At Hebrew Union College he came under the particular influence of Dr. Isaac M. Wise, president of the college, who died just prior to the ordination services of the class of 1900. Another professor, Ephraim Feldman, whose field was philosophy, had the greatest influence on Fineshriber. Fineshriber described him as a "master stylist in the writing of both English and Hebrew" and a "shy, spiritual man." Yet, like

Fineshriber himself, Feldman wrote little for publication and never collected the rare fugitive pieces he did write.[15]

Fineshriber was a popular leader at Hebrew Union College. He sang tenor in the glee club, played quarterback on the football team, was the pitcher of the "college nine," and was even considered quite a pugilist.[16]

In the fall of 1900 William Fineshriber accepted the pulpit of Temple Emanuel in Davenport, Iowa. Floyd Dell, a close friend of the rabbi while he lived in Davenport, said that the place had a "European" climate of opinion because "it was so largely German and Jewish, with an 1848 European revolutionary foundation, and a liberal and Socialist superstructure."[17] Dell, who wrote many novels as well as nonfiction, became the famous editor of *The Masses* and *The Liberator*. He introduced the personage of his friend, the "eloquent young Reform rabbi," into a number of his books. In his "autobiographical" novel *Moon-Calf* he makes the "discovery" that the young rabbi "was not a preacher at all, he was a scholar."[18] Dell describes the sessions in which he and the rabbi would sit "drinking beer" and discussing the great questions.[19] It is interesting that the young rabbi of *Moon-Calf* preaches a sermon on Heine. Dell's book of essays, *Looking at Life*, was dedicated to "Rabbi William Fineshriber, friend of truth and wisdom."[20]

Another Davenport friend who introduced the personality of the rabbi into her work was Susan Glaspell, who later won the Pulitzer Prize in 1932 for her play, *Allison's House*. In *The Road to the Temple*, "an intellectual young man whose mind could indeed play" with ideas (i.e., Fineshriber) and the author's husband "talked Nietzsche," "delighting in there having come at last a German philosopher who smiles, whose heavy marching native language dances for him and grows deft." She remarks that Nietzsche is only for "the energetic, the playful and the free."[21]

In 1911 Rabbi Fineshriber became assistant rabbi of Children of Israel in Memphis, Tennessee. When Dr. Max Samfield died on 28 September 1915, Fineshriber became rabbi.[22] Although small in number, Memphis Jews had played an important role in the city's history. In education, law, medicine, business, charitable enterprises, and culture, they were highly visible. Fineshriber's rabbinic predecessors—Jacob Peres, Simon Tuska, and Max Samfield—had all been community activists, honored by Memphis for their eleemosynary, cultural, and literary contributions. For example, banner newspaper headlines announced the death of Samfield. To commemorate the loss to Memphis, the streetcars were stopped for ten minutes.[23]

Thus the Memphis pulpit was an ideal location for Fineshriber; he encountered an audience that was highly receptive, expecting a rabbi to share his wisdom. His quick wit and talent for extemporaneous speaking were impressive (he rarely required any notes or special preparation).[24] Dr. Julian Feibelman of New Orleans, who served as Rabbi Fineshriber's assistant in Philadelphia, recalled his remarkable facility of expression. "You could wake him out of a sound sleep and ask him to speak on Einstein's Theory of Relativity and he would charm you with what he had to say."[25] Fortunately the newspapers loved him and quoted him frequently; otherwise, the historian would be hard-pressed for documentation.

The issue of women's rights was an early concern of Fineshriber, even though the vast majority of the "best element" of Fineshriber's Memphis contemporaries (religious and lay) were decidedly antifeminist. Active in the Equal Suffrage Association, he was the first man in the tri-state area (Arkansas, Mississippi, and Tennessee) to plead for the cause, itemizing the injustices suffered by women.[26] Grace Prescott, in her study of the suffrage movement in Memphis, describes him as "one of the most forceful speakers in the city for universal suffrage."[27] At a 1913 meeting of the Equal Suffrage Association he stated, "Equal suffrage is no longer a matter of speculation. Such forces are being marshalled together by women that within a few years equal suffrage will be granted by the United States, and the states slow to act will be forced to give in."[28]

When two Memphis suffrage clubs sponsored a women's day at the 1913 Tri-State Fair, the featured speakers representing Louisiana, Arkansas, Mississippi, and Tennessee were all females, with one exception: Rabbi Fineshriber.[29] Closing a rally in Court Square, held on 2 May 1914, he pleaded: "Taxation without representation is tyranny. . . . Woman has been taxed severely, and it is not a question of financial burden. For ages woman has borne the burden. . . . [The] purpose of this meeting . . . is to shock the people of Memphis into a realization that the question of equal suffrage is not child's play. We are to show the citizens of Memphis that this is no parlor game. Women seeking the right to vote have the backing of the best element among men and of the church."[30]

Shortly after his arrival in Philadelphia in 1924, Fineshriber was asked by an *Inquirer* reporter about the state of female morality. He replied that a "bare leg or cigarette never made nor marred anyone's morality. Right thinking and right doing lie wholly within ourselves."[31] As an advocate of women's rights and in line with his contemporary, Denver judge Ben Lindsey, he anticipated attitudes two generations hence. A headline dated 14 December 1927 suggests this modernity: "Com-

panionate Marriage [i.e., living together] Endorsed by Fineshriber. Former Memphis Rabbi Says Freedom of Woman Makes It Necessary to
Acknowledge Rights and Privileges."[32]

Rabbi Fineshriber's advocacy of human rights extended to other repressed members of society, including African Americans. At the time
of his arrival, about 75,000 blacks lived in Memphis, constituting 40
percent of its population. This was a period of transition in the mid-
South. Thousands of native-born Memphis blacks migrated to northern cities. At the same time thousands of newcomers arrived from rural
Mississippi, Tennessee, Arkansas, Alabama, and Louisiana. As historian
David Tucker put it, "All the roads in the Mid-South led to Memphis,
a bustling river town and the home of Beale Street."[33] Everything was
available, from religion to vice. Although many blacks were poor and
employed in the typical service occupations, jobs in the lumber industry,
railroad yards, cooperage plants, and public schools were plentiful.
There were black lawyers, doctors, and druggists, black newspapers, and
black banks. A small middle class competed with Jews and Italians, owning groceries, restaurants, drugstores, laundries, funeral homes, and sa-
loons.[34]

The black middle class endorsed mayoral candidates and asked for
their fair share of urban services. But they were restrained in their demands because they controlled fewer voters than the Crump machine.
Working with saloon keepers and ward bosses, the machine paid the
two-dollar poll tax for many blacks, registered them, and cast their
votes. Memphis was the only major southern city where African Americans were never disfranchised after Reconstruction.[35]

It is not surprising that black clergy tended to follow the accommodationist line advocated by Booker T. Washington. The age of accommodation had begun in the 1890s. Outspoken Reverend B. A. Imes, "who
saw God leading America into an integrated society," left Memphis.[36]
Like journalist Ida B. Wells, who had so eloquently attacked the practice of lynching, black pastors who criticized the prevailing dispensa-
tion were driven out of town, never to return. Memphis black clergy
did not plead for an integrated society but adjusted to the status quo,
advising African Americans to follow the Christian way of life in order
to win over the whites by their fine example. The city was left "without
even the most mildly militant of black clergymen."[37] At the end of the
1930s, black scholar Ralph Bunche criticized the Memphis black clergy,
"The Negro preachers of Memphis as a whole have avoided social questions. . . . They have preached thunder and lightning, fire and brimstone
. . . but about the economic and political exploitation of the Negro in
Memphis they have remained silent."[38]

On 22 May 1917 there occurred what Kenneth T. Jackson called "one of the most vicious lynchings in American history."[39] Without a trial Ell Persons, an African American man accused of raping and then decapitating a sixteen-year-old white girl, was burned alive before 15,000 witnesses. After the immolation the heart was cut out and the dismembered remains were scattered among a group of blacks and then displayed for public perusal. The event was anticipated in the press for several days without a word of alarm or admonition uttered. The day after the lynching one newspaper ran a banner headline above the name of the newspaper, which read "Persons Burned Over Saturated Pyre." Under the heading "Lynch Bulletins" appeared grotesque descriptions of the preparations for the lynching more bizarre than anything Franz Kafka or Oliver Stone ever imagined.[40] They illustrate the barbarous mentality Fineshriber would challenge:

> Two trucks loaded with bottled drinks did a landoffice business at the scene of the lynching. The thirsty thousands soon depleted the supply.
>
> Several "gallant" members of the mob strove to open up an unobstructed view of the negro's burning body for women who were unable to get close enough to witness the affair. The attempt failed because of the jam around the pyre.
>
> Conspicuous among the mob were several venders of sandwiches and chewing gum. Their sales were enormous.
>
> Of those who remained throughout the night, some were singing practically all the time.
>
> Women with children in their arms stampeded with several hundred men to rush for souvenirs. Bits of Person's clothing were snatched from his burning body and the huge rope with which he was first secured was cut into shreds.
>
> Broken down automobiles lined the roads from the scene all the way to town. Owners were unable to get service from Memphis, negro chauffeurs fearing to appear in the vicinity.

Without considering the danger to himself and his congregation William Fineshriber exercised what he considered his duty to speak out. He recalled his horror and dismay and the steps he took to awaken the conscience of the community. "[I] went back to my home and wrote a note to the congregation, called a meeting of my congregation and said we ought to be the first to state publicly what we think about the horrible thing of burning a Negro. . . . I knew the editor of the *Commercial Appeal* [C. P. J. Mooney] very well. He was a member of a group that I belonged to [the Egyptians] and so I had perfect facilities to meet him and talk to him. And I told him about it and he wrote a very fine editorial about the thing, saying what a shame it was that the city of Memphis had been disgraced by someone burning a Negro."[41]

A notice of the congregation's meeting and protest appeared in the *Commercial Appeal* on 23 May. On 24 May about twenty clergymen representing several Memphis clerical associations met at the chamber of commerce.[42] At this meeting Dr. T. E. Sharp, president of the Protestant Pastors Association, presided, and Rabbi Fineshriber acted as secretary.[43] Fineshriber asked the newspapermen to leave the room so the ministers could deliberate privately. Six African American ministers were present but remained silent during the proceedings. After the meeting was concluded, copies of the resolution that had been endorsed by the clergymen were "handed out to the newspapers by Rabbi Fineshriber":

> We, the clergymen of the city of Memphis, met in solemn assembly, do hereby resolve that we, as clergymen and citizens, confess our dereliction of duty in not having warned an inflamed public against mob violence when it was apparent to every reader of newspapers that preparations had been made for a lynching. . . . We furthermore resolve that it should be brought home also to the consciences of other representatives, men and leaders of the community, that they, too, failed in their duty; and by inadequate preparations to resist their anarchic designs to take the proper measures to defend the dignity and majesty of the law and our civilization; and that the conscience of the community had been dulled to the apprehension of the enormity of such lynchings and their accompanying degeneracies.
>
> We call upon the citizens of this community to put away the false theory that lynchings are deterrents to crime, to realize that mob violence saps the foundation of democracy, law and civilization; that we cannot rear our children in safety if we set the example of law breaking and give it our sanction. We appeal for the continued extension of mental, moral, industrial and spiritual education of the negro as the most effective deterrents of crime. We appeal to our fellow citizens to stand together as one in behalf of a law abiding, law enforcing and law respecting community.[44]

Fineshriber "argued and pleaded" with C. P. J. Mooney, editor of the *Commercial Appeal*, the largest newspaper in Memphis, "until I was able to convince him that it was the duty of the newspaper to fight such brutality."[45] The resulting 25 May editorial was extremely mild and cautious; however, the newspapers published the much more forceful statement of the Memphis clergy the same day.[46]

Fineshriber's attacks on racism and bigotry continued into the 1920s. He was the only Memphis clergyman with the courage and conviction to criticize the Ku Klux Klan, even from the pulpit. An announcement of his intentions to "preach on the Ku Klux Klan" appeared in the *Commercial Appeal* on 12 October 1921. The article mentioned that "it is believed the nature of the lecture will attract a great many people to the Temple, aside from members of the congregation." Apparently Fineshriber's sermons on important social issues were now considered community events.

The sermon was reported in an article headlined "Fineshriber Assails 'Mob Law' of K. K. K." According to the reporter, the rabbi denounced "the Ku Klux Klan as an organized mob fostering the survival of the Anglo-Saxon race in America, even unto the exclusion of all other Americans." He then "prescribed tolerance and brotherly love as the only effective antidotes to be used by right thinking people against the klan, in order that the constitutional rights of Americans may be upheld." Many of Fineshriber's remarks were highly palliative and must have pleased the conservatives. He defended the original Klan created after the Civil War to cope with vagrancy and vandalism: "There is no use to discuss the present Ku Klux Klan until we look a bit into its history. It was taken from the old body who were determined that the negro should not wield the sceptre of government over the white man. . . . Owing to the attitude of the federal government after the Civil War, an appeal to it would have been futile. The klan was therefore the inevitable step. It served its purpose admirably. It functioned with a certain amount of law and decency."

Obviously Fineshriber's views of the first Klan expressed the prevailing historical sentiments of his day. Accurate histories of the first Klan did not then exist. From such obeisant observations, however, he lured his audience away from old formulas towards logical reasoning.

America is largely made up of Anglo-Saxons. The Ku Kluxers consider themselves 100 per cent Americans. The idea behind the organization, if it is sincere, is a reflection of the old notion that the minority must be hated by the mob until it is stamped out. Let us pray that the world has been sufficiently enlightened through the great struggle of war to make us realize that might is not right and that the glamor of a white robe does not take the place of justice meted out through the regular channels of law in the courts. . . .

The policy of the Ku Klux Klan would tear down order and substitute mob law, when there is no occasion for it. It is a menace to
the principles of Americans and far more dangerous than Bolshe-
vism. Let us hope that right thinkers let it be dissolved naturally
and without force. Education, not force, is the cure.

Fineshriber was well aware that the words "Bolshevik" and "Jew" were
considered equivalent by many Americans of that time.

The revised Klan arrived in Memphis early in 1921, rapidly grew in
membership and activities, and made its first public appearance in the
Armistice Day parade, less than a month after Fineshriber's speech.[47]
The rabbi subsequently continued his war with the Klan from his pulpit
and from the lecture platforms of various organizations.[48] In an interview made six weeks before his death at age eighty-nine, he relived vivid
memories of his struggle and the danger he courted.[49] Threats had been
made against him as well as his wife and two young sons. When asked
about these threats, he replied, "[Yes,] my younger brother, who is dead,
came to Memphis at that time, saw the situation and said, 'You're aw-
fully cocky. I am very much afraid you will run into trouble.' He said,
'I am going to leave a little reminiscence with you,' and he gave me a
pistol. The reason he gave me the pistol was because we had beds on the
back porch of our house. . . . The children and we slept on the porch
facing our yard. And he said, 'This is a very dangerous thing you are
doing. Someone might come up; that's why I am giving you the pistol.' " Then he added with a smile, "I still have the pistol. I haven't used
it, but I still have it."

In 1921 Rabbi Fineshriber's friend and confidant C. P. J. Mooney
launched an attack on the Klan through editorials, articles exposing the
financial irregularities of the KKK, reports of Klan and anti-Klan activities around the country, and front-page cartoons by J. P. Alley.[50] Irish
Catholic Charles Patrick Joseph Mooney knew that the KKK in the
mid-South directed its most vicious attacks at the Catholic Church.
Others joined the anti-Klan phalanx, including Episcopal Bishop F.
Gailor (a close friend of Fineshriber), who denounced the Klan on 26
December 1922 as "the curse of the country."[51]

Under Mr. Crump's aegis the political establishment of Memphis,
including Mayor Rowlett Paine, hated the Klan. Crump's machine
benefitted from the infamous Memphis red-light district, accepting
contributions from madams. The Klan, representing itself as the purest
expression of white Protestantism, did not hesitate to condemn Crump
as a "wet" with lax moral standards. The elections of 1923 proved to be
a disaster for the Klan when all its candidates (except one) were soundly

defeated by the Crump machine. Subsequently the KKK lacked political power in Memphis. In 1923 the Pulitzer Prize was awarded to the *Commercial Appeal* for its courageous campaign against the "Invisible Empire."[52]

That Memphis was perhaps unique in its relatively unified and successful assault on the Klan does not vitiate Fineshriber's actions. He acted as the catalyst and stood out among the clergy. Fineshriber had taken a statesman-like position, for a wise statesman pursues lofty ideals but knows what is possible and what is impossible. He had a sense of timing. If Fineshriber had spoken out openly for equality, he, like his black equivalents, would have been "driven out of town." Instead his acceptance grew with each successive campaign for justice.

Fineshriber made positive, concrete suggestions for how the unfortunate conditions of the African American might be ameliorated. His excellent rapport with the business community enabled him to gain an audience. Addressing the Memphis realtors, for example, he offered them the kind of paternalistic advice that would receive a decent hearing: "[Solving] the problem of better homes for the negro population is a matter that will eventually have to be looked into by the realtors. This can be done in such a way as to make the community a better place in which to live. Every man is the product of his environment, and by putting the colored people on a higher plane of living, the beneficial results will fall to the city itself."[53] Once again the persuasive orator was moving white Memphians in the right direction by using language they could accept without squirming.

Fineshriber also helped raise funds for the African American community as he did for the Catholic community and others. For instance, on 9 December 1923 he gave what was advertised as a "Grand Lecture under the auspices of the Howe Choral Class" (a well-known black choir) at the African American St. John's Baptist Church. At this meeting funds were collected to run the church for a year.[54]

Had Fineshriber remained in Memphis longer than a dozen years he undoubtedly would have returned the focus of his attention to advance the interests of African Americans. Following the KKK campaign Fineshriber used his remaining Memphis tenure to open Memphis's eyes to the plight of many others. Addressing the Masons on 7 October 1921, he spoke of the extensive unemployment in Memphis and expressed chagrin and shock at "the great mass of indifferent citizenry."[55] He spoke sympathetically for the World War I veterans' compensation act, more commonly called the "Bonus Bill."[56] He was the first Memphian to express the need for tariff revisions and the cancellation of the European debt reparations, which played havoc with the world economy.[57]

While in Memphis Fineshriber worked for a great variety of worthwhile philanthropic organizations crossing denominational lines. He was an active Rotarian, Shriner, and member of the Scottish Rite. Civil organizations that benefitted from his efforts included the Drama League (he served as vice president), the Little Theatre movement, the Nineteenth Century Club, the Home of the Good Shepherd, Southwestern College, and the Boy Scout movement.[58] He was instrumental in creating organizations and institutions that would foster thoughtful reform. For instance, he was a charter member of The Egyptians club (the name was proposed by him because ancient Memphis was in Egypt). This "club for the discussion of scientific, religious, economic and other topics pertaining to the welfare, culture and happiness of the people" was founded in 1911 and still publishes papers read by members.[59]

The 11 July 1924 newsletter of the Memphis Rotary Club illustrates why the community valued Fineshriber's participation in service organizations:

> Our own Bill Fineshriber, who has been called to the City of Brotherly Love, will sing his swan song to us.
>
> It is strictly against our idea of good government to speak well of any except the dead, but in this instance we cannot refrain from mounting the rostrum to tell the suffering world that we regard Bill Fineshriber as typifying all that is high and noble in the human race.
>
> When Bill speaks, it is like the soft cadence of music. He has the knack of saying something, and always saying it beautifully. Of course, there are only a few of us who can follow the trend of his discourse, but we know the rest of you like it too. We never saw such a little squirt so burdened with brains and culture as Bill is. It will be a shame for Bill to waste his eloquence on a Philadelphia congregation asleep in the temple. But we nevertheless wish him much health, happiness and success in the Third City.
>
> We have another Ku Klux in Rotary who has a brilliant mind. We refer to Charles Haase.[60]

The ironic KKK attribution to two Jewish Rotarians is a telling example of Fineshriber's having defused the power of the Klan.

In Fineshriber's brief tenure as rabbi of Congregation Children of Israel, a new temple was built, the congregation doubled in membership, and the religious school grew from 100 to 550. His contributions to the work of B'nai B'rith, the Associated Jewish Charities, the Jewish Neighborhood House, the Young Men's Hebrew Association, and the Jewish Chautauqua movement were significant. He held offices in several of these organizations.[61] Rabbi Fineshriber also taught courses at the University of Tennessee at Knoxville (summer school) and lectured at Tulane, Harvard, and Peabody.[62] His lectures in Memphis covered a range of subjects, including "In Defense of Germany," urging that America remain neutral in World War I (later published by The Egyptians club); a well-publicized series of lectures defending the theory of evolution, which were well attended by Memphians of all persuasions and quoted in detail in the newspapers; and lectures on many literary figures, including Shaw, Molnar, Tolstoy, O'Neill, and Kipling. To reach an even wider audience he spoke in such places as Helena, Arkansas; Shreveport, Louisiana; and Chicago, Illinois.[63]

When Fineshriber left for Philadelphia, the themes of "race tolerance" and "brotherhood" appeared repeatedly in the many tributes showered upon him. Memphis knew full-well Fineshriber's stance on lynching and the Ku Klux Klan. His brave words and actions were part of the recent past, not ancient history. An article dealing with Fineshriber's final sermon at his temple concluded, "Dr. Fineshriber has invariably placed the value of action above preaching. It has been his aim to teach Memphis racial and religious tolerance. He is a man of great stature and a spiritual leader of rare dedication."[64] Editorials commending Fineshriber, especially for his civic leadership, appeared in both city newspapers.

In those things that concern the welfare of the city Dr. Fineshriber has been a leader and a builder. He is a man of ripe scholarship and he will be equal to the duties that will fall to him in his new field. Philadelphia is a city wherein scholarship and culture are evaluated at their real worth.

. . . Few men have been more closely identified with the moral and intellectual advancement of the community and the promotion of worthy and deserving enterprises. . . . He is a strong champion of justice and fair play. All men would be better if they would keep before them the ideals that he has as his standard. . . . He possesses the gift of being at the same time a powerful and convincing speaker. Few communities have many such men. No community has enough of them. For many he has changed the standard of values.[65]

This "standard of values" was beautifully enunciated in Fineshriber's farewell address in the Pantages Theater for an audience of two thousand, a cross section of Memphis. The invitation to the event stated, "This will be a community service, thus emphasizing that element in Fineshriber's work which has so endeared him to the people of Memphis of all races and creeds." The article reporting on the address, headlined "Rabbi's Farewell Is Tolerance Plea: Forget Hate That Memphis May Grow Urges Fineshriber," read: "[Memphis] will never rise to her predestined height if the reactionaries rule. The wiseacres who hark back to the good old times are enemies of Progress. . . . The spirit of ferment and unrest can be seen in Memphis now. Thank God for that, for that spirit is necessary for the growth of cities. . . . There are those who view with alarm any new movement. They are the ones who shut their eyes to the world's advance. They are spiritually and mentally dying or dead. . . . The spirit of false Americanism must be replaced by real Americanism of the kind that realizes that America was discovered, colonized, and developed by men of all races and creeds."[66]

Two weeks later Fineshriber was quoted in the *New York Herald-Times* from a speech he made in Atlantic City, echoing verbatim the stirring final words of his Memphis farewell.[67] Yet another "farewell," this time to Prescott, Arkansas, reiterated the brotherhood theme: "I have tried to get people of all races and creeds to love one another."[68]

An article in the *Philadelphia Inquirer* containing Fineshriber's inaugural sermon as head rabbi of Keneseth Israel Congregation in Philadelphia was headlined "Time of Segregations Is Past" and read: "[And,] finally, it [the synagogue] must be a Place of Meeting for All Peoples. The time is past for segregations and for clans. God created the human race; human races are the invention of man. To be hospitable, to be democratic, in short, to love our neighbors as ourselves, is a fundamental doctrine of the synagogue."[69]

It would not be an exaggeration to say Fineshriber ministered to the whole community. He believed in a pluralistic, intellectually "open" society and fought against any kind of religion by edict. Thus he considered blue laws "damnable." He noted, "To attempt to legislate goodness and religion into society is vicious in its conception and damnable in its results."[70] Faced with the insular mentality of Memphis, he never spoke condescendingly. Instead he charmed Memphians to bring out the best in them, and they adored him for his candor although they didn't always understand him. When asked what Memphis needed most, he answered, "a university or two."[71] This was a diplomatic answer given the dearth of learning Memphis exemplified. In 1927 Temple University of Philadelphia, a Baptist institution, awarded Dr. Fineshriber an honorary doctor of divinity degree because of his "service and impartial sympathy that knows no distinction of race, color, or creed."[72] No comparable Memphis institution existed to recognize his work for civil rights.

Had Fineshriber remained in Memphis and had another racial crisis occurred, he would no doubt have spoken out, as was his wont. It was a pity for Memphis that he (all too human) left for a higher-paying and larger pulpit. (Fineshriber's successor, Harry T. Ettelson, continued the tradition of public service. In an interview in 1968 he recalled the biracial meetings of the Cross-Cut Club, an interdenominational organization of Memphis clergy. Ettelson initiated the contacts with the black ministers. Ettelson's successor, James Wax, would revive the more activist role of Fineshriber, heading the ministers' association in a time of racial strife.) When Fineshriber left Memphis, he was praised by everyone from Mayor Rowlett Paine on down for "being an influential factor in the development of the moral and social life of the city."[73] The fact that he was able to challenge racial prejudice and bigotry and be praised to boot was remarkable.

II

THE HEYDAY

This section juxtaposes an initial essay that questions the motivation, commitment, and involvement of Jews—rabbis in particular—in the modern civil rights movement with a series of case studies that document widespread, albeit varied, participation with roots deep in Jewish tradition and historical experience.

Under what pressures did the rabbis work? What were their relationships to their congregants, other clergy, and members of the general community? What factors in their backgrounds, experiences, and personalities influenced their choices? How did their thoughts and actions compare with those of others in their communities and elsewhere? What were their survival mechanisms? Can an individual's impact be measured? By what standards can people decades later evaluate? With such extensive variation, can one really speak of "the South"? These are but some of the questions alluded to here that require continued study.

"Hamans" and "Torquemadas":
Southern and Northern Jewish Responses
to the Civil Rights Movement, 1945–1965

MARC DOLLINGER

Marc Dollinger offers a problematic view of Jewish participation in the struggle for black civil rights, reflecting the interpretations of Leonard Dinnerstein and especially John Bracey, Jr., and August Meier. In this view, although some northern and southern Jews participated actively in a positive way, most adapted to the racial mores of their time and place and strove first and foremost for acceptance. Reminiscent of Martin Luther King, Jr., Dollinger implies that those who believed in racial justice and yet remained largely silent were perhaps as much if not more of the problem than the outright racists. What is the responsibility of those who remain silent out of fear or simply apathy? This is a question of strategy as well as values and deserves further scrutiny.

In 1963, at the height of the civil rights movement, Rabbi Richard Winograd, interim director of University of Chicago Hillel, journeyed to Birmingham, Alabama, to protest racial segregation. Local African American leaders hailed the rabbi as a man committed to high moral ideals, but the Jewish community opposed Winograd's effort and criticized him for his high-publicity venture. "I had the feeling," the rabbi explained in reference to two great villains in Jewish history, "that we somehow were the Hamans and Torquemadas" to southern Jews.[1]

Although one might expect a spiritual leader to admonish his southern coreligionists for their stand on civil rights, Winograd refused. "I was not fully convinced," he explained, "that we had a right to place the Jewish community of Birmingham in a more dangerous position than we are willing and able to place ourselves." From a moral point of view the rabbi believed "the scales were very even." Instead of lamenting southern Jewish recalcitrance, Winograd was pained about "the circumstances which had led to pitting Jew against Jew."[2]

The Chicago Hillel director understood that in the South public support for black equality threatened to undo generations of peaceful coexistence between southern Jews and their white neighbors. Jews south of the Mason-Dixon line lived in a climate of fear and intimidation. Synagogue bombings, threats of economic boycott, and violence directed against civil rights workers convinced most southern Jews to follow less confrontational strategies. A 1961 poll, for example, revealed that 97 percent of the northern Jewish population registered its approval for the landmark *Brown* decision whereas a substantial 40 percent of southern Jews considered the ruling "unfortunate." A majority of southern Jews believed that desegregation was moving too quickly and criticized "Yankee agitators" and "northern do-gooders" for interfering. Southern Jews had been acculturated into an American culture foreign to their northern coreligionists. They belonged to the South, and if they wanted to succeed in their America, they had to remain sensitive to the attitudes of those in the surrounding community.[3]

Winograd's Alabama experience captured the complex and sometimes contradictory Jewish attitudes toward the civil rights movement. On one hand, the rabbi's visit demonstrated northern Jewish commitment to racial equality. Scores of Winograd's rabbinic colleagues and thousands of lay Jews punctuated their support for the civil rights movement by traveling south and participating in rallies, marches, and political protests. On the other hand, by empathizing with the painful moral dilemma facing southern Jews, Winograd defended more than just his Birmingham coreligionists: he offered an unwitting defense for a northern Jewish community caught in its own debate concerning the wisdom of civil rights reform in the South and later in the North. Despite the impressive public efforts of many Jewish liberals in the civil rights struggle, even northerners wavered in their commitment to racial equality.

Between 1945 and 1954 northern Jewish support for racial equality could best be described as ambivalent. In the decade after the *Brown* decision, northern Jews balanced their commitment to the civil rights movement against their desire to succeed in segregated suburban hometowns. The confrontation in Birmingham represented more than just intrareligious squabbling over the best civil rights strategy: it revealed how southern and northern Jews linked their own successful acculturation to the legal status of the nation's African American minority.[4]

For Winograd and his northern brethren, support of the civil rights movement in the South meant more than opposition to Jim Crow and a desire to extend constitutional protections to all Americans. By marching in protests, registering voters, or casting ballots for pro–civil rights politicians, northern Jews enjoyed the opportunity to advance a model of pluralist democracy that validated their own rapid rise to the American middle class. The civil rights movement reaffirmed the viability of the American Jewish experience and established Jews as a model ethnic minority. In just two generations northern Jews managed impressive successes in business, exerted political influence in local and state elections, and finally began breaking through the quota barriers at the nation's leading colleges and universities. The image of another ethnic minority denied basic civil rights struck a sensitive chord. Although their position proved naive and often paternalistic, most northern Jews believed that the elimination of racist barriers in the South could offer African Americans their own version of Jewish American success just as it guaranteed a pluralist society amenable to continued Jewish mobility.

Southern Jews and the Civil Rights Movement

The story of southern Jews and the civil rights movement begins with the Jews' distinctive acculturation in the American South. In the antebellum period German Jews settled throughout the South, establishing themselves as leaders in merchandising and trade. They adapted to the larger non-Jewish white community, enjoying both material prosperity and social acceptance. As late as the 1940s the South boasted the lowest rate of anti-Jewish discrimination in the country. Although incidents such as the Leo Frank hanging in 1915 kept them aware of their own marginality, southern Jews escaped most of the ideological anti-Semitism that swept the urban North and the agricultural Midwest in the late nineteenth and early twentieth centuries.[5]

Maintaining good relations with the surrounding white community proved crucial to the physical as well as economic well-being of southern Jews. Geographic and demographic factors insulated northern Jews from much of the ugliness of racial politics, but southern Jews lived a more vulnerable existence. In 1964 Jews in Birmingham, Alabama, numbered only 4,000 among an overall population of 630,000. Their rabbi lamented that they were "very very vulnerable." Montgomery claimed 1,800 Jews among a population of 134,000. Other southern towns numbered similarly small Jewish communities.[6]

By the end of World War II southern Jews faced a critical dilemma:

how to respond to the growing calls for racial equality. Established southern Jews counted themselves as sons and daughters of Dixie and remained recalcitrant. In Jackson, Mississippi, for example, they assimilated to such a large degree that their rabbi considered them "indistinguishable in ideology" from the surrounding community and "as racist as any white non-Jew." Montgomery Jews advertised their affiliation with the White Citizen's Council "in an attempt to show that they are at one with the majority viewpoint in the Gentile community." They claimed that their actions sought "to inhibit the growth of anti-Semitism." The local Jackson newspaper boasted that "today many a fine Jewish leader is part of the southern resistance. Jackson's citizen's council, outstanding in South and Nation, points to them with pride." Even rabbis from long-established southern families defended the distinctive "southern way of life," took issue with northern Jewish critics, and defended the racial status quo.[7]

Other southern Jews, many of whom had only recently moved from the North, pressed for change. In the rabbinic community some championed the civil rights cause at great risk to themselves, their families, and their congregations. Others distinguished between what they called a private commitment to racial equality and their public responsibility to protect their synagogue membership from the considerable wrath of the larger white community. In all cases, southern Jews faced the difficult task of choosing between racial equality for blacks and their own physical, economic, and social well-being.

Incidents of anti-Semitism remained rare through the end of World War II, but by the 1950s the association of northern and some southern Jews with the civil rights movement precipitated an increase in violent anti-Semitism. At Temple Beth-El in Charlotte, North Carolina, eleven sticks of dynamite were found in November of 1957. Within eight months similar incidents occurred in Gastonia, North Carolina, and Birmingham, Alabama. On 16 March 1958 Miami's Beth-el Congregation rocked as a bomb exploded, and the congregation's rabbi, Abraham Levitan, received threats not to preach about integration. Rabbi Jacob Rothschild of Atlanta acknowledged that a bombing of his synagogue in October 1958 occurred in part "because I was so obviously identified with the civil rights movement."[8]

Although most non-Jewish white civil rights leaders in the South condemned the bombings, they did little to alleviate fears within the southern Jewish community. Bombings waned in 1959 but increased again in the 1960s. In addition to threats of physical violence, public support for the civil rights struggle opened southern Jews to threats of economic boycott from white customers, but any refusal to join the movement invited action from African American customers. When Martin Luther King, Jr., organized a picket line around a store in Birmingham, Alabama, the community's rabbi, Milton Grafman, appealed to the civil rights leader for understanding. During a meeting between the local clergy and civil rights organizers, Grafman explained that his congregants were "caught in a vise between the Negroes and the Whites—they couldn't win for losing." Although northern Jews spent the first fifteen years of the civil rights movement observing from afar, southern Jews struggled in the eye of the storm.[9]

As Isaac Toubin explained in the *Southern Israelite*, "Jews who espouse and defend the cause of civil rights jeopardize the security of isolated Jewish communities in the South, threaten their social integration and economic position, and ultimately even their physical safety." "The Jew in the South," one rabbi explained, "despite his long residence in the area and the high place he has attained in communal life, remains insecure." When pressed on the civil rights question, he explained that "the vast majority, however doubtful they may be about the morality of segregation, will neither express integrationist sentiments nor identify themselves with an integrationist movement." Southern Jewish survival demanded acceptance of the status quo.[10]

Nevertheless, by adopting the racial attitudes of the larger white society, southern Jews invited criticism from the African American community. When asked about the role of southern Jews in the civil rights movement, Aaron Henry, Mississippi's NAACP director, explained that "the image of the Jew in national civil rights activity has not rubbed off on the Jewish population of Mississippi. There is little difference, if any, between the Gentile White and the Jew in their treatment of the Negro." For Henry the indifference of southern Jews to racial equality "was the greatest surprise of my civil rights career." Reverend Fred Shuttlesworth condemned southern Jews for refusing to use their considerable economic power to help end segregation. "The Jewish people could have done more, since they had control," he wrote to a young rabbinic student in 1965; "if the Jewish people actually were . . . actively committed to crusading and would apply their economic power to it, you would do it overnight." In a letter to Birmingham clergy, Martin Luther King specifically criticized the southern Jewish community for feigning support for racial equality by supporting slow, measured change: "I have almost reached the regrettable conclusion," he wrote, "that the Negro's greatest stumbling block in the stride toward freedom is not the White Citizen's Councilor or the Ku Klux Klanner, but the white moderate who . . . constantly says, 'I agree with you on the goal you seek, but I can't agree with your methods.' "[11]

The Southern Rabbinate

The southern Jews' overriding security concerns prevented even those who considered themselves liberal, especially rabbis, from acting publicly. "The whole Jewish community might become a target for antagonism," one such Jew explained; "other Jews would fear that one was risking the status of the entire ethnic group, and many local Jews felt that no one had any right to upset the delicate balance whereby Jews had been treated well and accepted generally as fellow southerners."[12] Southern rabbis occupied a precarious position in southern Jewish life. Their self-selection as guardians of ethics and morality demanded understanding for black inequality, yet the congregants they were hired to serve often insisted on keeping "politics off the pulpit." Rabbinic attitudes about the civil rights movement tested the relative strength of traditional Jewish values against the realities of southern living.

A few rabbis, transplanted by and large from the North and filling posts in the urban South, managed a vigil in defense of racial equality. Rabbi Jacob Rothschild of Atlanta's Reform congregation, himself victimized by white racists when his synagogue was bombed in 1958, criticized the delaying tactics of those, including President Eisenhower, who believed that "you can't legislate the hearts of men." That argument, voiced by self-described civil rights moderates, amounted in Rothschild's estimation to "as specious a statement as ever beguiled the soul." "Laws do not wait for general acceptance," he implored, "they stimulate and coerce a way of life that is better." Arthur Levin, the regional director of the Anti-Defamation League (ADL) in the South from 1948–1962, hailed another religious leader, Charles Mantinband, as an "example of a rabbi who was outspoken and who made no compromises with his conscience and his congregation." Malcolm Stern, a colleague of Mantinband's, called him "a quiet self-effacing individual whose fervent belief in the equality of mankind led him, as the rabbi of Hattiesburg, Mississippi, to take the presidency of that state's Council on Human Relations."[13]

Most, though, fearing retribution from both the white community and their own congregants, refused to take public stands on the issue of civil rights. William Malev, a Houston rabbi in one of the South's largest synagogues, explained that in communities where congregants opposed integration, "the rabbis have not spoken out, and to have done so would have been to invite resentment and anti-Semitism, if not, indeed, violence towards the Jewish community." Rabbi Moses Landau, spiritual leader of the Jews in Cleveland, Mississippi, explained that "if you are going to take sides and agitate, you accomplish nothing, except the hostility of the people." Landau believed that if he had decided to support the civil rights movement, that support "would have been limited to twenty-four hours." After that single day, he stated, "I wouldn't be there in the state anymore." With the prevailing segregationist mentality, Landau argued, "the Jewish community could not exist, could not exist, if they were in any way involved in the civil movement."

In 1957 Rabbi Eugene Blachschleger of Montgomery said that he "made no public pronouncements on this subject [desegregation] either from my pulpit or in the columns of our daily press." Rabbi Martin Hinchin of Alexandria, Louisiana, refused to discuss civil rights from the pulpit as well. "I have my own ideas," he acknowledged, but "I don't foist [them] upon my own congregation . . . because I don't want to harm the Jewish community in any way, shape, or form."[14]

In a 1965 interview Hinchin stated that he "would like to see, of course, the Negro to have fair treatment, in all respects." Yet, he added, "he's going to have to earn it to a certain degree himself." The Alexandria rabbi adopted the prevailing belief that "you can't legislate sociology," and advocated a measured response to racial inequality. The African American, Hinchin affirmed, "is going to have to prove himself—through education, through his own morals (which he will do, but it's going to take time)."[15]

Some rabbis adopted the prevailing status quo belief in racial separation. Still, only a few, willing to break with the tradition of keeping personal political opinions private, chose to articulate their attitudes publicly. One who did, Malev of Houston, challenged the validity of the northern Jews' morality-based defense of racial equality. Malev employed segregationist language to redefine traditional notions of Jewish social action and advance a southern interpretation of Jewish ethical responsibility. He showed how spiritual leaders could fashion ethical and moral principles to their own particular needs. Although Malev did not say so explicitly, his opposition to desegregation demonstrated that the expression of Jewish political behavior owed more to conditions in the surrounding community than it did to any unchanging traditional imperative for Jewish social action.

Rabbi Malev took aim at one of the northern Jewish community's most progressive organizations, the American Jewish Congress, which at the time had announced an integration plan to build new schools in fringe locations between white- and black-populated areas. "The purpose" of such a plan, Malev insisted, "would be to *make sure* that white and colored children attend the same schools." Echoing southern segregationists, Malev objected to the fact that desegregation was "not to take place naturally and normally in the community in which white and colored children live, but they are actually to be compelled by city ordinance to go to the same schools, even where the natural centers of population do not indicate it." The rabbi reminded his civil rights coreligionists that there existed "no constitutional principle which decrees that integration must be compulsory for white and colored people." Pointing to the letter of the law, Malev noted that the Supreme Court "only stipulates that there can be no compulsory segregation, but certainly no one can argue that we must, by law, compel white and colored children who live in different neighborhoods and who could ordinarily attend their own schools to go to integrated schools, despite the fact that they do not live in the neighborhood and are not interested in attending such integrated schools." For the Houston rabbi, attempts such as the one by the American Jewish Congress had "not helped the cause of desegregation, and certainly has not made the Jew more popular among his neighbors."[16]

Malev expanded his opposition to civil rights reform by claiming that desegregation orders violated ethical law. "The reason why the Supreme Court decision on desegregation confronts such difficulties in the South," Malev contended, "is because the law is not acceptable to many thousands of southerners." The rabbi argued that because the white masses opposed federal orders, they bore no responsibility to adhere to them. This argument, a misinterpretation of Rev. King's contention that God's law superseded the immorality of Jim Crow, ignored the injustices of segregated education and conflicted with what northern Jews considered the very meaning of prophetic Judaism.[17]

Few scenes evoked as much fear and hostility in southern Jews as the sight of northern Jews proclaiming their support for the civil rights movement. Even those southern Jews who offered private support for racial equality objected to the high-profile tactics of their northern coreligionists, especially when those tactics were planned with no thought for the precarious position of the local Jewish community. "The participation of our 'defense' organizations," Malev explained in reference to the American Jewish Congress, the ADL, and the American Jewish Committee, "is not an advantage but a liability to the Jewish communities in the South." Malev complained that these Jewish bodies represented only northern interests and failed to understand the unique position of southern Jews. The rabbi criticized the apparent ignorance of the offending Jews, whom he claimed "speak with arrogance, looking down their noses at the backward and timid southern Jews and sometimes commit blunders because of their incomplete knowledge of the situation."[18]

In a few cases southern Jewish attacks on their northern coreligionists bordered on the personal. When the Reform rabbinate's governing body, the Central Conference of American Rabbis (CCAR), went on record in support of equal employment opportunities for blacks, conference member Rabbi Grafman bolted. "My colleagues who have shouted the loudest," he insisted, "have not been willing to take southern pulpits—period." Grafman continued to argue that northern rabbis spoke from high morals but lived for material success. "They like their fifteen and twenty-thousand-dollar pulpits," he explained. Grafman finished his condemnation with a rhetorical challenge to CCAR: "If you are truly sincere about your prophetic Judaism, then you would not hesitate to take a pulpit in Gadsden, Alabama, for $9,000 a year. This is what a prophet does. But he has no right to tell somebody else to commit economic suicide unless he's willing to make a sacrifice himself."[19]

The Freedom Rides

Tensions between the two communities peaked in the summer of 1961 as dozens of northern Jewish volunteers traveled to Mississippi as part of the freedom rides. "The Jews of this Mississippi town are not happy that I am here," one Jewish activist wrote; "too many of us civil rights workers are Jews it seems." In Birmingham Rabbi Grafman condemned the freedom riders for upsetting the balance between Jews and their white neighbors. "He doesn't have to live with these people," Grafman explained in reference to a northern activist, "but we do, and our people have got to live with them." When Martin Hinchin was asked whether freedom riders visited his town of Alexandria, Louisiana, he responded, "No, thank goodness," explaining that the volunteers were adding "salt to the wounds" and "not helping the situation one bit."[20]

Northern Jewish participation in the freedom rides threatened local southern Jews. At a time when even some African Americans protested the confrontational tactics of the freedom riders, southern Jews trembled at the thought of white reprisal. In many places freedom riders faced physical assault from angry whites, and in the worst scenes, segregationists lit fire to freedom buses, forcing protesters to flee for their lives. While the buses would continue rolling from town to town, many argued, the local citizenry remained to face the ire of segregationist whites.

After southern law enforcement officials arrested scores of freedom ride protesters, dozens of northern Jews sat in southern jails awaiting trial. Their families and friends back home contacted a local rabbi, Perry Nussbaum of Jackson, Mississippi, to enlist his support. Rabbi Roland Gittelsohn of Boston as well as Henry Schwartzchild, the executive director of a congregation in Glencoe, Illinois, asked Nussbaum to visit congregants jailed at the prison in nearby Parchman. Schwartz-child alluded to his own skeptical preconceptions of the southern Jewish community: "I wish I could be sure that a rabbi in Israel would not need my reminder or urging to do this act of simple compassion and sympathy with an obviously just cause." Invoking his own southern experience, Schwartzchild explained that he "came to Jackson expressly and pointedly as a Jew" and hoped "that the local rabbi, if not his community, would have the courage to *visit* the jail [Schwartzchild's emphasis]."[21]

Nussbaum responded by visiting Parchman and several other local prisons to assist the Jews detained there. Correspondence followed between the rabbi and the families of those arrested. In late July Nussbaum solicited the help of his colleagues by penning a confidential letter inviting them to a meeting to coordinate jail visitation. "Since my return last Saturday," he wrote in reference to his most recent visit, "I have been involved in getting permission to bring spiritual guidance to the Jews involved (averaging about 20 so far). As you will expect, it took a lot of talking with the authorities concerned, but I insisted on our rights as Jews, regardless of the nature of the 'crime' and as Rabbis, regardless of our position on the subject of segregation."[22]

Nussbaum enjoyed little support from his southern colleagues. Rabbi Moses Landau of Cleveland, Mississippi, condemned Nussbaum for his violation of the South's unwritten rules on issues of race. Landau saw no reason for a meeting of rabbis and opposed any jail visitations by uninvited rabbis. "I well understand why the authorities were surprised and indignant and that you had to do 'a lot of talking and insisting on our rights as Jews' when you injected yourself into a situation without being called upon to do so," he wrote as he chastised Nussbaum; "it is clear from your letter that neither the authorities nor the prisoners have asked for any spiritual help." Landau appealed to Nussbaum to consider the welfare of his congregants. "It is your privilege to be a martyr," he insisted; "there are dozens of vacant pulpits. You can pick yourself up within 24 hours and leave. Can you say the same of the about 1000 Jewish families in the state? I am paid by my Congregation, and as long as I eat their bread, I shall not do anything that might harm any member of my Congregation without their consent."[23]

Allan Schwartzman of Greenville, Mississippi, echoed Landau's sentiments. Schwartzman could not agree "in the unilateral action" taken by Nussbaum, noting that most of the freedom riders "have the wherewithal to pay their fines and be on their way back home, were it not for the cause they seemingly espouse." The Greenville rabbi questioned the wisdom of such involvement in the race issue: "I am wondering whether we as local rabbis would not be harming our people, our positions as rabbis in our communities, and the good work that we are doing in the racial problems of Mississippi," he wrote, "by 'going to bat' for these temporary inmates."[24]

Although some rabbis did volunteer to visit the jails, Nussbaum canceled his proposed meeting for lack of interest. At his own congregation, the board of directors consented "uneasily" to the visits with the stipulation that it be done, according to Nussbaum, "without identification of my congregation." Several congregants threatened to resign their temple memberships, and others registered their disapproval with the local sheriff. The freedom rides continued but without the support of most southern rabbis.[25]

Northern Jews and the Civil Rights Movement

Northern Jews chronicled impressive feats in the struggle for civil rights. Leaders of northern Jewish organizations waged legislative battles on Capitol Hill, and their constituents around the country supported the Student Non-Violent Coordinating Committee, the Congress of Racial Equality, and the National Association for the Advancement of Colored People. Jewish students comprised roughly two-thirds of all the white freedom riders in the summer of 1961 and more than a third of the volunteers for the 1964 Mississippi voter registration campaign. When freedom riders traveled through the South to test complicity with federal desegregation laws, 62 percent of the northern Jewish community approved, and an astonishing 96 percent backed President Kennedy's decision to send United States marshals to Montgomery, Alabama. Northern Jewish representation in the struggle grew so strong that one historian referred to the postwar period as the "Jewish phase of the civil rights revolution."[26]

Despite their overwhelming support for the civil rights struggle in the South, however, northern Jews struggled with the same acculturative forces that limited southern Jewish activism. Between 1945 and 1954, when the political spotlight shone away from the civil rights issue, northern Jews often sacrificed their defense of racial equality in favor of political programs that would speed the Jews' social and economic mobility. Even in the glory years between the *Brown* decision and passage of the landmark Civil Rights Act of 1964, northern Jews, striving for inclusion in their new middle-class suburbs, emulated the race-based policies of their larger communities.

When the civil rights movement focused on northern urban racial inequality in the years after 1965, all but the most ardent Jews faced the uncomfortable realization that they had journeyed much closer to the southern Jewish position on civil rights than they ever anticipated. As Rabbi Winograd's experiences implied, the public divisions between these two groups of American Jews grew more from a common desire for security and success in American life than from any basic moral difference between North and South.

The tough moral choices confronting southern Jews from the very beginning of the civil rights movement came to northern Jews at a much slower, measured pace. Northern Jews had enjoyed the privilege of waging a principled campaign against racial injustice at a time when the specter of Jim Crow remained a thousand miles away. Despite their geographic isolation, however, northern Jews still refused to tackle the most pressing problems: some of their efforts, including a campaign to secure a federal antilynching law, proved anachronistic; others, including support of "Truman's Committee on Civil Rights" and plans to end segregation in education, restaurants, and places of business, focused on Jewish as well as African American imperatives.[27]

The Antilynching Campaign

The northern Jewish campaign against lynching targeted what had been one of the worst violations of civil rights in the American South. Typified by trumped-up charges of sexual aggression by black men against white women, incidents of lynching had been used historically to scare the southern black community into compliance with the Jim Crow system. Northern Jews considered the practice of lynching southern blacks an ugly form of racist brutality and a flagrant violation of human rights. They looked to a federal antilynching law as an important and obvious first step to preserve the constitutional rights of the nation's black citizens.

The Jewish communal campaign came years too late. Jewish efforts to provide legal protection against lynching proved symbolic at best: they did not effect meaningful change. By the early 1950s, lynching as a means to intimidate African Americans had all but disappeared in the South. Antilynching legislation would have proved more effective fifty years earlier, when the number of these brutal acts reached all-time highs.

Still, the campaign offered important clues to understanding Jewish liberalism in the postwar years. Antilynching legislation reaffirmed two beliefs fundamental to Jewish politics: confidence that an expanding federal government could be harnessed to ameliorate injustices perpetrated on the state and local level and optimism that the Jewish American experience could be replicated for other minorities. By viewing their own acculturation through the lens of southern blacks, Jews understood both the potential for social mobility and its serious limitations. The absence of a federal law banning lynching reminded the Jewish community of its enviable position in American life. Securing at least basic legal protections for African Americans reaffirmed the Jewish community's optimistic appraisal of American life.

The American Jewish Congress took the lead in the antilynching campaign and pressed for immediate federal action to address an issue once considered a state matter. It held that the selective nature of lynching violated African American rights under both Article 4, which provided for a republican form of government, and the Fourteenth Amendment, which guaranteed legal equality to all citizens. Under those circumstances federal intervention was not only permitted but required. In testimony before Congress, Albert E. Arent, chairman of the American Jewish Congress's executive committee, explained that lynchings "occur where the local community is unwilling to accord to underprivileged groups the equal rights which our federal Constitution guarantees." According to Arent the purpose of lynching was "to keep the weaker group 'in its place' by the imposition of special punishments and penalties applicable only against that group." He demanded congressional action to counter "private arbitrary mob rule" and to guarantee African American citizens their constitutionally protected "republican form of government, with its safeguards of due process and equal treatment."[28]

American Jews maintained great faith in the federal government's ability to insure civil protection. When southern lawmakers pointed out that lynching remained a state issue by constitutional mandate, Jewish leaders balked. Joseph B. Robison, an attorney and lobbyist for the American Jewish Congress, explained that "neither kidnapping nor theft raises a problem of immediate Federal concern. The crimes covered by the [antilynching] case bill do." Robison delineated the difference between lynching and other criminal acts. He explained in his congressional testimony that the proposed law would limit federal intervention "to two types of illegal conduct. The first is violence prompted by the race, religion, or ethnic origin of the victim. The second is violence aimed at preventing fair trial and punishment of persons charged with a crime." From a legal point of view, Robison concluded, "both of these offenses undermine constitutional provisions which the federal government is required to enforce."[29]

Truman's Committee on Civil Rights

Northern Jews enjoyed a modicum of support at the federal level when President Harry Truman assembled his "President's Committee on Civil Rights." The Jewish community, represented on the committee by Rabbi Roland Gittelsohn, welcomed the administration's action as an important step in realizing full civil equality. The American Jewish Congress called for the body to enact "basic legislation to protect and extend democratic rights for all minorities." It repeated its call for a federal anti–poll tax law, a federal antilynching law, and fair employment practices reform and included appeals for an end to education and housing discrimination.[30]

In the winter of 1947 the president's committee released its findings to the public. It called for strengthening the civil rights section of the Justice Department, the creation of a special FBI unit trained in civil rights work, and a permanent commission on civil rights in the executive branch. The committee asked Congress to pass laws to increase penalties for civil rights violations, eliminate poll taxes as a requirement for voting, and end segregation in the U.S. military. It called on states to create permanent civil rights commissions analogous to those in the federal government and asked the American people to participate in "a long term campaign of public education to inform the people of the civil rights to which they are entitled and which they owe to one another." It attacked the Jim Crow system, pointing to segregation as "the cornerstone of [an] elaborate structure of discrimination against some American citizens." The committee rejected the rationale behind the Supreme Court's *Plessy v. Ferguson* decision, dismissing the argument that a segregated school "simply duplicates educational, recreational, and other public services." Instead, it blasted the "separate but equal" doctrine by calling it "one of the outstanding myths of American history" and concluding that "it is almost always true that while indeed separate, these facilities are far from equal."[31]

With little surprise the northern Jewish community offered unqualified support for the committee and its findings. The Truman committee embodied the highest northern Jewish civil rights ideals. American Jews could look to the White House for reassurance: the president of the United States welcomed their vision of a pluralist nation guaranteeing equal rights to one of its most beleaguered minorities. Even though many in the civil rights movement questioned Truman's resolve, his effort and his decision to include a leading rabbi on the committee reaffirmed the Jewish community's optimistic national vision.

Stephen S. Wise announced that the president's committee had "performed a great service for the people of America" and that its recommendations would translate into "a more fruitful and more abundant life for all Americans." Wise, speaking on behalf of the American Jewish Congress but representing the views of all the major Jewish organizations, urged the president to "continue the life of the committee" so that it could "press forward for adoption of its recommendations." Aware of the difficult legislative battles awaiting in Congress, Wise focused on Truman himself, asking for "no delay in the adoption of those recommendations which require no more than administrative action by the President and the executive departments of the Government."[32]

Northern Jewish liberal support of antilynching and anti–poll tax measures complemented the Jewish community's own goal of social inclusion. A society that protected African Americans from arbitrary violations of civil rights, Jewish leaders never tired of explaining, also guaranteed the sanctity of Jewish rights. As Cincinnati's Jewish Community Relations Council (JCRC) explained, "The society in which Jews are most secure is itself secure, only to the extent that citizens of all races and creeds enjoy full equality." Throughout the early postwar period, though, continued anti-Semitic discrimination reminded American Jews that their rights still needed protection. Although northern Jews could pride themselves on their commitment to racial equality at a time before the issue rose to national political prominence, they tempered their support when African American equality conflicted with efforts to halt domestic anti-Semitism. This apparent retreat did not signal an abandonment of black equality. Instead, it reflected the roots and limitations of Jewish liberalism: each time Jewish leaders favored anti-Jewish discrimination efforts over antiracism campaigns, they reaffirmed the centrality of Jewish acculturation in their postwar liberal politics. Jews wanted African Americans to follow in their footsteps, but they also wanted their own path free of discriminatory obstacles.[33]

Federal Aid to Education

A classic case of competing interests arose in the spring of 1947, when Rabbi Stephen S. Wise testified before the Senate subcommittee on education in support of a federal aid-to-education bill. The New York rabbi and head of the American Jewish Congress cherished the public school system and credited it for elevating American Jews in just two generations from immigrant status to full-fledged citizens. Public schools symbolized the successes of the American Jewish past and offered hope for future achievement. In the postwar years, the importance of a quality primary and secondary education grew as more and more graduate and professional schools opened their doors to previously excluded groups. In the eyes of the Jewish community, public schools acted as a social leveler, giving less-advantaged Americans the linguistic, social, and educational skills necessary for social advancement.

Southern legislators, fearful of opening the doors of their segregated schoolhouses to Washington's influence, voiced their opposition to the proposed laws. They considered federal support for state schools a threat to the racial status quo. Without even raising a specific objection to the Jewish community's goals of stronger public education, southern lawmakers complicated Wise's political strategy. Ideally, the New York rabbi would have wanted to argue for stronger public schools as a Jewish leader concerned about his constituents. By introducing race into the equation, the southerners forced Wise to comment on an unrelated topic, namely, Jewish communal attitudes toward segregated schools in the South.

Wise tried to navigate a moderate course through the shoals of American racial politics. If he honored his commitment to racial equality and refused to allow the southern amendment, he doomed the bill's chances for success. If he sidestepped the thorny issue of segregation in southern schools, he would at best delay the question of racial equality until a later date. Wise and the American Jewish community chose the latter.

Although he began his testimony by condemning state-mandated segregation, Wise fell in line behind southerners who demanded that federal aid to education not be used "as a means to attack the segregated school system." Wise assuaged his potential critics by invoking the "separate but equal" doctrine of the Supreme Court's *Plessy v. Ferguson* case. "So long as the law guarantees that States having segregated school systems do not discriminate financially against children in minority schools," Wise affirmed, "we believe that the bill should be supported." Wise, like most liberals of the era, lobbied for the political success of his favored bill instead of waging a more difficult defense of racial equality.[34]

Jewish leaders sometimes downplayed American racism during efforts to dramatize the seriousness of anti-Semitism. In the aid-to-education bill, southerners forced Jewish leaders to decide between two alternatives, yet in the years after that debate, representatives of Jewish organizations echoed Wise's argument without an imminent political threat. American Jews articulated their political views on the basis of their own American experience. Most times, the Jewish community could link its liberal reform campaign to the civil rights struggle because they both shared common roots and goals. When Jews confronted anti-Semitic discrimination, though, they employed the most powerful arguments available, even when those arguments compromised the fight for racial equality. Although they did not intend to polarize the black and Jewish communities, Jewish leaders illustrated how competing social and economic needs pit two allies against one another.

The National Community Relations Advisory Council (NCRAC), for example, took Wise's argument to its logical conclusion. It held that because racism enjoyed widespread social acceptance, "employers have frequently been willing to admit to a discriminatory policy and to face frankly the question of a change in such a policy." In relation to their own community, though, the NCRAC argued that "almost without exception, however, employers are unwilling to admit to a discriminatory policy against Jews and can point to some Jewish employment in their firms as evidence of a fair policy." The national umbrella organization concluded that although "the presence or absence of Negro employees in a plant is easily observable, no such visible check of Jewish workers is possible."[35]

Other Jewish organizations employed similar logic in their calls for antidiscrimination reform. Cincinnati's JCRC echoed its national body's position in a letter it sent to the governor of Ohio. It contended that "the task of fact-finding with respect to employment discrimination based upon religion is substantially more difficult than discrimination based upon race." Citing information such as "name, place of residence, birth place of parents," on job applications, the JCRC hoped to convince the state's chief executive that potential employers could easily identify and discriminate against Jews "without asking an applicant direct questions as to his religious affiliation." Although employers certainly could use biographical information to discriminate against Jews, the JCRC's argument ignored the very powerful and much more effective means employers used to keep African Americans off their payrolls.[36]

Fair Employment Practices Commission and the Race Question

When Jews battled for the creation of a fair employment practices commission (FEPC) to check discrimination in hiring, they took overt steps to distance themselves from the race issue as well. In its own publicity the NCRAC declared that "FEPC does not promote social equality." It wanted detractors to know that their main concern was job opportunity, that "the bill has nothing to do with personal or social relationships." Irving M. Engel of the American Jewish Committee assured Congress that "no proposed law, either state or federal, suggests that any employer is compelled to hire Negroes, Mexicans, Italians, Catholics, Jews, or members of any other racial, religious or national group." Engel, along with most American Jews of the time, opposed hiring quotas of any kind and used that to reassure critics that FEPC would "not confer special privileges on minorities." The Jewish community believed in merito-cratic hiring. It based its reform programs on the principle of equal op-portunity. As the NCRAC explained, "Pay the Negro good wages for his work, give him the opportunity to demonstrate his own capacity to learn, work and earn, [and] give him his constitutional rights, and you have solved this so-called race problem." Although these reform efforts eased discrimination against Jews, they did not translate into similar gains for the African American community.[37]

The *Brown* Decision

Successes with the Truman committee and fair employment practices paled in comparison to the far-reaching impact of the Supreme Court's landmark ruling in the *Brown* case. On the afternoon of 17 May 1954, after more than a year of tense deliberations, the court handed down its decision in the case of *Brown vs. Board of Education, Topeka, Kansas*. Chief Justice Earl Warren, who labored for months to secure a unani-mous ruling, distilled the complex legal argument into one question: "Does segregation of children in public schools solely on the basis of race, even though the physical facilities and other 'tangible' factors may be equal, deprive the children of the minority group of equal educa-tional opportunities?" In a moment long awaited by all civil rights ac-tivists, Warren responded, "We believe that it does."[38]

The African American community hailed the decision. "When the Supreme Court came out with the *Brown* decision in '54," Bayard Rustin remembered, "things began rapidly to move. Some of us had been sitting down in the front of these buses for years, but nothing had happened. What made '54 so unusual was that the Supreme Court in the *Brown* decision established black people as being citizens with all the rights of all other citizens." "*Brown*," according to one historian of the period, "heightened the aspirations and expectations of Afro-Americans as nothing ever had before."[39]

White southern reaction ranged from passive complicity to outspo-ken opposition. Polls indicated that only 20 percent of non-Jewish southern whites backed the Court ruling. Although Mississippi senator James O. Eastland proclaimed that the South "will not abide by nor obey this legislative decision by a political court," most segregationists believed that the decision would have little immediate impact. They pointed with hope to the court's ambiguous request that integration occur "with all deliberate speed" and remained confident that the local school districts and judges trusted with enforcement responsibilities would find creative ways to bypass the desegregation ruling.[40]

In Washington the executive and legislative branches refused to carry the civil rights banner. Wary of losing white southern voters, President Eisenhower offered neither "approbation nor disapproval" of *Brown*. In fact, the chief executive disagreed with the whole notion of legislating social change and often reminded his audiences that he did not "believe you can change the hearts of men with laws or decisions." The U.S. Congress refused to draft meaningful civil rights legislation, and many of its members made clear their opposition to integration. Senator Richard Russell of Georgia called the *Brown* decision "a flagrant abuse of judicial power." Virginia senator Harry Byrd denounced the desegregation order as "the most serious blow that has ever been struck against the rights of the states." In the legislature's most public act of defiance, a group of 101 southern congressmen drafted a "Declaration of Constitutional Principles" in March of 1956 demanding noncompliance with the Court order.[41]

Northern Jews rejoiced after the *Brown* ruling. Court-ordered desegregation dovetailed with all the political priorities of northern Jews: African Americans enjoyed civil protections promised them a century earlier, government acted aggressively to protect its citizens, and Jews could rest in a nation that would adhere to its constitutional promises. At its convention only days after the historic ruling, the Conservative movement's Rabbinical Assembly congratulated "the Supreme Court of the United States on its historic decision." In November of 1954 the Conservative movement's National Women's League pledged "its wholehearted cooperation in the effort that lies ahead." The Reform movement's rabbinic organization announced that it "views with satisfaction the historic decision of the United States Supreme Court which outlaws segregation in the field of public education." It hailed the ruling "as a profound victory of our prophetic tradition and as eloquent expression of the faith of all Americans in the basic justice of our democratic system."[42]

Henry E. Schultz, chairman of the ADL, announced that "the court's decision will wipe out the anachronistic 'separate but equal' doctrine that has been nothing more than a legal cover for the imposition of second-class status on millions of Negro citizens. The people of the South, white and black," he declared, "will be better for it." He boasted that at B'nai B'rith's 1953 Supreme Lodge convention, a resolution was passed demanding "equality of opportunity on an integrated and non-segregated basis for all, regardless of race or religion, everywhere in our country."[43]

The American Jewish Congress, responding to the southern states' opposition to the ruling, "urged the use of full powers and influence of the federal government to obtain prompt and full compliance with the decisions of the United States Supreme Court condemning state-imposed racial segregation." The National Women's League called on "the United States Congress to pass legislation eliminating discrimination because of race, creed, political belief, or national origin in transportation facilities, hotels, restaurants, places of amusement, hospitals and other institutions serving the public." The American Jewish Committee boasted of its close involvement "with the Supreme Court decision," noting that "not only were we active, along with our organizations, in the filing of an amicus brief, but we contributed materially to the social theory upon which the desegregation decision was based."[44]

The *Brown* decision inspired American Jews to step up their campaign for racial equality. In the decade prior to the landmark Supreme Court case, American Jews divided their time between several social action causes. Efforts to eliminate anti-Jewish discrimination through a federal FEPC topped the Jewish agenda, and concern about civil liberties infractions and immigration reform in the aftermath of the Holocaust commanded its own share of the Jewish community's limited resources. The easing of anti-Jewish discrimination and renewed national attention on American racism turned the tide in favor of race reform and inspired one ADL official to declare that "desegregation in the public schools is 'human relations problem number one.' "[45]

The *Brown* Decision in the South

Throughout the South school officials enacted laws aimed at neutralizing the effects of *Brown*. "As long as we can legislate," one southern white boasted, "we can segregate." The pupil-placement law, for example, permitted southern school officials to consider "the psychological effect upon the pupil of attendance at a particular school." Upheld by the Supreme Court, the ordinance gave white southerners the discretion to limit student transfers and maintain existing racial divisions in their schools.[46]

Desegregation stood at a standstill as the Jewish community readied itself for a long battle. Four years after the *Brown* decision, little more than 25 percent of the school districts had complied with the desegregation orders, and seven states still held fast to racial segregation. The five worst states could not count a single black alongside whites in the elementary grades, high school, college, or graduate school. The American Jewish Congress blasted congressional indifference. "Almost four years after the Supreme Court declared that state-imposed segregation in public schools deprives Negro school children of equal protection of the laws," it affirmed in testimony before a House judiciary subcommittee, "the responsible officials of the states in which these children live are continuing to deny them their declared rights." "Today," the American Jewish Congress concluded, "equal protection of the laws is a meaningless formula for millions of Negro school children."[47]

Northern Jews and Suburbanization

Despite their unprecedented and impressive commitment to the civil rights struggle, northern Jews remained vulnerable to the same acculturative forces that checked their earlier efforts. Ironically, just as some northern Jews sacrificed their time, money, and safety fighting for racial equality in the South, their Jewish friends and neighbors back home acquiesced to the prevailing racial status quo in an attempt to enjoy the hard-fought privileges of middle-class American life. By the late 1950s northern Jews had taken advantage of both the postwar economic boom and the easing of restrictive housing covenants to move from their urban ethnic enclaves to the new American suburbs. Country clubs and vacation resorts lifted their Gentiles-only policy. Political and business leaders welcomed Jews into their civic organizations. The Jewish community responded with religious programs to promote interfaith dialogue and educational activities aimed at bridging the cultural gap between Jew and non-Jew. Northern Jews lived side by side with their Christian neighbors, relished their new social status, and shared in the prevailing consensus mentality.[48]

Nevertheless, acceptance into the surrounding non-Jewish society mandated that Jews adopt the prevailing social attitudes as well. In the postwar urban North, that meant racial separation. Although northern racism lacked the legal backing characteristic of the Jim Crow states, segregation, nonetheless, remained the rule. Jewish children attended majority white schools, their parents joined racially segregated social organizations, and Jewish groups adopted whites-only policies in their community centers, playgrounds, and swimming pools. Unwittingly, northern Jews had become part of the very system they were condemning.

Northern Jews followed the precedents of their larger communities, emulating race-restrictive policies in their own programs and activities. In Cincinnati the Jewish neighborhood playground association adopted the larger community's policy of excluding blacks from their facilities. When a group of African American women in Cincinnati confronted the Jewish community on the issue, Richard Bluestein acknowledged that the problem of Jewish exclusion of blacks had become "increasingly acute," and he promised to search for ways to preserve "the good reputation of the entire Jewish community with Negroes and with the liberals of the city." Mike Israel of the JCRC, himself a staunch supporter of the civil rights movement, acknowledged that in Cincinnati "there was a strong feeling that as Jews we had enough trouble, we should not get involved in black problems."[49]

In St. Louis Herman Kaplow observed a trend away from racial inclusion. "Perhaps as part of the total and gradual process of acculturation," he explained, "the idea developed that it would be in the best interests of the Jewish community for Jewish centers to serve non-Jews." When centers began to accept non-Jews, Kaplow pointed out, "they did so, in most instances, following the precept of the majority community—whites only." The Jewish compulsion to adopt the broader racial status quo plagued communities across the country. In 1951 the ADL released a survey of Jewish community centers in forty-two leading cities. Of the thirty-five facilities that allowed non-Jews, twelve refused to admit blacks.[50]

Northern Jews had little trouble identifying racism in the South, especially when opponents of black equality worked segregation into their local codes and defied federal laws. Racial separation in the urban North, home to the vast majority of American Jews, created more difficult and complex problems. Not only did northern segregation lack legal sanction, making it harder to eliminate, but it enjoyed at least tacit approval from the Jewish community. Restrictive housing covenants limited African American access to most suburbs, creating segregated neighborhoods and reinforcing existing inequalities. With the concept of neighborhood schools entrenched in the American educational system and with white officials assigning black and white pupils to different schools, northerners achieved the same racial separation as their southern counterparts without all the legal complications. "The process of suburbanization," one writer noted, "was strengthening the de facto basis for racial segregation even as judicial rulings, militant protest, congressional action, and executive intervention were weakening its de jure basis."[51]

Eliminating racism in the urban North proved as difficult for American Jews as efforts to end Jim Crow in places such as Mississippi and Alabama. "When most Negroes lived in the rural areas of a generally impoverished South," two ADL observers noted at the time, "it was possible to think of discrimination as a parochial problem and so more or less disregard it. But this attitude is no longer possible."[52]

The American Jewish Congress warned that "when the Supreme Court held that racial segregation of children in public schools 'has a tendency to retard the educational development of Negro children,' its finding was not limited to one part of the country." More and more, American Jews understood Charles Silberman's observation that "the racial crisis will not be solved in Selma or Birmingham or St. Petersburg. It will be solved, if it is to be solved, in New York, Chicago, Philadelphia, Detroit, Rochester, Syracuse, Kansas City, Los Angeles—and in the suburbs of those cities."[53]

Geographic Mobility in the African American Community

The northern civil rights movement gained momentum in the wake of wide-scale demographic changes in the African American community. Between 1950 and 1960 the black population of New York increased 46 percent. Chicago recorded its gains at 65 percent, and in Philadelphia the black population grew 41 percent. Washington D.C., Los Angeles, and Milwaukee all experienced similar increases. By 1960 nine million African Americans, half of the U.S. black population, resided outside the eleven southern states. New York counted one million black residents. Chicago and Detroit boasted respective African American populations greater than Atlanta and Birmingham. The majority of American blacks lived in urban centers, and whites outnumbered blacks in the suburbs by a ratio of thirty-five to one.[54]

The recent arrivals tended to crowd into predominantly black public schools. In Chicago 87 percent of the city's African American elementary school students attended virtually all-black schools. Thirty-eight elementary schools in Philadelphia listed their African American student populations at 99 percent. Similar situations existed in Los Angeles and New York. Pupils in these schools did not enjoy the same quality of education as students in white schools. In New York, for example, the Commission on Integration reported that schools in African American neighborhoods of greater New York "have tended to be older, less well equipped and more crowded than the schools in the white neighborhoods; the quality of the teaching provided in these predominantly colored schools has also suffered."[55]

Integration in the Urban North

Northern Jews faced a dilemma similar to the one confronted by Stephen S. Wise in his 1947 response to the federal aid-to-education bill, only this time the segregated schools opened for classes in the northern Jews' own communities. Just as Wise balanced Jewish support for public education against the need to end segregation in the southern states, northern Jews faced the impossible task of protecting the quality and integrity of their neighborhood schools without appearing to abandon the cause of racial equality. The complementary goals of supporting a pluralistic society and fostering Jewish mobility evolved into competing aims. Pluralism demanded integration, but Jewish mobility demanded the best public schools.

Middle-class suburban Jews opted for a middle road in the northern desegregation crisis. They opposed legal segregation as it was defined in the South, but they held firm in their support for neighborhood schools and in their opposition to mandatory integration. Although their ambivalence was qualified to some degree by the fact that their college-age children participated in numerous grassroots civil rights campaigns, the Jews' position translated to an acceptance of the racial status quo and an unwillingness to attack northern racism with the same zeal they had used against the South. Once the civil rights movement focused on the North, its meaning to many urban Jews changed. For many northern Jews, the struggle for racial equality in the South fostered a benevolent self-image. The later civil rights movement, on the other hand, threatened public schools and challenged two generations of successful Jewish acculturation to American life.

Working-class Jews objected to northern civil rights reforms with even greater vigor than their wealthier coreligionists. Whereas middle- and upper-class suburban Jews did fear the effects of court-ordered integration or the loss of their neighborhood schools, urban-dwelling Jews lived on the civil rights front lines. They resided in older neighborhoods, most often targeted for desegregation, while suburban Jews managed to insulate their communities from government action. What remained a principled debate for middle-class Jews evolved into a nuts-and-bolts question for urban Jews. Abandoned, many believed, by upwardly mobile white-collar Jews who moved their homes, synagogues, and Jewish institutions out of the old neighborhoods, the working-class Jewish community fought to retain its traditional communal structure. Repudiation of northern liberal civil rights reform reaffirmed the connection between Jewish acculturation and political persuasion. Working-class Jews lived within a different American milieu, and their rejection of liberalism reflected their divergent American experience.[56]

National Jewish self-defense organizations feared the conflict created by the northern civil rights movement. In St. Louis a local federation executive affirmed that the covert discrimination typical of northern communities was "still very much a part of the attitudes and feelings of the white population generally." Nathan Edelstein of the American Jewish Congress worried in 1960 that the increased contact between blacks and Jews had "been largely ignored [by the Jewish community] and its implications are not too well understood." "Today, as the urbanized Negro reaches out for the better things of life—better housing, better schools," John Slawson of the American Jewish Committee explained, "the whites with whom he competes are often Jews. We see this happening in New York and other cities as well, where conflicts over de facto segregation in the schools are creating new tensions."[57]

The continuing exclusionary practices of some Jewish organizations forced the NCRAC to remind their constituents of appropriate racial policy. "The commitment of the Jewish community to racial equality," it advised, "can be advanced by Jewish organizations, agencies, and institutions through their scrupulous adherence to racially nondiscriminatory practices in their own operations." The American Jewish Congress, frustrated by growing apathy in the North, lamented that their "appeals to moral excellence . . . have evoked only indifference, often hostility." Those young Jews who stepped up their civil rights work during this period affiliated with secular organizations such as the Student Non-Violent Coordinating Committee and the Congress of Racial Equality, whose youthful membership, goals, and strategies paralleled their own American experience.[58]

"Jews and Negroes," Slawson admonished, "are coming more and more into contacts for which neither group is properly prepared." The American Jewish Committee leader advised his brethren to proceed with greater caution. "Certainly we must continue to help clear the Negro's path to equal opportunity," he advised in 1959, "but let us not delude ourselves that the special roadblocks standing in our way will thereby automatically be removed." Slawson anticipated a declining role for Jews in the struggle for racial equality. "With newfound strength emerging from the Negro's own ranks, and with powerful community groups aligning themselves on his side," he concluded, "the moment may be at hand for us to deal more closely, but of course not exclusively with our specifically Jewish problems in the field of civil rights."[59]

Jewish middle-class support of civil rights activities started to wane in the mid-1960s. By 1964 the American Jewish Congress, a voice of the most progressive middle-class northern Jews, lamented that "more and more Jewish voices are being heard expressing the white community's prevalent fear of the advent of the Negroes in their schools, their neighborhoods and their society." It pointed to New York City's Parents and Taxpayers Association, which, it explained, "has been formed to fight the (minimal) integration program of the schools proposed by the Board of Education [and] enjoys much local Jewish support." The American Jewish Congress observed an uncomfortable abandonment of traditional Jewish support for civil rights. "Sadly," it concluded, "even liberals are attracted by the proposition that education can be separate and equal, and all that is required is the upgrading of slum schools."[60]

School Segregation, Northern Style

Attempts to inspire widespread Jewish interest in the northern civil rights movement failed. As early as 1961 the American Jewish Congress labored to solve the northern segregation crisis in a way that respected the needs of both blacks and Jews. In their study *School Segregation, Northern Style*, Will Maslow and Richard Cohen took chief aim at school officials who manipulated the letter of the law to evade desegregation rulings. They condemned local administrators who "took the easy way out" by remaining "color-blind in the belief that as long as they could not be accused of listing race formally as a school entrance requirement, they had no legal responsibility toward enforcing the desegregation decision of the Supreme Court."[61]

Maslow and Cohen saw little difference between northern and southern segregation. "The fact that school segregation in the South is imposed by racial laws and in the North by school districts," they explained, "makes it nonetheless segregation for Negro children living in the Bedford-Stuyvesant section of Brooklyn or in Philadelphia, Los Angeles, or other metropolitan centers of the North." They also understood, however, that any viable integration plan needed to respect the neighborhood school, which most Jews supported and which Maslow and Cohen called "probably the biggest single obstacle facing any local school board determined to eliminate school segregation."[62]

They proposed a four-point plan that kept neighborhood schools intact and featured permissive busing, open enrollment, building of new schools, and realignment of school districts to ameliorate segregation. With permissive busing, students in overcrowded black schools were allowed to transfer to underutilized white institutions. Akin to the permissive busing plan, open enrollment permitted any students, white or black, in overcrowded schools to transfer to schools with space available. Open enrollment fulfilled both the letter and the spirit of integration rulings. White students in overcrowded schools could transfer, if they wished, to under-enrolled schools. "Since the program does not rest on a racial or ethnic base—and because it can also be defended as a device to prevent overcrowding," its two proponents boasted, "this approach appears to be impervious to legal attack as discriminatory or unconstitutional." To counteract the natural segregation of racial housing patterns, Maslow and Cohen supported efforts to build new schools in "fringe" areas midway between black and white residential areas. Although this policy threatened to postpone needed improvements in black schools by channeling capital to fringe areas, it emerged as a viable compromise adopted by the city of New York.[63]

The practice of gerrymandering school districts underlay Maslow and Cohen's final and most complicated point. "If racial integration is to be achieved," they argued, educators would have to strive for "racial balance, with school district lines drawn to foster rather than hinder integration." In New Rochelle, New York, for example, creative use of school boundaries dating back to 1930 created an almost all–African American elementary school. White students residing in black neighborhoods were allowed to transfer to other schools, but black students were refused permission to switch classes, regardless of availability.[64]

The NCRAC offered only qualified support for the American Jewish Congress program. Although it supported plans to build fringe schools, it refused to consider any solution that compromised the concept of neighborhood schools. "We regard the neighborhood school as having important educational values," the Jewish umbrella organization affirmed, including "accessibility to pupils, encouragement of after-school association among pupils, [and] convenience of parent participation in school activities." "No specific group," it claimed, had "any special right, legal or otherwise, to enrollment in any school."[65]

The efforts of the American Jewish Congress and others to invent acceptable integration plans ended in frustration. Fewer and fewer Jews shared the American Jewish Congress's civil rights conviction. With the rise of Black Power and the systematic purges of whites, most of the younger grassroots Jewish activists turned away from the movement. Their parents, content with the legal changes secured in the movement's southern campaign and frustrated by the complexity of the race problem in the North, responded to the American Jewish Congress plan with indifference. The very tone of the black-Jewish relationship changed. For Herman Kaplow, the director of the St. Louis Jewish Federation, that meant putting an end to the paternalistic racial attitudes shared by many American Jews. It was time, Kaplow believed, to let go of the civil rights movement and leave its future in the hands of the African American community. In a striking reversal of the Jews' earlier universalist argument, Kaplow reminded his coreligionists that "it is not the responsibility of a Jewish agency to meet Negro needs *unless it also serves the total general community* [Kaplow's emphasis]."[66]

The American Jewish community grew smaller during its twenty-year involvement with civil rights. The dramatic regional differences between Jews faded as northern Jews faced the same charges of hypocrisy and callousness usually reserved for their coreligionists to the south. When northern Jews clashed with their southern brethren in Mississippi and Alabama, they did it with an understanding that both longed for the most elusive prize in all of Jewish history: inclusion in and acceptance from the greater society. The civil rights movement taught Jews that there were many "Americas," each with its own character and each demanding different and sometimes conflicting attitudes from its citizens.

Civil and Social Rights Efforts of Arkansas Jewry

CAROLYN GRAY LeMASTER

Carolyn Gray LeMaster traces the efforts of a series of rabbis who served in a state with a very small Jewish population. In Arkansas, as in other states where civil rights were linked with labor activities, issues of race and class were almost inseparable. Although congregants often advocated silence, one civil rights activist succeeded another, and the rabbis saw their activities mirrored by committed Jewish laypersons and by ministers from other denominations. They were never totally isolated. They worked through their pulpits to sway opinions and through ministerial associations and public boards to change policies. LeMaster demonstrates how individuals served as role models for others who consciously followed their paths. All of these support systems eased the way for reform. This essay raises a peripheral issue begging for further study. Jewish women appear to have been less reluctant to speak out than the men. Although some of the women's actions had impact on their husbands' occupations, they may have felt freer to act because repercussions were less likely. Could Jewish women have been that independent, or did their actions reflect what their husbands believed and might have done under other circumstances?

The history of Arkansas Jewry provides a revealing case study of Jewish efforts to procure social and civil rights for all peoples. This chapter presents information on the subject from the turn of the century to the 1950s and then gives an account of the Jewish involvement in integration efforts that began in 1957 with the crisis at Little Rock's Central High School.[1]

Part I: Early Jewish-Black Relations in Arkansas

Although few early records exist to chronicle how rabbis who served in Arkansas responded to civic and social rights, data have been uncovered on two that bear mentioning: Rabbi Ephraim Frisch of Pine Bluff and Rabbi Samuel Teitelbaum of Fort Smith. Rabbi Frisch (1880–1957), a native of Shubocz, Lithuania, was brought to America by his parents as a child of eight. After graduating from the University of Cincinnati and Hebrew Union College he served his first rabbinate at Temple Anshe Emeth, Pine Bluff, from 1904 to 1912. While there he became friends with Isaac Fisher, a young black educator who was selected as principal of Branch Normal College (now the University of Arkansas at Pine Bluff). The school was part of the Arkansas Industrial University in Fayetteville but was located at Pine Bluff, closer to the blacks it sought to serve.

Fisher, a talented graduate of the Tuskegee Institute in Alabama, encountered opposition from disgruntled blacks of Pine Bluff who resented his being named to replace a popular local black as well as his emphasis on industrial education as a way of raising the quality of life for African Americans. Fisher envisioned new departments for the school—one for home economics and one for agriculture that would include a dairy as well as classes on making bricks, harnesses, and shoes—and instruction in printing and in music. Although the white press of Pine Bluff spoke well of his efforts, he was later opposed by whites who were jealous of his success and by others who resented his requests for funds to improve the school. One of the latter was Jeff Davis, Arkansas's governor from 1901 to 1907.[2] Fisher's career at Branch Normal ended in June 1911 when he resigned after his work at the school was virtually ended by opposition and by the limits a white system placed on black education.

Several prominent white citizens of Pine Bluff protested the treatment of Fisher that led to his resignation. His longtime friend, Rabbi Frisch, sent to the local *Pine Bluff Commercial* a letter of support that was published in May 1911. In defending Fisher, Rabbi Frisch noted that his leaving would "result in great damage to our state" and that Fisher had inculcated "a high standard of integrity, industry, and decorum among his people." Rabbi Frisch had often visited Branch Normal and was familiar with Fisher's efforts. The young educator was capable of doing "some half dozen important things exceptionally well," Rabbi Frisch wrote in his letter. The rabbi noted that he could not understand the politics played out in Pine Bluff and Little Rock that purposely sought to discredit Fisher's work; he was "not given a square deal by the authorities."[3]

When Isaac Fisher sought positions elsewhere, Rabbi Frisch wrote several letters of recommendation for him. In one of these he noted that it was "political juggling" by the white county superintendent who "interfered too much in Fisher's work" and by another white who had been "jealous of the black educator's remarkable success" that caused Fisher to resign.[4]

Rabbi Frisch left Pine Bluff in 1912, a year after Isaac Fisher's departure. The rabbi then served congregations in New York until 1922, at which time he became spiritual leader of Temple Beth-El at San Antonio, Texas. There he increased his efforts for civil rights and liberties and in so doing almost lost his pulpit in 1937. That year, when some one thousand workers (including a number of minorities) were discharged, a one hundred–member committee of the San Antonio Worker's Alliance was sent to the local Works Progress Administration office to protest. Allowing them no hearing, the office's director instead called the police, who, "with blows and curses, kicked them [members of the committee] down five flights of stairs." Not content with such mayhem, the police went to the Workers' Alliance hall and proceeded to kick and beat those found there. They also destroyed a typewriter, a piano, tables, and 250 chairs. It was noted at the time that only a "meager reaction" was forthcoming from area churches and their leaders regarding the events. The one lone religious voice mentioned was that of Rabbi Frisch, who, when the local press would not publish in full his "vigorous protest," published it at his own expense and distributed it to local leading citizens. Many in his congregation were not pleased with his stand or his efforts; however, one member, Sidney Berkowitz, championed the rabbi's cause and encouraged him in it.[5] Rabbi Frisch kept his pulpit and continued his efforts for social and civil justice. He was active for many years in the affairs of the Central Conference of American Rabbis, serving as an editor of its yearbook, chairman of the social justice commission, and chairman of the committee on church and state.[6]

Rabbi Frisch's tenure in Arkansas overlapped with one of the state's most outstanding figures, Judge Jacob Trieber (1853–1927), who was decades ahead of his time regarding civil rights for blacks. In 1900 Trieber was appointed federal judge of the Eastern District of Arkansas by President William McKinley and thereby became the first Jew in America to hold a federal judgeship. He was born in Raschkow, Germany, and educated there until age fourteen, when he immigrated with his family to America. The family lived in St. Louis one year, then moved to

Helena, Arkansas. Trieber began his career as a store clerk but also studied law at night under Judge M. L. Stephenson, a former justice of the Arkansas Supreme Court. Trieber helped organize the First National Bank of Helena in 1887 and served as its president. He was elected to Helena's City Council in 1882 and was named superintendent of the state census in 1890. He was elected treasurer of Phillips County in 1892 and was appointed U.S. district attorney for the Eastern District of Arkansas in 1897.

As a federal judge Jacob Trieber presided over many cases that stemmed from problems with the railroads, bootlegging, and racial prejudice. The latter particularly concerned him because he had come from a childhood in which he had seen the intolerance racism spawned. He also was aware of the treatment of blacks in the South, and he became an expert on the legal status of blacks in Arkansas before the Civil War. He later wrote "one of the most concise . . . presentations of the subject" that had ever appeared in print.[7] He was touched by the tragic lynching of blacks in Arkansas and the South and commented on one occasion that "people wouldn't know there is anything in Arkansas except murders and demagoguery."[8] He said that although the country as a whole was growing, Arkansas was asleep, "regardless of its great natural resources."[9] Believing that all men deserved equal justice, he maintained that racism harmed the state in many ways. He said that demagoguery was the worst foe of free institutions and that reason would "eradicate prejudice and follow the precepts laid down in that divinely inspired instrument, the Declaration of Independence."[10]

Acknowledging the racist thinking and attitudes of the day, he noted that prejudices would not be overcome easily, and he believed that eradicating them should not be done by abuse or force.[11] His honor and integrity, together with his outspokenness for justice, gained him the respect of all and helped soothe racial tensions. It was said of him that he impressed "all his hearers with a feeling of fairness seldom exhibited."[12] As his days on the bench of the federal court progressed, Judge Trieber showed by his rulings what fairness under the law meant. He was familiar with the actions of white racists, known as "whitecappers," from the time he had come to Arkansas as a teenager. In 1903 a group of whitecappers began efforts in Poinsett County to rid the county of all blacks. Even a detective, J. F. Brown, was murdered when he investigated one of their attacks on a black family. Soon after, more than a dozen whitecappers demanded that the Davis & Hodges sawmill replace eight recently hired black workers with whites. Subsequently, indictments were sought against fifteen whitecappers by the United States attorney in a case known as *United States v. Hodges*. In *United States v. Morris* indictments were also sought against twelve others for terrorism in Cross County. The cases were extremely serious, for in the state's area of jurisprudence since the Civil War, Arkansas had been seen as "unwilling and unable to prevent whitecapper violence and racism."[13] The problem had been exacerbated when the state had passed laws promoting racial discrimination and segregation. Only the federal law could be used against such actions dealt with in the *Hodges* and *Morris* cases, and at that time the federal law was unsettled. In Judge Trieber's charge to the grand jury, he said that federal law stated the seriousness of having two or more individuals to "conspire to injure, oppress, threaten, or intimidate any citizen" in exercising freely any right or privilege given him by the United States Constitution. He observed that, since the Thirteenth Amendment was ratified,

> slavery has ceased to exist in this country and every citizen is entitled to enjoy those rights which are inherent in every free man. Without enumerating what all of these rights are, it is sufficient to say that among them are, in language of the Declaration of Independence, the cornerstone of our republican form of government, the following: "That all men are created equal; that they are endowed by their Creator with certain inalienable rights; that among these are life, liberty and the pursuit of happiness." The right to own, hold, dispose, lease and rent property, either real or personal, and to perform honest work for support of himself and his family are natural rights belonging to every free man, without any statute or written law. Deprive a man of these rights and he ceases to be a free man. Congress, in order to leave no doubt on that subject, has enacted statute[s] [protecting these rights]. . . . Under these acts, the court charges you . . . that it is unlawful for two or more persons to conspire for the purpose of preventing by force, threats or intimidation any citizen . . . from renting lands and cultivating the same, or performing any honest labor, when hired to do so, on account of being a . . . citizen of African descent.[14]

The grand jury indicted the twenty-seven defendants two days later. Although the defendants sought to have the indictments dismissed, Judge Trieber overruled and declared his *United States v. Morris* opinion: "Congress has the power, under the provisions of the thirteenth amendment, to protect citizens of the United States in the enjoyment of those rights which are fundamental and belong to every citizen, if the deprivation of these privileges is solely on account of his race or color, as a denial of such privileges is an element of servitude within the meaning of that amendment. . . . That the rights to lease lands and to accept employment for hire are fundamental rights, inherent in every free citizen, is indisputable."[15]

After evidence was presented to the jury in the *Hodges* trial in March 1904, Judge Trieber instructed the panel that the case questioned whether each citizen, white or black, had the right "to work for a living, to engage in the pursuit of happiness and a livelihood . . . [and] whether right and law should prevail or the unlicensed mob."[16] The jury found three leaders of the group under indictment guilty; the others were found innocent.

The Arkansas press supported Judge Trieber's opinion in the *Hodges* case, and it was well received by the public. Such a ruling coupled with a positive attitude seemed to bode well for black employment opportunities in the state. Optimism was short-lived, however, when, on 28 May 1906, the United States Supreme Court overruled *Hodges*. The ruling held that "the federal courts lacked jurisdiction to protect blacks from racially motivated discrimination by private individuals, no matter how severe. The Court reasoned that the ability to earn a living was not a fundamental right of citizenship protected by the thirteenth amendment, and that extending protection to blacks against racial discrimination would be a form of improper reverse discrimination against whites. The Court further stated that the punishment of such wrongs as were charged must be sought in the state courts."[17]

Despite Judge Trieber's keen insight into civil rights and his attempt to correct the wrongs of racism, the Supreme Court's shortsightedness soon bore bitter fruit. The whitecappers' numbers and their "violent racism grew exponentially." In 1915 the Ku Klux Klan was reorganized, and by the early 1920s the racist group had become a national organization of some six million. For the next fifty years "the *Hodges* case became the rod and staff of those who denied that the federal government had the authority to intervene in race relations."[18] No comprehensive protection guarded "against racial discrimination in employment" until the Civil Rights Act of 1964 was enacted. At long last Judge Trieber's ruling on the Thirteenth Amendment and the Civil Rights Act of 1866 was vindicated.

Judge Trieber also handled other civil rights cases. These included a 1905 challenge to the Arkansas poll tax amendment that had been enacted in 1893 to suppress the black vote. Trieber ruled in *Knight v. Shelton* that the poll tax amendment of 1893 was invalid because it had not won the necessary majority vote. His ruling held, but the victory was short-lived. The Arkansas legislature again enacted a poll tax amendment in 1909, and it did receive a majority vote. Another civil rights case arose in 1905 when several men were accused of keeping black individuals in a state of peonage. When the blacks had attempted to leave such conditions, the men had them arrested and returned them to a state of peonage. Judge Trieber saw justice served in the case when a sixty-count indictment was returned by the grand jury against nine of the accused. But again such efforts were thwarted, this time by the United States Supreme Court in *Clyatt v. United States,* in which the constitutionality of the peonage laws was upheld. That ruling helped spawn the notorious "Elaine Race Riots" in Arkansas in 1919. At that time black sharecroppers sought to unionize, and a small race war erupted. Almost twenty people were killed, mostly blacks. Subsequently 120 blacks were indicted, and six were eventually sentenced to death. As a result of Judge Trieber's ruling in the *Moore v. Dempsey* case, however, the death sentences were commuted to prison sentences. Also during that period Judge Trieber had several blacks, whom he knew were innocent of any wrongdoing, quietly released.[19]

Judge Trieber was an advocate of rights not only for blacks but also for women. He became a popular speaker for women's groups during the years before the ratification of the Nineteenth Amendment. He appealed to the Constitution itself, which he often quoted. In a speech to the Political Equality League in 1914, he said that "a woman is a person and should be entitled to all the rights guaranteed by the Constitution to a male person."[20]

Rabbi Samuel Teitelbaum was born in Galicia, Austria-Hungary, in 1900 and, like Rabbi Frisch, was brought to America by his parents when he was eight years old. The family settled in St. Louis, where young Samuel attended public school as well as a Talmudic yeshiva. He received a bachelor of arts degree from Harvard University in 1922, spent one year at Washington University Medical School, and in 1927 was graduated with a master's degree in Hebrew literature from the Jewish Institute of Religion in New York. Immediately after his graduation he began to serve the United Hebrew Congregation of Fort Smith, Arkansas, and remained there until entering the U.S. Army as a chaplain in 1942.

In mid-February of 1935, after the relief wages of unemployed miners of the Fort Smith area were cut, the miners formed a parade through the Fort Smith business district. (Before the wages were lowered, the miners had received between fifteen cents and thirty cents an hour.) Those affected by the cuts included 3,300 persons on relief rolls and 1,150 who were housed and fed by the transient bureau.[21] These miners included whites and minorities. On 19 February seven individuals who had been arrested in connection with the "strike" were indicted on various charges; some were jailed.[22] During these tumultuous times organized labor groups often called on Rabbi Teitelbaum to support their causes. He usually consented, incurring resentment from many of his congregants as well as others of the community. At one point local law officials issued an order to search the rabbi's home for "radical literature," but a "Southern red-necked ex-sheriff" who was friendly to the rabbi prevented the search. (The law official, "Pink" Shaw, was described by the rabbi as a "man of integrity and fearless." At one time a Fort Smith mob threatened to lynch a black teenager accused of raping a white woman, but Shaw stood in front of the crowd and prevented it; a white male was later found to be guilty, and the black was acquitted.)[23] Rabbi Teitelbaum could well have been in physical danger for his efforts on behalf of the unemployed workers. After the Reverend A. B. Jones of Atlanta came to Fort Smith and visited one of the workers' jailed leaders, Rev. Claude C. Williams, Jones was taken from his hotel room, driven twelve miles north of Van Buren, beaten, and left by the side of the road.[24]

Rabbi Teitelbaum was asked by his congregants to desist from his overt efforts or resign his position, and he "suffered many days of anguish" before seeking encouragement from his friend and mentor, Rabbi Stephen S. Wise of New York. After chronicling the events in a letter to Wise, Rabbi Teitelbaum received a reply from the venerable scholar: "Our poor Jewish people . . . are so nervous and timid and panicky that they imagine they will be safer, that is how they will put it to themselves, if they let you go."[25] Rabbi Wise encouraged his friend to resign his position rather than recant his views or deeds. When the United Hebrew Congregation Board voted on whether to retain Rabbi Teitelbaum, his contract was renewed by a one-vote majority.[26]

Social action was not the only area that created problems for Rabbi Teitelbaum with his congregants or with Fort Smith citizens. When he had first come to Arkansas, he was told of the proper decorum in white-black relationships (actually, he was apprised of the many Jim Crow laws). He was told to call blacks "boy" or "girl" (never "gentleman," "sir," "mister," "lady," "miss," or "mrs."). He was never to shake hands with blacks, eat with them, or admit them by the front door. Rabbi and Mrs. Teitelbaum managed, however, to do the exact opposite of these "laws." On her work day the Teitelbaum's black maid ate lunch at the table with them, and the rabbi shook hands with blacks in public and called them respectful names. As the first white clergyman to respond when invited to black pulpits, Rabbi Teitelbaum joined forces with a local Catholic priest, and the two men succeeded in a campaign to allow blacks to use public library books (although they could not use the library facilities). The rabbi welcomed enthusiastically a group of blacks to a festival service in the temple, where a succah was set up on the pulpit platform. The blacks had come to see the service, they said, as they planned one for their own sanctuary. On seeing the guests, the temple's president angrily asked what the "niggers" were doing there and proceeded to ask them to leave. Rabbi Teitelbaum chided him: "This is a house of worship and Jewishly and morally it must be open to everyone." He told the president that if the blacks left he would leave with them. They were allowed to stay, and the congregants who attended seemed pleased to share their worship service with strangers.[27]

During the 1930s a Bi-Racial Committee was established in Fort Smith, and Rabbi Teitelbaum served as one of its members. The first meeting, held in the prestigious Goldman Hotel, consisted of white members only, despite the fact that it was called biracial. When the rabbi asked why there were no blacks, the hotel manager stated that the "colored people are natural servants; they're not capable of anything requiring mental and intellectual capacity." When the rabbi asked about such talented men as Booker T. Washington and George Washington Carver, he was told, "They're exceptions." The rabbi also raised such issues as integrated public education and the use of the public library, but the issues were tabled. Only a few members attempted to maintain the Bi-Racial Committee, and it ceased to function. Rabbi Teitelbaum continued his involvement with the black clergy, who regarded him and the local Catholic priest as their only friends among the religious sector. At one time when the rabbi spoke in a black church, the black minister asked why no white congregations would invite blacks to speak in their houses of worship. The rabbi approached his board on the matter but was "told in no uncertain terms that the congregants would walk out of such a service."[28]

At one time an agent of the Anti-Defamation League (ADL) of B'nai B'rith visited Fort Smith and told Rabbi Teitelbaum that he should "refrain from getting involved in social and political issues, that these [were] to be left to the ADL, and that in the South Jews in general and their communities should avoid such 'entanglements.' " The rabbi ignored this counsel, and his stubborn tenacity in holding the course for civil and social rights he felt were true to biblical teachings eventually saw results.[29] In the late 1930s he visited the Cooper Clinic in Fort Smith, which had specialists in a variety of medical fields. As he walked through the lobby, he witnessed a phenomenon he had not seen in the South before: both black and white patients sat together in the waiting room. Dr. Davis Goldstein, a well-known dermatologist and member of United Hebrew Congregation, held the rabbi responsible for the change.

"You, rabbi, did this to me, and I did it to my colleagues. . . . You motivated me to realize that 'colored people' are human beings and must be treated as such." Several years later, when Rabbi and Mrs. Teitelbaum visited Fort Smith after the U.S. Supreme Court ruling on integration, he found a significant segment of the Jewish community to be the boldest and staunchest open supporters of desegregation. They lauded him for being ahead of his time.[30]

One of Rabbi Teitelbaum's congregants at Fort Smith, Rose Weinberger, had a heart for others as large as his. Born in Harrisburg, Pennsylvania, Rose Sherman Weinberger had come with her husband in 1931 to Fort Smith, where they had four children. Her guiding principle was "Godliness is helping others." On arrival in Fort Smith Mrs. Weinberger began almost immediately a life of service to the community. She became the first Jewish member on the board of the Young Women's Christian Association (YWCA) in that city, and her initial responsibility with the group was in helping young women find jobs. She provided clothes for some of them and contacted local businesses for jobs, scholarships, and references. Her concern for minorities prompted her to help establish a YWCA branch for black women and a nursery for black children. When she found that blacks were not admitted to the two local hospitals, she worked with Dr. Charles Holt to found the Twin City Hospital for them. She helped establish a library for blacks at Lincoln High School because they were not allowed to use the city's public library facilities at the time. She also encouraged the collection of food, toys, and clothing for blacks, particularly during the Christmas season.[31]

During the 1930s and 1940s Rose Weinberger was also active in the Arkansas Jewish Assembly, an organization that served as an umbrella group to strengthen Judaism in the state. Another member of the assembly, Harry Solmson, Sr., a Little Rock insurance executive who served as a president of the association, was particularly interested in the plight of poor minorities, especially during the trying days of the Great Depression. In 1933 he formed Arkansas Farm Homes, Inc., a limited dividend corporation in which he planned to use five thousand acres of his father-in-law's property (the Henry Myar estate) west of Camden to create a modern farm colony for blacks. One hundred farms were to be located on fifty-acre tracts, each having a house, barn, and woven-wire fence. Annual payment would have been $125, which would have included payment on principal, interest, insurance, and taxes. Although the project was accepted by the state housing board and the federal government, lack of funds during the depression prohibited its implementation.[32] Solmson died in 1939, never having seen his dream fulfilled.

Like Solmson other Jewish businessmen sought to help blacks. Two of these were Leonard and Gus Ottenheimer, owners of a garment manufacturing plant in Little Rock. In the early 1940s the brothers contacted several black ministers and professionals, telling them that if they would provide good workers the Ottenheimers would furnish a place for them to work. At the time, integrating black and white workers was not considered feasible, so the Ottenheimers did what they thought was fair. They opened another facility (known as the Rocket Plant) and equipped it with the exact equipment used by white workers; earnings were the same. The experiment was a success, and the Rocket story was publicized nationwide. Magazine and newspaper articles chronicled its history, and one of the nation's largest needlecraft manufacturers came to see if one of its factories could be started in the South. A central Arkansas black newspaper editor wrote in 1948 that the employees of the Rocket Plant were concrete examples of democratic ideas. "Strange as it may seem to some of us," he wrote, "this decent and commendable employment project of our race group is a reality, in one of the leading industries of Greater Little Rock."[33] The managers of the factories were never accused of favoritism by any white or black employees. By 1952 the Ottenheimer Plant No. 1 included more than five hundred employees, and the Rocket Plant had more than two hundred fifty.[34]

These examples give insight into how some rabbis and a few Jewish individuals helped to seek or promote equality for blacks. For the most part, however, the Jewish community accepted the status quo and did not openly oppose the Jim Crow laws. Although they might not inwardly agree with such actions, they condoned at least tacitly those of the dominant culture.

Part II: Little Rock's Integration Crisis and Its Aftermath

One of the hottest news topics of September 1957 was the campaign to integrate Central High School in Little Rock, Arkansas. Much has been written about that epochal time, and a made-for-television movie starring Joanne Woodward highlighted events surrounding it. What has not been chronicled is the account of the immediate and subsequent Jewish response to that crisis.

The explosive events of September 1957 at Central High had been preceded three years earlier by the United States Supreme Court decision in *Brown v. Board of Education* to outlaw segregated school facilities. After that ruling several school districts in Arkansas began quietly integrating their schools. In 1955, however, trouble regarding integration developed in some western Arkansas counties such as Lawrence and

Crawford. By 1956 political resistance to integration mounted in the state.[35] In February 1957 the state legislature met to consider four bills that sought to ensure segregated schools. Without debate the bills passed the house 88–1, but because of growing opposition, particularly among religious groups, the state's senators voted 16–15 for a public hearing.[36]

The hearing was held the evening of 18 February. A number of the bills' proponents and opponents presented their cases. Those speaking for segregation included a former Arkansas governor and the pastor of a black Baptist church in Little Rock. Those speaking against it included Baptist, Methodist, Catholic, and Presbyterian ministers from across the state, many of whom came with delegations from their churches. One of the prominent speakers against the bills was Rabbi Ira E. Sanders, spiritual leader of Reform Temple B'nai Israel of Little Rock. Rabbi Sanders, an eloquent orator and respected leader in religious and civic affairs, gave an impassioned plea that the bills be defeated.

Rabbi Sanders said that the four bills, conceived to circumvent the highest legal authority of the land, would "never stand the test of time." He noted that "higher than the legal law of the land stands the moral law of God, which operates slowly but surely." Justice would prevail in the end, he said. Knowing that he was speaking mostly to Christians or to those who were familiar with the Christian Bible, the rabbi spoke from their frame of reference: "When Jesus died on the cross, he repeated those immortal words: 'Father, forgive them, for they know not what they do.' Legislators! may future generations reading the statute books of Arkansas's laws not be compelled to say these words of you. For the sake of the glorious heritage Arkansas may yet give our beloved America, defeat, I pray you . . . these four measures, and the God of all men will bless your handiwork."[37]

Response to Rabbi Sanders's speech included both applause and boos.[38] Nevertheless, his stirring words as well as the pleas of the bills' other opponents had little effect on the senators; with minor concessions, all four bills passed handily. Governor Orval E. Faubus signed them into law on 26 February.[39] Rabbi Sanders's photo was included with the newspaper article on the hearing, and the resolute expression on his face gave evidence of his commitment to the civil rights of all peoples. His speech and his stand simply followed the pattern he had established since assuming the pulpit of Congregation B'nai Israel in 1926.

Rabbi Sanders had been born in Rich Hill, Missouri, in 1894 and educated in the public schools of Kansas City and Cincinnati. He received his rabbinical degree from Hebrew Union College in 1919 and served congregations in Allentown, Pennsylvania, and New York City before accepting the pulpit of the Little Rock congregation. His interest lay in social work, and in 1927 he founded the Little Rock School of Social Work and served as its dean. He also served as president of the Little Rock Council of Social Agencies from 1927 to 1929.[40]

Rabbi Sanders had been in Little Rock only a short time before he became galled at the South's infamous Jim Crow laws, which among other indignities relegated blacks to separate seating in public places. He was particularly incensed when he rode the streetcar one day from his residence to the temple at Fifth and Broadway. After getting on the car, he sat at the back next to a black man. The conductor told him that in the South the colored and white did not sit together. An argument ensued, and the rabbi later conceded that the conductor won the battle in the war of words. Rabbi Sanders got the last word, however, and in his pulpit lambasted the Jim Crow laws and predicted that they would be abolished within the next twenty-five years. The incident initiated Rabbi Sanders's crusade against sectional prejudices and discriminatory laws.[41]

Rabbi Sanders fought prejudices of all kinds. When Alfred "Al" Smith, a Catholic, ran for president in 1928, the rabbi announced in the temple's weekly bulletin that he would speak on "Shall We Elect a Roman Catholic President?" Two prominent men of his congregation urged him not to discuss such a highly volatile subject from the pulpit. One of them offered a one-hundred-dollar check for books for the temple's newly established library if he would refrain. The rabbi's outraged reply was, "Do you think I would sell myself for a mess of pottage?" He gave the sermon to a crowded auditorium, and the state Democratic party asked for permission to publish his lecture.[42]

In his mission against social injustices of any kind, Rabbi Sanders believed he emulated the prophets of old. He later commented that justice and fair play flamed in his heart like a "burning fire shut up in my bones."[43] In 1937 he helped found the Urban League of Little Rock, which sought equality for the community's black citizens. He served on its board for twenty-five years, in both executive and advisory positions. While initially trying to establish the league, Rabbi Sanders had difficulty finding any other whites who would serve with him, but he finally found two. He noted that it later became fashionable for the white community to be on the board, especially after Winthrop Rockefeller was appointed to the organization's national board of directors.[44] Rabbi Sanders organized and was chairman of the Pulaski County public welfare program (forerunner of the federal Works Progress Administration). He also helped found and presided over the Arkansas Human Betterment League and was a founder of the Arkansas Lighthouse for the Blind. Through subsequent years he served on numerous boards of humanitarian, civic, and religious organizations. His untiring efforts of service for minorities brought him honors on a number of occasions from the black community. He received honorary doctorates from the University of Arkansas and Hebrew Union College and received the Humanitarian Award from the Arkansas Council on Brotherhood of the National Conference of Christians and Jews (NCCJ).[45]

Because he pursued for all people the social justice that is embedded in Judaism, Rabbi Sanders never sought to be liked, only respected.[46] When he spoke against the bigoted measures about to be passed in 1957, he was certainly not a latecomer in his overt public stand. As had Rabbi Jacob Rothschild of Atlanta, Rabbi Sanders had spoken out for the equality of blacks "long before it became fashionable."[47] His unswerving stand for social justice during the thirty years prior to 1957 had earned him the respect of his congregation as well as that of the community at large.

The passage of the repressive bills in February 1957 emboldened Governor Faubus and his segregationist followers, and the trouble at Central High School began that fall. Gradual integration, beginning with nine black students, had been planned that year by the Little Rock School Board. On 2 September, avowing he was acting to keep the peace, Governor Faubus called in the armed National Guard, who were instructed to stop the blacks from entering Central High. Faubus removed the Guard on 21 September, and after a mob formed, President Dwight D. Eisenhower placed the Arkansas National Guard under federal control and sent the 101st Airborne Division of the U.S. Army to help control the situation. The president also called for a day of prayer. Rabbi Sanders joined a group of Arkansas leaders headed by Episcopal Bishop Robert R. Brown to propose a Columbus Day prayer rally, called a "ministry of reconciliation."[48] Temple B'nai Israel joined with more than forty-five other houses of worship in the event in which some five thousand people participated. About five hundred met at the temple.[49] Later, when the temple received a bomb threat for a particular Sunday morning, Rabbi Sanders refused to be intimidated, and he held Sunday school as usual. A few brave mothers brought their children to the classes, which proved to be uneventful.[50]

Rabbi Sanders and his involvement in the school crisis garnered national attention in newspapers and magazines, and he received correspondence from individuals statewide and nationwide congratulating him on his endeavors. A telegram from Rabbi Maurice N. Eisendrath, then president of the Union of American Hebrew Congregations

(UAHC), was one of the many that offered encouragement. Eisendrath noted that he was going to "recommend to the National Board of UAHC a mobilization of Reform leadership . . . [and] urge efforts similar to [Rabbi Sanders's] in communities throughout the nation, both North and South." He commended Rabbi Sanders and his colleagues for their "vivid demonstration of the need to apply" the mandates of the day "to the realm of social action."[51]

Rabbi Sanders, as a Jew, was not alone in his involvement in the Little Rock school crisis. Attorney Henry Spitzberg and a number of the city's Jewish women joined with many other concerned citizens in seeking peaceful solutions to integration. Spitzberg, who had begun practicing law in Little Rock in the early 1920s, was one of several attorneys engaged by Little Rock school superintendent Virgil Blossom during the integration crisis. Spitzberg strongly supported the Supreme Court decision and trusted that its implications would help change race relations in the South. He fought for the schools both in the legal field and in action groups that arose.[52]

After Governor Faubus closed Little Rock's high schools in September 1958 to avoid integration, many of the city's civic and religious leaders sought ways to reopen them. Rabbi Sanders met openly as well as in private with like-minded people in the community; together, they helped lay the strategy that would reopen the schools.[53]

Soon after the schools had been closed, three Little Rock women—Adolphine Terry, Vivion Brewer, and Velma Powell—founded the Women's Emergency Committee to Open Our Schools (WEC).[54] The organization quickly grew to include a membership of some one thousand women, most of whom were wives of young businessmen and professional leaders. A substantial number—more than sixty-five—of Reform Jewish women became strong workers in the organization's campaigns. Among these were Josephine Menkus, Jane Mendel, Rosa Lasker, Carolyn Tenenbaum, Ruth Kretchmar, and Alice Back.[55] One of the most active and effective WEC workers was Irene Samuel—wife of local Jewish practitioner Dr. John M. Samuel—who served as WEC's executive director and was considered the group's "organizational genius."[56] Mrs. Samuel later said that had it not been for the help of the many Jewish women, the organization would not have been as effectual.[57] Many of these women worked behind the scenes. Marilyn Siegel, for example, although dying of cancer, raised financial support for WEC from her sickbed.

After the contracts of forty-four teachers and employees of the Little Rock school system were not renewed in the spring of 1959 because they did not support segregation, an action group called Stop This Outra-

geous Purge (STOP) was initiated by several professionals and businessmen of the city. The organization drew support from a cross section
of Little Rock citizens, and many of its male members were husbands of
WEC members. For the most part the businessmen who actively worked
in STOP were the second-rank executives. The city's "real economic
power center gave its approval to STOP only in its tacit permission to
the younger executives and in its financial support of the movement."[58]
Business leadership of the community entered the organization in
blocs—the banks, department stores, and groups of doctors and den-
tists. STOP efforts were successful, and the contracts of all purged
teachers and employees were reinstated. In June 1959 a federal court
ruled that the school closing laws were illegal, and the school board announced that the high schools would reopen that fall. Officers of the
STOP campaign conceded that the group's success belonged to the
work of WEC members. STOP members changed the organization's
name to the Committee for the Peaceful Operations of the Public
Schools, and Irene Samuel was appointed one of its four leaders.[59]

Much of the support from the business community in Little Rock
toward school integration was done behind the scenes because a boycott
list was being circulated. Some of the city's Jewish businessmen favored
integration, but they followed the trend among other such Jews in the
South at the time, privately working with the Christians of like mind
"yet letting few know of their efforts."[60] Other prominent Jewish businessmen and professionals, however, set themselves up as an "advisory"
committee for consultation to the Jewish community as a whole. Actually, it was in essence a censorship group "to keep certain things out of
the press." Although the group did not view itself in a censorship capacity, "its mere existence had a silencing effect on many members of
the Jewish community."[61] In referring to the dominant Jewish response
to the crisis, Rabbi Sanders said, "The Jewish people have always been
lackadaisical when confronted with a social problem." Many followed
the trend of other community leaders, he said, and "were committed to
the status quo."[62] In retrospect we can see that the crisis in Little Rock
erupted so suddenly and violently that few were prepared to cope with
it intelligently. An atmosphere of fear took control, and this fear permeated the Jewish community as well.[63] Although the Jews as an organized
group did not adopt an official position on integration, many non-Jews
presumably believed that the Jews did take a side. This belief stemmed
from the fact that Rabbi Sanders was considered the recognized leader
among them and campaigned to enforce the law of the land.[64] Such an
attitude no doubt was reinforced by the many Jewish women who be-

came active and public in their support of the U.S. Supreme Court decision.

For the most part members of Little Rock's clergy followed the trend of the businessmen, with just a few taking effective action. Among the clergy only eight innovators in race relations could be found in the entire city, and Rabbi Sanders was counted among them. It was known that he used his pulpit to condemn Jim Crow laws and lash out at bigotry and prejudice. He later said that he received little opposition from his congregation for his efforts.[65] The most outspoken of the eight innovators, Rev. Dunbar Ogden, pastor of the medium-sized Central Presbyterian Church and president of the Little Rock Ministerial Association, was not so fortunate. He lost his pulpit because of his actions. His dismissal no doubt helped rationalize and explain the inaction of some of his colleagues.[66]

As Rev. Mr. Ogden and others discovered, serious consequences awaited many who chose to stand for social justice during that tumultuous time. The medical practice of Dr. John Samuel, whose wife Irene was in the forefront of the WEC campaign, suffered greatly. Dr. Samuel had resumed his practice in Little Rock after serving in the U.S. Army during World War II and continued his custom of maintaining an integrated patient waiting room. When segregationist sentiment escalated during the 1950s, some of Dr. Samuel's patients protested at having to share his waiting room with "niggers." He lost so much of his practice that he considered leaving Little Rock.[67]

Pine Bluff attorney Sam Levine was outspoken during the school crisis and was another who paid dearly for his stand. Levine served in both the state house of representatives and the state senate, beginning in the 1930s. He again served in the senate during the crucial years of 1957 and 1959. One of the outstanding moments of his career came in 1959 on the closing day of the general assembly. He filibustered for thirty-three minutes, killing an administration bill that would have packed the Little Rock School Board with supporters of Governor Faubus. This occasion marked but one of very few defeats suffered by Faubus-supported bills in the state legislature.[68] Although Levine had distinguished himself during his long legal career, this incident, which was said to have saved Arkansans "from [their] fevered selves and from [their] politicians," ended his role in government.[69] Levine, who was said to have had the biggest vocabulary in Pine Bluff and the poorest clients, was ahead of his time. He did not run for the legislature again, but he did run for a chancery judgeship in Jefferson County. Although the lawyers of the county backed him, his opponent used anti-Semitic tactics, even painting swastikas on his posters. Levine lost in a primary runoff by ten votes, but in the general election he quietly backed a former opponent, who won the race.[70]

In 1963 the Committee on Race and Religion was formed, and members of different groups met to try to bring factions together. That year the Panel of Americans was established, which succeeded the Women's Emergency Committee. Members of the organization included Catholic, Protestant, Jewish, Oriental, and black individuals. These formed groups of five, one from each background, who spoke at churches, schools, and civic gatherings and gave five-minute summations of the ways in which they had encountered prejudice. It was the first such panel in the South and was well received by its audiences.[71]

After crosstown busing was initiated in 1972 to integrate all of Little Rock's public schools, more than fifty of the city's schoolteachers requested help to ensure a smooth transition. In response Jane Mendel, a member of Temple B'nai Israel, founded the Volunteers in Public Schools (VIPS) program, which began with sixty-seven participants. Mendel was named "Woman of the Year" by the *Arkansas Democrat* in 1973. She was also instrumental in forming the Interfaith Sensitivity Council on the Holocaust in 1979 and was active in numerous civic causes. In 1983 the Little Rock School Board and the VIPS Board established the Jane Mendel Award to be given annually to an outstanding volunteer.[72] By 1987 the VIPS program included more than three thousand workers.

Rabbi Sanders assumed the office of rabbi emeritus of Congregation B'nai Israel in 1963 but continued his community involvement. Speaking to a civic club in 1965, he said that the abolition of racial injustice was the greatest challenge facing America.[73] He remained active in humanitarian, civic, and religious causes until a few years before his death in 1985.

Rabbi Sanders was succeeded in his pulpit in 1963 by Rabbi Elijah E. Palnick, a Canadian native and Hebrew Union College graduate who had served congregations in Alabama and Florida before coming to Little Rock. Rabbi Palnick came at a time when the city and the state were still feeling the aftereffects of the integration crisis, and brotherhood was at a low state. Even the Little Rock Ministerial Alliance had its constitution changed in order to exclude Rabbi Sanders, who had committed so much of his time and efforts to his community. Jews as well as blacks were excluded from the "social bastions," and such actions were condoned (and at times even encouraged) by some of the city's ministers.[74] As a young man of twenty-eight, Rabbi Palnick quickly entered into the religious and civic life of Little Rock and the state. He assumed a leadership role in the Committee on Race and Religion (later known as the Greater Little Rock Conference on Religion and Human Relations), serving with other religious leaders of the city. One of his first efforts in Little Rock was to have his temple host the committee's interfaith, interracial report session. Approximately four hundred church leaders attended the meeting.[75]

Orval Faubus, Arkansas's governor from 1955 to 1967, was still firmly entrenched in power when Rabbi Palnick came to Little Rock, and one of the last areas of the state to be integrated was the state capitol. Rabbi Palnick and his family marched with a group to the capitol to protest the segregation of its rest rooms and other facilities, which were afterwards integrated.[76] The rabbi worked with others in implementing the desegregation plan proposed by Little Rock's school superintendent, Floyd Parsons. He also served on a secret negotiating committee that consisted of about twenty-five of the city's businessmen, educators, professionals, and religious leaders. Four blacks served on the committee: Dr. Roosevelt D. Crockett, president of Philander Smith College from 1961 to 1964, dentist Dr. G. T. Freeman, optometrist Dr. W. H. Townsend, and L. C. Bates. The purpose of the committee, headed by Edward "Ed" Penick, Sr., board chairman of Worthen Bank, was to resolve the problem of desegregating the downtown businesses and other public facilities. (No outlying malls had developed in Pulaski County, and the business district centered in the downtown area.) The strategy was to begin with the tastefully furnished, whites-only, ladies' parlor and rest room of the Gus Blass Company, the city's largest department store. A boycott of the store by blacks, encouraged by the white members of the committee, quickly led to a solution, and the integrated facility was the group's first victory. The Blass store then hired black clerks and later added black cashiers as well. Other downtown stores soon followed suit.[77]

Rabbi Palnick was active in the Arkansas Council on Human Relations and later served as its state chairman. Such councils were formed in the 1950s in eleven southern states as biracial groups with the single purpose of encouraging dialogue between men and women of goodwill of all races. Arkansas's council was chartered in 1955, and Ozell Sutton was its executive director when Rabbi Palnick came to Little Rock. Elijah Coleman, principal of Townsend Park High School in Pine Bluff, succeeded Sutton as executive director. Rabbi Palnick was one of several white members of the council who traveled with Coleman statewide to set up biracial committees. Later, voter registration became another thrust of the council. Rabbi Palnick traveled the state for four years, becoming acquainted with blacks and whites throughout. He stayed

Arkansas Council on Human Relations Meeting, 1970; *(l-r)* Rabbi E. E. Palnick, civil rights activist attorney John Walker, Elijah Coleman, Irene Palnick (courtesy of Rabbi E. E. Palnick).

in the homes of such blacks as the Colemans, Dean D. J. and Georgia Albritton in Pine Bluff, and Dr. Harry P. and Margaret McDonald in Fort Smith. He also stayed at black hotels such as the Arkansas Baptist Hotel in Hot Springs. In Fayetteville he stayed with University of Arkansas professors Morton Gitelman and Otto Zinke, who were white, and Marion "Nip" Smith, who was black. In Jonesboro he became well acquainted with activist Alan Patteson, Jr., a radio station owner and a white liberal Catholic.[78]

The council helped in desegregating Little Rock restaurants, and the strategy was a peaceful one. About thirty eateries cooperated in setting up a pilot program in which two blacks would eat at a specific place for two weeks and then would write up any reactions. For example, Dr. W. H. Townsend and a black attorney were assigned to the popular Franke's Cafeteria, located on downtown Capitol Avenue. They ate there at noon each day, sitting at a large table. No matter how crowded the facility became, no one would sit with them until about ten days into their assignment. A white gentleman sat with them and asked if and at what time they would be there each day. They told him, and thereafter he sat with them. It broke the ice, and others joined them as well. Such efforts were successful elsewhere, and the same strategy was used in integrating the city's theaters and other facilities.[79]

Rabbi Palnick became one of the most outspoken voices against what he perceived as social and civil injustices. In November 1970 when some contributors to the United Fund had become perturbed because the Legal Aid Bureau (a member of the fund) was involved in integration and worked with an organization that led a series of demonstrations at the state welfare department and the Pulaski County welfare department, the fund considered cutting off support to Legal Aid. Rabbi Palnick strongly criticized the possibility, arguing that Legal Aid "provided legitimate redress for some of [the city's] neediest citizens." He faulted some of the wealthy, who "in a fit of pique" sought to take away a basic service to the city's poor. Not mincing words he said, "It is really so shortsighted as to be unspeakable."[80] The rabbi pursued equal employment opportunities for blacks just as forcefully. In 1970 he urged the Governor's Council on Human Resources to take a stand in urging more opportunities for blacks in the state highway department. At the time the department had 3,796 employees, only 62 of whom were black. Although the council did not act on the rabbi's suggestion at the time, by 1986 when the rabbi left Little Rock, the ratio of employees of the highway department was 476 minorities (which were mostly black) out of a total of 3,954.[81]

Rabbi Palnick was elected chairman of the Citizens Advisory Committee when it was appointed by the Little Rock City Manager Board in the 1960s. The purpose of the committee was to identify blight problems—faulty sewer facilities, poor street lighting, inadequate play areas for children, for example—and recommend priorities to overcome the problems. It was also to study the needs for a downtown civic center.[82] Dr. Townsend was elected vice chairman of the committee, and he and the rabbi worked with the city's department heads to discuss the concept of a new era. For example, they had several sessions with the Little Rock Police Department, explaining that a change of attitude was necessary for a peaceful climate to develop (this included eliminating the use of the term "boy" when speaking or referring to blacks). At one time Dr. Townsend and the rabbi were almost arrested by the police when they championed the cause of a young black man who identified an officer who, he alleged, had beaten him. The officer attempted to sue Rabbi Palnick and Dr. Townsend, but the business community intervened on their behalf. Dr. Townsend was one of many who joined a sit-in to help integrate lunch counters, at which time more than two dozen blacks were arrested.[83] Dr. Townsend, Dr. Freeman, and Ozell Sutton, executive director of the Arkansas Council on Human Relations, joined together to form the Council on Community Affairs (COCA), which selected two representatives from each county in Arkansas that had a heavy black population. These members brought the problems of their communities to COCA in Little Rock and were given assistance and information. When Winthrop Rockefeller became governor, he addressed the committee's issues, and most of them were solved under his administration. Rabbi Palnick served on the Governor's Council on Human Relations.[84]

After the initiation of President Lyndon B. Johnson's "war on poverty" in the mid-1960s, an office of the Economic Opportunity Agency (EOA) was established in Pulaski County. Rabbi Palnick was appointed by the United Way as a member of the EOA board, where he served as chairman of the personnel committee. The rabbi met with open opposition on the board in January 1970 after two prominent businessmen, William F. "Billy" Rector and Everett Tucker, Jr., were appointed to the EOA board. The two businessmen brought a split on the board. They were appointees of local government officials and business groups, as opposed to those who were from religious and charitable groups and the poor. Rector and Tucker had previously called some federal agencies, including the EOA, "nonessential" and had recommended that some be reevaluated and perhaps eliminated. There was a verbal clash at the January meeting between Rabbi Palnick and Rector concerning the selection of a new executive director of EOA. (Governor Rockefeller had appointed EOA's director, William L. "Sonny" Walker, director of the state Office of Economic Opportunity; it was the first time a black had been named head of a major state department other than state institutions for blacks).[85] The rabbi and his committee supported Willie D. "Bill" Hamilton, a black Little Rock educator who had been on the EOA staff since 1966; Rector and Tucker supported Virgil F. Gettis, an Atlanta urban affairs coordinator. Hamilton won the position, but Rabbi Palnick lost his place on the EOA board. He returned to it that October, however, as a representative of the Opportunities Industrialization Center.[86]

Rabbi Palnick opposed Rector again in 1971 after the latter served as a leader in a drive to build a private school in west Little Rock. The Pulaski County EOA voted unanimously to oppose any private school established to avoid integration. Ironically, it was Rector who seconded the vote, saying that the new school (known as Pulaski Academy) was not being built to avoid integration but to avoid busing. He noted that if the school should be censored, then other private schools, such as Catholic ones, should be as well. He said that Pulaski Academy would be open to all races. Rabbi Palnick accused the new school's leaders of having a "pagan strain" in civic thought and charged them with racially dividing the community.[87] He spoke to the Little Rock Rotarians in July

1971 and, rebuking parents who helped establish private schools in order to keep them "lily-white," said they would be teaching their children lessons "more vivid and lasting than any that were taught in their houses of worship."[88] After his "stinging rebuke" regarding Pulaski Academy, a reader of a local newspaper's "Answer Please!" column asked if the rabbi's house of worship or his own neighborhood were integrated. The answer to both questions was "no," although the rabbi said that few blacks had chosen Judaism, and any were welcome.[89]

Rabbi Palnick was an active participant in the annual memorial services for the Reverend Martin Luther King, Jr. In 1969 he was one of the principal speakers at such a service, held at the state capitol. At that time the rabbi compared King to Moses, "who refused to be a prince in safety . . . and stood up to Pharaoh." King, like Moses, "did not go into the Promised Land, but only saw it from a distance, leaving it to those who followed" to make the dream real for themselves.[90]

In June 1968 Rabbi Palnick was elected first vice president of the Greater Little Rock Ministerial Alliance. At that time the group was encouraged by its outgoing president, Rev. Lloyd A. Hunter, to become a social action force for the good of the community. The incoming president at the time was Rev. N. Mitchum, pastor of the Bullock Temple CME Church. Hunter said that the organization had been evading the real issues confronting the group and that their meetings had a "stifling business-as-usual air."[91] Rabbi Palnick and other like-minded religious leaders joined forces in helping make a difference in social action. His wife, Irene, joined him in his efforts and served as a member of the United States Commission on Civil Rights during the 1970s and 1980s.[92] She also was active in the League of Women Voters when it began a two-year study of the social welfare services available to Pulaski County residents.[93]

Unlike the women, the male membership of Temple B'nai Israel took little action in social and civil rights activities. Phil Back was one of the few helpers who encouraged Rabbi Palnick; he even attended Ku Klux Klan rallies and took down license plate numbers. In retrospect the rabbi said he had no open opposition to his activities from his congregants. He believed this was because they knew his teachings on social justice were taken directly from the biblical prophets. He did receive veiled criticism in other ways, however, that centered on personal attributes—how he dressed, how he cut his hair, how he looked. And in 1973 the congregation's president, Arnold Goodman, felt compelled to send a memo to the temple's members in response to questions about why the rabbi was out of the city so often. Goodman supplied a list of committees, many of which had to do with civil and social rights, on which the rabbi was actively involved, and he chronicled a number of the rabbi's accomplishments and honors.[94]

Rabbi Palnick served on numerous boards besides those already cited. He was president of the Southwest Region Association of Reform Rabbis and a member of UAHC's Social Action Commission, and he represented Arkansas at the White House Conference on Children. For his humanitarian and social work, he received the NCCJ's 1982 Humanitarian Award from the Arkansas Council on Brotherhood. He was also honored by several Little Rock African American churches. The blacks acknowledged the Jewish involvement and the financial support that came from that community. They appreciated the fact that the Jewish and other clergy could and would say things publicly that blacks could not say for themselves and stated, "We always knew we had the goodwill of the Jewish community."[95] In his article "Southern Jewry and the Desegregation Crisis," Leonard Dinnerstein mentions that perhaps "six to ten" southern rabbis "worked diligently to promote the cause for civil rights."[96] Certainly Rabbis Sanders and Palnick should be counted among that number.

During the 1970s and 1980s Rabbi Palnick was particularly active in interfaith projects. In all his efforts in Little Rock, he was careful to work with a cadre of other like-minded clergy and laypersons. In 1980 he was elected chairman of the Interfaith Denominational Executive Roundtable, which included leaders of Catholic, Protestant, Jewish, and Islamic faiths. He and Rev. James R. Bullock, Jr., assistant pastor of Second Presbyterian Church, started an ecumenical Thanksgiving service in November 1980 that has continued through the years. He actively worked with the Arkansas Council of Churches, founded in 1955, when in 1983 it became the Arkansas Conference of Churches and Synagogues and included the Arkansas Union of American Hebrew Congregations.[97]

Rabbi Palnick was pleased that at least 80 percent of his congregation's children remained in public schools. The rabbi's own children, son Lazar and daughter Rachelle, attended public schools, and Lazar, at the age of six, became a plaintiff in a lawsuit that sought to integrate all the city's public schools. His dad, along with other spiritual leaders and social activists, moved to intervene in the Little Rock school case, then known as *Clark v. Board of Education of the Little Rock Public Schools.* This was the second phase of a lawsuit that had begun in 1956 as the *Cooper v. Aaron* case (of Central High School fame). The group that Palnick joined moved to intervene on behalf of white students who wanted an integrated education. Although federal Judge J. Smith Henley denied them intervener status, they could participate as *amici curiae* (friends of the court). Later, when the schools were integrated, white students who were sent to Booker Junior High on Little Rock's east side were able to see discrimination firsthand. The school had been built about the time that Henderson Junior High was built on the city's west side. Henderson had movable walls, air conditioning, carpeting, and "all kinds of incredible facilities; Booker was bare bones—hot as hell in summer, cold in winter—an eye opener for those who rode the bus and saw what it was like."[98]

As a child Lazar Palnick's first introduction to a courtroom had been in regard to social action. It made a deep impression on him, and he went from being a child going to court to promote school integration to an adult working on such cases. Within a year of his graduation from the University of Arkansas School of Law in 1982, he joined the law firm of prominent Little Rock black activist John Walker. While with Walker he served as the coordinating attorney in some sixty to eighty cases throughout the state. He handled the daily affairs of the Little Rock school case and played a major role in achieving a historic settlement in 1991. His first three voting rights cases, *Sherpell v. Humnoke School District*, *Smith v. Clinton* (which involved the legislative seats in West Memphis in the state house of representatives), and *Lewellen v. Raff* (which covered civil rights leaders running for the state senate), were all successful. The cases marked the beginning of the elimination of major civil rights barriers to black voting in Arkansas. The cases later became the precedent the courts used to declare the entire voting process in east Arkansas unconstitutional and to require reapportionment. The success in the Humnoke case was used as a national precedent in applying the voting rights act to all school districts.[99]

Both Rabbi Palnick and his son Lazar made a difference in social and civil rights before leaving the state—Rabbi Palnick in 1986 when he accepted the pulpit of Albany Hebrew Congregation in Georgia and Lazar in the late 1980s when he married and moved to Pittsburgh. When the rabbi was queried in the 1980s about how he viewed the current status of humanitarian affairs in the state, he said he believed they had seen progressive growth for a while but had begun to slip. On the positive side, he noted that there were no barriers to black or Jewish opportunities, but he also feared that the worsening economic situation of the haves and have-nots might cause additional problems.[100]

Presently there is still wrangling in the courts over the public schools of Little Rock and Pulaski County implementing the terms of the 1991 settlement. Are they working in accordance with the settlement? Are they integrated enough? Is the ratio of blacks to whites equitable? How much consolidation is necessary? And white flight from Little Rock has progressed through the years. Much remains to be done regarding race relations. The Jim Crow laws are gone, however, and the various races can mingle as they will. The redneck bigot does not openly show his or her face, and bigotry is not taught from the pulpit of some churches as it once was. There has been a quantum leap forward in such areas compared to the pre-1957 days. The concerted efforts of both Jews and non-Jews, blacks and whites, working together toward justice for all humankind, are largely responsible for bringing this about.

Rabbi Sidney Wolf: Harmonizing in Texas

HOLLACE AVA WEINER

The story of Rabbi Sidney Wolf offers numerous variables to the kaleido-scopic picture. Corpus Christi boasted a triracial population and an exten-sive military presence. Its lone rabbi mingled easily with the Christian com-munity and served, to a large degree, as the representative Jew for half a century. He achieved positive results through ministerial associations, boards, and quiet brokering, taking the concept of brotherhood beyond racial boundaries in a region where racism, discrimination, and segregation were the rule.

Depression-era Corpus Christi was three towns, not one. On the wrong side of the tracks sat Colortown where blacks, then 5 percent of the city's thirty thousand residents, subsisted in dilapidated rental hous-ing.[1] There was the barrio—poor-to-modest dwellings throughout the west side—a sector that was home to Hispanics, the 45 percent of the populace who labored in the fields, on the docks, and in the trenches digging ditches.[2] The most visible stretches of the city were white, from the sun-bleached beaches hugging the horseshoe bay to the Victorian homes on the bluff overlooking a harbor where oil tankers arrived to gorge their holds with newly discovered crude oil.[3]

Cut off from the rest of Texas by 150 arid miles that ended at the Gulf of Mexico, Corpus Christi seemed the center of a universe, the largest city in a vast farm and ranching region that reached to the Mexi-can border. It was a county seat where "colored" signs directed blacks to the balcony at the movie theater and custom steered Hispanics there.[4] Although the populace was divided racially, segregation and isolation fostered self-sufficient, tight-knit communities. The League of United

Latin American Citizens, which grew into a nationwide organization, began here in 1929.[5] The NAACP chapter that started in the late 1930s produced statewide leaders.[6] Among the white population that governed the town, both Jews and Gentiles, natives and foreign-born mingled on a first-name basis in the shops, on the docks, at the country club, and at the Rotary.[7]

Into this tripartite world in the summer of 1932 arrived Rabbi Sidney Abraham Wolf, a recent graduate of Hebrew Union College, the Reform Jewish seminary in Cincinnati. Texas had not been first choice for the Cleveland-born Wolf, a musically inclined fellow who had hoped for a Midwest pulpit with a first-class organ. Rather, south Texas was his only alternative. Three months past his ordination and still without a congregation, he jumped at the offer from seventy Jews in Corpus Christi for a three-month trial at $31.25 a week. This rabbi remained the next fifty years.[8]

The 25-year-old rabbi was no stranger to auditions. A musician by feel and theologian by training, he had paid his way through seminary as a piano man performing everything from boogie-woogie to Bach in barrooms and ballrooms. Harmony was his forte, improvisation his gift.[9] Still, he was caught off guard by the south Texas environment. His three-day trip by steam train to Corpus Christi ended in culture shock. To this sun-baked coastal city, a casual summer resort, the rabbi wore striped woolen trousers, a high-collared white shirt, and a thigh-length frock jacket. He also carried an umbrella. "This is a rainless town," the rabbi wrote years later in his memoirs. "I must have presented quite a figure.[10]

Although Jews were no rarity in Corpus Christi—the first had settled there in 1858, six years after the city was chartered—a rabbi was an oddity in the region. No rabbi had ever stayed any longer than the Ten Days of Repentance.[11] Yet here was Sidney Wolf—blue-eyed, brown-haired, with a slight build, a warm smile, and a theatrically resonant voice—ready to settle in and ride the circuit. Because the closest full-time rabbis were hours away in San Antonio, Houston, and Galveston, Wolf availed himself for weddings and funerals to the handful of Jewish families living in outlying towns such as Sinton, San Diego, Falfurrias, and Alice. He was likewise on call for the Christian community if need be for counseling.[12] When he was invited to speak one night in the neighboring farm community of Bishop, he grew alarmed as he drove into town and was met by a blanket of darkness. Only one light was on in the town—inside the Methodist church where the rabbi was sched-uled to speak and where the entire populace had gathered for his standing-room-only address. The whole town had turned out to see what in the world a rabbi was.[13]

Local Jews surprised Wolf as well although in other ways. His congregation of seventy souls was relatively well-to-do. Congregants' stores lined bustling Leopard Street. Some had homes dotting the prestigious bluff and ranches extending for miles into the Rio Grande Valley.[14] Nevertheless, the synagogue to which they escorted him occupied an inconspicuous corner at Eleventh and Craig Streets and was, in his words, a "simple shack" built in 1930: "[To] heat the structure there was a potbellied stove and for cooling, a few well-placed electric fans. . . . On Sunday mornings when the children met for classes, we managed somehow to divide the one room into classrooms with burlap curtains for walls. There were no screens on the windows and the pews consisted of hard folding chairs. A pump organ that wheezed more than it gave any semblance of musical sound was played to accompany a choir. . . . There I stood then on Sabbath Eves attired in a frock coat and striped trousers which I had purchased at a chain store in Cleveland for the great sum of $22.50. With a *pince nez* on my nose."[15]

For his first wedding service four months later at Temple Beth El, the diminutive rabbi mounted a platform to appear as tall as the bride and groom. For his own wedding he returned to Cincinnati and married Sara Phillips in June 1933. Sara—slender, stately, blond—shared the rabbi's love of music. The couple had met two years before when he and other students at Hebrew Union College visited her home to hear her father's recording of Tchaikovsky's Fourth Symphony.[16]

For Sara and Sidney the music faded in January 1936. Pregnant with their first child, she traveled from Texas back to Ohio and into the bitter cold for the final weeks of her pregnancy. Six days after the birth of a son nicknamed "Pinney," short for Phineas, Sara died of double pneumonia.

The rabbi, who stood sentry at her deathbed, was devastated yet could not linger to mourn. He had two weddings scheduled the next weekend in Texas. He left the infant in the care of his mother-in-law, missed his son's bris, and dispiritedly made the slow train ride back home. "It seemed that my own little private world had come to an end," he wrote three decades later. "Disconsolate, I returned to Corpus Christi a crushed and devastatingly lonely man."[17]

During that bleak winter, the rabbi was comforted by his Episcopal colleague and neighbor, the Reverend William Capers Munds, rector of the Church of the Good Shepherd. Like the rabbi, Munds was from Cleveland; like the rabbi, he had an extensive collection of classical recordings; and like the rabbi, his Sunday afternoons were free.

"We used to meet on Sunday afternoons to play records," says church member Arthur Elliott, an oil company accountant at the time. "The rector had a good phonograph, a Victor. It was a big box. Sidney would explain what the record was, the circumstances under which that symphony was composed. Then we would play the music."[18]

Wolf, a child prodigy at the piano, could have chosen a musical career. The oldest of three children, born on 8 December 1906, he was the offspring of a Polish father and Lithuanian mother, immigrants to America who spoke Yiddish at home and made a living as wholesale grocers. They started his piano lessons when Sidney was seven and encouraged him to stick with music, but while a senior at the Cleveland Jewish Center in 1923 and 1924, Sidney earned marks high enough to win him several books on Jewish law and lore. He devoured these books and also participated in a series of debates on the question "Was the European Ghetto Beneficial or Harmful to the Jewish Spirit?" The young musician had been introduced to the possibilities of a Judaism that reached beyond that of his introspective, Orthodox upbringing with its emphasis on religious rituals and dietary laws. He was drawn to the notion of a more secular life and a career as a community-oriented rabbi.[19]

During his senior year of soul-searching, two classmates, Rudolph Rosenthal and Albert Goldstein, gradually convinced Sidney Wolf to join them in applying to Hebrew Union College and a career in the Reform rabbinate. Part of the application process required a recommendation from a local Reform rabbi. The first rabbi whom Wolf visited berated him for forsaking his traditional Orthodox Jewish upbringing. His second try at a mentor led him to Rabbi Abba Hillel Silver, who extended the warmest of receptions.

Wolf matriculated at Hebrew Union College with the expectation of blending religion with music. He worked part-time, playing organ at a small synagogue in Hamilton, Ohio, and had a scholarship at the college's conservatory of music. He supplemented his income by playing at roadside honky-tonks and organizing impromptu concerts in the dorm. His serious attention focused on synagogue music. His thesis delved into the compositions of nineteenth-century German Judaic composer Louis Lewandowski.[20]

Few in Corpus Christi cared. His congregants were part Orthodox, part Reform, and most kept their shops open on Saturday—the Jewish Sabbath and the busiest trade day of the week. Wolf had left an environment rich with rabbis and remnants of Old World culture and been transplanted into a relative frontier where revivals and itinerant Bible

Belt evangelists were the norm. To Texans accustomed to twangs and harangues from the pulpit, the young clergyman with the Midwest accent seemed a moral mix of mainstream America and ancient tradition. He was in a prime position to become an arbiter between groups.

In 1934 the rabbi and the Reverend Munds held the city's first annual interfaith Thanksgiving service—a gathering so remarkable in its day that it was subsequently written up in *Time* magazine. In the 30 November 1936 edition of the news weekly, an issue that featured Marlene Dietrich on the cover, the religion page pictured Rabbi Wolf and the Episcopal reverend. Side by side they stood—the rector in a robe, the rabbi in his frock coat. The accompanying article spotlighted their joint Thanksgiving worship experiment, the first interfaith Thanksgiving service in what has become a tradition in Corpus Christi.[21]

> Down an Episcopal church aisle in Corpus Christi, Tex., this week was to march a Jewish rabbi bearing a Menorah or seven-branched candelabrum. An Episcopal rector was to read from the Reformed Jewish prayer book. The rabbi in turn was to pronounce the solemn syllables of the King James version of the New Testament. Cheek by jowl in the church pews would sit Episcopalians and Jews. . . . Decorated by its women's Guild and the Jewish Sisterhood of the Temple, Episcopalians and Jews acting as ushers, the day's offering to go to the needy of both congregations, and the sermon to be preached by the rabbi. His subject this week: "True Brotherly Love." Corpus Christi's inter-faith venture, probably unique in the U.S., owes much to the calibre of its brotherly shepherds. Rector Munds, 44, is president of the city's Community Chest, its Planning Commission and chairman of the Boy Scouts. Rabbi Wolf, 30 next month, is a Rotarian, member of the Civic Music Association, chairman of the county Red Cross.[22]

Praying together was one thing. Socializing on the golf course or at the Rotary was fine too. The liberated rabbi drew the line, however, at intermarriage: "Marriage is in itself such a complex relationship that different religions merely contribute to the problems of adjustment. . . . A couple who has a mixed marriage is welcome to participate in the affairs of the temple, however."[23]

In 1937, as he concluded his year of mourning, Sidney Wolf looked around and noticed no less than forty-two bachelors in his congregation. The rabbi, young and single a second time around, realized that eligible women were few, particularly among the minuscule Jewish community. To ease his loneliness and that of his single, male congregants, he launched a so-called bachelors club for the purpose of "pooling our problems, hopefully to attract the attention of eligible young ladies."[24] He spread the word through the Jewish grapevine. The result: Jewish girls came by train on weekends from San Antonio, decked out in wide-brimmed hats, cloth gloves, and tailored Kelly-girl suits. The men and women picnicked. They danced. And they paired off into couples.

The matchmaking worked for so many that by the summer of 1937 the bachelor club was disbanding, the rabbi still unattached—until his high school friend Rudolph Rosenthal, by then a Cleveland rabbi, interceded with the address of a Jewish girl from a musical family in Louisiana. After an initial exchange of letters, the rabbi took a night train 450 miles to Lafayette, Louisiana, to meet his blind date. It was love at first sight. A five-month courtship and a forty-six-year marriage followed.[25] The woman the rabbi met in Lafayette was a spunky native of Chantilly, France, twenty miles outside of Paris. She was the youngest of five sisters, born in 1912 and named Bertha Rosenthal but called "Bebe" because she was the baby of the bunch. Bebe had grown up in a house filled with music and intellectual stimulation. Her paternal grandfather was a champion chess player. Her mother taught piano in France, then America. Two of her sisters moved to Louisiana as young adults to live with relatives, and when Bebe's father died in 1933 the rest of the family migrated to the bayou region.

Unlike the rabbi's first wife, Bebe was dark-haired and dark-eyed, with a foreigner's flair for turning a phrase. In her tongue the local Loaves & Fishes soup kitchen was "fishers and loafers." She joined the board of Planned Parenthood, and when her husband delivered an unpopular sermon—promoting birth control in 1947 or opposing the Vietnam War in the 1960s—she bluntly assessed the reaction: "Not everybody loved it."[26] When she was invited to teach sex education to the most unruly class of teenagers at the temple, the rabbi's spouse let parents and religious educators know she would teach on her own terms: "There is nothing going to be hidden. We are going to talk about homosexuals . . . IUDs . . . pulling out. . . . We are going to be embarrassed. We are going to get used to it. Children love frankness and honesty."[27]

Bebe came from a community-oriented background. Outwardly, her family was more French than Jewish and more musical than anything else. Once Bebe met Sidney, they played duets at the keyboard, and they played in concert, their own, for as long as they both lived.

As newlyweds they had planned an extended six-month honeymoon in Texas without Sidney's two-year-old son. But when Bebe realized the tot's caretaker-grandmother in Cincinnati was disabled by arthritis, and

Rabbi Sidney Wolf *(center)* visiting the Cole School, Corpus Christi, Texas, 1938 (courtesy of The Dr. Frederick McGregor Photo Collection of the Corpus Christi Museum).

that Sidney carried a weight of guilt concerning the separation from his child, the new bride said, enough. Three months after their marriage in June 1938, the rabbi retrieved his child. Bebe said it was her decision. She had "cleaned up his life and put everything back together."

Bebe was no straitlaced cleric's wife, and Sidney was no typical Bible-thumping clergyman. Clearly, they were an intellectual couple with their feet on the ground, a renaissance pair who found richness in a rural county seat. With Bebe and two-year-old Pinney's arrival in Corpus Christi, the Wolf home became a veritable synagogue annex and cosmopolitan community center. In their home Catholic sisters broke matzo with Jewish families at Passover seders. Here ministers gathered informally for discussions, philosophic and pragmatic. Here, in the 1950s and early 1960s, late at night the phone might ring: a black physician, fear in his voice, would ask the rabbi's help in admitting a sick patient to a hospital that allowed no African Americans on staff. With a few phone calls the rabbi could quietly oblige.[28]

The Wolfs' busy, white, neocolonial home on tree-shaded Leming Street also afforded privacy. A hallway bisected the house, separating the bedrooms from the living room, dining room, parlor, and study. The hallway could be shut off from the communal areas, allowing Bebe, Pinney, and later Joanne (born in 1940) to retreat into their own space no matter who had come to call. The rabbi found ultimate privacy in his backyard, where he built a greenhouse and cultivated orchids.[29]

As Bebe and Sidney settled into the rhythm of married life, the winds of war were blowing across Europe. In 1934 the first of thirty-five refugee families fleeing the Nazi terror came to Corpus Christi.[30] The reality of impending war hit home for the rest of Corpus Christi in March 1941 when Congress created the Naval Air Station, the world's largest such facility, at the southern entrance to Corpus Christi Bay.[31] As men in uniform from all races and all parts of the nation streamed into town, the population doubled and the community's sophistication broadened. Rabbi Wolf volunteered his services as auxiliary chaplain, welcoming servicemen to his home for weekend open houses and performing Jewish weddings in the parlor.

The base's military chaplains were invited into the Corpus Christi Ministerial Alliance, which Wolf had helped launch in the late 1930s. These clergy met monthly to share a meal or a topic of interest and to monitor the pulse of the community. In 1944 this cross section of ministers felt racial resentments stir when black and Hispanic soldiers were refused service at Anglo restaurants and stores. To "prevent and alleviate friction," the ministers created an eleven-member Corpus Christi Inter-Racial Commission to "get quickly to the bottom of many minor misunderstandings."[32]

War united Corpus Christi—and divided it. During one of the Rotary's Thursday meetings at the old Plaza Hotel, Rabbi Wolf bristled when a fellow Rotarian declared that "the Jews should buy more war bonds. If they did not, then Hitler would come over here and give Sidney Wolf a pick axe and order him to dig." As Wolf rose to counter the speaker, a minister restrained him. Instead of the rabbi taking issue, a prominent businessman stood to brand the remarks out of order and in conflict with the spirit of Rotary International.[33]

Although Jews represented less than one half of 1 percent of the city's population, 10 percent of the local boys in uniform were Jewish. When the war took the life of Mayor Robert T. Wilson's son, the rabbi mourned with the Protestant mayor. And in postwar 1946 when the rabbi convened a banquet at the Driscoll Hotel to raise money for Europe's displaced Jews, he invited the mayor to offer the customary greetings to the Jewish community. Rabbi Wolf wrote that instead of platitudes, the mayor, "in a subdued but deeply moving voice, pledged $5,000 in memory of his beloved son who had lost his life on the battle-fields of Europe . . . whereupon it seemed as if the whole crowd rose en masse to its feet to follow the Mayor's example, raising its pledges to meet an astronomic sum"—$126,611.[34]

By then the rabbi's reputation extended beyond the region's pulpits and reverberated deeply within the secular community. Ever certain that music nourishes a community's soul, the rabbi had been instrumental in founding the Corpus Christi Symphony in 1945. The orchestra made its debut in the seaport's largest hall, a six-hundred-seat auditorium at Corpus Christi High School. The symphony's founding president was the rabbi. Its program annotator was the rabbi. Its radio promoter was the rabbi. "This is Sidney Wolf, your musical companion," he would say over the local airwaves. When the symphony performed Prokofiev's *Peter and the Wolf*, the rabbi delivered the narration in his recognizable bass voice that the local music critic deemed "as good as any movie star's."[35]

That deep voice resonated across the city into its segregated pockets. To the black community, Rabbi Wolf was a rare friend, a prominent white man who dialogued with their ministers, spoke at youth group functions and purchased uniforms for youngsters in the African American Boy Scout troop. "I remember the first Boy Scout shirt and tie I ever owned. Rabbi Wolf went and bought it," says James "Jimmy" Wagner, a Corpus Christi native and NAACP leader born in 1925. "My mother was a domestic. She couldn't afford it. . . . The Jewish community was always a friend of the blacks here in Corpus Christi. It was a tradition, and the forerunner of that was Rabbi Wolf. He would make the first move. He wouldn't wait 'til somebody asked him."[36]

Hispanics benefitted from the rabbi's presence as well. "Although he kept a low profile, he was well-known in town and respected as a humanitarian," recalls Dr. Hector P. Garcia, a physician and the founder of the American G.I. Forum, a national Hispanic civil rights organization begun in Corpus Christi in 1948. "[I] know a lot of people he helped. Any time the poor people needed help with money or jobs or food, we would send them to the rabbi. He was always responding. He was one of those people who served everybody, not just the people he was representing. . . . He accomplished perhaps more than we did because of his position as a religious man."[37]

Hispanics had long believed themselves at the bottom of the heap. Despite their numbers they had no clout. In roadside cafes waiters ignored them. At harvest time, regardless of age or experience, they earned ten cents an hour picking onions, cotton, or spinach. Maternity wards relegated Hispanic mothers to beds on a screened-in porch rather than allowing them to share a room with an Anglo patient. Even in death south Texans with Mexican surnames were buried in segregated sections of cemeteries and often barred from funeral parlor chapels.[38] "They didn't think much of us," says retired Judge Hector De Pena, who was born in the Rio Grande Valley in 1914. "We were considered inferior. They used to be called 'greasers' because their jobs made them sweat. Then we were 'Mexicans.' We were humble. We didn't speak out. World War II changed things. We found out we were just as good and maybe even better."[39]

During the postwar era Hispanic and African American soldiers who had fought for their country returned home to Corpus Christi less complacent than before. They now believed they merited some degree of equal treatment. Jimmy Wagner remembers being discharged from the Marines, returning to his hometown, and walking into the Christian-owned Perkins Brothers department store to buy a pair of shoes. "They were not friendly. They said, 'Boy. What you doin' here?' I walked out, went to Lichtenstein's, and was treated courteously. I remember that just as plain as day."[40]

Lichtenstein's was Corpus Christi's Jewish-owned department store, the prestige place to shop, and the first Corpus Christi retailer to promote blacks from positions as janitors to jobs as mail clerks and salesclerks in the ladies' clothing department. Competing retailers slowly followed suit.

The rabbi perceived other ways to mix. In 1948 he began taking his teenage students on annual tours of St. John Baptist Church, an African American institution. Architect Jack Solka, then a Jewish confirmation student at Temple Beth El, remembers vividly the impression these visits made in an era when waiting rooms, water fountains, benches, and lunch counters remained segregated. "Rather than the typical blond angel, the angels on the wall at the church were black," Solka recalls. "It made me wonder and think. It was a real amazement on my part."[41]

The rabbi sought to stir similar interracial thinking among adults in his congregation. One Friday night in 1950, during the oneg shabbat reception following worship services, Rabbi Wolf suggested featuring a black minister on his pulpit in observance of Brotherhood Week. Bebe Wolf remembers: "Some people said 'Why be the first one, rabbi?' Others said it was not the right time. Afterward I asked him, 'Sidney, what are you going to do?' And he said, 'I've already done it!' "[42]

The following Friday evening a black minister, the Reverend Sidney R. Smith of the First Congregational Church, preached from the pulpit at Temple Beth El. With the minister were his wife, Beulah Smith, and the choir she directed at the segregated Solomon M. Coles High School. Smith was a northern-bred, mainstream minister, the most middle-of-the road choice the rabbi could have selected for the interracial debut. Still, some congregants boycotted the temple that Friday night. Others refused to sit in the same pew with "the Negro guests" (as they were called). L. A. Train, then a teenager, remembers some people giggling at the gospel mannerisms of the choir and the repeated rounds of "Hallelujahs."[43]

The rabbi carried on. The student gospel choir returned year after year for subsequent Inter-Racial Relations Sabbaths but with different speakers, among them local NAACP president Dr. H. J. Williams, a physician denied membership in the Nueces County Medical Society from 1956 until 1963. (It was Williams whom the rabbi quietly helped with hospital admissions.) Another year the headliner on the pulpit was dentist H. Boyd Hall, the state's NAACP president and an outspoken activist who integrated Corpus Christi's prestigious Ocean Drive in 1954 but not without a lawsuit against a home builder.[44]

Thelma Spencer Caesar, who sang the "Hallelujah Chorus" with the black choir and who graduated from Coles High School in 1953, looked forward to the annual engagement: "[The] synagogue had the handsomest men and the people were so friendly. People would introduce themselves—Mr. Grossman, Mr. Kane, the Wolfsons. . . . It sort of gave you a good feeling that these people knew something about what you were going through. I started doing reading to find out why they didn't celebrate Christmas."[45]

Caesar, now an administrative assistant at St. John Baptist Church Day Care Center, appreciated the rabbi's year-round presence in the black community. "You saw him in different places, he and his wife." When Caesar and other black students sought to integrate the Y-teens social organization, she remembers that Bebe Wolf, a YMCA board member, endorsed the change.

When African Americans sought to integrate the city's municipal golf course in the early 1950s, Sidney Wolf pushed the measure through while sitting on the Park and Recreation Department Board. In 1953, when Wolf's friend Dr. H. J. Williams, then president of the local NAACP, complained to the park board that blacks were still barred from golf course concessions, locker rooms, and showers, Wolf was irate: "[It] is my opinion that everybody should be allowed free use of the golf course, regardless of whether he is white, brown or black. We don't hesitate to collect taxes from everybody. . . . These men are only asking for elementary rights. They want to be able to buy a Coke or use a locker. . . . It is not for us to feel that we can grant or withhold these rights at our own discretion."[46] Wolf's motion to integrate golf course amenities passed unanimously.

Local Del Mar Community College quietly integrated that same year when a black student applied to the freshman class. The rabbi, aware of the tension the application sparked, waited in the wings to ease the transition. No difficulties arose, however, and other African American freshmen successfully applied.[47] The following year, when the United States Supreme Court ruled that public schools must desegregate, Corpus Christi's citizenry was not as compliant. Token integration and quiet resistance ensued for the next fourteen years—until Hispanics and blacks filed a federal class action suit financed by the United Steel Workers Union.[48]

Sensing the emerging civil rights movement and the need to enlighten the community, Wolf and four other ministers created the Association of Congregations in 1956. The new group's agenda was to put Corpus Christi on the national lecture circuit and host prominent civil libertarians who might broaden the community's soul.[49] Among the charter members of the lecture association was the Reverend Dr. Alfred Swearingen, who had recently moved from a congregation outside Princeton, New Jersey, to Corpus Christi's Parkway Presbyterian Church. Swearingen recalls that he was skeptical about accepting a pulpit in south Texas: "When I was interviewed for the church, I contacted Wolf and the others (Rev. Oliver Harrison at First Christian Church, Rev. Harold T. Branch at St. John Baptist, and Rev. Joseph Brown at The Church of the Good Shepherd) to get a bearing on the sociology and the theological disposition of the community. . . . It's Bible Belt basically and still is. . . . I did find pretty rigid evangelical fundamentalism somewhat rampant in that era. Before I made the jump I wanted to be sure I could survive in that atmosphere. . . . They said, 'Hey, we need ya.' I got stirred up. It was kind of a missionary enterprise in my perspective."[50]

Swearingen, now retired and teaching at elderhostels in Santa Fe, New Mexico, declared the speaker series a popular success: eight hundred to one thousand people attended each lecture in the Ray High School cafeteria, and twenty-one ministers eventually joined the association. "It was an era when the church could be influential," Swearingen says. "When I look back to this era in Corpus Christi, there was a vision and a theological and spiritual sensitivity to effect what was best for the larger society of Corpus Christi."

Not all was upbeat, however. "We were getting negative feedback from a number of our communicants," Swearingen says, recalling his one-on-one conversations with the rabbi. "We had to continually sit down and educate and persevere and talk about where we were coming from ethically and theologically." There were no threats on the clergy, he says; rather, those who disagreed with the move toward racial equality greeted the religious leaders coldly. Sometimes children were more persuasive than men of the cloth. When the adult speaker series led to ecumenical spinoffs among youth groups, Swearingen recalls, "we had some young people converting their parents to a better viewpoint."[51]

"All of this was most unusual in Corpus Christi, as well as for the South as a matter of fact," recalls the Reverend Harold T. Branch, minister at St. John Baptist for thirty-two years. Branch, who in 1971 became the first black elected to the Corpus Christi City Council, credits the rabbi for many of the city's racial strides: "[He] was sort of a pioneer. He lived on the growing edge of his community. If he felt something was right, he would move ahead and do it believing it would win out over the opposition. . . . He was a sharp thinker on his feet. He was good at repartee. He could come back. It was captivating when he would start speaking at meetings and public forums. . . . Our paths just crossed so many times in the course of our lives. He had tremendous compassion for people of all strata. He was at home with all people."[52]

Wolf was there when the NAACP fought for urban renewal—demolition of dilapidated housing leased by blacks from absentee landowners. The controversial push to accept federal funds won city council approval twice during the 1950s and 1960s but went down to crushing defeat in voter referendums. "There was racism in the vote," Wagner insists.[53]

The push for public accommodations in the mid-1960s fared better. Tactics changed. Anglos, energized by church leadership, went with black friends to lunch counters and movie theaters.[54] Rabbi Wolf, Dr. Swearingen, a handful of their colleagues, and scores of their congregants joined blacks in a march around city hall. A public accommodations ordinance followed in December 1964. Still, as late as 1967 Hispanics who worked at the local post office could not get jobs at customer windows nor haircuts from Anglo barbers. "There were very clear lines and divisions in this community," recalls Corpus Christi attorney Tony Bonilla, a former national president of the League of United Latin American Citizens. "There was a lot of dialogue that took place. Rabbi Wolf's work was subtle. He was not out to make a name for himself as some kind of a hero or community healer or compromiser. He just did it quietly. He was always available. He was always on call."[55]

Hispanics and blacks counted on the rabbi's moral suasion and city hall connections to secure Anglo backing for broader representation. Because Jewish merchants and ranchers had deep roots in the region and were part of the city's infrastructure, they mingled among the wealthy Protestants. Wolf saw to it that Jewish connections became a bridge for others. A relentless push continued for triethnic representation on city boards and commissions.

"Rabbi Wolf was a link between the Hispanic community and not only the Jewish community but, in a way, the establishment," Bonilla says. Twice, when Bonilla was invited to Israel as part of a Hispanic delegation, the Jews of Corpus Christi helped underwrite his trips.

"Sidney Wolf was a leader who could bring people together. He had a certain goodness about him. He was very bright yet not considered egotistical, arrogant, or self-centered as many intellectuals are inclined to be. It was possible for him to open doors with the establishment. Rabbi Wolf, by his quiet, moral leadership did a lot to help Corpus Christi find its soul."[56]

Twice Rabbi Wolf seriously pondered leaving Corpus Christi: once after his first wife died, to be closer to his infant son, and later during the war years when a Toronto synagogue offered him a larger pulpit in a more culturally sophisticated region.[57] By then the rabbi was entrenched in south Texas and committed to the wartime effort at the naval base. His oldest son, Pinney, seemed pure Texan, and daughter Joanne was starting school. Bebe "never heard any regrets" about the decision to stay.

When the rabbi retired from the pulpit in June 1972 the bishop of Corpus Christi presented him with a zucchetto—a pink skull cap that is the mark of a Catholic prelate. By then Wolf was the region's senior clergyman in both age and tenure. In his newfound spare time the retired rabbi turned his energy toward the Mexican-American community by teaching Latinos, age seventeen to sixty-five, to read and write at the public school's adult learning center. He indulged himself by creating a course he called "Perceiving Music" for the two local colleges. "I loved to teach rather than preach," he said.[58]

Wolf had had his fill of obligatory pastoral duties. "Visiting the sick, comforting the bereaved . . . are Mitzvos [commandments] incumbent upon every Jew," he wrote in his memoirs. "This is not, in my view and many others in the rabbinate, the prime function of the Rabbi. The Jewish ministry is not a priesthood or pastoral office. Rather it is one of educating, counseling and service to the community and congregation in many directions for the promotion of the well-being of both the Jewish people as a whole and the general community."[59]

When Rabbi Wolf first moved to Texas from Ohio, he led a congregation of fewer than eighty. At first he was a curiosity, but soon he became a key player, whether imitating a wolf at a children's concert, bringing people together at Thanksgiving, or marching for public accommodations.

Three months before the rabbi's death from cancer in February 1983, the Corpus Christi City Council, by then presiding over a town of 231,000, proclaimed a "Rabbi Sidney Wolf Day."[60] The Cleveland-born rabbi who came to Corpus Christi for a three-month tryout had found his calling in a town named for the body of Christ.

Rabbi David Jacobson and the
Integration of San Antonio

KARL PREUSS

Karl Preuss's essay, like Weiner's study of Sidney Wolf, illustrates the expe-rience of a minor participant far from the center stage. Like Wolf, Jacobson worked closely with other activists in a triracial society with an important military component. Unlike Wolf, however, Jacobson served a community with a tradition of rabbinic leadership.

Southern Jews today may admit with some discomfort that many of their ancestors tended to reflect local attitudes about blacks. Thus, ac-cording to one estimate, perhaps a quarter of southern Jews owned slaves. In his *History of the Jews in America*, Howard M. Sachar lists several prominent Jews who supported the southern cause during the Civil War and served in various high-ranking government positions. Judah P. Benjamin, for example, served in several offices for the Con-federate States.[1]

Although Texas was a part of the Confederacy, it is perhaps more difficult to make similar generalizations about Jews who lived in that part of the South. Many of the newcomers to Texas after it became a state in 1845 were Germans who gravitated toward the free soil ideology of the Republican party. Some of these Germans were also Jewish, and, like their more established southern cousins, they usually reflected the prevailing attitudes of their adopted culture. As a result, southern Jews and the recently arrived German Jews of Texas often did not see eye-to-eye on the question of abolition.

Even during the years preceding Texas statehood, Germans settled in central and southern Texas in appreciable numbers. By 1850 one es-timate placed the German population of San Antonio at two-fifths of the total. Another observer placed the German population of San Antonio in the mid-1850s at three thousand, one third of the city's population.[2]

Few Germans in Texas held slaves. In fact, many Anglo-Americans in the 1850s regarded Germans as "damned Dutch abolitionists." According to historian Terry G. Jordan, this image resulted partly from an 1854 convention held in San Antonio during which a small group of German intellectuals passed a resolution condemning slavery. Census figures tend to support the view that Germans were not likely to be owners of slaves. In 1850 the number of Germans who owned slaves in certain east Texas counties in the major plantation area along the Brazos River amounted to only 9 percent. Among the Anglo-American population the figure was 59 percent. In 1860 the figure for German slave holders was 4 percent, for Anglo-American slave holders 72 percent.[3]

What these figures would have been among those Germans who were Jewish is uncertain; however, because Jewish attitudes toward slavery generally reflected those of the larger culture, it is likely that the views of Jewish Germans regarding slavery were similar to the views of non-Jewish Germans. Moreover, most Jews gravitated to urban areas where they established themselves as retailers and merchants. The need (perceived or real) for slaves among these small businesses would have been minimal. This condition seems to have been the case in San Antonio, although the Moke brothers were local dry goods merchants who also dealt in slaves.[4]

Jesse D. Oppenheimer, born in 1870 into a prominent San Antonio family from Bavaria, recounted in 1963 that Jews in San Antonio in 1870 said they had been pleased that the Confederacy and its peculiar institution had suffered defeat. As for those Jews (including Oppenheimer's father and uncle) who joined Confederate forces, they did so, he said, out of loyalty to the land rather than as a statement of support for the southern cause.[5]

No figures exist for the early Jewish population of San Antonio. By 1856, however, there were enough Jews in the city to organize the Hebrew Benevolent Society to assist in Jewish burials. A Prussian named Louis Zork was a charter member. He had been active in San Antonio in 1847 as a Mason and established a grocery store that he advertised in 1851 as having "prices 20% cheaper than any other store in the city."[6] Later Zork got involved in banking and real estate.[7] Other names on the charter included Morrison, Schwartz, Steinback, Feinberg, and Meyer, most of them Jewish Germans involved in retail or trade. Many of these men actively participated in the German community socially and joined

German institutions such as the Turnverein besides becoming members of the Masonic Order.[8]

As the Jewish community in San Antonio matured, it grew in population and financial resources sufficiently to establish a synagogue. The resultant Temple Beth-El was established in 1874 as a charter member of the recently organized Union of American Hebrew Congregations, an umbrella organization for Reform houses of worship. The dedication of Temple Beth-El was a community event. Jews and Christians alike participated, and the Jewish choir was augmented by local church choirs and German singing societies. While Temple Beth-El's second building was under construction in 1902, the congregation held services in a Baptist church across the street. Temple Beth-El reciprocated. Numerous Christian congregations have held services at the Reform synagogue over the years up to recent times.[9]

The Reform movement to which Temple Beth-El belonged departed sharply from Jewish tradition. It focused on ethics rather than the laws and rituals of Judaism.[10] Its universalism found expression in a sometimes aggressive social activism in the civil rights movement of the 1960s.

Rabbis who officiated at Beth-El reflected the outward direction of the Reform movement and involved themselves and their congregation in the larger, non-Jewish community. For example, Rabbi Samuel Marks, spiritual leader of Temple Beth-El from 1897 to 1920, was particularly active in the civic life of San Antonio. At the opening of the Empire Theatre in December 1914 he was present with other civic leaders and delivered the benediction. In 1917 Rabbi Marks described himself as "a prominent—perhaps the most prominent—ecclesiastical figure in the state."[11] Even discounting for hyperbole, the statement is at least a remark on the rabbi's perception of his role outside the local Jewish community. The *Houston Post* wrote of Rabbi Marks that "the utter harmony which the local Jewish community enjoys with its Gentile neighbors, and the respect accorded them, may be traced to the effects of the personality and strong influence of Rabbi Samuel Marks."[12]

Another active rabbi, Ephraim Frisch, championed labor rights during his tenure at Temple Beth-El from 1923 to 1942, at a time when publicly supporting these causes was decidedly unpopular.[13] David Jacobson, who had served with Frisch for several years as associate rabbi, commented that the incumbent rabbi had done a great deal in the community for labor relations. The life of laborers in south Texas was of particular concern to Frisch. Some members of the congregation believed that Frisch had, in Jacobson's words many years later, "gone beyond what he should have done in taking the side of the pecan workers and speaking very harshly of the employers."[14] William Sinkin, one of Frisch's supporters at Temple Beth-El and a prominent businessman in San Antonio who participated in the civil rights struggle, remarked that the rabbi was "a strong, courageous voice for social justice, and he laid the foundation for Temple Beth El's role in integration."[15]

David Jacobson arrived at Temple Beth-El in 1938 to serve as associate rabbi with ailing Rabbi Frisch. Like many Reform rabbis of that time, Jacobson had been brought up in an Orthodox home, although in this case it was the home of his grandparents and his aunt and uncle. They had moved the infant from Cincinnati, where he was born in December 1909, to their home in Indianapolis after his mother died in an accident. Despite his status as a virtual orphan, Jacobson recalled many years later, his life as a child was a happy one in which his family encouraged him to develop his interests in reading and writing. While attending the Arsenal Technical High School in Indianapolis, he worked as a staff writer for the *Indianapolis News*. Because the young Jacobson was so bright, school authorities promoted him to higher grades ahead of his classmates.[16]

After leaving high school Jacobson attended classes concurrently at the University of Cincinnati and Hebrew Union College. Jacobson graduated younger than most of his peers but found few opportunities for a position during what he described as "the very bottom of the Depression." His mentor, Dr. Julius Morgenstern, president of Hebrew Union College, recommended that Jacobson take a position in Mason, Iowa, one of the few communities that was then searching for a rabbi.[17]

Jacobson, however, expressed a preference for study in England and soon found a position as rabbi of the West Central Liberal Congregation of London while he worked toward his Ph.D. at Cambridge. The congregation was founded by Lily Montagu, whose father, Sir Samuel Montagu, had been a leading philanthropist in Great Britain and an important figure in London's Orthodox community. Although Jacobson believed that the two were devoted to each other as father and daughter, he was aware of their intense and unyielding clashes regarding Orthodox and Reform Judaism.[18]

Less strident was Claude Montefiore, another philanthropist and a scholar who had played a leading role in Britain's Reform Jewish community. Montefiore was a liberal man much predisposed to St. Catherine's College at Cambridge, which he helped to support with his considerable wealth. With his encouragement Jacobson enrolled there and earned his doctorate under the guidance of Stanley Arthur Cook, the internationally known biblical scholar.

After completing his studies at Cambridge, Jacobson returned to Indianapolis where he reestablished himself in the city's small Jewish community. As assistant rabbi at the local Reform synagogue, he spoke from the pulpit on a monthly basis. Otherwise he found little to do. The rabbi there, Jacobson later recalled, demanded little of him.[19]

In 1938 Temple Beth-El in San Antonio invited Jacobson to serve as associate rabbi while the ailing Frisch took a lengthy convalescent leave. Like Frisch, Jacobson assumed early on an activist role in the community. Soon after Jacobson arrived in San Antonio, Mayor Maury Maverick, Sr., appointed him chairman of a commission to examine the economic and social health of the city. Jacobson obtained the mayor's agreement to engage the American Public Welfare Association to make an in-depth survey of San Antonio. Jacobson then supervised the project, known as the Citizens' Welfare Survey Committee, which combined the resources of local, state, and federal welfare agencies.

The results of the survey, conducted from July through September 1940, were discouraging. The city, as most observers could affirm, was plagued by social ills, including juvenile crime, lack of street lighting, no electricity in large parts of the Hispanic community, and one of the highest rates of tuberculosis in the country. Out of this survey came a number of institutions, such as the Community Chest (now the United Way) and the Community Welfare Council.[20]

Before much could be done about these problems, however, the nation was plunged into war. Rabbi Jacobson volunteered to serve as a chaplain in the navy. He departed for Houston to apply for his commission and was then assigned to the Potomac River Naval Command. Jacobson later commented that one of the valuable experiences he had enjoyed while in the navy was the chance to fraternize with members of the non-Jewish clergy. During official visits to Quantico, Virginia, for example, he usually had dinner with a Catholic priest, "a splendid individual who confided in me many of the problems he faced."[21]

Following the war Jacobson was reunited with his wife, Helen, and their young family. Jacobson had married Helen Gugenheim six weeks after having first met her in San Antonio in 1938. On his return to San Antonio in 1945 as rabbi of Temple Beth-El, he discovered that the war had transformed the city, which had been home to four air force bases and an army post. These bases later played a pivotal role in the struggle for black civil rights. Indeed, a first step was taken by Brig. Gen. Russell I. Oppenheim, a relative of Helen's who had returned from Europe to assume command of Kelly Air Force Base, an air logistics center in San Antonio. One of General Oppenheim's first acts as commander was to hire a black secretary. The act was unprecedented, but no one launched a serious objection.[22]

Despite President Harry S. Truman's prohibition in 1948 of racial discrimination in the armed forces and in federal hiring, treatment of blacks as second-class citizens remained a fact of life in San Antonio. According to Helen Jacobson, at the end of the war there were *no* integrated facilities in the city. Although blacks were able to attend shows at the Majestic Theater, they were consigned to "nigger heaven," a balcony far to the rear and in the upper reaches of the theater where visibility was poor. Blacks sat in the rear of buses. They could shop at department stores, but they were not permitted to eat at lunch counters or restaurants patronized by whites. There were some cases of what was known as "vertical integration." That is, blacks could be served only if they were willing to remain standing. Presumably owners and managers of food-serving establishments designed this stratagem so they could assert that they were in some sense integrated.[23]

Libraries were also segregated. The Carver Library was the only branch of the city library system open to blacks. During the late 1940s Helen Jacobson was on the library's board of directors. She recalled years later that a librarian in Houston wrote to the San Antonio library inquiring about its policy regarding African Americans. Until late May 1949, when the topic came under discussion, the library board had evidently not given the matter official consideration. The letter generated discussion at a board meeting on 31 May 1949, after which a fellow board member, Dr. John McMahon, moved that the library be open to all, irrespective of race or creed. Mrs. Jacobson and others seconded the motion. The integration took place quietly and without incident.[24]

Later, in June 1954, under pressure from Henry B. Gonzalez, a San Antonio lawyer with growing political clout, the city passed an ordinance integrating all municipal golf courses, parks, and swimming pools. De facto segregation of the swimming pools persisted, and the city issued another ordinance, with stronger wording, in 1956. This time it also included city buses, which at that time were run by a private company. As part of his support for Gonzalez, who graduated from the city council to an eventual seat in Congress, William Sinkin hosted fund-raising dinners. It is a comment on David Jacobson's standing in the community that when these dinners occurred, Gonzalez insisted the rabbi be present.[25]

Meanwhile, several Supreme Court rulings after the war began to overthrow the Jim Crow laws. In 1950, for example, the Court ruled in

Sweatt v. Painter that a separate law school for blacks at the University of Texas in Austin had failed to provide equal treatment because, among other reasons, its policies included arbitrarily separating black law students from white colleagues with whom they would likely interact after leaving law school. Failure to include blacks in on-campus professional and social activities denied them the educational benefits and prestige that were freely available to white students.

The landmark case most identified with the postwar civil rights movement, however, was *Brown v. Board of Education of Topeka, Kansas* in 1954. In this case the Supreme Court ruled that racially segregated schools were inimical to equality and mandated that they be integrated. In the ensuing months San Antonio's school districts gradually desegregated. The following year in Alabama, the black community organized the Montgomery bus boycott to protest the city's refusal to allow blacks to sit where they wanted on public transportation.

As in the rest of Texas and the South, blacks in San Antonio remained segregated despite the presence of relatively few blacks in the city. With the exception of public parks mentioned above, restaurants, lunch counters, theaters, and other public places continued to be segregated. One longtime resident of San Antonio observed that there were no facilities for black travelers along the route that stretched from San Antonio to El Paso, a distance of some 550 miles through one of the remotest and most inhospitable areas of the southwest.[26] Noteworthy, however, and in sharp contrast to practices in some other southern states was that most blacks in Texas were allowed to vote in at least some elections: "If a Negro paid a poll tax, he could vote without hindrance or let. His vote, except in a few areas, could not be decisive, particularly in a one-party state. Black votes could swing close state elections, as in 1960, but little else."[27]

Although it will come as no surprise that most Texans were not keen on the civil rights movement, it did not arouse the rancor and sometimes murderous hatred that it did in states such as Alabama and Mississippi. When the Supreme Court unanimously rescinded "separate but equal" Jim Crow laws in *Brown v. Board of Education,* most Texans seemed to take little notice.[28] One observer in 1962 wrote a summary of these events to the American Jewish Committee in Dallas. "When the *Brown* decision was handed down by the Supreme Court in 1954," he wrote, "there was little stir locally."[29]

As the civil rights struggle heated up, some community leaders in San Antonio redoubled their efforts to achieve social justice for the disadvantaged. San Antonio's Robert E. Lucey, an energetic and sometimes acerbic Catholic archbishop who in 1963 delivered the benediction at

Lyndon Baines Johnson's presidential inauguration, decided six weeks before *Brown v. Board of Education* that the parochial schools of San Antonio would be integrated. There were admittedly few blacks in the city's parochial schools (101), but Archbishop Lucey's was the first diocese in Texas to integrate. Some would argue later that Lucey's decision was an important first step in the peaceful integration of San Antonio.[30]

Archbishop Lucey's personality, style, and standing in the community stood in sharp contrast to Rabbi David Jacobson's. As archbishop, Lucey was spiritual leader to San Antonio's 195,000 Catholics.[31] Jacobson's flock numbered scarcely more than seven hundred individuals, and he was the spiritual leader of only Temple Beth-El, which was unaffiliated with the still smaller Conservative and Orthodox Jewish communities.[32]

When Pope Pius XII elevated Robert Lucey to archbishop in 1941, *Time* magazine asserted that Lucey was "the most socially conscious New Dealer in the Roman Catholic hierarchy."[33] President Franklin D. Roosevelt telegraphed his congratulations. In contrast, when Jacobson arrived at Temple Beth-El as associate rabbi, the event went largely unnoticed.

Aside from considerable public exposure, Lucey also had a strong, combative personality that attracted attention and sometimes undermined his effectiveness. Lucey's biographer recounted an address the archbishop made to the Texas legislature's housing committee in the early 1950s. "He was very authoritarian," a legislator revealed later, "talking to the committee as if he were giving orders to it. He was laying down the social order of the Church, no question about it, but he was doing it in a very authoritarian manner. Telling, not asking. I know I resented it . . . and that was one of the reasons I voted against him."[34] Some of Lucey's detractors referred to him as the "red archbishop."[35]

Archbishop Lucey counted Rabbi Jacobson among his closest colleagues. They shared common values, worked together on social issues, routinely discussed matters on the telephone, and socialized at each other's homes. Unlike Lucey, Jacobson was not confrontational, but he could be direct. His general style and approach to a problem was to be cordial and persuasive. He was not one to man the picket lines; he was nonetheless a tireless soldier for social justice. At a time when blacks were expected to sit at the back of buses, drink from separate drinking fountains, use separate toilets, and accept without complaint routine discrimination, Rabbi Jacobson invited black leaders to speak from his pulpit at Temple Beth-El. Further, he and Helen invited black guests into their home and welcomed them to dinner at their front door. No one in the Reform community seemed to object to their rabbi's unusu-

Rabbi David Jacobson, his wife, Helen, and Archbishop Robert E. Lucey pose at a dinner in 1963 commemorating the twenty-fifth anniversary of Jacobson's arrival at Temple Beth-El in 1938 and his marriage to Helen that same year (courtesy of Zavell Smith Photographer).

ally gracious treatment of blacks. If anything was ever said, it never reached the ears of the Jacobsons.[36]

Another clergyman who played an important, perhaps critical, role with Lucey and Jacobson in the peaceful integration of San Antonio was Everett Jones, bishop at St. Mark's Episcopal Church in downtown San Antonio. Jones was good friends with both the Jacobsons and Archbishop Lucey. They socialized with each other and shared interfaith interests and common values. Harold Gosnell, who worked under Jones for twenty years and succeeded him as bishop, described his mentor as a quiet man with an engaging sense of humor.[37] The Jacobsons found him similarly appealing. David Jacobson underscored that Bishop Jones was a warm and influential human being and one of the most impressive and beloved clergymen in San Antonio.[38] A lack of sources will likely prevent his full story from being told, but one contribution by Bishop Jones that will be remembered is the Ecumenical Center for Religion and Health. During 1967 Bishop Jones and Rabbi Jacobson cooperated to establish the Ecumenical Center at the South Texas Medical Center in San Antonio, where religion and medicine could assist each other in the healing arts. As part of its mission the Ecumenical Center continues to host speakers, train chaplains, promote educational programs, and offer counseling.

Because they worked so closely together for integration and the welfare of the larger community, Jacobson, Jones, and Lucey became known in some circles as the "big three." Conventional wisdom among those who knew these men is that they were key players in the peaceful integration of San Antonio.[39] Indeed, Jacobson related later how the three of them discussed important matters among themselves and then informed the press of what they had in mind. In this way, Jacobson said, they served as the conscience of the community.[40]

On 10 March 1960 Rabbi Jacobson and several other San Antonio clergymen met with a number of San Antonio businessmen to discuss how they could desegregate their establishments. Chairing the group was the Reverend C. Don Baugh, a Protestant minister then serving as executive director of the San Antonio Council of Churches. Baugh's recollection is that he was "the one who first had the idea of our community gearing for action,"[41] a point of view that does not enjoy unanimous acceptance. Baugh did, however, play an important role and helped to galvanize action.

In February, Baugh wrote later, he had sought the cooperation of Mayor J. Edwin Kuykendall, city manager Lynn Andrews, and Dr. James Laurie of the chamber of commerce to convene and chair sessions to discuss ways to desegregate the city. According to Baugh these civic leaders begged off by saying they thought that religious leaders should play this role.[42] Because these civic leaders declined to become involved in the segregation issue, Baugh turned to his religious colleagues and convened the meeting of 10 March that included Rabbi Jacobson.

Besides Baugh and Jacobson about seven other clergymen attended, representing the Catholic community, the San Antonio Baptist Association, the San Antonio Council of Churches, and the San Antonio Community Welfare Council. Also included in the meeting were managers from a number of San Antonio businesses that Baugh thought would most likely be approached by the black community—Joske's, Sears, F. W. Woolworth, S. H. Kress, and others.[43]

No black representatives were present at the first meeting because, as Baugh tells it, the participants from the business community wanted the freedom to air their feelings about integration and their role in it. In retrospect Baugh conceded that not to have included representatives from the black community must have made his efforts seem patronizing. Excluding blacks led to complications.[44]

Because the black community had been unaware of Baugh's efforts on its behalf, on 13 March (a Sunday) the local chapter of the NAACP announced from the Second Baptist Church that it would demonstrate if businesses that NAACP representatives had approached would not desegregate by the following Thursday. Except for Sommers Drug Company, all of the businessmen present at Baugh's meeting had been approached by the NAACP, and all had already set a policy against serving food to black customers. The businessmen had not met with Baugh, however, in response to the black ultimatum but rather to his earlier request to deal with integration. This fact was lost when someone in the group (evidently) leaked news of the meeting to the press.[45]

At a later secret meeting with the clergymen on 15 March, businessmen again aired their concerns about integration. Any kind of disturbance, they agreed, threatened a loss of income. One manager related how a business in another community had lost "several hundred thousand dollars" in one month because of a single small incident. And what would happen to the first business to integrate? Would it be overrun with black patrons? How would the established white clientele react? One clothier said that white women seemed to have no problem trying on girdles and hats that presumably had been tried on by black customers. If white women could tolerate this level of intimacy (some could not), what objection could they have to sitting next to a black person at a lunch counter?

After five hours and forty-five minutes of discussion, and twenty-five gallons of coffee, all the business leaders present, except the one from Joske's, agreed to integrate their lunch counters the next morning, 16 March. Someone from the group contacted four black ministers and invited them to come to the meeting.

One of these ministers was the Reverend Samuel H. James of the Second Baptist Church. He had a close relationship with Jacobson. Not present for reasons that remain unclear was the Reverend Claude Black of Mount Zion Baptist Church. Black, an intelligent and articulate spokesman for the African American community, would later play a role in black/white relations as San Antonio's first black city councilman. His own view of Baugh's committee was critical. He believed that integration had to be secured by the force of law rather than by a simple handshake. If the businessmen present at Baugh's meeting could volunteer to integrate, what was to prevent them from quietly reneging? Although Black was not present at Baugh's meeting to voice his objections, his arguments became known in the local press, where he was sometimes identified as a "radical" spokesman for the black community.

Besides James, the other black leaders at Baugh's meeting were the Reverend P. L. Wood, district superintendent of the West Texas Conference of the Methodist Church; S. J. Davis, a prominent civic leader and comptroller of St. Phillip's College; and James Taylor, Catholic layman, funeral director, and friend of the Jacobsons. These men agreed to the committee's request that there would be no demonstrations for thirty days during which time Joske's, which had been dragging its feet, would decide on what course to take regarding integration. Baugh announced the agreement to the local press.

The role that Rabbi Jacobson played in these deliberations was that of bridge-builder. Jacobson was a mediator. In fact, an agreement between the management of the printing trades in San Antonio and the printing union provided for Jacobson's role as a mediator in labor disputes. Later Jacobson served as an arbitrator for other organizations in San Antonio, in other parts of Texas, and in Louisiana. He sought accommodation and compromise without sacrifice of principle. In addition, Jacobson had already devoted much time to the NAACP and other black organizations to promote interracial harmony. Claude Black, himself an outspoken proponent of civil rights for African Americans, said many years later that Jacobson had been a friend to the black community when white friends were scarce. Furthermore, he thought Jacobson had an approachable personality and that the rabbi was seemingly less inclined than some other Jewish leaders to take issue with the theological differences that have traditionally divided Christians and Jews.[46]

In any event, assured that he had the support of the black community, Baugh issued a statement to the press that starting on the morning of 16 March, a Wednesday, several downtown stores would open their eating facilities to blacks.[47] Joske's asked for a thirty-day moratorium to reconsider its policy. The *New York Times* reported the story on the front page of its Sunday issue.[48]

Baugh's committee had scored an important victory, "the first full desegregation, using the voluntary method in a major Southern city," as Baugh later wrote.[49] The major lunch counters in downtown San Antonio had agreed to serve blacks. Nevertheless, other important work lay ahead. To assure that there was no backsliding, Baugh sent a memo to churches and other congregations in the city asking their ministers and religious leaders to issue a statement of support for the recent integration. Baugh's memo was the product not so much of his own concern but of the several businesses who agreed to integrate. They feared a white backlash. And what would happen, they asked, if one of them were to hold out or renege? This did not happen. The lunch counters were not overrun by black patrons, and those blacks who did eat at the newly integrated lunch counters seemed to receive the same treatment as white customers.[50]

With this much accomplished, Baugh and his committee launched a second phase of lunch counter integration aimed at remaining holdouts in the city. He convened another meeting on 30 March 1960 and invited the same clergy and businessmen who had attended the meeting on 15 March. In addition to these original attendees, the committee invited the managers or owners of several other eating establishments who continued to resist integration. Among these were John Lee of Luby's Cafeterias, a chain headquartered in San Antonio, and Earl Abel, owner of a popular San Antonio restaurant located near the boundary of Alamo Heights, an incorporated community within San Antonio that was home to much of the city's gentry. Although no hostilities erupted at the meeting, some of these owners and managers made clear their determination to hold out against integration.[51]

Meanwhile, Paul Cheatham, Jr., president of San Antonio's Community Welfare Council, had called a meeting for 27 April. Fifty prominent businessmen had agreed to serve on an interracial committee. Twenty-six actually showed up. It was, said Baugh later, the first of many such experiences. Civic leaders agreed to serve on committees but in fact resisted taking any responsibility. This vacuum of responsibility would have to be filled largely by Baugh, Jacobson, and the few other members of the community who were committed to social justice.[52] The eighty-member Inter-Racial Committee, as the group became known, was too unwieldy and needed direction by a smaller steering committee. Three members of the black community served with C. Don Baugh, David Jacobson, and several others in this capacity.[53]

In January 1961, as chairman of the large Inter-Racial Committee, Baugh decided to break it up into nine subcommittees that would focus on such areas as churches, restaurants, theaters, city employment, and housing. The committee experimented with this arrangement for about a year, but Baugh believed that one of the biggest problems the committee had to face was the lethargy that followed the successful integration of downtown lunch counters in March 1960. Joske's had resisted integration for three months and (perhaps unintentionally) made itself a symbol of resistance. When Joske's finally capitulated, Baugh wrote later, "the desegregation of their facilities brought a final lethargy that almost buried all future efforts and motivation for desegregation."[54]

The episode that shocked the city back to its senses took place at the Broadway Theater in Alamo Heights, just down the street from Earl

Abel's Restaurant, another holdout against integration. On 11 April 1961 two officers in the Cambodian armed forces who were students at Lackland Air Force Base had been invited to dinner at the home of a prominent San Antonio family. After dinner the two officers and their hosts decided to see a movie at the Broadway Theater. The theater manager would not allow the two officers to see the movie because he thought they were black. As it happened, one of the officers was a member of the Cambodian royal family. His sister was the queen. When the report of how these officers had been treated reached the royal family, the response was explosive. Officials in Washington made certain that San Antonio, home to five major military installations, understood that there would be no repetition of the incident. In Baugh's words: "Business and civic leaders suddenly grew very interested in the work of the Inter-Racial Committee!"[55]

That interest seems to have been short-lived, however, for in 1962 the steering committee became the de facto Inter-Racial Committee because the larger eighty-member committee had been unresponsive to the demands of integration. The "new" thirteen-member committee included Rabbi Jacobson, C. Don Baugh, and the individuals who had long been committed to social justice. At this point, the committee apportioned the names of major restaurants to its members, who would try to persuade the restaurants to integrate.

At least one of these meetings took place in the home of William and Faye Sinkin. William Sinkin, who had supported Frisch when he served as rabbi at Temple Beth-El, now allied himself with the synagogue's new leader, Rabbi Jacobson. Sinkin and the Reverend Claude Black of Mount Zion Baptist Church decided to take on the lunch counter at Kress's Department Store. Years later Sinkin retold the story. He and Black visited the lunch counter and sat for twenty minutes without being served. Eventually, the manager told them that they would not be served until Black stood up (a case of "vertical integration"). The minister quietly rejected the demand. Black suggested that the manager call his home office and explain that his unwelcome patrons would sit all day at the lunch counter or until they were served. "Some of those folks out there [black patrons in the department store] are my church members. You wouldn't want to drag me out in front of them would you?" According to Sinkin, the manager said nothing but returned after twenty minutes to ask, "What will you have?" Black and Sinkin returned after a few days and were served without incident.[56]

A week or two later Sinkin joined G. J. Sutton in a similar endeavor. Along with the Reverend Claude Black, Sutton was one of the most powerful spokesmen in San Antonio's African American community.

The restaurant they visited was Casa del Rio, one of the busiest in town. Once they were seated, the two men waited for an hour. Sinkin began to get nervous and sweaty. He wanted to leave. Sutton would not hear of it: "We shall sit here until we are served." The manager, who had been Sinkin's friend, took him aside and spoke frankly. "You know I can't serve a nigger." Why couldn't the men just leave and avoid an incident? Leaving, however, was out of the question. The men waited. Eventually, they were served, but (as Sinkin recalled) "in a very hostile manner." As they left the restaurant Sinkin told Sutton that he was too emotionally drained to think about returning to test their success. "Oh, yes, we are coming back," insisted Sutton. "How do you think I felt for all these years?" The men did return and were promptly served without incident.[57]

Jacobson recounted similar efforts in which he was himself involved. Although integration was important, the actual means he used to achieve it were, he believed, not that significant. It was a simple matter, he recalled many years later, to break down the resistance. What he usually did, he said, was simply visit the establishment and explain that the moral thing to do was to integrate. Sometimes he took a black friend to a restaurant where they would sit down and ask to be served. Jacobson's recollection is that these simple tactics were usually effective. He believed that his prominence in the community as a rabbi gave him the moral authority that an ordinary layperson would have lacked. As for the threat of arrest or other ill treatment that characterized attempts at integration in other parts of the South, that, said the rabbi, was out of the question.[58] By 9 February 1962 the Inter-Racial Committee was able to send out letters of appreciation to some thirteen restaurants in San Antonio that had agreed to open their doors to black patrons. Rabbi Jacobson was personally involved in the integration of Luby's, La Fonda, and Earl Abel's, among others.

Not all restaurants that Jacobson approached succumbed to his moral suasion, however. Helen Jacobson recalled at least one instance when her husband left a restaurant on Broadway in Alamo Heights without having been able to persuade the establishment to integrate and indeed was refused service when he entered with a black friend. At the other end of the spectrum, however, the owner of Luby's Cafeteria actually thanked Rabbi Jacobson for breaking down racial barriers. Years later Jacobson recounted the event to a local newspaper: "[We] were there for a very long time without being waited on, so I went to the waiter and insisted he serve us. I was stubborn about it. Later on, the top official of that restaurant chain told me, 'I didn't want to [open the restaurant to blacks], but I've discovered how right you were, and we should have

done it on our own long ago.' "[59] The introduction of black patrons had
in no way inhibited business, and the fears that some businessmen had
privately voiced, such as a white backlash or being overrun with black
customers, never materialized. Furthermore, a number of restaurants
decided to integrate on their own.[60]

Efforts to integrate the city continued into the spring of 1962. In
April and May, Baugh later reported, hotels began to serve all guests
who were in the military or who were at the hotels as part of a convention. In June the hotels expanded their acceptance of black guests to
those who registered in advance. By the end of the year major hotels in
San Antonio dropped all restrictions on black guests.[61]

Details about Rabbi Jacobson's role in this process of integration remain unclear because of the paucity of documentation. Recollections
from that time are now vague and uncertain, and out of deference to
those who were reluctant to be among the first to integrate, the press
gave the matter a low profile. There was never any court action or public disturbance; the integration of San Antonio proceeded quietly and
without event. For that reason alone the story is worth retelling because
it provides a marked contrast to how events unfolded in such Deep
South cities as Montgomery and Selma. Rabbi Jacobson himself never
kept a record of his effort to bring about integration. "It wasn't a big
deal," he once announced to the author over lunch. This self-effacing
rabbi was indeed one of the "quiet voices."

Nonetheless, it is fair to conclude that Jacobson played an important,
perhaps critical, role. He was San Antonio's key Jewish advocate of integration, a role he could not have played without at least the tacit support of Temple Beth-El, which he continued to serve until his retirement in 1976. Bob Rosow, former president of Temple Beth-El and
longtime friend of the Jacobsons, commented to a local newspaper in
1988 that "while almost every other major city in the nation was torn
asunder by the fight over desegregation," owing partly to Jacobson's efforts, "there was none of that in San Antonio."[62]

In January 1989 the city's African American community recognized
Jacobson's work on its behalf by conferring on him the Martin Luther
King, Jr., Distinguished Achievement Award. Jacobson's support of
the black community was not confined to his efforts to integrate San
Antonio in 1960. Besides having been a longstanding member of the
NAACP, Jacobson was chairman of the scholarship committee for the
Martin Luther King, Jr., Memorial City-County Commission and
served as board member with a score of other philanthropic and chari-
table institutions that benefitted San Antonio's citizens, both white and
black. The rabbi also helped to establish a Jewish/black dialogue in San

Antonio. Helen Jacobson, also active in social causes, had served as chair of the United Negro College Fund campaign.[63]

Rabbi David Jacobson was much more than simply spiritual leader of San Antonio's Reform Jews. His willingness to participate in the larger, non-Jewish, community and his friendship with prominent political and ecclesiastical figures such as Henry B. Gonzalez and Robert E. Lucey allowed Jacobson to speak with greater authority than if he had merely carried the Jewish flag in the civil rights struggle or represented solely Jewish concerns. Rabbi Jacobson spoke with a moral authority that transcended sectarian issues. A tradition of activist rabbis in a city that viewed its ministers as leaders and was willing to bend with the times contributed to gradual, peaceful change.

The Prophetic Voice: Rabbi James A. Wax

PATRICIA M. LAPOINTE

Several southern cities impacted by the civil rights movement had great hopes for gradual reform given recent alterations in municipal government structure. Memphis was one of these cities. Expectations were shattered, however, when a businessman/mayor refused to compromise on an issue that linked race with economic inequities. James Wax, sometimes fiery in temperament when faced with injustice, joined a line of rabbis willing to speak out. He, too, had role models of an independent, socially conscious rabbinate, and he, too, worked closely with other clergy in a leadership capacity. On 31 March 1995, Rabbi Harry K. Danziger, Wax's successor, commented at a conference in Memphis on southern rabbis and black civil rights:

> *People like Rabbi Wax saw the moments that brought them such public notice and eventually adulation as, in fact, tragedies. Rabbi Wax believed so deeply . . . that reasonable people of good faith could sit down and work out the very worst of society's problems. The fact that the situation had come to his standing up publicly before TV cameras and confronting the mayor of the city or that the clergy marched on the office of the mayor was no triumph for him. Anyone who thinks about the advocates of what they called prophetic Judaism knows that the great prophets of chastisement like Jeremiah and Rabbi Wax's role ideal, Amos, never wanted to get up before the people and say what they had to say. They only did it because there was no other choice and because God commanded it. I believe that Rabbi Wax would gladly have given up the public praise he received had people of good faith using reason sat down behind closed doors and worked things out.*

Late on the evening of 4 April 1968, a stunned nation learned of the death of Dr. Martin Luther King, Jr., his life cut short in Memphis by a then unknown assassin. The grief and rage of many black Americans erupted in riots across the country. A grim President Johnson, joined by political and civil rights leaders, called for calm amid increasing violence.[1]

In Memphis, Mayor Henry Loeb continued his "no compromise" stance in the fifty-three-day-old sanitation workers' strike that had brought Dr. King to Memphis and a martyr's death.[2] On Friday morning a memorial service for Dr. King was quickly organized by the Memphis Ministers Association and held at St. Mary's Episcopal Cathedral. The association was headed by Dr. James A. Wax, senior rabbi of Temple Israel, the city's oldest Jewish congregation.[3]

Following the service the clergymen gathered in the cathedral crypt for the reading of a prepared statement urging the mayor to take immediate action to resolve the workers' grievances and peacefully end the strike. On vote the statement was approved, and the ministers left the cathedral to march to the mayor's office. Solemnly, some 250 clergymen, headed by Rabbi Wax and William A. Dimmick, dean of St. Mary's Cathedral, marched in pairs—black and white—through strangely quiet streets cordoned off by hundreds of helmeted police and national guardsmen with drawn weapons.[4]

The mayor's office was under tight security, and a shotgun lay on the floor under his desk.[5] In a room crowded with police officers, ministers, and television cameramen, the Reverend Bill Aldrich read the prepared statement urging Loeb to end the strike. It was followed by an impassioned plea for justice by the Reverend James A. Jordon, pastor of the historic Beale Street Baptist Church.

Deeply moved by his own emotions and the gravity of the situation, Rabbi Wax faced Mayor Loeb and in an admonitory voice recalling the prophets of old said: "We come here with a great deal of sorrow and frankly with a great deal of anger. What has happened in this city is a result of oppression and injustice, the inhumanity of man to man, and we have come to appeal to you for leadership in ending this strike. There are laws greater than the laws of Memphis and Tennessee and these are the laws of God. We fervently ask you not to hide any longer behind legal technicalities and slogans but to speak out at last in favor of human dignity."[6] That moving, extemporaneous statement was carried on local and national television. It provoked a firestorm of response—some supportive—most full of hate and racism.[7] What circumstances had brought this man of God to the most dramatic moment in his life?

James Aaron Wax was born 20 December 1912 in St. Louis, Missouri, the first son of Morris and Rose Edlin Wax. The family moved soon after to the small town of Herculaneum, a center for lead mining located on the Mississippi River thirty miles south of St. Louis. Morris opened a dry-goods business and took an active part in his community, serving several terms on the local school board as well as working actively for the Democratic party. For most of their years of residence in Herculaneum, the Waxes were the only Jewish family in town.[8]

Although growing up outside a traditional Jewish setting seems an unlikely beginning for one who later chose to enter the rabbinate, the experiences of these formative years were important in shaping the social awareness that influenced the life of James A. Wax. In a company-owned mining town that opposed organized labor, he learned about issues that affected the working class. As a champion high school debater, Jimmy Wax developed skills that would serve him well in the pulpit. On several occasions, he was invited to speak at local churches, and he became adept at interacting with the Christian community. The easy social relationships of small-town life helped the young Wax develop the openness and warmth that was such an asset in working with people from all walks of life.

In the early 1930s, while a student at Washington University in St. Louis, Wax was strongly influenced by the sermons of Rabbi Ferdinand Isserman of Temple Israel in that city. Stressing the ethical values of Judaism and its strong commitment to social justice, Isserman challenged his temple youth to take an active role in alleviating injustice.[9] Although Wax had been considering a career in law or politics, inspired by Isserman and encouraged by a hometown Methodist minister, he chose the rabbinate as a means to achieve social justice through spiritual leadership.[10]

Isserman and Wax were among those Reform rabbis who followed the path of social justice activism marked out by Stephen Samuel Wise, foremost early-twentieth-century Reform rabbi. In a 1975 sermon marking the centennial of Stephen Wise's birth, Dr. Wax affirmed that "Wise's interest transcended the Jewish people and thus he sought to correct injustice wherever it might be found. He was a courageous champion of social justice . . . the model which we Jews might well set for ourselves: loyal to our own people, faithful to our religious heritage, concerned about the plight of mankind."[11]

Financial constraints of the depression required Wax to transfer from Washington University to Southeast Missouri State College, where he received his B.A. in 1935. With Dr. Isserman serving as his mentor, Wax applied for entry into Hebrew Union College in Cincinnati. Lacking a background in Hebrew, Wax took intensive course work in the language to prepare himself for admission to the college. An outstanding student, Wax received the bachelor of Hebrew letters degree in 1939 with honors as the top student in Hebrew. Two years later he was awarded the master of Hebrew letters degree.

Ordained to the rabbinate just a few months before America's fateful entry into World War II, Jimmy Wax had hoped to enter the chaplaincy program but was turned down for military service. Between 1941 and 1945 he served congregations in St. Louis, Missouri, and Glencoe, Illinois. While interim rabbi at North Shore Congregation Israel, James Aaron Wax married Helen Louise Goldstrom. The ceremony took place at the bride's home temple in Baltimore. Rabbi and Mrs. Wax later had two sons, Jonathan I. and James A., Jr.[12]

In 1946 Wax was called to be associate rabbi of Temple Israel in Memphis, one of the largest Reform congregations in the South. Following the retirement of Dr. Harry Ettelson in 1954, Wax was named senior rabbi. At his installation service, he pledged that "this pulpit shall ever be concerned with the problems of life. Whatever affects human beings, children of God, shall be of utmost concern. I shall make no distinction by virtue of religion, nationality, or race, for we are all children of one God."[13] He honored that pledge throughout his ministry.

Commitment to human rights formed the foundation of Wax's long years of ministry and community service. This commitment was clearly articulated in an address he made to the National Federation of Temple Youth on 2 March 1946. Wax pointed out that from its inception, the federation had been concerned with social justice, and he emphasized that "the preservation of peace in the world depends ultimately upon the degree of justice which is practiced by the citizens of [each] country." Among the urgent social needs he discussed were full employment at fair wages, facilities to provide for the health and well-being of individuals, decent housing, and equality of African Americans. Wax asserted: "Despite the fact that eighty years have passed since the Negro was emancipated, he remains for all practical purposes a degraded and oppressed people and the task of conferring the rights to which he is legally and morally entitled rests upon us." Wax affirmed that Judaism adopted a broad view of morality and considered every problem of society a moral problem, showing "concern for the relations between man and man as well as the relationship between man and God." Significantly, he admonished other rabbis to speak out "with vigor, with clarity, and if need be, with courage upon current social problems."[14] Rabbi

Wax spent a lifetime living out that philosophy through forceful, vigorous sermons, challenging public messages, and actions that gave substance to his words.

In many respects the late 1940s and the 1950s were good years in Memphis, marked with postwar growth and economic prosperity. These were years when Rabbi Wax showed his concern for the disadvantaged and victims of social injustice through organizations that worked to meet human need. He was committed to improving and extending health care, recognizing that those who lived on the economic fringe, especially blacks, had limited access to medical assistance. His compassion for the mentally ill and impaired placed him in the forefront of organizations seeking to serve these often-neglected members of society. In the early 1950s Wax was an organizer and president of the Memphis Mental Health Association, which had as a major goal the establishment at the state level of a separate board for the supervision of mental health facilities.

In 1953 Governor Frank G. Clement appointed Wax a trustee and member of the newly formed Tennessee Mental Health Commission. Wax worked tirelessly to improve professional services and the quality of care for the mentally impaired. Never hesitant to take a strong stand on behalf of those who had no champion, Wax challenged the political interference of Governor Ray Blanton, who in 1975 fired the medical director of Western State Hospital at Bolivar, Tennessee, because of local patronage pressures. During a committee hearing on the matter, Wax was moved to righteous indignation by the governor's action and in a face-to-face confrontation heatedly charged Blanton with political manipulation that threatened the hospital's accreditation.[15] A *Memphis Commercial Appeal* editorial commended Rabbi Wax for his principled stand in the "confrontation with Governor Ray Blanton over the political patronage mess at Western State Hospital."[16]

Concerted efforts by the Memphis Mental Health Association to secure a new psychiatric hospital for the city succeeded when the Tennessee Psychiatric Hospital and Institute opened in the medical center in May 1962.[17] A new hospital activities facility constructed in 1982 was dedicated as the James A. Wax Building in recognition of Rabbi Wax's outstanding service to the mental health field.[18]

When Dr. Wax retired from the state board in 1984, a resolution commending his thirty-one years of selfless service read in part: "Now, therefore, be it resolved by the Board of Trustees of the Department of Mental Health and Mental Retardation of the State of Tennessee, that we salute the Honorable Rabbi Wax for his fervent dedication to the cause of improving the mental health, alcohol and drug, and mental retardation care system and pray that his retirement from the Board will not lessen his advocacy for these principles."[19]

In other health care areas, Wax supported from the outset efforts to fund the building of the now world-famous St. Jude Children's Research Hospital, the dream of entertainer Danny Thomas. Wax also served on the boards of the United Cerebral Palsy Association, the Shelby County Tuberculosis Association, and the Mid-South Center Council for Comprehensive Health Planning. In addition, he worked to obtain employment for the mentally and physically handicapped.

As a respected member of interfaith organizations such as the National Conference of Christians and Jews and the Memphis Ministers Association, Dr. Wax was a bridge-builder of understanding and cooperation between religious bodies. This ability to inspire unity is exemplified in his faculty appointment to the Memphis Theological Seminary, where he served as an instructor in Hebrew studies from 1972 to 1985. A school of the Cumberland Presbyterian Church, Memphis Theological Seminary was committed from the outset to ecumenical outreach, and Rabbi Wax was instrumental in this intent. At Rhodes College (formerly Southwestern at Memphis), Dr. Wax was the distinguished lecturer on Judaism for eleven years. This lectureship was endowed by the Jewish Chatauqua Society.

The recipient of several honorary degrees, Rabbi Wax was awarded the doctor of Hebrew letters in 1966 by Hebrew Union College for outstanding contributions to the field of religion. His service to the Memphis community was recognized in the awarding of the doctor of humanities degrees by Christian Bothers University in 1975 and by Rhodes College in 1978.[20]

Message of Judaism, Dr. Wax's weekly program broadcast over radio station WMPS from 1961 to 1978, was well received; to many in the community, he represented the Jewish voice. He later appeared as a regular panelist on the WREG television program *What Is Your Faith?* Not only did Wax build bridges between Christian and Jew, he also sought to strengthen smaller Jewish groups in Memphis. To that end he worked toward the establishment of a Conservative synagogue and gave generous assistance to Rabbi Arie Becker when Congregation Beth Sholom undertook the building of a new sanctuary.[21]

While faithfully carrying out the pastoral duties of a large congregation, Wax was also active in local and national Jewish endeavors. In 1971 he was instrumental in forming the Memphis Rabbis Association, organized to promote the welfare of the Jewish community.[22] Wax rendered distinguished service to Jewish education, letters, and religious organizations, including long tenure on the board of governors of Hebrew Union College, the Central Conference of American Rabbis (treasurer), the Southwest Conference of American Rabbis (president), the executive council of the American Jewish Historical Society, and the American Jewish Committee.

In March 1956 the *Tri-State Defender*, the Memphis black weekly newspaper, honored Wax for his "consistent effort to bring about peace and harmony between the races."[23] Rabbi Wax was a frequent speaker at high school and college interfaith services, often appearing on programs at black schools. In January 1956 he spoke on Judaism at Rust College in Alcorn, Mississippi, and participated in discussion sessions with students and faculty. Two months later, as a matter of principle, Wax withdrew from a Religious Emphasis Week speaking engagement at Mississippi State College, following action taken by the Right Reverend Josiah G. Chatham, pastor of St. Richard's Church in Jackson, Mississippi. Wax's only public comment was that he had decided not to speak after "careful consideration of the restrictions on subjects which would be discussed."[24] The action of Rabbi Wax and Rev. Chatham followed the highly publicized withdrawal of all clergy who had been scheduled to speak during the February 1956 Religious Emphasis Week at the University of Mississippi. The unanimous action of these clergymen, one of whom was Rabbi Milton Grafman of Birmingham, Alabama, came in protest to the university's cancellation of its invitation to the Reverend Alvin Kershaw, a white minister associated with the NAACP and an outspoken opponent of segregation.

Significant accomplishments in obtaining civil rights for black Memphians resulted from the work of the Memphis Committee on Community Relations (MCCR). Created in late 1958 by a group representing a cross section of the city's leadership, the organization received its charter from the state of Tennessee in January 1959. Its primary objective was to end segregation in Memphis without the violence that marked such efforts in so many southern communities. In a letter to prospective founding members, Lucius E. Burch, Jr., well-known attorney and a principal organizer of the MCCR, pointed out that "the increasing wave of bombings, violence, threats, and demonstrations [are] bound to worry every thoughtful citizen." He noted that suspicion and tension were increasing between black and white citizens because there was no adequate forum for discussing problems that needed to be addressed, and Burch underscored the fact that the only articulate leaders were the extremists of both races.[25]

Quietly and with little or no publicity, the MCCR provided the forum where white and black Memphians were able to work cooperatively to secure desegregation of public facilities. Prominent citizens

were chosen to head committees on public transportation; public libraries and museums; public colleges, universities, and schools; public playgrounds, parks, and zoo; and public housing.[26] The work of this organization was so successful that the Kennedy administration sent observers
to Memphis to study the methods used by MCCR to end segregation in
public facilities with a minimum of community opposition.[27]

After the process of desegregating public facilities was on its way
to full realization, the MCCR, recognizing that the black citizens of
Memphis were vastly underrepresented in public office, lobbied elected
officials to appoint blacks to governmental boards and committees. This
pressure was followed by MCCR support for qualified black candidates
seeking elected office. In the late 1960s MCCR focused its efforts toward providing improved economic opportunities and job training for
black Memphians. Three targeted areas included access to more and
higher-paying jobs, elimination of fraudulent lending practices (which
especially affected blacks), and involvement of neighborhood merchants
in social work that benefitted their customers.[28]

Rabbi Wax served as secretary of the MCCR until its demise in the
1970s. At least three of the prominent business executives associated
with MCCR were Temple Israel members. As the owners of large Memphis corporations, their leadership in desegregating employment in
their own companies was extremely important in bringing about civil
rights in the work place. In the midst of his work with the MCCR,
Rabbi Wax was asked to serve on Mayor William B. Ingram's Community Action Committee. Initiated in January 1965, its stated purpose
was the development of a community-wide antipoverty program, with
job training for young blacks. The mayor sought federal funding
through the Office of Economic Opportunity to implement the Community Action Committee's programs. Because Mayor Ingram was
politically controversial, other agencies in the community, notably the
Memphis Chapter, Tennessee Council on Human Relations, objected to
mayoral control of federal funds.

In August 1965 Rabbi Wax was named chairman of the Community Action Committee's policy committee, most of whose members
were black. In spite of external conflict Wax's committee established a
number of beneficial programs. Although community activists were in
agreement with Community Action Committee objectives, their disagreement concerning control of federal funds and the selection of committee members brought an end to the organization. The committee was
formally dissolved in January 1966.[29] In his notification letter to Dr.
Wax, Mayor Ingram wrote: "The programs which you have promoted
and established in our City have received nationwide recognition for

their efficiency and creative ideas. Thousands of children and parents have benefitted from these programs and our City is a better place in which to live. There is no way that I can adequately express my heartfelt appreciation for your loyalty to the City of Memphis in the many hours of toil and frustration that have been yours in an attempt to move this program forward. The City of Memphis is deeply indebted to you, and I am personally indebted to you."[30]

Wax was also active in other organizations working for civil rights, among which were the Tennessee Council on Human Relations, the west Tennessee chapter of the American Civil Liberties Union, and the Memphis Urban League. That his membership in these groups was substantive and not merely in name only is affirmed in a letter written to Wax by J. A. McDaniel, director of the Urban League. Asking for Wax's assistance in obtaining vocational guidance for black students, McDaniel wrote: "Your help is needed and is always greatly appreciated."[31]

An important civic undertaking to which Rabbi Wax contributed much time and energy was the Program of Progress, a reform movement organized to restructure local government. The city's progressive leaders believed that the commission form of government, which had been dominated by the old Crump political organization, was a major handicap in the move toward civil rights for black citizens. The Program of Progress was a broadly based cooperative effort forged from a "wide power base [that included] the predominant Negro leadership, labor, the Republican leadership, the New Guard Democratic machinery, the Chamber of Commerce, the old reform movement, and a smattering of prominent clergy and social leaders."[32] Many key leaders in the Program of Progress were major activists in the Memphis Committee on Community Relations. A successful referendum on 8 November 1966 secured the adoption of the mayor-council system of city government, scheduled to become effective in January 1968.[33]

The first mayor elected under the new municipal government plan was Henry Loeb III, and three of the thirteen council members who took office with him were black. Their election had come about with the support of those activists working for civil rights. In his inaugural remarks Loeb said: "There is a new spirit in the community . . . and a new sense of purpose. These are indeed fitting companions for the new form of government which begins today."[34] Rabbi Wax gave the invocation at the public swearing-in ceremony on 1 January, prayerfully asking that "our leaders will always place human values above material consideration. May the welfare of all our people be their purpose and concern."[35] A brief three months and five days later, Rabbi Wax faced Mayor Loeb in an extraordinarily dramatic confrontation.

The administration of Mayor Henry Loeb was marked by one of the most traumatic events in the nation's history as well as by the most significant labor action in the history of Memphis. More than a labor action, the sanitation workers' strike proved to be a watershed event in the civil rights struggle.[36]

When he took office in January, Loeb was an experienced public servant, highly educated, personable, and well liked in the white community. He came from a prominent Jewish family and was associated in their business, Loeb Enterprises.[37] At the inaugural ceremony Judge Marion Boyd praised Loeb as a man who would measure up to his vast responsibilities and display courageous leadership. Barely in office a month, Loeb faced a major strike against the public that was prolonged by his opposition to negotiation and strong antiunion position. Loeb's refusal to negotiate with the strikers reinforced the belief of most in the black community that he was a racist.[38]

In Memphis city sanitation workers were the lowest paid group of public employees. Commonly referred to as garbage men, 90 percent of these workers were black. The workers did not receive any overtime or holiday pay, and it was not until the 1950s that they were provided with health insurance. Renewed efforts to unionize the bulk of the sanitation workers through the American Federation of State, County, and Municipal Employees were initiated early in 1968.[39] Prior efforts to unionize these men had met with strong resistance and hostility in a city with a long history of opposition to organized labor. There were "only 40 dues-paying members out of 1,300 sanitation employees when union president T. O. Jones called a strike meeting in February 1968."[40]

The deaths on 31 January of two sanitation workers who had been crushed in a faulty garbage compressor provided the catalyst for the 12 February strike. This forceful action was not only a response to the death of fellow workers but was also an explosion of pent-up frustration resulting from years of subsistence pay and unresolved grievances. Only after the sanitation workers' strike was well under way did national union leaders become involved in the Memphis labor action.[41]

From the outset of the strike Mayor Loeb adamantly refused to negotiate with local organizers, striking workers, or others in the community. Loeb repeated emphatically that the strike of public employees was a violation of state and municipal law, and he staunchly refused to discuss union representation until the men returned to work. Throughout the strike the city attorney, Frank Gianotti, provided strong support for

Loeb's position and backed him all the way on "no work—no negotiations."[42]

An article in the *Wall Street Journal* on 8 March stated that "Mayor Loeb has become the prime target of the strikers who accuse him of 'superciliousness and intransigence.' Although he advocated racial equality as a mayoral candidate last November, few Negroes forget his championing of segregation in 1959 when he was first elected [mayor]." Jesse Turner, Sr., a director of the local NAACP, was quoted as saying that "Henry Loeb has done as much to unify Memphis Negroes as any one man could do. His attitudes have given us something to rally around."[43]

Unfortunately, escalating tensions in the sanitation strike might have been fueled by both city newspapers. Some have claimed that most news coverage ignored the real issues that had brought about the strike and that the reporting provided racially slanted headlines, cartoons, and editorials that described the strike as the work of labor radicals and blacks determined to get their way at the expense of the public good.[44] Rather than calling for outside arbitration and reasoned negotiation, the newspapers supported the "absolute law and order" stance of Mayor Loeb and the police department. The black community was further angered when Loeb authorized the use of mace and tear gas to stem violence when on 28 March a protest march led by Dr. King got out of control and rioting and looting ensued.

Most individuals in positions of civic responsibility totally misjudged the volatility of the strike and failed to heed those voices warning that the city was sitting on a powder keg with a short fuse. In this rancorous situation the Memphis Ministers Association sought to provide a forum for discussion and, hopefully, the means to end a strike that was becoming increasingly bitter and racially focused.

In May 1967 Rabbi Wax had been elected president of the Ministers Association. He was the only Jewish clergyman in the organization, and his election marked the respect and esteem in which he was held by his colleagues. The group elected James W. Lawson, Jr., a black Methodist, as vice president and Joseph Eckelkamp, a Franciscan priest, as secretary-treasurer. It was the first time that either a black or Catholic had been chosen for an elected office.[45] Although there were some African Americans in the Ministers Association, most of the city's black clergy belonged to the Interdenominational Alliance.

In a report to Rabbi Richard G. Hirsch of the Religious Action Center in Washington, Wax noted that after taking office as president of the Ministers Association, he strengthened the Social Action Committee and also appointed a Committee on Race Relations. Seeking ways to end discrimination and prejudice, the biracial committee drafted a statement, "An Appeal to Conscience," that appeared as a paid advertisement in Memphis newspapers on 4 February 1968, a week prior to Race Relations Sunday. Wax wrote that his "feelings of opposition to the Mayor became rather strong" when Loeb ignored a request from the Race Relations Committee asking that he issue a mayoral proclamation supporting "an end to racial discrimination in all areas of human experience." Wax noted that because Loeb was the city's elected leader, his failure to support the ministers' statement elicited strong feelings of resentment from members of the committee.[46]

On 16 February Rabbi Wax was contacted by black ministers, who asked for his help in resolving the strike. Accompanied by members of the Race Relations Committee, Wax met with P. J. Ciampa and other national union leaders who had come to Memphis in support of the sanitation workers. Wax and his committee urged that the strike be deferred for several weeks to allow for serious negotiation. This the national representatives of the American Federation of State, County, and Municipal Employees were unwilling to do, fearing that such action would cause the union to lose face. Rabbi Wax then offered to host a forum at which the mayor and the union leaders could discuss an equitable settlement of the workers' demands.

A meeting was set for Sunday evening, 18 February, at St. Mary's Episcopal Cathedral. Jerry Wurf, president of the AFL-CIO American Federation of State, County, and Municipal Employees, had arrived in Memphis late Sunday night and, after a briefing by his men, joined the local union leaders gathered at St. Mary's.[47] In an extremely ironic situation a Jewish national labor leader confronted a mayor who had been born into the Jewish faith and was identified as a Jew in a meeting arranged and mediated by a Jewish rabbi. The talks, with the local press sitting in at Loeb's insistence, went on until 5 A.M. on Monday, the nineteenth. Loeb would not talk directly to the national union representatives; thus, the mediator was required to repeat all statements, lengthening the discussions and fraying tempers.

The meeting resumed Monday afternoon at St. John's United Methodist Church. Nothing was resolved. Later, the white ministers met with their black colleagues to attempt some constructive solution to the impasse. Rabbi Wax noted in an oral history interview of May 1968 that these meetings were made difficult by the strained circumstances under which they took place.[48] As spokesmen for the sanitation workers, the black ministers reflected the hostility and resentment resulting from the breakdown of communications with city officials, increased police force used against the strikers, and Loeb's opposition to unionization. As the strike continued, racial animosity increased.

Rabbi Wax, president of the Memphis Ministers' Association, appeals to Mayor Loeb for racial justice (courtesy of *The Commercial Appeal,* photograph by Robert Williams).

Because of the black-white tensions in the community, Rabbi Wax called a meeting of the Ministers Association for Wednesday afternoon, 3 April 1968, at St. Mary's Cathedral. Representatives of both ministerial groups were present. Feelings ran high among the black ministers, who demanded action—not calm deliberation. Angry accusations were made. Rabbi Wax, whose forte was reasoned discussion, found himself in a lions' den of seething emotions and volatile rhetoric.

The group met again the following morning at Mason Temple, a black church in the Beale Street area. By that time tempers of most black ministers were at the boiling point. The white clergy had seriously underestimated the overwhelming frustration and anger these black ministers brought to the meeting, and they were not prepared for the demand that the group immediately march to the mayor's office. Although the Ministers Association had previously approved a march, the group felt such action would only further anger the white public and be counter-productive to any negotiated settlement of the strike. Most white ministers, including Rabbi Wax, declined to join the march.[49]

The shocking assassination of Dr. King on Thursday evening, 4

April, left the city stunned and terrified. The efforts of the Ministers Association to provide a forum for ending the strike were overridden by the enormous tragedy of Dr. King's death. The strike was finally settled on 16 April when the sanitation workers gained union recognition and other benefits.[50] The strike united the black community in Memphis as nothing else had in the city's history.

In the fall of 1968 Charlotte M. Davis, a member of the social science department of Clark College in Atlanta, wrote the following letter:

Dear Rabbi Wax:

This has been a year right out of the book of Job for most of us. I want to tell you that the only thing of it I remember clearly, sharply, and positively is the little minute on television I nearly missed. As long as a man can and will stand up and speak as you spoke, I guess I can keep doing my work and have faith in the future. You spoke in the finest tradition of the prophets, a tradition that belongs to both you and me. I know that our God is proud of you, and I thank you for giving me something to face 1969 with. Some men can speak for one, some for a few, but you spoke for all of us who hope for justice to tyrants everywhere.[51]

In his letter thanking Ms. Davis for her encouraging remarks, Rabbi Wax responded: "The quest for justice has never been easy, but with faith in God one is moved to search for righteousness. It is my deepest hope and prayer that justice will come to all of God's children. To me this is the essence of our great moral codes."[52]

The events of early 1968 had shocked, saddened, and scarred the city; nevertheless, there were positive results in spite of the tragedy and turmoil. Memphians were forced to deal with long-ignored racial injustice. People of goodwill across the city united in a process of healing and forgiveness.

A decade later in February 1978, Rabbi Wax was presented the National Human Relations Award by the Memphis Round Table of the National Conference of Christians and Jews. He was honored by religious and civic leaders from all parts of the city and state, including Tennessee senators Howard Baker and Jim Sasser. In accepting the award, Wax said: "It belongs to the 250 Christian ministers who stood side by side with me in struggles for racial equality." He expressed his "deepest thanks to the Christian people of this city for the kindness and friendship they have shown me for more than 30 years." Leo Bearman, one of the evening's speakers, told the audience of more than eight hundred: "We at Temple Israel want to tell you how proud we are that you chose our rabbi, our friend, one we hold in highest esteem, for this honor."

Judge W. Otis Higgs, Jr., prominent black jurist and civic leader, saluted Wax for his great courage and for having taken unpopular stands on racial equality during the struggle for civil rights.[53]

The Temple Israel trustees adopted a formal resolution recognizing the great honor Dr. Wax had received. It read in part:

> As in the intimacy of a family, among our Congregation, the achievements and honors which come to one of our members are a genuine satisfaction to all of us. Especially is this the case when our spiritual leader, Rabbi James A. Wax, is chosen to receive the Brotherhood Award annually presented by the National Conference of Christians and Jews. To Temple Israel, men, women, and children alike, the continued striving of Rabbi Wax for understanding and accord among all elements of our society is a matter of current and constant awareness. He has, by precept and example, demonstrated to us for 32 years the teachings which are the essence of prophetic Judaism and which, indeed, shall be the guides by which men come to peace in a troubled world. . . . We are especially grateful for the years we have had with our beloved Rabbi and his conscientious ministry to us and to our entire community. In sharing him with all the citizens of Memphis, we the congregational family of Temple Israel, recognize that he has fulfilled that sublime mandate spoken by the Almighty to Abraham, "Be thou a blessing." The life of Rabbi James A. Wax and his work in Temple Israel and in all of the community to which he has ministered have been a rich and bountiful blessing.[54]

A few weeks later Wax retired as senior rabbi of Temple Israel, having served his congregation and his city with zeal and faithfulness, but his interest in the welfare of the community continued unabated. From 1978 to 1989 Dr. Wax served as acting rabbi at Temple Beth El, a small congregation in Helena, Arkansas. While preaching the Yom Kippur sermon on Friday, 6 October 1989, he spoke about the moral right of all citizens—especially the poor and elderly—to receive decent, affordable health care. The old fire was present and the voice strong. Suddenly stricken, he could speak no more. James Aaron Wax died 17 October 1989, his last public utterance having been consonant with a life dedicated to ministry and to serving all God's children.

Epilogue

Rabbi Wax understood that the struggle for justice and human rights for all people is never easy and that the battle is ongoing. The unstinting service he gave his community was recognized with awards and honors that read like a who's who of public service. He left as a legacy many things that his family, his congregation, his friends, and his city cherish, among which was his moral leadership during a time of great trial when the social fabric of this nation was nearly rent in two.

Deeply committed to his own religious heritage, Rabbi Wax also made lasting contributions during his forty-three years in Memphis as a builder of interfaith communication and understanding. Innate kindness and integrity, combined with a strong desire to serve the total community, enabled him to work constructively across racial and religious lines.

As a young man Jimmy Wax had entered the rabbinate with a vision for social justice in the context of Reform Judaism. The year 1968 placed him squarely in one of the country's major civil rights actions. His courageous leadership at that time was but one manifestation—albeit a dramatic one—of a lifetime of serving others.

His death was widely mourned in the community, and the *Memphis Commercial Appeal*, as well as the publications of religious and service organizations, noted his many contributions to improving the quality of life in the city.[55] Congressman Harold Ford, the first African American elected to the House of Representatives from Memphis, called Rabbi Wax the conscience of the city. The editor of the Catholic diocesan newspaper affirmed that "Memphis lost a great force for justice when Rabbi James Aaron Wax died last week," and the writer recalled the patience, compassion, love, and faith that characterized Wax's work.[56] It was a life that had been dedicated in the fullest measure to carrying out the admonition of the prophet Amos: "Let justice roll down like waters and righteousness like an ever-flowing stream."

Rabbi Grafman and Birmingham's Civil Rights Era

TERRY BARR

The civil rights movement reached an apex in Birmingham as it had in Memphis, virtually simultaneously with a change in municipal government. Yet unlike James A. Wax, Milton Grafman served in a city with a rabbinic tradition of circumspect social consciousness and a strong tendency toward racial intransigence. He chose to walk his way through the civil rights era with careful steps. Caught in a middle ground, he was shocked when the Reverend Martin Luther King, Jr., used him and his coworkers as symbols of the failure of the gradualist approach. In a controversial article published in the June 1994 issue of the Journal of American History, *Michael J. Klarman has argued that moderate racial change was indeed occurring in such southern cities as Birmingham prior to the* Brown *decision of 1954. Changes were sluggish and local, however, and King and his lieutenants recognized the need for confrontation to obtain national support and federal assistance. Given strategic considerations, then, the moderation that individuals such as Rabbi Grafman saw working and wanted to continue to pursue would be counterproductive. Klarman quotes Wyatt Walker as stating with hindsight, "We knew that when we came to Birmingham that if Bull Connor was still in control, he would do something to benefit our movement. We didn't want to march after Bull was gone." Terry Barr's story of Grafman raises numerous "what ifs": What if King had waited until after Connor had been removed from office? What if the gradualist approach had been allowed to take its course? What if Grafman and others had been willing to take more dramatic steps? What if a James Wax, Jacob Rothschild, or Charles Mantinband had occupied a Birmingham pulpit? Historians can resort to hindsight when grappling with such questions but with little hope of reaching any more than controvertible hypotheses.*

In mid-twentieth-century Birmingham, Alabama, the drama of racial segregation took center stage. Although many groups were involved, it is perhaps hardest to define the role of individuals who took a gradual approach out of fear of what might happen to the community if it were confronted too dramatically. Attempting to straddle the fence, these individuals sometimes met criticism from many directions. In hindsight, even the historian might question whether these gradualists did or said the right things.

Such was the case of Milton L. Grafman, rabbi emeritus of the oldest of Birmingham's three Jewish congregations, Temple Emanu-El. Rabbi Grafman's religious and civic role in Birmingham spanned six decades, and although he was instrumental in pushing his own congregation and Birmingham citizens of all backgrounds to be more tolerant and accepting human beings, and although he instituted and served on numerous biracial committees, he was uncomfortable about his legacy.[1]

To him, Birmingham in the early sixties was a "no-win situation."[2] To take any stand in Birmingham during the civil rights era that even remotely suggested a willingness to talk to black leaders and end segregation left him (or any white person for that matter) open to recrimination, threats, and possibly violence, yet not siding fully with Dr. King in those days left him vulnerable to charges of bigotry. He remembered that years after the Birmingham struggles of the early sixties, at the closing of temple service a visitor had asked, "You were the one at the Birmingham jail, weren't you?" referring to the fact that Rabbi Grafman and seven other Birmingham clergy had written an open letter to Birmingham's blacks asking that they not follow Dr. King. This letter precipitated King's famous "Letter from Birmingham Jail."[3]

Beginnings and Birmingham

Milton Grafman was born in Washington, D.C., on 21 April 1907 but spent most of his childhood and adolescence in Pittsburgh, Pennsylvania. As a freshman at Fifth Avenue High School, Grafman took an advanced ancient history course and joined in a decision with his classmates that deeply affected him: "[I] was raised in Pittsburgh and went to integrated schools in the public school system. At that time, though, not only didn't blacks and whites socialize; neither did Christians and Jews. [In the ancient history course] . . . our teacher instituted something called 'socialized recitation.' Every two weeks the class elected a program committee to study assignments and make up questions to ask in class. The class was overwhelmingly white, though it had a few blacks in it. But I'll never forget that for the first president of the class committee, we elected a black student. His name was Robert Seal."[4]

Rabbi Grafman also recalled a senior English class assignment to write about where they hoped to be in fifteen years. Unbeknown to the class these essays were to be printed in the yearbook. As part of his response Grafman wrote, "It has always been my desire to see justice prevail, and for this reason, I trust that the future will find me in one of the two positions best suited to attain this end—at the bar or in the pulpit."[5] Initially it seemed that the legal profession might win Grafman's services; however, after he received his B. A. from the University of Cincinnati in 1926, his older sister persuaded him to enter Hebrew Union College "to at least find out about the rabbinate."[6] And find out he did, becoming an ordained rabbi in 1933. After serving as rabbi in a Lexington, Kentucky, temple from 1933 to 1941, Grafman was offered the position of rabbi at Birmingham's Temple Emanu-El. He arrived there on 8 December 1941.[7]

Grafman had vowed to "become a chaplain behind the lines," a vow that proved prophetic far beyond the literal war to which he was referring.[8] His own role as rabbi to Birmingham's oldest synagogue demanded of him civic responsibilities that sorely tested his spirit. Since the late nineteenth century Birmingham has been a racially and ethnically diverse city. Its booming steel industry attracted workers of varied backgrounds through the first half of the twentieth century. Since the beginning of the twentieth century Birmingham's Jewish community has also been strong. Congregations K'nesseth Israel, Temple Beth El, and Temple Emanu-El represented Orthodoxy, Conservatism, and Reform, and many of the members of these congregations were successful merchants.

Birmingham also had its share of problems, and the Ku Klux Klan was one of the biggest. In 1922 "the city's Robert E. Lee Klan alone boasted 10,000 members and was the largest Klavern in the South. Furthermore, there was a total of 20,000 Klansmen in Birmingham in the general population of 217,500 people. Jews constituted only 1.84 percent of the local citizenry whereas the klansmen constituted more than 9 percent of the city's populace." During this time "Klan whippings, floggings, and kidnappings . . . were commonplace." Although Jews were almost never the target of Klan violence, the climate of fear worked on the psyches of Birmingham's Jews. After a hiatus, by the late 1940s Klan activity rose again to quell demands for black equality.[9]

Even before the upheavals of the civil rights era, Grafman began addressing social and religious issues. The first of these struggles was within his own ethnic community. In the face of the Holocaust and even though the Central Conference of American Rabbis in their 1938 Columbus platform had reversed the long-standing position of the Reform movement on Zionism, many southern Reform Jews continued to reject the concept of a Jewish state. This position held true in Birmingham as elsewhere. From 1945 to 1948 Rabbi Grafman participated in the Zionist movement "to the distaste of a number of his congregants who were associated with the anti-Zionist American Council for Judaism." Along with sixty-eight other "locally active Zionists," he signed a full-page ad in a local newspaper asking the federal government "to tell the British Government to stop this ghastly mockery . . . [and to] carry out without further delay the recommendation of the 100,000 refugees (to Palestine). And for God's sake stop this regime of brutality and repression in Palestine."[10]

When the state of Israel was established in May 1948, the Birmingham Zionists, including Grafman, celebrated. As has been observed, however, they also misjudged the viability of the partitioning of Jews and Arabs. Grafman was optimistic: "I feel the partition scheme will work out and that the threats of the Arabs will prove to be just threats. While there may be some violence, I don't believe there will be either Civil War or major strife between the Jews and Arabs in the Holy Land. I feel that Palestine Jews and Arabs will work out their destiny together."[11]

The rabbi's hope, in its idealism, foreshadowed other Grafman visions. Rabbi Grafman also worked to improve Jewish-Christian relations. In 1943 he founded the Institute on Judaism at Temple Emanu-El "to help educate Christian clergy about the Jewish faith." He may also have been instrumental in broadening the scope of what was then the Protestant Pastors' Union, which changed its name to the Ministers' Association of Greater Birmingham after his arrival in 1951. He later became the first and only rabbi elected as its president.[12]

Such improved relations between Christians and Jews existed alongside anti-Semitic sentiment. In the late 1940s and 1950s, during the McCarthy anti-Communist hearings and the beginning of the civil rights movement, Rabbi Grafman found himself the target of anti-Semitism.

In 1955 Dave Campbell, host of a popular radio call-in talk show, asked Grafman to be his substitute host for that evening's nine-to-midnight slot. Grafman "didn't want to do the show at first" because he thought it would be "opening a can of worms." Nonetheless he agreed. All went well until 11:00 when an unidentified caller asked, "Who are the biggest and worst traitors in America?" implying Julius and Ethel Rosenberg. When Grafman identified Benedict Arnold as one, the caller interrupted him: "C'mon Rabbi, you know what I mean." As the caller became "abusive," Grafman tried to calm him. Without warning, the station engineer, who was new on the job, pulled the plug, and for the next three minutes listeners heard only static. Grafman urged the engineer to put the show back on because cutting the caller off was, in Grafman's view, "the worst thing to do." The engineer listened to Grafman's plea, and though Grafman received another bad call, soon numerous calls of support poured in, ending the show on a decidedly edgy but hopeful note.[13]

That same year Rabbi Grafman was invited to speak at the University of Mississippi's religious emphasis week. One of the other speakers was an Episcopal priest, the Reverend Kershaw from Ohio, who had recently won a large cash prize on *The $64,000 Question*. The university canceled Kershaw's appearance when it heard of his intention to donate a share of his winnings to the NAACP. Grafman not only withdrew from the event in protest, but he also successfully urged the other participants to follow his lead. When this story appeared in the Birmingham newspapers, Grafman received hate calls. One caller insisted that he "haul [his] ass back North with the rest of the nigger-lovers." The rabbi obtained a police whistle and blew it into the phone on receiving such calls.[14]

Another confrontation occurred when the Ku Klux Klan wanted to set up an exhibit at the 1964 Alabama State Fair held at Birmingham's Fair Park. Grafman, feeling that such an arena was "an inappropriate location for a Klan exhibit since thousands of children would see it," made a motion at the National Conference of Christians and Jews that that body ask the Fair Authority to bar the exhibit. Their request was granted. The Klan threatened the rabbi and his congregation with a million-dollar lawsuit charging libel. Although Grafman considered this a "publicity stunt," and although the charges were dropped, the rabbi lived under this and similar threats throughout the 1960s.[15]

Birmingham in the 1960s, Part One: Denial and Bombs

In 1963, at the height of the Birmingham desegregation demonstrations, Jews constituted "approximately one-half of one percent of the total county population."[16] In the late spring of that year Rabbi Richard Winograd, who had come to Birmingham along with eighteen other outside rabbis to support the "Birmingham Negroes," observed that "the Negroes to whom [they] spoke seemed to sense that 'the Jews are not fully white men.'" He further noted that "one Negro said to him, 'A Jew can't make a good racist.'"[17]

For blacks Birmingham was a nightmare in many ways: Blacks accounted for 40 percent of the city's population but were three times less likely than white residents to hold a high school diploma. Only one of every six black employees was a skilled or trained worker, whereas 75 percent of the white population fell into this group. The median annual income for blacks was three thousand dollars, less than half of what white's earned. Singer Nat King Cole [a native of Montgomery, Alabama] had been beaten on stage during a 1956 Birmingham performance, and on Labor Day, 1957, a carload of drunken whites had grabbed a black man off a street corner, taken him to a country shack, and castrated him.[18]

Martin Luther King, Jr., described an entirely segregated city in which the NAACP had been outlawed by Birmingham officials in the 1950s for being a "foreign corporation. From 1957 through January of 1963, while Birmingham was still claiming that its Negroes were 'satisfied,' seventeen unsolved bombings of Negro churches and homes of civil rights leaders had occurred."[19]

One of those whose home and church had been bombed was the Reverend Fred Shuttlesworth, founder of the Alabama Christian Movement for Human Rights (which replaced the outlawed NAACP) and leader of Birmingham's black activists. After Shuttlesworth's house was bombed, *Pittsburgh Courier* columnist Trezzvant W. Anderson asked, "Were there any arrests? . . . You can bet your life there were not. . . . The Reverend Mr. Shuttlesworth himself was chained and whipped on a public street by a white mob at Phillips High School when he took his children there in 1957 to seek to enroll them [in the white school]. His wife was stabbed during the same incident with white cops present. Has anybody been convicted? No indeed."[20]

In the early 1960s, *New York Times* reporter Harrison Salisbury visited Birmingham and wrote a series of articles that documented the fears of Birmingham's black and Jewish citizens. Salisbury reported that "volunteer watchmen stand guard 24 hours a day over some Negro churches. Jewish synagogues have floodlights for the night and caretakers. Dynamite attempts have been made against the two principal Jewish temples in the last 18 months."[21]

In one of its many disingenuous refutations of Salisbury's points, a *Birmingham News* editorial argued: "There have been no dynamite attempts in Birmingham in the last 18 months. The only such attempt at Temple Beth-El occurred April 28, 1958, when this community was shocked by an unsuccessful attempt to dynamite the house of worship." The *News* also complained about Salisbury's reporting that "his [Bull Connor's] men apprehended two young men with an old-fashioned

hearse in which dynamite and anti-Semitic literature were found. They
had parked beside a synagogue and told a negro watchman they were
going to blow the place up. But the young men did not go to prison.
They were freed on their own recognizance by the judge when the witness did not appear."[22] Neither the witness nor the rabbi had been told
the case was coming up.

The *News*'s rejoinder was that "no dynamite was found in the hearse.
The Negro watchman was present at the trial in which the two young
men were given jail sentences of 180 days each, with the sentences suspended on condition they leave Birmingham."[23] According to historian
Mark Elovitz, the fears of Birmingham Jews were further confirmed
when, in mid-October of the same year, the janitor of Temple Emanu-El
was accosted by two men in a car: "You'd better get out of here—this
will probably be the next temple to be bombed." The two men were
caught. They told police they were members of "the National States
Rights Association," an anti-Jewish, anti-Negro organization. These incidents ceased but the concerns remained.[24]

Rabbi Grafman and the Birmingham Jewish community faced still
more threats in the following decade. In 1963 "the KKK conducted a
large mass meeting on the outskirts of Birmingham. As a result of this
and a stepped-up campaign to distribute anti-Jewish and anti-Negro
hate literature by the National States Rights Party (50,000 copies of the
'Thunderbolt,' a white supremacist paper, were printed), local synagogues and the Jewish Community Center were placed under 24-hour
surveillance by employed policemen and prowl cars."[25]

Rabbi Grafman remembered Harrison Salisbury's visit vividly. The
rabbi shut his door because he did not want to alarm his secretary with
a recounting of the threats to Temple Emanu-El and to himself that he
was about to relate to Salisbury.[26] In his article Salisbury stated, "In
Birmingham neither blacks nor whites talk freely. A pastor carefully
closes his door before he speaks. A negro keeps an eye on the sidewalk
outside his house. A lawyer talks in the language of conspiracy."[27] Grafman believed he was the "pastor" mentioned in this article.[28]

Birmingham in the 1960s, Part Two:
Wallace, Letters, and More Bombs

In January 1963 Alabama's newly elected governor, George Wallace,
gave his infamous inauguration speech, crying out for "segregation now,
segregation tomorrow, and segregation forever." Days later eleven Alabama clergymen including Rabbi Milton Grafman responded in the
Birmingham News:

It is clear that a series of court decisions may soon bring about the desegregation of certain schools and colleges in Alabama. Many sincere people oppose this change and are deeply troubled by it. As Southerners we understand this. We nevertheless feel that defiance is neither the right answer nor the solution. And we feel that inflammatory and rebellious statements can lead only to violence, discord, confusion and disgrace for our beloved state. We therefore affirm and commend to our people: (1) That hatred and violence have no sanction in our religious and political tradition. (2) That there may be disagreement concerning laws and social change without advocating defiance, anarchy and subversion. (3) That laws may be tested in courts or changed by legislation but not ignored by whims of individuals. (4) That constitutions may be amended or judges impeached by proper action, but our American way of life depends upon obedience to the decision of courts of competent jurisdiction in the meantime. (5) That no person's freedom is safe unless every person's is equally protected. (6) That freedom of speech must at all costs be preserved and exercised without fear of recrimination or harassment. (7) That every human being is created in the image of God and is entitled to respect as a fellow human being with all basic rights, privileges, and responsibilities which belong in humanity.[29]

The clergy advocated obedience to court decisions and that "all people of goodwill . . . join us in seeking divine guidance as we make our appeal for law and order and common sense."

On the following Sunday the editorial writer for the *Birmingham News*, acknowledging that it is "not easy to challenge a minister" when he speaks about knowing "the ultimate spirit in which all problems of human relations must be solved," proceeded to challenge the clergy. The editorialist agreed that Wallace's speech was "defiant" but "left it to the citizen's own judgment whether it was 'inflammatory' or 'rebellious.'" The writer lamented that no other prominent voices were speaking out on any aspect of this issue but then chastised the clergy for asking that people who do speak out should be able to do so "without fear of recrimination or harassment. [The] clergymen place a condition which should not be expected. There is ample freedom to speak. But he who speaks must anticipate, if he is saying the unpopular, recrimination, even harassment. That is the root-cause of near-silence—few dare risk expressing a contrary point of view."[30] Three months later Birmingham felt the power of two converging forces that would alter life there irrevocably: the newly instituted mayor-council form of city government (formerly, city government had been run by commission); and the nonviolent, mass demonstrations led by Martin Luther King, Jr., and the Southern Christian Leadership Conference (SCLC). Ever since the mob violence led by the Klan in collusion with city police against the 1961 Freedom Riders, prominent white merchants led by Chamber of Commerce president Sidney Smyer had discussed ways of getting rid of Commissioner of Public Safety Eugene "Bull" Connor without launching a direct campaign against him. Their solution was to eliminate the office: "Over months of meetings with lawyers, teachers, civics professors, and assorted do-gooder groups, they developed the idea that Birmingham urgently needed a modern 'mayor-council' form of government."[31] After a successful petition drive a special election was called, and "a year and a day after Connor had been re-elected with the largest vote in history [61 percent], a majority of the people in this city voted to terminate his office."[32] Undaunted, Connor ran for the newly created office of mayor and lost in a runoff on 2 April to Albert Boutwell. Connor, however, launched a court battle to be allowed to complete his original term of office.[33]

As the political maneuvering transpired, the Reverend Fred Shuttlesworth and the Alabama Christian Movement for Human Rights (ACMHR) organized student sit-ins at downtown department stores and met with white business leaders to try to break the barriers around public facilities. These leaders included Smyer and representatives from the major stores: Sears, Loveman's, Newberry's, Greene's, Woolworth's, and Pizitz. Loveman's and Pizitz, two of the largest, were founded by local Jewish merchants. Although a segregationist, Louis Pizitz had been a longtime supporter of southern black institutions.[34] He and the representative from Loveman's played crucial roles at the meeting. Initially, after an awkward silence, Loveman's spokesman offered to "desegregate" his store's water fountains. Shuttlesworth countered that the black citizens were "past water now. We have to have toilets." Another painful silence ensued, and then black negotiator and businessman A. G. Gaston turned to Loveman's representative and said, "You know, your daddy and I got started in business about the same time. And you know you got your start among the Negroes like I did. We got our money together. And most of our customers are Negroes. And it looks like you could do something." After yet another silence, Shuttlesworth turned to Louis Pizitz: "Mr. Pizitz, the last time, they arrested two students in your store. This time it's gonna be different. Martin Luther King and I are gonna sit on your stool, and we aren't gonna walk out. They're gonna have to drag us out. And the press will be there. And you'll be out of business all over Alabama." While Shuttlesworth and Pizitz "glared" at each other, Loveman's representative responded: "Wait a minute. . . . I can just call the maintenance man and just paint over the ["whites only"] sign in the restroom."[35] The impasse had been broken under pressure.

After defeat in Albany, Georgia, King and the SCLC, at Shuttlesworth's urging, were preparing to make Birmingham the next battleground.[36] The city fathers solicited Shuttlesworth's advice on how to keep King out of Birmingham. He responded, "Well on your slogan at the airport, you say 'It's So Nice to Have You in Birmingham.' . . . We think that means King, too."[37] Although Rabbi Grafman was not a part of these negotiations, his position on desegregation and the ways in which it should be carried out would soon be known. For their part the merchants would make no promises on the rapidity of public desegregation, so Shuttlesworth and King agreed to start the demonstrations after the mayor's election of 2 April 1963.[38] Clearly, King's entrance into Birmingham would affect all parties to these negotiations; his departure from Birmingham just as clearly left Birmingham's citizens—black and white, Jewish and Christian—with the burden of living up to, and living with, the coming changes.

From 6 April to 10 April the SCLC and ACMHR conducted sit-ins and demonstrations and launched an economic boycott that sought to pressure the city into granting six specific desegregation goals.[39] Bull Connor, still commissioner of public safety, confronted the demonstrators at every turn. Dr. King was faced with the problem of whether to continue the demonstrations when, on 10 April, an Alabama circuit court judge granted an injunction "naming 133 civil rights leaders whom he forbade to take part in or encourage any sit-ins, picketing, or other demonstrations. The list included King, [Rev. Ralph] Abernathy, and Shuttlesworth." After agonizing deliberations, caused by the near bankruptcy of the SCLC coffers and the fact that to that point King's tactic of filling the jails was not succeeding, King decided to subject himself to arrest on 12 April, Good Friday. On that date Dr. King, Abernathy, and fifty other demonstrators were jailed, and King was placed in solitary confinement.[40]

On the following day the *Birmingham News* printed an open statement by eight of the eleven clergymen who had called for "sanity" after Governor Wallace's inauguration speech. Once again, Rabbi Milton Grafman was one of the authors of the statement. Reminding the citizens of Birmingham of the clerics' previous call for peaceful settlement of disputes and obedience to court decisions, they noted that there were "indications" that all citizens of Birmingham have an "opportunity for a new constructive and realistic approach to racial problems," by which they meant the new city government. The letter continued:

> However we are now confronted by a series of demonstrations by some of our Negro citizens, directed and led in part by outsiders. We recognize the natural impatience of people who feel that their hopes are slow in being realized. But we are convinced that these demonstrations are unwise and untimely.
>
> We agree rather with certain local Negro leadership which has called for honest and open negotiation of racial issues in our area. And we believe this kind of facing of issues can best be accomplished by citizens of our own metro area, white and Negro, meeting with their knowledge and experience of the local situation. All of us need to face that responsibility and find proper channels for its accomplishment.
>
> Just as we formerly pointed out that "hatred and violence have no sanction in our religious and political traditions," we also point out that such actions as to incite to hatred and violence, however technically peaceful those actions may be, have not contributed to the resolution of our local problems. We do not believe that these days of new hope are days when extreme measures are justified in Birmingham.[41]

The authors "commend[ed] the community as a whole, and the local media and law enforcement officials in particular, on the calm manner in which these demonstrations have been handled . . . [and] urge[d] these same officials] to remain calm and continue to protect our city from violence, urging our own Negro community to withdraw support from these demonstrations, and to unite locally in working peacefully for a better Birmingham." Finally, the letter advocated that "rights . . . denied [be] pressed in the courts . . . and not in the streets" and that all citizens should "observe the principles of law and order and common sense."[42]

One's views of Rabbi Grafman and the cosigners of the letter will be largely determined by one's reading of this letter. The white-controlled mass media supported the letter. *Time* magazine agreed with the white clergy, calling the SCLC's protests "poorly timed" and adding that "to many Birmingham Negroes, King's drive inflamed tensions at a time when the city seemed to be making some progress, however small, in race relations." The *Washington Post* and the *New York Times* expressed similar sentiments.[43] Many white moderates in Birmingham, including former mayor David Vann (1975–79), applauded the letter. Vann, who was attempting to negotiate an end both to the demonstrations and to segregation, commented recently that he had "agreed with the clergy's letter," especially because of the change in city government: "I wanted to go forward with the democratic process to see what could be done with it. Hundreds and hundreds of black people had worked very hard on the problem of getting Bull Connor defeated." Many of these citizens, Vann asserted, did not want King's presence because they, too, did not want to disrupt the process already begun. About Rabbi Grafman, Vann noted, "What the clergy was saying was often unpopular with its parishioners. Dr. King couldn't understand what they were saying. But no one was more hurt than [Grafman] by King's letter [from the Birmingham jail]. Rabbi Grafman is anything but a bigot. He was a critically important leader who had a great moral commitment to end segregation . . . [during the days] of the Bull Connor show. He said to me once that 'segregation is just not the Christian thing to do.' He is one of my favorite folks. He's a saint."[44]

Many black ministers, agreeing with moderate whites, hoped that once the city election was decided in Albert Boutwell's favor that "both the merchants and the city government would grant some of the movement's requests without demonstrations being necessary."[45] The Reverend Ed Gardner, cofounder of the ACMHR, noted that King "never did get" some black people involved until the "final demonstration" in May.[46] A. G. Gaston, perceived by many as the black business leader in Birmingham, called for "all the citizens of Birmingham to work harmoniously together in a spirit of brotherly love to solve the problems of our city, giving due recognition to the local colored leadership among us." According to historian Taylor Branch, Gaston's statement "took no notice of King or the demonstrations."[47] Even the Reverend John T. Porter, King's protégé and former assistant pastor at Dexter Avenue Baptist Church [King's former congregation in Montgomery], whom King had just installed personally in a Birmingham pulpit [Sixth Avenue Baptist], initially declined his support because he considered Fred Shuttlesworth "an unstable dictator."[48] Black leaders in Birmingham greatly respected Shuttlesworth's "courage," but they did not "universally" praise his "judgment and emotional stability."[49]

Despite the qualms of some local black leaders, Dr. King had mass black support and decades of discrimination against blacks to justify his actions. Thus, when handed the open letter from the white Birmingham clergy, he responded with the "Letter from Birmingham Jail." As Branch observes, King was aware that these were the same "liberal clergymen" who "had risked their reputations" in responding to Wallace in January: "Yet, after all the beatings and threats, King felt that they had

not risked themselves for true morality . . . [and] could not make themselves state forthrightly what was just. Instead, they stood behind the
injunction and the jailers to dismiss his spirit along with his body."[50]

In his famous letter King said that he wanted to "confess to his Jewish and Christian brothers" that he had "almost reached the regrettable
conclusion that the Negro's greatest stumbling block in his stride toward freedom is not the White Citizens' Council or the KKKer, but the
white moderate, who is more devoted to 'order' than to 'justice' . . . who
lives by a mythical concept of time and who constantly advises the Negro to wait for a 'more convenient season.' "[51] He spoke further of his
disappointment at being labeled an "extremist," asserting that he stood
between the forces in the black community of "complacency" and of
"bitterness and hatred." He roundly denounced the white clergy for
their commendation of the Birmingham police.[52] King lieutenant Wyatt
Walker argued at a mass meeting on the day the clergy's letter was published that "it was hard to believe that the white churchmen were being
anything other than disingenuous by publicly reprimanding the black
leadership for Birmingham's lack of biracial negotiations."[53]

Some of Birmingham's current black leaders still feel the sting of the
white clergy's words and lack of action. Abraham Woods, president of
Birmingham's chapter of the SCLC, said in 1992 that if Grafman and
the other clergy "wanted justice and equality, they wanted it without
plowing up the field. They wanted it without the thunder and lightning." Reverend John Cross, pastor of the Sixteenth Street Baptist
Church in 1963 when it was bombed by Klansmen, added that he
"doubted if the eight ministers were unequivocally committed to ending racial injustice."[54] Reverend Fred Shuttlesworth was more definite
about Grafman and the other Birmingham clergy:

> [It was] good that [Grafman] said something . . . spoke out
> [about Wallace], [but it was] nothing special. Many clergy are al-
> ways on the wrong side, going the wrong way. It's tragic that the
> clergy is far behind in leading people and in trying to mold and
> shape opinion for righteousness. The rabbi thought he was making
> history and he was, but it was the wrong kind. So he would speak
> out, but when it came to acting, to raising people's consciousness
> out of the status quo and into acting against injustice, he wouldn't
> be for that. Most high churchmen want to sit back and not be with
> the people. But they should get out and march with the people. In
> Birmingham, people were afraid of offending others. One white
> preacher said that if he preached the real truth, he wouldn't have a
> pulpit. I said, "Try it one time; you'll find another pulpit." Yes,

I think Rabbi Grafman is a bigot. Jesus would classify him as a bigot, and other preachers too. If people think that simply going to each other's churches is something, then I say it's much ado about nothing. People ought to live and work with one another every day. Sunday A.M. is still the most segregated time of the week.[55]

Grafman argued in response that all the clergymen were asking was that the black leadership wait until the desegregation legislation could be passed by the newly elected, more moderate [but of course still white] city government.[56] The argument here, of course, centers on the wait-and-see gradualist approach of the white moderates versus the equality-now argument accompanied by the necessity of pressure espoused by Dr. King and the SCLC. Would the legislation have been forthcoming? Would gradual integration have taken place? No one knows. Dr. King and Rabbi Grafman were hurt by each other's letter. Dr. King felt rebuked and "condemned" by the clergy's letter and responded accordingly. Rabbi Grafman believed that King "did a great disservice" to the clergy who wrote the letter. He asserted that "everyone who signed that statement agreed with the 'Letter from Birmingham Jail' even if they questioned King's tactics."[57]

David Vann says of that era in Birmingham that "it's difficult to be judgmental about anything."[58] It is easy to say now that the justice of King's cause prevailed over the clergy's position. Exactly what cost, however, would the ministers have paid if they had sided wholeheartedly with Dr. King, the SCLC, and the ACMHR? In the face of potential violence, just how patient would Grafman's congregation have been with him had he linked himself more closely with integrationist forces? Finally, the rabbi and other clergy would be staying in Birmingham to live with their congregations, friends, and enemies after King departed.

Grafman maintained that his congregation stood solidly behind him during these times—that after neither public statement (to Wallace nor to King) did he receive a single word of condemnation from his congregation, although they were "leery about their security and that of the temple." Conclusions about such uniform reaction range from the complete support of a congregation for its rabbi to the reality that although many Jews would similarly disagree with Wallace, so would many of Grafman's congregation disagree with King's tactics and with his cause. Grafman's deepest sympathies lay with the white Christian ministers, however, because if they took "a pronounced stand supporting the marches in Birmingham, they might split their congregations."[59]

Still, the clergy's open letter did cause problems for Rabbi Grafman with Jewish people outside of Birmingham. Most of the hate mail that he received came from "New York . . . from other Jews."[60] Many said that he "had betrayed his faith and asked how a rabbi acquainted with the persecution of his own people could side with hatred and bigotry."[61] Today, however, he is strongly defended by Birmingham Jewish leaders such as Karl Friedman and Mark Elovitz. Friedman, a prominent lawyer in the city, recently remarked, "In 1960 or '61, Rabbi Grafman, who was a member of the interfaith Birmingham Minister's Council, insisted that the council break the color line, and it did. He instituted at Temple Emanu-El a conference to teach other ministers, including black ministers, about Judaism. [In the civil rights struggle] he was trying for compromise, and some of these compromises weren't fully acceptable to blacks. It's simply not true that he's a bigot."[62] Elovitz, former rabbi at Birmingham's Temple Beth El and author of *A Century of Jewish Life in Dixie,* added that Rabbi Grafman was "anything but a bigot . . . [but rather was] enlightened, social-minded, and interested in the well-being of all peoples. People who say that he's a bigot are ignorant, uninformed. Saying that he's a bigot is a vicious canard."[63]

One of the other authors of the clergy's open letter, Episcopal Bishop George Murray, recalls Grafman's telling him in those days that "in defending the rights of blacks," he was "also defending the rights of Jews. If people are allowed to move against one group, we're all in danger." Murray remembers just how prophetic Grafman's words were. Out of town when the Birmingham demonstrations began, Murray returned to see an article in the Birmingham papers quoting U.S. Attorney General Robert F. Kennedy asking Dr. King to delay the demonstrations in order to give Birmingham's new government a chance to work. Murray arranged a meeting with Dr. King and white leaders at his office to persuade King to cancel the demonstrations. To the best of his memory, he believes that King sent Shuttlesworth to represent him. In any case King's representative said, "If you're here to join us, welcome, if not, I might as well go home." Thus, the meeting ended abruptly. "Everyone else was afraid to have such a meeting for fear of bombing," Murray declared. "I was glad that Dr. King attained his objectives. They were my objectives too. But I would still object to the tactics used," he said, referring specifically to using school children to march in subsequent demonstrations. Murray stressed that he "knew how many KKKers were around" and that every night he "checked the shrubbery" outside his house. He, too, received phone threats from callers he suspected were Klansmen. Eventually he took his name off the mailbox and moved his children's beds from their rooms to the center of the house in an effort to protect them from a potential bomb.[64]

Another clergyman who signed the letter to King reacted more strongly than Grafman and Murray to the "Letter From Birmingham Jail." After Bishop C. J. Carpenter, whose name was first on the clergy's open letter, read King's letter, he remarked to George Murray, " 'This is what you get when you try to do something. You get it from both sides. George, you just have to live with that.' Carpenter felt abused and misunderstood for his efforts. The clash of emotion turned him . . . into a more strident Confederate."[65] Years later, after Carpenter's death, Grafman met with Carpenter's son, who told him that after the letter, his father received mail branding Carpenter the "Apartheid Bishop."[66]

Although several of the clergy received threats and hate mail, one wonders why Grafman, particularly, risked speaking out at all during these chaotic, often violent, years. When asked this question recently, Grafman responded that during the civil rights struggle of the early sixties, his mind reverted back to the election of the black student Robert Seal as president of the first program committee for his high school ancient history class. He simply couldn't forget Robert Seal.[67]

If, as representing white moderate forces and Birmingham's Jews, Grafman was being pressured from Dr. King on one side and the KKK on the other, soon he and the rest of Birmingham's Jews had to face a force from a new direction: "In the predawn hours of May 8, 1963, nineteen Conservative rabbis deplaned at Birmingham's Municipal Airport intent upon 'employing a unique and highly imaginative way of asserting . . . their determination to be . . . an influence in the arena of American social conflict.' "[68] During the meeting of the Rabbinical Assembly in New York, the rabbis concluded that they must "meet the responsibility of encouraging Jews to help Blacks" by joining the protest movement.[69] Birmingham's Jewish leadership believed that Jews "ought to stay out of the desegregation fight on the ground that it is a 'Christian problem' between whites and Negroes and not simply a racial problem."[70] Furthermore, the local Jewish Community Council worried that the visiting rabbis' presence might unleash serious anti-Semitism because many in Birmingham would conclude that the integration fight was being led by Jews.[71]

Karl Friedman remembers that a delegation of local Jewish leaders met the nineteen visiting rabbis at the airport. According to Friedman, Rabbi Grafman, acting as a spokesperson, tried to explain to the visitors the problem gripping Birmingham and the need for moderation.[72] The Birmingham Jewish leaders stated that "a settlement seemingly was in the making, that from all appearances the rabbis' presence in Birmingham could accomplish nothing, could possibly muddy the waters, could reflect most unfavorably on our Jewish community, since the bigots have repeatedly claimed that the integration movement was a Jewish-Communist inspired movement . . . [and] that the Jewish community, through individuals, not as any organized group, was working through organized and recognized committees, for a peaceful settlement of our racial problems."[73] The Birmingham group tried to convince the visiting rabbis to "confer with someone from [their] group," before marching.[74] Karl Friedman remembers, however, that some of the nineteen, such as Rabbi Richard Rubenstein of Pittsburgh, were "unreasonable . . . and were determined to march with the blacks. They really made a mess of things."[75] Of course, these visitors' entrance into Birmingham's civil rights struggle caused confusion and embarrassment among local Jewish leaders; however, the visiting rabbis' presence focused national attention, again, on Birmingham—surely a positive result. Former Birmingham mayor David Vann recalls that the coming of the rabbinic marchers proved to be "very sensitive" for Rabbi Grafman and his relation to his own congregation.[76] How many in his congregation wondered—in light of the visiting rabbis' willingness to stand with Birmingham's black citizens and the local Jewish leaders' opposition to doing so—whether Grafman was truly committed to the civil rights cause?

While in Birmingham the visiting rabbis attended an inspirational service at the Sixth Avenue Baptist Church, wearing their rabbinical attire and leading songs in Hebrew. Rabbi Alex Shapiro said from the pulpit that "I have never been moved more deeply in my life" by the courage of Birmingham's black community. He added that "as Jews who had seen the Germans overrun Europe, they [the nineteen rabbis] hoped always to lend succor against oppression anywhere." Some of the visiting rabbis spent the night at the A. G. Gaston Motel, which, they were told, was a violation of a city ordinance because the Gaston Motel was a black establishment and thus was barred from accepting white customers.[77]

At a meeting between Birmingham's Jewish leaders and the visiting rabbis on the day after the march, however, some of the rabbis "indicated that their visit to Birmingham was a mistake," that "sitting in convention assembled is one thing, and being exposed to the raw facts of life is yet another thing." On the following day, the rabbis decided "to return to their homes since they wanted to be home for the Sabbath."[78] Although in a written account of this event Birmingham's Jewish leaders acknowledged the visiting rabbis' "sincerity and sense of dedication," and that their visit "created a reservoir of good will among the Negroes," these visitors, according to the Birmingham Jewish leaders, "did not create [the same] good will among the whites." Instead, "the advent of the rabbis . . . created a spirit of helplessness in the Birmingham Jewish community," and it "will be a long time before [the] ill will and hostility will be dissipated."[79]

The mass march on 7 May (ironically, the day before the nineteen rabbis arrived), where Bull Connor unleashed police dogs and fire hoses on the marchers, proved to be the straw that broke segregation's back in Birmingham. Three days later an accord between Birmingham's blacks and whites was announced: "The merchants [many of whom were Jewish] agreed to desegregate lunch counters and hire black workers. . . . Bull Connor . . . demanded to know the names of the businessmen who had secretly negotiated the truce."[80] Obviously, then, King's tactics worked. How much longer would segregation have been the rule in Birmingham if he and his lieutenants had not acted? Shortly thereafter, the U.S. Supreme Court recognized Albert Boutwell and the new city council as the legitimate governing body of Birmingham.[81]

From Sixteenth Street to Sixth Avenue to Washington

On 9 September 1963 a court order declaring that Birmingham must integrate its schools was put into effect. Governor Wallace and Mayor Boutwell had stalled the opening until the Alabama courts ruled on new evidence of the "inherent differences in the races," and during their stalling the schools had opened and closed several times with white students also staging a sit-in at Boutwell's office to protest integrated classes. Only days before the opening a bomb destroyed the home of prominent black lawyer Arthur Shores. Simultaneously Wallace officially declared his presidential candidacy.[82]

On Sunday morning, 15 September, the Sixteenth Street Baptist Church, site of the first demonstrations the previous spring, was bombed. Many people in Sunday school classes were injured; four young girls were killed.[83] Dr. King returned to Birmingham on 18 September for the mass funeral of three of the bombing victims.[84] The Reverend John T. Porter, minister of the Sixth Avenue Baptist Church where the funeral was held, recalls that the service saw "the largest outpouring of clergy across Christian-Jewish lines dressed in clergy garb ever before or since. . . . I felt great joy in seeing the togetherness of leaders of the religious community, but great sadness that it took this event to bring us together."[85]

Among the clergy attending was Rabbi Milton Grafman. Reverend Porter commented recently that "Rabbi Grafman is one of the progressive leaders of the community. He played a delicate role in keeping communication established over the years in relation to the black community. Overall, the Jewish community had more acceptance from the black community. Grafman was quite effective in walking the thin line between traditional groups and the minority communities who wanted change. The presence of the rabbis [at the funeral] wearing their rabbinical garb was very strong, very noticeable."[86] Rabbi Grafman recalled: "[I] called Rev. Porter and asked if there would be places for [the white clergy] at the funeral. He said he would reserve places for us. The funeral was an unnerving experience, and six hours later I had to deliver a sermon, for it was the beginning of Rosh Hashanah. During the Kaddish I said the names of the girls who were brutally murdered. I then threw away my notes and proceeded to excoriate the congregation for the next forty-five minutes for its sins of omission and commission concerning segregation and the treatment of blacks in our community."[87] Temple Emanu-El once more received a bomb threat.[88] At the Rosh Hashanah service the following morning Rabbi Grafman again chided his congregation for living in a city where "white doctors hire Negroes only as receptionists . . . and merchants refuse to employ black sales people." Subsequently congregants wrote him thanking him for giving them a "well-deserved kick in the pants."[89]

Grafman also asked the congregation to join him and eleven other religious and civic leaders in contributing to a memorial fund they had established to pay for the victims' funerals, for the wounded's hospital bills, and for the rebuilding of the Sixteenth Street Baptist Church. His congregation responded enthusiastically.[90] Grafman became a trustee of this fund, which also helped black and white victims of the random violence that occurred in the wake of the church bombing.[91]

Given the recent events, President Kennedy agreed to meet with three different delegations to discuss Birmingham's problems. The first delegation was composed of Dr. King and black leaders from Birmingham. This delegation requested that federal troops be dispatched to help maintain order and keep integration alive. Kennedy refused and, instead, sent two white "personal emissaries" to mediate the city's racial problems—former army secretary Kenneth Royall and former West Point football coach Earl Blaik.[92]

Next, a five-man committee of white Birmingham officials met with the president. They argued that Birmingham was making progress but that the constant criticism from northerners and "outside agitators such as Martin Luther King" compounded the problem. Kennedy urged them to take concrete steps to end tensions by hiring "Negro sales clerks . . . or at least one black policeman . . . [and by holding] biracial negotiations with local Negro leaders." The Birmingham officials "parried each salvo," however, ultimately agreeing only to "support" the Blaik-Royall advisory mission.[93]

On 23 September 1963 the third delegation, composed of "six prominent Alabama clergymen," including Bishop George Murray and Rabbi Milton Grafman, visited President Kennedy.[94] Murray remembers asking the president if there weren't anything he could do "to make Dr. King move more peacefully." According to Murray, Kennedy replied, "Everyone thinks Martin Luther King and I stand together on everything. But I asked him to modify his tactics on two occasions, and he defied me both times. I'm not ready to put the office of the president on the line again to be defied."[95] Murray also reported that JFK asked them if they "couldn't do more to get black police officers hired." The clergy answered that it was "hard to find [a black person] who wanted the job or who could pass the civil service exam." Then, Murray recalls, Rabbi Grafman asked, "Mr. President, could you get a black FBI man assigned to Birmingham?" Kennedy reportedly "grinned" and said, "They're awful hard to find."[96]

Returning to Birmingham Rabbi Grafman met with Blaik and Royall.[97] The Kennedy mediators were endorsed publicly by A. G. Gaston and Arthur Shores, who also "denounced" King after King vowed to return to Birmingham unless the "minimal conditions that President Kennedy had tried to sell [to the white civic delegation]" were met.[98] These conditions were that the city "hire Birmingham's first black policeman; issue a public call for law and order; demand the withdrawal of the provocative Alabama state troopers; and institute good-faith negotiations with the black community."[99] Although not all of King's demands were met, he did not return.[100] The Blaik-Royall mission "never came close to formulating a report," recommending only that "calm" be the prescription for Birmingham.[101]

Eventually Birmingham achieved integration in all public facilities. Today the city has a black mayor, though it has seen its white population flee mainly to the southern suburbs. Former predominantly white sections of the city such as the West End are now almost wholly black. Many schools have resegregated given the realities of community makeup. Such ongoing racial recalcitrance was clearly evidenced in 1990 when professional golf's PGA Championship was scheduled to be held at Birmingham's Shoal Creek Country Club—a club that had no black members. Shoal Creek founder Hall Thompson was quoted as saying that the club "would not be pressured into accepting black members." Along with other Birmingham citizens Rabbi Grafman protested the club's refusal to desegregate: "It's created, I believe, a tension between many of both races, which had been diminishing over the years. My personal feeling is that Birmingham had improved its race relations over the years where we really could be envied by other cities and other communities. This [event] has really set us back."[102]

Helping to improve community and race relations was Rabbi Grafman's goal throughout his tenure in Birmingham. In 1970 Grafman and Temple Emanu-El offered the use of the temple's facilities to Dr. J. Herbert Gilmore, pastor of the First Baptist Church of Birmingham, and three hundred of his parishioners when they walked out of their church because of its refusal to admit two black women as members.[103]

In June 1979 a white Birmingham police officer, George Sands, shot and killed a young black woman, Bonita Carter. The circumstances of the case were murky, and the black leadership of Birmingham, led by then city councilman Richard Arrington and the SCLC's Rev. Abraham Woods, believed this to be another case of police brutality. Woods and other ministers "called for a permanent civilian-police review board."[104] Mayor David Vann, realizing that the city council's "routine call for an investigation of Bonita Carter's shooting" was an inadequate measure, made a "historic move" and called for the formation of a blue-ribbon citizens' committee to probe the shooting and make recommendations.[105]

Vann remembers that he appointed this committee based on the advice of Operation New Birmingham, a biracial group that has met every Monday morning since the early 1970s.[106] Vann's eight-person committee consisted of four blacks and four whites, including Rev. Ed Gardner, cofounder of the ACMHR, and committee chair Rabbi Milton Grafman. There was a precedent for Grafman's being named to the committee as he was also named in the mid-1960s by then mayor Boutwell to the first Birmingham biracial Community Relations Committee.[107] Grafman believes that the makeup of Vann's committee ensured "impartial hearings" and that these hearings were "fairly and openly held," although ultimately the committee "was unable to reach a finding" about the actual circumstances of the shooting.[108]

Numerous factors impeded the review board's ability to reach conclusions.[109] Nonetheless, the committee, led by Grafman, did prodigious work: "If the thousand pages of committee hearings did not resolve every question of Bonita Carter's killing, they did help many readers fix in their mind a picture of what took place on the night of 22 June."[110] The very existence of the committee drew "mixed reaction from the black community."[111]

In 1979 newly elected mayor Richard Arrington reappointed Grafman to the Police-Community Relations Committee, saying that Grafman "has a high level of credibility among all segments of the community—blacks as well as whites. He has a long record of working to bring about change and a reputation for being concerned about justice." In 1983 Grafman received the Liberty Bell, given by the American Bar Association, for his contributions to community relations.[112] The Reverend John T. Porter of Sixth Avenue Baptist Church believes that such efforts led to the interfaith and interracial conferences between his church and Temple Emanu-El that still continue today.[113]

Rabbi Grafman's position as, arguably, the Jewish leader in Birmingham afforded him some degree of choice during the civil rights struggle. He could have remained silent, but he knew that the discrimination that directly affected Birmingham's black community had also to a smaller extent affected Birmingham's Jews. Ultimately, not to speak out against segregation, as he said to Bishop George Murray, might lead to further discrimination.

Rabbi Grafman was motivated also by a respect for fairness, justice, and equality. Nonetheless, Birmingham was a concrete situation, and Grafman's choice of defending abstract principles caught him between the reality of Martin Luther King's civil disobedience campaign and the refusal of Bull Connor, George Wallace, and others to change.

Rabbi Milton L. Grafman died on Sunday, 28 May 1995, in Birmingham. About his life "longtime Temple Emanu-El member" Emil Hess said, "During the civil rights years, [Grafman] was part of a small group of clergy who lent their efforts to trying to ameliorate the problems. . . . It was not a popular effort, and very few clergymen were involving themselves in it."[114] The Reverend Abraham Woods, president of the local SCLC, remarked that he "respected Mr. Grafman even though he [Woods] was disappointed in the action the white clergyman had taken. . . . 'I consider him to have been one of our great assets.' "[115] Jonathan Miller, now the rabbi at Temple Emanu-El, said of this era in Grafman's life: "Rabbi Grafman was not looking to stop the civil rights movement. . . . He wanted the change to come not through demonstrations on the street, but through the processes of civil government that were moving at a very rapid pace."[116]

Divided Together: Jews and African Americans in Durham, North Carolina

LEONARD ROGOFF

Unlike most other documented southern communities with a Jewish presence, Durham lacked a long-term and powerful German Reform base. Evolving from East European labor-class roots, many members of the Jewish community interacted directly with African Americans of equal or higher status. Durham's uniqueness was compounded further by the introduction of transplanted Jewish intellectuals into the local university ranks. In this maelstrom all sorts of variations appeared: bilateral coalitions, Orthodox and Conservative activism, reticence to act, Jewish/black political and business leadership. The economic history of the city and common class interests served as major factors in the relations among Jews, blacks, and the general community.

The Jews of Durham, North Carolina, occupied a middle ground between the African American and white Christian communities. Though Jews did not suffer the legally sanctioned, racial prejudice accorded blacks, their religion and foreign origins cast them as outsiders. The Jews' history of poverty and discrimination made many Jews sympathetic to blacks, but they were cautious to express that sentiment. Though they acceded to the racial codes, Jews in their personal relations with African Americans often sought to ameliorate the harsher aspects of segregation. A few Jews became civil rights activists, but none joined the rabid segregationists. Jews tended to be racial moderates, and Durham's rabbis reflected these community values.

Relations between Jews and blacks in Durham were in large measure shaped by the city's economic history. Durham, which was not incorporated until 1869, was the prototypical New South city. In the postbellum years Durham Station grew from a whistle stop into a major mill and market center. As the subsistence farming yielded to cotton and tobacco, agricultural markets opened. Railroad connections to Richmond and Baltimore spurred the growth of commercial networks. A lone prewar tobacco company increased to more than a dozen in 1872, dominated by the factories of Blackwell's Bull Durham and Washington Duke and Sons. The tobacco industry provided seed money for banks and textile mills. The number of local businesses exploded from five in 1866 to one hundred in 1880.[1]

The city's population grew nearly tenfold in the decade after 1870, reaching 2,041 in 1880. African Americans, many of whom were former slaves, flocked from the countryside to work in factories and homes. Starting in 1874, Jewish merchants, mostly of German origin, arrived from Richmond and Baltimore to serve the newly urbanized population of workers and managers as well as the farmers drawn to the Durham markets. This small community of a half-dozen merchants was overwhelmed in the early 1880s by more than a hundred "Russian" Jewish immigrants brought from New York by Duke and Blackwell to roll cigarettes in their factories. Virtually all these Jewish proletarians left Durham by 1886, but they created a Jewish critical mass that drew a steady stream of East European peddlers and storekeepers. The Jewish population increased from perhaps forty in 1880 to about two hundred in 1900, peaked around five hundred in 1910, and then settled at three hundred fifty in 1920, where it remained until the 1950s. In 1884 the Jewish community established the Cemetery Society, and two or three years later Orthodox Jews organized the Durham Hebrew Congregation.[2]

Class would unite Jews and African Americans in Durham even as race would divide them. In the earliest days Jews and blacks, bound by poverty, lived in proximity to one another. The Jewish Pine Street ghetto abutted the African American community of Hayti. These neighborhoods were in the Bottoms, a low-lying, gullied area of shacks, dumps, and warehouses near the tobacco factories. A red-light district flourished nearby. Wealthier white people, including the town's few German Jews, lived on higher ground closer to the Main Street business district. As early as 1883 immigrant Jews began opening "mom and pop" grocery stores in Hayti; these Jews became the only whites to live in the black neighborhood. Jewish grocers purchased produce from black farmers, and several Jewish tobacco workers listed their boarding places in city directories at "colored" restaurants.[3]

Newspaper accounts after the turn of the century reported minor scraps between the two groups. Several Jewish storekeepers were charged with receiving stolen goods from blacks or overcharging black customers. Blacks occasionally assaulted Jews, and Jewish storekeepers kept guns under their counters. These incidents increased early in the century when a cocaine epidemic sparked a crime wave. Nevertheless, such conflicts, according to newspaper reports, were not commonplace; they were outnumbered, in fact, by accounts describing disputes among Jews.[4]

Jews by virtue of their race had certain economic advantages. In the tobacco factories Jews held the higher-paying, skilled jobs as cigarette rollers. Blacks were relegated to unskilled labor such as hauling tobacco. Jews hired African American domestic help for insignificant wages. The Reverend Kolman Heillig, a Lithuanian immigrant who was drawn to Durham in 1892 to serve as the town's first rabbi, employed a black houseworker, a man the children knew as "uncle," who slept under the porch with the cow. From the first, black maids worked in Jewish homes, and several Jews recalled being raised by an "Aunt Molly" or an "Aunt Zola," black women who became "family." Some of these workers even picked up a few words of Yiddish and learned the arts of making chopped liver or setting a Passover table.[5] For the most part Jews and African Americans knew each other as employer and employee, merchant and customer, or landlord and tenant.

Pauli Murray, the noted black writer, lawyer, and Anglican priest, recalled that in the Durham of her childhood, in the years before World War I, blacks and whites "lived close together, and, within limits of the strict racial code, considerable familiarity existed in their dealings with one another." Murray included Dora and Moses Greenberg, Lithuanian immigrants and pillars of the Orthodox synagogue, among the whites whose "humanity" overcame the "walls of segregation." Her family shopped at the Greenberg grocery up the hill from her home. Murray's uncle, Rev. Small, knew Hebrew, "which made a bond between him and the Jewish family." (Murray's memoir confirms a legend in the Jewish community about an African American who once walked into the synagogue and began reading the Torah in Hebrew.)[6]

The attorney Benjamin Lovenstein, the Greenberg's son-in-law, made a career defending African Americans in the early 1900s. Known in the black community as "Mr. Holstein" or "the Hebrew lawyer," he gained considerable notoriety for his defense of a black man named Major Guthrie who had been convicted of murder. Lovenstein threw himself into the "moneyless job" of securing a pardon for Guthrie, organizing a statewide petition campaign, and personally appealing to the governor. After the fourth of Lovenstein's black clients was acquitted, the *Durham Morning Herald* reported disapprovingly that the attorney was "delighted."

Lovenstein served the black community because, like the Hayti merchants, he was too poor to choose his clientele. He once refused to represent a black man who had also hired a black lawyer. The newspaper noted that even Lovenstein "drew a color line." Lovenstein was committed to justice for African Americans, driven by a sense of his own "humble origins" as the son of impoverished immigrants, but his advocacy of civil rights did not necessarily mean that he endorsed social equality.[7]

The peddler Morris Witcowsky, who worked northern North Carolina, claimed that the Jewish peddlers "were probably the first white people in the South who paid the Negro people any respect at all." He addressed his black customers as "Mr. and Mrs.," never as "aunt and uncle." He kept a credit "book on the shvartzers [*sic*]" but insisted the term meant no disrespect.[8] Sam Margolis, the son of a Hayti grocer, recalled how his father's life was saved by a black railroad fireman who intervened when his father was caught in a street fight, an event that made Margolis a lifelong friend of blacks.[9] Jews raised in Hayti recalled many neighborly courtesies that passed between Jews and blacks. When Israel Gordon, a "well known Jewish merchant" of Hayti, was mugged in 1938, the *Carolina Times,* the local African American newspaper, reported, "Many have expressed their regrets," observing that Gordon was "highly respected and much liked." Neil Johnston, a Durham African American, recalled that the Jews "always treated us different, even if it was just a smile in passing. We never really saw them the same as we saw the other whites."[10] The sense of Jews as friends of blacks was reinforced by the Rosenwald Fund, which in the 1920s rebuilt eight Durham County schools.

The theme of uplift, the aspiration to join the middle class, united elements of both communities. Durham's unrelenting New South business ethic inspired blacks and whites alike. The city earned the reputation as the "Negro Wall Street," praised by both Booker T. Washington and W. E. B. Du Bois for its "hands off attitude" toward black aspirations. In 1898 African American businessmen had founded the North Carolina Mutual Life Insurance Company, which spawned the Mechanics and Farmers Bank ten years later.[11] Jewish grocers and dry-goods shop owners turned readily to the bank for its liberal credit policies. Some immigrants, such as grocer Morris Katz, who spoke halting English, also felt more socially comfortable dealing with the black bankers than with the downtown white financiers. Jews and African Americans found open routes to upward mobility in Durham. The city with the support of the Dukes prided itself on its "live and let live" tolerance, its "different" race relations.[12]

Unlike the African Americans who created corporations, immigrant Jews found prosperity through individual enterprise in retail trades and real-estate investment. After arriving in Durham most Jewish artisans, peddlers, and storekeepers left poverty behind them in a decade or two, becoming a petite bourgeoisie, and a smaller number accumulated considerable wealth. The money from their businesses financed purchase of their stores and homes and then was invested in rental properties, often in African American neighborhoods. Second-generation Jews began the typical occupational climb from retail trades into the professions. Jewish students excelled in the public schools and then continued their education at Trinity College (after 1924, Duke University) in Durham or the University of North Carolina in nearby Chapel Hill.

Booker T. Washington had urged blacks to "imitate the Jew," but in Durham Jews borrowed the theme of uplift from African Americans.[13] In 1910 Dr. James Shepard, a pharmacist, founded the National Religious Training Institute and Chatauqua for the Colored Race, which evolved in 1925 into North Carolina College for Negroes, the nation's first state-supported liberal arts college for blacks (and in 1969 into North Carolina Central University). In 1912 the Durham Hebrew Congregation appointed a committee "to make arrangements for a Jewish training school in this city."[14] The project was never launched, but it was probably encouraged by Rabbi Abram Simon, who served on the board of trustees for Dr. Shepard's National Training Institute. Dr. Simon, a native of Memphis, Tennessee, was a graduate of the University of Cincinnati, having received his ordination in 1894 from Hebrew Union College and a doctorate from George Washington University in 1917. In 1904 he was appointed rabbi of the Washington Hebrew Congregation.[15] Rabbi Simon was a frequent visitor to Durham, where he was welcomed in both the Durham Hebrew Congregation and the African American White Rock Baptist Church. His involvement in African American education—coming at the very time when liberal Jews were joining blacks to form the NAACP—was part of an emerging national black-Jewish alliance.

Dr. Simon had similar messages for both his Jewish and black audiences. In October 1909 he spoke at the Durham synagogue on "the duty of the Jew in the small community," calling for a progressive clergy who could educate their people. At White Rock Dr. Shepard introduced Dr. Simon as "the foremost rabbi in the Jewish church in America." Simon's speech had a touch of Du Bois and Washington; he called on the blacks to pursue industrial education but also to aspire to the genius of Plato, Darwin, or Shakespeare. He endorsed Shepard's call for an educated black clergy as the vanguard of racial progress. In 1911 Rabbi Simon returned to Durham, and once again Jews crowded into the black church's front rows, which had been reserved for whites. In his address Rabbi Simon quoted Jesus and St. Paul. As Jew and Christian sought common ground in the spirit of the social gospel, Jesus' Hebrew origins were often cited. After the speech Rabbi Simon went to a B'nai B'rith dinner and spoke at the synagogue.[16]

Rabbi Simon was an American-born Reform Jew of German origin in contrast to most Durham Jews, who were East European and nominally Orthodox. Simon's appeal was to the congregational modernists. In 1921 when Durham Hebrew Congregation dedicated its new synagogue, renamed Beth El, Rabbi Simon was invited to deliver the keynote address. Early Durham rabbis, like many early African American ministers, tended to be self-declared clergymen. These "reverends" lacked semicha (ordination), and they supported themselves as grocers, cheder (Hebrew school) tutors, and ritual slaughterers. The pay was low, the turnover high. Yiddish-speaking immigrants had limited ability to reach out to the Gentile community. Not until about 1913 would Durham have a fully ordained clergyman, Rabbi Abraham Rabinowitz, and he was a Polish immigrant whose semicha came from an Old World yeshiva. Clannish and traditional, their family bonds tightened by Yiddishkeit, local Jewry had tenuous communal relations with the Christian community, white or black.

In 1937 Rabbi Israel Mowshowitz arrived at Beth El Congregation as Durham's first American-born rabbi. A graduate of Yeshiva College, Rabbi Mowshowitz was "modern Orthodox" in his religious orientation, and he was more interested in establishing ties to the non-Jewish community. He counted among his friends the "outstanding black minister" Rev. Miles Mark Fisher of White Rock. Rev. Fisher, who held a doctorate from the University of Chicago, and Rabbi Mowshowitz, a doctoral candidate in psychology at Duke University, both exemplified the new, college-educated, professional clergy advocated by Drs. Simon and Shepard. Each was civically involved and politically progressive. Rev. Fisher, who had come to Durham in 1933, founded an NAACP chapter and embarked on an ambitious social justice program, opening the church to labor organizers and challenging the conservative business leadership of White Rock. For Race Relations Sunday in 1943 Rabbi Mowshowitz delivered a sermon, "On Common Ground," to an interracial, interreligious gathering at Temple Baptist Church. This ecumenical program, which the newspaper described as "unique" for Durham, was a local event for National Brotherhood Week sponsored by the National Conference of Christians and Jews. Rabbi Mowshowitz described his relations with the black community as "excellent."[17] (Rev. Fisher's daughter, Ada, a physician, would later convert to Judaism and join Durham's Judea Reform Congregation.)

At White Rock Jews met Durham's black business elite. Within the confines of a segregated society Jewish and African American leaderships developed a cooperative, mutually supportive relationship. When Jews built their synagogue in 1921, C. C. Spaulding and Dr. Aaron Moore of North Carolina Mutual contributed, even as Jews donated to the building of black churches.[18] Church-building in the South—including synagogues—was a civic duty that crossed racial and denominational lines. Throughout its history Beth El Congregation turned to Mechanics and Farmers Bank for loans to help it through its perennial financial crises. In 1939, when European Jewry became endangered, Spaulding and banker J. H. Wheeler organized a campaign in the African American community to raise funds for the United Jewish Appeal. In the 1940s Emmanuel J. "Mutt" Evans, a downtown merchant and president of the synagogue, headed the steering committee to raise funds for Lincoln Hospital, which served the black community. When Evans chaired the Community Chest in 1948, he became the first white person to attend the kickoff banquet in the black community. In 1957 local Jews were able to build their new synagogue because of liberal credit terms that Mechanics and Farmers Bank extended to them.[19]

Despite the relations between Jewish and African American business elites, Jews as middle-class citizens remained separate from the mass of the city's black poor. Before World War I, Jews had moved from their Pine Street ghetto to a downtown neighborhood on Roxboro Street, anchored by the cathedral-style Beth El Synagogue. This "ghetto without walls," never a wholly Jewish neighborhood, bordered white working- and upper-class residential areas.[20] The Jews' rise to prosperity was only temporarily derailed by the depression. The resiliency of the tobacco industry and the ongoing construction of Duke University, the result of a 1924 bequest of forty million dollars, allowed the town to withstand the depression relatively well. A local World War II army base, Camp Butner, would also boost local businesses. New Jewish migrants, mostly northerners, flowed into town to open stores, their numbers replacing the second-generation youth who typically departed in pursuit of education and careers. In the late 1930s a small Jewish faculty presence, particularly in medicine and the sciences, also began to establish itself, some of whom were European émigrés.

With the founding of a Hillel Foundation in Chapel Hill in 1936,

Reform and Conservative rabbis first arrived in the area. The Hillel rabbis, who also were responsible for the Duke campus in Durham, tended to be political and religious liberals dedicated to interfaith efforts. In his New Year's message of 1944 Hillel director Rabbi Maurice Schatz, evoking the destruction of European Jewry, linked Jewish survival to progressive politics: "By our unreserved identification with liberalism and all humanitarian causes we can hope to recoup our incalculable losses of the past decade and emerge in our historic role of champions of forlorn hopes and unpopular causes."[21]

As university towns, Durham and nearby Chapel Hill contained a citizenry that was more cosmopolitan and racially tolerant than was typical of the state or the South generally. Chapel Hill especially was regarded as a bastion of southern liberalism. The Jewish student presence at the University of North Carolina had become significant in the 1930s under the enlightened leadership of university president Frank Graham, who in 1933 forced the resignation of a medical school dean who admitted that he had kept a Jewish quota. (Graham, however, was not prepared to admit Pauli Murray to the University of North Carolina graduate school when she applied.[22]) Most Jewish students were drawn South by sports, easier admission standards, and a desire to escape city life, but the university's reputation for liberalism also brought a number of activists.[23] In the 1930s University of North Carolina student Bill Levitt, leader of the Marxist Carolina Youth Federation, helped form a two-man picket line in front of segregated Durham stores. Another University of North Carolina student, Sidney Rittenberg, son of the Charleston, South Carolina, mayor, was a disciple of Frank Graham who quit school in 1940 to work in the labor and civil rights movements. New Yorker Allard Lowenstein chose to attend Chapel Hill in 1945 so that he could participate in the civil rights struggle.[24]

Campus liberals lived at the fringe of the established Jewish community, and their activism was contrary to the caution southern Jews more generally expressed. With the postwar suburban ascendancy, Jews and African Americans no longer lived in such proximity. The advent of supermarkets put an end to the Jewish Hayti grocers, and urban renewal in the 1950s and 1960s dislocated many downtown businesses. A black neighborhood began encroaching on the Roxboro Street Jewish enclave, and it deteriorated as homes were divided into boarding houses. In 1957, in a symbolic move, the Jews abandoned their downtown Orthodox synagogue and built a multipurpose, Conservative "Synagogue-Center" in the Trinity Park suburb, several blocks from the Duke campus.

Nevertheless, even as Jews and blacks were segregated in their schools and residences, Jews often depended on black trade in their businesses. Their stores sold uniforms for maids and millworkers. With its black enterprises and sizable middle class, African Americans possessed considerable economic power in Durham. At one point North Carolina Mutual Life Insurance was the largest black-owned corporation in the country. North Carolina College spawned an educated elite. Black executives were welcomed to the local Rotary Club and had access to city government. Whites cooperated with the moderate black leadership, knowing that behind that leadership more militant blacks were pushing harder to desegregate. Class resentments divided the African American community. The black middle class had a vested interest in stability, representing a moderate force that had improved its position within the status quo.

Jewish merchants, balancing their principles and interests, sought to accommodate blacks within the limits of segregation. Jewish merchants hired black clerks well before such practice had become acceptable among white Gentile storekeepers. In New York and Detroit in the 1930s and 1940s, by contrast, blacks rioted against Jewish merchants who refused to hire blacks.[25] Jews customarily gave their black employees more responsibilities than was conventional—including having them wait on customers—rather than just assigning them menial chores.[26] The Evanses' United Department Store had more liberal check-cashing policies for blacks than did other stores, permitted them to try on clothes, and provided rest rooms for them. In the 1950s, when a county judge told the Evanses that their biracial snack bar violated state segregation laws, the Evanses removed the seats, integrating their establishment through a legal technicality. (Harry Golden saw this case as a precedent for his Vertical Integration Plan, noting that southern laws typically permitted blacks and whites to stand together but not to sit together.[27]) In the context of the times these practices represented significant symbolic steps. Mary Mebane, an African American writer from Durham, recalled in her autobiography that the Evanses' luncheon counter was the only place in downtown Durham where she could eat without suffering the indignity of segregation.[28]

Certainly for some Jews blacks were no more than "schvartzes," and their interest in blacks was their potential for profit. A Jewish woman expressed shock at walking into a store and overhearing the owner, a European-born merchant, shouting racial epithets into the telephone to a tenant who owed him back rent. Another well-to-do merchant observed that he did not give his maid sick pay because he did not want to encourage her to be shiftless. One Durham-born merchant and landlord commented, "We never had no trouble with them until they started integrating, and then we started having trouble."[29] Some Jews owned sub-

stantial real estate in black neighborhoods, a custom that was not confined to Jews and included much of the town's business and political
leadership. Several times, in cases that drew newspaper headlines,
prominent Jews were accused of owning substandard housing, charges
that were vigorously denied.[30] Occasionally bad feelings prevailed. Several Jewish grocers in Hayti received threatening letters from blacks
who disliked having white merchants in their neighborhoods. The Jews
hired an attorney who was able to squelch any problems.[31]

"No matter how much we may have sympathized with the blacks,"
recalled pawnbroker Leon Dworsky, "we had to protect our own positions first."[32] As much as Jewish businesses catered to black trade, they
were even more dependent on white millworkers who worked in the
downtown factories near their stores. The merchants feared a "redneck"
backlash, a threat made all the more real by occasional Ku Klux Klan
marches. A rabbi, stopping at a newsstand, overheard several factory
workers remark that the murdered Mississippi civil rights workers
Chaney, Schwerner, and Goodman had gotten exactly what they deserved. A swastika was carved on a door of Beth El, and a brick was
thrown through a window during a Sabbath sermon. Despite the Jews'
initial outrage, however, they downplayed the incidents, not wishing to
publicize acts that they regarded as the works of extremists rather than
as an expression of community sentiment.[33] Their anxieties were triggered for the most part by economic concerns, not by fear for personal
safety.

The response of North Carolina to the civil rights movement generally, and Durham and Chapel Hill specifically, was moderate. Community pressures that drove some Jewish businessmen in the Deep South
into the White Citizens Councils were not felt locally. The state's political leaders feared that the racial violence provoked by massive resistance would hinder the economic development that they saw as North
Carolina's salvation. In 1948 North Carolina had elected as governor
W. Kerr Scott, whose "Go Forward" campaign had launched civic and
educational improvements—including the appointment of an African
American to the state board of education. In 1954 Governor Luther
Hodges, a former bank president, declared that North Carolina would
comply with federal court decrees, yet the state put the brakes on "all
deliberate speed" by granting public funds to students who attended
alternative schools.

The desire to temper white anger and to comply with federal mandates led to token integration. In the 1950s white flight took hold in
Durham, and school enrollment became predominantly black. Desegregation made progress in the 1960s, but court-mandated integration

was not implemented until 1970. Under court order, the University of North Carolina had begun to desegregate its law, medical, and graduate schools, and black undergraduates were first admitted in 1955. Duke University, threatened with the loss of federal funding, integrated its graduate student body in 1961 and its undergraduate school a year later (apparently dropping its religious quota at the same time).[34]

In February 1960 African American college students at North Carolina A&T University began a sit-in at a lunch counter in nearby Greensboro, accelerating the protest movement that would racially transform the South. A week later sit-ins began in Durham and shortly thereafter in Chapel Hill. Durham and Chapel Hill were rocked by street demonstrations and mass arrests. Violence simmered without exploding as sit-downers were dragged to arrest, sometimes under a hail of spit and curses. The desegregation of Chapel Hill was especially bitter—a demonstrator was doused with ammonia—because of the college town's pretense of liberalism. In Durham the black financial and political leadership was a moderating force, although militants pressed forward with street demonstrations and legal suits to force desegregation. Chapters of the Congress of Racial Equality, the NAACP, and the Student Non-Violent Coordinating Committee were active locally, and the town was visited by James Farmer, Roy Wilkins, and Martin Luther King, Jr. The local Congress of Racial Equality chapter was led by Floyd McKissick, a nationally known civil rights activist and first black graduate of the University of North Carolina Law School.[35]

In Durham political power oscillated between a black-white liberal alliance and a white conservative bloc. The Durham Committee on the Affairs of Black People, founded in 1935, was a force in city politics, especially when allied with labor unions or the university community, both of which tended to be especially liberal. Although Durham voted for segregationist gubernatorial candidates, in 1949 it first elected a moderate as mayor. He appointed a biracial group of labor and business leaders to the Citizens for Good Government Committee that included John Wheeler, an African American banker, and E. J. Evans, president of the Merchants Association. In 1950, when a mayoral candidate withdrew, Wheeler, on behalf of the committee's black faction, pressed Evans to run for mayor.

Evans aligned himself with Democratic party progressives such as Kerr Scott who were challenging the machine politics of entrenched white conservatives. Evans, an alumnus of the University of North Carolina, must also have taken a cautionary lesson from former university president Frank Graham, who lost a 1950 United States Senate primary in an infamously racist, red-baiting campaign.

Evans ran against James R. Patton, a conservative corporation lawyer. In his campaign literature Evans called for "harmony," asking the voters to reject "prejudice, bigotry and hypocrisy." The newspaper described his campaign of "Equal Representation for All People" as "controversial," and advertisements appeared warning against black bloc voting.[36] Evans, northern-born but southern-bred, proudly listed his presidency of Beth El Congregation and chairmanship of the state United Jewish Appeal among his qualifications. Southerners, he thought, respected church work.[37] In the election Evans won black electoral districts by margins of twenty to one; the *Durham Morning Herald* headlined "Negro Vote Elects E. J. Evans."[38] Evans would be elected mayor six times. In each campaign—even when he was unopposed in 1953 and 1955—extremists attacked him on both racial and religious grounds. The Ku Klux Klan telephoned threats to his home. Once, after being tipped off by an informer, the family retreated to a motel to avoid a possible bombing. Evans was attacked constantly by segregationist publisher Wimpy Jones, who in his populist *Public Appeal* reprinted *The Protocols of the Elders of Zion* and linked Evans to the "communist" NAACP.[39]

As mayor, Evans appointed the city's first black policemen, firemen, and municipal supervisors and pushed for an urban renewal authority that won federal grants for low-income housing. In 1957 he instituted the biracial Committee on Human Relations. Evans remained true to his principles as a peacemaker, but the civil rights movement grew increasingly militant; a 1950s liberal was a moderate by the 1960s as black power advocates spurned the patronage of whites. Evans recalled one incident when the police called his home to inform him that a sit-in was taking place at the downtown Woolworth's. He rushed to the store and assured the black demonstrators that he would press their demands with the business leaders if they would end their protest. They left, but that night windows were smashed up and down Main Street. In 1961, in his last campaign, Evans was "surprised" to find himself opposed by a sharply divided Durham Committee on Negro Affairs.[40] Evans's opponent, J. L. Atkins, was supported by Durham's labor movement. He, too, advocated racial and political reconciliation, and the *Carolina Times* described "both candidates as equally satisfactory" and "two proven friends of the race."[41] Despite the loss of the black leadership's support, Evans ran well in African American districts and won by his largest margin in six elections.

Some older Jews of the immigrant generation at first expressed anxiety about his political ambitions, but the Jewish community eventually supported him with pride. Having a Jewish mayor had symbolic importance as a sign of Jewish acceptance in Durham. In the postwar years local Jewry was solidly middle class. Dispersing in the suburbs these American Jews no longer seemed so different from their Gentile neighbors. When they dedicated their new temple in 1960, they published a credo stating that their synagogue embodied both the "spiritual truths of Hebrew culture and religion and the dynamic impact of the teachings of American democracy."[42] Mindful of the Holocaust, Jews redoubled their interfaith efforts in the postwar years, and rabbis regularly appeared before school assemblies and church congregations. Brotherhood became America's civil religion.

Over generations the Jewish community was acculturating if not assimilating. With the aging and dying of the immigrant generation the Jews had abandoned their traditional East European Orthodoxy for a distinctly American Judaism. In 1948 Beth El Congregation, after considering ten candidates, hired its first Conservative spiritual leader, Rabbi Simon Glustrom. Rabbi Glustrom held a B.A. and teaching certificate from Yeshiva University. These credentials reassured the Orthodox, even though Glustrom had done his rabbinical training at the Conservative Jewish Theological Seminary. He was a native of Atlanta, and the synagogue board cited his "Southern background" as a special qualification.[43]

Rabbi Glustrom, still in his twenties, was racially as well as religiously liberal. After eight years in New York the rabbi and his wife Helen, a Canadian, felt "culture shock" living in a place where rest rooms and drinking fountains were marked "white" and "colored." They found blacks no less than whites had internalized the status quo. "We had a maid—she was a lovely person—who insisted on coming in the back door," the rabbi recalled; he was "very pained" that she would not enter through the front. African Americans tended to be "in a very subservient position" and "by and large . . . were very quiet" in the late 1940s and early 1950s, he noted.

His congregants "very much accepted" prevailing racial codes and attitudes. Once the rabbi invited an African American Sunday school group to Friday night services, but he encountered resistance, most notably from the cantor, who had come to Durham from Macon, Georgia. "When he turned around and saw the black children, he was startled," Rabbi Glustrom recalled, and "it threw him off completely." The cantor remarked, in Hebrew, that the blackness made him think it was midnight. Some congregants believed that the rabbi was "too liberal" and "too aggressive," that he was "moving too fast" in opening the congregation to African Americans, but the criticism never reached the point where his tenure was threatened, and his contract was renewed. Although the congregants were "quite conservative" on racial issues, the rabbi quickly added that "they weren't rednecks." He found local Jews to be warm and welcoming. "Most of the congregants were storekeepers who wanted peace and quiet," Rabbi Glustrom reflected, and they certainly would not have wanted the white Christian community pointing at Jews as civil rights advocates. Rabbi Glustrom did remember some congregants, mostly recent northern émigrés who were professionals or affiliated with Duke, who were "amenable to change." E. J. Evans, the Rabbi noted, "wanted to create a different [racial] climate."[44]

The community's Jewish and southern identities came into conflict in 1954 when the congregation interviewed a candidate for rabbi. The candidate "seemed to be the ideal for our community," a congregant recalled, and had passed the board and congregational reviews. At a final interview the board discovered that the rabbi, a northerner, was a member of the NAACP, and he declared his intention to continue his civil rights activism in Durham. The board members agreed with him, but they acted on their fears. In 1954, the year the Supreme Court had shaken the South, not even Durham's white Christian ministers had committed to civil rights. "There was a lot of discussion. We felt he was right," the congregant reflected, "but what were we going to do?"[45]

Instead, the congregation hired Rabbi Louis Tuchman, an Orthodox rabbi who had previously served in Charleston, South Carolina. Rabbi Tuchman, a graduate of Yeshiva University, was chiefly concerned with preserving the congregation's Orthodoxy and in Jewishly educating an Americanized youth. "Traditional synagogues in general didn't have many relationships with other religious movements" white or black, Rabbi Tuchman reflected, noting that Orthodoxy lacked the ecumenical outreach of either Reform or liberal Conservative Judaism. Except for an annual brotherhood week, the rabbi had very few interactions with the non-Jewish community generally, and "none whatsoever" with the African American community specifically. "We had a fine relationship [with African Americans] as individuals—there was no problem—but as far as a communal relationship, in my time we didn't have that," Rabbi Tuchman recalled. "We went our own way."

"Like everyone else," the Tuchmans hired African American women to clean their home and to care for the children. Relations were always "very good," the rabbi observed, adding that he paid their social security. The houseworkers were trusted with the keys to the home and came and left as they pleased. He recalled one incident when the family took their houseworker with them on a vacation. A motel owner refused to give the woman a room, suggesting that she sleep in the car. "We said nothing doing; she's with us," the rabbi explained, and the family continued north until they found a motel that would accommodate all of them.[46] If Jews were not openly integrationist, they still held personal feelings that ameliorated some of the harsher effects of institutional racism.

When civil rights did become a public issue, Tuchman, like other North Carolina rabbis, took an integrationist stance. In August 1955 Governor Hodges in a radio and television report to the state called on both races to maintain school segregation voluntarily. The North Carolina Association of Rabbis, acting in concert with Christian governing bodies, responded immediately by passing a resolution informing the governor of "its whole-hearted support of the Supreme Court decision calling for de-segregation in the Public Schools." The rabbis stated, "We dare not permit the existence of laws which discriminate against any human being." The rabbis urged the governor to act "without undue delay." A year later the rabbis passed a second resolution calling for "a swift end to segregation."[47]

In his Purim sermon of 1957 Tuchman lectured on "the problem of desegregation": "Purim teaches us that we must oppose all attempts at stifling man's freedom and his right to enjoy that freedom. . . . As Jews . . . we must speak out clearly and forcefully whenever the freedom of any individual is threatened." He repeated this theme on Hanukkah: "[If] we circumvent or pretend that it doesn't exist, then the problem of integration will not disappear. We must thrust ourselves into the fray and proclaim for every man his God given right to bask in the warm rays of freedom and equality.[48]

Rabbi Tuchman was Beth El Congregation's last Orthodox rabbi. With the move to the suburban synagogue in 1957, it broke definitively with its Orthodox legacy and a year later hired a Conservative spiritual leader, Rabbi Herbert Berger, who served until 1978. Though a native of Cleveland, Rabbi Berger had southern credentials, having previously held pulpits in Memphis and Savannah. A Conservative rabbi of Orthodox background, Rabbi Berger was a graduate of Yeshiva College, the Hebrew Theological College in Chicago, and the Jewish Theological Seminary. He had been a Hebrew school principal, a Hillel adviser, university lecturer, and army chaplain. While serving in Durham, he earned a doctorate in educational psychology at the University of North Carolina. By professional training he sought to resolve conflict and find commonalities with all disputants.

Rabbi Berger had been raised in an integrated, middle-class neighborhood in Cleveland. He was by temperament a tolerant man, committed to interfaith efforts. In 1960 at the synagogue dedication, the rabbi issued a statement of welcome titled "One God and One Humanity," affirming a "fellowship of righteous people of all faiths and creeds."[49]

But Rabbi Berger was not a man who courted controversy, and he sought to accommodate himself to his congregants on racial as well as other issues. He was sensitive to the anxiety they pointedly expressed about an economic backlash from whites if Jews were to become publicly identified with civil rights. Their attitude was "not to rock the boat," the rabbi recalled. He noted, however, that these same Jews also felt "closely allied" with blacks in rejecting inequality.[50]

Rabbi Berger recalled efforts at rabbinical conventions to sign up rabbis to march with Martin Luther King, Jr. "I did not want to," he reflected. "I felt constrained. My congregation would be upset. I didn't want to fly in their faces." The rabbi did invite Professor Richard Cramer, a Chapel Hill activist, to speak to the congregation on civil rights. Privately, he expressed to Cramer his difficulty in speaking out when one prominent member, a real-estate developer who was a former state chairman of the United Jewish Appeal, was a slumlord.[51] Still, Rabbi Berger joined the town's African American leaders at Rotary meetings, where he delivered invocations, and at interfaith lunches. At E. J. Evans's home he met African American bank and insurance executives. Once again, class lines brought blacks and Jews together. "We felt honored blacks associated with us," Rabbi Berger remembers, noting that the African Americans he met were wealthy, educated, dignified people. Blacks were welcomed into the synagogue for interfaith services. At the invitation of the synagogue's custodian—the Reverend Pete Brodie, an African American minister—Rabbi Berger preached at a black church, with the apparent blessing of his congregants.[52] Southern neighborliness prevailed.

With a Jewish mayor and a large African American middle class with a vested interest in stability, local Jews "did not feel personally threatened" by the civil rights movement, according to Rabbi Berger. In 1963 Rabbi Berger added his name—along with several dozen other Jews, most of whom were affiliated with Duke—to those of nearly seven hundred Durham residents who made a "pledge of support" to merchants who "adopt a policy of equal treatment to all without regard to race."[53] This public endorsement of integration, published on a full page in the *Durham Morning Herald*, was intended to reassure storekeepers and restaurant owners who feared the economic consequences of desegregating.

Rabbi Ephraim Rosenzweig, the Hillel director who arrived in 1952, offered an instructive example of a rabbi who suffered when he did exceed community caution on racial matters. A native of Cincinnati, Rabbi Rosenzweig had been raised in the values of classical midwestern Reform Judaism, a religious milieu shaped by the Pittsburgh Platform. Rosenzweig cited as an inspiration for his liberalism his attendance at the religious school of Rabbi David Philipson, the distinguished civic and rabbinic leader who had served as the Platform's secretary. He also credited his racial tolerance to his Russian-born parents, who welcomed into their home his African American friends at the University of Cincinnati. After ordination from Hebrew Union College, Rabbi Rosenzweig served as director of community relations for B'nai B'rith and the American Jewish Committee in Montreal before coming to North Carolina. Imbued with a universalist outlook, the rabbi was an internationalist who invited Muslim and Christian students to Hillel for services and folk dancing.

Rabbi Rosenzweig encountered trouble with the state's B'nai B'rith hierarchy in the late 1950s when he took the unusual step of hiring an African American woman as secretary at Hillel's Chapel Hill headquarters. He also added his name to a list of local clergy who publicly called for integration. A Durham Jewish lawyer, who served as state B'nai B'rith president, was intent on finding communists and fellow travelers, and he turned his sights on the liberal Rosenzweig. Businessmen from Raleigh, Greensboro, and Charlotte warned him that his actions were endangering their businesses. Moreover, they admonished him that the state's B'nai B'rith members would withhold funds from Hillel because of his stand. The Jewish academic community rallied to his defense, and a contingent of Duke and University of North Carolina faculty appealed personally on his behalf to the national B'nai B'rith office in Washington. "The national office was supportive," Rabbi Rosenzweig recalled, "but I had to live with the local situation." Hospitalized with ulcers, his health deteriorating from the pressures, he resigned in 1962. The local Jewish community, however, demonstrated their support by asking Rabbi Rosenzweig to take over the pulpit of Durham's newly organized Judea Reform Congregation. Rabbi Rosenzweig remained a social activist, and his congregation was committed to civil rights. Recognizing that Jews and African Americans did not know each other, the rabbi and a black Baptist minister, the Reverend Mr. Mosley, organized a series of social gatherings that brought their two congregations together.[54]

Sam Gross, a New Yorker who joined the Duke faculty in 1960, offered an outsider's perspective on the Jewish community's attitude toward civil rights: "The [Jewish] townspeople for the most part were much more sympathetic to the black community than the white Christian community, but still maintained some of the ethos of the white establishment." Gross observed that "there was a large number of Jewish people involved in the elimination of racial segregation," including both academic and business people, native southerners and northern émigrés.[55]

Some members of the established community did take public stands in support of civil rights. In Chapel Hill Harry and Sybil Macklin's kosher-style deli was the first restaurant in town, if not the state, to desegregate, and it became "a guerrilla command post" for civil rights demonstrators. A prosegregationist radio announcer, Jesse Helms, denounced the place over the air.[56] Hazel Gladstein Wishnov, whose family had settled in Durham in the 1880s, joined the NAACP while living in the North. Returning to Durham she became a social worker and protested segregationist practices at her agency. Molly Freedman, a Durham merchant's wife, received heated criticism when she accepted and welcomed black delegates to a convention of the North Carolina Council of Women's Organizations in Chapel Hill.[57]

The Durham B'nai B'rith Lodge brought a series of civil rights advocates to town, including attorney Morris Abram in 1956 and Harry Golden, Charlotte's inimitable raconteur, whose *Carolina Israelite* newspaper was outspokenly integrationist. In October 1960 the lodge honored Walter Hicks and J. H. Wheeler of the Mechanics and Farmers Bank. Howard Lewis, a Veterans Administration optometrist who chaired the local Anti-Defamation League, organized a program on the writings of William O. Douglas with Duke law professor Melvin Shimm leading a discussion on civil rights in North Carolina.[58]

The integrating of Durham coincided with its evolution from a New South industrial town into a Sunbelt research and academic center. In 1958 the Research Triangle Park was established, drawing international computer and pharmaceutical firms. Both Duke and the nearby University of North Carolina at Chapel Hill emerged as institutions of national rather than just regional stature. A once-isolated, provincial Piedmont mill-and-market town became increasingly cosmopolitan. The Jewish community grew and changed accordingly as small-town merchants yielded in number to doctors, professors, engineers, and retirees. Chapel Hill Jews, negligible until the 1950s, exceeded Durham's in the 1970s though Jews in the two towns, united by their synagogues and a Jewish federation, considered themselves one community. The Jewish population expanded from 545 in 1964 to 1,955 in 1984.[59] As was true for the community as a whole, local Jewry was now culturally and religiously pluralistic. In 1961 the town's few Reform Jews, their numbers augmented by Sunbelt émigrés, had founded Judea Reform Congregation.

Unlike the established merchants who depended on public goodwill for their livelihoods, the faculty and professionals were salary earners who had the security of their campuses, hospitals, or research firms. Professionally mobile, they claimed no local past, nor did many foresee a future for themselves in the South. They were southern only by geography, not by culture. These academic émigrés tended to bring their liberalism with them.

Jews most commonly participated in civil rights as liberals—signing petitions, serving on panels—rather than as militants committing acts of civil disobedience. Jewish students and faculty joined the protest lines in front of hotels, theaters, and restaurants. Larry and Miriam Slifkin, native small-town southerners who had moved to the area in the 1950s as research scientists, picketed theaters and restaurants. She was motivated in measure by the example of her immigrant parents, storekeepers in Alabama, who practiced racial tolerance. Richard Cramer, a sociologist at the University of North Carolina, served as the first faculty advisor to the campus NAACP. Several Duke faculty families, the Grosses and Kornbergs among them, kept their children in a desegregated Durham public school where they were virtually the only whites to remain. The children were taunted as "honkies," Hudi Gross recalled. "It was a very trying period."[60] University of North Carolina professor Dan Okun served as chairman of the Committee of Concerned Citizens that sought to mediate between the Congress of Racial Equality and town government on integrating Chapel Hill's public accommodations.

At the community's fringes some Jewish activists did cross the line into civil disobedience. In 1964 a Chapel Hill judge sentenced six Jewish protestors to jail for sitting in, blocking traffic, and resisting arrest. Rosemary Ezra, a Californian who came to the area as a Congress of Racial Equality field worker, was sent to Women's Prison for six months by a judge whom she thought anti-Semitic. She was unable to pay her five-hundred-dollar fine because she had mortgaged her car and home to finance her civil rights work. Joseph Tieger, a Duke student and member of the Congress of Racial Equality, had in the judge's words the "dubious distinction of having the most arrests in Orange County" for civil rights. His twenty-three arrests earned him a twelve-month sentence.

Lowenstein, who returned to the area in the 1960s, plotted strategy and organized street demonstrations. The governor denounced Lowenstein by name as an outside agitator, and Wimpy Jones cursed the "New Yorker" in print as "the chief instigator . . . the cheapest little Jewish agitator we ever know [sic]."[61] These activists did not cite a specifically

Jewish motivation for their commitment. Ezra was "not connected to the Jewish community" in her civil rights work.[62]

Women often took leadership roles. Lucy Handler, a Duke faculty wife who came in 1938, was a founder and longtime president of the Durham League of Women's Voters, one of Durham's first integrated organizations. Dorothy Blum, a socialist since her student days in Germany, helped organize black youth groups, tutoring students at a segregated high school and starting the Progressive Teenagers Group at a black church. Charlotte Levin, a University of North Carolina faculty wife, toured schools, churches, and social clubs as a member of the multiracial, interdenominational Panel of American Women. For her work in support of civil rights she recalled several bigots who pointedly told her that "all Jews are nigger lovers." Levin, too, was motivated by childhood memories of her father, a merchant in Troy, North Carolina, who would bring wagon loads of toys to the African American poor on Christmas.[63] At historically black North Carolina Central University the only two white faculty to be granted emeritus status were both Jews, Ernst Manasse and Nell Hirschberg. Manasse, a German émigré from the University of Berlin, had been hired by Dr. Shepard in 1939 after applying to more than one hundred colleges in a desperate attempt to escape Nazi Europe.[64]

Postscript

With the Sunbelt transformations the area became less distinctly southern, more demographically mainstream American. The local Jewish population more than doubled in the 1980s, reaching 3,358 in 1991. Of the nearly thirteen hundred Jewish families in Durham-Chapel Hill, only about fifty persisted from the older community.[65] Jewish population growth was one element of an emerging multiethnic South. The Asian and Hispanic population also grew rapidly, and African Americans continued their reverse migration from the North.

The area was more liberal, more cosmopolitan than was typical of the South. In 1969 Chapel Hill became the first predominantly white town in the South to elect an African American as mayor when Howard Lee won office. In 1989 Durham elected African American Chester Jenkins mayor. Jews won election to city councils in numbers well beyond their proportion; invariably, they were liberals allied with African American factions. In 1991 Chapel Hill elected a Jewish mayor, Kenneth Broun. The former dean of the University of North Carolina Law School cited his work training black lawyers in South Africa as a credential and was endorsed by the NAACP. Jews headed social-justice groups such as the Interfaith Council and the North Carolina Civil Liberties Union; smaller numbers were prominent in radical circles. In 1979 three young Jews, members of the Communist Workers party, who worked in Durham's black neighborhoods as doctors and community organizers traveled to Greensboro for an interracial, anti-Klan rally. As they protested, Klansmen opened fire. Among the fourteen shot, two Jews were killed and another was wounded. The subsequent acquittal of the Klansmen outraged the local community and the nation; there was little sympathy for their radical politics.[66]

With the founding of the Durham-Chapel Hill Jewish Federation and Community Council in 1977, academic and professional Jews took the mantle of leadership from the established business community. The federation adhered to a liberal agenda on racial as well as other matters. The academic community also dominated the membership and leadership of the synagogues.

The community's liberalism was reflected in the pulpit. Judea Reform's Rabbi Rosenzweig had been succeeded in 1976 by Rabbi Eric Yoffie, a graduate of Brandeis University and Hebrew Union College-New York. Beth El's Rabbi Berger was followed in 1978 by Rabbi Steven Sager, a University of Maryland alumnus who received ordination from the Reconstructionist Rabbinical College in Philadelphia. Both were young, secularly educated, religious liberals who participated in interracial forums and dialogues. The most active civil rights leader was Rabbi John Friedman, a graduate of the Hebrew Union College-Cincinnati, who arrived at Judea Reform in 1980. Rabbi Friedman served as president of Durham Congregations in Action, a social justice agency, and worked assiduously to forge personal and institutional ties with black Christian and Muslim clergy. For his activism Durham's Martin Luther King Committee awarded Rabbi Friedman its "Keeper of the Dream" award. When the Durham community was torn by the racially divisive issue of merging city and county school systems to promote integration, Jews led panels endorsing it, and both Rabbis Sager and Friedman signed a statement declaring a "merged school system is good for all."[67]

The celebrated breakdown of the black-Jewish civil rights alliance was not felt locally although local Jews were well aware of the national mood. Incidents between the communities were isolated and not generally expressive of community feeling. Nation of Islam adherents appeared occasionally on local campuses, rankling Jews, but African American anti-Semitism did not establish itself on local campuses. Once a black labor leader complained about Jewish administrative domination of Duke University Hospital. With such small Jewish numbers, however, the conditions that created black-Jewish turf wars in Chicago or New York—conflicts concerning neighborhoods, economic control, government funding, or political redistricting—did not exist locally. The campuses were racially torn by strikes by cafeteria workers and housekeepers and by the building of black student unions, but these disputes did not have a specifically Jewish dimension. To forestall potential problems, Jewish groups renewed efforts to open dialogues with local African Americans. Interracial programs became regular features of campus and community calendars.

In 1985 the Black-Jewish Roundtable formed to discuss issues of common interest. Topics focused on such issues as South Africa, school tracking, and affirmative action. In contrast to neoconservative trends, local Jews strongly endorsed minority quotas. From the Jewish perspective the African Americans seemed more interested in political action than in a dialogue for mutual understanding. As was true of the past, the interchanges drew largely from academic and political elites without involving the broader communities. The roundtable waxed and then waned.[68]

With integration, relations between Jews and African Americans were recast. Jews and African Americans worked together in offices, classrooms, and laboratories, but only a few committed individuals built personal relations beyond their institutional ties. Mindful of the tensions that divided Jews and African Americans nationally, local Jews, for reasons of both principle and self-interest, remained liberal on racial issues. Clergy and community leaders sought to bridge the gap through interfaith programs and issue-based forums. Neither community, however, saw Jewish-black relations as a pressing local issue.

Even as Jews and African Americans were divided in Durham by race and religion, they found common ground in class-related issues. In the early years of Durham, Jews and African Americans, sharing poverty, lived closely together. Within the confines of a segregated society the Jewish and African American civic and religious leadership found common ground on issues of mutual benefit. Jews accommodated themselves to southern racial attitudes and practices even as they expressed goodwill toward the African American individuals they knew as customers and employees. Southern neighborliness was capable of overriding racial barriers. Confronted with the challenge of civil rights, Jews were primarily concerned with maintaining their hard-earned civic and economic standing. Recent migrants, many of whom were drawn south to work in the universities, were more forcefully liberal, though few became civil rights militants.

Community values were reflected in the pulpit. The early Orthodox rabbis were traditional East European immigrants concerned with internal communal and congregational affairs. They had less interest in or ability to communicate with the larger non-Jewish communities of either race. As local Jewry acculturated over generations, the congregation evolved from its immigrant Orthodox legacy. The new American-born, university-educated rabbis who ascended to the pulpit tended to be politically progressive and more civically involved. Still, no matter how tolerant the rabbis may have been personally on racial matters, they were constrained by the conservatism of their congregants. As the South integrated and a culturally mainstream Sunbelt community emerged, rabbis and African American clergy forged relations, but the two peoples remained socially and residentially apart.

Big Struggle in a Small Town:
Charles Mantinband of Hattiesburg, Mississippi

CLIVE WEBB

Dedicated with love to Sally Rippin, my guiding star
throughout the writing of this article.

*Charles Mantinband is one of the best-known southern Jewish activists in
the civil rights struggle. In this essay Clive Webb describes the many pressures
exerted to silence his voice. Hatemongers clearly created a climate of fear.
Much of this story concerns the rabbi's relationship with his congregation.
Although the author does not identify avowed segregationists in the congregation and notes that many agreed with Mantinband's opinions, the intimidation factor was so high that the tension level between congregation and rabbi
remained at a fever pitch. Mantinband adjusted as best he could without
compromising his activism. Although the fear and insecurity of the Jewish
community has been noted many times, few stories are as poignant as those
of Mantinband here and of Perry Nussbaum in the next selection.*

Whether or not the desk sergeant had been dozing, he must have been
wide awake within moments of answering his phone. The distressed
caller on the other end of the line exclaimed that he had just been startled from his sleep by a "loud explosion." The time was 3:37 A.M. By
daybreak a crowd of onlookers, newspaper reporters, and politicians had
gathered outside the Jewish Reform Temple on Peachtree Street as fire
workers made their way through the smoking debris. Damage would
eventually be calculated at more than two hundred thousand dollars.
The bombing of the Atlanta Temple on 12 October 1958 was the fourth
such attack since March. Another three synagogues during the past year
had been saved only because dynamite placed by terrorists failed to ex-

plode. The bombings caused windows to shatter, walls to collapse, and ceilings to come crashing down. Moreover, they shook to the foundations the belief of many southern Jews that they could continue to evade the intense political turmoil that erupted in the wake of the *Brown* decision.[1]

Several days after the Atlanta bombing, and some 350 miles away in Hattiesburg, Mississippi, Rabbi Charles Mantinband was walking home from town when he came upon the recently retired mayor. "You know, Rabbi," remarked the former mayor with a knowing smile, "I've told my friends that they need not go to such lengths as bombing the temple. We all know who the troublemaker is and they could just go after him." Reaching into his jacket pocket, Mantinband removed a small notebook and pen and began to record a verbatim account of the conversation. When asked what he was doing, the rabbi replied that the notes would be sent to his attorney, "so that if anything happens to me they will know the source." His interlocutor, looking a little flustered, asked forgiveness, insisting that he had only been joking. "I'm not," replied the rabbi firmly. "See you again."[2]

Rabbi Mantinband had not exactly gotten himself into trouble again. The fact was that he had never been out of it. His public stance against segregation had made him a target of local authorities anxious to keep tabs on his every movement. Someone sat round the clock at the bus stop opposite the rabbi's home, monitoring his comings and goings. His mail had invariably been opened by the time he arrived at the post office to collect it. Mantinband's wife, Anna, remembered how the watcher at the bus stop once followed her onto the bus itself and seated himself right beside her even though the bus was only half full. "I see the reverend is taking a trip," he began immediately. "I seed him get into a car with a New York license yesterday. I got a little book; I know every move the reverend makes."[3]

Judging simply by appearances, one might have had difficulty understanding how anyone could think Charles Mantinband dangerous. Standing roughly five feet ten inches, the portly, bald rabbi usually dressed in a smart suit and looked out at the world through a pair of small-framed spectacles. What comes to mind is the kind of wise old owl that inhabits children's storybooks. Mantinband's demeanor was no less affable. Soft-spoken, he was always courteous in conversation, even with his opponents. "He always had a friendly smile on him," reflects Joseph Brunini, a Roman Catholic bishop from Jackson and an associate of Mantinband's.[4] That Mantinband never stopped smiling was testament to his strength of will. So crippled was he by arthritis that at times he was forced to perform his duties from a wheelchair.

Rabbi Mantinband had enjoyed a long and varied career before he became spiritual leader of Temple B'nai Israel in Hattiesburg in 1951. He was born on 2 April 1895, "long, long ago," as he liked to joke. Almost unique among those rabbis who placed themselves in the front line during the civil rights struggle, Mantinband was a native southerner. Men like Jacob Rothschild in Atlanta, Perry Nussbaum in Jackson, and Ira Sanders in Little Rock came to the South as outsiders, untainted by the region's racial prejudices. Mantinband's upbringing was quite different. His family having returned from New York to Norfolk, Virginia, while he was still a small child, Mantinband grew up with an unquestioning acceptance of the racial teachings he received both at home and in the classroom. "My early schooling and social life was in a segregated society," conceded the rabbi. "After considerable struggle I learned to exercise control in my attitude and make no distinction between one man and another."[5]

That struggle began when Mantinband returned North in search of a college education. According to his wife, Anna, when the young Mantinband enrolled at the City College of New York, he "found himself in a class seated alphabetically next to a black student." Physically repulsed, Mantinband "promptly walked out of the room in protest." Once his instructor managed to confront him on the issue, he advised the resentful student to change his thinking or withdraw from college. It was warning enough. When the class next convened, Mantinband had taken his seat alongside the black student. He never looked back.[6]

Having been ordained at Rabbi Stephen S. Wise's Jewish Institute of Religion in New York City, Mantinband went on to serve a number of congregations in both the North and South. The most recent of these had been in what is known as the tri-cities—Florence, Sheffield, and Tuscumbia—in Alabama. During this time Mantinband first began to get actively involved in the race issue, becoming one of the prime movers in the Alabama Council on Human Relations.

By the time Mantinband had arrived in Hattiesburg, he had long since come to believe that Jews could offer a unique contribution to the civil rights movement. The social activism inherent in the teachings of Reform Judaism committed Mantinband and his coreligionists to the struggle for worldly perfection. Racism was just one of the obstacles to be overcome if that state were ever to be reached. Jews also knew better than anyone what it meant to live as a persecuted minority. They could not, in all conscience, be anything but acutely sensitive to the plight of others who remained targets of oppression the world over. "Judaism is committed to the principle of the equality of all men under God," explained Mantinband. "Motivated, therefore, by our Jewish background and teaching, and ever mindful of Israel's persecution and disability throughout the ages, we Jews are sensitive to the suffering of all victims of injustice and exploitation."[7]

Jews were not only able to empathize with African Americans, however; they offered an example of how to combat oppression. With so many others ready to attack them, Jews had come to realize that they could ill afford to fight among themselves. Mantinband pointed to the way in which Jews had turned inward, creating a cohesive community based on mutual cooperation. It was a lesson from which he believed African Americans could learn a great deal. "The Negro, no less than the Jew, must learn to 'know himself, to accept himself, to improve himself,' " opined Mantinband. "Respect for authority, a sense of discipline, a need of dedication, a spirit of sacrifice, co-ordination and co-operation, patience, faith, an optimistic outlook on life, all these under God's providential care, are necessary. They are to a large degree still lacking in the Negro world."[8]

Mantinband perceived his own contribution to the civil rights movement as an educational one. Through article writing and speech making he sought to enlighten both his own congregation and the larger public concerning the virtues of racial integration. This enlightenment would, he hoped, create a climate conducive to calm discussion and help lay the foundations on which political leaders could build.

Such an approach relied on two factors. The first was an appeal to people's better nature. The second was time. In Mantinband's mind direct action precluded both. When a representative from the New Orleans office of the Anti-Defamation League, an organization that advocated direct action, traveled to Hattiesburg on a fact-finding mission, he reported that Mantinband "does not fully agree with us." Nonetheless, the two men had struck up a "good working relationship." Mantinband's conviction remained that, although their hearts were in the right place, marchers and demonstrators ended up doing more harm than good. Their confrontational tactics only served to antagonize southerners, instinctively hostile to "outside" interference, perhaps even turning moderates into extremists. "We have applauded the objectives of the Freedom Riders," the rabbi commented in one of his published articles, "but have not been certain about the wisdom of their strategy. My feeling is that, in the final analysis, the struggle must be carried on by local leadership, white and Negro, Christian and Jew, on the home front— working despite fear of reprisal." Mantinband adhered rigidly to this philosophy throughout his years in the small town of Hattiesburg.[9]

Hattiesburg is located in the Piney Woods region of southern Mississippi. Its initial settlement came about when William Harris Hardy, a lumber and railroad magnate, selected the site for a station along the proposed Meridian-to-New Orleans route of his New Orleans and Northeastern Railroad. When the line was completed in 1883 Hattiesburg became fully incorporated as a city. During the next several decades the community flourished, thanks to its chief industries: transportation, turpentine manufacture, and a yellow-pine lumber mill.

After an initial boom, the population had become fairly stable by the mid-twentieth century. According to the census of 1960, Hattiesburg had 34,989 inhabitants. Of these, about 20 percent were African American.[10] The city's Jewish population comprised some fifty families, the heads of whom were mostly engaged in the retail trade. "I would say that over 50 per cent of the businesses downtown were owned by Jewish families. . . . I mean, whole blocks," affirms Leonard Auerbach, himself a real-estate owner. At the turn of the century Jews began settling in Hattiesburg. The local B'nai B'rith lodge was founded in 1908. Not until seven years later, on 5 September 1915, was congregation B'nai Israel organized, its first services being held at the Oddfellows Hall. Finally, in 1919, came the completion of Temple B'nai Israel's edifice, Hattiesburg's only synagogue.[11]

Seldom victims of overt prejudice, Hattiesburg's Jews were often among the leading lights of the city's white community: well-educated, well-liked, and well-off. "For the most part," attested Rabbi Mantinband, "they were upper middle class." Festering in their minds, however, was the fear that their acceptance was conditional. "Part of the price Jews paid for the high degree of acceptance and success they had achieved," Murray Friedman once observed of the Deep South, "was that they had to conform to the region's racial patterns." The Jews of Hattiesburg were no exception. Only so long as they continued to appear just like their white neighbors would they remain safe from recrimination. On the issue of race, especially, they had long since learned to keep their mouths shut.[12]

Such anxieties were not entirely unfounded. The state of Mississippi was the heart of the massive resistance movement. It was during July 1954 that the first White Citizens' Council was founded in the city of Indianola. The council posed an enormous potential threat to white moderates. As writer David Halberstam observed, anyone who took up a position in support of the Supreme Court decision faced "an organized network of groups consciously working to remove dissenters—his job and his family's happiness may be at stake." Although the council never officially sanctioned anti-Semitism, the idea that Jews masterminded the civil rights movement gained considerable currency among some of its members. "I am not anti-Semitic," exclaimed Robert Patter-

Rabbi Charles Mantinband stands in front of the ark at the 1960 confirmation class, B'nai Israel, Hattiesburg (courtesy of Carol Mantinband Ginsburg and William Mantinband).

son, founder of the first Citizens' Council, "but I am against any man or group [that] aids and abets the NAACP which is trying to destroy our way of life."[13]

As a college town Hattiesburg was perhaps more liberal than most other communities in Mississippi, but opposition to integration was still intense. The *Hattiesburg American* responded to the *Brown* ruling by observing that "the Supreme Court has come up with its most stupid decision. . . . The decision is bound to create embarrassment and distress, and will hinder, instead of help, race relations." The greatest threat to the Jewish community, however, lay some thirty-five miles to the north in the city of Laurel. There lay the headquarters of the White Knights of the Ku Klux Klan of Mississippi, under the leadership of its founder and first Imperial Wizard, Sam Bowers, Jr. The last thing Hattiesburg's Jews wanted to do was fuel Bowers's fanatical conviction that the civil rights movement was "a Jewish-communist conspiracy" operated from Washington as part of a larger struggle to seize control of the United States.[14]

The threat of personal danger obliged Mantinband himself to act always with the utmost caution. When the local newspaper, the *Hattiesburg American*, ran an editorial denouncing the NAACP as "the greatest obstacle in the advancement of the colored people of the south," an enraged Mantinband sat down at his typewriter and pounded out an emotional rejoinder. Condemning the racial violence that threatened to engulf Mississippi, and in particular the murders of Emmett Till and Mack Parker, the letter then singled out the real enemy of African Americans.[15] "The Citizens' Council and Sovereignty Commission," exclaimed Mantinband, "more and more resemble the gestapo of the Nazis."

Established in 1956, the State Sovereignty Commission employed secret investigators to inquire into "subversive activities." It filed the names of all Mississippians suspected of sympathizing with the civil rights movement. One of the first names filed was Charles Mantinband. He was identified by the commission in 1956 as a codirector of the Mississippi Council on Human Relations. So thick was the air of suspicion in Mississippi against the civil rights movement that the council was soon suffocated. Between 1957 and 1961 it was entirely inactive. That Mantinband was one of only five whites identified with the organization made his name all the more conspicuous. The risk involved in criticizing the commission was immense, as Mantinband well knew. Realizing as he did that "to expose oneself in print is to invite embarrassment if not violence," the rabbi chose not to sign the letter with his own name. In a determined effort to disguise his identity, and perhaps also to lend the letter greater legitimacy in the eyes of those he was attacking, Mantinband referred to himself as "A God-fearing Christian citizen."[16]

Such a maneuver was typical of the way Mantinband, as something of a marked man, struggled to regain his anonymity. Whenever the rabbi passed any of his black friends on the street, he kept his eyes staring straight ahead for fear that even the most casual nod might raise suspicion against him. "Please know that during the past two years I have been a rather lonesome and isolated creature," he once confessed sadly to Dr. Kenneth Clark. "If the Negro citizenry of the Magnolia State is aware of my presence and influence, I scarcely hear about it." Indeed, interviews with J. C. Fairley, erstwhile leader of Forrest County's NAACP, and Charles Phillips, his right-hand man, revealed that neither man had ever heard of Mantinband.[17]

Anxious as he was to avoid publicity, however, there were times when Mantinband did emerge from behind the scenes to stand in the harsh glare of the spotlight. His unhappy involvement in the Clyde Kennard affair was perhaps the most compelling occasion.

Clyde Kennard had served as a paratrooper in Germany and Korea for ten years before returning to his Mississippi home. With money saved during his military service, Kennard bought some land just outside Hattiesburg and helped his parents to set up a chicken farm. Kennard himself then traveled north to pursue an education at the University of Chicago. When his father took ill and died, the dutiful son returned home to help his mother maintain the farm. He had not, however, given up all thoughts of a college education. With the credits gained during his time in Chicago, Kennard attempted in September 1959 to enroll at what was then known as Mississippi Southern College, now the University of Southern Mississippi. There was just one problem. True to the tenets of Jim Crow, Mississippi Southern College accepted white students only. And Clyde Kennard was black. Kennard was informed that the state would cover his expenses at any northern college of his choice. Under absolutely no circumstances, though, would he be admitted at Mississippi Southern.

Kennard was nothing if not persistent. The following year he reapplied for admission. This time, however, he came up against not just the college authorities but the combined forces of the state of Mississippi. As the date of Kennard's interview with college president William D. McCain drew nearer, the State Sovereignty Commission began to call his friends in the hope that they might persuade Kennard to withdraw his application. The calls were unsuccessful, as were the efforts of Governor James P. Coleman to have the college issue a letter rejecting Kennard's admittance because of alleged "deficiencies and irregularities" in his application papers. Kennard arrived at Dr. McCain's office at 9 A.M. on 15 September 1960. This arrival, however, was not before he had been hotly pursued by two police officers, who later charged that he had been "driving at a terrific rate of speed."

The interview with Dr. McCain was entirely unproductive. Afterwards Kennard was escorted back to his car via a side door so as to dodge waiting reporters. There to greet him were the two police officers, who arrested Kennard not only for speeding but for the possession of two cartons of whisky that had apparently been found in the car.[18]

Rabbi Mantinband had first met Clyde Kennard during one of the latter's visits home from Chicago. The two had enjoyed many a conversation, Kennard being invited inside whenever he passed by the Mantinbands' home. Mantinband was intensely suspicious of the charges against his friend, not least the one for possessing whiskey, because he knew Kennard to be a teetotaler. There were others who shared his conviction that Kennard had been falsely accused. Lou Ginsberg, one of Mantinband's congregants, recalled how she and her husband, Herbert, had been visiting the district attorney at his home one night when they heard of Kennard's arrest. "And I said, 'Oh Jimmy, you know he didn't do that. Y'all were just doing that 'cause he's trying to get into Southern.' And Herbert gave me a nudge I should be quiet."[19]

Mantinband could not keep silent. Almost immediately he volunteered his services as a character witness at the trial. The rabbi was joined by another member of his congregation, department store owner Dave Matison. Matison's credentials were not altogether exemplary, however. According to one source, he had earlier offered to pay Kennard's tuition at another college so long as he did not try to enter Mississippi Southern.[20] In the event, there was nothing that either Matison or Mantinband could do. Before anyone had even set foot in the courtroom, Justice of the Peace T. C. Hobby called aside the two men, urging them to "go on home, boys. You can't help this bird. We're going to throw the book at him." The defendant's own behavior did not improve matters. Perhaps because he had lost all hope of being acquitted, Kennard, who had earlier denied the allegations, said nothing in his own defense. Hobby wasted no time in fining him five hundred dollars for illegal transportation of alcohol and another one hundred dollars for reckless driving.[21]

The Mississippi Supreme Court set aside Kennard's conviction twelve months later in September 1961. By that time, however, Kennard had experienced another brush with the law, one that would scar him permanently. This time he was arrested as an accessory to the theft of twenty-five dollars' worth of chicken feed at the Forrest County Cooperative warehouse. Johnny Lee Roberts, an employee at the warehouse, admitted to the crime but insisted that Kennard had bought the chicken feed from him, knowing that it was stolen. Judge Stanton A. Hall sentenced Kennard to seven years' hard labor at the state penitentiary. Roberts received a suspended sentence.[22]

During the lonely days in his cell as he awaited trial, Kennard re-

ceived strength and support from a number of friends, among whom
was a certain rabbi. "When he was behind bars in Hattiesburg," Mantinband later reported, "I brought him Gibbons' *Decline and Fall of the
Roman Empire*, which for him was spiritual nourishment." Nor did the
visits end once Kennard had been convicted and relocated to the state
penitentiary. According to Esther Shemper, the rabbi "used to go visit
him all the time."[23] Still, Mantinband had been unable to do anything
to clear his friend's name, and he was utterly powerless to alter the subsequent course of events. While serving the second year of his sentence,
Kennard developed cancer. Despite his rapidly deteriorating health,
prison authorities refused his transfer to a hospital. As public pressure
began to mount, Governor Coleman eventually intervened. According
to a scathing Mantinband, "The governor became a hero and saint, by
commuting his sentence." Clyde Kennard died of intestinal cancer on
4 July 1963. He was thirty-eight. Not until years later, long after Mantinband's own death, would the truth of his having been framed by the
state authorities come to light.[24]

The intransigence of organized officialdom was upsetting to Mantinband but not altogether surprising. What shocked and saddened him
most was the attitude of his own congregation toward the civil rights
issue. Among Hattiesburg's Jews was an instinctive support for the
Brown decision. This was as true of those born and bred in Mississippi
as it was of those who had only recently settled in the South. Leonard
Auerbach, whose parents moved to Hattiesburg long before he was born,
asserts that the Jews were much more enlightened on the racial issue
than their Gentile neighbors. "I really think so," he remarks. "I don't
recall ever having any problems [with the decision]." His claim is borne
out by a report filed by a representative from the Anti-Defamation
League who met with Jewish leaders in Mississippi during March and
April 1958. Jews in Hattiesburg, he wrote, were "rather calm about the
segregation-desegregation situation and although we discussed it at
length at the meeting there was no excitement with the whole evening
going off very calmly."[25]

Ironically, however, those most naturally sympathetic to Mantinband's cause became in many instances some of his staunchest adversar-
ies. Fear of violent reprisals, both real and imagined, resulted in repeated efforts by the congregation to censor their rabbi whenever he
involved himself in the race issue.

In February 1956 Mantinband traveled to Alabama State College for
Negroes to attend the annual meeting of the Alabama Council on Human Relations. The rabbi had been invited to offer his observations of
the race problem in Mississippi. Speaking before an integrated audience

of three hundred people, Mantinband started with a passionate defense of the NAACP, which had come under fire the previous night at a state-wide rally of the White Citizens' Council. Mississippi senator James Eastland had alleged that the NAACP was a Communist-front organization, one of many such groups mentioned on a list held by the attorney general's office. "I have the attorney-general's list in my coat pocket," exclaimed Mantinband, reaching for the paper and holding it aloft, "and the NAACP's name is not on it." Then, turning to the main theme of his speech, the rabbi testified to the loneliness suffered by those individuals scattered across Mississippi who were willing to speak out against segregation. "My offense is great; it smells to heaven," he remarked, quoting from *Hamlet*. The speech received enthusiastic applause, leaving Mantinband with the feeling of a job well done as he journeyed home later that night.[26]

The following morning as he sat down to breakfast and unfolded his newspaper, Mantinband was struck with horror. There on the front page of the *Hattiesburg American* was the headline "Local Rabbi Says Race Relations Stink." Throughout town, members of Mantinband's congregation were choking on their cornflakes as they stared in disbelief at the paper. It didn't take long for the phone to ring. The temple board had appointed a five-man delegation to call on the rabbi and to urge him to refrain from any further public statements about the integration issue. Mantinband listened quietly as he was told that he had no right to jeopardize the security of Hattiesburg's Jews by acting as he did. Then, smiling graciously, he replied that he would gladly comply with the board's demands. Asked when, he continued: "The day I die."[27]

The board was not amused. A second meeting was convened; this time virtually the entire congregation attended. Julius Rosenthal, a rabbi from upstate New York who at one time exchanged pulpits with Mantinband for a month, described the charged atmosphere: "A lynch mood was in the air. . . . Many attacks on the Rabbi came from those who had long been silent or had even been his apologists."[28]

Although Mantinband kept his job, he drew little consolation from the arguments of his supporters. Some argued that the congregation should think first and foremost of the rabbi's virtues as a spiritual leader. Failing that, a decision to fire Mantinband might cause the congregation even greater problems because a replacement might be difficult to find. "The national association of Reform rabbis would probably make it difficult for [Hattiesburg] to secure another man," explained Julius Rosenthal, "and it is hard enough for such a small, out-of-the-way congregation to attract a rabbi without this."[29]

As Rabbi Mantinband's civil rights career began to blossom, his congregation endeavored to prune its growth, even to uproot it. During the next seven years he found his authority challenged, his activism criticized, and his opinions censored. In the summer of 1958 Mantinband and his wife flew to Europe for a much-needed vacation. The rabbi had recently assumed the chairmanship of the Mississippi Council on Human Relations. He nonetheless welcomed the prospect of leaving the race problem behind for a few short weeks.

No sooner had Charles and Anna left town than "a prominent temple member" received an ominous communiqué from the local White Citizens' Council. The congregation must seize this opportunity to remove the "mischief-making rabbi," demanded the letter, or "we cannot be responsible for the consequences." No one who read the letter was prepared to find out exactly what those consequences were. "They were afraid of what would happen," recalls Esther Shemper. "You know, they were bombing the temples and individual homes if necessary, and they were afraid it would happen to us." Members of the congregation immediately set about planning a surprise welcome home for the rabbi.[30]

On this occasion it was only the intervention of a local Catholic clergyman that saved Mantinband. Having learned of the emergency meeting called by the board of B'nai Israel, Monsignor Martin ensured that he received an invitation of his own. Commending Mantinband's courage, the monsignor invited those assembled to recognize the basic humanity of the rabbi's stance on civil rights and to "hold up his hands." This they reluctantly agreed to do. Mantinband had been let off the hook. It would not be long, however, until the congregation once again cast their reels out after him.[31]

Mantinband was not without ardent supporters within the congregation. "He was a very intelligent man," enthuses Marvin Reuben. "Very liberal, particularly where integration was concerned. He was far ahead of his time." Reuben himself stood on the front line during the desegregation crisis. As general manager and co-owner of WDAM TV, he was responsible for a series of outspoken editorials that supported the Supreme Court's *Brown* decision and denounced extremists like the Klan who would do anything to prevent its implementation. Unfortunately for Reuben the kind of people he attacked over the airwaves were unlikely to express their disgust by simply switching channels. Instead, they decided to pay the station a number of visits, leaving their own unique brand of calling card: acid poured over the car owned by Reuben's wife, crosses burned outside the building, and the shooting down of the station tower. Although Reuben claims to know who the culprits were, no one was ever convicted. An already frightened Jewish community became almost completely paralyzed. As Maury Gurwitch, a local shoe store owner observes: "Marvin was constantly threatened. He was a very brave soul to step forward. We merchants were locked in place downtown, and we really were hesitant to speak out."[32]

Alarmed at the attacks against Reuben, the congregation inevitably stepped up its opposition to Mantinband. The rabbi was especially criticized for socializing with African Americans. Because the Mantinbands lived directly across the street from the temple, the congregation worried that it, too, would be identified with these integrated get-togethers. The state senate had also passed an act in March 1956 that removed tax exemptions on all property owned by churches or religious groups who used "all or any part" of their facilities on a nonsegregated basis. Compliance with both custom and the law was the primary concern of the temple's board of directors. When one member reminded Mantinband that the house was temple property and threatened to have him evicted, the rabbi was stirred to an unusual display of anger. Warning his adversary not to interfere with his personal life, Mantinband joked coldly: "If they came into your store to buy a refrigerator, you'd be delighted to see them."[33]

The arguments did not end there. Mantinband had been a popular speaker at black colleges since the early fifties, before the *Brown* decision was passed. On one occasion representatives from B'nai Israel paid the president of one of these colleges a visit and asked him not to invite Mantinband to any future engagements. When the visit yielded no result, the temple leaders turned to the rabbi himself. Mantinband was asked, respectfully but firmly, if he would cease all further contact with the colleges. The rabbi, as always, was extremely diplomatic in his response. Only after he had sat patiently, listening to each and every argument put forward by the board, did he respond. "I told them I would [agree]," he later wrote, "on condition that I also refuse invitations to white colleges and be allowed to inform the authorities why." The subject was never discussed again. Then there was the twenty-five-hundred-dollar gift bestowed on B'nai Israel by "a national foundation" in honor of Mantinband's "sane approach and wisdom in dealing with the race issue." Reluctant to accept what it considered such a controversial award, the board only relented when Mantinband threatened to resign, which for purely pragmatic reasons, they were reluctant to see him do.[34]

The situation was always the same. The congregation was convinced that with every action he performed in support of racial equality, the rabbi was punching holes in the flood barrier that kept their neighbors' anti-Semitism in place. "Grudgingly, they concede that my position is morally correct and consistent with the noblest teachings of Judaism," recorded Mantinband in his diary. That did not prevent him from seeking legal advice about the security of his job, despite the fact that he had been granted tenure.[35]

The only solution Mantinband found was simply never to tell his congregation what he was up to. Should the temple's members find out through some other source, so be it. Mantinband would deal with such situations as they arose. In the meantime he would simply get on with the task at hand. "One time when I was [temple] president," remembers Maury Gurwitch, "he said, 'I'll be gone a week,' and I turned on the television and saw him in Miami at some big convention with Martin Luther King."[36]

The lack of like-minded spirits within his congregation might have been offset were Mantinband able to look for comfort from other Jews, and in particular his fellow rabbis, throughout the rest of Mississippi. Sadly this was not the case. "I feel that the sins of these colleagues of mine are the sins of omission rather than commission," Mantinband once wrote to Harry Golden, celebrated editor of the *Carolina Israelite*. "I suspect that they comfort themselves by feeling they are influential and useful behind the scenes, and play it safe and cozy."[37]

The one friend Mantinband had within the local rabbinate was Perry Nussbaum of Jackson. Initially, Nussbaum was extremely reluctant to involve himself in the race issue. According to Mantinband he was "a sort of Johnny-come-lately." It took great perseverance on Mantinband's part, for instance, to recruit Nussbaum as a member of the Mississippi Council on Human Relations. Only after several years of polite but persistent invitations to join did Nussbaum agree to do so. Nussbaum was right to be fearful, however. His involvement in civil rights issues eventually resulted in both his home and temple being bombed.[38]

Nonetheless, the relationship between the two rabbis blossomed. Both regularly attended the social science forums organized by Dr. Ernst Borinski at Tougaloo College, a black institution in Jackson. Borinski was a German Jewish immigrant who had fled to the United States after the Nazis invaded Austria in March 1938. He had accepted a teaching position at Tougaloo in 1947. The social science forums provided an opportunity for an integrated audience to meet and socialize. As Ed King, erstwhile chaplain of Tougaloo, states: "It was a place that a few white liberals could speak." Among the celebrated speakers who accepted invitations to lecture at Tougaloo were Ralph Bunche, James Baldwin, and Pete Seeger. Attendance at the social science forum was not without its risks, however. Sovereignty Commission investigators stood outside the college gates, writing down the license numbers of anyone who came to the Wednesday night meetings. Death threats were received—through the mail, over the phone, even in person. By the late fifties, fears for personal safety had forced the suspension of the forums.[39]

Mantinband and Nussbaum still corresponded. To some extent Mantinband had served as Nussbaum's mentor on civil rights, so it was no surprise that the Jackson rabbi should turn to his friend when his congregation rose in revolt against him. Among Nussbaum's congregants many opposed integration as a matter of principle. This was particularly true of Sidney Rosenbaum, president of Jackson's B'nai B'rith lodge and a man "whom I had taken to task last Spring for having a Citizens' Council program." Nussbaum did not appeal directly to Mantinband for advice on how to deal with his predicament. Just sharing similar experiences with a fellow rabbi may in itself have proved therapeutic.[40]

Among other Mississippi rabbis was an extreme reluctance to become involved in the integration struggle. Far from supporting Mantinband, one rabbi even openly cheered on the other side. Benjamin Schultz of Temple Beth Israel in Clarksdale became the favorite rabbi of segregationists throughout the South for his oft-quoted remarks on the lesson the rest of the nation could learn from Mississippi. Applauding the state's struggle against the incursions of both the federal government and world communism, Schultz called upon "the dedicated clergy of our state and the South generally to demand that our Northern preachers fight the Cold War for America, even if it means less time for them to attack the South." Schultz was clearly dancing to a different tune from Mantinband. Mantinband himself endeavored to struggle on, although there were times when he came close to being seduced by dreams of an easier life. As he acknowledged to one friend: "There are temptations for a Rabbi to desert the scene and go into less turbulent pastures."[41]

That Mantinband did not succumb to such temptations was in part due to his plugging into an informal network of southern liberals who provided a system of mutual support. Whenever the deluge of criticism threatened to engulf Mantinband, he could always count on a friend for encouragement. Harry Golden was one such friend. So too was P. D. East, infamous editor of the *Petal Paper*. East's newspaper, which he ran from his own home in Petal, a small community on the outskirts of Hattiesburg, was a beacon shining through the murky fog of lies and distortion pumped out by the Mississippi press. Similar in style to Golden's *Carolina Israelite*, the *Petal Paper* prescribed laughter as the best remedy against the ills of segregation. Mantinband loved it. According to one letter he wrote to East, the rabbi would "practically memorize" each and every issue. To express his gratitude, and also to help spread East's integrationist message, Mantinband distributed copies of the paper "judiciously" to friends and associates he thought sympathetic to the civil rights struggle.[42]

Such allies as Mantinband had, however, were scattered throughout Mississippi and the rest of the South. When the rabbi turned to other clergymen in his hometown, the response was less than enthusiastic. Sunday mornings in Hattiesburg did not start with the preacher stirring his congregation and shaking the church walls as he railed against the evils of Jim Crow. The most dramatic display of racial solidarity that the city's clergy could muster was the inclusion of a local black gospel choir during observance of Race Relations Sunday, held once every February. "It was a gesture," sighed Mantinband in retrospect. "Not very useful." The rabbi's relations with Hattiesburg's religious leaders were largely amicable. Indeed, in the early 1960s he was elected president of the Hattiesburg Ministerial Association, an honor that Mantinband believed helped to calm his congregants' fears about their continued acceptance by the rest of the white community. Still, Mantinband's election was achieved in spite of, rather than because of, his stance on civil rights. The rabbi's hard work over the years raising money for charity, particularly through his involvement with the Rotary Club, tended to outweigh people's perception of him as a troublemaker. "I believe that if a rabbi lives in a community long enough," Mantinband asserted, "and earns the reputation for hard work, integrity, and public service, people will tend to say, 'Well, he may be a bit queer and out of step, but let him alone. He's a good fellow.' "[43]

Eventually, however, the pressure became more than Mantinband could bear. When the rabbi was offered a new congregation in Longview, Texas, he did not hesitate long before handing in his resignation notice. The official reason for the Mantinbands' departure was that they wanted to be closer to their daughter and grandchildren, who lived in Shreveport, Louisiana, just across the border from their new home. As attractive an enticement as this might have been, however, the couple would likely never have moved were it not for the ceaseless barrage of criticism. "They made it so miserable for him," asserts Esther Shemper, "that I think actually in a way they did ask him to leave." Lou Ginsberg, a fellow member of B'nai Israel, confirms this. Mantinband's critics had tried so often to clip his wings that eventually he just had to fly away. "He wanted to leave," she adds succinctly, "because the congregation was not happy with him." When Mantinband received the first George Brussel Memorial Award "for distinguishing service to the cause of individual freedom and social justice along inter-faith and inter-racial lines" at a ceremony in New York in April 1962, he did so knowing there were few in his congregation with whom to share the honor.[44]

On 19 February 1963 a farewell banquet was held in honor of Mantinband as part of National Brotherhood Week. Mayor Claude Pittman presented the rabbi with the key to the city before an audience of some seventy-five persons. "It has been a great joy to know and work with you and to live here," enthused Mantinband, apparently without irony. "As we leave, we carry away the happiest of associations." Not everyone was so willing to enter into such a spirit of conciliation, however. Rabbi Leo Bergman, who attended the banquet as a representative of the National Conference of Christians and Jews, recalled that all kinds of people were present: college presidents, clergymen, business leaders, and journalists—almost everyone of importance, that is, except for Mantinband's own congregation. "The best brains of the Jewish community were there, but how few they were in contrast!" remarked Bergman. "Later I learned that it had been difficult to interest the Jewish group."[45]

When Rabbi Mantinband moved to Longview in March, he was saying goodbye not only to his congregation but his most active days as a civil rights advocate. Only three months later he was one of some two hundred clergymen from every faith invited by the Kennedy administration to attend a White House conference on "present aspects of the nation's Civil Rights problem."[46] The rabbi also continued to serve on the board of the Southern Regional Council until 1971. Despite an unfailing commitment to the cause of racial equality, Mantinband would find the next decade relatively quiet. Ironically, the year after his departure Hattiesburg became a focal point of the voter registration campaign known as Freedom Summer. The arrival of northern volunteers, many of them Jewish, the establishment of Freedom Schools, the demonstrations outside the city courthouse—all of this the Jews of Hattiesburg would have to face without the rabbi.[47] As for Mantinband himself, waning involvement in civil rights can be explained in part by his advancing years coupled with his gradually failing health. By the time he died on 3 August 1974 he had been blind for a number of years. This blindness was somewhat ironic for a man whose vision of brotherly and sisterly love among all people had sustained him through all the personal and political turbulence that had marked his career in Mississippi.

What Price Amos?[1] Perry Nussbaum's
Career in Jackson, Mississippi

GARY PHILLIP ZOLA

Perry Nussbaum led a peripatetic career that ultimately brought him to Mississippi. He attempted to inculcate Jewish traditions among his congregants, fight anti-Semitism, and create organizational ties crossing many boundaries. In a pattern reminiscent of Max Heller's, key events seemingly transformed Nussbaum into an activist whose Jewish identity intertwined with his stand on civil rights for African Americans. Gary Zola's study traces the man and the forces that pushed and pulled him in many directions.

Perry E. Nussbaum (8 February 1908–30 March 1987) retired from the active rabbinate in August 1973. His retirement was a bittersweet event for him and for his congregation, Temple Beth Israel of Jackson, Mississippi. Nussbaum was admired and resented. On the one hand, he had unquestionably revivified Jewish life in the capital city of Mississippi and, in the process, left a lasting impression on the community. As one congregant noted, "He made the Jew in Jackson Jewish-conscious. . . . He left a Jewish heritage to [the congregation]."[2] On the other hand, Nussbaum's rabbinate in Jackson coincided with the compulsory dismantlement of segregation in the South—a societal transformation foisted on an unwilling white populace by the federal government. As a leading spokesman for Mississippi's Jewry during this explosive period, Nussbaum became a human lightning rod in one of the state's stormiest periods.

Actually, the emotional pot boiled over six years earlier. On 18 September 1967 a bomb destroyed a significant portion of Beth Israel's newly dedicated house of worship. Two months later, on 22 November, the temple's parsonage—the rabbi's home—was bombed. These bombings marked, in effect, the climax of tensions that had built up for more than a decade; most Jews believed the bombings constituted segregationist retaliation for the rabbi's high-profile crusade on behalf of civil rights. Nussbaum did not agree. He blamed the events on a community thoroughly contaminated by anti-Semitism and bigotry. So from 1967 on, spent, discouraged, and weary from the tumult, both Nussbaum and his congregation awaited his retirement.[3]

At the congregational banquet honoring the rabbi on his retirement, Mississippi's governor William Waller told the assembly that Nussbaum had taught the community a great deal about human relations and that history books would someday record the rabbi's influence on the state. Nussbaum was dubious. As he put it many years later: "I can't be persuaded that anybody is interested in Mississippi any more."[4]

Nussbaum's role in that tempestuous period of Mississippi's history has indeed begun to emerge in recent years. To some Nussbaum was a prophetic teacher of Jewish morality, the custodian of his congregation's spiritual and moral values. Others remember him as an "arrogant, ornery, impetuous" man whose reckless crusading endangered the synagogue and its members. One fact is obvious: Perry Nussbaum's career in Jackson illustrates the formidable challenges faced by southern rabbis who dared to speak out against the South's steadfast commitment to segregation.[5]

Who was Perry Nussbaum? Later in life, Nussbaum mused: "I do not know why I became a rabbi . . . and a Reform rabbi to boot." This wisecrack may have been Nussbaum's way of saying that his childhood did not project him naturally into the Reform rabbinate. Raised in Toronto, Ontario, he was the son of working-class Galician immigrants. He and his family attended a small Orthodox synagogue in which he became a Bar Mitzvah. Nussbaum first encountered Reform Judaism shortly after his graduation from Toronto's Central High School of Commerce. Unable to gain acceptance to the Chartered Accountants of Toronto (which he attributed to his being a Jew), Nussbaum worked as the secretary to Rabbi Barnett R. Brickner of Holy Blossom Synagogue.[6]

One morning while taking dictation, Nussbaum offhandedly asked Brickner if he should consider entering the rabbinate. Brickner's answer was encouraging: "Perry, you'll be a damned fool if you don't." Such encouragement from a man like Brickner, a capable orator and a dedicated pastor, persuaded Nussbaum to apply to his rabbi's alma mater, the Hebrew Union College (HUC) in Cincinnati. To become eligible for admission to a university in the United States, Nussbaum spent an additional year in Toronto completing the prerequisite course work. He began a combined course of study as an undergraduate at the University of Cincinnati and the Hebrew Union College Preparatory Department in the fall of 1926.[7]

Although the program normally required eight years, Nussbaum successfully earned both his undergraduate diploma and his rabbinic ordination in seven. In his own words his accelerated curriculum was not the result of native brilliance; he simply could not afford the cost of an additional year of study. As a student at the University of Cincinnati, Nussbaum earned an unremarkable record. He excelled, however, in his Hebraic studies at HUC. To earn supplemental income Nussbaum put his secretarial skills to good use by working as a stenographer for some of the professors. He also profited from the practice of typing, duplicating, and selling his lecture notes to underclassmen. Completing his academic requirements for ordination a semester early, Nussbaum asked for and received permission to work full-time for several social welfare agencies in Cincinnati. He seriously considered enrolling in a social service school after ordination but in the end decided to take a pulpit.[8]

During his student years Nussbaum corresponded with Rabbi Ferdinand Isserman who succeeded Brickner at Holy Blossom. Isserman—a man intensely committed to interfaith work and described by one colleague as "a living embodiment of the prophetic principles of justice, mercy, and peace"—may very well have served as an early role model for the young Nussbaum. Although he established cordial relations with the younger, American-born faculty members, most of Nussbaum's teachers would not have voted him most likely to succeed. By his own admission Nussbaum "was never a diplomat." He had little capacity for catering to superiors—even those who might be in a position to further his career. This fact may very well explain why he was the last member of the class of 1933 to be offered a position by HUC president Dr. Julian Morgenstern. With no other choice, Nussbaum became the rabbi of Beth Israel Synagogue in Melbourne, Australia.[9]

Nussbaum summed up his brief stint in Australia with characteristic directness: "I came, I saw, I failed." Promoting an embryonic Reform Judaism in Australia, overwhelmed as it was by Orthodoxy, proved too much for the neophyte rabbi. Looking back from the vantage of forty years, he attributed his lack of success to inexperience. Before ordination his only practical training consisted of two High Holy Day student assignments. Dr. Morgenstern's assessment of Nussbaum's potential, however, was entirely different; he counseled the young rabbi to pursue another career. Nussbaum persevered. Morgenstern grudgingly offered him a High Holy Day pulpit in Amarillo, Texas, and suggested that he try to make the post into a permanent position. Nussbaum decided to do just that.[10]

His frustrating experience in Melbourne presaged Nussbaum's first two peripatetic decades in the rabbinate. In 1937 Nussbaum jumped at a chance to leave Amarillo and assume a pulpit in Pueblo, Colorado, where he also taught public speaking and served as a part-time librarian at a local college. While on a speaking engagement in El Paso, Nussbaum met his future wife, Arene Talpis, a schoolteacher. In 1941 he became the rabbi of Temple Emanu-el in Wichita, Kansas.[11]

Like many of his rabbinic colleagues, Nussbaum joined the army chaplaincy in 1943 and remained in uniform for the duration of World War II. Three years later, in 1946, he became Rabbi Abraham Holtzberg's associate in Trenton, New Jersey. He could not stand the post. He left in less than a year, saying: "Holtzberg didn't want an associate—he needed a secretary." From Trenton Nussbaum moved to Temple Emanu-El of Long Beach, New York, where he hoped to settle permanently. His professional troubles persisted. The three years he spent in Long Beach were filled with belligerent bickering and petty political infighting. With his wife's mental health and spirit in a precipitous decline, Nussbaum resigned abruptly and accepted a call to Temple Anshe Amunim in Pittsfield, Massachusetts. Pittsfield provided Nussbaum with "more of the same."[12]

Why were Nussbaum's congregational stints so transitory? To be sure, Nussbaum moved to new pulpits during the early years of his rabbinate to procure more desirable working conditions. Most rabbis were eager to advance themselves to larger congregations that were capable of providing a more generous financial package and better working conditions. Moreover, many rabbis longed for the opportunity to fraternize with other rabbinic colleagues in cities with a larger Jewish population. Such communities, usually found in major metropolitan areas, also typically possessed the potential for growth as well as an array of Jewish activities and institutions that were lacking in smaller cities. Clearly, Nussbaum's sequential moves reflect an effort to improve his professional circumstances.

Nevertheless, professional improvement only partially explains his rabbinical transience. Even his admirers conceded that "rabbinic life did not always come easy to Perry." Nussbaum's forceful and outspoken personality seems to have been an ongoing source of controversy, and his direct manner was often perceived as brusqueness. Although he was a man with a "warm heart," he had a "mental toughness" that some congregants found disagreeable. He clung to his principles, yet this very integrity was often taken to be a form of inflexibility.[13]

Nussbaum has been described as a "difficult personality," a man who "had a way of irritating people." Indeed, to this day he is remembered by some surviving members of his congregation in Jackson as a "headstrong" and "abrasive" individual. Traces of this quality emerge from Nussbaum's correspondence. In one instance, an out-of-town college instructor, referring to himself as "a wandering Jew from New York," wrote to express his disappointment that the rabbi had offered a blessing at the meeting of the United Givers Fund—a philanthropic fund that evidently doled out some of its proceeds to segregated facilities. The Jackson newcomer scolded Nussbaum for blessing a fund that supported "the obnoxious doctrine of race exclusion." Nussbaum pinned the man's ears back: "The 'wandering Jew from New York' has much to learn about the problem of Jewish survival in this part of the country. . . . [You] . . . ought to do some self-tutoring about the facts of Jewish life while devoting [yourself], as you do, to the problem of education of our Black young people."[14]

Nussbaum recognized his shortcomings. When he sent a copy of his biographical resume to a colleague, he scrawled a tongue-in-cheek note on the last page: "I should have started out this Biography with the statement: 'Nussbaum has never been a diplomat. . . . As a rabbi he has never had any tact.' " At times the interpersonal demands of the rabbinate frustrated him. He once remarked that "sermonizing to Am Ha-aratsim [ignoramuses] and acting as a 'rebbe' [rabbi] to their children didn't provide much incentive to maintain interest in Rabbinics." When an organizational position at the Union of American Hebrew Congregations (UAHC) in New York opened up, Nussbaum seriously considered leaving the pulpit. He told Maurice Eisendrath, president of the UAHC, that he had long insisted his forte lay in organization and administration. "I believe," he wrote Eisendrath, "those who have had any kind of intimate contacts with me will support me in this [contention]."[15]

Nussbaum's weaknesses, however, were offset by his many abilities. He was a learned man who once described himself as "studiously inclined, but never a brilliant scholar." He continued studying independently after ordination. While in Pueblo he nearly completed the residence requirements for a Ph.D. in history. His move to Wichita, however, prevented him from completing the curriculum. He enjoyed teaching and was considered by some an outstanding instructor. The few articles he published prove he possessed a forceful, even inspirational, style of writing. He excelled especially in the composition of original prayers—several of which gained praise from colleagues—that periodically appeared in the temple bulletin.[16]

Nussbaum was also a capable orator. A non-Jew who heard Nussbaum preach at an interfaith Thanksgiving Day service praised the rabbi for his eloquence: "No other clergyman in Jackson could have approached your finesse in meting out encouragement & yet in scotching any thought of complacency or self-congratulations by the sated majority." After hearing Nussbaum speak in Atlanta, the consul general of Israel complimented the rabbi on his "penetrating analysis," calling the lecture a "most impressive exposition" and a "masterpiece."[17]

Besides his intellectual strengths, Nussbaum was also an effective pastor. Writing to an older colleague he displayed real compassion for congregants whose daughter planned to marry a non-Jew. He wondered whether he should consent to marry the couple and "give the poor parents a modicum of 'nachas' [pleasure] out of a daughter, and hold them positively and without bitterness within the Temple." On another occasion Nussbaum remembered holding the hands of a twenty-year-old Jewish cadet who crashed his plane on base during a World War II training flight. After the boy's death he wrote: "As that young Jewish boy lay dying, I breathed a prayer not only for the repose of his soul but also for that mother and father who as yet were unaware that their son was making the supreme sacrifice in behalf of his country. I put myself in their place—rather, I put my own members in their place—and wondered about the reservoir of courage and spiritual strength we all should be developing during this trying period."[18] Though his outspoken, direct manner rankled some congregants, Nussbaum clearly had a great deal to offer as a learned, hardworking, and honest individual and a deeply committed Jew.

What brought Nussbaum to Jackson? In June 1954 Nussbaum attended the convention of the Central Conference of American Rabbis (CCAR) in Pike, New Hampshire. There he chatted with his former classmate and friend, Rabbi Nathan Perilman of Emanu-El Congregation in New York City. Perilman had just returned from Jackson, Mississippi, where he had been the featured speaker at a farewell banquet for the synagogue's retiring rabbi, Meyer Lovitt. Perilman raved about Mississippi's capital: "[Meyer Lovitt] has been there for twenty-five years. It's a wonderful congregation. There they'll appreciate you. The South is known for its respect for its rabbinical leaders. You can do as little or as much as you want to. Jackson is beautiful—wide streets, clean, a wonderful Southern city. Perry you'll like it. Take Arene and your daughter down there—and drink mint juleps the rest of your life."[19]

After twenty-one years of a revolving-door rabbinate, Nussbaum was ready for the kind of position Perilman described. Nussbaum and his wife longed for stability and, as they phrased it, some "rest and relaxation." Nussbaum decided to apply for the pulpit immediately, and he flew down to interview the following month. The rest and relaxation he expected Jackson to provide eluded him.[20]

Throughout the South 17 May 1954 became known as "Black Monday." On that day, just three months prior to Nussbaum's interview at Beth Israel, the Supreme Court ruled in *Brown v. Board of Education of Topeka, Kansas* that racial segregation of public schools was unconstitutional. The Court's decision was a watershed event for the nation.

White southerners were bitterly opposed to the new policy. As one writer noted, "The return of General Sherman and the Union Army, it seemed, could not have unified southern opinion more." Most of the region's white citizenry resolved to maintain segregation at all cost. Robert "Tut" Patterson, for instance, was so distressed by the Court's ruling that he could not sleep all that night. Fearing "for his young daughters," Patterson promptly organized "the first chapter of the Citizens' Council—a segregationist committee [composed] of white businessmen." Though Citizens' Council chapters cropped up throughout the South, Jackson's chapter was especially well-organized and influential. Most white southerners had no intention of capitulating to the Supreme Court.[21]

It is difficult to overstate the level of fear and mounting hysteria that engulfed the Jewish communities of the South during this period, and Jackson was no exception. As with all who did not fit the white Christian Protestant mold, Jews were aliens in southern culture. Because a fair number of southern Jews owned retail stores of one kind or another, assimilation and patronization were essential to their economic survival; they wanted desperately to avoid offending their customers—white and black. So *Brown v. Board of Education* placed many Jews in an awkward predicament. Some Jews criticized segregation; others passionately defended the status quo. Most Jews, however, simply wanted to avoid getting caught in the cross fire of tremendous societal disruption.[22]

Adding insult to injury was the fact that northern Jews were quick to hail the Supreme Court's decision. National Jewish organizations such as the Anti-Defamation League, the American Jewish Committee, and the American Jewish Congress aggressively proclaimed the need to dismantle segregation in the South. These efforts unnerved southern Jews. Admonishing a northern visitor from the Anti-Defamation League, one southern woman said, "Every time one of you makes a speech, I'm afraid my husband's store will be burned up." Such apprehensions were hardly unfounded. In 1958 a series of bombings in southern synagogues gave substance to the fear that any connection between Jews and the struggle for black equality would result in the destruction of Jewish businesses and the loss of Jewish lives. Rabbis who openly denounced segregation found themselves besieged on two fronts; not only did they merit the scorn of segregationists, but they also inflamed the passions of their own flocks. It did not take an outsider long to recognize that Jewish life in the Deep South had a character all its own.[23]

By July 1954 the implications of the Supreme Court's recent decision on school desegregation were already a top-priority issue for Jackson's Jews. The rabbi in Jackson certainly needed to be a broad-minded and tolerant man, yet congregants also wanted a rabbi who understood the importance of circumspection and discretion. As one southern woman explained, "We have to work quietly, secretly. We have to play ball." It is no surprise, therefore, that the very first question the rabbinic search committee posed to Nussbaum when he arrived for his interview was "Doctor, what's your position on school desegregation?" Nussbaum's reply was easier said than done: "I consider myself a liberal," Nussbaum told them, "but I have always been careful not to get my people into trouble."[24]

Clearly, the candidate's self-professed liberalism concerned the search committee. Nevertheless, it ultimately decided to rely on Nussbaum's assurance that he had no intention of jeopardizing the community's safety. When the committee offered him the position, he accepted. He resigned from Pittsfield and moved down to Jackson in the fall of 1954. Nussbaum struggled mightily to live up to his promise as he began a tenure that he would characterize many years later as "the roughest and toughest and most involved . . . of my rabbinical career."[25]

Nussbaum's first few years in Jackson were remarkably tranquil—especially in relation to the controversies that eventually erupted. Beth Israel was a small congregation; Nussbaum served one hundred families. The rabbi was expected to conduct Friday evening services, supervise the Sunday school, and offer moral support to the sisterhood. Highly assimilated (a large proportion of the congregation put up Christmas trees in their homes), the congregation shunned traditional Jewish ritual of any sort. In Nussbaum's opinion some members of his new congregation were "anti-Hebrew, anti-Israel, anti-everything!" To redress this situation Nussbaum introduced Hebrew studies, an ambitious program of Bar Mitzvah, and an annual program of adult education.[26]

Nussbaum also discovered that many of his wealthiest congregants were involved in the American Council for Judaism. The council was an anti-Zionist organization founded in 1942 by a group of Reform rabbis who were initially opposed to the establishment of Israel and what was called the "Zionist domination of American Jewish life." After Israel's independence the organization continued to advocate Judaism as a religion of universal values and not a nationality. Nussbaum was firmly opposed to the council's stance, and from the moment he arrived in town he prohibited so-called Councillites from meeting inside the temple. As Nussbaum later recalled, his policy "left its scars."[27]

With characteristic vigor he threw himself into communal affairs outside of the synagogue. He joined the boards of numerous philanthropic agencies including Rotary, Shriners, Family Service Society, the Salvation Army, and the Mississippi Association of Mental Health. Mendall M. Davis, general manager of the Jackson Chamber of Commerce, invited the new rabbi to become a member. Graciously accepting the offer, Nussbaum assured Davis of his willingness "to serve the city and the Chamber." Invoking the words of the prophet Jeremiah, Nussbaum provided Davis with what he hoped would be his watchword while in Jackson: "Seek the peace of the city."[28]

Throughout his rabbinate Nussbaum had enjoyed interfaith work, and he looked forward to similar activities. His positive relations with Christian clergy in former congregations frequently provided him with an oasis of professional fulfillment in a desert of interpersonal conflict that often existed within his own congregation. Nussbaum was amazed to discover that, contrary to common practice in the North, ecumenism in Jackson did not include the rabbi.

The transplanted northerner quickly learned that, in Mississippi, religion was a dominating influence. Mississippians of the 1950s and 1960s prided themselves on being devout Christians. At that time Protestantism of the evangelical variety was overwhelmingly dominant. One author's recollections of religious life in Philadelphia, Mississippi, serve as an apt generalization for the state as a whole: "There was often anguish when a Catholic married into a fine old Protestant family. . . . There was not much difference between the Protestant denominations in the county. . . . We all interpreted the Bible literally and subscribed to the hellfire-and-brimstone preaching of fundamentalism."[29]

Religious leadership played a dominant role in the political life of the state, especially in the matters of race relations and the civil rights movement of the 1960s. Christian leaders invoked their interpretation of the Bible to justify the world view of the white southerner. Political convictions, too, were typically founded on Christian teachings. Describing the cultural milieu during the period, one Mississippian observed, "Politics, economics, education, moral actions, as well as contemplation and reflection, [were] parts of spirituality."[30]

The tacit alliance between the Protestant fundamentalist churches and the state was keenly felt in the capital city. Nussbaum was fond of comparing the city's leading Protestant churches to the Russian Orthodox Church before the 1917 Revolution. The practice of excluding the rabbi from the forum of religious dialogue was a "barometer of the esteem in which his religion was held." For Nussbaum, this behavior was pure religious chauvinism, a medieval relic and a confirmation of the fact that, in Mississippi, Christianity and Judaism were not on equal spiritual or political footing. One of Nussbaum's priorities soon became, as he phrased it, "to storm the thick and high walls of Protestant fundamentalism in the Bible Belt."[31]

Finding himself excluded from the ranks of the Jackson Ministerial Association, Nussbaum tried to cultivate alternative avenues for interfaith communication. He welcomed the opportunity to participate in the local Army Reserve chaplains group where he nurtured a small group of friends who remained close associates throughout their careers. These bi-monthly gatherings provided the solitary rabbi with a "wonderful escape from reality" and a recreational outlet. "While others went fishing or played golf," Nussbaum recollected, "I played soldier."[32]

Collaborating with a small number of like-minded Christian colleagues, Nussbaum helped to establish a Jackson Interfaith Fellowship that sponsored monthly programs aimed at exploring issues of religious differences and similarities. In 1968 the fellowship was superseded by the Greater Jackson Clergy Alliance, the first racially integrated association of Protestants, Catholics, and Jews in Mississippi. As an extension of the alliance, a state-wide association—the Mississippi Religious Leadership Conference—was established the following year. As Nussbaum pushed unflaggingly for Jewish inclusion, his efforts slowly began to pay dividends. Including the rabbi on committees dealing with religious concerns eventually became *de rigueur* in Jackson. He never tired of speaking at churches, at dedication ceremonies, and at ecumenical gatherings in the hopes of proving that "Judaism was also alive and viable in the community."[33]

Assailing anti-Semitism in Mississippi culture was another one of Nussbaum's dogged pursuits. Throughout his career he ardently condemned expressions of anti-Semitism and prejudice as un-American. As early as 1938 a young, outspoken Rabbi Nussbaum urged a community forum in Pueblo to oppose those "isms" that threatened American principles of freedom: Nazism, fascism, fanaticism, despotism, and anti-Semitism. While serving in Pittsfield he carried on a "one man campaign" to guarantee that the Jewish children enrolled in the prestigious Cushing Academy were entitled to be excused from classes on the High Holy Days. His concern about anti-Jewish sentiment is documented in a scrapbook of newspaper articles he collected over the course of his career. The majority of these clippings concern matters of religious liberty. In his own speeches Nussbaum inveighed regularly against the use of prayer in public schools, Christian proselytism, and anti-Jewish hatemongers.[34]

Being the Bible Belt's primary defender of the Jewish faith became a full-time undertaking for Nussbaum. His first major battle took place in October 1957. A local congressman, Thomas G. Abernathy, brought the name of a certain "leading communist" to the attention of the House of Representatives. Abernathy informed his colleagues that this man, a Jew named Israel Cohen, had published a circular outlining a Jewish conspiracy to take over the world and promote "the advancement of the American Negroes." In fact, Abernathy's disclosure was yet another rehashing of the well-established canard espoused in the anti-Semitic classic, *The Protocols of the Elders of Zion*.

Nussbaum was outraged. He wrote Abernathy a tactful letter in an attempt to educate him as to the anti-Semitic history of this forgery. Nussbaum urged him to eliminate mention of this false document from the annual bound issue of the Congressional Record. Abernathy declined. When Nussbaum wrote again and insisted that the congressman withdraw mention of the fabrication, Abernathy responded angrily. He told Nussbaum that the Jewish community was full of communists who intended to bring the South to its knees. At this juncture the rabbi's wealthy congregants—Abernathy's financial supporters—intervened and assured him that they would see to it that Abernathy was educated quietly.[35]

Jackson's new rabbi could not abide by the customary slights and indignities to which the local community had grown accustomed. The Jackson Country Club maintained an unofficial policy of excluding Jews from membership; Nussbaum waged a "one-man battle" against this practice in spite of the fact that his vocal opposition annoyed some members of his congregation.[36]

Sometime early in 1964 Nussbaum had a boisterous confrontation with author and emcee Clayton Rand over what Nussbaum considered to be the toastmaster's blatantly anti-Semitic after-dinner "humor." Speaking before the Jackson Rotaries, Rand, who specialized in so-called "good ole boy" humor, let loose a barrage of ethnic jokes that he hoped would please and delight the local crowd. Nussbaum and his wife were in the audience, and they found nothing funny about Rand's monologue. Nussbaum considered the emcee's jokes an insult and expressed his indignation in writing: "Mrs. Nussbaum and I were made sick, literally, by the time you were through, despite our own sense of humor.

Jackson Rotarians will tell you I am not lagging in this respect. . . . I must insist that your references to Jews—at least four times—are more natural to an audience of anti-Semites than to Jackson Rotarians."[37]

Nussbaum sent copies of his letter to all of the directors on the Rotary Board—local and national—and published it in the temple's bulletin as well. Before long the matter attracted a good deal of attention in the local media. Rand wrote Nussbaum on four separate occasions angrily accusing the rabbi of being a troublemaker. Rand maintained that the whole business was attributable to one simple fact: "the Jackson Rabbi did not have a sense of humor." Regardless, Nussbaum achieved his objective; rabbis in other southern cities subsequently wrote to assure him that the controversial toastmaster had stopped using the offensive material.[38]

Nussbaum's primary effort to strengthen Jewish life in the state expressed itself through his work with a union of Mississippi Jewish congregations. Within months after his arrival in Jackson, Nussbaum contacted all of the Jewish congregations in the state and invited them to band together for the purposes of intragroup communication and education. On Sunday, 15 May 1955, twenty-five delegates convened in Jackson and formed the Mississippi Assembly of Jewish Congregations. Nussbaum, its initiator and convener, was elected president. The assembly met annually to discuss issues of local concern and, intermittently, to hear lectures given by visiting colleagues. The group's most successful endeavor was its sponsorship of an annual statewide teacher training conference, which brought leading Jewish scholars from around the country into contact with the state's rabbis and laity.[39]

Nussbaum apparently hoped the assembly would go beyond its educational endeavors and play a helpful role in the area of interfaith dialogue. He quickly learned, however, that most of the member congregations wanted nothing to do with Nussbaum's ecumenical interests. When he invited a non-Jewish speaker to address the assembly in 1958, Rabbi Alexander Kline of Clarksdale objected: "Perry, we love you," Kline wrote his colleague in Jackson. "Just forget about interfaith. We need faith. We are with you in everything you do to deepen Jewishness . . . in Mississippi." The assembly lasted several years, succumbing ultimately to the consequences of inner rivalries.[40]

What was Nussbaum's position on the debate concerning desegregation in the South? Although he recognized the rectitude of the Supreme Court's ruling, initially he had no intention of taking a leadership role in the area of race relations. Writing to his colleague Julian B. Feibelman of New Orleans in 1955, Nussbaum outlined his position: "Ever since the era of Father Coughlin, I have consistently refused to take the leadership in race relations, on the ground that if the dominant group in the community doesn't publicly affirm leadership then the minority representative doesn't get very far—and such activity often as not boomerangs on your own people." So for his first few years in Jackson, Nussbaum's activities in the area of civil rights consisted of efforts to establish ties with moderate clergy and politicians who were likely to share his apprehension regarding the powerful influence of what he called the "extreme right." He hoped to make progress by using associational tactics that were, in his own words, "sub rosa." As long as the congregation was not associated with any of these endeavors "all was fine."[41]

He did not, however, neglect the issue when addressing his congregation. In his sermon for the Jewish New Year in 1955, Nussbaum did indeed preach on the incendiary issue. He told the congregation that he believed the High Holy Day liturgy could be likened to a personal advertisement column that reads: "I believe in God . . . [but] who will help me maintain my belief in my fellowman?" Musing over who, in contemporary society, might be inclined to ask such a question, Nussbaum offered his listeners several possibilities. Could the ad have been placed by the Jew who suffered from anti-Semitism? Or could it have been written by an alienated modern Jew who no longer believed in the teachings of tradition? Finally, Nussbaum wondered: "Was the Ad inserted by an American Negro?"

The rabbi told his congregation that a "thoughtful American whose skin is of a different hue than ours" was entitled to ask that question "out of sheer desperation." For where else was the Negro to turn today if not "to the religious conscience of American men and women?" Then Nussbaum drove his controversial lesson home by stressing the common bonds of understanding that linked Jews and blacks: "[The Negro] believes, as you and I have been taught, that God has made man in His image. There is nothing in his Bible to the contrary. He believes, as you and I have been taught, in the innate goodness of every man, whoever he is and whatever he is. He believes what you and I as Jews have hungered for ourselves during 1900 years of history—that every man has a natural right to share in God's gifts: the right to lift himself, and to give his children the best possible training; the right to economic security; the right to political equality."[42]

While he was prodding his congregation, Nussbaum tried simultaneously to give northerners a picture of the southern Jew's frightfully difficult political dilemma. In 1956 the UAHC magazine, *American Judaism,* published a symposium on the question "Do Temples Belong in

Politics?" As one of the contributors, Nussbaum acknowledged that neither rabbis nor congregations can divorce themselves from the great issues of the day. He warned readers, however, to be wary of pronouncements in the name of Judaism that have "deteriorated into bandwagon-climbing bombast, which, for all its golden-tongued oratory, is blind to some realities." With regard to Mississippi, Nussbaum maintained that all Jews—even his own congregation—must be advocates of freedom and equality for everyone. Nevertheless, "the headline hunters are still with us!" he declared. Paraphrasing the Psalmist, Nussbaum cautioned Jewish crusaders to " 'take heed to their words'—especially when these words reach outside the congregation": "[And,] may I add that some conscientious adherents of the Jewish faith in my own state who have to live with the profoundest political problem in the South since Reconstruction devoutly wish our coreligionists elsewhere might exercise a greater degree of circumspection."[43]

Later that same year Nussbaum participated in a CCAR forum that dealt with a similar theme: "The Southern Rabbi Faces the Problem of Desegregation." Nussbaum pleaded with his colleagues not to judge the southern Reform rabbis without first considering the difficulty of their plight. He and his other colleagues in the Deep South were striving to preserve, under terribly difficult circumstances, "the fundamentals of Judaism . . . not [only] the one area that apparently some . . . colleagues assume to be the paramount and salient one in the contemporary fight to preserve American Judaism." The southern rabbi's first concern, he told them, was to his own people. Having said this, Nussbaum assured his colleagues that he and many other southern rabbis were trying to make progress in the realm of civil rights, but "so much of what we do and say cannot be publicized." He closed his presentation with a biting question aimed at his northern colleagues who continually voiced their outrage at the "sins of Dixie": "There are some pulpits opening up this year in Mississippi. Anybody want to be a candidate?"[44]

During his first few years in Jackson, Nussbaum was even unwilling to criticize publicly those rural Jews who joined the segregationist Citizens' Councils. In his opinion "[these Jews] would have to make up [their] own mind[s] . . . because not belonging to the Citizens' Council [in certain rural areas] would mean complete social ostracism, all kinds of boycotts, financial handicaps, [etc.]."[45]

Many of his northern counterparts, however, had no patience for what they considered Nussbaum's rationalizations. Concerned about his reputation in the North, Nussbaum continually disavowed the suggestion that, once comfortably ensconced in Jackson, he had "gone the way of the Citizens' Councils." Such accusations were patently false, Nussbaum insisted. His critics could not even begin to fathom the depth of emotion these issues provoked in his adopted region. Did they understand that most members of his congregation wanted their temple to withdraw from the UAHC, the B'nai B'rith, and other national organizations? Did they know that a very significant percentage of Jackson's Jews were anti-Negro in every respect? Did they care that these were the very people who control the congregations in Mississippi and elsewhere? If the northern Jews truly understood these realities, they would not be so quick with their condemnations.[46]

Nussbaum was criticized for agreeing to speak on the campus of the University of Mississippi in 1955. The school's board of trustees screened all speakers brought to campus in order to censor antisegregation presentations. A clergyman, Alvin Kershaw, was not permitted to participate in Religious Emphasis Week because he had contributed to the NAACP. Religious leaders throughout the nation heaped scorn on the university and urged clergy to boycott the campus. Nussbaum decided to go to "Ole Miss," however, and use the occasion to preach on Amos. He urged his listeners to examine the principles of justice and righteousness in their own community.[47]

Some months later when Rabbi James Wax of Memphis threatened to bring Nussbaum before the CCAR Ethics Committee for offering to go to the school after Wax had refused to violate the boycott, Nussbaum emotionally defended his decision to speak. He insisted that he had not "surrendered an iota of more than twenty years of dedication to prophetic principles about social justice." His goal was to find a way to teach those principles in the sui generis environment of Mississippi. "There is no other state like Mississippi," he told Wax. He assured his colleague that he was "desperately trying to maintain Jewish principles about race relations without contributing to a potentially explosive situation that undoubtedly will make scapegoats of the Jews."[48]

Three incidents occurred between 1957 and 1961 that transformed Nussbaum's attitude about confronting social justice and civil rights issues. First, Nussbaum's level of discomfort with the daunting success of the Citizens' Councils throughout the South and, especially, in Mississippi, intensified in the wake of a report he received from S. Andhil Fineberg of the American Jewish Committee in New York. Fineberg distributed a questionnaire about Citizens' Councils to Jewish leaders throughout the South, and Nussbaum agreed to participate in the survey. Shortly thereafter, Fineberg shared the disturbing results of his research in a report distributed in October 1957. Fineberg's survey demonstrated that the Citizens' Councils were becoming more numerous, more powerful, and more dangerous than had been previously thought.[49]

Of particular concern was the ever-growing influence of the council chapter in Jackson led by the powerful newspaper editor William J. Simmons. By 1958 the Jackson chapter had built up a card file containing the racial views of nearly every white person in the city. One contemporary observer remarked that the Jackson council had "created a climate of fear that has strait-jacketed the white community in thought control enforced by financial sanctions." Nussbaum seemed to sense danger in the air for the Jewish community. He wrote to the regional director of the UAHC, Robert Schur, and urged him to convene a strategy-planning meeting of the rabbis in the Deep South. Nussbaum's colleagues told Schur the meeting was unnecessary.[50]

The Fineberg report contained an ominous warning that must have spoken to Nussbaum's conscience. It noted that the proliferation of these councils was due, in part, to the widespread tendency of many citizens to steer clear of the segregation controversy: "The tendency among those who fear they may be victimized is . . . to act as though the controversy over desegregation does not exist." Such an attitude, Fineberg warned, was especially perilous and a potentially costly one for southern Jews to embrace. In a powerful comparison between the Jew and the black, Fineberg remarked, "The situation resembles that which confronted the Jews of the United States when Nazi inspired anti-Semitism was highly troublesome. As was then the case, a program of public education on a large scale is necessary." It is likely that Fineberg's forceful allusion to the European Holocaust forced Nussbaum to reevaluate his "sub rosa" approach to dealing with the controversy.

The first opportunity to change his strategy arose when the local B'nai B'rith lodge invited a member of the Jackson Citizens' Council to address them during one of the group's meetings. Nussbaum castigated the lodge from his pulpit and in public. On the well-attended holiday of Yom Kippur, the rabbi urged his congregation to neither join the Citizens' Council nor attend its meetings. From the pulpit he reminded his people that despite the rationalizations of some Christian religious leaders the Hebrew Bible did not sanction racial discrimination.[51]

A second transforming development occurred on 12 October 1958: the bombing of The Temple in Atlanta. Early that same year Jewish institutions in Nashville, Miami, and Jacksonville were bombed. There were unsuccessful bombing attempts in Charlotte and Gastonia, North Carolina, and Birmingham, Alabama. Irwin Schulman, regional director of the Anti-Defamation League, issued warnings to rabbis throughout the South. He urged them to request closer supervision by local police and offered them practical advice on how to reduce the potential of a bomb attack. When news of the bombing in Atlanta broke, Nussbaum was, as he later recalled, "scared stiff."[52]

The next day Nussbaum expressed his alarm in a temple bulletin column titled "It Can Happen Here." He informed his congregation that if a large and prominent congregation in a city like Atlanta could be attacked, then certainly their own synagogue was at risk. Influenced by the contents of Fineberg's analysis, Nussbaum told his people they could not save themselves by burying their heads in the sand.[53]

Some of Nussbaum's northern colleagues read his bulletin with interest. They wrote to congratulate him for having the courage to speak out. The article's impact in Jackson, however, was far from favorable. Somehow, a copy ended up in the secular press. The city's leadership expressed indignation at the rabbi's innuendos. Was the rabbi trying to rabble-rouse? Did he not realize that his words were besmirching the city's reputation? How could Jackson's rabbi have so little faith in his own community?[54]

The article and resulting tumult provoked Nussbaum's first major congregational battle. At the next board meeting resolutions were proposed that would require the rabbi of Temple Beth Israel to obtain approval from the board *before* expressing himself in public. Nussbaum understood that the intent of these proposals was "to cut me down to size, and to let me know that I will not be reelected [as rabbi]." The rabbi's supporters tried to reassure him that they had the votes to defeat the resolutions. And they did. Still, Nussbaum anguished over the emotional rift the controversy caused. Even though he won the vote, he lamented privately: "Whatever the outcome I will still be the loser."[55]

The entire experience left Nussbaum dazed and discouraged. He knew that some congregants would not approve of his action, but the intensity of their opposition—the attempts to muzzle him by resolution—caught him off guard. He wrote to several colleagues as an emotional release and to solicit counsel. In a letter to Rabbi Jacob J. Weinstein of Chicago, Nussbaum bared his soul: "[All] I know is that for four years I have desperately tried to keep my mouth shut in public, while boring from within. . . . I thought that my own people were fully appreciative of the lengths to which I had gone to present the case of the Southern Jew in the forums of the 'North,' [though] I have repeatedly said to my congregation that with all our problems I will not let them resign from Judaism and the Jewish people. . . . But it all adds up to this. . . . Behave, or else!"[56] In the wake of this unnerving controversy Nussbaum tried to behave and "keep his mouth shut." Three years later, however, he found himself thrust onto the center stage of yet another civil rights drama.

The third watershed event took place during the summer of 1961. In December 1960 the *Boynton v. Commonwealth of Virginia* decision effectively desegregated all vehicle terminals regulated by the Interstate Commerce Commission. The Congress of Racial Equality decided to test the federal government's commitment to the Supreme Court's ruling by sponsoring "Freedom Rides." The first call for Freedom Riders went out in March 1961. Seven blacks and six whites volunteered to ride two buses into the terminals of several southern cities. Speeches and rallies were planned along the way, and the final stop was to be held in New Orleans on the anniversary of the *Brown v. Board of Education* decision.[57]

Predictably, the "Freedom Riders" encountered bitter and, in some instances, violent opposition throughout the South; consequently, some civil rights leaders were prepared to halt the rides temporarily. Student leaders of the Congress of Racial Equality, however, refused to back down, and they called on college students to give up their summer vacation to participate in the rides. They promised to "fill Mississippi's jails" with Freedom Riders. Though they may not have achieved this goal, literally hundreds of activists—many of them collegians—rode integrated buses to Jackson. On arrival, they were arrested, tried, convicted, and unless they posted bond, sent to prison.[58]

Nussbaum left Jackson in mid-June 1961 to attend the CCAR convention in New York City and vacationed with friends back east. Nussbaum later recalled that he did some "real soul searching" while he was away from Jackson. During the convention he heard three impassioned presentations at a "social justice" seminar that clearly moved him. He read newspaper editorials on the Freedom Riders who had already begun to descend on the South. He knew that many of these crusaders were young Jews. "I returned to Jackson with the die cast," he recollected, "I would not turn my back on Jews." When Nussbaum returned to Jackson on 22 July, a stack of letters awaited him from rabbinic colleagues and worried parents asking him to visit their congregants/children— Freedom Riders incarcerated in the Mississippi State Penitentiary in Parchman. Nussbaum responded immediately.[59]

Due to the highly charged political atmosphere, Nussbaum needed to obtain special permission to visit the Jewish prisoners confined in both the Jackson city and county jails. Authorities were hesitant to acquiesce. "Perry," the county sheriff moaned, "how can you want to have anything to do with those nuts?" Nussbaum refused to back down. He insisted on his right as a clergyman to visit his coreligionists and provide them with "spiritual guidance . . . regardless of the nature of the 'crime.' " "I am worried about you," the sheriff rejoined.[60]

On Thursday 27 July Nussbaum drove 125 miles to visit another group of Freedom Riders incarcerated at the state penitentiary in Parchman. Surprisingly he found the Hinds County sheriff, who had jurisdiction over Parchman, much more amenable to these pastoral visits. Taking advantage of the apparent goodwill, Nussbaum notified the official that he or some other rabbi would be visiting the Jewish prisoners weekly. The next day he sent a confidential circular to all of his colleagues in the vicinity informing them of developments and urging them to attend a meeting in his home to discuss "the Chaplaincy phase for the Freedom Riders' incarceration."[61]

Ironically, the most ardent resistance to this effort did not come from Nussbaum's laity but his own colleagues. Evidently, Nussbaum and his lay leaders arrived "uneasily" at an agreement that enabled him to proceed with his visits to prison. Most people assumed that rabbis were obligated professionally to visit Jewish prisoners no matter what their crime. Nussbaum informed his congregation of his activities and promised "to work out this program on my own, without identification with the congregation." Secrecy was of paramount importance. Had his activities attracted public attention, Nussbaum later observed, "this would have been the last straw for my own people." Perhaps this explains why, in the midst of the Freedom Riders affair, Nussbaum met with Congress of Racial Equality attorney William M. Kunstler in an effort to dissuade Jewish clergymen from participating in future Freedom Rides.[62]

Although a few colleagues responded positively to his circular, others bluntly informed Nussbaum they wanted absolutely nothing to do with the imprisoned Freedom Riders. Moses M. Landau of Cleveland accused Nussbaum of injecting himself into a matter that did not concern him. He saw no reason to visit the prisoners because, he incorrectly contended, neither they nor the prison authorities asked for visitations. As if he were oblivious to the point of the Freedom Rides, Landau reminded Nussbaum that these prisoners did not need to remain in prison and that they could be set free if their families sent them money for bail.[63]

Allen Schwartzman of Greenville echoed Landau's contention that these prisoners could gain immediate release if they paid their bail. He also believed it would be unwise for the state's rabbis to set up a chaplaincy rotation unless either the prisoners or the prison authorities made an official request. Schwartzman was concerned that by visiting these individuals, rabbis would jeopardize the security of the local Jewish community and "the good work that we are doing in the racial problems of Mississippi by 'going to bat' for these temporary inmates."[64]

These reactions made Nussbaum "heartsick." He wrote Landau and Schwartzman immediately and pointed out that (a) as a rabbi, he did indeed have an obligation to become involved in the matter, and (b) all Jews in institutional situations are entitled to spiritual guidance, whoever they are. He added, in unmistakable exasperation, that he assumed that of all people rabbis would recognize the appropriateness of this task. Nussbaum insisted these were special circumstances that called for special effort. He sensed he was doing something important, even historical: "There is a story to be told," he told Landau and Schwartzman, "but I am not looking for publicity."[65]

Until the High Holy Days Nussbaum assumed personal responsibility for visiting the Freedom Riders. For many of these young and inexperienced prisoners, he was their only contact with the outside world. They were not permitted to have exercise or fresh air. While at Parchman he offered personal counseling to all those who requested it, Jew and non-Jew alike. He brought them toiletries and cigarettes. He also conducted brief worship services. On several occasions, when Nussbaum told the female guards that he would lead a Jewish service in the prison's chapel, they ushered in all those females who volunteered to attend: Jew, non-Jew, white, and black. Years later Nussbaum asserted with pride that the prayer services he led at Parchman may have been the first racially integrated worship to take place in the history of Mississippi.[66]

Most important, he served as a "conveyor belt" to the outside world—carrying mail and personal messages in and out of prison. As a time-saving device Nussbaum drafted a form letter he used to communicate promptly with parents. Besides a few confidential communications with his Mississippi colleagues, Nussbaum made every effort to keep his activities a secret in Jackson. The administrative costs (viz., gasoline, postage, long-distance telephone calls, and so on) and secretarial duties were his responsibility; he could not call on the temple for support of a project such as this. During the course of a few weeks Nussbaum mailed more than sixty-five form letters. Besides his weekly drive to Parchman (nearly two hours each way) and his visits to the Jackson prisons, Nussbaum set aside another half-day each week to handle the voluminous correspondence with worried parents and interested colleagues.[67]

Nussbaum hardly anticipated the avalanche of praise that fell on him because of his efforts to help the imprisoned Freedom Riders. Literally hundreds of letters poured in from across the nation—kudos from all kinds of people. A temple administrator from Chicago wrote, "I know under what pressures and circumstances you must be working, and you have my genuine admiration." A non-Jewish professor from San Francisco State College told the rabbi that in the 1880s his maternal grandfather, a prominent citizen of Odessa, used to protect Jews from marauding Cossacks by hiding them in his home. The grateful father of an incarcerated Freedom Rider added, "Of course, he never thought that in the life of his great grandson you [a Jew] would play such an important role [in our family]. Human existence is so strange!" The young wife of a jailed minister asked the rabbi to pray for her husband from whom she had not heard in a month. "May God bless you & your great work," she wrote Nussbaum.

The father of a young Jewish coed assured Nussbaum that he had been in touch with many people throughout the course of the Freedom Riders' ordeal, and all "speak of you in glowing terms." On her release the young woman wrote Nussbaum herself: "Your visits really brightened our Thursdays; I have a great deal of respect for you." Rabbis from all over the country complimented Nussbaum on his chaplaincy effort. His neighbor, Sidney Goldstein of Meridian, effused: "Blessings on you! You make me feel very proud that the rabbinate comes up with people like you!" One of the most moving letters came from the father of a jailed rabbinical student: "[I] admire men who practice what they preach; that they do so under difficulty makes it even more impressive. . . . I admire your courage more than I do that of my son and his friends who face only the loss of 39 days while you face the social pressures of your community and your service to it. . . . Believe me, Rabbi, there are many Jewish hearts who are proud of these young men and women, and would be even more so of *you*, if I were free to tell them. . . . That you are willing to drive those long miles every Thursday is to me the living reality of what our prophets preached and you are practicing."[68]

By mid-September most of the Freedom Riders had either posted bail or completed their sentences. Nussbaum's home became a meeting place for them on their release and when they appeared in Jackson months later for their court appeals. At one of these gatherings a group of Freedom Riders presented him with a *Mogen David* (Star of David) fashioned out of cement from a cell wall at the Parchman penitentiary. Nussbaum proudly displayed that memento in his study.[69]

Life in Jackson calmed, and Nussbaum resumed his regular routine. Yet his furtive efforts on behalf of the young, idealistic Freedom Riders during the summer of 1961 left their imprint on Nussbaum's conscience. Despite the hazards, the experience proved to be spiritually fulfilling. The long drives to Parchman, the counseling sessions, the letter-writing to parents and colleagues, the many affirmations that he was doing something heroic, even prophetic—all of these factors convinced him that he had done justly. After the Freedom Riders' summer, Nussbaum changed. He worried less about trying "to keep his mouth shut in public" and more about "boring from within."[70]

Outside activists continued their incursions into the segregated South. The Council of Federated Organizations, a newly established umbrella organization, managed to harness the energies of numerous civil rights groups throughout the nation to insure that "freedom riders" from the North would return to Mississippi in the summers of 1962, 1963, and 1964. National civil rights leaders were deeply concerned that local activists would "disappear" into the swamps of Mississippi unless volunteers from the North were present to lend constant support and encouragement. Desegregation of public accommodations, however, was no longer the primary mission. Instead northern volunteers pursued an intensive voter registration campaign. Their strategy was straightforward: the power of the ballot would, ultimately, break open Mississippi's closed society.[71]

The three young volunteers who were martyred in the summer of 1964—Michael Schwerner, James Chaney, and Andrew Goodman— were part of a massive volunteer effort called the Mississippi Summer Project. By targeting Mississippi, the most openly segregationist state in the South, the organizers of the Summer Project hoped to expose the cruelty of day-to-day life to both the nation and the federal government. Most white Mississippians resented the summer intruders intensely and castigated the volunteers as a group of "beatniks and wild-eyed left wing nuts." Newspaper headlines and editorials repeatedly warned the interlopers that "Mississippians Will Not Be Run Over." An "invasion frenzy" swept across the state during these years. Amidst this atmosphere, local Mississippians who dared to defend let alone justify the goals of the civil rights workers found themselves facing more opposition and peril than ever before.[72]

During these tumultuous years Nussbaum emerged as one of several religious leaders in Jackson who spoke on behalf of tolerance, fellowship, and compassion. He collaborated with a handful of Protestant clergy who, for the first time, openly challenged Mississippi's racial *modus vivendi*. Roy Clark, pastor of the Capitol Heights Methodist Church, Moody McDill, pastor of the Fondren Presbyterian Church, Ed Harrison, rector of St. Andrew's Episcopal Church, Don Thompson, minister of the Unitarian Fellowship, and James Wrotens—one of Nussbaum's closest personal friends and a Methodist preacher who headed the Department of Religion at Millsaps College—were among the first of Jackson's clergy to openly condemn segregation. McDill organized the first interfaith (though not initially interracial) worship service in the city.

Thompson, who survived an attempt on his life, was the first white minister to be physically attacked by extremists. Heartened by these comrades, Nussbaum began to participate in their initiatives. He quickly became "a compulsive speaker" on the heretofore contaminated theme: "brotherhood."[73]

In January 1963 twenty-eight young Methodist ministers in Mississippi issued a "Born of Conviction" statement that appeared in the pages of the *Mississippi Methodist Advocate*. In their proclamation the clergymen affirmed their belief in freedom of the pulpit, the brotherhood of humankind, and the opposition to the proposed closing of public schools in response to the federal government's integration requirements. Then, on 12 June 1963, Medgar Evers, field secretary for the NAACP and the best-known black leader in Mississippi, was assassinated. The brutal killing of this young black father stirred the conscience of dozens of Christian clergymen. Evers's murder convinced them that the time to fight the extremists had arrived. The most prominent figure in this circle of religious penitents was the Reverend William B. Selah, the distinguished pastor of Galloway Memorial Methodist Church, the oldest Methodist church in Jackson.[74]

The fate that befell these new advocates of brotherhood and equality served as a sobering lesson for any prospective crusader who may have considered joining them. Literally all of Nussbaum's circle of support—including most of the twenty-eight Methodist ministers—were soon compelled to leave the state. Their prophetic message had been flatly rejected. Most unnerving of all, the eminent Dr. Selah, pastor of his church for eighteen years (and only a few years away from retirement), was pressured to resign when his congregation refused to support him in his call to permit blacks to attend services in their church. Even sixty-eight-year-old Rabbi Charles Mantinband of Hattiesburg, Mississippi, an early opponent of segregation and one of Nussbaum's few rabbinic colleagues, was pressured to leave his pulpit after eleven years and relocate to Longview, Texas. One of the very few in the circle to remain in the city, Nussbaum was dazed by the apparently insurmountable strength of segregation's advocates.[75]

Writing about the defeat of these liberal clergymen in the pages of the *CCAR Journal*, Nussbaum expressed his frustrations and anxieties, openly describing himself as the only survivor of this group. He reminded his rabbinical colleagues of the dangers an outspoken rabbi faced in the South: "There is no fooling around with white supremacist members who are 'out to get' the pastor," Nussbaum wrote. "So this survivor is running scared." Repeating his long-held conviction that northerners had no idea whatsoever how desperately complex and difficult a situation he faced in Jackson, Nussbaum asked his readers a series of rhetorical questions: "[What] is your considered counsel now for that sole survivor? . . . What will happen when the vicious among the extremists begin the refrain, 'what kind of rabbi have you got?' . . . Tell me, colleagues, how did Isaac feel when that knife was poised above his head? . . . A solution to this problem of this last survivor, who has it?"[76]

Despite these discouraging developments Nussbaum did not retreat from his new leadership role. He found himself "unable to stay away from the increasing challenges to me as a religious teacher in the area of race relations." In 1964 he became a founding member of the inter-faith "Committee of Concern," a group that raised funds to rebuild dozens of small black churches that had been destroyed by bombs throughout Mississippi. Not only did he not conceal his role in this project, he actually wrote to the UAHC in New York to solicit contributions from its member congregations. Likewise, the local Anglo-Jewish press, *The Southern Israelite,* ran an article describing Nussbaum's efforts. Despite some local opposition to the committee's work, more than $200,000 was raised. A few years later Nussbaum helped to organize the Greater Jackson Clergy Alliance and the Mississippi Religious Leadership Conference, both of which provided ecumenical venues for white and black religious leaders to meet and discuss views on a wide range of contemporary concerns.[77]

It is interesting that Nussbaum repeatedly praised his congregation for not using the same "sordid expediencies" that ended the careers of his Christian colleagues. Perhaps he hoped that by reminding his people that they were open-minded and long-suffering the power of suggestion would inspire them to live up to his expectations. He persistently reminded his congregation that their rabbi must remain true to his convictions even though they appeared controversial to some. He also thanked his community for understanding his moral imperative to preach Judaism's fundamental principles—"God's fatherhood and Human brotherhood, whatever man's skin color, politics and economic status." Remember, he told them, "I am only human. . . . For the feathers that inevitably were ruffled, I ask forgiveness."[78]

By 1966 Nussbaum had begun to sponsor annual "Clergy Institutes," day-long series of lectures given by a scholarly rabbi or professor. For the first time, local black ministers were invited to attend these institutes that were held at Beth Israel. When Temple Beth Israel dedicated its new building in March 1967, neighboring ministers (the site of the new building was adjacent to two Protestant churches) and other church leaders took part in the ceremonies. Despite opposition from some temple members, Nussbaum invited black leaders to the dedication. At Nussbaum's insistence the temple became one of the few religious buildings in the white community to house interracial gatherings. These initiatives were radical in segregation-bent Jackson, and many members of the Jewish community worried about the consequences. For them, the terrifying events of 1967 vindicated their insistence that the rabbi had taken them too far too fast.[79]

Tensions in the Jewish community came to a head with the bomb attacks on Temple Beth Israel and the Nussbaum home. Although much has been written about the bombings themselves, the repercussions of the attacks have not been fully explored. Officially, the congregation continued to express support for Nussbaum in the aftermath of these attacks, but some members of the congregation were fed up with the controversial rabbi. "If only the rabbi had kept quiet. . . . If only he hadn't gone to all those meetings," they would say. "The rabbi is untactful, divisive, and getting old." They approached Nussbaum privately and urged him to leave town for his own sake and for his wife's sake. "There are so many better pulpits [for you]," they advised him. After the temple was bombed, the board of trustees voted not to allow non-Jewish groups (by this, they meant the rabbi's interracial gatherings) to use the temple unless the meeting had prior approval from the board itself. Nussbaum bitterly resented the board's decision. He interpreted the policy as a vote of no-confidence in his moral leadership.[80]

Hearing that he was to blame for the communal catastrophes was more than Nussbaum could bear. Contemporaries observed that "the bombings seemed to crack open [in the rabbi] a reservoir of bitter feelings" about the congregation and the community. He scolded those who blamed the victim. "My so-called civil rights activities are to blame for the bombings!" He declared indignantly, "People who make such statements are the same people who believe that the 'solution to the Jewish problem' is always the successes or failures of the Rabbi."[81]

Nussbaum saw the bombings as none other than the "fruits of viciousness which is standard operating procedure down here." He told his congregation that the true source of this brutality was the malevolent cliques in southern society: "the KKK, the John Birchers, and a host of anti-everything that is not white, Protestant, native Mississippi." When, on the morning after the bombing, prominent members of the city's clergy and social gentry strode up his driveway to offer the rabbi their sympathies, he told them bluntly that they were the ones who, in large part, were responsible for these calamitous acts. From the ranks of respectable citizens such as themselves, he told them, the Klan

Bishops of Mississippi attaching their gifts of Mezuzot to new synagogue of Beth Israel
Congregation, Jackson, Mississippi, March 1967; *(l-r)* Episcopal John M. Allin, Roman
Catholic Joseph B. Brunione, and Rabbi Nussbaum (courtesy of American Jewish Archives,
Cincinnatti, Ohio).

and the Citizens' Councils received encouragement and finances during
the years of terror.[82]

As far as Nussbaum was concerned, white Christians who refused to
take their religious teachings seriously were especially culpable. A leading Southern Baptist minister who had come to Nussbaum's home to
express his sympathy concerning the bombing was told to spare his regrets. "If you really want to show your sympathies," Nussbaum lectured
the minister, "then tear up whatever you're preparing for your sermon

next Sunday morning and speak to the people in the front pews about their culpability in everything that's happened not just to me . . . but to the blacks and their churches over the years."[83]

A few days after the bombing Nussbaum resigned from the Rotary Club where he and the other community leaders had met for nearly fourteen years. Nussbaum's opponents interpreted the rabbi's resignation from Rotary as an act intended to add insult to injury. Despite appeals from the community the rabbi refused to reconsider his decision. Nussbaum expressed regret concerning these displays of pique years later. Justified or not, his hotheaded conduct in the aftermath of the bombings diminished his standing among Jackson's social elite. He never reestablished his "hard won community status" as a result of his behavior in the wake of the bombings.[84]

Nussbaum decided to leave Jackson. Although he was nearing retirement, he could not conceive of remaining in its environment. He believed he had performed "over and above the call of duty as a rabbi," and he wanted to get out. When, in the wake of the bombings, UAHC president Maurice Eisendrath asked if there was anything he could do for Nussbaum, the rabbi asked him to "find something, preferably non-pulpit, for a man and his wife who still have the best years of their life (hopefully), who jump every time they hear a creak." He wrote several colleagues in hopes of becoming their assistant. There were no takers for a sixty-year-old rabbi. A few years prior to the bombings, the congregation had granted Nussbaum a contract to age sixty-five. With no other viable options Nussbaum ended up staying in Jackson until he and his wife retired to San Diego in 1973, where they remained until his death.[85]

Eulogizing Nussbaum before the CCAR, his successor in Jackson characterized the former rabbi as an unpopular hero. His unflagging frustrations came from the fact that he had involuntarily become an advocate for *two* unpopular causes. First, Nussbaum consistently championed social justice to the Jews of Jackson, Mississippi. Nussbaum defended southern Jewry and tried to interpret the complex nature of Jewish life in the Deep South to Jews in the North who responded with little sympathy or patience. Second, his social rights activism intensified steadily during a painful and angry era of anti-integration sentiment in the region. Thus the rabbi found himself battling opponents on multiple fronts. He wrestled with his people who were fundamentally content with the sociopolitical status quo in Mississippi, with segregationists, and "with all the experts on Judaism and the Jewish Problem [outside the South] with special reference to Social Justice." Aligning himself as he did with unpopular positions, Nussbaum was destined to lead an isolated rabbinate.[86]

As early as 1963—long before the climactic bombings—Nussbaum sensed his fate. Because of time, place, and conscience, he was convinced that his was to be the lonely path of principle. He hoped, however, that one day the historical record would evaluate him more favorably than did his peers: "[History] will testify and some of his contemporaries on the inside of things, he hopes—as the [Hebrew Union] College Archives will reveal after he has gone to the yeshivah shel maleh [the academy in heaven] . . . that at no time did he fail to rise to the challenges of these years, within and without the congregation. . . . He hardly ever was tactful about the lessons of the 'six millions' and the evils of procrastination."[87]

Perry Nussbaum was a reluctant prophet—a man "who didn't want to be a hero." Reluctant or not, the prophet in any age is rarely a popular human being. That was, as the rabbi undoubtedly knew, the price of being Amos.

III

MEMOIRS

Historians must evaluate personal accounts with care. Often individuals record events and thoughts placing themselves in the best possible light. Then, too, memories do not necessarily serve well when looking back three and four decades. Such memories, like historical interpretations, can be clouded by intervening events. Nevertheless, reminiscences can provide information and insights that may otherwise be unavailable. As the years pass it becomes more important to record the memories of those directly involved in events so that their insights are not lost to future generations. This section includes the memories of two rabbis of the era and the spouse of a third. Each examines emotions and events not recorded elsewhere.

Jacob M. Rothschild:
His Legacy Twenty Years After[1]

JANICE ROTHSCHILD BLUMBERG

Rabbi Rothschild was one of the best-known southern supporters of black rights. Like other civil rights activists, he was subjected to threats, and his congregation was bombed even though it was located in one of the more cosmopolitan and moderate cities of the region. Janice Rothschild Blumberg's essay demonstrates that Rabbi Rothschild, too, preferred to work behind the scenes and through the Christian clergy and clerical organizations whenever possible. Confrontation, as Rabbi Danziger observed, symbolized failure. Rothschild's story also illustrates limits to coalition building. When conflict about methods arose, even long-term associations could be severed, leaving a well-intentioned individual in distress.

When Jacob M. "Jack" Rothschild (1911–1973) chose the rabbinate as his lifework he did not think specifically of race relations as a central part of that activity. Growing up in the Reform congregation Rodeph Sholom in Pittsburgh, he had been influenced by the forthright sermons of his own rabbi, Dr. Samuel Goldenson, against exploitation of labor in the steel industry and by the extraordinary courage of his father's sister and her husband, Rabbi Samuel Mayerburg, in actively opposing the Pendergast machine in Kansas City.[2]

He was attracted by the teachings of the Prophets and viewed the mission of a twentieth-century American rabbi primarily as an obligation to lead others in applying those precepts to the issues encountered in daily life. Nevertheless, he often commented that had it not been for civil rights, he didn't know what he would have accomplished in his career. "I was lucky enough to be in the right place at the right time," he observed.[3]

Perhaps luck did play some part in it. As the first Jewish chaplain exposed to combat in World War II, he survived Guadalcanal and later an extended bout with malaria. Returning to civilian life in April 1946, he had the good fortune to be offered, and the good judgment to accept, the position of rabbi of Atlanta's Hebrew Benevolent Congregation. Whether this was indeed good fortune or good judgment, however, was open to question at the time and for some years thereafter.

The Atlanta of 1946 was a completely segregated city of about five hundred thousand, an estimated twelve thousand of whom were Jewish. The Temple, as the city's one Reform congregation was popularly known, consisted of some four hundred families and a rabbi emeritus who had ruled with an iron will for fifty-two years, exemplifying the worst as well as the best elements of Classical Reform. He had a long-standing reputation for harsh treatment of his younger colleagues and strong antipathy to the idea of retirement. His behavior toward his successor bore this out.[4]

Culture shock added further difficulty to Rothschild's adjustment in his new job. The degree and impact of legally imposed racial segregation appalled the thirty-five-year-old rabbi, and some of the customs of southern Jewry, especially as practiced by the old-line families of his own congregation, surprised and dismayed him. The fact that he soon met and married a daughter of one of those families only exacerbated the problem, for the birth of their two children in rapid succession added financial and familial pressures to the already existing ones implicit in his position.

One major point in which the Jewish population of Atlanta differed from that of other cities with which Rabbi Rothschild was familiar was the degree of separation between its Orthodox and Reform communities.[5] Few members of The Temple made any effort to retain their predecessors' leadership in community affairs, and even fewer engaged in social relationships with those of other congregations. Likewise there was little rapport between the rabidly anti-Zionist martinet at The Temple and other local rabbis.

Rothschild entered into community affairs immediately, exhibiting an openness to Zionism as well as to other factors in Jewish life. Soon recognized for his organizational abilities, he rose quickly to community leadership, becoming president of the local B'nai B'rith and co-chairman (with then Orthodox Rabbi Harry H. Epstein) of the United Jewish Appeal in 1950 and president of the Atlanta Jewish Federation in 1954.

Although Rothschild eschewed his predecessor's emphasis on being an "ambassador to the Gentiles," he by no means ignored that aspect of his job. He lost no time in affiliating actively with such organizations as the Atlanta Council of Human Relations, Georgia Council of Human Relations, Southern Regional Council, Urban League, and the National Conference of Christians and Jews, for which he had been a regular "Brotherhood Month" speaker in Pittsburgh during his tenure there as assistant to Rabbi Solomon B. Freehof prior to World War II. He established his own outreach program to non-Jewish Atlantans in the form of a day-long Institute for the Christian Clergy, hosted by The Temple each February—Brotherhood Month—featuring a recognized Jewish scholar giving an in-depth lecture on some aspect of Judaism. It was in these arenas that Jack Rothschild made his initial contacts with the men and women who would later be his colleagues in the struggle for civil rights.

In the beginning, however, his participation in the larger community was secondary to what he saw as the immediate needs of his congregation. His first objective was to bring it into the mainstream of Jewish life, often noting that whereas his predecessor's mission had been "to turn his Jews into Americans," his own was "to turn his Americans into Jews." His initial priorities were education, Temple-oriented youth activities, and reviving meaningful elements of ritual in home and synagogue.

So revolutionary did these measures seem to the majority of The Temple members that a reference to racial injustice in his 1947 Rosh Hashana sermon went apparently unnoticed.[6] Early causes célèbres arose because of such items as his name appearing with those of leading Christian clergymen protesting the fact that the state capitol was being held by two men each claiming to be governor, a McCarthy-era witch hunt against an employee of the Jewish social service agency who was seen at a party also attended by an acknowledged communist, and an acknowledged Zionist becoming president of the sisterhood.[7]

From the outset Rothschild had demanded and received freedom of the pulpit. Still, it is doubtful that he would have been able to speak out on civil rights as he did without carefully preparing his congregation to accept it. The trial and lynching of Leo Frank, one of their own, in 1915 had left longtime members of The Temple with a paralyzing fear of Gentile disapproval.[8] With an unusually perceptive worldview and a sharp sense of his listeners' tolerance for controversial views, Rabbi Rothschild gradually accustomed his congregation to hearing his opinion on the segregation issue by speaking of it at least once during each High Holy Day season and on two or three other occasions every year.[9] As a result of both this persistence and the rapid growth of the congregation to more than one thousand families, by the time the civil rights issue heated up with the 1954 Supreme Court decision on *Brown*, he had gained sufficient support to sustain his advocacy of compliance with it.

It is difficult if not impossible for anyone who did not experience those times to realize the absurdities resorted to by some of those who opposed equal rights. Rothschild listed two of the more incredible news items in his 1948 Yom Kippur sermon: (1) an armed white man went to the home of a black man who had dared to vote, killed him, and won acquittal on grounds of self-defense; (2) summoned to a meeting of college presidents in Georgia, three blacks were chased out of the town by Klansmen wielding a fiery cross because the blacks had sat at the same conference table with their white colleagues (the blacks had been housed and fed in private homes rather than in dormitories with the others).

In response to these items Rothschild told his congregation that by delaying the implementation of civil rights "we invite the outside interference that we fear." He appealed to his members' pride of heritage— both southern and Jewish—in his plea for "enlightened action." He told them, "We have a greater responsibility. . . . It becomes increasingly obvious that unless decent people take up the burden, the South faces a return to the most primitive kind of bigotry and race hatred."[10]

He approached the subject of oppression not only with discretion but with a large measure of compassion for the sufferers whose rights were being denied as well as for the oppressors themselves, whose attitudes had been deeply ingrained from birth and therefore could not be easily altered. In 1952, as churches and homes of black leaders throughout the South were being bombed, he grasped at a straw of optimism in a message to students at Morehouse College by suggesting that such atrocities might indicate that the hard-core haters were becoming desperate.[11]

On the Yom Kippur immediately following the Supreme Court decision he acknowledged that Jews in the South faced a delicate problem: "[A] way of life, a pattern of behavior is being threatened. I firmly believe that no one outside the South can fully appreciate the cataclysmic changes—emotionally and spiritually—that the implementation of the [*Brown*] decision will require. . . . Generations of indoctrination must be erased." He hastened to say, however, that the difficulty of the problem in no way absolved anyone from the duty to face it and added that, although it was not specifically a Jewish problem, it was an issue rooted in the moral law of all religions. He confronted those who glibly repeated the cliché "religion and politics don't mix" with a reminder that the Ten Commandments were examples of religious laws later enacted into political law.

In that same sermon he directed darts of sarcasm toward those who advocated closing the schools to avoid integration. "What man of intelligence," he asked, "burns down his house to rid himself of an unwanted guest? . . . [Such action is] all the more foolish when we don't even know if the visitor is welcome or not because we've never really had him in our house—as an equal, that is." He then reassured his listeners that the change would not come all at once or immediately but little by little, "a few parents . . . sitting down together to discuss protection for their children at a dangerous intersection, a handful of people talking over together free clothing for needy children or common problems of health and hygiene." Thus, a gradual rapport would be built "upon which the idea of common schools will no longer loom so menacing and foreboding."

Ever practical in his approach, he conceded that it would be foolish "to storm the deeply rooted ramparts of tradition in the vanguard of the attack, alone and without preparation" but suggested four steps that could be easily taken:

1) . . . Recognize the issue as a religious one and not leave it to the secular organizations of Jewish life to deal with alone.

2) . . . Form study groups to learn what Judaism has to say on the subject and to acquaint ourselves with the basic facts of black history.

3) Organize a Social Action Committee within the congregation in order to keep abreast of developments and have an authorized voice for public statement.

4) . . . As individuals, join the non-sectarian groups already established and dealing with the issue.[12]

Innocuous enough? Not in 1954 Atlanta. The Temple Board voted down his plea to establish a social action committee, though it did agree to leave him unhampered in his effort to accomplish the same purpose without officially organizing one.

Rothschild tried again in a sermon during the next High Holy Days, listing a few items from recent newspapers:

A White Citizens Council in Alabama advocated that all music written, played by, or in the idiom of blacks be banned.

A telephone company in Mississippi was ordered to segregate all party lines.

The attorney general of Georgia recommended that it be made a crime punishable by death to aid a federal officer in enforcing any law tending to break down segregation in the South.

The president emeritus of Georgia State College for Women, a deeply revered educator, was stripped of his title and threatened with loss of his pension because as chairman of the Georgia Interracial Committee he had publicly advocated "moderation and discussion" in regard to compliance with the Supreme Court decision.[13]

The Temple board, paralyzed with fear, again refused to sanction a committee on social action, although they did endorse a "Public Affairs" committee. When told that the rabbi intended to preach compliance with the Supreme Court decision, a good friend of the Rothschilds and sisterhood leader expressed the prevalent attitude: "What does he want to do to us? Start the Frank Case all over again?"[14]

Jack Rothschild's sense of humor was one quality that superseded all others as a not-so-secret weapon against bigotry and fear. This humor was particularly effective one morning in 1955. An elderly congregant, often a vituperative adversary, called to protest a projected sisterhood luncheon at which a distinguished black clergyman and educator, Dr. Benjamin E. Mays, was scheduled to speak on "The Moral and Legal Aspects of Desegregation."

"Don't you know that integrated eating is against the law in this state?" the caller railed.

"You must have been misinformed," the rabbi responded calmly. "The Sisterhood luncheon isn't going to be integrated."

His adversary, taken somewhat aback, asked if that meant that the speaker in question had "considerately" declined to join the ladies for lunch, planning to arrive only in time for the program.

"Not at all," Rothschild told him. "Both Dr. and Mrs. Mays will be our guests for lunch, but they will be seated at the center of the head table and all of 'us white folks' will be segregated around them."

The luncheon took place as scheduled without incident and with a capacity attendance.

It should be noted that this was probably not the first time that "integrated eating" took place at The Temple social hall but only the first time that the fact was widely publicized. Rothschild's day-long Institute for the Christian Clergy had never excluded African Americans. The exact year when they began attending is uncertain, which indicates the degree of ease with which this potential hurdle was passed. The same is true for the annual day-long sisterhood event for Christian women held in conjunction with the Clergy Institute. This was regularly attended by a capacity crowd of churchwomen, usually including Mrs. Martin Luther King, Sr.

Well aware of this extreme sensitivity on the part of many members of The Temple, Rothschild tempered his candor with discretion, never forgetting his guiding maxim—that once a leader gets too far ahead of his flock, the flock cannot follow. On at least one occasion he declined a specific request to speak on civil rights. It came—perhaps surprisingly—from the Lions Club of Cartersville, Georgia. He gave the following explanation: "While I agree that the subject . . . ought to be dealt with in civic groups, I am not at all sure that I as an outsider would do well to come in and speak on so controversial an issue. I would think that leadership in this cause, which is indeed a worthy one, ought to come from members of your own community.[15]

Although he could have been expected to speak more freely to audiences outside the South, he did not say anything from those platforms that he had not already said from the bima of his own sanctuary. When in 1955 he spoke at New York's Central Synagogue, he remarked that current attempts to muzzle dissent in the South reminded him of the situation in a totalitarian state. Northern editors found the statement sufficiently daring to sensationalize their reviews of it with bold-face captions.[16] Rothschild, responding to a reporter for a southern Jewish weekly who asked him if his board had ever tried to stop him from making such statements, said truthfully that they had not but conceded that they "might not be so happy about getting all this national publicity."[17]

In dealing with southern audiences outside of Atlanta the rabbi had to use an extra portion of discretion, yet he still persisted in speaking his mind. In 1956 he told a B'nai B'rith assembly in Jackson, Mississippi, that "[injustice,] inequity, inequality, the failure to achieve human rights anywhere challenge the basic principles of Judaism. . . . And we cannot evade or escape what it says. Even when we live in the South and are faced with a decision that has distressed and outraged large numbers of our fellow Southerners. . . . Unless we are willing to admit our status as second-class citizens—a fact which I, for one, deny—then we have the need, the right, and the responsibility to state what our religion says about the problem. . . . There is no uniquely Jewish point of view. But there is a religious point of view . . . and we look to similarly motivated men of all religions by whose side we can stand."[18]

His outspokenness disturbed many of his rabbinical colleagues throughout the South, some of whom made their feelings known to him directly. At a meeting of the southeast region of the Union of American Hebrew Congregations in 1956, delegates reacted with near hysteria to the keynote address, an uncompromising statement on civil rights by Rabbi Roland B. Gittelsohn of Boston. They expressed their fear of pogrom-like action on the part of segregationists with such phrases as "blood will run in the streets," "hooded monsters," and possible "evisceration." Rothschild, after delegates voted down a resolution that he considered innocuous, asked what sort of resolution they would endorse. He was told "none," whereupon the rabbi of a large congregation in Alabama added, "I wouldn't risk one hair on the head of one of my members for the life of every shvartzeh in this state."[19]

Saddened and dismayed by such attitudes, he nonetheless declined to condemn these rabbis and accepted with sympathy the position of those in small communities whose exposure to violence and pressure was much greater than his own. To one such colleague from another city in Georgia, an old friend who had written imploring him "to lead the red-hot boys to be a little more prudent and cautious," he replied with a reminder: "We Jews expect others to risk their lives for us just because it is right." He then asked, despite the special risk imposed by anti-Semitism, "[How] can we condemn the millions who stood by under Hitler or honor those few who chose to live by their ideals . . . when we refuse to make a similar choice now that the dilemma is our own? . . . When you—and many others in the South—seek to silence those who would speak out, then you really do more than just remove yourselves from the battle. You also seek to deny the right of those who want to act with courage to do so." Although he thought he had been circumspect, in any case he would not desist. He concluded: "[If] this is dangerous, then I shall have to live dangerously. Because, I firmly believe that this is my responsibility as a rabbi. And even if I weren't a rabbi, it would be my responsibility as a human being. . . . Don't think that I like endangering the security of our institutions—and even my family—God forbid. But I'm here, and life requires it—and so be it."[20]

Only a few months before, in response to the 1957 Little Rock High School debacle, eighty members of the Atlanta Christian Council issued a statement specifying six points on which their religion had spoken indisputably on civil rights: 1) freedom of speech, 2) obedience to the law, 3) preservation of public schools, 4) racial "amity" as exemplified in the golden rule, 5) maintenance of communication between the races, and 6) the guidance of prayer. Despite a carefully worded disclaimer assuring readers that the signatories spoke only for themselves and not for any church or other group, only eighty of the many hundreds of members dared to sign.[21]

Jack Rothschild had long advocated such a statement, helped to write it, and praised it both in his weekly sermon and in a follow-up article for the *Atlanta Journal and Constitution*. He did not sign the document, however, even though the ministers offered to tone down their Christian rhetoric because he knew that the statement must be couched in the most christological terms to appeal most effectively to the broadest possible Christian audience.

The statement came to be known as the Ministers' Manifesto. Mild as it was it served as the first tentative crack in the wall of silence that had surrounded Christian moderates in Atlanta. The Atlanta newspapers supported it by inviting various ministers to write their views on the subject. Jack Rothschild's article, later reprinted in *The Congressional Record*, received a boldface caption across the page, announcing, "Rabbi Rothschild Speaks. Moses, Prophets, Jesus Fought to Erase Inequality."[22]

Rothschild's nadir of discouragement with the course of events probably occurred in May 1958 after a wave of terrorism against Jewish institutions swept the South. He observed that there was no logical pattern to the choice of targets. Some were in cities where no Jewish leader had spoken out, yet in at least one city, Nashville, where a rabbi had been outspoken, a synagogue other than his own was bombed. He concluded with a truism paraphrased thirty years later on stage and screen by the chauffeur in *Driving Miss Daisy:* hate is hate, and violence is directed against all minorities when it becomes possible and fashionable to use it.

Earlier in the same sermon Rothschild had observed that most people chose to ignore the subject of race relations, presumably on the premise that if they talked about it they, too, would be bombed. Addressing the possibility of such violence occurring in his own city, he said he was encouraged to think that Atlanta's mayor and law enforcement officers would never be parties to creating an atmosphere conducive to such acts. "We must resolve not to surrender to violence," he told his congregation. "Or submit to intimidation."[23]

Five months later he and they were put to the test. On Sunday morning, 12 October 1958, forty sticks of dynamite ripped through the side of The Temple virtually destroying the religious school, offices, and assembly hall. Five known neo-Nazis were quickly indicted for the crime, one of them tried twice and acquitted (the first trial ending in a hung jury), the others released for lack of evidence. All five were kept under surveillance for a sufficient length of time to prevent further violence.[24]

Following the bombing, extremely stressful days were intensified by threats to the rabbi's home and family. Nevertheless, Jack Rothschild steered a steady course through stormy seas of press, police investigation, and details of everyday temple business, which included a campaign for funds to enlarge the religious school, a project scheduled to be launched at the very time the bombing occurred. He made certain that every temple event took place according to schedule at an alternate location as needed, the only exception being cancellation of religious school classes on the morning of the bombing itself. Not only were services held in the sanctuary on the following Sabbath, but the announcement appeared on the bulletin stand close to the street in time for motorists to read it on their way to work Monday morning. His sermon was titled "And None Shall Make Them Afraid."[25]

Throughout the ordeal the Rothschild sense of humor helped maintain balance. When awakened by a telephone call minutes after falling asleep at 3:00 the next morning, he detected that his wife, who had answered the phone, was having no success in getting rid of the caller. Taking the receiver, he learned that the caller was a reporter for a morning newspaper.

"What can I do for you?" asked the rabbi, whereupon the reporter asked, "Was that Mrs. Rothschild I was talking to?"

Rothschild replied, "If it wasn't, do you think I'd tell you?"

A day later a reporter informed Rothschild that a temple in Peoria, Illinois, had been bombed and asked if he had any message for the rabbi there. He said, "Welcome to the club"—and caught himself just in time to add "Don't print that!"

Among the thousands of letters he received from all parts of the world after the bombing, the most poignant ones were those written by African Americans. Without exception they were sympathetic, some containing contributions and some serving as bitter reminders of the much more numerous and devastating terrorist acts perpetrated against members of their own community, which received no notice at all from "white" America much less the sympathy and attention being showered on The Temple.[26]

Jack Rothschild's unflinching integrity was never more apparent than then, when he was approached with numerous opportunities for personal aggrandizement and material gain. In the months immediately following the bombing he refused the many invitations he received to lecture in other cities or write about the bombing for major publications. The affairs of his congregation were his primary responsibility, and he affirmed that priority by the choices he made.

The cause of justice gained three major advances as a result of the bombing and the instinctive response of two key political figures. First, Atlanta mayor William B. Hartsfield made an impromptu statement to the media, focusing attention on the atmosphere of hate and disdain for the law that had permeated the South. Hartsfield was among the first to arrive at the scene and told reporters, "Whether they like it or not, every political rabble-rouser is the godfather of these cross-burners and dynamiters who sneak about in the dark and give a bad name to the South."[27]

Hearing this along with news of the bombing as they headed for church on Sunday morning, an overwhelming number of Atlantans—indignant at the thought that anyone would desecrate a house of worship in their city—expressed horror and sympathy for the Jewish community. For members of The Temple this unprecedented show of support finally exorcised the lingering trauma engendered more than forty years before by the trial and lynching of Leo Frank.

Second, President Dwight D. Eisenhower happened to be in New York the morning of the bombing and, understanding the political advantage implied by having such a Jewish audience, reacted to news of the bombing with a statement to the effect that he was ordering the FBI to assist local law enforcement agencies in solving the crime and prosecuting those responsible.[28] This led to mandatory intervention of the FBI in subsequent cases throughout the South, which helped put an end to the bombings. Rothschild wrote to the president thanking him for his prompt, "forthright" response to the bombing and urging him to convene a White House conference on law and order. Ike's only response was a letter stating that the conference was being given "careful consideration."[29]

The third and most significant result of the bombing, as far as religious leaders were concerned, was that it blew open the wall of silence behind which many otherwise progressive people had taken refuge. Now guided by the statements of their mayor and their president, these previously muted moderates finally found the courage to speak. Three weeks after the bombing the eighty daring clergymen who had signed the blandly worded Ministers' Manifesto the year before were joined by 232 others—including all Atlanta rabbis—in issuing a much stronger and more detailed document. It called for organized, open discussion of the school situation (state legislators had voted to close them if ordered to integrate) and asked that the governor appoint a citizens' commission to hold hearings throughout the state to ascertain the true feelings of most citizens on the matter. Eventually this was done.[30]

At about this time a few ministers of both races organized a "nonorganization," referred to simply as "the dinner group." It had no officers, no program, no official agenda but met every other week to develop friendships and keep open the lines of communication. Occasionally the group invited members of the white business establishment to the meetings.

Among those who attended regularly were the presidents of Morehouse College, Spelman College, and Atlanta University, and the distinguished minister of Ebenezer Baptist Church, Dr. Martin Luther King, Sr. When his son, Dr. Martin Luther King, Jr., relocated to Atlanta in 1960, the great civil rights leader also joined the group, thus beginning a personal friendship with the rabbi.[31]

A major question for Jewish institutions in early 1960 was whether to permit the use of their buildings for substitute schools if the public schools were closed (as they had been under similar circumstances in other southern cities and were specifically destined to be—by government statute—in the state of Georgia). A guiding influence on the Community Relations Committee of the Atlanta Jewish Community Council, Jack Rothschild played a major role in formulating its statement of policy on the issue: 1) to deny occupancy to those who would use them to circumvent the Court order, 2) to offer occupancy in cases where "the only purpose is to meet the needs of children locked out of public schools," 3) to insure that classes held under the latter conditions would be private and nonsectarian and not be considered an adequate or permanent substitute for public schools, and 4) to make no public statement implying the availability of the buildings prior to the closing of the school. The Atlanta rabbis as a group prepared a separate statement that they designated Rothschild to read at the committee hearings being held statewide to explore the matter.[32]

The Rothschild sense of humor came into practical use during the winter of 1960 at the height of the public school controversy. Roy Harris, a powerful state politician, had openly suggested carrying out a campaign of annoyance against anyone who advocated keeping schools open in the face of court-ordered integration. As a result the Rothschild home was repeatedly bombarded with telephone calls in which the caller would hang up as soon as someone answered. These calls would often recur throughout the evening and frequently prevented sleep throughout the night. Not wishing to have his telephone number changed or unlisted, Rothschild devised a better plan. The next time he was awakened by such a call he immediately dialed Harris's home. When a sleepy male voice answered, the rabbi announced cheerily, "I just want to let you know, Roy, that your boys are on the job." That ended the late-night "Harrisment."

School integration was the crisis issue and therefore the aspect of civil rights that most urgently needed to be addressed, but Jack Rothschild constantly reminded his audiences of the broader issue of human justice. He told a national assembly of Jewish teenagers meeting in Atlanta in 1960 about Martin Luther King, Jr., and the direct action technique, likening it to the personal commitment demanded by their own

Jewish faith. He read them a statement in which students at the pre-dominantly black Atlanta University Center had listed the goals of their race in the movement to obtain human rights.[33] On Rosh Hashana that year he told his congregation about a new school building elsewhere in Georgia that remained empty despite dire need for such facilities be-cause it had been built "in the wrong place for children with the wrong color of skin." On Yom Kippur, the day set aside for atonement, he said that public education was only the immediate question. The much more fundamental one concerned human dignity and equal rights for all. He used the biblical parallel of Jonah—who fled in panic when God chal-lenged him—to accuse his congregation and whites in general of taking refuge behind whatever shelter they could in the hope of avoiding total surrender. "As we flee from the moral commitment," he said, "we pre-tend that our use of the law makes us law-abiding citizens, facing up to our great decision. But in our hearts we know that we use the law as a legal means of evading what is right."[34]

The effect that such statements had over the years is indicated by the volume of Jewish participation in Atlanta's signal event of the civil rights reform—the peaceful integration of its public schools. As the rabbi noted, "Almost without exception the Jews of Atlanta stood up for and out as champions of the liberal cause." Many had been leaders in HOPE (Help Our Public Schools), the coordinated effort for influenc-ing the public to support open school legislation, and in OASIS (Or-ganizations Assisting Schools in September), the coalition working to effect peaceful transition when it occurred. All of the city's synagogues belonged to OASIS, as did the Jewish Community Council with all its constituent organizations.[35]

OASIS designated subcommittees to give special attention to youth-serving agencies, to supply speakers and trained discussion leaders, and to work individually with civic, neighborhood, and church groups. A committee on religion prepared material for clerics of all denomina-tions and sponsored a citywide observance of "Law and Order Sabbath" immediately before the day set for school opening. OASIS organized almost one thousand citizens to sign "A Layman's Letter to His Child" that appeared in the Sunday papers the day before. Leading citizens taped spot announcements that saturated the air waves. A woman be-longing to The Temple headed the public relations committee, which successfully arranged for the "care and feeding" of the hordes of re-porters who came into Atlanta to cover the event. The committee also helped prevent the occurrence of any of the excesses known to have taken place recently at the University of Georgia when two black stu-dents entered that institution.

Personal efforts on the part of Atlanta Jews were typified by the actions of the rabbi's mother-in-law, Carolyn Oettinger, who lived across
the street from one of the high schools destined to receive African
American students. When the names of the three students were announced some weeks before opening day, she called their parents and
invited them to come with their children to her home one afternoon for
"cokes and cookies." Her reason, she said, was "to let them know they
had a friend nearby, in case they needed one."

In his sermon the following Rosh Hashana Jack Rothschild described
his feelings as he watched from her driveway the emotion-filled scene
of three teenagers being escorted by government authorities into the
school. After likening it to the Akeda story, the sacrifice of Isaac, he
said: "A lump rose up in my throat too big for me to swallow. . . . Why?
Because these, too, were Abraham's child. Because another human sacrifice had been broken down. Because they dramatized another victory of the human spirit. Because despite the color of their skin they
were just three more children of the living God. And I began to wonder
what all the preparation had been for, all the dedicated labor of so many
dedicated people, all the careful planning, all the logistics of a battle. It
was so simple, after all. Three children went to school. All they really
needed was for our hearts to go with them."[36]

The Rothschild "connection" with Martin Luther King, Jr., grew
into a personal, family friendship when the rabbi's mother-in-law
chanced to meet Dr. King and learned that his wife was a musician,
which she herself was also. She immediately arranged a dinner at her
home to introduce them to her children and several other people, black
and white.

Shortly thereafter the demonstration against segregated facilities at
Rich's Department Store took place, leading to King's first arrest and
incarceration in early November 1960. Rothschild, out of the country at
the time and returning after the crisis had passed, had no opportunity
to help resolve the situation. His family and many of his congregants,
however, vented their indignation by temporarily ending their long-
standing relationships with Rich's. A member of The Temple, attorney
Morris B. Abram, played a major role in the drama by initiating a series
of calls to then presidential nominee John F. Kennedy. These calls led
to the release of Dr. King and possibly also to Kennedy's successful
candidacy.[37]

The controversy at Rich's was still boiling when Rothschild returned
to Atlanta, and because the store's board chairman, Richard R. Rich,
was also a member of The Temple, there were those who urged the rabbi
to speak to him about settling the dispute. The rabbi explained why he

did not do so in a letter he wrote to the department store executive in March 1961, after the conflict was resolved. Rothschild congratulated Rich on having done the right thing, adding that he had not interfered because he knew that "there was no more decent and liberal member of our community than you and I couldn't see how my voice could do anything but add to the problems with which you were faced and the struggle to find a solution to them."[38] This followed the rabbi's customary procedure of speaking out only to the extent that he felt was efficacious, trusting those with a reputation for progressiveness and sincerity (such as Dick Rich) to exert the utmost effort in quietly effecting the necessary change.

A poignant reminder of the lingering prevalence of segregation occurred a few months later when the Rothschilds invited the Kings to a small dinner party at their home. Dr. King, apologizing for arriving late, explained that he was unfamiliar with the neighborhood and, because of poor street lighting, had had to ask at another house which one belonged to the rabbi. "But I was careful not to embarrass you with your neighbors," he quickly added. "I let Coretta go to the door so they would think we were just coming to serve a party."

As might have been expected, the conversation soon gravitated to the recent attacks on Dr. King and the dreaded possibility that a future one could be fatal. Modestly, the great civil rights leader joked about "having trouble keeping up with my reputation." Eventually his wife interjected seriously, "If it's worth doing, it's worth the price we may have to pay."

Jack Rothschild continued his relentless verbal attack on bigotry, moving on from integration of public facilities to the fundamental issue of human rights. At Passover he cited the great Negro spirituals based on the Exodus from Egypt to remind his congregation that the current struggle was "not merely a matter of sitting in classrooms or at lunch counters" but a manifestation of the basic human drive for freedom.[39]

At about the same time he told a predominantly black audience at Atlanta's Interdenominational Theological Center that the agony being witnessed among whites and blacks alike is man's recognition of his own inability to live up to the best of himself. He referred to the progress made in Atlanta as "superficial and grudging" and "for all the wrong reasons." The knowledge of this situation, he declared, "gnaws at our consciences and destroys the inner fibre of our being."[40]

With the opening of schools in 1962 attention focused on the attempt of James Meredith to enroll at the University of Mississippi. Rothschild, in a Rosh Hashana sermon, contrasted the reaction of those who upheld the recent Supreme Court decision outlawing prayer in the public schools with that of the fundamentalists who opposed it, reasoning that happiness would be attainable for everyone only when they realized that "one man's joy" need not be predicated on another's sorrow. He applied the thought to the racial struggle, telling the true story of a sheriff in a small Georgia town who stated with sincere naivete, "We never had no trouble here before. These nigras lived like we wanted them to for a hundred years—and everyone was happy." Rothschild commented that this was probably the most honest appraisal he had heard on the subject because the sheriff obviously never understood how miserably unhappy the blacks really were. The rabbi then added that "a sorry quirk of human nature" led people to rest their own nobility on the debasement of others. He concluded that we "must strive to understand that what drives us to seek the flowering of the human personality drives them as well. And what limits us, likewise limits them."[41]

Between the Holy Days, the Sabbath of Repentance coincided with the weekend on which the clergy of Oxford, Mississippi, had called for an observance repenting the bloody riot that took place when Meredith appeared on campus. In his sermon Rothschild stressed the religious aspect of the situation, asserting that prayers of repentance were useless without follow-up actions. "If the church is going to be a significant influence in our world," he declared, "it had better start working on the issues of its own day."[42] He continued to highlight the theme of social action—always basic to his belief—in his public statements throughout the following years. On one occasion he was quoted in the *Atlanta Constitution* as having said that churches and synagogues had been "woefully inadequate" in coping with the problems and that government officials should use their prestige to rally leadership in the quest. Two years later Georgia governor Carl Sanders asked him to suggest possible appointees to a committee established for that purpose.[43]

Speaking to many congregations in the North during 1962 and 1963, Rothschild reported that southern Jews, for the most part, were reacting well to the changes taking place in their region. He explained that for many it was an act of heroism "just not to join a White Citizens' Council." He praised the many southern Jews who had become active in the cause of human rights and assured his audiences that while the southern Jew may be "uncomfortable, uneasy, even fearful . . . he is essentially brave."[44]

In an undated manuscript published in the *Southern Israelite* in August 1963, Rothschild analyzed the prevailing attitude of southern Jews. Balancing their vulnerability against their underlying empathy with the plight of other minorities, he concluded, "The Southern Jew seems ready to admit that this is an area in which religion cannot keep silent.

. . . He now takes the stand that the struggle . . . doesn't really involve him as a Jew at all—it involves him only as an American!" Rothschild considered this a potentially dangerous position, threatening the establishment of a dichotomy between patriotism and Judaism in which the assumption would be "that there are two separate compartments of his [the southern Jew's] life—one Jewish and the other American. . . . That when his fellow-citizens look at him, they must distinguish between him as a Jew and him as an American. He would have them blame his Americanism if he does anything they don't like—and credit his Judaism when they are pleased. But what if they come to the opposite conclusion—as well they may?"[45]

Rothschild received a prepublication copy of Martin Luther King's memorable letter from the Birmingham jail, presumably from the author himself. He responded immediately, praising it as "the most moving and significant document I have yet read," adding, "I hope you plan to give it wide distribution. I, myself, have taken the liberty of making copies available to Ralph McGill and one or two of my own interested laymen." He read the letter to his congregation as part of a subsequent Friday evening sermon.[46]

In line with his personal policy against grandstanding, Rothschild did not participate in the Freedom March of 1963. The *New York Times* reported "favorable mention" of the march in sermons by several southern rabbis, quoting Rothschild's statement that one of the results of it must be "the recognition by religious organizations of their responsibility to carry out the intent of the law."[47] On Rosh Hashana he spoke of it again, remarking that many whites seemed to be threatened by the fact that blacks were finally demanding their full share of American citizenship, "as though what the Negro seeks would decrease the white man's share in America, as though his being for himself means that he is against you . . . [but] it is not necessary to destroy another in order to safeguard self."[48]

On the following Sunday he heard that Birmingham's Sixteenth Street Baptist Church had been bombed, killing four young girls in their Sunday school room. Rothschild immediately wrote to the pastor of the church, expressing his horror, sympathy, and outrage.[49] Once more the violence had occurred on the eve of the Jewish Sabbath of Repentance, giving Rothschild the opportunity to ask in his sermon, "What repentance is there for us in the murder of four children in a church?" Again he thundered that it was not enough to say we were sorry. "We must do something," he exclaimed. "Oratory is not enough."[50]

Temple members responded by contributing thirty-five hundred dollars in the first two weeks to help restore the church and by continuing to send donations for many weeks thereafter. The letters that accompanied these contributions, many of them from children, testified to the results of Rothschild's advocacy among his own congregants.[51]

Another interesting indication of the congregation's feelings came about as a result of the rabbi's teenage daughter having been seen "sitting in" with a racially mixed group of girls at a downtown lunch counter. One member of The Temple, on hearing of the incident, called the rabbi's wife to protest and subsequently resigned from the congregation. Rabbi Rothschild later delighted in recounting his board's reaction. When the resignation was announced and the routine motion to "accept with regret" was made, someone else proposed that in this case the phrase "with regret" be omitted. The substitute motion passed unanimously, and the member received a letter stating that the board regretted the member had failed "to learn the lesson of Judaism taught by our rabbi in word and deed" and agreed that, this being so, the family would be happier elsewhere.[52]

As the focus of civil rights activism moved on to the desegregation of restaurants and housing, Jack Rothschild served as vice president of the Atlanta Council of Human Relations. In this capacity he had to deal with complaints from citizens who feared their neighborhoods would be targeted for "blockbusting." Such fears were heightened by newspaper reports sensationalizing whatever news or pseudo-news could be extrapolated from proceedings of the council, however preliminary or tentative the conclusions might be.[53]

In early 1964 Atlanta mayor Ivan Allen asked the rabbi to address a meeting of the restauranteurs and hotel owners who still refused to change their "whites only" policy. Urging them to do so from a moral point of view, Rothschild opened his remarks with flattery, referring to them as "intelligent and successful businessmen." Then he admonished them: "You throw up your hands in horror at the prospect of either a Federal or local public accommodations law. We don't need it, you say. We'll do it ourselves. But you don't—and you have no intention of doing it. You're just buying time. How, then, can you avoid helping make the passage of just such a bill inevitable? You deplore direct action, picketing, selective buying and all the rest. You say: we will work it out at the conference table. So you confer and appoint committees—and nothing happens because you don't really intend for anything to happen. But you know that your dalliance will bring about the very direct action that you deplore. Then you'll capitulate. After your city has been torn apart by dissension." He concluded that he had long since despaired of convincing them on moral grounds of the need for change but that they should at least recognize the practical grounds for such need.[54]

That same year at a Rotary Club meeting he warned: "Time is running out for us. . . . The Negro is becoming more impatient and less willing to wait quietly and peacefully for the fulfillment of glib promises smoothly made but that we don't really mean to keep. . . . Moderate leaders are being goaded into action by younger, more impatient voices."[55]

He told an audience of mostly white church women that although he could appreciate the real gains made, especially in Atlanta, much of the success looked better than it really was. "Until we are ready to make a soul-centered commitment, our best efforts will result only in the kind of 'tokenism' that is so prevalent today. Thus far, we have erected a facade of equality that we know is a lie." He reminded his listeners that the direct-action technique had come into practice precisely in order to fight the perversion of statutes, such as the antitrespass law, that were being used to prevent blacks from exercising their civil rights.[56]

One downtown restaurant in particular, targeted for sit-ins by the Student Non-Violent Coordinating Committee, was subjected to excessively filthy trashing perpetrated under the umbrella of nonviolence. Rabbi Charles Mantinband of Mississippi, a courageous advocate of civil rights whom Rothschild deeply admired, asked the latter what he thought of the sit-ins and related matters. Rothschild replied that the sit-ins, planned to coincide with the visit to Atlanta of a United Nations subcommittee, were "bad enough" although "nothing to compare" with the demonstrations in Mississippi and Alabama. He stated further: "[I] have objected rather strenuously to the tactics that were employed and therefore am somewhat persona non grata with the movement. To begin with, I object to the objectives. S.N.C.C. set out to 'destroy the image of Atlanta' . . . by creating an impression that the Atlanta police were as brutal as the Birmingham police and there was no difference between them and any other southern law enforcement officers. I have long held no brief for the 'image of Atlanta' and have said repeatedly that the image is better than the fact. But I don't see the purpose of undoing what little has been done by deliberately exacerbating the situation."

He added that although the demonstrations tended to be disruptive and were sometimes "unnecessarily extreme," in general he believed they were valid because almost nothing had been accomplished without some sort of pressure. He thought the sponsors made a tactical error in permitting such disruptiveness, but, on the whole, he believed they had made "comparatively few mistakes in a very delicate situation."[57]

In November 1963 Jack Rothschild participated in the first of two memorable banquets at which he introduced his friend, Dr. Martin Luther King, Jr. The occasion was the biennial convention of the Union of American Hebrew Congregations, meeting in Chicago. Rumors had spread beforehand indicating that some of the southern delegations planned to walk out. Rothschild, referring to that aspect of the convention in an article written some years later, commented that the members of his own congregation "accepted it [his introduction of King] as an honor . . . and were almost annoyingly complacent" about his part in the proceedings.[58]

There were no walkouts from the huge, crowded ballroom where the banquet was held. The evening's only flaw was that too many speakers had been scheduled before Dr. King, and the one immediately preceding him held the platform for an excruciating forty-five minutes. By the time Jack Rothschild began his introduction it was 11:30 P.M. He condensed his prepared remarks to a fraction of their original length and quickly elicited laughter by claiming that King had spent so many nights in jail that people spoke of him as one celebrity who had given out more fingerprints than autographs.[59] King asked appreciatively for a copy of these remarks.

Slightly more than a year later Jack Rothschild again introduced his friend, this time at a banquet that attracted worldwide attention. It was the dinner given by the city of Atlanta to honor Dr. King after he received the Nobel Prize for Peace. A group of African American leaders had asked the rabbi, along with publisher Ralph McGill, Archbishop Paul Hallinan, and Dr. Benjamin Mays, to organize and chair such an event, the likes of which had never before been attempted in the southern city.

It was no small undertaking to organize an integrated public banquet in Atlanta in December 1964 (it actually took place on 27 January 1965). Delegates from the Southern Christian Leadership Conference, which Dr. King headed, wanted to use the occasion to raise funds for the organization. Rothschild opposed the idea on the grounds that the city's tribute to its first Nobelist should not be diluted by other considerations. His view prevailed.

Meanwhile, Mayor Ivan Allen presented the idea to Atlanta's "power structure," the informal group of business leaders without whose endorsement no event had ever successfully taken place in the city. They refused to endorse it. Allen, however, on reporting this to the committee, offered to back the event to the extent he could if the committee decided to proceed with the dinner despite the negative response of the "Establishment."

The group proceeded but not without further road blocks. Ralph McGill, normally a tower of strength, was restrained from active participation because of a lawsuit pending against his newspaper, the *Atlanta Constitution*. Archbishop Hallinan became very ill and could offer little more than moral support (a tremendous asset, however, because it ensured the support of the Catholic community). FBI chief J. Edgar Hoover, determined to discredit King, sent agents to the archbishop in the hospital in a desperate but vain attempt to persuade him—on the basis of alleged marital infidelities committed by the civil rights leader—to withdraw his support of the dinner. That left all decisions, arrangements, and public relations problems to Dr. Mays and the rabbi. Fortunately they had excellent assistance from Don McEvoy, regional director of the National Conference of Christians and Jews, and Helen Bullard, the public relations executive who had directed Ivan Allen's mayoral campaign.

One crucial point of assistance was effected by Ralph McGill. McGill appealed to his friend Robert W. Woodruff, retired president of Coca-Cola and unrivaled "guru" of the Atlanta business establishment. The story, as understood and repeated by Rabbi Rothschild at the time, was that Woodruff, on learning that Atlanta business leaders had rejected support for the dinner honoring King, sent word to those leaders to the effect that, if Atlanta jeopardized the company's fragile relations with its third-world clients by embarrassing Coca-Cola, the company might have to move its corporate headquarters to another city. Mayor Ivan Allen in his autobiography attributes the conversation to himself and Paul Austin, then president of Coca-Cola. Whatever the case, the outcome is indisputable: Coca-Cola turned the tide for support of the dinner by the white establishment.

The success of the event—the first racially integrated public dinner ever held in the city—is well documented. A capacity crowd of almost fourteen hundred filled the city's largest hotel ballroom, with more than one thousand having been turned away. The Ku Klux Klan and a segregationist restauranteur picketed outside the building, but neither that distraction nor continuous rain dampened the spirit of the evening. Jack Rothschild, as master of ceremonies, expressed the prevailing sentiment in his introductory remarks: "You—rich and poor, Jew and Christian, black and white, professional and lay, men and women from every walk of life—you represent the true heart of a great city. You are Atlanta. You—and not the noisy rabble with their sheets and signs now slogging sullenly the sidewalks beyond these doors. Here is a truth we must resolve never to forget. Let none of us ever again fear to summon this truth so simply, so eloquently and so forcefully brought home to us tonight by our presence here."[60]

Dr. King echoed this sentiment in a letter of thanks to the rabbi. He wrote that it was a testimonial not only to himself but "to the greatness of the City of Atlanta, the South, the nation and its ability to rise above the conflict of former generations and really experience that beloved community where all differences are reconciled." In a postscript he added, "I will never forget the great role you played in making the testimonial the great success it was."[61]

Archbishop Hallinan wrote from his hospital bed, complimenting Rothschild on "the magnificent program" and added, "This affair would not have come off at all had it not been for you, the Negro religious and academic leaders, & the Catholic cooperation."[62]

These expressions of praise and gratitude marked the high point of Jack Rothschild's career and a major turning point in the progress of Atlanta, his adopted city. More challenges awaited, however.

Rothschild had long advocated the establishment of a Community Relations Commission in Atlanta, appointed by the mayor. The commission finally came into being in 1967, with him as its vice chairman and his close friend Rev. Samuel Williams as chairman. Their first action was to hold hearings in neighborhoods where existing conditions threatened to spawn trouble. Angered and frustrated by hearing firsthand reports of people forced to live in inadequate housing—with faulty sanitation and unlighted, unpaved streets—Rothschild transmitted his feelings to his congregation through sermons, especially those delivered on the High Holy Days. Recognizing that racial restrictions lay at the base of the problem, he encouraged those from his own congregation who were attempting to create a biracial neighborhood, but he felt even more frustrated and angry at the limited success they were having.[63]

Even more discouraging were allegations of anti-Semitic statements by leading members of Dr. King's Southern Christian Leadership Conference. On being informed of them Rothschild wrote to King that he could not believe such pronouncements could represent the position of the organization. The civil rights leader replied with a five-page letter in which he tried to explain the remarks, primarily on the basis that they were taken out of context.[64]

Seven months later Martin Luther King, Jr., was assassinated. Jack Rothschild was asked that night to appear on television to memorialize him. Later that evening he visited the King home, where he was warmly received by Coretta, alone and apparently deeply appreciative of his visit. Surprisingly, he did not receive an invitation to the funeral. Mu-

Rabbi Jacob M. Rothschild with Dr. Benjamin E. Mays, president of Morehouse College, receiving Clergyman of the Year award of the National Conference of Christians and Jews, 1968 (courtesy of Janice R. Blumberg).

tual friends in the black community, unable to believe that this was intentional, inquired and learned that it was indeed the case. Too many celebrities had to be accommodated in the limited seating inside the church. The following Sunday evening, when the combined clergy of Atlanta paid its respects to King in a memorial service at the Episcopal Cathedral of St. Phillip, Jack Rothschild was designated to deliver the eulogy. Parts of it were later broadcast on national television on Harry Reasoner's segment of *60 Minutes*.[65]

As the growing militancy of the Black Power movement formed a breach between blacks and their allies in the struggle for racial equality, Rothschild became more discouraged but continued to speak out—to blacks and whites alike—decrying separatism on the part of either race. He had long predicted that time was running out for white Americans to resolve their racial problems, and he now spoke of the need for African Americans to renew their patience in order to solidify the gains that had already been made. When, in November 1968, he expressed these sentiments at a meeting of the Hungry Club—prominent black businessmen and professionals with whom he had long been on friendly terms—he was hissed and booed for the first time in his life. In his introduction he had said, "I want freedom for all Americans—and I want it now. But I am convinced that the way to achieve those goals is not to destroy the fabric of American democracy." He had also acknowledged the "justifiable scorn which greets any plea for patience" yet declared that he could not accept any form of apartheid, even a voluntary one, as a solution to the inequities existing in American society. In his conclusion he said, "I don't like being told it's not my fight. It is. . . . As a Jew, I have a commitment to justice and dignity and equality. And as a Jew, I am not going to forgo my religious commitment in the face of black separatism any more than we Jews withdrew from the battle in the face of white segregationism."[66]

Rothschild's candor apparently cost him the warm acceptance he had enjoyed previously in the black community. Among its newspapers only the conservative *Atlanta Daily World* reported the speech in a favorable light.[67] Two weeks later, when the Anti-Defamation League of B'nai B'rith honored the rabbi with an award, not one of his many African American friends attended, although many had recently attended a dinner of tribute to him by the National Conference of Christians and Jews. His friendship with the King family, Dr. Mays, Andrew and Jean Young, Sam and Billie Williams, and a few others remained, but he was no longer embraced as an ally by the black community in general.

Jack Rothschild continued to attack infringements of civil rights and liberties. In speaking to rabbinical students at Hebrew Union College–Jewish Institute of Religion, he reflected on the responsibilities of a rabbi as he saw them: "[A] rabbi must have a deep dedication and a pervading commitment to the ideal of equality and dignity for all men. He must be prepared to involve himself in every facet of community life that will translate that commitment into the minds and hearts of those he would lead. . . . It is the rabbi's responsibility to teach his congregation—and let Christians know—what Judaism has to say on the great moral issues that confront mankind. . . . There is great joy and satisfaction to be derived from the changing attitudes of large segments of . . . society and from the knowledge that what once had been a lone and lonely voice has become one with a swelling chorus. . . . What seemed impossible then, has partly at least been achieved. That is something— but not nearly enough."[68]

Those words, spoken in November 1970, might have served as his epitaph. Among the mourners who packed The Temple sanctuary for his funeral three years later were leaders of both communities, black and white. Prominent among them were then Governor Jimmy Carter and Rosalyn Carter, Congressman Andrew Young, Dr. and Mrs. Martin Luther King, Sr., Coretta Scott King, and Maynard Jackson, who had just been sworn in as mayor of Atlanta—the first African American to be elected to that office. The presence of these luminaries spoke eloquently of Jack Rothschild's accomplishments as a rabbi in the struggle for civil rights.

The Year They Closed the Schools:
The Norfolk Story

MALCOLM STERN

One of many controversial areas concerning the civil rights era was the relationship between southern and northern Jews. As national Jewish organizations advocated integration and northerners marched, many southern Jews asked the "outsiders" to stay out of their communities because of fear and differences concerning tactics. Often northern Jews could not understand how their southern brethren could remain apparently silent about a moral issue. In this article the late Malcolm Stern reflects on how northern Jews failed to understand when Jews in the South attempted to maneuver through numerous treacheries on the path to civil rights. What some viewed as a tactic to avoid integration was intended as a temporary expedient toward implementation of the Brown *decision.*

Looking back over my pre-Norfolk experiences I am astonished to realize how many of them prepared me, a Yankee, for the civil rights era in the South. I was born and reared in Philadelphia. All my grandparents were American-born; their parents and some of their grandparents were immigrants from German states. My father, an aesthete, left his family's hide and tallow business to purchase a farm in suburban Philadelphia, where he dabbled in farming, playwriting, and painting. My mother, whose two uncles were in Hebrew Union College's first graduating class, was a trained librarian. Prior to her marriage she had introduced children's storytelling into the Philadelphia Free Library system. Later she served our temple library and became a religious school-teacher. After a brother was killed in World War I, she helped to organize the Women's International League for Peace and Freedom. Her love of children extended to leadership in the Jewish Family and Children's Service and, for the last decade of her life, to the ownership and directorship of Camp Accomac, a leading Jewish girls' summer camp in Maine.

In 1922 and in 1925, my parents took us to Europe. In the latter year, my brother and I spent seven months in a Swiss boarding school where we were exposed through our roommates to different cultures, including Italian, Hungarian, and Egyptian.

When Dad moved us to the farm in 1923, we children transferred from a private school organized by my parents' Jewish friends to a school attended by the children of millworkers. In our new school my brother and I were the only Jews. Anti-Jewish epithets often greeted us, and on several occasions crosses were burned in open fields adjacent to ours. My parents helped us interpret the epithets and kept from us the fact that the crosses were a protest against us, the first Jews in that neighborhood.

From my infancy onward we had help in the house. The same year my brother was born, Annie Shorter, a superb cook, moved into our house. Annie was black, a native of Hagerstown, Maryland, who told us of grandparents who had been slaves. She remained with our family for thirty years and had an important influence on my brother and me because we often spent more time with her than with our busy parents. She was strict and not always sweet, but we loved her.

Not long after our migration to the suburbs, the local movie theater was showing a film we boys wanted to see, and our parents arranged for the farmhand to drive Annie and us to the theater, despite Annie's protest. We learned the reason for her objection when the theater manager objected to admitting a black. When she pointed out that she had us in her care, he reluctantly allowed the three of us to sit in the back row. That was my first exposure to "Jim Crow"—in the North! Our public school was integrated, and I was friendly with the one black girl in the class, who may have been the only black child in our neighborhood. I certainly was aware of the larger community's prejudice toward blacks.

I encountered more blatant aspects of such prejudice as a rabbinical student sent to conduct holiday services in a variety of Virginia towns and in West Point, Georgia. I was bothered by the "Whites Only" signs that segregated railroad station waiting rooms and other public facilities. I found the southern Jews whom I met most congenial. The majority of them had black servants, obsequious but not apparently unhappy in their roles. One vivid image survives in my memory from my visit to Petersburg, Virginia, where I was entertained by an elderly couple, once-wealthy Richmonders, who had been reduced by the depression to living in their summer "shack." They were lovingly attended by an elderly black couple, who grew the vegetables and raised the chickens on which they all subsisted. What shocked me most was the stream of profanity that punctuated their mistress's conversation, but it seemed so much a part of her personality that no one paid much attention.

My first rabbinic post, as assistant rabbi in Reform Congregation Keneseth Israel in my native Philadelphia, brought me into contact with Fellowship House. Founded and directed by a remarkable Quaker woman, Marjorie Penney, Fellowship House occupied an abandoned firehouse in a rundown section of North Philadelphia, about one mile from the more prosperous area where our temple was located. Into this house Marjorie invited interested groups of all races and creeds in an effort to develop outreach projects into the schools that would foster interracial activities. At one point I volunteered to bring members of our temple's young married group to produce an interracial seder. My wife and I worked with other Fellowship House people—black, yellow, and white—to prepare the food. As the time to begin the service drew near, one of the blacks announced, "Well, we're all ready, but where's the rabbi?" He was astonished to learn that the rabbi had been working beside him all day.

In 1943 I entered the Army Air Corps as a chaplain and spent eight months in Nashville, Tennessee, and eleven months in Montgomery, Alabama, and acquired an even more intensive view of southern living. I found Nashville far more progressive and liberal in its attitudes than Montgomery. Although some of the Montgomery Jews we met had attended the better Ivy League colleges, I commented to my northern friends, "They hadn't had a thought since the Civil War." One Montgomery Jewish housewife did have the temerity to write letters to the editor of the local newspaper on a variety of subjects. In one she protested that "so few of the Negro homes have indoor plumbing." The editor responded by suggesting that the lady's husband, a prominent landlord of many Negro homes, might well take the lead in rectifying the lack. There were no more letters of protest from this lady.

As a consequence of these and other experiences I found few surprises when in 1947 I moved from Philadelphia to become rabbi of Congregation Ohef Sholom in Norfolk, Virginia. The community to which I came was ideologically similar to the one that I left in that both espoused Pittsburgh Platform Reform Judaism, what has come to be called "Classical Reform." It was assimilationist, dominated by third-generation American Jews whose aspirations were more social than Jewish. Many yearned for acceptance by the non-Jews and bragged about their non-Jewish friends, even though they were excluded from their social clubs. Exclusionist social patterns were also reflected in the German Jewish community. During my seventeen years at Ohef Sholom, no one could be elected president unless he (no women, then) had grown up in the congregation. A separate German Jewish country club had died during the depression rather than open its doors. The town club was originally German Jewish but gradually extended its membership.

My congregants were largely motivated by a single question: "What will the Gentiles say?" Anti-Semitism was a major concern. Even in 1947 the Martha Washington Hotel in neighboring Virginia Beach, where many of my members had summer homes, could announce on its highway billboards, "Christians only."[1] One of my major missions during my seventeen years there was to persuade the congregation that the beauty and joy of Jewish observances in the temple and in their homes would make them more, not less, acceptable to their neighbors.

Everyone who could afford it had black help in their homes. Blacks often resided in the homes where they worked, and relationships with their white employers were usually affectionate, albeit paternalistic on the part of whites. Ill or aging retainers were looked after. *Driving Miss Daisy* was as much a portrait of some of my membership as it was of the Atlanta temple's.

The major difference between life in Philadelphia and that in Virginia seemed to be the pace. There was a leisurely, gracious quality in Norfolk that encouraged a very active social life. People in the South had time for the amenities. Members of the established community knew one another. Even though Norfolk boasted a population of more than three hundred thousand—with about ten thousand Jews among them—the core of business leaders and professional leaders were frequently friends as well as civic associates. Membership in the Rotary Club gave one automatic communal leadership, so my name was proposed by a member and I was promptly elected. This event put me on a first-name basis with the mayor, federal judge, and director of public safety among others. Out of deference to my rabbinic position they might have referred to me as "Doctor," but throughout the South first-naming is common; it crosses generations and, as southerners say, "makes everyone kin."[2]

Religion is strong in the South. Belonging to a congregation is important. Your neighbors, your business associates, and anyone you meet socially are quick to inquire with which church you are associated (a synagogue is frequently called a church, even by Jews in the South). Newcomers to the community are immediately solicited for church membership. During my seventeen years in Norfolk, Christian colleagues would often send me the name of a Jewish family newly arrived in their neighborhood.

This pigeonholing of people by religion understandably makes Jews self-conscious. Throughout my Norfolk tenure, from 1947 to 1964, I sensed that the majority of my congregants had the feeling that non-Jews would not let them be anything but Jews. This was borne out by the Moses Myers House, erected in 1797 by Norfolk's first permanent Jewish settler.[3] Moses' descendants intermarried and have been Episcopalians for five generations. To old-guard Norfolkians they are still Jews.

This rather lengthy prologue sets the stage for what Norfolk, its Jews, and I went through in the civil rights era.

The *Brown v. Board of Education of Topeka, Kansas* Supreme Court decision of May 1954 affirmed the principle that "separate but equal" violated the constitutional rights of blacks. The court demanded the integration of schools with what the enforcement decree called "all deliberate speed."

Good race relations were already a matter of pride in Norfolk. At the 1954 convention of the Central Conference of American Rabbis, I told a session that Norfolk was atypical of the South. I mentioned fifteen interracial projects or organizations already in place. Among them was a 1951 Brotherhood Week Service I had arranged in our temple, despite the qualms of a number of our members. They were not opposed to interracial activities; their major concern was whether such activities—if publicized—might engender anti-Semitism. For this service I had assembled an interracial choir trained by the minister of music of the neighboring Methodist church. The sermon was delivered by Dr. Samuel Proctor,[4] then president of Virginia Union University, a black divinity school in Richmond. Fifty-five of my members joined a large interracial gathering that filled our pews. A number of other temple members admitted that they had taken advantage of a concert scheduled that evening to absent themselves.

Among Norfolk's other organizations at that time was the Interracial Ministers Fellowship that met monthly for lunch in one or another of the members' church or synagogue. When it was our turn I had no difficulty in finding members of my sisterhood willing to prepare and serve the lunch, although these members were admittedly those on the more liberal end of the spectrum. A number of them were active in the Women's Council for Interracial Cooperation that met regularly at the YWCA and sponsored projects to improve race relations.

I had hoped to create a Fellowship House in Norfolk and had actually explored using an abandoned school building in a black area that bordered downtown. It was symptomatic of worsening race relations that by 1958 my dream building had become a ruin. The Supreme Court decision produced a determination on the part of most southern communities to preserve segregation.

That same year, 1954, had seen Norfolk shaken when a black family that had moved into a white area had its home firebombed. Rev. Moultrie Guerry, a highly respected white Episcopal minister, went into the area and held meetings aimed at interracial understanding. From this incident and others like it came a Study Committee on Housing in which I participated. We learned quickly that Norfolk desperately needed decent housing for blacks and that the stumbling block was availability of financing. I wrote to Adlai Stevenson, who was in the midst of his campaign for president of the United States, urging a solution to this problem (see appendix A). His failure to be elected was only one reason why many years passed before mechanisms could be established in the South to overcome the problem of financing for black would-be homeowners and other problems of discrimination.

The growth of segregationist sentiment made it increasingly difficult for the interracial ministers' group to find meeting places. The determination of a few of us kept the group going, and my temple continued to take its turn as host. The YWCA was pressured by the Community Fund, one of its major sources of income, to evict the Women's Council for Interracial Cooperation. They found a meeting place in the Jewish Community Center.

Into this tense atmosphere in the spring of 1958 came the first of a series of lawsuits brought by the NAACP demanding the admission of Norfolk's black students into the white junior and senior high schools nearest to their homes. In June 1958 federal judge Walter Hoffman ruled that qualified black students had to be admitted. A total of 151 black students applied. The Norfolk School Board devised a set of guidelines that in effect rejected all the applicants. After Judge Hoffman reviewed the guidelines, he determined that seventeen black students met the criteria that would integrate them among ten thousand white junior and senior high school students.

More than a year earlier the Virginia state legislature had enacted what the state's political boss, Senator Harry Byrd, called "massive resistance laws." Under these laws any school that became integrated was to be closed and placed under the direct jurisdiction of the governor. As a consequence Norfolk's schools were caught between the federal court order to integrate and the state law that threatened to close the schools.

To most of the people with whom I conversed at that time it seemed

Malcolm Stern, 1964 (courtesy of Louise Stern)

unthinkable that public schools could be shut down or that anyone would even want to close them. How naive we were! Long after the schools failed to open you could hear the comment, "They can't do this."

Scheduled for 8 June 1958 was the annual joint service of my temple and Ghent Methodist Church across the street. As was our long-standing custom, the visiting clergyman preached. I decided to express my strong feelings about the vise in which our citizenry had been placed. In a statement, often quoted, I declared, "If we don't rise above our partisan feelings of segregation versus integration, we shall have disintegration of our public schools." I pleaded with the combined congregation to put their religious principles into action and to prevent what had already happened in Little Rock, Arkansas, where a high school had been burned because of Governor Faubus's intransigence.

At the close of the service I stood at the church door to greet the departing congregation. The first person to reach me was Judge Hoffman, an elder of the church. He looked haggard. His decision to integrate the schools had brought down on him a storm of attack: threats, late-night phone calls, and other acts of harassment. As he shook my hand with warm approval for my message, I commented, "I may get tarred and feathered for what I said." He responded, wryly, "If it's any consolation, I'll be ahead of you."

To my intense gratification, although a few individuals, both Jewish and Christian, walked past me with tacit disapproval, the majority expressed gratitude for my having enunciated what was foremost on their minds. Two days later at Rotary, one of the Christian community leaders who had been present said to me, "Malcolm, what we need is a community meeting at which all legal angles of this school situation can be aired so that the people can know where they stand." This coincided so strongly with my own thinking that I penned a letter to the mayor and city council with an outline of how such a meeting might be handled (see appendix B). I disseminated copies, along with a cover letter, to a number of business and professional leaders whom I considered fair-minded on the subject (see appendix C).

Soon thereafter, as I was preparing to leave for my summer vacation, I received a phone call from Mayor Duckworth. "Malcolm," he said in a friendly tone, "you have a good idea but it won't work. The City Solicitor says that state laws, not city ordinances, are in control, so we can't call for a referendum."

Four days after I left town the story of my effort made the newspapers.[5] The prointegrationist *Virginian-Pilot* had banner headlines: "RABBI SUGGESTS PUBLIC MEETING AND REFERENDUM." The article gave full details with the mayor's comment that it would not work. The prosegregationist *Ledger-Star*'s headline read: "MAYOR TURNS DOWN PROPOSAL FOR OPEN FORUM." The accompanying article emphasized the impracticability of my suggestion but gave no details. Two days later the *Virginian-Pilot* editorialized that I was a citizen of goodwill, but the public forum would not work because extreme partisans would probably drown out moderate voices. The editorial ended with my prophecy of disintegration of the schools.

I was out of the city for five weeks and received a number of letters from congregants, not one of which mentioned the newspaper articles, so I knew that they were trembling. I assumed that the articles might have evoked some act of anti-Semitism, but on my return I learned that nothing, pro *or* con, had appeared in print. My congregants' fears were realized, however, on Labor Day when *The Virginian*, an anti-Semitic hate-sheet, was distributed to many Norfolk homes including mine. It stated that the president of the NAACP was a Jew, and hence all Jews were involved in this Zionist-Communist-Negro conspiracy to take over America.[6] When one of Norfolk's reactionaries attempted to quote the hate-sheet's statement in the record of the city council, Alan Hof-heimer, a past president of my congregation and a leading attorney, per-suaded the mayor to delete it. The mayor commented, "But you know that the president of the NAACP is a Jew." "Yes," retorted Alan, "but if he were a member of your Presbyterian church would you feel respon-sible for him?"

Norfolk schools were scheduled to open on 8 September 1958. To forestall the problem while awaiting a court decision, the school board postponed the opening until the twenty-second. On the eighteenth a federal circuit court ruled that the seventeen black children had to be integrated. A further delay and an appeal made it evident that the white junior and senior high school would not open.

A small group of individuals led by Professor Robert Stern had been working all summer in a vain effort to influence state and local leaders to prevent school closing.[7] At a meeting in Bob's home we agreed that the time had come for more concerted action. We created a Committee for Public Schools to enlist community support. By this time both sides of the issue were clearly defined: public schools with token integration versus segregation at any cost. When the schools failed to open, several pro–public school groups issued full-page advertisements in the local papers.

In the meantime the openly segregationist Tidewater Educational Foundation had advertised that they were starting private schools and invited parents to enroll their children. They also solicited public school teachers who were under contract and receiving salaries, inviting them to teach. With rare exceptions the teachers refused to teach for the foun-dation, which began approaching churches for the use of their facilities. The Presbyterians took the lead in issuing a state-wide proclamation urging their churches not to lend their facilities to segregationist private schooling. The Episcopalians and Baptists followed suit as did some other denominations. No synagogue was approached, but the Norfolk synagogues agreed that they would not submit were an invitation to be forthcoming.

When it became certain that Norfolk's white junior and senior high schools would not open, parents began looking for alternatives. A num-ber of children were sent to adjacent county schools on payment of a fee. South Norfolk, with a population decidedly prosegregationist, could not prevent the enrollment of Norfolk students, but they made it difficult by holding classes for outsiders from 4:00 P.M. to 9:00 P.M.[8]

Other groups of parents began rounding up high school teachers to give specific courses in their homes, but it soon became obvious that no home could hold all the students desiring to attend these tutoring groups. An appeal was made to churches and synagogues for space. Three sets of parents, including Lester Sherrick, the president of our temple, appealed to our board of trustees to open our facilities to tutoring groups. I consulted an assistant superintendent of schools, known to be prointegrationist. He stated that the school administration approved any arrangement that would keep teachers teaching and students in school. He shared my view that extending hospitality to the tutoring groups would prevent the expansion of the segregationist foundation. Those Jewish leaders who felt that any private schooling was a bow to segregation and would reduce the pressure on the authorities to reopen the schools were finally persuaded by anxious parents, and all four synagogues in town began hosting tutoring groups. This evoked an inquiry from the Commission on Social Action of the Union of American Hebrew Congregations (see appendix D).

In the interim petitions were circulated designed to have the city council apply to the governor to return the schools to local jurisdiction so that they could be reopened. On 30 September 1958 an overflow crowd attended the weekly meeting of the city council. Several neighborhood groups, frustrated that their PTAs were being dominated by segregationist voices, brought petitions urging the council to invoke that portion of the state's "massive resistance" legislation that allowed a municipal government to petition the governor. The president of the integrated Protestant Ministers Association read a strong appeal from his group, ending with the statement, "[If] there is anything that we ministers can do, please call on us." At this comment, Mayor Duckworth let it be known, for the first time in public utterance, where he stood: "The best thing you preachers can do," he responded angrily, "is to tell those seventeen niggers to go back where they belong and we'll open the schools tomorrow." Completely stunned, the minister took his seat. Later in the meeting he gained the floor again and, admitting his astonishment at the mayor's retort, added, "Mr. Mayor, I could not in good conscience leave this assembly today without stating that I couldn't go to those seventeen Negro children. You can't halt progress. Even if those seventeen withdrew, there would be seventeen others to take their place."

The mayor replied, "I don't know why the NAACP picked on Norfolk. We've done more for the Negro than any city in the South. We've cleaned out the slums and treated them decently. The Negroes pay only 5 percent of the taxes and occupy 75 percent of the jail space."[9] I sat glued to my seat, eager to retort but realizing the futility in that atmosphere. An Episcopal minister rose to defend the blacks. To him the mayor responded, "I can't understand why it is only since the Supreme Court decision you ministers have jumped on the bandwagon of integration." Replied the minister, "Your Honor, I can speak for myself and say that I was born with the idea." That minister was Peyton Randolph Williams, whose Virginia forebears were closely related to Thomas Jefferson.

Reports of the council meeting appeared in the afternoon paper and were spread by word of mouth. A Jewish Community Council meeting held that evening was equally tense. A resolution was introduced calling on all those who might be spokesmen for the Jewish community—obviously the rabbis—to refrain from making any public pronouncements on the school issue. I listened carefully to the wording of the resolution. In the light of the city council meeting and well aware of my members' fears of anti-Semitic reprisals, I voted with them for the resolution. One Conservative and one Orthodox rabbi who until that moment had done nothing publicly on the matter were the only voters against the resolution. Understandably, they took the resolution to be an affront to their freedom of speech.

I explained my vote that Friday night from my pulpit. I told the congregation that I heard their urging. They all knew that I was for integration of the schools, so at that moment I had no intention of making any public pronouncements. However, I added, should some situation arise in which my voice and my position might be useful, I would not be muzzled.

Our temple held its board meetings on Friday nights following services (a futile attempt to induce all board members to attend worship). Ohef Sholom also had a long-standing tradition that the rabbi did not attend board meetings.[10] I subsequently received a call from the temple president, who was very much in sympathy with my views, inviting me to lunch with him. At the lunch he reported that at the board meeting he had been handed a petition signed by five members, the number required by the temple's constitution, to call a special board meeting to censure me for speaking out on the subject. When I assured him that I would submit any future pronouncement to him and to Vice President Albert Hofheimer, another sympathetic board member, before going public, he persuaded the petitioners to withdraw.

It soon became obvious that the city council would not act against the Byrd machine and its massive resistance. Our Committee for Public Schools tried appealing to leading businessmen and professionals who proved even more fearful. To support its stand the city council called for a November referendum scheduled two weeks after Election Day. A young woman doctor from north central Virginia, Dr. Louise Oftedal, mother of five children and a political tyro, challenged Senator Byrd's seat in Congress. The Byrd machine ran scared enough to issue an order to the polls on Election Day that armed forces personnel and their families, about one-fourth of Norfolk's population, would not, as theretofore, be permitted to vote unless their annual poll tax had been paid.[11] This order created an uproar until it became obvious that Byrd was winning. Then the restriction was withdrawn.

Our Committee for Public Schools realized that our only hope for reopening schools lay in court test cases. Twenty-three Norfolk parents, unable to find a Norfolk lawyer willing to undertake the case, secured an Arlington attorney. They filed suit in the Virginia State Supreme Court, claiming that their children's right to a public education was being denied. The case, *Ruth Pendleton James et al. v. J. Lindsay Almond et al.* took time.[12]

Nineteen fifty-nine arrived. The tutoring groups had been proceeding fairly well, and parents were becoming complacent. They pointed to the advantage of small classes without behavior problems. The problem kids were on the streets. As the second semester approached, the parents were all too ready to continue the tutoring arrangements. The teachers were less happy. The tutoring groups had them running all over town. One of my religious school teachers taught English and Latin. She was teaching one session at our temple and other classes in a variety of churches. With the end of the semester the teachers' contracts and salaries would end.

In the meantime Gabriel Cohen, editor of *The Jewish Post and Opinion,* had visited Norfolk, interviewed a Conservative rabbi, and reported to his readers that the local rabbis had done little about the school situation. Understandably, this evoked a protest from me (see appendix E). His article may have inspired the rabbi he interviewed, Joseph Goldman, then president of the Tidewater Rabbinical Association, to call a meeting of Norfolk rabbis, Christian ministers, and public school administrators. Out of this gathering came a widely circulated statement, largely framed by me, warning parents that if the schools did not reopen, many teachers would seek posts elsewhere because their salaries would end with the semester. We pointed out that the tutoring groups offered no applied sciences, making the students ineligible for college admission. We added that church and synagogue facilities were being overtaxed.

By 19 January 1959 the parents' suit—defeated in state court but appealed to federal court—brought an end to massive resistance laws. A defiant Norfolk City Council announced that it would withhold funds from any school that became integrated. Governor Lindsay Almond appeared on television with an impassioned statement in which he said, "We have only begun to fight."

At long last Norfolk's business community awoke to reality. Business was falling off. Since September's school closing, navy families had been requesting and receiving transfers to other bases. An advertisement, signed by one hundred business leaders, including four Jews, appeared in the press, stating, "Although we prefer segregation, the best interests of the community will be served by reopening the public schools." Their phraseology made it clear that they did not want to antagonize their many customers who were strongly segregationist.

A lawsuit against the city council was followed by a session of the state legislature at which Governor Almond capitulated. He told the legislature that he would go to jail to maintain segregation, but he felt that it would be a foolish gesture in view of federal pressure to integrate. Announcing the demise of massive resistance, he stated that schools would be reopened in Norfolk and in other Virginia communities that had also been integrated by federal courts.

It was a tense weekend for all of us. On Saturday, 31 January, my wife and I were driving home from Sabbath worship. As we approached Maury High School, one of the two white high schools about to be integrated, we were horrified to see the effigy of a black man hanging from a tree in the schoolyard. As soon as I reached home, I telephoned Calvin Dalby, the director of public safety, who urged me to keep the matter quiet while he had the effigy removed. We succeeded in avoiding any public notice of the matter.[13]

Everyone was concerned that violence might attend the 2 February opening of the integrated schools. At the suggestion of the temple vice president, Albert Hofheimer, the Kiwanis-sponsored high school leadership group, the Key Club, issued a paid advertisement in the Sunday *Virginian-Pilot* on 1 February. The president of the Key Club, Ronnie King, happened to be Jewish. He had been one of four Jewish youngsters among a group of Norfolk teenagers interviewed on national television by Edward R. Murrow. Ronnie secured the signatures of Key Club leaders and helped frame their pronouncement to the effect that the eyes of the world were on Norfolk's teenagers, whom they urged to return to school with decency and good behavior. Their advertisement attracted national attention and evoked a letter of commendation from President Eisenhower.

Members of the clergy offered to usher the black students into the former white schools, but the director of public safety issued an order that only those adults who had official reasons to enter schools were to be permitted to do so.

While police stood twenty-four-hour guard duty at the schools, 2 February came and went. Except for a hoard of media photographers from everywhere, it proved (to everyone's relief) to be a day without incident.

Two days later I spoke to Jane Whitehill, a junior at Granby High. Janie, whom I had confirmed a year earlier, had been outspokenly integrationist when she was interviewed on Murrow's program. I asked her how integration was proceeding. Only one lone black girl had been admitted to Granby High. Janie told me that on the first day of regular classes, she and a group of her Jewish friends had entered the cafeteria and seen the black girl by herself in the cafeteria line. They invited her to join them for lunch. This evoked cries of "nigger-lover" from passersby. There seem to have been no other difficulties.

Even before our Norfolk schools reopened, I recognized that there would be die-hard segregationists in Norfolk. On 27 January I sent a letter to Governor Almond (see appendix F), and copies to our state senator and representative, urging that for the sake of peace in the public schools, qualified private schools should receive financial underwriting. I received warm acknowledgments from all three. Evidently the legislature shared my views, for one of its first enactments was to allocate $250 a year to any parent who could prove that his child was seeking private schooling to avoid integration. This law remained in force for several years until integrated schools became the norm.

That battle was not easily concluded. The city council brought countersuits, as did the commonwealth's attorney. The NAACP had to fight them in court to prevail in the long run. So far as I was aware, Norfolk's Jews accepted the integration of the schools without vocal opposition and, for the most part, with considerable relief. From then on, if the matter came up in conversation, my congregants tended to extol my role and seemed grateful for my leadership through a difficult period.

At the height of the fray I said from my pulpit, "If the South ever relaxes on interracial relations, the blacks will get a better deal in the South than in the North." That prophecy seems to have been validated when Virginia became the first state to elect a black governor.

Appendix A

August 20, 1956

Hon. Adlai E. Stevenson
Libertyville, Ill.

Dear Mr. Stevenson:

As one of many who hopes to see you in the White House next year, I am deeply aware of how thorny a problem the segregation issue is in your campaign. I beg leave to present to you the following suggestion, which may prove helpful to you as well as to the Southern communities:

One of the few areas in which whites and Negroes can be brought together amicably in most Southern communities is on the question of housing opportunities for Negroes. I refer not to government-owned housing, but rather to private-enterprise developments. The most bitter segregationists recognize the need for providing suitable housing for Negroes so that they will not spill over into white residential areas; and those of us who are more sympathetic to integration have been striving to assure decent housing for Negroes.

The biggest obstacle to the development of rental and sales housing has been the securing of financing by any would-be developers. Corporations, both North and South, have proved reluctant to extend credit. The Eisenhower administration recognized this and set up the Volunteer Home Mortgage Credit Program with regional offices in 16 cities. I have been unable to ascertain whether any constructive help has been forthcoming from this Program. Here in Norfolk, I know of no instances in which it has proved helpful.

My knowledge of all this has come form a Study Committee on Housing formed locally as the result of an explosive series of incidents following the sales of homes to Negroes in a former white area nearly two years ago. Our Committee, meeting without publicity, is a voluntary assemblage of clergy, real estate brokers, college professors, and interested leading citizens of both races.

It would be our hope that within the framework of Democratic policy there might be developed a free-enterprise credit program, with government underwriting, that would assure to would-be developers of Negro real estate such funds as would be needed to set up apartment projects and private homes for sale or rent to Negroes.

Hoping that you will find it possible to further this idea, and wishing you every success in your campaign, I am

Your sincere admirer,

Rabbi Malcolm H. Stern

[NOTE: This letter was never acknowledged.]

Appendix B

A SUGGESTED BLUEPRINT FOR A PUBLIC FORUM ON THE PUBLIC SCHOOLS

Proposed Title: A CALL FOR THE QUESTION

Time: Early in August, with as much advance publicity as possible.

Place: Arena or Center Theater, with either radio or television coverage. (NOTE: In case of overflow crowds, both halls could be used with amplification from one to the other.)

Participants on the Program:

Presiding: A city judge, who would outline the purpose of the meeting and would rule "out of order" any questions or statements of an incendiary nature.

Representation from the City Council & City Administration, especially the Mayor and City Attorney.

Representation from the Board of Education: Chairman, Superintendent, and Attorney.

Representation from the State: Commonwealth Attorney, State Board of Education.

Representation from the Federal Judiciary: preferably Judge Hoffman.

Purposes of the Meeting:

1. To inform the citizens of Norfolk as to the facts in the present school situation.

2. In view of the facts presented—to preserve the school system.

3. To avoid debate on the merits of either segregation or integration, but to elicit practicable suggestions from the citizenry-at-large.

4. To ascertain the will of the community as to whether it wishes its schools open or closed under existing laws.

5. To make use of the strength of the democratic process.

Program:

Call to Order by Presiding Judge.

Singing of "America" and Invocation.

A statement of facts from each of the four bodies whose representatives are listed above, in which each tells what it can and cannot do.

A 10 minute break, during which Ushers will pass slips of paper to those desiring to write in questions. It is suggested that the Ushers be members of the clergy. The questions will be passed to the Presiding Judge who will read off those which he deems fit and direct them to the appropriate member of the panel. Suggestions for solution may also be written on the slips, but should be marked SUGGESTION to differentiate them from the questions which could be disposed of first.

If deemed advisable, this meeting could be followed by a referendum, at the earliest practicable date. The referendum would place before the people the various possibilities of procedure arising from the public meeting, and would give those in authority the democratic sentiment of the people of Norfolk.

Appendix C

June 13, 1958

Dear Friend:

I am addressing this to you as one of a group of people interested in and perturbed about the present school situation.

I enclose a copy of a proposal I have sent—with a covering letter—to Mayor Duckworth and City Council. Should this proposal receive favorable action, it will need your help, and even if it does not reach fruition, there is something that you can do about the school situation.

I feel that you agree that it would be a great disaster for our city schools to close—even for the briefest period. Here are some valid reasons—in addition to the more obvious ones:

1. Private schools in the Norfolk area have reached their capacity of students. Private school administrators have been put in the uncomfortable position of having to discriminate against some people; this is inevitable under present conditions.

2. High school graduates are finding college entrance increasingly difficult. Can we afford to penalize our local high school students through closed schools, when this might endanger their standing for college admission?

3. Some parents have already spoken of sending their children to relatives or to private schools out-of-state. This means breaking up families—not an ideal state.

I have been greatly encouraged to write to the City Council and to you by my experience of last Sunday. I preached to Ghent Methodist Church, and in the course of my remarks I stated that it is time to rise above our partisan views of segregation vs. integration to prevent disintegration in our schools—and incidentally, in our homes. The enthusiastic response to my appeal—mostly in the form of gratitude for my utterance of the things that are in most people's minds—emboldened me to proceed as I have.

Will you, in pulpit, in social conversation, and by any other means at your disposal, encourage people to speak up for keeping our schools open? And should the public meeting take place, please urge right-minded people to turn out in full force.

I shall be out of the city from June 18 to July 16, but on my return I pledge to do all that I can to further the above.

With grateful thanks for any attention that you may give this important matter, I am

Cordially,

(signed) Malcolm
Malcolm H. Stern
116 Elwood Avenue
Norfolk 5, Virginia

Appendix D

October 2, 1958

Mr. Albert Vorspan
Union of American Hebrew Congregations
838 Fifth Avenue
New York 21, New York

Dear Al:

In response to your inquiry regarding the tutorial program in Norfolk churches and synagogues, may I give you the following information:

1. The overwhelming majority of Norfolk Jews have whole-heartedly supported in every feasible way the local attempts by the School Board and others to comply with the Supreme Court decision. They have given no support to the pronouncedly segregationist Tidewater Educational Foundation (hereafter T.E.F.).

2. The T.E.F. for several months has been announcing that it would obtain facilities and accredited teachers for private segregated schools in the event that our public schools were closed.

3. When the closing of schools became imminent—within the last two weeks—groups of parents began organizing private tutorial groups with accredited secondary teachers. Many of these parents have indicated that they wish no dealings with the T.E.F. They started groups in private homes but these soon became too large and too complex for any home to handle. As a result, they began pressuring churches and synagogues for available space.

4. At a meeting of our Temple board held last Friday night, a number of our community leaders endeavored to uphold the principle that tutorial groups would lift the pressure for the reopening of public schools. This had been my own thinking until I consulted good friends in the public school administration who are announced liber-

als. They feel that the private tutorial groups serve the following purposes:

(a) They keep the pupils in education and off the streets.

(b) They keep teachers teaching.

(c) They imply, in essence, a protest against the T.E.F. since the majority of the teachers prefer working under these private auspices.

5. Our facilities and those of the majority of churches and synagogues have been granted to these private groups of parents rent free. The only stipulated costs to the parents are the custodian's fee and compulsory insurance for each child.

6. Churches and synagogues are cooperating in exchange of students with resultant excellent public relations. A number of our leading ministers have joined with the rabbis in emphasizing that the tutorial groups have no official connection with the house of worship and have no denominational segregation, preserving the "separation of church and state."

7. The facilities that have been granted in most churches and synagogues have been made available with the stipulation that they will close immediately upon reopening of public schools. This of course would be necessary since the tutorial groups are using only teachers under contract to Norfolk Public Schools.

8. It should be pointed out that many individual Jews (including myself) have been actively identified in the formation and activities of the Norfolk Committee for Public Schools. We have not allowed the tutoring groups to let us relax in our effort to reopen the schools.

For the rest of the picture, I refer you to the press coverage.

Trusting that the above fills you in on our picture, and assuring you of my desire to offer any further information that you may request, I am

Sincerely yours,

(signed) Malcolm
Rabbi Malcolm H. Stern, D.H.L.

Appendix E

December 26, 1958

Mr. Gabriel Cohen, Editor
National Jewish Post & Opinion
P.O. Box 1633
Indianapolis 6, Ind.

Dear Gabe:

I'm delighted that your weekend in Norfolk has made you an expert on the Jews of Norfolk and their attitudes toward the school situation! When you suggest that the local rabbis have done little about the situation, you are guilty of both bad reporting and failure to read your press exchanges.

The enclosed article appeared originally in the Philadelphia *Jewish Exponent* and was copied verbatim by the Denver *Intermountain Jewish News*. (copy attached)

Your Cleveland correspondent, Jackie Caplan, interviewed me last June on the subject of the Jews of Norfolk and the school question. Whatever became of her article, or didn't you bother to read it?

If you wish to know what one Norfolk rabbi has done in the light of the present circumstances, I refer you to the following press articles (I'm sorry that I have no copies to send you):

Norfolk *Virginian-Pilot*, June 24, 1958, back page headline article: "Public Forum on Schools Proposal Sent Council"

ibid., June 25: an editorial on same

New York Post, June 25, small item: "Rabbi Seeks to Save Norfolk Integrated Schools"

Richmond News-Leader, June 25: "Rabbi Asks Referendum on School Issue in Norfolk"

There are other articles, but they are in the hands of an attorney who has been working with the Norfolk Committee for Public Schools (in which many local Jews are taking an active part), the organization that has been fighting to have the schools reopened and integrated.

At least two of Norfolk's rabbis, Dr. Paul Reich and myself, have been in the forefront of interracial cooperative activities through the years.

The next time you visit Norfolk, I trust that you will secure all the facts and not just some limited group opinions before sitting in judgment on an entire community.

Sincerely,

(signed) Malcolm H. Stern
Rabbi Malcolm H. Stern, D.H.L.

Appendix F

January 27, 1959

The Hon. Lindsay Almond, Governor
Executive Mansion
Richmond, Virginia

Dear Sir:

In the interest of peace as well as public education in Virginia, may I urge upon you and upon the Legislature the following actions:

1. Permit those localities, now required by federal law to do so, to re-open their schools without further interference.

2. Allocate special funds to properly qualified corporations which will permit them to operate segregated schools, provided that they can demonstrate to the State Board of Education their ability to equip and staff such institutions.

Although I personally am opposed to segregated schools, I believe that in the present stormy atmosphere that pervades our Commonwealth, such institutions will syphon off those who might cause trouble in the public schools.

You will indeed demonstrate real leadership if you accede to these proposals. You will bring peace to troubled communities. Public schools can resume their normal functions, while those who insist on segregation will also be provided for.

Respectfully submitted

(signed) Malcolm H. Stern
Rabbi Malcolm H. Stern, D.H.L.

A Personal Memoir

MYRON BERMAN

Rabbi and historian Myron Berman identified with the civil rights struggle through early experiences in the North. His most dramatic direct involvement occurred relatively late. A Conservative in Richmond, he served as a Jewish spokesperson and clergyman attempting to bring harmony with justice out of confrontation and to forge personal and professional bonds for progressive growth.

A northerner by birth and through attitudes conveyed by upbringing, I served as rabbi of Temple Beth El in Richmond, Virginia, for twenty-eight years, from 1965 to 1993. Reminiscing about the motivation that led me to a career in the rabbinate, I fondly recall the weekends spent with my grandfather in Temple Gates of Prayer, a Conservative synagogue in a quiet neighborhood in Flushing, New York. My parents, although ethnically oriented, were not particularly observant because of an almost seven-days-a-week commitment to a grocery store in another community. Major factors in stimulating my desire to learn more about Judaism included my affinity for my grandfather and the prestige I felt as a six-year-old attending adult services and the third Sabbath meal. These early years of my life were also influenced by a sexton, the Reverend I. Rosenbaum, who eventually taught me not only the Haftorah and Torah cantillations but also the traditional singing modes of the Sabbath and High Holy Day services.

Perhaps because of these influences and the fact that I lived in a non-Jewish area in another part of Queens, I continued my Jewish studies at the Florence Marshall Hebrew High School. We met for two afternoons a week in the late afternoon and for four hours Sunday morning. All classes were held in Hebrew. During the first year of my attendance at Hebrew High School, I turned thirteen. Additional impetus for continuing my Jewish studies came from remarks made to me in Hebrew during my Bar Mitzvah ceremony by Rabbi Abraham Dubin of Temple Gates of Prayer—words that were rather flattering to a young teenager.

Included in my background was attendance at a racially integrated high school in Elmhurst, New York. Following graduation I attended City College of New York in the daytime and, simultaneously, the Seminary College of the Jewish Theological Seminary two nights a week and four hours on Sunday afternoons. City College in the late forties was a pressure cooker of ideals, ideologies, and intellectual competition. Its population was largely Jewish children of the lower and lower-middle classes. It was a secular atmosphere; in the liberal arts department, ideas predominated over economic concerns. Every protest group was represented on the campus. The two professors whose personalities and intellectual approaches have remained with me were Drs. Oscar Janowsky and Robert Morris, later of Columbia University.

At the Seminary College my enthusiasm for Jewish studies was further stimulated. All lectures were conducted in Hebrew by instructors such as H. L. Ginsberg, the biblical scholar, philosopher Abraham Heschel, and historian Abraham Halkin. Attending both City College and Seminary College was exhausting, but my experience at the Seminary College was infectious because Zionism and the allure of a Hebraic atmosphere provided not only inspiration but exposure to a wide cultural background as well.

I graduated from City College in three-and-one-half years but still had half a semester to complete at the Seminary College. I enrolled at Dropsie College in Philadelphia, then an independent graduate institution in Semitic studies. Dropsie attracted me with its remarkable array of Semitic experts who made my frequent trips to Philadelphia worthwhile.

I entered the rabbinical school of the Jewish Theological Seminary in 1949, still undecided about my future career. At that time some of the greatest minds in the Jewish world were assembled at the seminary. Besides Ginsberg and Heschel there were Dr. Mordecai Kaplan and Dr. Louis Finkelstein among others. Of particular influence in my life was the religious philosophy of Dr. Kaplan, which was permeated with ethical idealism and a world outlook overlaid by a scientific attitude. He educated a generation of students devoted to the proposition of the compatibility of Judaism with the complexities of the modern world.

Simultaneous with my entry to the seminary, I enrolled in the graduate department of history at Columbia University, a leading center of historical research. Dr. Salo Baron had a tremendous impact on my life. His doctoral seminar was inspiring, as was the variety of courses he offered. Among Columbia's intellectual lights were Professors Henry Commager, Robert Morris, Dumas Malone, and William Leuchtenberg. It would have been difficult not to absorb a love of history listening to the lectures of those stellar historians.

While I was a freshman in the rabbinical school, the Korean War erupted. Dr. Finkelstein gathered students and faculty in a special assembly and announced that the Conservative movement had made a commitment to supply chaplains for the armed forces. Although the media continually reflected the reality of the overseas engagement of the United States in the Far East, the war still seemed rather remote to students. On graduation from the seminary in June 1953, I immediately enlisted in the U.S. Air Force and was commissioned a first lieutenant. During two years of service many of my social attitudes developed. While serving in Roswell, New Mexico, I became acquainted with the problems faced by Latino Americans. The *bracero,* or "wetbacks," as many of these migrant workers were called, created for me an awareness of the plight of peoples with whom I had never come into contact.

This awareness intensified when I was sent overseas. One of the most illuminating experiences of my career occurred during a lecture in Niigata, Japan, a small university city in the northwest corner of Honshu. I was asked to lecture to a freshman English class on the subject of Judaism. After spending considerable time articulating the history, customs and ceremonies, and ideas of Judaism, I concluded by referring to the insignia of the Jewish chaplain, the Ten Commandments. When I had completed my remarks, I noticed one young man in the rear of the classroom fervently raising his hand. Prefacing his remarks by a statement that my lecture had been enlightening and thoroughly understandable, he then asked a startling question: "Chaplain, what kind of Christian are you anyway?" Despite our three thousand years of history, Jews were no different from Christians in the mind of this educated Japanese student. His query served to stifle whatever chauvinistic American and/or Jewish sentiments I may have harbored.

On leaving the chaplaincy in 1955 I completed my graduate work at Columbia and served as rabbi of a small New Jersey congregation. From 1958 to 1965 I became assistant and later associate rabbi of Temple Beth El in Cedarhurst, New York, where ramifications of the civil rights movement began to affect the community in a variety of ways. During the synagogue's early involvement with the civil rights movement, Wyatt

Tee Walker, an official of the Southern Christian Leadership Conference, appeared at the synagogue pulpit. It was at that moment in history when cooperation between black leadership and the Jewish community was forged.

Although the majority of the twelve-hundred-member congregation was either uninterested or perhaps even negatively inclined towards the civil rights movement, a significant element favored integration. An example of the latter was Everett Ruskay, grandson of Esther Ruskay, a founder of the National Council of Jewish Women, and father of John Ruskay, former vice chancellor of the Jewish Theological Seminary. At a reception held at the Ruskay home, we met Ruby Dee and Ossie Davis, who were soliciting contributions to the civil rights movement from the Jewish community.

In Cedarhurst I was in charge of the educational and youth departments. The cause of civil rights had a profound effect on members of our United Synagogue Youth group, and several members volunteered to participate in freedom marches in the South. For me, however, the emotional impact of the racial struggle reached a crescendo when in 1964 a memorial service for Michael Schwerner, Andrew Goodman, and James Chaney, the slain martyrs of the civil rights movement, was held in Hewlett High School. At the conclusion of the memorial service I asked one of the Jewish fathers, in light of the sad fate of his son, should he have encouraged him to make such a sacrifice? Without any hesitation, he replied: "I would tell him to do it again." I listened to his response with mixed emotions of admiration and disbelief. Although I could not commit myself to such a sacrifice, I marveled at this Jewish father's sense of social justice.

It was comparatively easy to deliver sermons and speeches on racial justice in Cedarhurst. Prior to my arrival in Richmond, however, I was advised not to stress this issue. Once, while a student, I had officiated at High Holy Day services of a small synagogue in Bishopville, South Carolina. This experience had been my first in the South and had solidified my conception of a region typified by plantation life. I had even had the experience of visiting a cotton plantation owned by a member of the Jewish community of Bishopville. Little did I expect that I would spend the majority of my rabbinical career in the capital of the Confederacy.

Arriving in Richmond in 1965 I was told of Virginia's massive resistance movement and the struggle to integrate lunch counters in the 1950s. The Civil Rights Act of 1964 had just been passed, but Thalhimer's Department Store, a chain owned by members of Beth Ahabah, Richmond's Reform synagogue, was the center of controversy because they upheld the state law barring integrated seating at their lunch counters. Although I chose the Richmond congregation as a career opportunity, it took many years of interaction with people and events to understand "the mind of the South."

On the one hand I found a bedrock feeling within the Jewish community of Richmond opposing integration and busing. On the other hand there had always been a cadre of southern Jews supporting civil rights either through individual efforts or through the Anti-Defamation League. Researching the history of Richmond Jewry I found that considerable support for the NAACP and the Urban League emanated from the Jewish community. This support often evoked negative reactions from the local press.[1] In March 1968 I heard a lecture by Dr. Martin Luther King, Jr., at the national convention of the Rabbinical Assembly. Referring to the tension between blacks and Jews, Dr. King condemned anti-Semitism as both irrational and immoral. He identified Israel as "one of the greatest outposts of democracy in the world" and called for a Marshall Plan for the Middle East.

Just a few short weeks later King's assassination shocked America. Fears arose in Richmond about the possibility of riots in the streets. I received a call from one of the Christian ministers in Richmond about a memorial prayer meeting, sponsored by the Richmond Area Clergy Association, to be held on the steps of the capitol as a symbol of communal unity in the face of tragedy. I agreed to attend. All that day, however, I received calls from friends warning me about the dangers of participating in such a gathering and advising me not to attend. Most of these callers were congregants or other members of the Jewish community concerned either for my safety or for the reaction of the general community to a rabbi's participation in such an event.

When I reached the capitol I found the grounds ringed by state and local police. There were fear and tension. I will never forget the thoughts running through my mind: Here we are, all standing together on the steps of the capitol of the Confederacy mourning the death of a black man. We looked at each other rather furtively, but our attention was directed even more apprehensively towards the crowd, as if we could prevent a sniper's bullet from snuffing out someone's life. Finally, about fifteen black and white ministers and myself (a tiny percentage of our six-hundred-member clergy association) joined hands and sang the civil rights anthem, "We Shall Overcome." That memory will remain with me forever.

I was thrust inadvertently into an even more personal involvement with the civil rights struggle in 1969. In April of that year James Forman issued the Black Manifesto on behalf of the national Black Economic Development Conference. The manifesto demanded reparation of five hundred million dollars from Christian white churches and Jewish synagogues for past injustices to the "black people." One month later James Corbett and Howard Moore appeared at the Second Presbyterian Church, the church that included worshippers from the most prominent families in Richmond, with their version of the Forman manifesto.

In his news conference Corbett declared, "The damage done to the black community by the historic patterns of racial discrimination has caused untold misery and moral and spiritual and economic suffering. This is particularly true in our city of Richmond, the symbol of Confederate oppression of black people." Referring to the churches and synagogues as possessors of "great wealth," the manifesto warned if monetary demands were not met, Corbett and others were prepared "to initiate other actions as deemed necessary." Corbett, an employee at the local bus station, had been unknown within the white community, but his remarks created quite a stir.

When the Reverend James Anderson, minister of the Second Presbyterian Church, presented the demands incorporated in Corbett's adumbration of the Black Manifesto to the regular meeting of the Richmond Area Clergy Association, a decision was made to call a special meeting of the organization on 2 June 1969. I was vice president of the group. On the eve of the special meeting I received a call from the association's president, Father John McMahon, who informed me that he would be unavailable to chair the meeting. I almost panicked. I was the only active rabbi in the association and contemplated historic precedents when Jews were placed in the midst of communal and national struggles and only succeeded in becoming scapegoats.

The next day was one of the most memorable days in my rabbinic career. The meeting of the Richmond Area Clergy Association was held at the First Baptist Church, the largest church in Richmond. Previous meetings were sparsely attended. Because of the publicity surrounding Corbett's challenge and the unrest within the community, the police, and (I suspect) the FBI, were out in full force. Credentials of all clergymen were checked prior to their entry into the vestry room. This was the largest assemblage of clergy ever experienced by the association.

No agenda had been planned for the meeting aside from the expected reaction to Richmond's version of the Black Manifesto. It was a catalyst of communal unrest. Included in the gathering were the extremes of the religious spectrum. Rednecked ministers from the southside proliferated alongside liberal Catholic and Protestant clergymen, together with a large representation of African American ministers.

While I opened the meeting with a prayer, my silent prayer was the hope that violence could be averted. Several speakers raised their hands, demanding to be heard. Sentiments ran the gamut, from outrage at the audacity of the Black Manifesto's proponents to sympathy with the plight of our minority population resulting from racial injustice.

Finally, the Reverend James Forbes, a black clergyman, now minister of Riverside Church in New York City, asked for the floor. He began by surprising the gathering with a recital of his background. He stated that he was a graduate of Union Theological Seminary in New York. He then chided the audience, claiming that he was not sure what manner of speech to adopt. He maintained that he could assume the stance of a learned professor from the North, speaking impeccable English. By the same token, because he was from the South he could imitate his less-educated brethren and dance as blacks had done during the slavery era. Suddenly he approached one of the ultraconservative white ministers and said to him, "Brother, pat me on the head and I'll do a dance for you—go ahead—don't be afraid!"

The audience was startled. They could not comprehend what had occurred. Reverend Forbes's remarkable performance had broken the ice. Instead of invective and threats, there was laughter and a willingness to listen.

While debate continued I appointed a subcommittee to articulate the feelings of the majority. Despite wide differences of opinion, the following resolution was adopted:

> Our black brothers have something against us. We are shocked and still uncertain about the way they have come. Yet we affirm that it may be a necessary way of God's coming to judge and help free us from racial attitudes that demean us.
>
> We firmly reject the revolutionary ideologies and racist theories contained in "The Black Manifesto."
>
> We are sharply critical of many aspects of "The Black Manifesto." But we are also critical of our own failures to respond adequately to the great moral crisis which racial injustice presents to our churches and synagogues, and to our nation.
>
> Therefore, we acknowledge the issues [of] which "The Black Manifesto" reminds us:
>
> 1. The involvement both past and present of white churches and synagogues in an unjust system in which the whites are too often the beneficiaries and the blacks are too often the victims.
>
> 2. The responsibility of the white churches and synagogues to assist the black community to build up what a system [of] racial

discrimination has prohibited.

Therefore, be it resolved that:

The President of the Richmond County Area Clergy Association appoint a committee, broadly representative of the membership of the association, to consult with representatives of the black community to identify specific areas in which the religious community may more effectively fulfill its responsibilities; and that this committee report back within two weeks with recommendations.

Two weeks later, I presided at a special meeting of the clergy association that issued a statement reflecting a compromise between the polarized elements of the religious community. It read in part: "We acknowledge our deep and grievous fault for failing to do justly towards our black brothers and other races and religious groups. We accept the concept of reparations in terms of making amends, but we reject any form of extortion." Extremism had been muted temporarily, but very few, if any, positive measures had as yet been proposed.

I felt a great deal of pressure because of the vulnerability of the Jewish community, comprising about ten thousand individuals, perhaps 2 percent of the population. By the 1960s the scions of the older, well-integrated German Jewish community had been superseded in number by northern migrants of East European origin. The Jewish community, which had been sharply divided along the lines of religious affiliation between Reform and Conservative elements, had just experienced a feeling of euphoria because of Israel's remarkable victory in the Six Day War. New, vigorous leadership emerged. The economically successful businessmen of East European origin and affiliated with the Conservative synagogue now allied with prominent members of the Reform synagogue of similar ethnic origin. Previously, the existence of anti-Semitism had been denied by the older, more assimilated part of the Jewish community. Now the new leadership confronted anti-Jewish prejudice, as they did other social issues, with a new sense of pride stimulated by Israel's role in world affairs. Symbolic of the transformation in Jewish attitudes towards both local and national issues was the change in nomenclature of the Richmond Jewish Community Council to the Jewish Federation of Richmond.

Still, there was an uneasiness in Richmond, reminiscent of past experiences, lest sons of Israel again become scapegoats between contentious segments within the community. As a self-protective measure a majority of the Jewish population preferred for Jews not to become involved in racial matters because they did not think of it as their struggle.

As the only active Jewish member of a six-hundred-member clergy association, I felt a sense of isolation, although two Reform, two Orthodox, and another Conservative rabbi were in Richmond at that time. Realizing that I was placed in a position of leadership more out of convenience than esteem, I had no alternative but to try to reconcile the various factions. Admittedly, anti-Semitism had always played a role in the South, disengaging Jews from the active role they had played in civic and social affairs in the previous century. Even so, Rabbi Edward Calisch, spiritual leader of Beth Ahabah for more than half a century, and Ariel Goldburg, his successor, had forged bridges to the non-Jewish community. Although the traditionalist Jew had questioned Rabbi Calisch's religious ideology and practice, the non-Jewish community had regarded him as the chief rabbi of the Jews. I was the beneficiary of Calisch's and Goldburg's experience, but I was apprehensive about the potential results of this new challenge.

As chairman of the Committee for Community Concern, I presided over a series of weekly meetings. One positive result of these gatherings was the forging of a sense of camaraderie among a group of religious leaders. Instrumental in creating this alliance was the cooperation of Bishop Walter Sullivan of the Catholic Diocese, Father N. Constantine Dombalis of the Greek Orthodox Cathedral, and Rev. Robert L. Taylor, an influential black Baptist minister. My friendship with these religious men has lasted more than a quarter of a century.

During the course of the next year committees were established to investigate racial attitudes within the religious community and to identify the needs of African Americans. Finally, in November 1969 the Richmond Area Clergy Association resolved to solicit funds to "help eradicate poverty within the black community of the Richmond Metropolitan area." The weekend of 1 March was set aside in all churches and synagogues for collection.

The final result of almost a year of weekly meetings was a proposal to allot funds for the creation of a series of day-care centers in the black community. More than thirty thousand dollars was eventually raised, but to our disappointment the funds were rejected by the black leadership as an inadequate response to the Black Manifesto.

The more militant element of the black leadership became increasingly insular during the next few decades. Most black clergymen centered their effort in their own religious associations, and the momentum for direct communal activity ceased to motivate the Richmond Area Clergy Association. The latter diminished in importance partially because of the nonparticipation of blacks and partially because of a committee created by the Virginia Council of Churches to deal with social issues.

Nonetheless, one positive result of this year of confrontation did emerge: the creation of a biracial nucleus of clergymen of varied backgrounds who had been thrust into a year-long effort to create racial harmony. The sense of personal rapport was to pay immeasurable dividends for the city of Richmond, which was about to face formidable racial and social crises during the next decades. Subsequently, when crises developed within the city, this group met regularly either in the office or home of Bishop Sullivan or Father Dombalis. Not only were civic issues such as poverty, the penal system, and the plight of the homeless discussed, but plans for representation at the city council, state legislature, or the office of the governor were also formulated. The existence of an interpersonal relationship without any intermediaries to call ad hoc meetings within twenty-four hours greatly facilitated this process. This close association has lasted more than a quarter of a century. Thus a unified voice often emerged through key press conferences that received city-wide attention.

One of my closest associations with the black community was through Dr. David Shannon, then president of Virginia Union University, one of the foremost black educational institutions in the South. Eventually, I received an appointment as adjunct professor for one semester in their graduate school of theology. Most of my students came from ultraconservative religious backgrounds and were quite reluctant to accept biblical criticism. They were eager, however, to learn Jewish interpretations of Scripture. Their reaction to me was rather impersonal until it was my turn to preach at the weekly convocation. When the service was concluded, one of my students paid me the ultimate compliment: "Rabbi, you preach just like a black minister."

Subsequently, because of my work in the Richmond Area Clergy Association, I was appointed to the board of a black senior citizens center in the heart of the downtown area. During this time I came into contact with several unusual people. I met well-educated black men and women whose desire for education emanated from parents who remembered slave experiences. Their efficient and well-managed operation of the senior center with but little assistance from the general community stood in sharp contrast to the perception of blacks that pervaded the white majority. One of the board members of the senior center was Willie Dell, former city councilperson and wife of a local black minister.

During the course of my communal involvement I became personally acquainted with Douglas Wilder, then state senator and later governor of Virginia. He was able to succeed to the highest elective post in a southern state that had proclaimed a policy of massive resistance to racial integration. Whenever he had the opportunity, Mr. Wilder always referred to his images of slavery.

Whenever I was involved with civil rights issues, I was always regarded as a representative of the Jews—sometimes the only one, although I did not possess such a title. At most, there were only six or seven rabbis in Richmond at any one time, and only the Reform rabbi and myself, a Conservative rabbi, enjoyed a period of career longevity. Although many members of my congregation were indifferent to civil rights issues and others militantly antagonistic, my involvement was tolerated. Many black ministers were pulpit guests. Through my insistence our synagogue was the first to participate in an interracial, interreligious program housing the homeless for one week.

Although southern rabbis differ widely in their religious and social attitudes, they all inevitably must confront the particularistic attitudes of southerners toward anti-Semitism and the aura of an all-pervasive Christian environment. Southerners have always manifested ambivalence toward Jews. On one hand, Southern Baptists, the religious majority in large segments of the South, regard Jews with favor as current manifestations of the "chosen" people of the Old Testament. Nevertheless, the stereotypes of Jews contained in the New Testament persist clandestinely if not openly. Many southern fundamentalist ministers are enthusiastic supporters of Israel but regard the return of the Jewish people to Israel as a precursor of the reappearance of their Messiah. The southern rabbi is often regarded as the embodiment of an Old Testament prophet, leading a flock of adherents who abide by all of the biblical and talmudic teachings. The southern rabbi is also assumed to possess a deep-rooted historic concern for minorities. I have also discovered, however, that in the South, he often plays the role of a neutral force between conservative Protestants and liberal Protestants and Roman Catholics. Still, whether speaking out for civil rights and social action or remaining deeply ensconced in internal religious matters, the southern rabbi is constantly aware of his congregation's concern for, and at times obsession with, their minority status.

The primary motivation for my participation in the struggle for civil rights and social action emanates from my perception and interpretation of our Jewish heritage. My experience in the military, conducting services in a chapel used by all three major faiths, and the role into which I was thrust in Richmond as coordinator of an interreligious, interracial task force for civil rights enlarged my philosophic perspective while affording me as much pleasure as inspiration. As a symbolic manifestation of interreligious and interracial cooperation, first names such as "Nick" (Father Dombalis), "Walter" (Bishop Sullivan), and "Bob" (Rev. Robert Taylor) have replaced formal titles in our conversation and correspondence. Even the Reverend Mr. Taylor, who formerly called me "Brother Berman," now refers to me as "Brother Myron."

IV

Father and son Howard and Micah Greenstein, serving pulpits in Gainesville, Florida, and Memphis, Tennessee, respectively, study the attitudes of Reform rabbis in the South during the 1990s. Their article describes changes in the relationship between blacks and Jews not only in the South but throughout America. As strained as emotions have become over specific issues, the rabbis perceive a more equal association in which each group speaks from positions of relative strength and independence, keeping doors open to cooperation as well. As modern ethnic communities, both emphasize internal concerns even while remaining involved in broader issues.

"Then and Now":
Southern Rabbis and Civil Rights

MICAH D. GREENSTEIN AND

HOWARD GREENSTEIN

The achievements of the civil rights movement in the South a generation ago present a curious paradox. On the one hand, the struggle in the sixties for racial equality in law, for which southern rabbis among others so bravely fought and sacrificed, has largely been won. On the other hand, although legislation has removed legal barriers to racial equality, it has only intensified an awareness of the gulf between goals and reality. In short, the work of the earlier civil rights movement is far from complete. Some goals have been achieved but many have not, and the eloquent dream that the Reverend Doctor Martin Luther King, Jr., proclaimed a generation ago has yet to be realized.

The glaring visual reminders of oppression and discrimination against people of color in public places have thankfully vanished. Discrimination in public facilities, public education, employment, and housing has been repudiated by law. Political representation of and by blacks in southern communities has mushroomed since the mid-1960s. Nonetheless, passage of civil rights laws banning discrimination in housing has not significantly altered the racial patterns of residential neighborhoods in the South. The economic disparity between blacks and whites has only worsened since that time. Illiteracy is widespread, poverty is still rampant, and welfare relief remains a prerequisite for the survival of a large segment of the black community.

Ironically, although the cause may be just as urgent as it ever was, the collective support for civil rights is not nearly as compelling. That contrast is especially pronounced among Jews. Probably no other single segment of American society demonstrated more vigorously its solidarity with black aspirations in the days of segregation and racial turmoil than the American Jewish community. In terms of both individual and organizational participation Jews were conspicuous in the struggle for justice and equality. A quarter century later the old alliances have weakened if not dissolved, and the old causes do not evoke nearly the same fervor. Time and circumstance have changed, and the consequences have sorely tested the depth of Jewish commitment to the African American struggle for equality.

When Histories Are Similar but Not Shared

Blacks and Jews have experienced similar histories of oppression and dispersion through the centuries. America, however, provided different challenges for each group. White American Jews were spared the legal restrictions imposed on people of color. Nonetheless, Jews were clearly not exempt from very hurtful and damaging discrimination. So-called gentlemen's agreements restricted the sale of real estate to Jews in certain neighborhoods. Discriminatory quotas in the more prestigious colleges and universities sharply limited Jewish enrollment. Restrictive policies in corporate business and industry curtailed employment for Jews, especially at the executive levels. Even in their leisure pursuits, Jews often traveled to resorts only to discover signs at the entrance that read, "No Jews Admitted" or "No Jews or Dogs Allowed."

Blacks and Jews were routinely condemned by the white majority, not for any particular action but for their mere existence. Anti-Semitism and racism meet in white hatred for whom blacks and Jews are, without necessarily any reference to what blacks and Jews do. The historical kinship between blacks and Jews, therefore, rests on a comparable though not identical understanding of what it means to be oppressed. In their zealous advocacy for minority civil rights, the outspoken southern rabbis chronicled in this anthology underscored a common memory of persecution and enslavement. These rabbis continually grounded their uncompromising commitment to the civil rights cause in the biblical citation "We too were slaves in the land of Egypt." From Atlanta and Alexandria to Birmingham and Baton Rouge southern rabbis reminded their respective communities of God's rebuke to the Israelites in the Book of Amos, "Are ye not as the children of the Ethiopians, unto Me, O children of Israel?"[1]

Clearly, however, similar experience is not the same as shared experience. Although American Jewry affirmed its solidarity with oppressed minorities by recalling its own enslavement in ancient Egypt, American Jews far surpassed their African American brethren in terms of socioeconomic well-being. For American Jews discrimination meant occasional rejection; for American blacks it meant human degradation. For American Jews discrimination was more feared than expected; for American blacks it was more expected than feared. For American Jews discrimination took the form of social and professional exclusion; for American blacks it took the form of radical isolation, segregation, and lynching.

Naked Self-Interest or Purely Humanitarian Concern?

An important question, in retrospect, is whether southern rabbis supported the civil rights struggle on purely humanitarian grounds or for the narrower purpose of eliminating anti-Semitism. In its public pronouncements the Central Conference of American Rabbis stressed unquestionably and in universalistic terms its unwavering defense of civil rights. It proclaimed at its 1961 convention, "We were gratified by the prompt action of the government in sending Federal marshals into Alabama to halt the violence against the Freedom Riders. Nevertheless, we do not believe that enough is being done, either through the use of law or by moral suasion. Tardiness in carrying on the fight against all forms of racial discrimination in national life can lead to further extremism, violence and disunity, and can all but destroy our claim to leadership of the free world. We therefore urge . . . that the blight of segregation be removed and deprivation of civil rights be ended as soon as possible."[2]

In 1963 this national association of Reform rabbis authorized the formation of a volunteer task force to increase rabbinic involvement in the civil rights struggle. More than 175 members of the Central Conference of American Rabbis stood ready to participate in any demonstration or "direct action" that would forward the struggle for racial equality.[3] The proceedings of the Central Conference of American Rabbis in the early-to-mid-1960s indicate that appeals for Reform rabbinic activity in the civil rights movement were part of a larger attempt to apply Reform Judaism's prophetic mission and ethos to the injustices facing American society.

Some writers have suggested that the black-Jewish alliance of the fifties and sixties was romanticized and exaggerated. In *Our Southern Landsman* Harry Golden observes that where Negrophobia remained most rigid, particularly in the states of Mississippi and Alabama, the Jewish communities, with the exception of a few embattled rabbis, remained silent.[4] Although there is no question that the "golden age" of partnership between blacks and Jews began after World War II, Golden questions whether the courageous actions of a few southern rabbis form a discernible pattern of leadership or whether their efforts are better understood as a series of isolated incidents.[5]

The truth is that southern Reform rabbis who did match their words with heroic performance risked more than their careers. They put their lives and the lives of their family members in jeopardy. Rabbis Charles Mantinband of Hattiesburg, Perry Nussbaum of Jackson, Milton Schlager of Meridian, and Jacob Rothschild of Atlanta, to name a few, all had to contend with violence and bigotry in response to their active support for civil rights. These rabbis and others like them took bold stands and opened their doors to integrated audiences in spite of denunciations and threats by white extremists.[6]

In Nashville, Tennessee, Rabbi William B. Silverman took a firm stand on the implementation of the Supreme Court decision on school desegregation and helped organize the Nashville Community Relations Council, a biracial group. When he announced that he would preach a sermon the next Friday night titled "We Will Not Yield," he received anonymous calls that The Temple would be bombed. And it was.

In 1954 in Atlanta The Temple president joined with Rabbi Jacob M. Rothschild in calling on members to vote against a proposed amendment to the Georgia constitution that would have obstructed school integration. One of the rabbi's sermons in support of civil rights was published in the *Atlanta Journal and Constitution* and by *The Congressional Record*. His synagogue was bombed in 1958.

Following the Atlanta bombing Rabbi Emmet A. Frank of Temple Beth El in Alexandria, Virginia, assailed the segregationist policies of Senator Harry F. Byrd and challenged the presumption that "Byrdliness is synonymous with Godliness."

In a letter to his congregation Rabbi Perry Nussbaum of Jackson, Mississippi, wrote, "Let all decent peoples stand up to bigotry and racism and demand that the authorities root out the vicious and despicable. . . . Judaism insists that we all share our blessings, the moral as well as the material."[7]

Jews and blacks also found common cause in combating the bigotry and brutality of the Ku Klux Klan, which rarely distinguished its loathing of Jews from its hatred of blacks. The 1963 murder of freedom riders Schwerner, Chaney, and Goodman, in Philadelphia, Mississippi, served as a heroic symbol of the solidarity of black and Jewish civil rights workers who sacrificed their own lives for the sake of freedom and justice for all. Nonetheless, in spite of such mutual support and common purpose, racial barriers persisted. Jews came to the defense of blacks, but rarely did they live with them. Jews clustered with their own in the more privileged neighborhoods, and blacks remained in the poorest parts of town.

The courageous southern rabbi who risked his life in defense of civil rights may have been geographically and socially removed from the blacks he defended; however, his own personal interaction with individual blacks—as domestics in his own household, as employees in his congregation, or as clerical colleagues and friends—helped him to defend their integrity and dignity as people whom he knew intimately. Furthermore, the southern rabbi's conviction to fight prejudice against all races and religions necessitated his involvement and commitment to the cause. The Judaism espoused by these predominantly Classical Reform rabbis shared a strong universalist element. Its spirit may be summed up tersely by the phrase "One God, One Humanity." These Reform rabbis were kindled by the flame of the prophets' passion, and they viewed their affirmation of the equality of the races as a religious imperative. Their courage and conviction is all the more remarkable inasmuch as most people preferred to accept the existing reality rather than change it.

Shifting Agendas

The promising initiatives of the civil rights movement undoubtedly produced major changes in the political and legal status of African Americans, who are now part of the fabric of American society. Those initiatives, however, especially as they apply to the black–Jewish alliance, have languished and unraveled. The explanation for this disappointing development cannot be assigned to any single cause. The shift in priorities in both communities is due to a complex of factors that even the most critical analysis could not have predicted a generation ago.

American Jews, for example, were bitterly disappointed in 1967 when Israel's desperate plight at the hands of combined Arab forces evoked little if any protest from the non-Jewish world. Jews were especially stunned at the silence of the black community. The Jewish community was infuriated when the United Nations Resolutions of 10 November 1975 proclaiming "Zionism Is Racism" elicited no protest or condemnation from the established black leadership in America. Jewish leadership was further outraged in August 1979 when America's UN ambassador, Andrew Young, a former civil rights leader, met secretly with Israel's avowed enemy, PLO hero Yasir Arafat, presumably in violation of United States foreign policy regulations.

At the same time, African Americans voiced increasing resentment toward Israel in its refusal to join the economic boycott against South Africa to protest apartheid. Advocates of black power in America accused Jews of hypocrisy in their opposition to affirmative action and preferential quotas and concluded that Jewish support for civil rights ended where their own self-interests began. Jews remained staunch allies in the voting booth; however, a larger number of Jews than ever before began shifting to conservative urban politics. Moreover, Jews were viewed as possessing tremendous power as the civil rights movement moved northward. It appeared as though black leaders such as Young were being forced to conform to Jewish interests and priorities. By the mid-1980s many blacks concluded that Jewish self-interest had replaced any notion of self-sacrifice.

The 1993 Survey of Southern Rabbis

In a 1993 survey mailed to 120 Reform rabbis in Alabama, Arkansas, Florida, Georgia, Louisiana, Mississippi, North Carolina, South Carolina, Tennessee, and Virginia, forty individuals responded, with at least one representative from each state. The dominant idea sounded by these contemporary rabbis is that today Jews and blacks face radically different agendas.

In the survey these Jewish leaders discussed the changes that have transpired in their communities between blacks and Jews since the early sixties and seventies. Many respondents were emeriti who had witnessed the civil rights movement firsthand from their southern pulpits. Others were newcomers who have immersed themselves in more recent attempts to revive black–Jewish relations in their respective communities. Regardless of demographics and years of experience, though, nearly every southern Reform rabbi emphasized that the present predicament facing blacks as a group is wholly unlike it was thirty to forty years ago.

Rabbi Stephen Fuchs at Temple Ohabai Shalom in Nashville, Tennessee, observes that "[Civil rights] issues are more complex today. Concern for equal access to restaurants and hotels has given way to more difficult issues like economic disparity and the indigenous poor. Jews and blacks seem to have less in common."[8] The statistics confirm Rabbi Fuchs's impressions. One-third of all black Americans and nearly half of all black children live in poverty today. Of all black infants 75 percent are born to unwed mothers, half of whom are teenagers. Nearly 25 percent of black men between the ages of twenty and thirty are in prison, on parole, or on probation. During the seventies and eighties murder and suicide were the chief causes of death for black males between the ages of fifteen and twenty-four.[9] The Reverend Jesse Jackson, among others, has pointed out that nowadays in America there are more blacks killed by blacks every year than were lynched by whites in more than two hundred years of slavery.

The impression given by many southern rabbis surveyed is that their congregants attribute the larger responsibility for these circumstances to the black community itself. Violence, crime, and delinquency are not believed to be maladies that whites or Jews have imposed on blacks. The prevailing attitude among most southern Jews, and probably most American Jews for that matter, is that these dreadful problems plaguing the black community cannot be blamed solely on others and must ultimately be reversed by blacks themselves.

Although there may have been major divergences between northern and southern Jewries with regard to race relations during the heyday of the civil rights era, survey responses of rabbinic leaders indicate very little difference between southern and northern perspectives on contemporary black-Jewish relations. This development may be due, in part, to the influx of northern Jews to southern Jewish communities. The sentiments of southern rabbis as expressed in the survey also contradict a widespread misperception among nonsoutherners that little has changed in race relations in the South during the last generation. Despite the smaller size and more diffused demographics of southern Jewry vis-à-vis northern Jewry, a number of respondents expressed the view that their congregants' attitudes toward race relations are scarcely different from that which they found in the northern Jewish communities they had previously served.

One issue that has sorely tested the black-Jewish alliances throughout the North and the South is affirmative action. Jews have always joined with blacks in denouncing bigotry and have spared no effort in promoting a society grounded in freedom and equal justice for all. At the same time, however, Jews throughout America have always emphasized meritocracy over preferential treatment. Quotas and numerical goals in the American Jewish experience meant automatic exclusion from elite universities and professional associations. The sampling of rabbis undertaken for this overview further suggests that the friction between affirmative action and meritocracy undergirds the reluctance among most southern Jews to line up on the side of affirmative action. They seem to applaud the avowed purpose of affirmative action but object to its application at their own personal expense.

The responses of the rabbinic survey suggest that race relations in general, and black-Jewish relations in particular, involve many shades of gray and are not the easily definable issues of yesteryear. The civil rights struggle in the fifties and sixties necessitated specific changes in both federal and state law. Now, at the brink of the twenty-first century, the issues are far less clear. "Twenty-five years ago," writes Rabbi David Ostrich of Pensacola, Florida, "the fight was for job opportunities and participation in civic and political affairs. Jews could join in supporting black aspirations. Today, the issues are murkier and revolve around affirmative action and the alleviation of poverty. Often Jews find themselves lining up against blacks [in specifics], even though they generally support black aspirations."[10]

In spite of the oppression and poverty facing black America thirty years ago, hope was still alive. This no longer seems to be the case in many parts of America, including the South. Julius Lester, a black literature professor at the University of Massachusetts and a practicing Jew, expresses this idea very well: "Many blacks cannot hope or dream today, because blacks no longer feel secure in their place on earth."[11] In his writings and lectures Dr. Lester argues convincingly that the sense of alienation, despair, and hopelessness, so pervasive in much of black America, is approaching a state of nihilism. Many African Americans, he submits, now believe in nothing and no one because they lack the most rudimentary skills for living. Many blacks, he contends, hate themselves more than they hate Jews, thus making the issue of black-Jewish relations a red herring in a much wider sea of collective discouragement and depression.

This sense of alienation and helplessness accounts for the seemingly irresistible appeal of a new generation of black militants and separatists. The inflammatory rhetoric of Louis Farrakhan and others who have preached the "lying and deceit" of Jews has galvanized disaffected black youth throughout America. As recently as 1992 Rev. Farrakhan was presented a key to the city and was awarded honorary citizenship to the city of Memphis by that city's first African American mayor, Dr. W. W. Herenton. This event caused a major rift in Memphis black-Jewish relations and was emblematic of the different agendas and concerns of each group.

A more promising southern episode in black-Jewish relations was the resilience of the New Orleans Jewish and African American communities following the divisive 1994 mayoral election. The hotly contested race pitted Donald Mintz, a leading member of the city's Jewish community, against Marc Morial, an African American state senator and son of former mayor Dutch Morial. A potential crisis in race relations erupted when a black college professor named Napoleon Moses was caught distributing racist and anti-Semitic flyers. Moses was living in candidate Mintz's home at the time, and the car he was driving was registered in the name of the candidate himself. Donald Mintz's campaign staff used the flyers to raise funds for their embattled candidate; however, the revelation of Moses' actions, and the perception that the Mintz campaign engineered a fund-raising campaign using the anti-Semitic leaflets as a tactic, shattered any trust that had previously existed between Mintz and the black citizenry of New Orleans.[12]

Rabbi Edward P. Cohn of New Orleans's Temple Sinai served as the chairman and only Jewish member of the New Orleans Human Relations Commission during the Mintz-Morial campaign. He attributes the black and Jewish communities' harmonious relations before and after this rocky episode to Dillard University's National Center for Black-Jewish Relations. Following the disclosure of the pamphlet distribution, many national commentators predicted a major rupture in black-Jewish relations. Rabbi Cohn never questioned the future of black-Jewish dialogue in New Orleans because of the strong links already forged between the two communities. He pointed to the insulating effect that resulted directly from regular and candid dialogue between black and Jewish communal leaders. "Throughout the campaign," Cohn declared, "we were determined that no one would put us at odds with each other."[13] Following his victory Mayor Morial spoke to small groups at area synagogues to reassure his Jewish constituency of their common agenda. The ongoing dialogue facilitated by the Center for Black-Jewish Relations at Dillard University made this and other reconciliation efforts possible between blacks and Jews.

New Orleans is a noteworthy exception to the norm. On the Jewish side of the dialogue, most Jews become enraged when popular black leaders make derogatory statements about Jews with barely a whisper of protest from the rest of the black community. Jewish leaders appear even more frustrated about the fact that many African Americans do not require their leaders to demonstrate tolerance and acceptance of others as a condition of their credibility. What many Jews fail to understand in this regard is that Jews look like white people and are therefore perceived to be the same as the rest of white America, if not worse. In the survey mailed to Reform rabbis throughout the South, numerous respondents confirmed this impression. Rabbi Donald Kunstadt at Springhill Avenue Temple in Mobile, Alabama, writes, "I do not believe there is a particular challenge to black-Jewish relations in our community. The question is a larger one of white and black relations. The Jewish community is only a sub-set of the white community."[14] Rabbi Cohn of New Orleans acknowledged the importance of periodic luncheon meetings between black and Jewish leaders but remarked that "everything between blacks and Jews, even under the best of circumstances, is primarily racial."[15]

The economic segregation between blacks and whites, and its resulting social separateness, widens the gap even further. As a significant segment of black America has spiraled downward due to crime, drugs, poverty, and illiteracy, Jews have been largely immune to these community afflictions. The vast majority of American Jews have achieved the highest level of socioeconomic success among all racial and ethnic groups. Even for the approximately 20 percent of the American Jewish community who find themselves in poverty, the assistance of Jewish agencies makes life bearable and livable. The general affluence of American Jewry enables the community to improve the lot of its most desperate members.

Discussion about "survival" for Jews, therefore, usually refers to the future survival of Jewish religion and culture rather than the present physical welfare of the Jewish people. This statement holds particularly true in the South, where Jewish communities are shrinking in size and in some cases disappearing completely. For many in southern black communities, however, survival is a matter of life and death in the here and now. The struggle for one's daily existence is an ongoing challenge for many African Americans.

The general inroads made by southern Jews in virtually every commercial, political, and social arena (with the possible exception of exclusionary country clubs) has further diluted the symbiotic bond between blacks and Jews in their collective quest for acceptance by the larger community. Although it is true that at one time blacks and Jews were indeed the most excluded and isolated groups, that common plight no longer exists in light of Jewish access to unprecedented opportunities in business, civic, and social affairs. The competition for power and changes in power in southern cities further shifts the historic alliance between blacks and Jews.

Accounting for the Changing Coalition

A number of significant factors explain the gradual but steady decline in the formal coalition between black and Jewish communities during the last generation. To begin with, both communities have become more insular. At the height of the civil rights era a shared goal of blacks and Jews was to forge partnerships for liberal reform. Now the immediate goal of each is to strengthen their respective communities from within. "Each community wants sympathy and understanding, yet each wants to handle its own affairs," writes Rabbi Arnold Fink of Alexandria, Virginia.[16] One signal of this inward shift is the existence of separate clergy associations for black and white ministers throughout the South. Southern rabbis are invariably members of predominantly white ministerial associations; black ministers tend to affiliate more closely with black clergy groups.

The insularity of the black community is understandable in light of the pressing social problems it faces. Southern blacks and their churches assign high priority to the fight against drugs, violent crime, homelessness, hunger, and infant mortality. For southern Jews and their synagogues today's major challenges focus on family solidarity, the threat of assimilation, mixed marriage, and Jewish continuity. The increasing prospect of a comprehensive peace in the Middle East, coupled with the decreasing threat of anti-Semitism for American Jews, has effectively removed the traditional external reinforcements of Jewish identity and accelerated the Jewish community's internal search for meaning and identity.

Unquestionably, sizable numbers of economically secure blacks and Jews place a high premium on the values they can mutually endorse, such as quality education, equal opportunity, and economic advancement. Even here, however, ethnicity often divides rather than unites. Jews contribute generously to increase black enrollments in prestigious colleges and universities as well as to remove barriers to professional attainment; however, members of both communities still seek their own fraternities and sororities, organizations, and neighborhoods. Blacks and Jews are clearly turning inward to ensure each community's continued survival instead of facing outward to emphasize the universal brotherhood of all religions and races.

Contemporary southern rabbis have not disavowed the humanitarian principles so many of their predecessors battled for a generation ago. They have, however, deemphasized the universal thrust of those principles for a number of reasons. First, many of the earlier goals and objectives to end legalized segregation have been realized. Equally important, and perhaps as a consequence of this fulfillment, agendas have changed to address newer and more urgent issues. In short, changing conditions have evoked reassessment on both sides.

This reappraisal is manifest in the debate concerning public and private schools within each community. In the early years of the civil rights struggle Jews and blacks united in the push for racial integration of public schools. A few decades later blacks and Jews have begun to raise serious questions about the merits of integrated schools. It is not uncommon to hear black educators argue that African American children may learn better with black teachers in schools run by black administrators. Similarly, Jewish day schools are on the rise. Once a principal advocate of public schools, the American Reform Jewish movement has activated its own national Jewish day-school program with such private schools emerging in southern cities large enough to sustain them.

Conclusions

In his excellent essay "The Role of the Rabbi in the South" Rabbi Malcolm Stern likens the role of the rabbi during the civil rights era to that of the biblical prophet.[17] The rabbi of the seventies, on the other hand, he characterizes as a facilitator, "challenging the interests and talents of his membership in creative Jewish directions." The rabbi's role has clearly shifted once again. The internalization of American Judaism has resulted in a renewal of Jewish ritual, larger emphasis on synagogue programming, and, generally speaking, a decreasing percentage of rabbinic time devoted to intergroup relations.

This is not meant to suggest the complete withdrawal of the southern rabbi from communal outreach efforts. Rabbis continue to serve as principal liaisons between blacks and Jews in the communities they lead. Southern rabbis, in particular, who serve in places with relatively small Jewish populations and even fewer Jewish professionals, typically occupy leadership roles in communal endeavors. Nonetheless, the vastly different transformations of Jewish life and black life in America since the heyday of the civil rights era have clearly resulted in shifting priorities for rabbis and black ministers alike. The pressing issues and concerns now facing each group are more divergent than similar.

It appears that renewed cooperation between southern blacks and Jews will be based as much on pragmatic survival issues as it will be on principled agreement. The near election of David Duke in 1992 made this ever clear. Mr. Duke's racist pronouncements, coupled with Klan death threats against Shreveport Rabbi Michael Matuson and black ministerial leaders, galvanized and united the Louisiana black and Jewish communities in ways reminiscent of the fifties and sixties. Nevertheless, this external threat to the welfare of southern Jews and blacks was a notable exception to the separate concerns facing each community internally.

Southern rabbis will continue to preach the prophetic vision and analogous histories of oppression that blacks and Jews share; however, whereas the battle for civil rights once filled the southern rabbi's daily agenda, nowadays it is clearly more peripheral. Black-Jewish relations and the fight for racial justice are two of many social-action issues today's rabbi would like to address. The competing demands on the southern rabbi's limited time outside the synagogue and Jewish world, how-

ever, make his predecessor's model of total devotion to intergroup relations difficult, if not impossible, to emulate. Although rabbis and black
leaders will continue to meet on matters of mutual concern, the radically different internal challenges facing each community will inevitably result in less interaction on day-to-day issues.

Notes

Introduction

Note: I express my appreciation to Berkley Kalin, Bobbie Malone, Abraham Peck, and the anonymous readers of the University of Alabama Press for their insightful comments on this chapter.

1. See, for example, Tony Martin, *The Jewish Onslaught: Despatches from the Wellesley Battlefront* (Dover, Mass.: Majority Press, 1993), and letters to the editor from Harold Brackman (p. 1332) and Eunice G. Pollack and Stephen H. Norwood (pp. 1332–34) in response to the review of Martin's book by Clayborne Carson in *Journal of American History* 82 (December 1995). See also Michael M. Cottman, "The Campus 'Radicals': Leonard Jeffries and Other Afrocentric Professors Refuse to Whitewash Their Lesson Plans," *Emerge* 5 (February 1994): 26–31.

2. Arnold Shankman noted for the period from 1880 to 1935, "Evidence indicates that the image of Jews held by Southern blacks was positive. . . . By no means did Jews and Southern blacks have a model relationship, but life in the South during these years was hardly ideal." The title of Shankman's book is indicative. Shankman, *Ambivalent Friends: Afro-Americans View the Immigrant* (Westport, Conn.: Greenwood, 1982); see also idem, "Friend or Foe? Southern Blacks View the Jew, 1880–1915," in Nathan M. Kaganoff and Melvin I. Urofsky, eds., *Turn to the South: Essays on Southern Jewry* (Charlottesville: University Press of Virginia for the American Jewish Historical Society, 1979), 105–23; and idem, "Brothers across the Sea: Afro-Americans on the Persecution of Russian Jews, 1881–1917," *Jewish Social Studies* 37 (Spring 1975): 114–22; Horace Mann Bond, "Negro Attitudes toward Jews," ibid., 27 (January 1965); David J. Hellwig, "Black Images of Jews: from Reconstruction to Depression," *Societas* 8 (Summer 1978); Robert G. Weisbord and Arthur Stein, "Negro Perceptions of Jews Between the World Wars," *Judaism* 18 (1969).

3. Historians of black-Jewish relations even disagree about definitions vital to an understanding of intergroup relations. Professors Bracey and Meier note, for example, "a mythological tone about what has been called the 'Black-Jewish Alliance' " (August Meier and John H. Bracey, Jr., "The NAACP as a Reform Movement," *Journal of Southern History* 59 [February 1993]: 23–24). See also idem, "Towards a Research Agenda on Blacks and Jews in United States History," *Journal of American Ethnic History* 12 (Spring 1993): 60–67.

4. In a presentation at the October 1993 meeting of the Southern Jewish Historical Society in Atlanta, Henry Green questioned Rabbi Leon Kronish's influence and thus raised the issue of the significance of "leadership" in relation to "followers." While Rabbi Kronish may have supported civil rights, many of his congregants did not. Conversely, they did not fire him. In many ways, an individual's influence is impossible to quantify. Two studies emphasizing the significance of moderate voices are David L. Chappell, *Inside Agitators: White Southerners in the Civil Rights Movement* (Baltimore: Johns Hopkins University Press, 1994) and John Egerton, *Speak Now against the Day: The Generation before the Civil Rights Movement* (New York: Knopf, 1994). Reform rabbis in the South since at least the late nineteenth century served as "ambassadors to the Gentiles." Translating Judaism to the Christian community and acting as the Jewish representative to the community were major aspects of the role. In this fashion a tradition of lay silence and rabbinic symbolic leadership existed and continued into the civil rights era. Malcolm H. Stern, "The Role of the Rabbi in the South," in Kaganoff and Urofsky, *Turn to the South*, 27; Gladys Rosen, "The Rabbi in Miami—A Case History," in Kaganoff and Urofsky, *Turn to the South*, 35, 38, 40. Rosen (p. 38) points to Rabbi Irving Lehrman of Miami's Temple Emanu-El as a rabbi who worked behind the scenes and through pronouncements in support of integration of the public schools and other civil rights issues. Although many of his congregants urged him to remain silent, the outside community viewed him as a moral leader.

Similar statements might be made for southern newspaper editors such as Ralph McGill, Harry Ashmore, and Hodding Carter. See John T. Kneebone, *Southern Liberal Journalists and the Issue of Race, 1920–1944* (Chapel Hill: University of North Carolina Press, 1985). Several of the journalists indicated that their positions were partly formed through early association with Jews. Ralph McGill attributed the broadening of his vision to his relationship (which began before World War I) with Rebecca Mathis (later Gershon) and her family in Chattanooga and to a Rosenwald Fellowship in 1937 (which took him to Europe). See McGill, *The South and the Southerner* (Boston: Little, Brown, 1964), 54 ff, and Ralph McGill to G. P. Lovell, 28 November 1966, Ralph McGill Collection, Special Collections, Woodruff Library, Emory University. Hodding Carter pointed to nine Jews who helped him to overcome his provincialism in *Where Main Street Meets the River* (New York: Rinehart, 1952), 186 ff. See also Harry S. Ashmore, *An Epitaph for Dixie* (New York: W. W. Norton, 1957).

Letters throughout the McGill Collection indicate that the "moderate" editors networked for mutual support and looked to each other as exemplars of courage and honor. Sylvan Meyer, editor of the *Gainesville (Georgia) Times*, although outside the "regulars" of "Pappy" McGill's group, still gained morale from McGill's example. Anne H. Meyer to McGill, 17 January 1969, McGill Collection. Meyer, a Jew, was among the earliest newspaper advocates of compliance with the *Brown* decision and received a Pulitzer Prize for editorials on civil rights. See Eli N. Evans, *The Provincials: A Personal History of the Jews in the South* (New York: Atheneum, 1973), 313. Another Jew, Louis Isaac Jaffe, editorial writer for the *Norfolk Virginia-Pilot*, won a Pulitzer in 1929 for his denunciation of the Byrd machine and lynching. John Hohenberg, *The Pulitzer Prizes*, cited in Stephen J. Whitfield, "The Braided Identity of Southern Jewry," *American Jewish History* 77 (March 1988): 376–77.

Did southern rabbis supporting civil rights network in the same fashion? Clive Webb researched relationships among Mantinband, Nussbaum, and Rothschild. He found an extensive correspondence between Nussbaum and Rothschild but only a few small notes between Mantinband and Nussbaum. He was not able to locate evidence of close contact between the latter and did not "know of Mantinband being in regular contact with any other rabbis in the region" (Clive Webb to Mark K. Bauman, 7 September 1994). Gary P. Zola, on the other hand, read all of the correspondence between Nussbaum and Mantinband during their years in Mississippi and found that "their letters were uniformly warm and mutually supportive." Mantinband, Zola concludes, had a "high regard and sympathy for Nussbaum." Mantinband had difficulty networking, however, because Hattiesburg was so isolated and he did not drive an automobile (Zola to Bauman, 10 November 1994).

These rabbis gained strength from each other's examples; nevertheless, one senses their feeling of isolation. Nussbaum, Rothschild, and Mantinband almost pleaded for support and assistance from their colleagues in the South although each recognized the reasons for reticence. Southern activists may have had more in common with northern liberals, but even so, southern rabbis were limited by northerners' lack of understanding (as the southern rabbis viewed it) of the conditions in the South. Even the most outspoken southern rabbis had difficulty dealing with what they perceived as northern condescension. The limitations of the networking may have weakened their ability to respond.

5. Steven Hertzberg, *Strangers within the Gate City: The Jews of Atlanta, 1845–1915* (Philadelphia: Jewish Publication Society, 1978); idem, "Southern Jews and Their Encounter with Blacks, Atlanta, 1850-1915," *Atlanta Historical Journal* 23 (Fall 1979): 21–22 (quotation). Malcolm Stern concurred with Hertzberg: "In the decades between the Civil War and World War II, no Southern rabbi seems to have made any attempt to deal with the race question. The fear of anti-Semitism, which reached its peak with the trial of Leo Frank in Atlanta in 1913, remained so pervasive throughout the South, that few (if any) Jewish laymen or rabbis would have had the courage to speak out on so unpopular an issue as the rights of blacks." Stern, "Role of the Rabbi in the South," 29–30. The articles in the first part of this anthology challenge these interpretations. See also Howard N. Rabinowitz, "Nativism, Bigotry and Anti-Semitism in the South," *American Jewish History* 70 (March 1988): 437–51; Stephen J. Whitfield,

"Jews and Other Southerners: Counterpoint and Paradox," in Kaganoff and Urofsky, *Turn to the South*, 76–104.

6. See Lunabelle Wedlock, "The Reaction of Negro Publications and Organizations to German Anti-Semitism," (master's thesis, Howard University, 1942); Bat-Ami Zucker, "Black Americans' Reaction to the Persecution of European Jews," Simon Wiesenthal Center *Annual* (1968): 177–97; Gabrielle Simon Edgcomb, *From Swastika to Jim Crow: Refugee Scholars at Black Colleges* (Melbourne, Fla.: Krieger, 1993).

    Occasionally Atlanta Jewry also became aware that not all Jews were white. Dr. J. Faitlovitch detailed conditions of Jews in what is now Ethiopia in 1915. Rabbi W. V. A. Franklin, identified as a "Falashan" or "Abyssinian" Jew, conducted services at a local congregation in 1942. Mark K. Bauman, "Centripetal and Centrifugal Forces Facing the People of Many Communities: Atlanta Jewry from the Frank Case to the Great Depression," *Atlanta Historical Journal* 23 (Fall 1979): 46; *Southern Israelite*, 1 May 1936, 8 January 1937, 23 January 1942.

7. Mark K. Bauman and Arnold Shankman, "The Rabbi as Ethnic Broker: The Case of David Marx," *Journal of American Ethnic History* 2 (Spring 1983): 51–52; Bauman, "Centripetal," 45–46; *Southern Israelite*, 18 February 1937; January 1924 diary entries, box 5, Rhoda Kaufman Collection, Georgia Department of Archives and History; Patricia E. Smith, "Rhoda Kaufman: A Southern Progressive's Career, 1913–1956," *Atlanta Historical Bulletin* 18 (Spring–Summer 1973): 43–50. Kaufman was forced to resign her position as head of the state welfare department later in the decade in response to Klan pressure.

    Jews who assisted African Americans were routinely praised for their efforts in the pages of the *Southern Israelite*. See for example the obituaries for Felix Warburg (5 November 1937), who left money to Fort Valley High and Industrial School and Tuskegee; Jennie Borochoff (22 January 1937), for whom "the lines of race, color and creed did not exist . . . in her work"; and Harry H. Smith (18 January 1946), the "Mayor of Decatur Street" (the largely Russian Jewish commercial section of Atlanta), who helped the needy regardless of race or creed.

    In Virginia, William Lovenstein, a prominent state legislator during the late nineteenth century, sponsored bills to assist African Americans. During the twentieth century Richmond Jews supported the Urban League and the NAACP. Berman, *Richmond's Jewry*, 235, 317–18. Lee C. Schloss, newspaper publisher and president of the Woodville, Mississippi, school board during the early 1890s, helped establish a black school with the financial support of the Rosenwald Fund. Leo and Evelyn Turitz, *Jews in Early Mississippi, 1840–1900* (Jackson: University Press of Mississippi, n.d.), 9–10.

8. *Southern Israelite*, 14 March 1930, 7 February 1969, 27 September 1944 (quotation), 14 September 1945, 26 January 1940; Mark K. Bauman,

"The Youthful Musings of a Jewish Community Activist: Josephine Joel Heyman," *Atlanta History* (September 1995): 46–59. The actions of Atlanta women were not unique. See Sarah Wilkerson-Freeman, "Two Generations of Jewish Women: A Heritage of Activism in North Carolina, 1880–1970," *SJHS Newsletter* (July 1989): 3–6. For background see Kathleen Atkinson Miller, "The Ladies and the Lynchers: A Look at the Association of Southern Women for the Prevention of Lynching," *Southern Studies* (Fall/Winter 1991): 261–80; Merl E. Reed, *Seedtime for the Modern Civil Rights Movement: The President's Committee on Fair Employment Practice, 1941–1946* (Baton Rouge and London: Louisiana State University Press, 1991).

9. The National Council of Jewish Women's program for 1936 advocated such a law, and the Executive Board (including Mrs. Ernest Horowitz of Atlanta) of the National Federation of Temple Sisterhoods endorsed the Costigan-Wagner antilynching bill. *Southern Israelite*, 15 November 1935, 14 February 1936, 26 January 1940, 9 August 1946 (quotation). The newspaper (8 March 1946) supported a citizen's committee under John A. Griffin established to educate the public on the terrible conditions in black schools to foster the passage of a bond issue. Advocating constitutional reform, the 10 January 1947 issue blasted late Georgia politico Eugene Talmadge and his son, "Haman," for bigotry in the gubernatorial election of 1946: "The un-Democratic, un-American and un-Georgian racial intolerance which swept him to his final victory was indeed the saddest commentary he perpetrated on this state."

On HOPE, see Paul E. Mertz, " 'Mind Changing Time All Over Georgia': HOPE, Inc., and School Desegregation, 1958–1961," *Georgia Historical Quarterly* 77 (Spring 1993): 47. Richmond, Virginia, Jews also supported the Urban League and NAACP, and the local Anti-Defamation League sponsored workshops on integration. Thalhimer's department store, a flagship like Rich's, was a target for demonstrators but later integrated under pressure. See Berman, *Richmond's Jewry*, 317–18.

Some historians have argued that southern prejudice against blacks shielded Jews in the region from overt anti-Semitism. Harry Golden, for example, wrote, "To a great extent the deep concern of the Southerner over 'the Negro' serves as a shock absorber for the Jewish minority." Harry Golden, *Our Southern Landsman* (New York: G. P. Putnam's Sons, 1974), 101.

10. Seymour G. Bottigheimer, rabbi of Temple B'Nai Israel, the oldest synagogue in Mississippi, invited George Washington Carver to give a sermon. Beth Israel's Rabbi Judah Wechsler supported the building of the first public school for blacks in Meridian in 1888. The school was named in his honor. Jackson-born rabbi Julian Feibelman invited Ralph Bunche to speak at Temple Sinai in New Orleans on an integrated basis when no one else in the city would. Turitz and Turitz, *Jews in Early Mississippi*, 17, 100, 125. Rabbi Ehrenreich of Congregation Beth Or in Montgomery,

Alabama, held discussions with former Columbia University president and political reformer Seth Low and Julius Rosenwald, president of Sears Roebuck, in 1915 to gain financial support for Tuskegee Institute and black higher education in the South generally. Byron L. Sherwin, "Portrait of a Romantic Rebel: Bernard C. Ehrenreich (1876–1955)," in Kaganoff and Urofsky, *Turn to the South,* 8. Harry Golden observed, "In all of the larger Southern cities, there are always a few Jews, calling themselves liberals, for whom the 'racial problem' is a major concern. Together with like-minded Gentiles—Protestant clergymen, Unitarians, Quakers, labor-organizers, writers, artists, scientists (many of whom also occupy a marginal social position)—and even some members of the Jewish proprietary class, they have welded themselves into a small but cohesive, active minority. Often the membership in this group cuts across racial lines and in some cities represents the only direct line of communication between the white and Negro races. . . . Such a liberal group may just 'talk,' or it may expand into an Urban League or some other well-defined educational or political organization interested in integration. . . . [The] Southern Jewish proprietary class . . . have maintained a strict neutrality." Golden, "Jew and Gentile in the New South," *Commentary* (November 1955): 412.

Writing in 1949 about the contemporary scene, David and Adele Bernstein found that "most Richmond Jews fall into what is now clearly an American Jewish pattern of liberal behavior as far as Negroes are concerned. The most striking case of tangible advancement in Negro-white employment practices is being conducted quietly and effectively by a Jewish merchant (who feels that its value would be vitiated by public discussion in the present experimental stage)." Bernstein and Bernstein, "Slow Revolution in Richmond, Va.: A New Pattern in the Making," *Commentary* 8 (December 1949): 539–46, repr. in Leonard Dinnerstein and Mary Dale Palsson, eds., *Jews in the South* (Baton Rouge: Louisiana State University Press, 1973), 262. For the story of Emanuel J. "Mutt" Evans of Durham, North Carolina, a successful merchant in a small town who catered to black customers, see Evans, *Provincials,* ix, 5–6, 28. See also Carolyn Gray LeMaster, *A Corner of the Tapestry: A History of the Jewish Experience in Arkansas, 1820s–1990s* (Fayetteville: University of Arkansas Press, 1994); Natalie Ornish, *Pioneer Jewish Texans: Their Impact on Texas and American History for Four Hundred Years, 1590–1990* (Dallas: Texas Heritage Press, 1989); and Leonard Rogoff's article in this volume.

11. For symposia, see "The Rift Between Blacks and Jews," *Time,* 28 February 1994, 28–34; "Blacks and Jews: The Politics of Resentment," *Reform Judaism* (Fall 1994): 10–18. Books include Paul Berman, ed., *Blacks and Jews: Alliances and Arguments* (New York: Delacorte, 1994) and Murray Friedman, *What Went Wrong? The Creation and Collapse of the Black-Jewish Alliance* (New York: Free Press, 1994). The exhibit "Bridges and Boundaries: African Americans and American Jews" opened at New York's Jewish Museum in 1992 and was reviewed by Giles R. Wright in *Journal*

of American History 82 (June 1995): 148–53. For earlier works see Shlomo Katz, ed., *Jew and Negro: An Encounter in America* (New York: Macmillan, 1967); Nat Hentoff, ed., *Black Anti-Semitism and Jewish Racism* (New York: Richard W. Bacon, 1969); Joseph R. Washington, Jr., ed., *Jews in Black Perspective: A Dialogue* (London: Associated University Press for Fairleigh Dickinson University Press, 1984); Stephen Steinberg, "Blacks and Jews: The Politics of Memory," *New Politics* 3 (Winter 1991): 64–70. The debate even crossed the Atlantic. See Nancy L. Green, "Juifs et Noires aux Etats-Unis: La Rupture d'une 'Alliance Naturella,' " *Annales, E.S.C.* (Mars-Avril, 1987): 445–64. Other notable works treating black-Jewish relations include L. D. Reddick, "Anti-Semitism among Negroes," *Negro Quarterly* 1 (Summer 1942): 112–22; Eugene I. Bender, "Reflections on Negro-Jewish Relations: The Historical Dimension," *Phylon* 30 (Spring 1969); Max Geltman, *The Confrontation: Black Power, Anti-Semitism, and the Myth of Integration* (Englewood Cliffs, N.J.: Prentice-Hall, 1970); Joseph P. Weinberg, "Black-Jewish Tensions: Their Genesis," *Central Conference of American Rabbis Journal* [hereafter *CCAR Journal*] 21 (Spring 1974); Philip S. Foner, "Black-Jewish Relations in the Opening Years of the Twentieth Century," *CCAR Journal* 36 (December 1975): 359–67; Isabel Boiko Price, "Black Response to Anti-Semitism: Negroes and Jews in New York, 1880 to World War II," (Ph.D. diss., University of New Mexico, 1973); Nicholas C. Polos, "Black Anti-Semitism in Twentieth-Century America: Historical Myth or Reality?" *American Jewish Archives* 27 (1975); Leonard Dinnerstein, ed., *Antisemitism in the United States* (New York: Holt, Rinehart and Winston, 1971); idem, *Uneasy at Home: Antisemitism and the American Jewish Experience* (New York: Columbia University Press, 1987); idem, *Antisemitism in America* (New York: Oxford University Press, 1994), (see esp. chaps. 9 and 10 and pp. 312–13, n. 1, for a description of some of the early questions raised about the existence of an alliance); Robert G. Weisbord and Arthur Stein, *Bittersweet Encounter: The Afro-American and the American Jew* (Westport, Conn.: Negro University Presses, 1970); Hasia R. Diner, *In the Almost Promised Land: American Jews and Blacks* (Westport, Conn.: Greenwood, 1977); Jonathan Reider, *Canarsie: The Jews and Italians of Brooklyn against Liberalism* (Cambridge, Mass.: Harvard University Press, 1985); William M. Phillips, Jr., *An Unillustrious Alliance: African-American and Jewish American Communities* (New York: Greenwood, 1991); James A. Jahannes, *Blacks and Jews: A New Dialog* (Savannah: Savannah State College Press, 1983); Abraham J. Peck, ed., *Blacks and Jews: The American Experience, 1654–1987* (Cincinnati: American Jewish Archives, 1987); Jerald E. Podair, " 'White' Values, 'Black' Values: The Ocean Hill-Brownsville Controversy and New York City Culture," *Radical History Review* 59 (Spring 1994): 36–59; Lenwood G. Davis, *Black-Jewish Relations in the United States, 1752–1984: A Selected Bibliography* (Westport, Conn.: Greenwood, 1984). Broader studies providing additional insights include Harold Cruse, *The Crisis of the Negro Intellectual* (New York:

William Morrow, 1967); Harold E. Quigley and Charles Y. Glock, *Anti-Semitism in America* (New York: Free Press, 1979); Kenneth D. Wald, *Religion and Politics in the United States,* 2d ed. (Washington, D.C.: CQ Press, 1992), 321–27.

12. Krause, "Rabbis and Negro Rights in the South, 1954–1967," *American Jewish Archives* 21 (1969), repr. in Dinnerstein and Palsson, *Jews in the South,* 360–85 (all of the quotations below are from this article); P. Allen Krause. "The Southern Rabbi and Civil Rights" (rabbinical thesis, Hebrew Union College-Jewish Institute of Religion, 1967). Krause's arguments, a quarter of a century old, were well taken. In many ways, this anthology supports his analysis even as it modifies it in detail. See also the classic, albeit impressionistic, Evans, *Provincials.*

13. See also "American Jewry Divided on Strategy," *The Reconstructionist* 34 (November 22, 1968): 4.

14. Theodore Lowi, studying the pseudonymous "Iron City" [Gadsden], Alabama, like Krause, described "new Jews" in marked contrast with "old Jews": "Typically, the new Jew can be pushed to concede the inevitability of desegregation; the old Jew can only be pushed to anger. Not a man on either side would join or otherwise condone a White Citizens Council. . . . But an old Jew, regardless of age, will use the rhetoric of states' rights, of *Plessy v. Ferguson,* and if pushed, of race superiority and biblical sanction. The new Jew will not. The old Jew either bears no sense of guilt on the matter, or deeply represses it. The new Jew is distinguished by a concern with and an only poorly repressed sense of guilt about Negro problems. The old Jews will make the inevitable adjustment to integration more easily and more quickly than their white Christian brethren, but they will verbally support segregation to the end. New Jews are less likely to verbally support segregation but will never openly support integration." Lowi, "Southern Jews: The Two Communities," repr. in Dinnerstein and Palsson, *Jews in the South,* 265–82; see esp. 277 (quotation), 281.

   For Lowi, Gadsden's old Jews had little association with Jews elsewhere, such as those in Birmingham who had been bombed in 1958 and to whom these old Jews refused financial assistance.

15. In virtually every instance, the rabbis worked closely with members of the Catholic priesthood. Because priests were appointed and transferred by the church hierarchy instead of their congregations, they may have experienced greater independence from local mores than the rabbis. The existence of Catholic private schools may have been another important variable. To this author's knowledge, neither the role of this group on behalf of black civil rights nor the interplay between southern Catholics and Jews, two minorities exposed to prejudice, have been explored in depth. Studies touching on these issues include Stephen Ochs, *Desegregating the Altar: The Josephites and the Struggle for Black Priests* (Baton Rouge:

Louisiana State University Press, 1990); Dolores Egger Labbe, *Jim Crow Comes to Church* (New York: Arno, 1978); Thomas Stritch, *The Catholic Church in Tennessee* (Nashville: The Catholic Center, 1987); Cyprion Davis, *The History of Black Catholics in the United States* (New York: Crossroad, 1990); Michael J. McNally, *Catholicism in South Florida, 1868–1968* (Gainesville: University of Florida Press, 1984); idem, "A Peculiar Institution: A History of Catholic Parish Life in the Southeast (1850–1980)," in Jay P. Dolen, ed., *The American Catholic Parish* 1 (New York: Paulist Press, 1987), 117–234; Charles E. Nolen, "Modest and Humble Crosses: A History of Catholic Parishes in the South Central Region," ibid., 235–323. Randall M. Miller graciously brought several of these works to the author's attention.

16. In the introduction to the section on "Jews and Desegregation," the editors wrote, "There are southern Jews who protest segregation, but fear of reprisal has silenced many of them. . . . On occasion individual southern Jews, laymen and rabbis alike, have spoken out boldly on the injustices of segregation, but they constitute a small minority of southern Jewry." Dinnerstein and Palsson, *Jews in the South*, sec. 5, esp. 305–6.

17. Leonard Reissman, "The New Orleans Jewish Community," *Jewish Journal of Sociology* 4 (1962), repr. in Dinnerstein and Palsson, *Jews in the South*, 288–306, esp. 303. See also Jack Nelson, *Terror in the Night: The Klan's Campaign against the Jews* (New York: Simon and Schuster, 1993). Variation is a constant in southern Jewish history. As illustrated throughout this anthology, community after community can be described as "unique." Morris N. Kertzer wrote, "If there are ten kinds of American Jews, there are twenty types of Southern Jews." Kertzer, *Today's American Jews* (New York: McGraw-Hill, 1967), 265.

18. See also Murray Friedman, "One Episode in Southern Jewry's Response to Desegregation: An Historical Memoir," *American Jewish Archives* 33 (November 1981): 170–83; Morton J. Gaba, "Segregation and a Southern Jewish Community," *Jewish Frontier* 21 (October 1954): 12–15. A tiny Georgia Jewish community separated from the national Anti-Defamation League of B'nai B'rith when the community considered the position of the latter detrimental. James Lebeau, "Profile of a Southern Jewish Community: Waycross, Georgia," *American Jewish Historical Quarterly* 58 (June 1969): 429–44.

19. Like many others, Fishman found that the few open desegregationists, more intellectual and isolated, were discouraged in their activities. Fishman, "Southern City," *Midstream* 7 (September 1961): 39–56, repr. in Dinnerstein and Palsson, *Jews in the South*, 307–33. The rabbi that Fishman's respondents referred to was probably Benjamin Goldstein of Temple Beth Or. See Dinnerstein, "A Neglected Aspect of Southern Jewish History," *American Jewish Historical Quarterly*, repr. in Dinnerstein, *Un-*

easy at Home, 92, and Mark Cowett's article on Morris Newfield in this volume.

20. Vorspan, "The Dilemma of the Southern Jew," *Reconstructionist* 24 (9 January 1959); repr. in Dinnerstein and Palsson, *Jews in the South*, 334–50, esp. 335–37. Works on synagogue bombings include Arnold Shankman, "A Temple is Bombed–Atlanta, 1958," *American Jewish Archives* 23 (May 1971); Nathan Perlmutter, "Bombing in Miami: Anti-Semitism and the Segregationists," *Commentary* 25 (June 1958): 498–503. See also Nelson, *Terror in the Night*.

21. Friedman discovered that the fear was well founded. Emmet A. Frank, for example, became the target of hate groups when he denounced Senator Robert Byrd and the other leaders of massive resistance for damaging the United States far more than any illusory communist conspiracy. Friedman argued that Jews through history tended to suffer during times of crisis and that the best answer for all would be the peaceful acceptance of integration. Murray Friedman, "Virginia Jewry in the School Crisis: Anti-Semitism and Desegregation," *Commentary* 27 (January 1959): 17–22, repr. in Dinnerstein and Palsson, *Jews in the South*, 341–50.

22. Greene, *The Temple Bombing* (Reading, Mass.: Addison-Wesley, 1996).

23. Lavender, "Jewish Values in the Southern Milieu," in Kaganoff and Urofsky, *Turn to the South*, 133. Eli Evans made the same observation in *Provincials*, 310–11. John Sheldon Reed found a correlation between southern Jewish opinions and those of middle-class non-Jews outside of the region with reference to the election of 1968. Reed did not deal directly with attitudes toward civil rights. Reed, "Ethnicity in the South: Observations on the Acculturation of Southern Jews," in Kaganoff and Urofsky, *Turn to the South*, 135–42.

24. Killian, *White Southerners* (New York: Random House, 1970), 70, 88.

25. Ringer, "Jews and the Desegregation Crisis," in Charles Herbert Stember et al., eds., *Jews in the Mind of America* (New York: Basic Books, 1966), 199, 201–2.

26. Hero, *The Southerner and World Affairs* (Baton Rouge: Louisiana State University Press, 1965), 163, 216–17, 475, 478, 482–84. See also Hero, "Southern Jews and Public Policy," in Kaganoff and Urofsky, *Turn to the South*, 143–50, esp. 144, 147.

27. Dinnerstein, *Uneasy at Home*, 94–95.

28. Dinnerstein, "Southern Jewry and the Desegregation Crisis, 1954–1970," *American Jewish Historical Quarterly* 65 (March 1973), repr. in Dinnerstein, *Uneasy at Home*, 132–45.

 The issue of the small number of native southern rabbis is raised below, but it is also noteworthy that rabbis who migrated to the South had a strong tendency to remain in the region and with the same congregation for virtually their entire careers (often several decades). For example, Ira Sanders served B'nai Israel of Little Rock from 1926 to 1963, and Julian Feibelman was rabbi of New Orleans's Temple Sinai from 1935 to 1967. See Evans, *Provincials*, 97.

29. Dinnerstein, *Antisemitism in America*, 175.

30. St. John, *Jews, Justice and Judaism* (Garden City, N.Y.: Doubleday, 1969), 297; cf. Weisbord and Stein, *Bittersweet Encounter*, 136.

31. St. John, *Jews, Justice and Judaism*, 298–99, 301–2, 306–7.

32. In his 1967 thesis Krause treated only Reform rabbis partly because of the lack of information and also because "there are simply not many non-Reform rabbis in the South." Charles Mantinband, "Mississippi: The Magnolia State," cited in Krause, "Rabbis and Negro Rights," 360 n. 1, 383. Even the total number of rabbis in the region is hard to place in perspective. In Atlanta, one of the most dynamic, least-provincial cities with a "significant" number of Jews, David Marx was the only rabbi employed by a Reform congregation during his active tenure as was Jacob Rothschild, his successor. Harry Epstein was the only rabbi leading a Conservative congregation for any significant period until the late 1960s. Only two other congregations (both Orthodox) in the city had long-term rabbis until the World War II era when one Orthodox congregation was added.

   The Central Conference of American Rabbis, the major organization of Reform rabbis, publishes a yearbook that includes materials on the annual convention with a listing of members by state. This list and those cited in the two succeeding notes, although not necessarily totally inclusive (rabbis might not have been members or may have been overlooked), should be extremely close to the actual number. The 1955 volume itemizes the Reform rabbis as follows: Alabama: 8 (includes two for the Mobile congregation); Arkansas: 5; Florida: 15 (includes a Hillel rabbi in Gainesville, one rabbi with no affiliation in Sarasota, and a rabbi emeritus in Miami Beach); Georgia: 8 (includes a rabbi emeritus in Atlanta and one rabbi employed by a Conservative congregation as an assistant also in Atlanta); Kentucky: 5 (includes two rabbis for a Louisville congregation); Louisiana: 12 (includes two New Orleans congregations with two rabbis and a rabbi emeritus in the same city); Mississippi: 11 (includes two rabbis in a Meridian congregation and a rabbi emeritus in Natchez); North Carolina: 10 (includes a Hillel rabbi in Chapel Hill); South Carolina: 6 (includes a rabbi without affiliation in Walterboro); Tennessee: 7 (includes three rabbis for one Memphis congregation); Texas: 21 (includes two rabbis and one emeritus rabbi for one Dallas congregation and two rabbis for a Houston congregation); Virginia: 10 (includes two rabbis without affiliations in Roanoke).

   Where two rabbis were listed for one congregation it is likely that one was serving as an assistant. In contrast to the number of Reform rabbis in the South, sixty rabbis were listed for California, forty for Illinois, and sixty-six for New York. *Central Conference of American Rabbis Yearbook* [hereafter *CCAR Yearbook*], vol. 64, ed. Sidney L. Regner (Philadelphia: CCAR, 1955). Bernard H. Rabenstein, reference librarian, Hebrew Union College–Jewish Institute of Religion, graciously provided assistance with this citation.

Obviously some rabbis moved in and out of the region and pulpit, and the number could have changed from year to year. Yet there was substantial continuity in many southern pulpits, and the number of rabbis (with the possible exception of Florida) before the late 1960s may not have been that different from the mid-1950s. Thus the 1954–1955 calculations are likely fairly representative of the number at any one time during the height of the modern civil rights era.

Besides referring to the small number of southern rabbis involved in civil rights campaigns without reference to the total number of southern rabbis, critics have noted that the activists, for the most part, were not born in the South. Although this author has been unable to quantify the total number of southern rabbis actually born in the South, it is likely that this number would be extremely small. In 1979 Jack D. Spiro wrote, "With the exception of very few of us (and I'm one of the exceptions), most rabbis are not Southerners." Spiro, "Rabbi in the South: A Personal View," in Kaganoff and Urofsky, *Turn to the South*, 42.

33. The numbers of Conservative rabbis listed by state are as follows: Alabama: 3; Arkansas: 0; Florida: 9; Georgia: 4; Kentucky: 1; Mississippi: 1 (a chaplain); North Carolina: 5 (includes two chaplains); South Carolina: 4 (includes one chaplain); Tennessee: 3; Texas: 9 (includes two chaplains); Virginia: 11 (includes two chaplains). Illinois, by comparison, had twenty-eight, Connecticut fourteen. Minnesota, with six, surpassed all but three southern states. A copy of the 1954 list from the *Proceedings* of the Rabbinical Assembly of America, the major organization of Conservative rabbis, was graciously provided by Professor Pamela Nadell.

34. The numbers of Orthodox Rabbis by state are as follows: Alabama: 0; Arkansas: 0; Florida: 6 (includes one without affiliation and one Hebrew academy principal); Georgia: 4; Kentucky: 2; Louisiana: 4; Mississippi: 0; North Carolina: 1; South Carolina: 4 (includes one without affiliation); Tennessee: 6; Texas: 7; Virginia: 5. Connecticut and Michigan, with ten Orthodox rabbis each, surpassed all southern states, and Missouri, with seven, equaled the highest. A copy of the *Rabbinic Registry* supplement was provided by the Rabbinical Council of America. This list does not include chaplains.

35. Mark K. Bauman, *Harry H. Epstein and the Rabbinate as Conduit for Change* (London: Associated University Press for Fairleigh Dickinson University Press, 1994), 74–78.

36. Joel Yor, "Witness for Freedom," *United Synagogue Review* (Summer 1963): 1; Harriet Stern typescript (in possession of author). One of the few southern Conservative rabbinic statements published in the era is William S. Malev, "The Jew of the South in the Conflict on Segregation," *Conservative Judaism* 13 (Fall 1958): 35–46. Malev, rabbi of a large Houston congregation, advocated moderation and understanding for the plight of southern Jews.

37. The editors of this anthology attempted to include as representative a sample as possible. Several dozen scholars in the field were solicited directly for contributions, and a call for participation appeared in national professional journals. Articles were sought treating Orthodox and Conservative, East European and Sephardic rabbis, rabbis from all of the southern states and from small and large communities, and rabbis who spanned the spectrum from segregationist to silent observer to integrationist. That such inclusiveness could not be accomplished reflects the lack of information available and the relatively few individuals conducting research in the area.

38. Janice Rothschild Blumberg, *One Voice: Rabbi Jacob M. Rothschild and the Troubled South* (Macon: Mercer University Press, 1985) and Greene's *Temple Bombing* are exceptions.

39. This recognition of Wise is somewhat ironic in that he straddled the fence on the issue of slavery and the Civil War, whereas his chief rival for leadership of the midcentury Reform movement, David Einhorn, championed abolition. See Max J. Kohler, "The Jews and the American Anti-Slavery Movement," *American Jewish Historical Quarterly* 5 (1897): 137–55; Bertram W. Korn, *American Jewry and the Civil War* (Philadelphia: Jewish Publication Society, 1951); idem, "Jews and Negro Slavery in the Old South, 1789–1865," *American Jewish Historical Quarterly* 50 (March 1961): 151–201; Sefton D. Temkin, "Isaac Mayer Wise and the Civil War," *American Jewish Archives* 15 (1963): 120–42; Isaac M. Fein, *The Making of an American Jewish Community: The History of Baltimore Jewry from 1773–1920* (Philadelphia: Jewish Publication Society, 1971); idem, "Baltimore Jews During the Civil War," *American Jewish Historical Quarterly* 51 (December 1961): 67–96.

40. Dollinger's essay is based on his doctoral dissertation, "The Politics of Acculturation: American Jewish Liberalism, 1933–1975," (Ph.D. diss., UCLA, 1993).

41. Rothschild's colleagues mixed similar emotions with understanding. See James A. Wax, "The Attitude of the Jews in the South toward Segregation," *CCAR Journal* 26 (June 1959); Elijah E. Palnick, "Southern Jewry and Civil Rights," *CCAR Journal* 13 (June 1965); and the series of addresses and articles by Rabbi Charles Mantinband appended to Anna Kest Mantinband, "Time for Remembering," Charles Mantinband Papers,

1923–1968 (American Jewish Archives, Cincinnati, Ohio, bound typescript).

42. Heschel is considered one of the giants of twentieth-century American Jewish social justice. Southern rabbis operated differently than did Heschel, however, so it is hard to determine if his example would have been followed. The number of Orthodox and Conservative rabbis educated in Europe who might have had European mentors also remains unknown. See Heschel, *The Insecurity of Freedom* (1959; repr., New York: Schocken, 1972); idem, *To Grow in Wisdom: An Anthology of Abraham Joshua Heschel,* ed. Jacob Neusner with Noam M. M. Neusner (Lanham: Madison Books, 1990); for the theological background of his positions see idem, *God in Search of Man* (New York: Farrar, Straus and Cuhany, 1955); idem, *Man Is Not Alone* (1951; repr., New York: Harper and Row, 1966).

Rabbi Max Heller, Zionism, and the "Negro Question": New Orleans, 1891–1911

1. The literature on southern dissenters is large and includes: C. Vann Woodward, *The Strange Career of Jim Crow,* 3d ed. (New York: Oxford University Press, 1974), 31–65; Charles E. Wynes, ed., *Forgotten Voices: Dissenting Southerners in an Age of Conformity* (Baton Rouge: Louisiana State University Press, 1967); Morton Sosna, *In Search of the Silent South: Southern Liberals and the Race Issue* (New York: Columbia University Press, 1977); Carl Degler, *The Other South: Southern Dissenters in the Nineteenth Century* (New York: Harper and Row, 1974); Hugh C. Bailey, *Liberalism in the New South: Southern Social Reformers and the Progressive Movement* (Coral Gables: University of Miami Press, 1969), 17–50; Harold W. Mann, *Atticus Greene Haygood, Methodist Bishop, Editor, and Educator* (Athens: University of Georgia Press, 1965); Arlin Turner, *George Washington Cable, A Biography* (Baton Rouge: Louisiana State University Press, 1966), 223; George M. Fredrickson, *The Black Image in the White Mind: The Debate on Afro-American Character and Destiny, 1817–1914* (New York: Harper & Row, 1971), 204–20; Mark K. Bauman, "Race and Mastery: The Debate of 1903," *From the Old South to the New: Essays on the Transitional South,* ed. Walter J. Fraser, Jr., and Winfred B. Moore, Jr. (Westport, Conn.: Greenwood Press, 1981), 190, argues that the presence of dissent was no aberration but an indication that there existed "a multitude of minds of the South."

2. Although Heller never met Cable, the rabbi was familiar with his work. In the memoir of her childhood, Heller's youngest child, Ruth Heller Steiner, recalled that in their home library, she first encountered Cable's novels, which made a "deep impression" on her, although the "negro problem" played a relatively small part in her consciousness as she matured. She admitted that "along with all of white New Orleans, we accepted as a fact of life the unbelievably low estate of half of the city; even

in our family, more conscious than most of social injustice, it impinged but seldom, and then only in the general terms of Father's convictions that the south was not doing its duty. Mother's dapper old dad, an unreconstructed rebel who lived with us for some years before his death, used to drive Father into a red but firmly controlled rage by expressing such sentiments as 'show me a nigger and I'll show you a thief,' " Ruth Heller Steiner, "Glimpses through the Mist" (American Jewish Archives, February 1965, revised January 1982, typescript [photocopy]), 9–10.

3. The term "best men" comes from John G. Sproat, *"The Best Men": Liberal Reformers in the Gilded Age* (New York: Oxford University Press, 1968).

4. Gary B. Cohen, *The Politics of Ethnic Survival: Jews in German Society: Prague, 1860–1914* (Princeton: Princeton University Press, 1981), 22–23; Cohen, "Jews in German Society," *European History* 10 (1977): 32; Hillel Kieval, *The Making of Czech Jewry: National Conflict and Jewish Society in Bohemia, 1870–1918* (New York: Oxford University Press, 1988), 10; Joy Jackson, *New Orleans in the Gilded Age: Politics and Urban Progress, 1880–1896* (Baton Rouge: Louisiana State University Press, 1969), 17, noted that New Orleans differed from the northern cities of that era because in New Orleans the immigrant groups never totally dominated a specific area of the city and that "the general tendency was toward integration rather than clannishness." Temple Sinai's receptivity to the Americanized Reform movement indicated that the members were among the most assimilated and most prosperous of the city's Jews. On the eve of Heller's arrival, approximately 58 percent of Temple Sinai's families owned or were partners in businesses that prominently featured their families' names. Cotton claimed approximately one-fourth of the congregants as factors, commission merchants, buyers, or those engaged in some form of processing, while nearly a third of the members dealt in dry goods, clothing, or furnishing goods, both wholesale and retail. By the turn of the century, over a third of Temple Sinai's members frequented the Harmony Club, a social gathering spot for Jewish business elites. Among those who left records of their occupations, only three of the 133 Temple Sinai members who appeared at a meeting two months before Heller's election worked as laborers, while 90 percent engaged in some form of commerce. New Orleans served as the hub of an intricate network of wholesale transactions between urban suppliers and peddlers or country-store owners in a sparsely populated rural hinterland upriver in Louisiana and Mississippi. Jewish merchants in New Orleans played dominant roles as wholesalers, factors, or commission merchants, and Temple Sinai's members, active in all three areas, clustered their businesses in the heavily trafficked areas of the French Quarter and the central business and warehouse district close to the river. Elliott Ashkenazi, *The Business of Jews in Louisiana, 1840–1875* (Tuscaloosa: University of Alabama Press, 1988), chaps. 1 and 4; Temple Sinai membership list, 28 November

354

1886, taken from Temple Sinai minutes, Temple Sinai Collection, Special Collections, Howard-Tilton Library, Tulane University, New Orleans [hereafter TSC], then traced through the New Orleans City Directories, 1886–1887, to provide an impressionistic economic and demographic overview. The Harmony Club's membership undoubtedly claimed more Sinai members in 1899 who were not included in the 1886 list, Louis W. Marcott, comp., *Membership Roster of New Orleans Clubs, 1899* (New Orleans: D. J. Searcy-Wm. Pfaff, Printers, 1899), Louisiana Collection, Howard-Tilton Library, Tulane University [hereafter Louisiana Collection].

5. Malcolm H. Stern, "The Role of the Rabbi in the South," in *Turn to the South: Essays on Southern Jewry*, ed. Nathan M. Kaganoff and Melvin I. Urofsky (Charlottesville: University Press of Virginia for American Jewish Historical Society, 1979), 23–24, noted that as Jewish southerners built their congregations, they were intensely aware of *"Mah yomru hagoyim?" ("What will the Gentiles say?"), which remained a primary concern in the region until after the establishment of the state of Israel; American Israelite,* 10 September 1886; Max Heller, "Why So Much Money?" Bulletin of the Isaac M. Wise Memorial Fund (New Orleans: issued under the patronage of Julius Weis, 1901), Louisiana Collection.

6. Max Heller, "A National Problem," *American Israelite,* 17 March 1904.

7. Gary Zola, "Reform Judaism's Pioneer Zionist: Maximilian Heller," *American Jewish History* 4 (June 1984): 375–97.

8. In his introduction to *The Crucible of Race: Black-White Relations in the American South since Emancipation* (New York: Oxford University Press, 1984), Joel Williamson defines three distinct "mentalities" in the mind of the white South—liberals, conservatives, and radicals. Liberalism was strongest during the 1880s when its adherents believed that the South had not yet given the Negro a fair chance to "absorb white culture." Although few, liberals were "articulate, highly energetic, and conspicuous," 5–6.

9. Barbara S. Malone, "Reform and Dissent: The Americanization of Max Heller, 1860–1898" (master's thesis, Tulane University, 1990), chaps. 1–3, passim; *Encyclopedia Judaica,* vol. 6, s.v. "Bernhard Felsenthal," by Stephen D. Temkin; Abraham J. Karp, *Haven and Home: A History of Jews in America* (New York: Schocken Books, 1985), 84–85; Emma Felsenthal, *Bernhard Felsenthal, Teacher in Israel: Selections from his Writings with Biographical Sketch and Bibliography by His Daughter* (New York: Oxford University Press, 1924), 23.

10. Malone, "Reform and Dissent," 1, 59–68; *Encyclopedia Judaica,* vol. 7, s.v. "James Koppel Gutheim," by Bertram W. Korn; Max Heller, "James Koppel Gutheim, A Memorial Address," *Jewish Ledger,* 22 May 1896.

11. Barbara S. Malone, "Reform and Dissent," chaps. 1–4, passim.

12. *Times-Democrat*, 2–4, 8, 22, 24 January 1890; *American Israelite*, 30 January 1890; *Jewish Chronicle* (New Orleans), 17, 31 January 1890; John Higham, *Strangers in the Land: Patterns of American Nativism, 1860–1925* (New Brunswick, N.J.: Rutgers University Press, 1955), 92; the Louisiana whitecapping incidents antedate those that William F. Holmes analyzed in Mississippi and Alabama, but similar economic frustrations undoubtedly triggered the outbreak of violence in northern Louisiana, Holmes, "Whitecapping in Mississippi: Agrarian Violence in the Populist Era," *Mid-America* 15 (1973): 134–48; "Moonshiners and Whitecaps in Alabama, 1893," *Alabama Review* (January 1981): 31–49; "Whitecapping: Anti-Semitism in the Populist Era," *American Jewish Historical Quarterly* 58 (March 1974): 244–61.

13. Moses Rischin, *The Promised City: New York's Jews, 1870–1914* (Cambridge, Mass.: Harvard University Press, 1962; repr., 1977), 19–75, passim (page references are to repr. edition); Irving Aarin Mandel, "Attitude of the American Jewish Community toward East-European Immigration as Reflected in the Anglo-Jewish Press (1880–1890)," *American Jewish Archives* 3 (June 1950): 28, "What really troubled the American Jewish community was the proverbial pauper class. These might conceivably remain permanent wards of the charitable societies, depleting resources, filling the charitable institutions, and perhaps even inciting anti-Semitism. American Jewry was very sensitive on this score." Attitudes among the New Orleans Jewish establishment paralleled those discussed in Robert Rockaway's study, "Ethnic Conflict in an Urban Environment: The German and Russian Jew in Detroit, 1881–1914," *American Jewish Historical Quarterly* 60 (December 1970): 133–50; *Times-Democrat*, 17 March 1891; *American Israelite*, 9 April 1891. *Daily States* quoted in the *American Israelite*, 9 October 1890, 12 November 1891. The Jewish community was careful not to exacerbate resentment against the immigrants, disturb the balance of labor, or perpetuate negative Jewish stereotypes. According to the *Times-Democrat*, 9 November 1891, "The scarcity of factories here" raised questions for the local Jewish community. "There was decided opposition to bringing immigrants here and making peddlers of them." Caution was also necessary not to attract "an influx of refugees to this city."

14. *Jewish Ledger*, 26 March, 16 April 1897.

15. "The World's Verdict. Rabbi Heller Discusses the Dreyfus Trial and Decision," *Daily Picayune*, 10 September 1899.

16. Carl E. Schorske, *Fin-de-Siecle Vienna; Politics and Culture* (New York: Vintage Books, 1981), 146–58; Schorske's outstanding account of Herzl's "conversion" to Zionism and subsequent founding of the contemporary Zionist movement has been instrumental in helping shape my understanding of Heller's turn to Zionism.

17. *American Israelite,* 1888–1890, passim, 31 October, 7 November, 1889, 10 December 1890. As editor of the New Orleans *Jewish Ledger* in 1896–97, Heller wrote many columns chastising what he considered predominant negative tendencies among assimilated Jews: an overemphasis on material possessions and excessive concern in courting favorable opinion from non-Jews; Sermon notes, 12 January 1890, Box 9, Folder 1, Max Heller Papers, American Jewish Archives, Hebrew Union College, Cincinnati, Ohio [hereafter MHP]; Heller kept the related themes of antimaterialism and social justice alive in sermons and editorial columns throughout his career. Some later examples include: "The Minister and the Business Man," *Temple Sinai Pulpit,* 7 November 1902; "The Elements of Business Morality," *Temple Sinai Pulpit,* 14 November 1902; Yom Kippur sermon, *Picayune,* 19 September 1904; "Dedications and Their Lessons," *American Israelite,* 18 October 1906; Rosh Hashanah sermon, *Times-Democrat,* 26 September 1908.

18. See William Ivy Hair, *Bourbonism & Agrarian Protest: Louisiana Politics, 1877–1900* (Baton Rouge: Louisiana State University Press, 1969); J. Morgan Kousser, *The Shaping of Southern Politics: Suffrage Restriction and the Establishment of the One-Party South, 1880–1910* (New Haven: Yale University Press, 1974), 152–65.

19. *Biographical & Historical Memoirs of Louisiana,* Vol. I (Chicago: The Goodspeed Publishing Company, 1892; Baton Rouge: A Classic Series Reprint, Claitor's Publishing Division, 1975), 520; *The Convention of '98* (New Orleans: William E. Myers, Publisher, 1898), 12–16; Kruttschnitt's mother was Jewish, but he was not reared in the Jewish faith. A successful attorney, Kruttschnitt also served as president of the local school board. Kruttschnitt obituary, *Daily Picayune,* 17 April 1906; E. B. Kruttschnitt to Max Heller, 21, 24 February 1898, Box 3, Folder 14, MHP; *Times-Democrat,* 4–28 February, passim; Heller's opening prayer was on 28 February, mentioned in the paper, 1 March 1898.

20. Fredrickson, *The Black Image in the White Mind,* 228–82; Thomas Gossett, *Race: The History of an Idea in America* (Dallas: Southern Methodist University Press, 1963), 84–122, 144–75; Heller, "Modern Intolerance," *Times-Democrat,* 19 February, 1898; I. A. Newby, *Jim Crow's Defense: Anti-Negro Thought in America, 1900–1930* (Westport, Conn.: Greenwood Press, 1965), 7–13.

21. Max Heller, "Modern Intolerance"; Cable, "The Freedman's Case in Equity," 7.

22. William I. Thomas, "The Psychology of Race Prejudice," in *The Development of Segregationist Thought,* ed. I. A. Newby (Homewood, Ill.: The Dorsey Press, 1968), 42–43; Louis R. Harlan, "The Secret Life of Booker T. Washington," *Journal of Southern History* 37 (August 1971): 393–94; Williamson, 111–39.

23. Booker T. Washington, "Taking Advantage of our Disadvantages," *AME Church Review*, April 1894, in Louis R. Harlan, ed., *The Booker T. Washington Papers*, vol. 3, 1889–1895 (Urbana: University of Illinois Press, 1974), 408–11.

24. August Meier, "The Paradox of W. E. B. Du Bois," in *Negro Thought in America, 1880–1915: Racial Ideologies in the Age of Booker T. Washington* (Ann Arbor: University of Michigan Press, 1963; repr., 1966), 182–83 (page references are to repr. edition), 190–206; Elliott M. Rudwick, *W. E. B. Du Bois: Propagandist of the Negro Protest* (New York: Atheneum, 1968), 36–37.

25. I. A. Newby, *Jim Crow's Defense; Anti-Negro Thought in America, 1900–1930* (Westport, Conn.: Greenwood Press, 1965), 7–13.

26. Jonathan Sarna has studied the literature on the psychological dynamics underlying conversion and finds that, most often, an emotional crisis precedes the conversion. "Converts to Zionism in the American Reform Movement," 9 July 1990. Typewritten manuscript [photocopy], 6–7, in possession of Bobbie Malone.

27. William Ivy Hair, *Carnival of Fury: Robert Charles and the New Orleans Race Riot of 1900* (Baton Rouge: Louisiana State University Press, 1976), 95–97. Interestingly, the only white person who had anything at all good to say about Robert Charles, the black man whose desperate murder of New Orleans policemen instigated the riot, was Hyman Levy. Although Hair does not mention it, Levy, a Dryades Street merchant from whom Charles bought clothes, was most likely a Jew.

28. Zola, "Max Heller," 375–97.

29. "Speaks on Atonement; Rabbi Heller Talks at Temple Sinai," newspaper clipping, hand-dated, "T. D. Sept 25," Box 14, Folder 2, MHP. Although Heller did not write the year on the clipping, the language and the incidents cited indicate that the sermon dated from the turn of the century; Open Letter Club postcards, George Washington Cable Collection, Box 125, SCHTL; Turner, *George Washington Cable*, 263–73, quote 264; Williamson, *Crucible of Race*, 104–7; Morton Sosna mentions that although Haygood, unlike Cable, refrained from attacking segregation, "he did argue that the debate over social equality was irrelevant" and maintained that black suffrage was just, *In Search of the Silent South*, 7.

30. "Scientific charity," as Roy Lubove describes in *The Professional Altruist* (Cambridge, Mass.: Harvard University Press, 1965), 6–7, had made its debut in the 1880s, raising the ideals of efficiency and organization over compassion. Heller's nemesis in this arena was Rev. I. L. Leucht, rabbi of Touro Synagogue in New Orleans and the chairman for the Committee on Charity and Relief for Touro Infirmary-Hebrew Benevolent Association, the institution responsible for the majority of aid to the indigent and immigrant Jews. Heller disagreed with Leucht's condescending treatment

of all those needing aid, Bobbie Malone, "Standing 'Unswayed in the Storm': Rabbi Max Heller, Reform and Zionism in the American South, 1860–1929" (Ph.D. diss., Tulane University, 1994), 66–69, 88–91, 158–71.

31. A *schlemiel,* or "Shlemihl" in Heller's phonetic spelling, is a Yiddish word for a "clumsy bungler" or fool, Fred Kogos, *A Dictionary of Yiddish Slang & Idioms* (New York: Paperback Library, 1967), 66; Clipping, "For a Community of Interest," *Jewish Daily News,* 25 August 1901, Box 15, Folder 2, MHP.

32. Francis G. Gaffey to Max Heller, 31 March 1900, MHP.

33. Fredrickson, *The Black Image in the White Mind,* 283–85, identifies the white moderate search for "interracial harmony and accommodation" as "accommodationist racism," a reaction against the "brutality" of the Darwinian racial extremists, and he sees these moderate Progressives as the natural heirs of the 1880s "paternalists" like Atticus Haygood.

34. In this passage and the following one, Heller is referring to social separation only in terms of intimate interpersonal relations, that is, interracial marriage. Elsewhere, he opposed intermarriage between Jews and Gentiles. His advocacy of "racial" separation was consistent, although such separation was voluntary only in the instance of Jewish-Gentile intermarriage.

35. Murphy quoted by Hugh C. Bailey, *Edgar Gardner Murphy, Gentle Progressive* (Coral Gables, Fla.: University of Miami Press, 1968), 59–61; Max Heller, "A National Problem," *American Israelite,* 17 March 1904.

36. Edgar Gardner Murphy, *The Present South* (New York: The Macmillan Company, 1904), 160–61; Max Heller, "A National Problem." The closest evidence that exists concerning Heller's attitude toward segregation is a letter that Louis Marshall, a national Jewish leader, wrote to Heller the following year. Marshall stated that he did not take "so hopeless a view of the future" as Heller, that he felt "the idea of segregation and autonomy" to be both "impracticable and contrary to the logic of historical development," Louis Marshall to Max Heller, 28 February 1905, Box 4, Folder 5, MHP. Whether Marshall was responding to Heller's fears about, or acceptance of, segregation, at this point, remains unclear.

37. Bailey, *Edgar Gardner Murphy,* 39; "Temple Sinai Holds a Touching Service," *Daily Picayune,* 20 September, 1901.

38. Edward Barnes to Max Heller, 21 September 1901, Box 1, Folder 4, MHP.

39. *Times-Democrat,* 9, 12 November 1904.

40. "The Negro Scholar and Gentleman," *Times-Democrat,* 17, 21 November 1904; "The Point of View," two newspaper clippings, unidentified [*Times-Democrat?*].

41. Louis R. Harlan, "Booker T. Washington's Discovery of the Jews," in *Booker T. Washington in Perspective: Essays of Louis R. Harlan*, Raymond W. Smock, ed. (Jackson: University Press of Mississippi, 1988), 154. Harlan also mentioned that Tuskegee's major white supporters in Alabama were Jews and that as early as 1905 a rabbi delivered the commencement address, 155–56.

42. "An Impudent Nigger," *Jewish Ledger*, 22 September 1905. While spending the summer of 1905 in Colorado, Heller wrote Stolz that he was reviewing *The Color Line*, a work by Tulane philosophy professor Benjamin Smith. Heller considered Smith one of the "broadest and deepest" scholars he had met, yet he never again referred to the work, a sustained polemic for white supremacy, Max Heller to Joseph Stolz, 18 July 1905, Box 8, Folder 7, MHP. In William Benjamin Smith's foreword to *The Color Line: A Brief in Behalf of the Unborn* (New York: McClure, Phillips & Co., 1905), x–xi, he states clearly that he is setting out to prove the "assumed inferiority of both the Negro and Negroid" and to refute the notion that this inferiority is "merely cultural and removable by Education of other extra-organic means." Their differing opinions on the racial question did not prevent Heller from enjoying Smith's friendship. When Smith retired from Tulane in 1915, Heller, who by then had been teaching Hebrew at the university for several years, chaired the resolution committee that paid tribute to Smith's career, Max Heller to R. K. Bruff, 6 November 1925; Max Heller to William Benjamin Smith, 10 November 1915, University Archives, SCHTL; on Thomas Dixon, see Fredrickson, 280.

43. "How to Meet Prejudice; An Interesting Sermon by Rabbi Max Heller," *Times-Democrat*, 16 February 1907; "Impressive Ceremonies Mark Eve of Atonement," *Times-Democrat*, 5 October 1908; Frances Joseph-Gaudet, New Orleans, to Max Heller, New Orleans, 11 October 1908, Letter signed, Box 2, Folder 16, MHP.

44. Max Heller, "Abraham Lincoln," *American Israelite*, 11 February 1909.

45. Max Heller, "Atonement Eve Address," *American Israelite*, 16 September 1909.

46. "Dr. Heller on 'Christmas Confusion'; The Doll and Toy Distribution," *Times-Democrat*, 30 December 1909.

47. "A Criticism of the Doll and Toy Fund," *Times-Democrat*, 30 December 1909.

48. "Dr. Heller's Position," *Times-Democrat*, 31 December 1909.

49. W. E. Myers, *The Israelites of Louisiana* (New Orleans: W. E. Myers, [1905?]), 83; interview with Bill Rosen, great-grandson of I. L. Leucht, New Orleans, April 1990; Malone, "Standing 'Unswayed,' " chap. 2–epilogue, passim; "Dr. Heller's Views," *Times-Democrat*, 1 January 1910.

50. "Rabbi Heller's Letter," *Times-Democrat*, 1 January 1910; "Another Letter from Rabbi Heller," *Times-Democrat*, 5 January 1910. The *Times-Democrat* was correct in its estimation of prevailing Jewish opinion. The *Jewish Ledger* roundly criticized Heller as well, 7 January 1910.

51. Valcour Chapman to Max Heller, 5 January 1910, Box 1, Folder 14, MHP. See also A. R. Perkins to Max Heller, 4, 5, 9 January 1901, Box 4, Folder 17, MHP; J. W. Hawthorn to Max Heller, 8 January 1910, Box 3, Folder 1, MHP.

52. *Times-Democrat*, 13 February 1911; *Daily Picayune*, 13 February 1911, clippings from scrapbooks, MHP; *Jewish Ledger*, 17 February 1911. Along with Heller, Central Congregational Church's guest speakers during 1910–1911 included W. E. B. Du Bois and Professor James H. Dillard, president of the Jeanes Fund and director of the Slater Fund, Central Congregational Church notes, Historical Events Notebook, Central Congregational Church of New Orleans records, Amistad Research Center, Tulane University.

53. *Times-Democrat*, 13 February 1911, *Daily Picayune*, 13 February 1911, clippings from scrapbooks, Box 15, Folder 5, MHP.

54. *Times-Democrat*, 13 February 1911; Meier, "The Paradox of W. E. B. Du Bois," 182–83; W. E. B. Du Bois, "Racial Prejudice," *Crisis*, 1 (April 1911): 6; Max Heller, "Manliness versus Prejudice," *American Missionary* (April 1911: 859–62).

55. Max Heller, "Manliness versus Prejudice," *American Missionary* (April 1911): 862.

Morris Newfield, Alabama, and Blacks, 1895–1940

1. See Mark Cowett, *Birmingham's Rabbi: Morris Newfield and Alabama, 1895–1940* (University: University of Alabama Press, 1986), chap. 1, passim.

2. Ibid., 7.

3. Ibid., 11–14.

4. Ibid., chap. 5, passim.

5. Ibid., 110–18.

6. Ibid., 21–28, 186.

7. Ibid., chap. 3, passim; Mayer U. Newfield, interviews by author, September 1979, March 1983.

8. Mark H. Elovitz, *A Century of Jewish Life in Dixie: The Birmingham Experience* (University: University of Alabama Press, 1974), 77, 118–19; Minute Books of the Community Chest, 1932; and Mayer U. Newfield, interview by author, Birmingham, Ala., 1979.

9. Cowett, *Birmingham's Rabbi*, chap. 2, passim.

10. See Thomas D. Parke, diaries, 1895–1923, Department of Archives and Manuscripts, Birmingham Public Library (entries for 15 April 1917, 30 September 1920, and 26 March 1917); Wayne Flynt, "Religion in the Urban South: The Divided Mind of Birmingham, 1900–1930," *Alabama Review* 30 (April 1977): 108–35; and "Religious Forum: Talk of Newfield, Edmonds, and Father Sands," n.d., in author's files.

11. See Cowett, *Birmingham's Rabbi*, chap. 6, passim.

12. See Blaine A. Brownell, "Birmingham: New South City in the 1920's," *Journal of Southern History* 38 (February 1972): 28–30.

13. See Wayne Flynt, "Organized Labor, Reform, and Alabama Politics, 1920" *Alabama Review* 23 (July 1970): 163–81; Philip Taft, "Labor Organization in Coal Fields," incomplete manuscript, Department of Archives and Manuscripts, Birmingham Public Library; and Malcolm C. McMillan, *Yesterday's Birmingham* (Coral Gables: E. A. Seeman, 1975), 38, 147.

14. Brownell, "Birmingham: New South City in the 1920's," 26–28.

15. Ibid., 30–33; and Virginia Van der Veer Hamilton, *Alabama: A Bicentennial History* (New York: W. W. Norton, 1977), 134.

16. David Chalmers, *Hooded Americanism: The History of the Ku Klux Klan* (New York: Franklin Watts, 1981), 8–21; William R. Snell, "The Klan in Jefferson County" (master's thesis, Samford University, 1967), 8; Kenneth Jackson, *The Ku Klux Klan in the City* (New York: Oxford University Press, 1967); and "Twice City Met, Beat Klan Down," *Birmingham News*, 19 December 1971.

17. George Tindall, *The Emergence of the New South, 1913–45* (Baton Rouge: Louisiana State University Press, 1967), 330; also see Irving Bernstein, *The Lean Years: A History of the American Worker, 1920–1933* (Boston: Houghton Mifflin, 1960).

18. James A. Head, Sr., interview by author, September 1979; Morris Newfield, "The Claims of Religion," *Birmingham Age-Herald*, 28 March 1920, and "A Matter of Conscience," undated clipping in *Birmingham Age-Herald;* Henry M. Edmonds, "Good Morning," *Birmingham Post-Herald,* 13 May 1960, copy in Edmonds Collection, Department of Archives and Manuscripts, Birmingham Public Library; "Religious Forum: Talk of Newfield, Edmonds, and Father Sands," n.d., in author's files.

19. See Newfield, "The Claims of Religion."

20. James A. Head, Sr., interview; and "Harry Mell Ayres," autobiographical sketch in Harry M. Ayres Collection, William Stanley Hoole Special Collections Library, University of Alabama Library, Tuscaloosa.

21. Mayer U. Newfield, interview, September 1979; and Henry M. Edmonds, "Beau Geste," *Birmingham Post-Herald*, n.d., Edmonds Collection, Department of Archives and Manuscripts, Birmingham Public Library.

22. Mayer U. Newfield, interview, September 1979.

23. Morris Newfield, "Industrial Relations," n.d., sermon delivered at Temple Emanu-El, in Newfield Collection, American Jewish Archives (hereafter AJA), Hebrew Union College, Cincinnati, Ohio.

24. Ibid.; "Federation of Nations," January 1919, and "Labels and Libels," n.d., located at AJA.

25. Morris Newfield to Edward L. Israel, April 1933, CCAR Collection, AJA. See also Jacob R. Marcus, interview by author, July 1981.

26. Simon Wampold to Edward L. Israel, 27 April 1933, CCAR Collection, AJA.

27. Morris Newfield to Samuel H. Goldenson, 21 July 1933, CCAR Collection, AJA.

28. See Dan T. Carter, *Scottsboro: A Tragedy of the American South* (New York: Oxford University Press, 1969), passim.

29. See Robert P. Ingalls, "Antiradical Violence in Birmingham in the 1930's," *Journal of Southern History* 47 (November 1981): 521–25; Mayer U. Newfield, interview by author, Birmingham, Ala., November 1980; and Buddy Cooper, interview by author, September 1979. Also see Carter, *Scottsboro.*

A Plea for Tolerance: Fineshriber in Memphis

This article is a revision of "Rabbi William H. Fineshriber: The Memphis Years," *West Tennessee Historical Society Papers* 25 (1971): 47–62.

1. Gerald M. Capers, *The Biography of a River Town: Memphis, Its Heroic Age* (Chapel Hill: University of North Carolina Press, 1939), 31.

2. Roger Biles, *Memphis in the Great Depression* (Knoxville: University of Tennessee Press, 1986), 14–16.

3. Ibid., 19.

4. Ibid., 18.

5. Robert A. Lanier, *Memphis in the Twenties: The Second Term of Mayor Rowlett Paine, 1924–1928* (Memphis: Zenda Press, 1979), 21.

6. John E. Harkins, *Metropolis of the American Nile: Memphis and Shelby County* (Woodland Hills, Calif.: Windsor Publications, Inc.), 126–27.

7. Berkley Kalin, "Art in the Sahara of the Bozarts: Culture Comes to Memphis," *Border States* (July 1974): 11–12.

8. In 1943 the congregation changed its name to Temple Israel. James A. Wax and Helen G. Wax, *Our First Century, 1854–1954* (Memphis: n.p., 1954), 52.

9. Babette Becker, "William Fineshriber," *The Papyrus*, 16 May 1924, 1.

10. *Commercial Appeal,* 18 November 1911.

11. Undated clipping of *Memphis Press* featured interview, headlined "Your Neighbors," Fineshriber folder, Mississippi Valley Archives Collection, University of Memphis (hereafter cited as MVC).

12. *Commercial Appeal,* 7 April 1921; also see "The Crucifixion: Who is to Blame?" (a sermon by Fineshriber), undated, MVC.

13. Interview of Mr. and Mrs. Abe D. Waldauer by author for the University of Memphis Oral History Office, 11 February 1968, MVC.

14. Interview of Rabbi William Fineshriber by author, Philadelphia, 1 December 1968, MVC. Mrs. Kurt Blum, Fineshriber's "adopted daughter," was present and assisted. Dr. Fineshriber died six weeks after the interview. Jacob Jacobson, *A Man Who Walked Humbly with God: 50 Years in the Rabbinate* (Philadelphia: n.p., 1950), 1–10. MVC.

15. Jacobson, 9.

16. Ibid., 10.

17. Floyd Dell, *Homecoming: An Autobiography* (New York: Farrar and Rineholt, 1933, 1961, 1969), 170.

18. Floyd Dell, *Moon-Calf* (New York: Sagamore Press, 1920), 248.

19. Ibid., 254–56.

20. Ibid., 253; Floyd Dell, *Looking at Life* (New York: A. A. Knopf, 1924). See also *Commercial Appeal,* 20 April 1924; book review headlined "Author Snickers at World," undated *Memphis Press* clipping; letters from Dell to Fineshriber. Poems by Dell dedicated to Fineshriber. Fineshriber folder, MVC. There are additional letters to Fineshriber and poems dedicated to Fineshriber in the American Jewish Archives (hereafter AJA).

21. Susan Glaspell, *The Road to the Temple* (New York: Frederick A. Stokes and Co., 1927), 137.

22. Minutes of the Board of Trustees. Children of Israel, 1885–1924. Entry for Fineshriber's resignation dates 10 April 1924.

23. *Commercial Appeal,* 29 September 1915.

24. The writer was fortunate to hear a recording of Fineshriber's high holiday sermon, delivered in October of 1950, when Fineshriber was seventy-two.

25. Interview by author for the University of Memphis Oral History Office, 8 November 1968. It is now a part of the MVC. Rabbi Feibelman served as Rabbi Fineshriber's assistant from 1926 to 1936. He later became rabbi of Temple Sinai, New Orleans, Louisiana.

26. Grace Elizabeth Prescott, "The Woman Suffrage Movement in Memphis: Its Place in the State, Sectional, and National Movements" (master's thesis, University of Memphis, 1963), 104–5.

27. Ibid., 92.

28. *News-Scimitar,* 20 October 1913.

29. Prescott, 106.

30. *Commercial Appeal,* 26 April 1914.

31. *Philadelphia Inquirer,* 9 November 1924.

32. *Commercial Appeal,* 14 December 1927.

33. David M. Tucker, *Memphis since Crump: Bossism, Blacks, and Civic Reformers, 1948–1968* (Knoxville: University of Tennessee Press, 1980), 14.

34. Tucker, *Memphis since Crump,* 14–18.

35. Harkins, 125.

36. David M. Tucker, *Black Pastors and Leaders* (Memphis: Memphis State University Press, 1975), 54.

37. Tucker, *Black Pastors and Leaders,* 52.

38. Ibid., 102.

39. Kenneth T. Jackson, *The Ku Klux Klan in the City, 1915–1930* (New York: Oxford University Press, 1967), 45.

40. *News-Scimitar,* 12 May 1917.

41. Fineshriber, interview, 1 December 1968.

42. *Commercial Appeal,* 15–25 May 1917. Also discussed in William D. Miller, *Memphis During the Progressive Era, 1900–1917* (Memphis: Memphis State University Press, 1957), 194.

43. *News-Scimitar,* 24 May 1917.

44. Ibid.

45. *Philadelphia Magazine,* October 1950.

46. *Commercial Appeal,* 25 May 1917.

47. Jackson, 46.

48. *Commercial Appeal,* 3 April 1922; clipping from *Memphis Press,* 3 December 1923. Fineshriber spoke out against Hugo Black's appointment to the Supreme Court in 1937. (Several clippings from the *Philadelphia Inquirer,* labeled October 1937, are in the Fineshriber file of the AJA.)

49. Fineshriber, interview, 1 December 1968.

50. *Commercial Appeal,* 12 October 1921; 16 October 1921.

51. Jackson, 47.

52. *Commercial Appeal,* 1 November 1953.

53. Ibid., 17 May 1924.

54. Announcement of event, Fineshriber file, AJA; *News-Scimitar,* 10 December 1923.

55. *Commercial Appeal,* 7 October 1921.

56. Ibid., 21 February 1922.

57. Ibid., 6 September 1923; the *Paducah Evening Sun,* 19 November 1923; *Forrest City Times-Herald,* 29 November 1923; *Shreveport Times,* 2 April 1924.

58. Waldauer, interview by author, 11 February 1968, MVC; *Commercial Appeal,* 15 April 1923, 25 April 1923, 22 April 1924, 30 April 1924, 16 July 1924; *News-Scimitar,* 25 April 1924.

59. "The Egyptians," *Constitution and Bi-Laws,* 1911, copy on file, MVC.

60. Copies of newsletter, AJA and MVC.

61. *Commercial Appeal,* 4 March 1922, 21 March 1922, 10 April 1922, 23 April 1923, 11 March 1924; *Jewish Exponent,* April 1924.

62. *News-Scimitar,* 30 March 1924.

63. *Commercial Appeal,* 23 October 1921, 1 January 1922, 19 March 1922, 30 March 1922, 1 April 1922, 8 April 1922, 22 April 1924, 25 April 1924, 16 July 1924; *Memphis Press,* 15 March 1922; *News-Scimitar,* 19 April 1924; *Nashville Banner,* 22 April 1924; *Chicago American,* 19 May 1919; *Chicago Tribune,* 17 May 1919; *Chicago News,* 19 May 1919; *Chicago Post,* 17 May 1919; *Chicago Examiner,* 17 May 1919; undated clippings from *Commercial Appeal* headlined " 'Liliom' Offers Subject for Enlightenment Talk," "Tolstoy Lecture Well-Received," and " 'Back to Methuselah' Finely Interpreted," Fineshriber folder, MVC; Minutes, Congregation Children of Israel, 2 June 1918, 6 June 1920. Interview of Mrs. Abe S. Goldsmith of Helena, Arkansas, by the author for University of Memphis Oral History Office, 29 June 1968, MVC. *The Jewish Spectator: Jewish Progress and Development in the South,* In Memoriam Max Samfield (Memphis, 1915), Thirtieth Anniversary Number 84. *The Jewish Spectator* was a journal of Jewish life and culture in the South. It was founded by Rabbi Max Samfield, Congregation Children of Israel. The first issue appeared 19 October 1885. There is only one copy of one issue extant. Xeroxed copy available, MVC.

64. *News-Scimitar,* 30 March 1924.

65. *Commercial Appeal,* 11 March 1924; see also 4 April 1924; *News-Scimitar,* 30 March 1924.

66. *Memphis Press,* 28 July 1924; the announcement of the event appeared in the *News-Scimitar,* 25 July 1924.

67. *New York Herald-Times,* 12 August 1924.

68. *Memphis Press,* undated clipping, Fineshriber folder, MVC.

69. Undated clipping, *Philadelphia Inquirer,* headlined "Rabbi Fineshriber Hits Segregations," Fineshriber folder, MVC.

70. Undated clipping, *Commercial Appeal,* headlined "Blue Laws 'Damnable,' " Fineshriber folder, MVC.

71. Undated clipping, *Memphis Press,* featured interview, headlined "Your Neighbors," Fineshriber folder, MVC.

72. *Press-Scimitar,* 23 June 1927.

73. *Press-Scimitar,* 30 March 1924.

"Hamans" and "Torquemadas": Southern and Northern Jewish Responses to the Civil Rights Movement, 1945–1965

1. Winograd, "Birmingham: A Personal Statement," 1963, p. 1, Miscellaneous File, Desegregation, American Jewish Archives (hereafter AJA), Cincinnati, Ohio. For a similar account, see Rabbi Andre Ungar of Temple Emanuel, Westwood, New Jersey, "To Birmingham and Back," in *Conservative Judaism* 18 (Fall 1963): 1–17.

2. Winograd, "Birmingham: A Personal Statement," 1.

3. Alfred O. Hero, Jr., "Southern Jews, Race Relations, and Foreign Policy," *Jewish Social Studies* 27 (October 1965): 216.

4. Defining the Jewish community has always been a challenge to historians. Studies that focus on the national Jewish leadership risk losing the subtle nuances of local community politics. Examinations of local Jews create demographic problems as researchers struggle to determine who qualifies as "Jewish." In this chapter the American Jewish community has been defined along organizational lines. By studying national organizations, their regional and local constituent groups, as well as the Jewish community's rabbinic and lay leadership, historians can sample reactions from the most vocal, organized, and influential cross section of American Jews.

5. See John Higham, *Send These to Me: Immigrants in Urban America* (Baltimore: Johns Hopkins University Press, 1984), esp. chaps. five, six, and seven.

6. Allen Krause, "The Southern Rabbi and Civil Rights" (rabbinic thesis, Hebrew Union College-Jewish Institute of Religion, 1967), 26. *World Almanac,* 1964, 261, cited in Krause, "The Southern Rabbi and Civil Rights," 20. Norfolk had 8,500 Jews out of 305,000 residents. In Jackson 150 Jewish families resided in a total population of 147,000. New Orleans boasted 10,000 Jews among an overall population of 627,000. See Krause, "The Southern Rabbi and Civil Rights," 18, 16–17, Leonard Reissman, "The New Orleans Jewish Community," *The Jewish Journal of Sociology* 4 (June 1962): 112.

7. While a sizable number of northern Jews migrated south in the years after World War II, they settled almost exclusively in more urban centers and remained far more liberal on race issues. A mail survey of Roanoke, Virginia, Jews revealed that more than 70 percent favored the *Brown* decision. Although these Jewish families enjoyed the protection of stronger communal organizations in the South's major cities, they remained susceptible to the overbearing power of the segregationists around them. Lawrence H. Fuchs, *The Political Behavior of American Jews* (Glencoe, Ill.: The Free Press, 1956), 108; Theodore Lowi, "Southern Jews: The Two Communities," *Jewish Journal of Sociology* 6 (July 1964). Even so, the postwar migration did little to change the character even of the South's larger centers. As late as 1958 a survey revealed that in New Orleans only 11 percent of the Jewish population had lived in the city for less than ten years. See Leonard Reissman, "The New Orleans Jewish Community," *The Jewish Journal of Sociology* 4 (June 1962): 113, cited in Krause, "The Southern Rabbi and Civil Rights," 12. Krause, "The Southern Rabbi and Civil Rights," 16–17. Alfred Hero, Jr., *The Southerner and World Affairs* (Baton Rouge: Louisiana State University Press, 1965), 490, cited in Krause, "The Southern Rabbi and Civil Rights," 17. Krause, "The Southern Rabbi and Civil Rights," 23, 24. *Jackson State Times*, Jackson, Mississippi, 24 October 1958, cited in Allen Krause, "The Southern Rabbi and Civil Rights," 17.

8. In a survey conducted between 1939 and 1946, Charles Herbert Stember reported that "southerners ranked lowest in anti-Semitic responses to six of nine questions," Charles Herbert Stember, *Jews in the Mind of America* (New York: Basic Books, 1966), 390. Most radical hate groups in the South included anti-Semitism in their rhetoric but rarely translated their words into action; see Arnold Shankman, "A Temple Is Bombed–Atlanta, 1958," *American Jewish Archives* 23 (November 1971). Leonard Dinnerstein and Mary Dale Palsson, editors, *Jews in the South* (Baton Rouge: Louisiana State University Press, 1973), 374.

9. Shankman, "A Temple Is Bombed–Atlanta, 1958." Gordon Gladstone, "Anti-Jewish Bombing Outrages in the United States, 1959–1970," unpublished paper, 1971, Box Number 518, AJA, Cincinnati, Ohio, 1–7. For the rabbi, King's critique of store owners implied deeper meaning. Grafman recalled, "I told him that in the city of Birmingham, when you talked about 'merchants' you might as well use the word 'Jew' and that there was certainly implied anti-Semitism here." Krause, "The Southern Rabbi and Civil Rights," 85.

10. Isaac Toubin, "Recklessness or Responsibility," *Southern Israelite*, 27 February 1959, 13–15, cited in Arnold Shankman, "A Temple Is Bombed–Atlanta, 1958." James A. Wax, "The Attitude of the Jews in the South

toward Integration," *CCAR Journal* 26 (June 1959): 18, cited in Krause, "The Southern Rabbi and Civil Rights."

11. Aaron Henry to Allen Krause, 22 July 1966, cited in Krause, "The Southern Rabbi and Civil Rights," 47. Fred Shuttlesworth to Allen Krause, Krause, "The Southern Rabbi and Civil Rights," 45–46. For King quotation see Krause, "The Southern Rabbi and Civil Rights, Part Two," unpublished paper, 1967, Box Number 1747, AJA, 309.

12. Alfred Hero, Jr., *The Southerner and World Affairs*, 490, cited in Krause, "The Southern Rabbi and Civil Rights," 17. Krause, "The Southern Rabbi and Civil Rights," 23, 24. *Jackson State Times*, Jackson, Mississippi, 24 October 1958, cited in Krause, "The Southern Rabbi and Civil Rights," 17.

13. Much of the material on southern rabbis has been gleaned from the rabbinic thesis notes of Allen Krause. Krause, a student at Hebrew Union College–Jewish Institute of Religion, Cincinnati, in 1967, researched and interviewed scores of Reform rabbis in the South. The timeliness of his interviews provides scholars with one of the few contemporary oral histories available on the subject of southern rabbis and civil rights. In order to protect his subjects from possible reprisals and to guarantee the highest possible level of candor, Krause agreed to restrict all scholarly access to his notes until the political climate changed. With the permission of Rabbi Krause and the director of the American Jewish Archives, Krause's confidential notes were released, for the first time, to the author. Notes from this section of the Krause thesis are listed as, "Krause, 'The Southern Rabbi and Civil Rights, Part Two.' " Krause, "The Southern Rabbi and Civil Rights," 145. Krause, "The Southern Rabbi and Civil Rights, Part Two," 317. Malcolm Stern, "Role of the Rabbi in the South," Nathan M. Kaganoff and Melvin I. Urofsky, editors, *Turn to the South: Essays on Southern Jewry* (Charlottesville: University Press of Virginia, 1979), 31.

14. Krause, "The Southern Rabbi and Civil Rights," 63, 62.

15. William S. Malev, "The Jew of the South in the Conflict of Segregation," *Conservative Judaism* 13 (Fall 1958): 36. Krause, "The Southern Rabbi and Civil Rights," 69–70, 78.

16. Malev, "The Jew of the South in the Conflict of Segregation," 39. In Birmingham, Rabbi Grafman acknowledged the need for desegregation but held firm to his conviction that integration should not be forced; see Krause, "The Southern Rabbi and Civil Rights," 82.

17. Malev, "The Jew of the South in the Conflict of Segregation," 39.

18. Ibid., 36–37.

19. Krause, "The Southern Rabbi and Civil Rights," 79.

20. Irene Paull, "My Grandfather's Ghost in Hattiesburg," *Jewish Currents*
    20 (January 1966): 13–14, cited in Krause, "The Southern Rabbi and
    Civil Rights," 238. Krause, "The Southern Rabbi and Civil Rights," 82,
    77.

21. Krause, "The Southern Rabbi and Civil Rights, Part Two," 285.

22. Ibid., 285, 287–88.

23. Ibid., 292.

24. Ibid., 291.

25. Ibid., 294. Sidney Goldstein of Meridian exclaimed, "Blessings on you!
    You make me feel very proud that the rabbinate comes up with people like
    you!" Charles Mantinband signaled his support by accepting the invita-
    tion to meet. In the end only Mantinband, Goldstein, and Irwin Schor
    of Clarksdale would have attended the proposed meeting. Krause, "The
    Southern Rabbi and Civil Rights, Part Two," 293, 292.

26. American Jews looked with pride on their historic commitment to racial
    equality. In 1909 they helped form the NAACP, and Joel E. Springarn
    served as its chairman for most of the years between 1914 and 1939.
    Wealthy German-American Jews sponsored numerous philanthropies that
    benefitted the country's black community. William and Julius Rosenwald,
    Herbert Lehman, and Felix Warburg all made generous donations to the
    NAACP. Julius Rosenwald established 5,357 black elementary schools in
    the South that by 1932 were credited with educating over 650,000 stu-
    dents, an estimated 25 to 40 percent of the black school-age population.
    See Jonathan Kaufman, *Broken Alliance: The Turbulent Times between
    Blacks and Jews in America* (New York: Scribners, 1988), 2, 30–31, 91; and
    *Justice, Justice, Shalt Thou Pursue, Resolutions on Social Action Adopted by
    the Constituent Bodies of the Conservative Movement in Judaism* (New York:
    Joint Commission on Social Action, The United Synagogue of America,
    n.d.), 7. See *American Jewish Year Book* (Philadelphia: Jewish Publication
    Society, 1959), 18. Martin Luther King's Southern Christian Leadership
    Conference as well as the Student Non-Violent Coordinating Committee
    and the Congress of Racial Equality received most of their financial sup-
    port from the Jewish community; see Kaufman, *Broken Alliances*, 19, 286.
    Jews represented 3.04 percent of the total 1958 U.S. population (of
    173,260,000 people, 5,261,550 were Jews). See Murray Friedman, *Uto-
    pian Dilemma: New Political Directions for American Jews* (Bryn Mawr:
    Ethics and Public Policy Center, 1985), 24. Hero, "Southern Jews, Race
    Relations, and Foreign Policy." For an overview of the African American
    struggle for racial equality, see Harvard Sitkoff, *The Struggle for Black
    Equality, 1954–1980* (New York: Hill and Wang, 1981). For a discussion
    of non-Jewish white liberals, read William H. Chafe, *Civilities and Civil
    Rights: Greensboro, North Carolina and the Black Struggle for Freedom* (New

York: Oxford University Press, 1981). For an oral history of the period, see Howell Raines, *My Soul Is Rested: Movement Days in the Deep South Remembered* (New York: Penguin Books, 1983) or Henry Hampton and Steve Fayer, *Voices of Freedom: An Oral History of the Civil Rights Movement from the 1950's through the 1980's* (New York: Bantam Books, 1990). For a history of the Student Non-Violent Coordinating Committee, see Clayborne Carson, *In Struggle: S.N.C.C. and the Black Awakening of the 1960's* (Cambridge, Mass.: Harvard University Press, 1981). The legacy of the 1965 Voting Rights Act is covered in David J. Garrow, *Protest at Selma: Martin Luther King, Jr., and the Voting Rights Act of 1965* (New Haven: Yale University Press, 1978). One of the few works on the early movement is Sitkoff, *A New Deal for Blacks* (New York: Oxford University Press, 1978). For information on the political behavior of non-Jewish liberals, see Morton Sosna, *In Search of the Silent South: Southern Liberals and the Race Issue* (New York: Columbia University Press, 1977). John T. Kneebone, *Southern Liberal Journalists and the Issue of Race, 1920–1944* (Chapel Hill: University of North Carolina Press, 1985). Thomas Krueger, *And Promises to Keep: The Southern Conference for Human Welfare, 1938–1948* (Nashville: Vanderbilt University Press, 1967). John A. Salmond, *The Conscience of a Lawyer: Clifford A. Durr and American Civil Liberties, 1899–1975* (Tuscaloosa: University of Alabama Press, 1990). Anne C. Loveland, *Lillian Smith, a Southerner Confronting the South: A Biography* (Baton Rouge: Louisiana State University Press, 1986). Ralph McGill, *No Place to Hide: The South and Human Rights* (Macon: Mercer University Press, 1984).

27. The American Jewish Congress led the Jewish community with a strategy combining grassroots activism with pressure on local, state, and federal government agencies. The American Jewish Committee and Anti-Defamation League opted for a more conciliatory approach, focusing instead on education and dialogue. See Friedman, *The Utopian Dilemma*, 23. For examples of the American Jewish Congress's strategies, read "Statement of Dr. Stephen S. Wise, President of the American Jewish Congress, On the Report of the President's Committee on Civil Rights," *CLSA Reports* (New York: American Jewish Congress), 1; and Will Maslow and Joseph B. Robison, "A Civil Rights Program for America," *CLSA Reports* (New York: American Jewish Congress), 7, repr. from *Lawyers Guild Review* 7 (May–June 1947). For background on the American Jewish Committee and ADL's strategy, see "Point with Pride, Accomplishments of the American Jewish Committee and Anti-Defamation League of B'nai B'rith," File of the Council of Jewish Federations and Welfare Funds, Box 7, AJHS, Waltham, Massachusetts, 5.

28. Will Maslow and Joseph B. Robison, "American Jewish Congress before Subcommittee of the Senate Committee on Judiciary, re: S. 42, S. 1352, and S. 1465, Bills to Protect Citizens and other Persons from Mob Violence and Lynching, February 2, 1948," *CLSA Reports* (New York: Ameri-

can Jewish Congress, n.d.), 2. Albert E. Arent, "Statement before the Senate Judiciary Sub-Committee Holding Hearings on S. 42, S. 1352, and S. 1465, Bills to Protect Citizens and other Persons from Mob Violence and Lynching," 1–3.

29. Joseph B. Robison, "Before the House Sub-Committee on the Judiciary Considering H.R. 3488, An Anti-Lynching Bill," 4 February 1948, *CLSA Reports* (New York: American Jewish Congress, n.d.), 6–7.

30. Will Maslow and Joseph B. Robison, "A Civil Rights Program for America," 8. The National Women's League of United Synagogue called on the Eighty-Third Congress to pass an anti–poll tax law, an antilynching bill, approve an FEPC, eliminate discrimination in the military, and end discrimination in places of public accommodation. See *Justice, Justice*, 9. For more information on the committee's recommendations, read *NCRAC Legislative Information Bulletin*, 15 December 1947, Number 6, New York, Special Collections Box A-83 1019, Klau Library, Hebrew Union College-Jewish Institute of Religion (hereafter HUC-JIR), Cincinnati, Ohio.

31. "Recommendations of the President's Committee on Civil Rights, October 29, 1947," *CLSA Reports* (New York: American Jewish Congress, n.d.). *NCRAC Legislative Information Bulletin*, 15 December 1947, Number 6, New York, p. 7, Special Collections Box A-83 1019, Klau Library, HUC-JIR, Cincinnati, Ohio.

32. "Statement of Stephen S. Wise, President of American Jewish Congress, On Report of the President's Committee on Civil Rights," 1–2, *CLSA Reports* (New York: American Jewish Congress). On 23–26 June 1952, the Conservative Movement's Rabbinical Assembly called for laws "to implement the program of the President's [1947] Committee on Civil Rights." See *Justice, Justice*, 10.

33. "Program of Action for the Cincinnati Jewish Community in the Present Race Relations Emergency," Appendix A, p. 3, Manuscript Collection 202, Box 16, Folder 4, AJA, Cincinnati, Ohio. "Program of Action for the Cincinnati Jewish Community in the Present Race Relations Emergency," 15 July 1963, p. 3, Manuscript Collection 202, Box 17, Folder 1, AJA.

34. "Statement of Stephen S. Wise, In Respect to Legislation for Federal Aid to Education, Before the Subcommittee on Education of the Senate Committee on Labor and Public Welfare (S. 80, 170, 199, 472), April 25, 1947," Papers of Stephen S. Wise, Box 64, AJHS, Waltham, Massachusetts. For a state-by-state breakdown of desegregation progress in elementary schools, high schools, and universities between 1954 and 1961, see *Statistical Summary of School Segregation-Desegregation in the Southern and Border States* (Nashville: Southern Education Reporting Service, 1961).

35. "Statement of Dr. Stephen S. Wise, President, American Jewish Congress, United States of America, Before a Sub-Committee of the Senate Committee on Labor and Public Welfare, Holding Hearings on S. 984, A

Bill to Prohibit Discrimination in Employment because of Race, Religion, Color, National Origin, or Ancestry, June 12, 1947," *CLSA Reports* (New York: American Jewish Congress, n.d.). "Recommendations on Scope, Methods, and Procedures Respectfully Presented to the President's Committee on Government Contracts by the Constituent National Agencies and Community Organizations of the National Community Relations Advisory Council," Manuscript Collection 202, Box 15, Folder 3, p. 2, AJA.

36. "Statement to the Governor's Commission on Civil Rights on Behalf of the Jewish Community Relations Committee, August 7, 1958," Manuscript Collection 202, Box 15, Folder 8, AJA. Similar strategies were employed by Irving Kane, chairman of the NCRAC in testimony before the Eighty-First Congress in May of 1949 and by a 1954 conference of public antidiscrimination agencies and private Jewish organizations. See "Statement Submitted by Irving Kane before the Eighty-First Congress: First Session, in the Matter of H.R. 4453 Entitled 'A Bill to Prohibit Discrimination in Employment because of Race, Color, Religion, or National Origin,' May 19, 1949," Manuscript Collection 202, Box 14, Folder 10, AJA, and *J.T.A. News*, 18 November 1954, Manuscript Collection 202, Box 15, Folder 3, p. 5, AJA.

37. *FEPC Reference Manual, 1948 Edition*, NCRAC, 64. "Statement of Irving M. Engel on Behalf of the American Jewish Committee to the House Committee on Labor and Education Subcommittee on Discrimination in Employment," 25 May 1949, Manuscript Collection 202, Box 14, Folder 10, p. 10, AJA *Colliers*, 28 July 1945, cited in *FEPC Reference Manual 1948 Edition*, 23.

38. Sitkoff, *The Struggle for Black Equality*, 21–22. See also Richard Kluger, *Simple Justice* (New York: Alfred A. Knopf, 1976).

39. Hampton and Fayer, *Voices of Freedom*, xxvii. Sitkoff, *The Struggle for Black Equality*, 23.

40. Only 8 percent believed that "every measure should be used to bring it [integration] about in the near future." Hero, "Southern Jews, Race Relations, and Foreign Policy," 216. Sitkoff, *The Struggle for Black Equality*, 23.

41. Sitkoff, *The Struggle for Black Equality*, 25, 26. After Congress refused to take serious steps to achieve racial equality, Henry Edward Schultz, national chairman of the ADL, complained that the 1959 congressional record was "highly disappointing." *National Jewish Monthly* 74 (March 1960): 30. Although Eisenhower did sign, on 9 September 1957, the first civil rights bill to be approved by Congress since Reconstruction, it offered only nominal changes in the status quo. See Sitkoff, *The Struggle for Black Equality*, 33, and *Not the Work of a Day: The Story of the Anti-Defamation League of B'nai B'rith* (New York: Anti-Defamation League), 49.

42. *Justice, Justice, Shalt Thou Pursue,* 12, 13. *CCAR Resolutions,* 1954, Microfilm 893, AJA.

43. *National Jewish Monthly* 68 (June 1954): 3.

44. *Congress Weekly,* 30 April 1956, 4, cited in Richard Lehrman, "The American Jewish Congress Weekly: A Study of Its Editorials—1955 through 1959," unpublished paper, Box Number 2389, AJA. "Justice, Justice," 14–18 November 1954, 13. Statement of Dr. John Slawson, Executive Vice President, American Jewish Committee, *American Jewish Year Book,* 1955, 631.

45. It also brought attention to injustices against other nonwhite minority groups. By 1957 the Reform movement's rabbinic body, the Central Conference of American Rabbis acknowledged the plight of nonblack minorities when it announced that "in calling for fuller justice and freedom for the Negro section of our population, our attention should at the same time be directed to all tragically neglected minority groups, such as the American Indians, Mexicans, Puerto-Ricans, and others who have been the victims of shameless expropriation and neglect, and who continue to be subjected to indignity and economic oppression." "CCAR Resolution," 1957, Microfilm 893, AJA. See the *American Jewish Year Book,* 1956, 511, *American Jewish Year Book,* 1959, 27, *American Jewish Year Book,* 1960, 13, *American Jewish Year Book,* 1961, 67, *American Jewish Year Book,* 1964, 15, 20. Alexander F. Miller, National Community Service Director of the ADL, *National Jewish Monthly* 69 (February 1955): 19.

46. Sitkoff, *The Struggle for Black Equality,* 27.

47. Sanford H. Bolz, Washington Counsel, American Jewish Congress, "Statement of the American Jewish Congress Submitted to Subcommittee #5 of the House of Representatives Committee on the Judiciary Holding Hearings on H.R. 10672, H.R. 12896, H.R. 13189, Relating to Civil Rights," New York, 9 July 1958.

48. For information on interfaith dialogue, see Albert I. Gordon, *Jews in Suburbia* (Boston: Beacon Press, 1959), Howard Singer, "The Rise and Fall of Interfaith Dialogue," *Commentary* 83 (May 1987): 50–55, Rodney Stark and Stephen Steinberg, "Jews and Christians in Suburbia," *Harper's Magazine* 235 (August 1967): 73–78, Lanie Sussman, " 'Toward Better Understanding': The Rise of the Interfaith Movement in America and the Role of Rabbi Isaac Landman," *American Jewish Archives* 34 (April 1982): 35–51. For evidence of educational activities, see "Point with Pride." For more on synagogue worship during this era, see Gordon, *Jews in Suburbia.*

49. Richard Bluestein to Charles Posner, 13 June 1950, Manuscript Collection 202, Box 14, Folder 16, AJA. *Oral History of Clarence E. Israel,* 27, Biographies File, AJA.

50. Herman Kaplow, "Jewish Federations, Their Agencies and the Integration Struggle," 3, Special Collections Box A-89 247, Klau Library, HUC-JIR, Cincinnati, Ohio. The report concluded that "in 23 the facilities were open to all regardless of race or creed, in 12 the facilities were open to non-Jews exclusive of Negroes, and in 7 the facilities were closed to all non-Jewish including Negroes." *Civil Rights in the United States in 1951, A Balance Sheet of Group Relations* (New York: American Jewish Congress and the NAACP, 1951), 111.

51. The rationale for neighborhood schools was best articulated by the Public Education Association, which listed five reasons for maintaining the system: "1. minimizing the distance from home to school, 2. avoiding traffic hazards and topographical barriers (ditches, steep hills, etc.), 3. taking advantage of convenient and accessible public transportation when necessary to use it, 4. utilizing school space and facilities to the maximum, 5. avoiding shifting pupils, thus ensuring continuity of instruction." See Will Maslow and Richard Cohen, *School Segregation, Northern Style* (New York: Public Affairs Committee, American Jewish Congress, 1961), 10. For a 1959 study detailing the attitudes of Americans, including Jews, toward integration, see Charles Herbert Stember, *Jews in the Mind of America* (New York: Basic Books, 1966), 200, table 115. Richard Polenberg, *One Nation Divisible: Class, Race, and Ethnicity in the United States since 1938* (New York: The Viking Press, 1980), 153.

52. George and Eunice Grier, *Equality and Beyond: Housing Segregation and the Goals of the Great Society* (Chicago: Quadrangle Books, 1966), 8. This book was commissioned by the Anti-Defamation League.

53. Will Maslow and Richard Cohen, *School Segregation, Northern Style*, 1. Charles Silberman, "A Jewish View of the Racial Crisis," *Conservative Judaism* 19 (Summer 1965), delivered in slightly different form to the 1965 Rabbinical Assembly Convention.

54. Washington D.C. increased by 47 percent, Los Angeles by 96 percent, and Milwaukee by 187 percent. George and Eunice Grier, *Equality and Beyond*, 6–7. Nathan L. Edelstein, "The Jewish Relationship with the Emerging Negro Community in the North," presented to the National Community Relations Advisory Council, 23 June 1960, p. 1, Special Collections Box A-89 310, Klau Library, HUC-JIR, Cincinnati, Ohio. Polenberg, *One Nation Divisible*, 150.

55. Maslow and Cohen reported that "in Los Angeles, 43 elementary schools have at least 85 per cent Negro attendance. More than one-third of New York's one million public school pupils are Negro or Puerto Rican, and there are 95 public elementary schools with Negro or Puerto Rican enrollments above ninety percent." Will Maslow and Richard Cohen, *School Segregation, Northern Style*, 3, 5.

56. For more on working-class Jews, see Jonathan Reider, *Canarsie: The Jews and Italians of Brooklyn against Liberalism* (Cambridge, Mass.: Harvard University Press, 1985), Yona Ginsberg, *Jews in a Changing Neighborhood: The Story of Mattapan* (New York: Free Press, 1975), J. Anthony Lukas, *Common Ground: A Turbulent Decade in the Lives of Three American Families* (New York: Random House, 1985).

57. Kaplow, "Jewish Federations, Their Agencies and the Integration Struggle," 1. Nathan L. Edelstein, "The Jewish Relationship with the Emerging Negro Community in the North," presented to the National Community Relations Advisory Council, 23 June 1960, p. 1, Special Collections Box A-89 310, Klau Library, HUC-JIR, Cincinnati, Ohio. John Slawson, "Basic Assumptions Underlying Jewish Community Relations Programs," p. 544, presented at the annual meeting of the National Conference of Jewish Communal Service, Pittsburgh, 29 May 1959, repr. from *Journal of Jewish Communal Service* 36 (Winter 1959): 111–19, cited in Graenum Berger, ed., *The Turbulent Decades, Jewish Communal Services in America, 1958–1978* (New York: Conference of Jewish Communal Service, 1980).

58. Herman Kaplow, "Jewish Federations, Their Agencies and the Integration Struggle," 4. *Congress Bi-Weekly* 31 (14 September 1964): 3.

59. John Slawson, "Basic Assumptions Underlying Jewish Community Relations Programs," 111–19.

60. *Congress Bi-Weekly* 31 (14 September 1964): 3. *Congress Bi-Weekly* 31 (25 May 1964): 3.

61. Public schools in the North, according to the American Jewish Congress lobbyists, justified their stall tactics by relying "on lower court decisions that the equal protection clause of the Fourteenth Amendment does not 'affirmatively command' integration but merely forbids the use of official or governmental powers to enforce segregation," Will Maslow and Richard Cohen, *School Segregation, Northern Style,* 4. In the 1896 *Plessy* case, Maslow and Cohen explained, Justice John Harlan "first used the phrase 'colorblind' to describe the classic legal concept which held that government must disregard a man's color in its relations with him. In terms of the choice confronting Northern school boards, however, being color-blind meant refusing to assume any responsibility for school segregation so long as it did not result from any school board policy or action." Maslow and Cohen, *School Segregation, Northern Style,* 4.

62. Maslow and Cohen, *School Segregation, Northern Style,* 1, 10.

63. Maslow and Cohen, *School Segregation, Northern Style,* 15. In New York City permissive busing was used to reassign 919 students from overcrowded classrooms in Bedford-Stuyvesant, Brooklyn, to available space in white schools in Queens. When a similar plan was instituted in Detroit, 1,200 students boycotted classes for three days to protest the new

students' arrival. A plan to move 794 students from East Harlem to Yorkville provoked little white opposition. Maslow and Cohen remained confident that "the initial tension that often accompanies such transfers can be reduced sharply or even eliminated," Maslow and Cohen, *School Segregation, Northern Style*, 14. New York instituted such a plan in the fall of 1960. "Under this program," Maslow and Cohen explained, "all pupils from twenty-one junior high schools with heavy concentrations of Negro and Puerto Rican students were given the opportunity to transfer to twenty-eight other schools that were being used at less than ninety percent of capacity," Maslow and Cohen, *School Segregation, Northern Style*, 14, 15.

64. Maslow and Cohen, *School Segregation, Northern Style*, 16. Between 1957 and 1959 New York City built fifty-four new elementary and intermediate schools. They put thirteen in predominantly black and Puerto Rican areas, seventeen in white neighborhoods, and twenty-four in fringe areas. Maslow and Cohen, *School Segregation, Northern Style*, 10. The New Rochelle case ended up in federal court where Judge Irving R. Kaufman ruled against the school district and demanded a viable plan for desegregation. See Maslow and Cohen, *School Segregation, Northern Style*, 7–8. The AJC, ADL, and American Jewish Congress filed briefs against the New Rochelle Board of Education. See "Joint Memo of American Jewish Committee and Anti-Defamation League from Sol Rabkin and Theodore Leskes," 14 September 1961, Papers of the Council of Jewish Federations and Welfare Funds, Box 19, AJHS, Waltham, Massachusetts. See also "De Facto Segregation in Public Schools: A Position Paper for the Guidance of Jewish Communities and Agencies" (New York: National Community Relations Advisory Council, 1964).

65. "De Facto Segregation in Public Schools," 3.

66. Herman L. Kaplow, Executive Director, St. Louis Federation, "Jewish Federations, Their Agencies and the Integration Struggle," 5.

Civil and Social Rights Efforts of Arkansas Jewry

1. Part of this chapter was given by the author as a paper at the Eighteenth Annual Conference of the Southern Jewish Historical Society, 7 November 1993, Atlanta, Ga. For further data on civil and social rights efforts of Arkansas Jewry, see Carolyn Gray LeMaster, *A Corner of the Tapestry: A History of the Jewish Experience in Arkansas, 1820s–1990s* (Fayetteville, Ark.: University of Arkansas Press, 1994).

2. Jeff Davis was well known for his racist views. At a speech given at Pine Bluff in 1904, he referred to "the race question, to nigger equality, to social equality" that he perceived as being forced on the people of the South by President Theodore Roosevelt. Davis railed that he stood for "a white man's government. . . . I say that nigger domination will never pre-

vail in this country . . . as long as shotguns and rifles are around loose and we are able to pull the triggers" (*Pine Bluff Graphic*, 1 September 1904).

3. Rabbi Ephraim Frisch's letter to the editor of the *Pine Bluff Commercial*, 31 May 1911, Isaac Fisher Papers, Box 1, Folder 1, Tuskegee University Archives; for more information on Isaac Fisher, see Elizabeth L. Wheeler, "Isaac Fisher: The Frustrations of a Negro Educator at Branch Normal College, 1902–1911," *Arkansas Historical Quarterly* 41 (Spring 1982): 3–50.

4. Frisch to Miss Linda Neville, Lexington, Kentucky, 14 November 1912, Isaac Fisher Papers, Box 1, Folder 2, Tuskegee University Archives.

5. John C. Granberry, "Civil Liberties in Texas," *The Christian Century*, 1326–27; Rabbi Ephraim Frisch, "The Police Raid a Blow at Civil Liberties"; Berkowitz to Frisch, 5 August 1937; Frisch to Berkowitz, 13 August 1937; Ephraim Frisch, Nearprint File, Biographies, American Jewish Archives.

6. Isaac Landman, ed., *The Universal Jewish Encyclopedia* 4 (New York: Universal Jewish Encyclopedia Company, 1948), 461.

7. "Treatise of Late Jurist on Negro Slavery Ranks Among Leading Studies of Subject," *Arkansas Gazette* article (full citation unavailable), Judge Jacob Trieber Papers, courtesy J. Marshall Trieber; Jacob Trieber, "Legal Status of Negroes in Arkansas before the Civil War," *Arkansas Historical Association* 3 (1911): 175–83.

8. Trieber to Col. H. L. Remmel, president of the Arkansas Board of Trade, 1901, Trieber Papers, courtesy J. Marshall Trieber.

9. Ibid., also quoted by Hon. Gerald W. Heaney, "Jacob Trieber: Lawyer, Politician, Judge," *University of Arkansas at Little Rock Law Journal* 8 (1985–86): 440.

10. *Memphis Commercial Appeal*, 19 September 1901.

11. Trieber to W. A. Webber, 12 June 1901, J. Marshall Trieber Papers; quoted by Heaney, "Jacob Trieber," 440–41.

12. *Osceola Press*, 27 October 1892.

13. Heaney, "Jacob Trieber," 443.

14. *Arkansas Gazette*, 7 October 1903, quoted by Heaney, "Jacob Trieber," 443–44.

15. 125 F. 322, 330–31 (E.D. Ark. 1903), quoted by Heaney, "Jacob Trieber," 444.

16. *Arkansas Gazette*, 18 March 1904.

17. Heaney, "Jacob Trieber," 448.

18. Ibid., 449.

19. J. Marshall Trieber, grandson of Judge Jacob Trieber, to author, 11 May 1984. Heaney, "Jacob Trieber," 449–54.

20. *Arkansas Gazette,* 12 April 1914.

21. *Fort Smith Southwest American,* 14 February 1935.

22. Ibid., 19 February 1935.

23. Rabbi Samuel Teitelbaum, "Remembering Struggles for Social Justice, Social Action, and Civil Rights in Fort Smith and Sebastian County, Arkansas, 1927–1942," courtesy Rabbi Teitelbaum.

24. *Fort Smith Southwest American,* 24 February 1935.

25. Teitelbaum to Wise, 25 March 1935, Fort Smith; Wise to Teitelbaum, 3 April 1935, New York.

26. Teitelbaum to author, 26 July 1993, Phoenix.

27. Teitelbaum to author, 21 June 1993, Phoenix.

28. Teitelbaum to author, 1 December 1993, Phoenix.

29. Ibid.

30. Teitelbaum to author, 7 June 1993, Phoenix. After World War II, Rabbi Teitelbaum served as a director of a Hillel Foundation in Illinois and as a leader in several pulpits in New York and Arizona until 1977. He continued to teach at several colleges and universities until he was well into his nineties, never ceasing his commitment to social and civil justice. He died in May 1994.

31. Rose Sherman Weinberger, interview by author, Fort Smith, Ark., 17 August 1982; *Fort Smith Southwest Times-Record,* 25 June 1978, 7 February 1982; *Arkansas Democrat,* 10 February 1986, 9 April 1986. Rose Weinberger helped initiate the Roger Bost School for the mentally retarded and developmentally disabled adults in Fort Smith, helped establish the Arkansas School of Nursing, founded the Fort Smith Junior Civil League, was president of the local United Service Organizations (USO), and assisted in forming county and state Democratic women's clubs.

32. Undesignated newspaper article, 21 October 1933, Harry B. Solmson, Jr., Papers, Memphis; Harry B. Solmson, Jr., interview by author, Memphis, Tenn., 9 May 1983.

33. *Southern Mediator Journal,* 2 July 1948.

34. Fay Williams, *Arkansans of the Years,* 2 (Little Rock: C. C. Allard & Associates, 1952), 256–57; Gus Ottenheimer, interview by author, Little Rock, Ark., 5 April 1984. The Ottenheimer plants were later sold to Sears-Roebuck.

35. John L. Ferguson and J. H. Atkinson, *Historic Arkansas* (Little Rock: Arkansas History Commission, 1966), 321–26.

36. *Arkansas Gazette,* 19 February 1957.

37. Copy of Rabbi Ira Sanders's speech to the state legislature, 18 February 1957, Rabbi Sanders Papers, B'nai Israel Archives, Little Rock.

38. *Arkansas Gazette,* 19 February 1957.

39. The four bills were: HB 322, which "would create a state sovereignty commission with many duties, the first of which would be to perform any and all acts and things deemed necessary to protect the sovereignty of Arkansas and other states from encroachments by the federal government"—this became Act 83 and was later repealed; HB 323, which "would make attendance not compulsory in integrated schools"—this became Act 84 and was later superseded; HB 324, which "would require persons and organizations engaged in certain activities to register with the state and make regular reports of their income and expenses" (it would apply particularly to the NAACP)—this became Act 85 and was later repealed; and HB 325, which "would allow school boards to use school money to hire lawyers for integration suits"—this became Act 86 and remains as part of Arkansas law (*Arkansas Gazette,* 19 February 1957, 27 February 1957; *Arkansas Code of 1987 Annotated,* Tables [Charlottesville, Va.: Michie Company, 1987], 260; *Arkansas Code of 1987 Annotated,* Vol. 4, Title 6 [Charlottesville, Va.: Michie Company, 1987], 271–86).

40. Ira E. Sanders and Elijah E. Palnick, *The Centennial History of Congregation B'nai Israel, 1866–1966* (Little Rock: n.p., 1966), 67. The Little Rock School of Social Work later became the University of Arkansas School of Social Work, and Rabbi Sanders taught in its sociology classes for 16 years.

41. Ira E. Sanders, "The Journal of a Southern Rabbi," unpublished memoirs of Rabbi Ira E. Sanders, 57.

42. Ibid., 58.

43. Ibid.

44. Ibid., 59.

45. *Arkansas Democrat,* 19 February 1986.

46. Sanders, "Journal of a Southern Rabbi," 65.

47. Leonard Dinnerstein, "Southern Jewry and the Desegregation Crisis, 1954–1970," *American Jewish Historical Quarterly* 62 (Sept. 1972–June 1973): 239.

48. *Arkansas Democrat,* 4 October 1957; *New York Times,* 4 October 1957.

49. *Arkansas Democrat,* 13 October 1957.

50. Rabbi Ira E. Sanders, interview by author, Little Rock, Ark., 25 March 1983.

51. Eisendrath to Sanders, 4 October 1957, Rabbi Sanders Papers, B'nai Israel Archives, Little Rock.

52. Tony Freyer, *The Little Rock Crisis: A Constitutional Interpretation* (Westport, Conn.: Greenwood Press, 1984), 46.

53. Sanders, "Journal of a Southern Rabbi," 71.

54. Lorraine Gates, " 'An Organization of Impeccably Respected Southern White Women': The Women's Emergency Committee and the Little Rock School Crisis," unpublished paper, 12 April 1993, courtesy Jane Mendel.

55. Businessman Phil Back, husband of WEC worker Alice Back, headed the Anti-Defamation League of B'nai B'rith in Arkansas at the time. He was more conservative than his wife and was a moderate leader during the school crisis. During the tenure of Rabbi E. E. Palnick, he became more outspoken and active in civil affairs.

56. Irving J. Spitzberg, Jr., *Racial Politics in Little Rock: 1954–1964* (New York: Garland Publishing Company, 1987), 21.

57. Irene Samuel, telephone interview by author, Little Rock, 11 October 1991. Irene Gaston Samuel was not Jewish; she was active at Temple B'nai Israel, where she and her husband attended. Her assessment of the signal work that was accomplished by Little Rock's Jewish women was confirmed in a conversation with Judge and Mrs. Henry Woods at the annual meeting of the Arkansas Historical Association, April 1994, at Helena, Ark. Mrs. Woods was an active WEC member.

58. Spitzberg, *Racial Politics*, 16–19.

59. Ibid., 111–12.

60. Elijah E. Palnick, "Southern Jewry and Civil Rights," *CCAR Journal* 13 (June 1965): 62.

61. Spitzberg, *Racial Politics*, 93.

62. Ibid., 93–94.

63. Ibid., 176.

64. Shimon Weber, "How Has the School Conflict Affected the Jews in Little Rock?" *Jewish Daily Forward*, 19 October 1957.

65. Thomas F. Pettigrew and Ernest Q. Campbell, *Christians in a Racial Crisis* (Washington, D.C.: Public Affairs Press, 1959), 30; Sanders, "Journal of a Southern Rabbi," 71; *Arkansas Democrat*, 9 April 1985.

66. Spitzberg, *Racial Politics*, 76.

67. Irene Samuel, interview; Spitzberg, *Racial Politics*, 154.

68. Spitzberg, *Racial Politics*, 108.

69. Patrick J. Owens, "The Gentleman Rebel," *ADL Bulletin* (Sept. 1965): 7.

70. Ibid.

71. Irene Samuel, interview; Spitzberg, *Racial Politics*, 153–54.

72. *Arkansas Gazette*, 3 July 1983, 1 June 1986; *Action*, Publication of the Jewish Federation of Little Rock, Winter 1986.

73. *Arkansas Democrat*, 9 April 1985.

74. *Arkansas Gazette*, 11 May 1982.

75. Spitzberg, *Racial Politics*, 151.

76. Rabbi Elijah E. Palnick, interview by author, Albany, Ga., 8 November 1993.

77. Palnick, interview; Dr. W. H. Townsend, interview by author, Little Rock, Ark., 24 January 1994.

78. Palnick, interview; Elijah Coleman, telephone interview by author, Pine Bluff, Ark., 20 January 1994.

79. Townsend, interview.

80. *Arkansas Gazette*, 19 November 1970.

81. "Makeup of the Workforce, 1986 State Highway Department Report"; Henry Droughter, section head, Equal Employment Opportunity Office, Arkansas State Highway Department, telephone interview by author, 25 January 1994.

82. "Rabbi to Direct Citizens Committee," undesignated newspaper article (full citation unavailable), Rabbi Palnick scrapbook, Albany, Ga.

83. Townsend, interview.

84. *Arkansas Democrat*, 27 November 1986; Townsend, interview. COCA was disbanded by its members after its missions were accomplished.

85. *Arkansas Gazette*, 11 November 1969.

86. *Arkansas Gazette*, 18 January 1970, 13 October 1970.

87. *Arkansas Gazette*, 13 July 1971.

88. *Arkansas Democrat*, 2 July 1971.

89. Ibid.

90. *Arkansas Gazette*, 8 April 1969.

91. *Arkansas Gazette*, 25 June 1968.

92. Louis Nunez, U.S. Commission on Civil Rights, to Irene Palnick, 30 November 1978; Bert Silver, U.S. Commission on Civil Rights, to Irene Palnick, 30 May 1985.

93. *Arkansas Gazette*, 6 April 1967.

94. Rabbi Palnick, telephone interview by author, 20 January 1994; "Memo from Arnold Goodman, President of Temple B'nai Israel, to the Congregation," 1973, Rabbi Palnick Papers, Albany, Ga.

95. Coleman, interview.

96. Dinnerstein, "Southern Jewry," 238.

97. *Arkansas Gazette*, 2 February 1980, 11 May 1982, 16 November 1985.

98. Lazar Palnick, telephone interview by author, Pittsburgh, Pa., 20 January 1994.

99. Lazar Palnick, interview.

100. *Arkansas Gazette*, 11 May 1982.

Rabbi Sidney Wolf: Harmonizing in Texas

1. Anne Train, group interview at home of Helen Wilk, Corpus Christi, Tex., 6 December 1993, notes in possession of author; Associated Press, "Increases Reported in Few Towns, Austin Leads with Corpus Christi Second in Percent of Gain," *Corpus Christi Caller-Times*, 14 July 1940; Cindy Tumiel, "H. Boyd Hall Led Fight on Segregation," *Corpus Christi Caller-Times*, 23 January 1983.

2. Paul Schuster Taylor, *An American-Mexican Frontier, Nueces County* (Chapel Hill: University of North Carolina Press, 1934; repr., New York: Russell and Russell, A Division of Atheneum Press, 1971), 92. According to Taylor, Corpus Christi's population in 1930 was 50 percent white, 5.1 percent "Negro" and 44.9 percent Mexican or people of "Mexican parentage"; Judge Hector De Pena, telephone interview by author, 17 August 1994, notes in possession of author; Gilbert Q. Casares, telephone interview by author, 18 August 1994, notes in possession of author.

3. Bill Walraven, *Corpus Christi: The History of a Texas Seaport* (n.p.: Windsor Publications, Incorporated History Books Division, 1982), 82; Anita Eisenhauer and Gigi Starnes, *Corpus Christi, Texas, a Picture Postcard History* (Corpus Christi: Anita's Antiques Word Shop Division, 1987), 44; *Heritage Park Corpus Christi. A Walking Tour* (Corpus Christi: City of Corpus Christi), publication number 86–051.

4. Jack Solka, group interview at home of Helen Wilk, Corpus Christi, Tex., 6 December 1993, notes in possession of author; De Pena, interview; Casares, interview.

5. Walraven, *A Texas Seaport*, 85.

6. Tumiel, "H. Boyd Hall Led Fight on Segregation"; Nick Jimenez, "Hall is Honored with King Award at NAACP Banquet," *Corpus Christi Caller-Times*, 11 May 1984.

7. George Farenthold, interview by author, Corpus Christi, Tex., 8 December 1993, notes in possession of author.

8. Sidney A. Wolf, "My Life and Career: Rabbi Sidney Wolf, June 13, 1972," *Our Golden Years. A History of Temple Beth El, Corpus Christi, Texas*, ed. Helen K. Wilk (Corpus Christi: Artcraft Printing, 1984), 74–75.

9. Ibid.

10. Ibid., 75–76.

11. Ruthe Winegarten and Cathy Schechter, *Deep in the Heart, the Lives and Legends of Texas Jews, a Photographic History* (Austin: Eakin Press, 1990), 42; Wilk, *Our Golden Years*, 8–15.

12. Ilene Wolf Goodman, interview by author, Houston, Tex., 18 September 1994, notes in possession of author.

13. Wolf, "My Life and Career," 76.

14. *Heritage Park Corpus Christi. A Walking Tour.*

15. Wolf, "My Life and Career," 76.

16. Maurice Nast, group interview at home of Helen Wilk, Corpus Christi, Tex., 6 December 1993, notes in possession of author; Wolf, "My Life and Career," 76.

17. Wolf, "My Life and Career," 76–77.

18. Arthur Elliott, interview by author, Corpus Christi, Tex., 8 December 1993, notes in possession of author; "Record Collectors Fall to Stereo, Give Rare 78 Albums to Del Mar," *Corpus Christi Caller-Times*, 15 November 1959.

19. Wolf, "My Life and Career," 74; Margaret Ramage, "Retirement Only a Beginning School, Civic Work Beckons Rabbi Sidney Wolf," *Corpus Christi Caller-Times*, 18 June 1972.

20. Sidney A. Wolf, "Op Lewandowski's Contributions to Modern Synagogal Music" (rabbinic thesis, Hebrew Union College-Jewish Institute of Religion, 1932).

21. Hortense Warner Ward, *A Century of Missionary Effort: The Church of the Good Shepherd, 1860–1960* (Austin: Press of Von Boeckmann-Jones Company, 1960).

22. "Love in Corpus Christi," *Time*, 30 November 1936, 53.

23. Ramage, "Retirement."

24. Wolf, "My Life and Career," 77.

25. Bebe Wolf, interviews by author, Corpus Christi, Tex., 7–10 December 1993, notes in possession of author.

26. Bebe Wolf, interviews by Helen Wilk, tape recording, Corpus Christi, Tex., 3 February 1991, tape in possession of interviewer.

27. Bebe Wolf, interviews by author.

28. Henry J. "H. J." Williams, folder of clippings from library files of *Corpus Christi Caller-Times*; Bebe Wolf, interviews by author.

29. Herbert Train, Anne Train, Maurice Nast, Katherine Nast, Jack Solka, David Lou Solka, L. A. Train, Rona Train, Helen Wilk, group interview at home of Helen Wilk, Corpus Christi, Tex., 7 December 1993, notes in possession of author; Bebe Wolf, interviews with author.

30. "New American Families Who Have Settled in Corpus Christi since Rise of Nazis," *Our Golden Years. A History of Temple Beth El, Corpus Christi, Texas*, ed. Helen K. Wilk (Corpus Christi: Artcraft Printing, 1984), 35.

31. Walraven, *A Texas Seaport,* 86.

32. "Organization of Inter-Racial Committee Completed Here," *Corpus Christi Caller-Times*, 12 November 1944 (Local History Collection, Corpus Christi Public Library).

33. Sidney A. Wolf, "Our Welfare Fund. 'He Who Is Gracious to the Poor Lends to the Lord,' " *Our Golden Years. A History of Temple Beth El, Corpus Christi, Texas*, ed. Helen K. Wilk (Corpus Christi: Artcraft Printing, 1984), 34–35.

34. Ibid.; Bebe Wolf, interviews by author.

35. Ralph Thibodeau, "Corpus Christi Symphony Orchestra," *Symphony Orchestras of the United States,* ed. Robert R. Craven (New York: Greenwood Press, 1986), 384–85; Ralph Thibodeau, interview by author, Corpus Christi, Tex., 8–9 December 1993, notes in possession of author.

36. James "Jimmy" Wagner, telephone interview by author, 13 January 1994, notes in possession of author.

37. Hector Garcia, M.D., telephone interview by author, 13 January 1994, notes in possession of author.

38. Casares, interview.

39. De Pena, interview.

40. Wagner, interview.

41. Jack Solka, group interview with author.

42. Bebe Wolf, interviews.

43. Herb Train, L. A. Train, group interview; Bebe Wolf, interviews.

44. Williams folder, *Corpus Christi Caller-Times;* Mary Gene Kelly, "Hall Says He Met Opposition to Race While Building Home," *Corpus Christi Caller-Times,* 2 June 1954.

45. Thelma Spencer Caesar, interview by author, Corpus Christi, Tex., 7 December 1993, notes in possession of author.

46. "Park Board Approves Full Use by Negroes of Facilities at Oso," *Corpus Christi Caller-Times*, 4 June 1954.

47. Rev. Harold T. Branch, telephone interview, 27 December 1993, notes in possession of author; Caesar, interview; Thibodeau, interview; Bebe Wolf, interviews.

48. Ed Deswysen, "Integration Suit has Changed His Life," *Corpus Christi Caller-Times*, 21 April 1970, Local History Collection, Corpus Christi Public Library; Georgia Nelson, "Judge Orders Unitary System," *Corpus Christi Caller-Times*, 5 June 1970, Local History Collection, Corpus Christi Public Library.

49. Rev. Dr. Alfred Frederick Swearingen, telephone interview, 20 August 1994, notes in possession of author.

50. Ibid.

51. Ibid.

52. Branch, interview.

53. Wagner, interview; Williams folder.

54. Swearingen, interview.

55. Tony Bonilla, telephone interviews by author, 13 January and 16 August 1994, notes in possession of author.

56. Ibid.

57. Bebe Wolf, interviews.

58. Lloyd Grove, "Students Honor Wolf as 'Greatest,'" *Corpus Christi Caller-Times*, 30 October 1976.

59. Wolf, "My Life and Career," 80.

60. Wilk, *Our Golden Years*, 80.

Rabbi David Jacobson and the Integration of San Antonio

1. See Howard M. Sachar, *A History of the Jews in America* (New York: Alfred A. Knopf, 1992), 73–77.

2. Terry G. Jordan, *German Seed in Texas Soil* (Austin: University of Texas, 1966), 54. In 1850 the population of San Antonio was 3,488; by 1860 it had grown to 8,235. Bureau of the Census, *United States Census Population: 1960, Texas, Number of Inhabitants*, "Population of incorporated places of 10,000 or more from earliest census to 1960," 23. Concerning Mexican immigration to South Texas see T. R. Fehrenbach, *Lone Star: A History of Texas and the Texans* (New York: Wings Books, 1968), 687.

3. Jordan, *German Seed*, 109–10.

4. Frances R. Kallison, "100 Years of Jewry in San Antonio" (master's thesis, Trinity University, San Antonio, 1977), 28; see also advertisement, *San Antonio Daily Herald,* 17 Dec. 1859.

5. Oral statements of Jesse D. Oppenheimer, 14 May 1963, cited in Kallison, "100 Years of Jewry," 31.

6. *San Antonio Ledger,* 5 June 1851, cited in Kallison, "100 Years of Jewry," 12.

7. Kallison, "100 Years of Jewry," 28; see also advertisement, *San Antonio Daily Herald,* 17 Dec. 1859.

8. Kallison, "100 Years of Jewry," 36.

9. *San Antonio Daily Express,* 11 Sept. 1875. Cited in Max Blumer, "The House of God," *Diamond Jubilee, 1874–1949* (commemorative brochure) (San Antonio: Temple Beth-El, n.d.).

10. See Michael A. Meyer, *Response to Modernity: A History of the Reform Movement in Judaism* (New York: Oxford University Press, 1988), 265–70.

11. Samuel Marks, "History of the Jews of San Antonio," *The Reform Advocate,* 24 Jan. 1914, 13.

12. Ibid.

13. Frances Kallison to author, 6 June 1993.

14. David Jacobson, interview by Francis B. Roser, San Antonio, Tex., 6 Feb. 1992, Bexar County Historical Commission.

15. William Sinkin, written remarks to author, 15 Jan. 1995.

16. David Jacobson, interview by Francis B. Roser.

17. Ibid.

18. Ibid.

19. Ibid.

20. Ibid.

21. Ibid.

22. Helen Jacobson, interview by author, 4 Jan. 1995.

23. Helen Jacobson, interview by author, 9 May 1994; Sinkin, interview, 15 Jan. 1995.

24. Helen Jacobson, conversations with author, 1994; Minutes, Board of Trustees, San Antonio Public Library, 31 May 1991.

25. C. Don Baugh, "A Report Covering the Efforts of Desegregating San Antonio, Texas, through the Voluntary Process, 1953–1960" (hereafter Baugh Report, Part 1), unpublished paper, Trinity University, spring semester, 1964, 6; Sinkin, interview, 15 Jan. 1995.

26. Helen Jacobson, conversation with author, n.d.

27. Fehrenbach, *Lone Star*, 683.

28. Ibid.

29. Henry E. Catto, Jr., to Gustav Falk, 13 Nov. 1962, Robert E. Lucey Papers, "Ecumenism" file, Catholic Archives at San Antonio.

30. Saul E. Bronder, *Social Justice & Church Authority: The Public Life of Archbishop Robert E. Lucey* (Philadelphia: Temple University Press, 1982), 69–70.

31. Bronder, *Social Justice & Church Authority*, 73.

32. Beth-El Congregation Minutes, 8 June 1932–11 May 1941, entry for 11 May 1938. Jewish congregations traditionally number their members by family. In 1959 Temple Beth-El was spiritual home to 707 families. There are no figures for the 1960s. Figures compiled in October 1994 by temple archivist Hilton Goldman from "Summary Reports and Analysis."

33. *Time*, 7 April 1941, cited in Bronder, 65.

34. Bronder, *Social Justice & Church Authority*, 73.

35. Sinkin, interview, 15 Jan. 1995.

36. Helen Jacobson, interview, 4 Jan. 1995.

37. Bishop Harold Gosnell, telephone interview by author, 12 Jan. 1995.

38. David Jacobson, telephone interview by author, 12 Jan. 1995.

39. William Sinkin, interview by author, 12 Jan. 1995.

40. David and Helen Jacobson, telephone interview by author, 12 Jan. 1995.

41. Baugh Report, Part 1, 3.

42. Ibid., 3, 9.

43. Ibid., 10.

44. Ibid., 12.

45. Ibid., 13–14.

46. Claude Black, interview by author, n.d.

47. According to the *San Antonio News*, F. W. Woolworth, Kress, Neisner's, Grant's, Green's, McCory's, and Sommers drugstores.

48. "Lunch Counters Integrated Peacefully in San Antonio," *New York Times*, 20 March 1960.

49. Baugh, "A Report Covering the Efforts of the Desegregation of San Antonio, Texas, through the Voluntary Process, March 1960 through July 4, 1963" (hereafter Baugh Report, Part 2), unpublished paper, Trinity University, 1964, 2.

50. Ibid., 5; *New York Times*, 20 March 1960, 1.

51. Baugh Report, Part 2, 9.

52. Ibid., 10.

53. Ibid., 11–12. The three members of the black community were S. J. Davis, educator; James E. Taylor, Jr., funeral director; and Valmo Bellinger, publisher.

54. Ibid., 4.

55. Ibid., 15.

56. Sinkin, interview, 15 Jan. 1995.

57. Ibid.

58. Helen and David Jacobson, interview by author, 9 May 1994.

59. "Jacobsons Aim to Defeat Bigotry," *San Antonio Express-News*, 16 Feb. 1989.

60. Ibid.; Baugh Report, Part 2, 17–18.

61. Baugh Report, Part 2, 19.

62. "Two to Be Honored for City Service," *San Antonio Express-News*, 4 Nov. 1988. See also Rosow's comments to the *San Antonio Light*, 3 Nov. 1988: "He [Jacobson] used his good offices to work out peaceful solutions to tough problems. He was one of the real leaders that kept San Antonio from exploding."

63. "Jacobsons Aim to Defeat Bigotry," *San Antonio Express-News*, 16 Feb. 1989; "MLK Award Is Presented to Jacobsons," *San Antonio Express-News*, 25 Jan. 1989; "Temple Beth-El to Honor Jacobsons," *North San Antonio Times*, 3 Nov. 1988; "50 Years of Service," *San Antonio Light*, 3 Nov. 1988; "2 to Be Honored for City Service," *San Antonio Express-News*, 4 Nov. 1988; "Rabbi Celebrates 50th Jubilee," *North San Antonio Times*, 10 May 1984; "Lecture Honors Jacobsons," *San Antonio Express*, 14 Oct. 1983; "Retired Rabbi Serves Temple in Abilene," *San Antonio Light*, 15 Feb. 1984; "Civic Leader Honored," *San Antonio Light*, 9 Oct. 1978; "Awards Recipient to Be Honored," *San Antonio Express*, 9 Oct. 1978; "Rabbi to Lead Welfare Session," *San Antonio Express*, 10 May 1977; "Jacobsons Mark a Milestone," *San Antonio Express-News*, 5 June 1976; "Temple to Honor Jacobsons," *San Antonio Light*, 16 May 1976.

The Prophetic Voice: Rabbi James A. Wax

1. "Dr. King Slain by Sniper, Looting, Arson Touched Off by Death," *Memphis Commercial Appeal*, 5 April 1968, 1; *New York Times*, 5–6 April 1968. President Johnson ordered troops into Washington to quell arson and looting.

2. Joan Turner Beifuss, *At the River I Stand: Memphis, the 1968 Strike, and Martin Luther King* (Memphis: B & W Books, 1985), 283. This well-

documented study of the strike is based in large part on interviews with those who were close observers or participants in the strike.

3. The Rabbi James A. Wax Collection, Memphis Shelby County Public Library & Information Center, Memphis, Tennessee. This essay draws in large part from papers in the Collection, donated by Wax in 1987. The Wax Collection contains a wealth of material on his involvement in a broad spectrum of community organizations. It includes sermons dating from 1939 to 1977, religious writings, correspondence from 1954 through 1984, photographs, awards, and ten large scrapbooks. Temple Israel was organized in 1853 as Congregation Children of Israel and chartered by the state in 1854.

4. Beifuss, *At the River I Stand,* 318–19. Beifuss gives the number as 300, Wax recalls 250. Not all white ministers joined the mile march from St. Mary's Cathedral to the mayor's office. Fearing the disapproval of their own congregations, as well as public censure, some ministers did not join the march. Although some members of Temple Israel disapproved of the march, they did support Rabbi Wax's decision to take a strong moral stand.

5. *I Am a Man: Photographs of the 1968 Memphis Sanitation Strike and Dr. Martin Luther King Jr.* (Memphis: Memphis Publishing Company, 1993), 114–15. Threatening telephone calls were made to the mayor's office and home. His wife and children were taken to a friend's home for safety.

6. Anthony Lucas, "Memphis Approves a Memorial Parade; Clergy and Teachers Assail Mayor," *New York Times,* 6 April 1968, 24. The statement made by Rabbi Wax appears in several sources with minor variations in the opening wording. Rabbi Wax repeated the statement made to the mayor in his Friday evening sermon on 5 April 1968: "Speaking this morning to the Mayor of our city, I said to him that I spoke with mixed emotions of sadness and anger, of deep righteous resentment, and the view which I expressed is the view of the clergy of the city of Memphis." Wax's sermon was a commemoration of the life and work of Dr. King.

7. Rabbi Wax received threatening telephone calls and hundreds of hostile letters, some of which were anti-Semitic as well as antiblack and/or anti-labor. Most of these letters were later sent to the American Jewish Archives and are not part of the Wax Collection.

8. Wax Collection, Box 6, Folder 12; Joan Turner Beifuss, "Profile: Rabbi James Wax," *Memphis Magazine,* February 1981, 39–45; Jay Hall, "A Man for All People," *Mid-South, The Commercial Appeal Magazine,* 26 February 1978, 8–10.

9. Rabbi Ferdinand Isserman was an outstanding role model for the young student. Throughout his rabbinical career, Isserman was a noted leader in interfaith and social justice action. His obituary in the *St. Louis Globe*

Democrat, 10 March 1972, noted Isserman's outstanding contributions to St. Louis during his thirty-three years at Temple Israel.

10. Wax Collection, Scrapbook 1; *Memphis Commercial Appeal*, 2 April 1954. Rabbi Ferdinand Isserman led the induction service when Wax was installed as Senior Rabbi of Temple Israel (Memphis).

11. Wax Collection, Box 3, sermon of 24 January 1975. See also Melvin I. Urofsky, *A Voice That Spoke for Justice: The Life and Times of Stephen S. Wise* (Albany, N.Y.: State University Press, 1982).

12. Helen L. Goldstrom, a native of Baltimore, was serving as executive director of the National Federation of Temple Youth in Cincinnati when she first met Rabbi Wax. Her loving and generous support of Rabbi Wax's ministry to both Temple Israel and the Memphis community was an important source of strength and encouragement in his work. Interviews with Helen Wax provided helpful insights into her husband's life and work.

13. Wax Collection, Scrapbook 4; *Memphis Commercial Appeal*, 2 April 1954.

14. "Social Justice," address to the National Federation of Temple Youth, Hebrew Union College, Cincinnati, Ohio, 2 March 1946, Wax Collection, Box 4, Folder 1.

15. *Memphis Press-Scimitar*, 30 October 1975; *Memphis Commercial Appeal*, 1 November 1975. A photograph in the *Commercial Appeal* caught Wax with eyes blazing as he told the governor: "The people of our state strongly disapprove of any political intervention in the operation of our hospitals." This incident, and other forceful actions taken by Wax on public issues, makes clear that his confrontation with Mayor Loeb in 1968 was not a singular occurrence.

16. *Memphis Commercial Appeal*, 2 November 1975. Governor Ray Blanton's administration was riddled with political corruption and scandal. In 1981 he was convicted of fraud and the illegal sale of liquor licenses and sentenced to prison.

17. *Memphis Commercial Appeal*, 26 May 1962. In 1977 the hospital was renamed Memphis Mental Health Institute.

18. Wax Collection, Scrapbook 8. The James A. Wax Building was dedicated 10 September 1982.

19. Wax Collection, Box 6, Folder 10. The resolution was dated 19 July 1984.

20. Wax Collection, Box 6, Folder 13.

21. Wax Collection, Scrapbooks 5 and 6. These books contain clippings and other information detailing Wax's close association with Rabbi Becker and Beth Sholom.

22. "Memphis Rabbis Form Rabbinical Association," *The Hebrew Watchman*, 24 June 1971, 1.

23. *Memphis Press-Scimitar,* 16 March 1956. Wax was one of five recognized for efforts in racial justice. Also honored was Dr. Paul Tudor Jones, senior minister of Idlewild Presbyterian Church and longtime colleague of Rabbi Wax in the civil rights movement.

24. *Memphis Commercial Appeal,* 17 February 1956. Rabbi Wax's withdrawal from the Mississippi State speaking engagement was also reported in *Social Action Review,* 4 March 1956.

25. Wax Collection, Box 5, Folder 7.

26. Ibid. Chairmen of the key MCCR committees deserve much credit for their work. They included Roane Waring, Jr., attorney, chairman of public transportation; Paul Tudor Jones, Idlewild Presbyterian Church, chairman of public libraries and museums; Dr. Laurence F. Kinney, chairman of the Department of Bible at Southwestern College (now Rhodes College), chairman of public universities, colleges and schools; Dr. Stanley J. Buckman, chairman of Buckman Laboratories and prominent philanthropist, chairman of public parks, playgrounds, and zoo; and Walter Simmons, head of the Memphis Housing Authority, chairman of public housing. Leaders of the black community active in the MCCR were Jesse W. Turner, Sr., banker and NAACP director; A. W. Willis, attorney; A. Maceo Walker, insurance company executive; Hollis F. Price, college president; Blair T. Hunt, educator and minister; Lt. George W. Lee, business and Republican party leader; and J. A. McDaniel, director of the Memphis Urban League.

27. Beifuss, "Profile: Rabbi James Wax." Beifuss points out that the successful efforts of the MCCR to end segregation in Memphis have never received proper recognition largely because they were overshadowed by the sanitation workers' strike and Dr. King's tragic death.

28. Wax Collection, Box 5, Folder 7; *Memphis Commercial Appeal,* 11 August 1967.

29. Wax Collection, Box 5, Folder 5.

30. Jonathan A. Wax, "Program of Progress: The Recent Change in the Form of Government in Memphis" (senior thesis, Princeton University, 1968), 31. Jonathan Wax wrote: "Another example of bickering during the Ingram administration was a fight for control of anti-poverty funds. Ingram sought control of the local committee, which had had no political domination. While he squabbled with Federal and local government officials and poverty workers, no anti-poverty funds entered Memphis for about a year." Community activists believed strongly that the mayor should not be the designated person to choose committee members or control the disbursement of federal funds because such power had great potential for political gain.

31. Wax Collection, Box 5, Folder 9.

32. Wax, "Program of Progress," 90–91.

33. *Memphis Commercial Appeal*, 9 November 1966.

34. *Memphis Press-Scimitar*, 1 January 1968, 1; *Memphis Commercial Appeal*, 1 January 1968, 1, 21. Loeb was sworn in as mayor at 12:01 A.M. on 1 January in a private ceremony at his home. The campaign between Loeb and incumbent mayor William Ingram had been heated, and Loeb said he feared last-minute appointments by Ingram. Ingram's support had come largely from working-class whites and the black community; Loeb's supporters were primarily conservative and affluent citizens.

35. Wax Collection, Box 4, Folder 9.

36. Denis Freeland, "Out of the Shadows," *The Memphis Flyer*, 1–7 April 1993, 10–12. On the twenty-fifth anniversary of the sanitation strike, Freeland discusses the PBS documentary *At the River I Stand*, written and produced by University of Memphis professors David Appleby, Allison Graham, and Steven Ross. The article notes that the documentary focuses on the importance of the strike as a major civil rights action that was eclipsed by Dr. King's assassination.

37. "Loeb: A Name by No Means Neutral," *Memphis Commercial Appeal*, 28 May 1990, A1. Loeb Enterprises included a large laundry, a chain of barbecue restaurants and drive-in grocery stores, and large real estate operations.

38. Jackson Baker, "Requiem for a Renegade," *The Memphis Flyer*, 17–24 September 1992. 12–13, 29. Henry Loeb died 8 September 1992. Baker's article reviews Loeb's career in politics, particularly the fateful events of 1968. Loeb had served as mayor in 1960 under the old commission government, resigning in 1963 to return to the family business. The black community had not forgotten that Loeb flatly turned down requests by leading citizens to integrate the city parks and museum and was known as a strong supporter of segregation.

39. Ibid.

40. "Ex-mayor Loeb, 71, Dies; Led City When King Slain," *Memphis Commercial Appeal*, 9 September 1992, A1.

41. Rabbi James A. Wax Interview, Sanitation Workers Strike Collection, University of Memphis Libraries, Mississippi Valley Collection, Memphis, Tenn., oral history transcript, file 178, tape 256.

42. *Memphis Commercial Appeal*, 19 February 1968, 1. Black council members sided with the strikers; conservative white council members supported Mayor Loeb. The more liberal members, working to take council action that would resolve the strike, were caught between the hostility of the strikers and their representatives and an inflexible mayor. Councilman and attorney Louis Donelson discusses this dilemma in chapter seven of *At the River I Stand*. The *New York Times* of 29 March 1968 reported: "Ef-

forts to settle the strike appear stalled. Mr. Loeb has been severely criticized for his role in the dispute, particularly for his refusal to recognize the union."

43. Norman Pearlstine, "Garbage Strike Piles Up Negro Unity," *Wall Street Journal*, 8 March 1968.

44. John Terreo, "Reporting by Memphis Newspapers Prior to the 1866 Race Riot and during the 1968 Sanitation Strike: A Historical Study" (master's thesis, University of Memphis, 1987). Terreo argues that biased reporting by the Memphis press contributed to two tragic events in the life of the city: the disastrous race riot of 1866 and the sanitation strike in 1968, the latter of which brought Dr. King to Memphis and his untimely death.

45. Wax Collection, Scrapbook 6.

46. Wax to Richard G. Hirsch, 29 May 1968, Wax Collection, Box 5, Folder 6. In a nine-page letter, Wax details his involvement in the sanitation strike. A separate three-page statement dated 1 July 1968 notes the Loeb family relationship with Temple Israel. Both Henry Loeb and his brother William were confirmed at Temple Israel, and their parents and grandparents are buried in Temple Israel Cemetery. The brothers married Christian wives. According to church records, on 28 January 1968, just weeks after becoming mayor, Henry was formally confirmed at St. John's Episcopal Church, where his wife Mary was a member.

47. Wax Collection, Box 5, Folder 5; Sanitation Workers Strike Collection, file 178.

48. Ibid.

49. Wax Collection, Box 5, Folder 5.

50. *Memphis Commercial Appeal*, 17 April 1968, 1. Dr. Ralph Abernathy was quoted as saying that "the sanitation workers' strike agreement is a significant breakthrough for justice of labor and for unions in the South [and is] a monument of victory for the individual sanitation workers."

51. Wax Collection, Box 5, Folder 9. The Reverend Brooks Ramsay, Baptist minister and social justice activist, called Dr. Wax's courageous assertion "one of the most powerful statements of justice and equality in our time."

52. Wax Collection, Box 5, Folder 5, 19 November 1968.

53. "Rabbi Wax Is Honored by Christians and Jews," *Memphis Commercial Appeal*, 21 February 1978; "Rabbi Wax Saluted for Service to City," *Memphis Press-Scimitar*, 21 February 1978.

54. Wax Collection, Box 5, Folder 5. The resolution adopted by the Temple Israel Trustees on 24 January 1978 was presented to Rabbi Wax at the Friday night service on 10 February 1978.

55. "Friends Recall Legacy of Wax: Rabbi Sought to Bridge Racial, Religious Division," *Memphis Commercial Appeal*, 19 October 1989, B1. Also

on that date, a lengthy editorial, "Good Citizen: Rabbi Leaves Example of Rich Life," cited his many contributions to the city.

56. Undated tribute to Rabbi Wax in the possession of Mrs. James A. Wax.

Rabbi Grafman and Birmingham's Civil Rights Era

1. Rabbi Milton L. Grafman, telephone interview by author, 27 November 1993.

2. Rabbi Milton L. Grafman, telephone interview by author, 2 June 1993.

3. Rabbi Milton Grafman, interview by author, 11 June 1993.

4. Ibid.

5. Grafman, interview, 27 November 1993.

6. Patsy Place, "Grafman: Age Was Ignored until He Retired," *Birmingham News*, 28 February 1986, 1C.

7. Mark H. Elovitz, *A Century of Jewish Life in Dixie* (Tuscaloosa: University of Alabama Press, 1974), 150.

8. Ibid., 151.

9. Ibid., 84–85.

10. Ibid., 143.

11. Ibid., 144.

12. Place, "Age Was Ignored," 1C.

13. Grafman, interview, 11 June 1993.

14. Ibid.

15. Ibid.

16. Elovitz, *Century of Jewish Life*, 174.

17. Ibid., 175.

18. Juan Williams, *Eyes on the Prize: America's Civil Rights Years (1954–1965)* (New York: Penguin Books, 1988), 181.

19. Martin Luther King, Jr., *Why We Can't Wait* (New York: Mentor Books, 1964), 48–49.

20. Cited in Williams, *Eyes on the Prize*, 181.

21. Cited in "Can This Be Birmingham? *New York Times* Slanders Our City," *Birmingham News*, 14 April 1960, 1.

22. Cited in "The Salisbury Case," *Birmingham News*, 8 May 1960, 22.

23. Ibid.

24. Elovitz, *Century of Jewish Life*, 168.

25. Ibid., 169–70.

26. Grafman, interview, 11 June 1993.

27. Cited in "Can This Be Birmingham," 1.

28. Grafman, interview, 11 June 1993.

29. "Eleven Religious Leaders Appeal for 'Sanity' in Desegregation Issue," *Birmingham News*, 17 January 1963, 1, 2.

30. "Should Ministers Speak," *Birmingham News*, 20 January 1963, B2.

31. Taylor Branch, *Parting the Waters: America in the King Years (1954–63)* (New York: Simon & Schuster, 1988), 420.

32. Ibid., 644; Williams, 183–84.

33. Williams, *Eyes on the Prize*, 183. Although "moderate" whites viewed Boutwell's election as a move away from division, King and his associates were convinced "that Albert Boutwell was, in Fred Shuttlesworth's phrase, 'just a dignified Bull Connor,' who was a consistent supporter of segregationist views. His statement a few days after election that 'we citizens of Birmingham respect and understand one another' showed that he understood nothing about two-fifths of Birmingham's citizens, to whom even polite segregation was no respect."

34. Elovitz, *Century of Jewish Life*, 126–28.

35. Branch, *Parting the Waters*, 645–46.

36. Howell Raines, *My Soul Is Rested: Movement Days in the Deep South Remembered* (New York: Penguin Books, 1983), 155.

37. Ibid., 156.

38. Ibid., 157.

39. David J. Garrow, *Bearing the Cross: Martin Luther King, Jr., and the SCLC* (New York: Vintage Books, 1988), 237. The six goals were desegregation of the store facilities, adoption of fair hiring practices by those stores, dismissal of all charges from previous protests, equal employment opportunities with the city government for blacks, reopening on a desegregated basis of Birmingham's closed municipal recreation facilities, and establishment of a biracial committee to pursue further desegregation.

40. Williams, *Eyes on the Prize*, 184, 186.

41. "White Clergymen Urge Local Negroes to Withdraw from Demonstrations," *Birmingham News*, 13 April 1963, 2.

42. Ibid.

43. Taylor Branch, *Parting the Waters*, 737.

44. David Vann, telephone interview by author, 12 June 1993.

45. Garrow, *Bearing the Cross*, 238.

46. Raines, *My Soul Is Rested,* 145.

47. Branch, *Parting the Waters,* 737.

48. Ibid., 704.

49. Garrow, *Bearing the Cross,* 237–38.

50. Branch, *Parting the Waters,* 738.

51. King, *Why We Can't Wait,* 84–85.

52. Ibid., 86–87.

53. Garrow, *Bearing the Cross,* 243.

54. William C. Singleton III, "Grafman Says He Was for Equality," *Birmingham Post-Herald,* 21 November 1992, C1.

55. Reverend Fred Shuttlesworth, telephone interview by author, 17 June 1993.

56. Grafman, interview, 27 November 1993.

57. Singleton, "Equality," C1.

58. Vann, interview.

59. Grafman, interview, 27 November 1993.

60. Ibid.

61. Singleton, "Equality," C1.

62. Karl Friedman, telephone interview by author, 1 July 1993.

63. Mark H. Elovitz, telephone interview by author, 15 June 1993.

64. George Murray, telephone interview by author, 15 June 1993.

65. Branch, *Parting the Waters,* 745.

66. Grafman, interview, 27 November 1993.

67. Ibid.

68. Elovitz, *Century of Jewish Life,* 170.

69. Friedman, interview.

70. Elovitz, *Century of Jewish Life,* 174.

71. Ibid., 175.

72. Friedman, interview.

73. Elovitz, *Century of Jewish Life,* 171.

74. Ibid.

75. Friedman, interview.

76. Vann, interview.

77. See Branch, *Parting the Waters,* 785.

78. Elovitz, *Century of Jewish Life,* 171, 173.

79. Ibid., 173–74.

80. Williams, *Eyes on the Prize*, 193.

81. Fred Powledge, *Free At Last? The Civil Rights Movement and the People Who Made It* (New York: Harper Perennial, 1992), 511.

82. Branch, *Parting the Waters*, 888–91.

83. Ibid., 891.

84. Ibid., 892.

85. Rev. John T. Porter, telephone interview, 12 June 1993.

86. Ibid.

87. Grafman, interview by author, 11 June 1993.

88. Ibid.

89. Ibid. Letter from congregant Jack Siegel in Rabbi Grafman's possession.

90. Ibid.

91. "Memorial Fund Will Aid Both White, Negro Victims," *Birmingham News*, 20 September 1963, 1.

92. Branch, *Parting the Waters*, 893.

93. Ibid., 896–98.

94. "JFK to See Delegation of State Clergy," *Birmingham News*, 21 September 1963, 1.

95. Murray, interview.

96. Ibid.

97. Grafman, interview, 11 June 1993.

98. Branch, *Parting the Waters*, 901.

99. Garrow, *Bearing the Cross*, 298.

100. Ibid., 303–5.

101. Branch, *Parting the Waters*, 909–10.

102. Michelle Chapman, "Racial Harmony Is the Responsibility of All Birmingham Residents," *Birmingham Post-Herald*, 16 July 1990, 1.

103. Elovitz, *Century of Jewish Life*, 153.

104. Jimmie Lewis Franklin, *Back to Birmingham* (Tuscaloosa: University of Alabama Press, 1989), 120.

105. Ibid., 55, 121.

106. Vann, interview.

107. Jay Hamburg, "Rabbi Grafman Awarded Liberty Bell," *Birmingham Post-Herald*, 4 May 1983, F1.

108. Grafman, interview, 11 June 1993.

109. Franklin, *Back to Birmingham*, 121–23. Vann refused to turn over the police report of Carter's shooting and Sands's personnel files, which Vann believed would not be legally admissible and would invade the officer's privacy. Sands did not testify before the committee, nor did other key witnesses to the shooting, one of whom was himself "subject to criminal prosecution for assault with intent to murder."

110. Ibid., 124–25.

111. Ibid., 125. Some thought it was formed only to give Vann a better chance at reelection. Others thought that the case was so clear-cut that there was nothing to review. Still others thought that the committee would serve only to "delay Sands' removal from the police force." Though Abraham Woods "initially disliked the idea of an inquiry board, since the facts of [the] case seemed clear to him," he "admitted upon reflection that he was 'beginning to see something' " in the board's creation and work. And future mayor Richard Arrington, at the time a black ally of Vann's, thought that "Vann's special committee . . . at least . . . conceded the important principle that an outside body could discover the essential facts of a controversial police shooting."

112. Kate Peirce, "The Communicator," *Birmingham Magazine*, August 1983, 63.

113. Porter, interview.

114. Greg Garrison, "Noted Civic Leader Rabbi Grafman Dies," *Birmingham News*, 29 May 1995, 1.

115. "Milton Grafman, Rabbi Who Opposed Protests, Segregation," *Atlanta Journal*, 30 May 1995, Metro Ed., B7.

116. Ibid.

Divided Together:
Jews and African Americans in Durham, North Carolina

1. Robert Kenzer, *Kinship and Neighborhood in a Southern Community: Orange County, North Carolina, 1849–1881* (Knoxville: University of Tennessee Press, 1987), 180. "Divided Together: Jews and African Americans in Durham, North Carolina" is based on research from the author's larger study, *Migrations: A Social History of the Durham-Chapel Hill Jewish Community.*

2. Levi Branson, *Branson's Business Directory* (Raleigh: Branson, 1884); *Hill's Durham City Directory, 1903–1904* (Richmond: Hill, 1903); *Report of the Building Committee of the Beth-El Congregation upon the Completion of the Beth-El Synagogue* (Durham: Beth-El Congregation, 1922).

3. See Branson, *Branson's Business Directory*, 1877, 1884, and 1890.

4. *Durham Morning Herald*, 16 August 1903; Jean Anderson, *Durham County: A History of Durham County, North Carolina* (Durham: Duke University Press, 1990), 262.

5. Ruth Simand Malis to Leonard Rogoff, n.d.; Eli Evans, *The Provincials: A Personal History of Jews in the South* (New York: Atheneum, 1976), 291–98.

6. Pauli Murray, *Song in a Weary Throat* (New York: Harper and Row, 1987), 33–34. Years later Murray, as an attorney, argued a case before the New York State Supreme Court; belatedly she recognized Justice Henry Clay Greenberg as the son of her former neighbor.

7. *Durham Morning Herald*, 13 June 1907, 5 January 1908, 14 March 1908, 4 February 1910, 23 February 1910; Meno Lovenstein to Leonard Rogoff, 18 October 1986.

8. Irving Howe and Kenneth Libo, *How We Lived: A Documentary History of Immigrant Jews in America, 1880–1930* (New York: Richard Marek, 1979), 328.

9. Sam Margolis, interview by Robert Klein and Karen Feldman, 25 March n.y. Oral history project at Beth-El Synagogue, Durham, N.C.

10. Quoted in Robin Gruber, "From Pine Street to Watts Street: An Oral History of the Jews of Durham, North Carolina." Oral History Seminar of Dr. Lawrence Goodwyn and Dr. Eric Meyers, Duke University, 49; *Carolina Times*, 22 January 1938.

11. Walter Weare, *Black Business in the New South: A History of the North Carolina Mutual Life Insurance Company* (Urbana: University of Illinois Press, 1973), 81, 120.

12. Anderson, *Durham County*, 163–64; William Boyd, *The Story of Durham: City of the New South* (Durham: Duke University Press, 1925), 161–62.

13. Leonard Dinnerstein, *Uneasy at Home: Antisemitism and the American Jewish Experience* (New York: Columbia University Press, 1987), 223.

14. *Durham Morning Herald*, 26 July 1912.

15. "Simon, Abram," *The Universal Jewish Encyclopedia*, ed. Isaac Landman (New York: The Universal Jewish Encyclopedia, Inc., 1943), ix, 545. Rabbi Simon would also serve as president of the Washington Board of Education (1920–1923) and of the Central Conference of American Rabbis (1923–1925). In 1925 the Hebrew Union College conferred on him a doctor of Hebrew literature degree.

16. *Durham Morning Herald*, 22 March 1911.

17. Israel Mowshowitz, taped answer to questionnaire by author, March 1987; *Durham Sun*, 13 February 1943; *Durham Herald-Sun*, 14 February 1943.

18. *Report of the Building Committee of the Beth-El Congregation upon the Completion of the Beth-El Synagogue.*

19. *Durham Morning Herald,* 27 May 1939.

20. Sigmund Meyer, interview by author, 25 September 1986.

21. "Durham, N.C.," *American Jewish Times* 10 (October 1944): 10.

22. Edward Halperin, "Frank Porter Graham, Isaac Hall Manning, and the Jewish Quota at the University of North Carolina Medical School," *North Carolina Historical Review* 67 (October 1990): 385–410.

23. Leonard Rubin, "On a Southern Campus: The Jewish Boy's Problem," *American Jewish Times* (April 1938): 30–31, 70.

24. William Levitt, telephone interview by author, 11 December 1992; Martha Holland, "Sidney Rittenberg, an American Perspective of China" (master's thesis, University of North Carolina, 1986); William Chafe, *Never Stop Running: Allard Lowenstein and the Struggle to Save American Liberalism* (New York: Basic Books, 1993), 29.

25. Henry L. Feingold, *A Time for Searching: Entering the Mainstream, 1920–1945* (Baltimore: Johns Hopkins University Press, 1992), 255.

26. Leon Dworsky, interview by author, 5 January 1987.

27. Harry Golden, "The Golden Vertical Plan," *New South* 11 (November 1956): 12.

28. See Evans, *The Lonely Days Were Sundays* (Jackson: The University Press of Mississippi, 1993), 52–53; Evans, *The Provincials,* 29; Mary Mebane, *Mary* (New York: Fawcett, 1981), 220.

29. Sam and Hudi Gross, interview by Naomi Klein, 26, 30 April 1986; Abe Stadiem, interview by author, 8 April 1992.

30. *Durham Morning Herald,* 12 May 1970, 13 May 1970; *Hashomer,* 20 May 1970; Barry Yeoman, "Landlord Hall of Shame," *North Carolina Independent,* 30 May 1991, p. 9. *Hashomer* was a Jewish student newspaper published on the Duke University campus. The *North Carolina Independent* is an alternative newspaper with a Jewish publisher; the reporter who made allegations of abuse against the Jewish landlord was also Jewish.

31. Gilbert Katz, interview by Robin Gruber, 25 January 1986.

32. Leon Dworsky, interview by Robin Gruber, 26 January 1986.

33. Rabbi Herbert Berger, telephone interview by author, 9 February 1994.

34. William D. Snider, *Light on the Hill: A History of the University of North Carolina at Chapel Hill* (Chapel Hill: The University of North Carolina Press, 1992), 246–49; Douglas M. Knight, *Street of Dreams: The Nature and Legacy of the 1960s* (Durham: Duke University Press, 1989), 97, 99.

35. Anderson, *Durham County*, 434–41.

36. E. J. Evans, "Dear Voter" Letter, May 1957; *Durham Morning Herald*, 1 June 1952.

37. Eli Evans, *The Lonely Days*, xxi.

38. *Durham Morning Herald*, 7 May 1951, 1 June 1952.

39. Eli Evans, *The Provincials*, 6, 11; *Public Appeal*, 1 March 1961, 28 March 1962.

40. *Durham Morning Herald*, 13 May 1961.

41. *The Carolina Times*, 20 May 1961. The Durham Committee on the Affairs of Black People had been renamed the Durham Committee on Negro Affairs.

42. Molly Freedman, "Know Your House of Worship," *Report of the Building Committee of Beth-El Congregation* (Durham: Beth-El Congregation, 1961).

43. Beth-El Congregation Minutes, 1948.

44. Simon Glustrom, telephone interview by author, 12 April 1994.

45. Leon Dworsky, interview by author, 5 January 1987.

46. Louis Tuchman, telephone interview by author, 12 April 1994.

47. "Resolutions of the North Carolina Association of Rabbis," *American Jewish Times-Outlook* (December 1955): 31.

48. Louis Tuchman to Jacob R. Marcus, 26 March 1957.

49. "Rabbi Herbert Berger," *American Jewish Times-Outlook* 24 (October 1958): 40; Herbert Berger, "One God and One Humanity," *Report of the Building Committee of Beth-El Congregation* (Durham: Beth-El Congregation, 1961).

50. Herbert Berger, telephone interview by author, 9 February 1994.

51. Richard Cramer, conversation with author, 26 May 1995.

52. Ibid.

53. Ibid.; *Durham Morning Herald*, 2 May 1963.

54. Efraim Rosenzweig, interview by Irene Zipper, 22 June 1986; Efraim Rosenzweig, telephone interview by author, 7 February 1994; Abraham Karp, *Haven and Home: A History of the Jews in America* (New York: Schocken Books, 1985), 93.

55. Sam and Hudi Gross, interview.

56. Roy Pattishall, "The Trouble with Harry's," *The Spectator Magazine*, 7 August 1986, 5.

57. Hazel Gladstein Wishnov, interview by Robin Gruber, 12 February 1986; Molly Freedman, interview by Naomi Kirshner, 1 April n.y.

58. Mrs. Sam Freedman, "Durham, N.C.," *American Jewish Times-Outlook* 21 (May 1956): 13–14; Mrs. Sam Freedman, "Durham, N.C.," 26 (December 1960): 17.

59. Beth-El Sisterhood Congregation Community List, 1964; Jacob Rader Marcus, *To Count a People: American Jewish Population Data, 1585–1984* (Lanham: University Press of America, 1990), 165–66.

60. Sam and Hudi Gross, interview.

61. *Public Appeal*, 20 April 1960.

62. John Ehle, *The Free Men* (New York: Harper and Row, 1965), 276, 287; *Morning Herald*, 2 April 1964.

63. Charlotte Levin, interview by Lori Posner, 10 April 1986.

64. Arthrell D. Sanders, "Former NCCU Prof Recounts Odyssey from 1937 Germany to Shepard's NCC," *NCCU Faculty Newsletter* 1 (Fall 1984): 3, 5.

65. Statistics are derived from lists maintained by Beth-El Congregation Sisterhood and the Durham-Chapel Hill Jewish Federation. A more scientific sampling was conducted in 1991 in *Retirement Planning Survey*, Durham-Chapel Hill Jewish Federation, Fall 1991. See also Marcus, *To Count a People*, 165–66.

66. Elizabeth Wheaton, *Codename Greenkil: The 1979 Greensboro Killings* (Athens: University of Georgia Press, 1987), 11–19; Eric Yoffie, interview by author, 21 July 1986.

67. Raleigh *News and Observer*, 30 April 1992.

68. See Rogoff, *Migrations*. See also Geoff Sifrin, "Relationships between the Jewish and Black Communities in the Chapel Hill-Durham Area," Community Relations Council Sub-committee on Black-Jewish Dialogue in Chapel Hill-Durham (November 1991); Durham-Chapel Hill Jewish Community Relation Council Minutes, 19 March 1990, 6 August 1990, 24 September 1991.

Big Struggle in a Small Town:
Charles Mantinband of Hattiesburg, Mississippi

1. Janice Rothschild Blumberg, *One Voice: Jacob M. Rothschild and the Troubled South* (Macon, Ga.: Mercer University Press, 1985), 80–82; Arnold Shankman, "A Temple Is Bombed–Atlanta, 1958," *American Jewish Archives* 33 (November 1971): 129–31. The successful terrorist attacks took place in Miami, Florida, and Nashville, Tennessee, on 16 March 1958 and again in Jacksonville, Florida, on 29 April 1958. Unexploded dynamite was discovered at Jewish institutions in Charlotte and Gastonia, North

Carolina, on 11 November 1957 and 11 February 1958 respectively and in Birmingham, Alabama, on 28 April 1958.

2. Anna Kest Mantinband, "Time for Remembering," Charles Mantinband Papers, 1923–1968 (American Jewish Archives, Cincinnati, Ohio, bound typescript), 70.

3. Ibid., 69.

4. Bishop Joseph Brunini, interview by author, 24 March 1994.

5. Charles Mantinband, "In Dixieland I Take My Stand," Charles Mantinband Papers (hereafter Mantinband Papers). The other southern-born rabbis who became involved in the civil rights struggle were Emmet Frank of Alexandria, Virginia, who grew up in Houston, Texas, and Julian Feibelman of New Orleans, a native of Jackson, Mississippi. On the latter, see Julian B. Feibelman, *The Making of a Rabbi* (New York: Vantage Press, 1980).

6. Anna Kest Mantinband, "Time for Remembering," 73.

7. Charles Mantinband, "A Message for Race Relations Sabbath 1962," Mantinband Papers.

8. Mantinband, "In Dixieland I Take My Stand."

9. Irwin Schulman to Alex Miller, 9 April 1958, Box 1, Folder 2, Anti-Defamation League of B'nai B'rith Records, 1946–1982, Amistad Research Center, Tulane University; Charles Mantinband, "Rabbi in the Deep South," *ADL Bulletin* 19 (May 1962): 4; Rabbi Charles Mantinband, "Jewish Communities in the South and the Desegregation Issue" (address at the Plenary Session, National Community Relations Advisory Council, Atlantic City, N.J., June 1956, Mantinband Papers, copy). Mantinband was typical of Southern rabbis—and of the region's white moderates generally—in opposing the confrontational tactics of Northern civil rights activists. Gradual change effected at the local level was considered by Southern rabbis to be the only means of ensuring a peaceful solution to the desegregation crisis. See Lawrence J. Goldmark, "Incident in Mississippi," *Jewish Digest* 19 (January 1974): 31; P. Allen Krause, "Rabbis and Negro Rights in the South, 1954–1967," *American Jewish Archives* 21 (April 1969): 37; William S. Malev, "The Jew of the South in the Conflict on Segregation," *Conservative Judaism* 13 (Fall 1958): 36–43; Albert Vorspan, "The Freedom Rides," *Jewish Frontier* (April 1962): 8.

10. P. D. East, *The Magnolia Jungle* (New York: Simon and Schuster, 1960), 13.

11. Leonard Auerbach, interview by author, 18 March 1994. At the time of the *Brown* decision, in 1954, the exact number of Jews who lived in Hattiesburg was 232. *American Jewish Year Book*, 1954, 8.

12. Charles Mantinband quoted in Allen Krause, "Interview Regarding the Role of the Rabbis in the Civil Rights Movement in the South," tape recording, 23 June 1966, American Jewish Archives; Murray Friedman,

"One Episode in Southern Jewry's Response to Desegregation: An Historical Memoir," *American Jewish Archives* 33 (November 1981): 171. On the compromise southern Jews were forced to make in order to secure their own socioeconomic status, see Leonard Dinnerstein, "Southern Jewry and the Desegregation Crisis, 1954–1970," *American Jewish Historical Quarterly*, 62 (March 1973): 232–33; Harry L. Golden, *Only in America* (New York: Permabooks, 1959), 126–28; Theodore Lowi, "Southern Jews: The Two Communities," *Jewish Journal of Sociology* 6 (July 1964): 110–12.

13. James Graham Cook, *The Segregationists* (New York: Appleton, Century, Crofts, 1962), 153–54; John Bartlow Martin, *The Deep South Says "Never"* (New York: Ballantine Books, 1957), 15.

14. *Hattiesburg American*, 17 May 1954. The career and ideological convictions of Sam Bowers are explored in Jack Nelson, *Terror in the Night: The Klan's Campaign against The Jews* (New York: Simon & Schuster, 1993).

15. Emmett Till, a fourteen-year-old African American from Chicago, came south to visit relatives in the Mississippi Delta in August 1955. Having allegedly whistled at a white woman in a grocery store, Till was savagely beaten before being shot dead. Having first mutilated the corpse, Till's murderers threw his remains unceremoniously into the Tallahatchie River. The resulting trial of two white men, which aroused national publicity, proved a classic example of racial injustice. Despite clear evidence of their guilt, the defendants were acquitted by an all-white jury. Robert Weisbrot, *Freedom Bound: A History of America's Civil Rights Movement* (New York: W. W. Norton & Company, 1990), 93–94. The murder of Mack Parker occurred less than four years later, in April 1959. Parker was arrested for allegedly raping a white woman. Abducted from his jail cell by a gang of hooded men, his scarred remains were eventually dragged by FBI investigators from the Pearl River, outside Poplarville, Mississippi. Although the FBI extracted confessions from three of the men who lynched Parker, and also identified his other assailants, the local prosecutor refused to allow the grand jury to read the report. The jury also snubbed FBI agents who volunteered their testimonies. Despite desperate attempts by the Justice Department to indict the accused men under weaker federal statutes, nothing could be done. Mack Parker's killers walked free. Taylor Branch, *Parting the Waters: Martin Luther King and the Civil Rights Movement, 1954–63* (London: Papermac, 1990), 257–58.

16. Charles Mantinband to the editor, *Hattiesburg American*, 21 January 1961, Mantinband Papers; Undated note on members of the Mississippi Council on Human Relations, Box 135, Folder 2, Paul B. Johnson Family Papers, McCain Library and Archives, University of Southern Mississippi. The State Sovereignty Commission is discussed in James W. Silver, *Mississippi: The Closed Society* (New York: Harcourt, Brace & World, 1964), 8; James W. Loewen and Charles Sallis, eds., *Mississippi: Conflict &*

Change (New York: Pantheon Books, revised edition, 1980), 257. The four other whites identified as members of the Mississippi Council on Human Relations were Bishop Joseph Brunini, also a codirector; Dr A. D. Beittel, president of Tougaloo College in Jackson; Mr. H. Power Hearn; and Rev. Murray Cox.

17. J. C. Fairley, interview by author, 19 March 1994; Charles Phillips, telephone interview by author, 19 March 1994.

18. Erle Johnston, *Mississippi's Defiant Years, 1953–1973: An Interpretative Documentary with Personal Experiences* (Forest, Miss.: Lake Harbor Publishers, 1990), 53–54; Monty Piliowsky, *Exit 13: Oppression and Racism in Academia* (Boston: South End Press, 1982), 22.

19. Lou Ginsberg, interview by author, 18 March 1994.

20. Ibid.

21. Anna Kest Mantinband, "Time for Remembering," 70–72; Johnston, *Mississippi's Defiant Years*, 54.

22. Piliowsky, *Exit 13*, 24.

23. Charles Mantinband to James Silver, 22 February 1963, Mantinband Papers; Esther Shemper, interview by author, 18 March 1994.

24. Mantinband to Silver.

25. Leonard Auerbach, interview; Irwin Schulman to Alex Miller, 9 February 1958.

26. *Montgomery Advertiser–Alabama Journal*, 12 February 1956.

27. *National Jewish Post and Opinion*, 14 February 1958.

28. Julius Rosenthal, "Mezuzahs and Magnolias," Mantinband Papers, 13–14.

29. Ibid.

30. Mantinband, "Rabbi in the Deep South," 3; Esther Shemper, interview.

31. Anna Kest Mantinband, "Time for Remembering," 68.

32. Marvin Reuben and Maury Gurwitch, interviews by author, 18 March 1994.

33. *Jackson Daily News*, 24 March 1956; Charles Mantinband, interview by Allen Krause.

34. Mantinband, "Rabbi in the Deep South," 3–4; Margaret Long, editorial, *New South* 17 (1963): 9; Benjamin E. Mays, president of Morehouse College, Atlanta, to Charles Mantinband, 7 May 1951; Robert Ogden Purves, Hampton Institute, Virginia, to Charles Mantinband, 10 May 1951; A. D. Beittel, Talladega College, Alabama, to Charles Mantinband, 12 May 1951, Mantinband Papers.

35. Charles Mantinband, "From the Diary of a Mississippi Rabbi," *American Judaism* 12 (1963): 9.

36. Maury Gurwitch, interview; Perry E. Nussbaum, Charles Mantinband, Jacob M. Rothschild, "The Southern Rabbi Faces The Problem Of Desegregation," *CCAR Journal* 14 (June 1956): 3.

37. Charles Mantinband to Harry Golden, 21 January 1961, Mantinband Papers.

38. Charles Mantinband, interview by Allen Krause.

39. Gabrielle Simon Edgcomb, *From Swastika to Jim Crow: Refugee Scholars at Black Colleges* (Malabar, Fla.: Krieger Publishing Company, 1993), 117–25; Ed King, interview by author, 23 March 1994.

40. Perry Nussbaum to Charles Mantinband, 22 August 1958, Mantinband Papers.

41. Silver, *Mississippi,* 131; Mantinband to Jacob Marcus [?], December 1960, Mantinband Papers.

42. Mantinband to P. D. East, 16 July 1960, 11 December 1959, Mantinband Papers.

43. Mantinband, interview by Allen Krause; "Rabbi in the Deep South," 4.

44. Esther Shemper and Lou Ginsberg, interviews; *Jewish Monitor* 14 (May 1962): 12–13; *National Jewish Post and Opinion,* 27 April 1962.

45. *Hattiesburg American,* 20 February 1963; Rabbi Leo Bergman, "Is there a Jewish Ku Klux Klan in Hattiesburg?" Sermon, 15 January 1965, Mantinband Papers.

46. Anna Kest Mantinband, "Time for Remembering," 76.

47. Hattiesburg's experience during the Freedom Summer is described in various works including Len Holt, *The Summer That Didn't End* (New York: William Morrow & Co., 1965); Mary Aickin Rothschild, *A Case of Black and White: Northern Volunteers and the Southern Freedom Summers, 1964–1965* (Westport, Conn.: Greenwood Press, 1982); and Elizabeth Sutherland, ed., *Letters from Mississippi* (New York: McGraw-Hill Book Company, 1965).

What Price Amos?
Perry Nussbaum's Career in Jackson, Mississippi

1. Nussbaum used this rhetorical question in place of the phrase "Sincerely yours" in a letter he wrote to several colleagues. In this letter he was soliciting advice and counsel in the aftermath of the first congregational crisis he endured as a result of his position on civil rights. See Nussbaum to Emil Leipziger, Sidney Regner, Jay Kaufman, and Al Vorspan, 23 October 1958, Rabbi Perry E. Nussbaum Papers (hereafter Nussbaum Pa-

pers), Miscellaneous Collection (hereafter Ms. Coll.) #430, American Jewish Archives, Cincinnati, Ohio (hereafter AJA).

2. Murray Polner, *Rabbi: The American Experience* (New York: Holt, Rinehart and Winston, 1977), 79.

3. Nussbaum repeatedly blamed the bombings on "bigotry and [the continuous] distribution of anti-Semitic literature." See untitled newspaper clipping, 6 December 1968, Temple Beth Israel *Bulletin*, 3 June 1968, and Nussbaum to Friends in the United States, 1 October 1967 (mimeographed letter), Nussbaum Papers, Ms. Coll. #430, AJA.

4. Nussbaum to Murray Polner, 20 November 1975, Nussbaum Papers, Ms. Coll. #430, AJA.

5. Jack Nelson's recent book on the Ku Klux Klan and the Jews titled *Terror in the Night: The Klan's Campaign against the Jews* (New York: Simon & Schuster, 1993) casts Nussbaum in a rather unfavorable light. Nelson portrays him as a difficult human being who had a knack for insulting people. Murray Polner's treatment of Nussbaum is a much more balanced presentation. See Polner, *Rabbi*, 69–114. Nussbaum is mentioned briefly in Leonard Dinnerstein, *Antisemitism in America* (New York: Oxford University Press, 1994), 190–93, and William M. Kunstler's *Deep in My Heart* (New York: William Morrow & Company, 1966), 58–59. See also Allen Krause, "The Southern Rabbi and Civil Rights" (rabbinic thesis, Hebrew Union College-Jewish Institute of Religion, 1967).

6. Perry E. Nussbaum, "Memoirs" (Nussbaum Papers, Ms. Coll. #430, AJA, n.d., typescript), 1; idem, "Biographical Sketch of Rabbi Perry E. Nussbaum" (Nussbaum Papers, Ms. Coll. #430, AJA, April 1967, typescript). On Rabbi Barnett R. Brickner, see Kerry M. Olitzky, Lance J. Sussman, and Malcolm H. Stern, eds., *Reform Judaism in America: A Biographical Dictionary and Sourcebook* (Westport, Conn.: Greenwood Press, 1993), 25–27.

7. Nussbaum, "Memoirs," 1.

8. Ibid., 1–2. See also Nussbaum, "Biographical Sketch," 1. In 1927 Nussbaum earned a B in English and math and a C in history at the University of Cincinnati. He scored a 96 percent in Hebrew and a 93 percent in Essentials of Judaism in the College's Preparatory Department. Cf. Nussbaum to Ferdinand Isserman, 8 February 1927, Nussbaum Papers, Ms. Coll. #6, AJA.

9. For quote on Isserman, see Julius Mark, "Memorial Tribute to Ferdinand Isserman," *Central Conference of American Rabbis Yearbook* (hereafter *CCAR Yearbook*), vol. 82, 169–70. See also Olitzky, Sussman and Stern, 99–101. Professor of Bible Sheldon H. Blank and professor of history Jacob Rader Marcus were two of Nussbaum's favorite instructors. Cf. Nussbaum to Isserman, 22 October 1926 and 23 September 1927, Nuss-

baum Papers, Ms. Coll. #6, AJA. See also Nussbaum, "Biographical Sketch," 1, 5; and idem, "Memoirs," 2.

10. See Nussbaum, "Biographical Sketch," 1–2, and idem, "Memoirs," 3. For a look at Nussbaum's attempt to defend Reform in Australia, see Perry E. Nussbaum, "Reform Judaism & Assimilation." Address printed by Beth Israel, Melbourne, Australia [1934?], Nussbaum Papers, Ms. Coll. #430, AJA.

11. Nussbaum, "Biographical Sketch," 2, and idem, "Memoirs," 3. On Nussbaum's stay in Wichita, see "Our Family Album" [1942?] in Nussbaum Papers, Ms. Coll. #430, AJA.

12. Nussbaum, "Biographical Sketch," 2. On his departure from Emanu-El of Long Beach, N.Y., Nussbaum informed the congregation that the prospect of uprooting his family was especially painful because they "wanted to settle permanently" in Long Beach. See Nussbaum to Members of Congregation Emanu-El, 3 February 1950, Nussbaum Papers, Ms. Coll. #430, AJA. In Pittsfield, Nussbaum was profoundly frustrated by financial trouble and worried that the congregation would not meet its annual budget. Writing to a member of the CCAR's Rabbinical Placement Commission he pleaded for consideration in getting a better pulpit: "I think I am justified in a 'promotion' to that type of congregation where I can bring to bear 20 years of experience and have the assistance and the security which other men of my generation now enjoy." Nussbaum to Jacob P. Rudin, 23 January 1953, Nussbaum Papers, Ms. Coll. #430, AJA.

13. Richard J. Birnholz, "Perry Nussbaum" (Memorial Tribute), *CCAR Yearbook*, vol. 97, 208–9.

14. For quotes on Nussbaum's personality, see Nelson, *Terror in the Night*, 32–33. For quotes related to the United Givers Fund, see Jack Sperling to Nussbaum, 24 October 1968, and Nussbaum to Sperling, 25 October 1968, Nussbaum Papers, Ms. Coll. #430, AJA.

15. See Nelson, *Terror in the Night*, 32–33, and passim. For Nussbaum's quote, see Nussbaum, "Biographical Sketch," 5, and Nussbaum to Maurice Eisendrath, 15 December 1952, Nussbaum Papers, Ms. Coll. #38, AJA.

16. Regarding Nussbaum's writing style, see idem, "Flying Up High Enough," *Southwest Jewish Chronicle* 17 (January 1943): 1. See also "And Then There Was One in the Capital City of Mississippi," *Central Conference of American Rabbis Journal* (hereafter *CCAR Journal*) (1 October 1963): 15–19; "Mississippi Rabbi Under Fire," *Reconstructionist* (12 December 1969): 21–24; and "The Southern Rabbi Faces the Problem of Desegregation—Pulpit in Mississippi Anyone?" *CCAR Journal* (June 1956): 1–3. For compliments on his original prayers, see David Lefkowitz to Nussbaum, 5 October 1962, Nussbaum Papers, Ms. Coll. #430, AJA. See Samuel R. Stone to Nussbaum, 12 March 1959; Levi Olan to Nuss-

baum, 23 October 1962; Lefkowitz to Nussbaum, 5 October 1962 (all in Nussbaum Papers, Ms. Coll. #430, AJA). In his memoirs, Nussbaum remarked: "I loved teaching on the college level." The religion department chairperson at Millsaps College told Nussbaum he was the "best instructor he had ever met." See Nussbaum, "Memoirs," 17 (Best Friends). See also untitled newspaper article dated 23 September 1972, in Nussbaum Papers, Correspondence file, AJA.

17. Roland E. Toms, M.D., to Nussbaum, 26 November 1970, and Moshe Gilboa to Nussbaum, 22 December 1970, Nussbaum Papers, Ms. Coll. #430, AJA.

18. Nussbaum to Abraham J. Feldman, 8 January 1952, Nussbaum Papers, Ms. Coll. #38, AJA. See also idem, "Flying Up High Enough."

19. Nussbaum, "Memoirs," 4.

20. For quote, see Nussbaum, "Biographical Sketch," 2.

21. Regarding the decision's effect on white southerners, see Seth Cagin and Philip Dray, *We Are Not Afraid: The Story of Goodman, Schwerner, and Chaney and the Civil Rights Campaign for Mississippi* (New York: Macmillan Publishing Company, 1988), 53–55.

22. For quote, see Polner, *Rabbi,* 80. On the insecurities of southern Jews and the impact of the 1954 Supreme Court ruling, see Dinnerstein, *Antisemitism,* 188–94; and Henry L. Feingold, gen. ed., *The Jewish People in America,* vol. 5, *A Time for Healing: American Jewry since World War II,* by Edward S. Shapiro (Baltimore: Johns Hopkins University Press, 1992), 40–43.

23. Dinnerstein, *Antisemitism,* 189–91. (For quote, see 191.) See also Shapiro, *A Time for Healing,* 42. In 1957 and 1958 bombings of Jewish institutions had occurred in Charlotte and Gastonia, North Carolina; Birmingham and Gadsden, Alabama; Nashville, Tennessee; Miami and Jacksonville, Florida; and Atlanta, Georgia. See Dinnerstein, *Antisemitism,* 190–94.

24. For quote, see Dinnerstein, *Antisemitism,* 193. See also Nussbaum, "Memoirs," 4, and idem, "Biographical Sketch," 2.

25. Transcript of "Oral History Memoir of Rabbi Perry Nussbaum" (5 August 1965), 2. Nussbaum Papers, Ms. Coll. #430, AJA.

26. Nussbaum, "Biographical Sketch," 4. See also Polner, *Rabbi,* 79, and Nelson, *Terror in the Night,* 34–35. For a history of Temple Beth Israel of Jackson, see Perry Nussbaum, "The Beth Israel of Jackson, Mississippi Story" (paper written for the centennial of the congregation's founding) in Nussbaum Papers, Ms. Coll. #430, AJA.

27. Nussbaum, "Biographical Sketch," 4.

28. Nussbaum to Mendall M. Davis, 11 October 1954, Nussbaum Papers, Ms. Coll. #430, AJA. See also Jeremiah 29:7.

29. Florence Mars, *Witness in Philadelphia* (Baton Rouge: Louisiana State University Press, 1977), 3–4.

30. Gayle Graham Yates, *Mississippi Mind: A Personal Cultural History of an American State* (Knoxville: University of Tennessee Press, 1990), 263–77. (Quote appears on 277.)

31. Nussbaum, "Memoirs," 2, 6 (Best Friends).

32. Ibid., 3.

33. Ibid., 6.

34. See Newspaper Scrapbook, Nussbaum papers, Ms. Coll. #430, AJA. See also Nussbaum to Levi Olan, 16 February 1954, Ms. Coll. #181, AJA.

35. See Newspaper Scrapbook, Nussbaum papers, Ms. Coll. #430, AJA, and Nussbaum, "Memoirs," 9–11 (Politics).

36. Transcript of "Oral History Memoir of Rabbi Perry Nussbaum" (5 August 1965), 2. Nussbaum Papers, Ms. Coll. #430, AJA.

37. Nussbaum's description of the controversy appears in Temple Beth Israel's *Bulletin*, 11 February 1964, Nussbaum Papers, Ms. Coll. #94, AJA.

38. Ibid. See also letters from Clayton Rand to Nussbaum, 13 February, 3 March, 17 March, and 22 December 1964, Nussbaum Papers, Ms. Coll. #430, AJA. Nussbaum was tireless in his defense of Jewish sensitivities. He was unyielding in his demand that state officials use the term "religious people" and not "Christians" when making official proclamations. When the Mississippi Council on Human Relations scheduled its annual meeting on a Friday evening, the Jewish Sabbath, Nussbaum complained to the council's executive director: "I have tried to establish among non-Jews an appreciation of Jews' right to their Sabbath and that they should not be put in a position of having to make a choice between their own religious loyalties and civic undertakings. . . . I tell you emphatically I consider the timing of such a program an affront to my religion and to those Jews who go to services and who have served the Mississippi Council on Human Relations." See Nussbaum to Mayor Russell Davis, 21 May 1970, and for quote see Nussbaum to Joan Bowman, 3 November 1971, Nussbaum Papers, Ms. Coll. #430, AJA.

39. Nussbaum, "Biographical Sketch," 3. See also George Hurtig to Nussbaum, 25 June 1955, Nussbaum Papers, Ms. Coll. #430, AJA.

40. Rabbi Alexander Kline to Nussbaum, 21 January 1958, Nussbaum Papers, Ms. Coll. #430, AJA. In his letter inviting a colleague to address the assembly at its annual meeting, Nussbaum advised the speaker to stick to parochial matters—Jewishly speaking. He informed the guest that the members of the assembly would prefer hearing about Jewish rather than non-Jewish issues. See Nussbaum to Julian Feibelman, 15 December 1955, Nussbaum Papers, Ms. Coll. #430, AJA. For more information, see

file on Mississippi Assembly of Jewish Congregations, Nussbaum Papers, AJA.

41. Nussbaum to Feibelman, 6 June 1955, and Transcript of "Oral History Memoir of Rabbi Perry Nussbaum" (5 August 1965), Nussbaum Papers, Ms. Coll. #430, AJA. See also Nussbaum, "Memoirs," 27 (Politics).

42. Perry Nussbaum, "Classified Information" (High Holy Day Sermon—1955), Nussbaum Papers, Sermon File, AJA. See also "The Essence of Brotherhood" (sermon delivered on 14 May 1958), Nussbaum Papers, Sermon File, AJA.

43. Perry Nussbaum, "Do Temples Belong in Politics?—A Symposium," *American Judaism* (Fall 1956): 17. See also Psalm 119:9. Mississippi's Reform Jews were well aware of the help provided to the NAACP by prominent northern Reformers like Jack Greenberg, Kivie Kaplan, and Al Vorspan of the UAHC. These outspoken interlopers came south regularly and, after completing their speaking circuit, returned home. Southern Jews insisted that their northern coreligionists did not take seriously the potentially disastrous ramifications their actions could wreak on the local community.

44. Perry Nussbaum, "The Southern Rabbi Faces the Problem of Desegregation," *CCAR Journal* (June 1956): 1–3.

45. Ibid. Nussbaum began collecting newspaper articles on the Citizens' Councils as soon as he arrived in Jackson. See his collection of newspaper articles, Nussbaum Papers, Ms. Coll. #430, AJA.

46. Nussbaum to Jay Kaufman, 20 January 1956, Nussbaum Papers, Ms. Coll. #430, AJA.

47. Nussbaum's message for the occasion was "The Essence of Brotherhood" (sermon delivered on 14 May 1958), Nussbaum Papers, Sermon File, AJA. For a chilling account of life on the campus of the University of Mississippi during this period, see James W. Silver, *Mississippi: The Closed Society* (New York: Harcourt, Brace & World, Inc., 1964).

48. Nussbaum to James Wax, 19 February 1956, Nussbaum Papers, Ms. Coll. #430, AJA.

49. S. Andhil Fineberg to Nussbaum, 29 October 1957, Nussbaum Papers, Ms. Coll. #430, AJA.

50. Silver, *Mississippi*, 10–11 and 41–44. See also Nussbaum to Robert Schur, 9 October 1957, Nussbaum Papers, Ms. Coll. #430, AJA.

51. Nussbaum to Leipziger, 23 October 1958, Nussbaum Papers, Ms. Coll. #430, AJA.

52. Irwin Schulman to Nussbaum, 30 March 1958, 23 June 1958, and 21 October 1958, Nussbaum Papers, Ms. Coll. #430, AJA. For quote, see tran-

script of "Oral History Memoir of Rabbi Perry Nussbaum" (5 August 1965), Nussbaum Papers, Ms. Coll. #430, AJA.

53. Temple Beth Israel *Bulletin,* 13 October 1958, Nussbaum Papers, Ms. Coll. #430, AJA.

54. *State Times,* 15 October 1958. See also James S. Ferguson to Nussbaum, 21 October 1958, George Lieberman to Nussbaum, 21 October 1958, Jacob J. Weinstein to Nussbaum, 27 October and 1 November 1958, and Nussbaum to Weinstein, 29 October and 3 November 1958, Nussbaum Papers, Ms. Coll. #430, AJA.

55. For a full discussion of Nussbaum's perspective on this controversy, see Nussbaum to Vorspan, 23 October 1958, Nussbaum Papers, Ms. Coll. #430, AJA.

56. Nussbaum to Jacob J. Weinstein, 29 October 1958, Nussbaum Papers, Ms. Coll. #430, AJA.

57. For the most complete history of the Freedom Rides to date, see August Meier and Elliott Rudwick, *CORE: A Study in the Civil Rights Movement, 1942-1968* (Chicago: University of Illinois Press, 1975), 135–58, and Mary Aickin Rothschild, *A Case of Black and White: Northern Volunteers and the Southern Freedom Summers, 1964-1965* (Westport, Conn.: Greenwood Press, 1982), 3–29. See also Howard Zinn, *SNCC: The New Abolitionists* (Boston: Beacon Press, 1964), Doris Yvonee Wilkinson, *Black Revolt: Strategies of Protest* (Berkeley, Calif.: McCutchan Publishing Corporation, 1969), and James Peck, *Freedom Ride* (New York: Grove Press, 1962).

58. Rothschild, *Black and White,* 11.

59. Nussbaum, "Memoirs," 21–26 (Politics). Letters came to Nussbaum from Rabbi Roland B. Gittelsohn of Boston, Mr. Henry Schwartzchild of Chicago, and Rabbi Martin Freedman, who was associated with CORE. See Krause, "Southern Rabbi," 284–85.

60. Nussbaum, "Memoirs," 22 (Politics). See also Nussbaum to Colleagues in Greenville, Greenwood, Clarksdale, and Cleveland, 28 July 1961, Nussbaum Papers, Ms. Coll. #430, AJA.

61. Ibid.

62. Nussbaum to Al Vorspan, 11 August 1961, Nussbaum Papers, Ms. Coll. #430, AJA. Kunstler briefly described his conversation with Nussbaum in the late evening of 24 August 1961. Kunstler cast Nussbaum in the role of a southern apologist expressing his fear that interfering northern rabbis would set off a rash of anti-Semitism in Jackson. In light of Nussbaum's activities on behalf of the Freedom Riders, Kunstler's characterization seems particularly stilted. Kunstler wrote that Nussbaum's appeal left him "extremely depressed" because, as a Jew, Kunstler always believed that "religious leaders, of all people, have an obligation to put

into practice the principles that fill their sermon." If Nussbaum did indeed make such an unfavorable impression on the lawyer, it is interesting that Kunstler wrote the rabbi the following year to ask that he look in on his daughter, who was to be attending nearby Tougaloo College for a semester. See Kunstler, *Deep in My Heart,* 59, and Kunstler to Nussbaum, 11 September 1962, Nussbaum Papers, Ms. Coll. #430, AJA.

63. Moses M. Landau to Nussbaum, 1 August 1961, Nussbaum Papers, Ms. Coll. #430, AJA.

64. Allen Schwartzman to Nussbaum, 2 August 1961, Nussbaum Papers, Ms. Coll. #430, AJA.

65. Nussbaum to Landau, 1 August 1961, Nussbaum Papers, Ms. Coll. #430, AJA.

66. Nussbaum to Jacob Rader Marcus, 23 October 1961, Nussbaum Papers, Ms. Coll. #430, AJA. See also transcript of "Oral History Memoir of Rabbi Perry Nussbaum" (5 August 1965), Nussbaum Papers, Ms. Coll. #430, AJA. Regarding the integrated services at Parchman, Nussbaum later recalled: "I was scared stiff, because that was the first time [integrated worship services took place in Mississippi] . . . If the word had gone out that the rabbi was going up there for the Negroes as well as the whites, my life would have been worth two cents."

67. Nussbaum to Marcus, 23 October 1961, Nussbaum Papers, Ms. Coll. #430, AJA. Whenever colleagues wrote to compliment Nussbaum on his effort, Nussbaum asked them to donate a small contribution from their discretionary funds to offset the costs he himself subsidized. He later remarked pointedly, "It is by no means insignificant that . . . when I asked colleagues to send me something to offset my expenses, that was the last I heard from them. I did get a contribution from Alfred Gottschalk of HUC-JIR (at that time dean) in L.A. from his own personal funds." See Nussbaum to Vorspan, 28 September 1961, Nussbaum Papers, Ms. Coll. #430, AJA.

68. Emphasis in original. Henry Schwartzchild to Nussbaum, 7 August 1961; George V. Sheviakov to Nussbaum, 16 August 1961; Marilyn Eisenberg to Nussbaum, 28 August 1961; Isadore Posner to Nussbaum, 6 August 1961, Nussbaum Papers, Ms. Coll. #430, AJA. More than all these encomia Nussbaum treasured the emotional words of praise he earned from his own twenty-two-year-old daughter, Leslie. See Leslie Nussbaum to Perry Nussbaum, August 1961, Nussbaum Papers, Ms. Coll. #430, AJA.

69. Nussbaum, "Memoirs," 26 (Politics).

70. Nussbaum to Weinstein, 29 October 1958, Nussbaum Papers, Ms. Coll. #430, AJA. (For quote in context, see note 56, above.)

71. John Dittmer, *Local People: The Struggle for Civil Rights in Mississippi* (Urbana: University of Illinois Press, 1994): 103, 118–19; Nicolaus Mills,

Like a Holy Crusade: Mississippi 1964—The Turning of the Civil Rights Movement in America (Chicago: Ivan R. Dee, 1992): 15–25; Judea B. Miller, "Not for Thee to Complete," *CCAR Journal* (Winter/Spring 1995): 13–20.

72. Mills, *Holy Crusade,* 107–10. See also note 55, above.

73. Nussbaum, "Memoirs," 1–30 (Best Friends). On Harrison and Clark, see Silver, *Mississippi,* 55–59, 208. Nussbaum refers to himself as a "compulsive speaker" in his article "And Then There Was One in the Capital City of Mississippi," *CCAR Journal* (October 1963): 18.

74. Silver, *Mississippi,* 58–60. Nussbaum, "Memoirs," 12–13. Nussbaum wrote a beautiful and prescient letter of condolence to Mrs. Evers: "I pray to the Lord that you will continue to have the same courage in the days ahead that you must have had these past years. I pray for your children. May they mature proud in the knowledge that their father was tireless and fearless in behalf of the American dream. Some day, when the history of these times in Mississippi and Jackson is honestly and fully set down, the name of Medgar Evers, martyr, will be a symbol and an example of those human qualities which, God help us, so few now display." See Nussbaum to Mrs. Medgar Evers, 12 June 1963, Nussbaum Papers, Ms. Coll. #430, AJA.

75. Nussbaum, "Memoirs," 10–17. On the twenty-eight Methodist clergy and Selah, see Silver, *Mississippi,* 58–60. In 1965 Nussbaum noted that Jewish students attending Tougaloo College brought a black student to Sabbath Services at Temple Beth Israel. The students sat down next to a congregant who was, according to Nussbaum, a "real racist." Although some of his members had threatened to eject any black who attempted to enter the temple, the student sat through the service without incident. Had congregants attempted to remove the young man, Nussbaum contended he would have told them what he thought of them "right in the middle of the service." See transcript of "Oral History Memoir of Rabbi Perry Nussbaum" (5 August 1965), 39–40. Nussbaum Papers, Ms. Coll. #430, AJA. On Mantinband see Anna Kest Mantinband, "Time for Remembering," Charles Mantinband Papers, 1923–1968 (American Jewish Archives, Cincinnati, Ohio, bound typescript), 57–74; and Krause, "Southern Rabbi," 154–64.

76. Nussbaum, "And Then There Was One," 17–19.

77. Transcript of "Oral History Memoir of Rabbi Perry Nussbaum" (5 August 1965), 39–40. Nussbaum Papers, Ms. Coll. #430, AJA. Nussbaum, "Memoirs," 25–30. See also Al Vorspan and Balfour Brickner to members of the UAHC Social Action Commission, 5 October 1964, and Balfour Brickner to UAHC Regional Directors, 7 October 1964, Nussbaum Papers, Ms. Coll. #430, AJA. *The Southern Israelite,* 25 December 1964, David Ben-Ami Collection, Correspondence File, AJA. Nussbaum served as the president of the Greater Jackson Clergy Alliance in 1971. Moses

Landau expressed opposition to Nussbaum's high-profile fund-raising on behalf of black churches. He told Nussbaum that his notoriety was likely to have a negative impact on the Jews living in the Delta region of the state. Nussbaum, however, refused to concede: "I just cannot be convinced," he wrote Landau, "that Jewish participation in helping to rebuild churches—even Negro—is dangerous to Jewish well-being." See also Nussbaum to Landau, 7 January 1965, Nussbaum Papers, Ms. Coll. #430, AJA.

78. "Report of Dr. Perry E. Nussbaum, Rabbi of Beth Israel Congregation," 3 May 1964 and 2 May 1965, Nussbaum Papers, Ms. Coll. #430, AJA.

79. Nussbaum, "Memoirs," 6–7 (Best Friends). See also Nelson, *Terror in the Night*, 45–48.

80. A significant portion of Nelson's book, *Terror in the Night*, is a reconstruction of the bombings. Cf. Polner, *Rabbi*. See also Temple Beth Israel *Bulletin*, 3 June 1967, and Nussbaum's letter "To Our Friends" (Nussbaum Papers, Temple Beth Israel File, AJA, 1 October 1967, mimeographed).

81. Nussbaum to Polner, 20 November 1975, Nussbaum Papers, Ms. Coll. #430, AJA. Nelson, *Terror in the Night*, 73. Temple Beth Israel *Bulletin*, 3 June 1967, Nussbaum Papers, Temple Beth Israel File, AJA.

82. Nussbaum, "To Our Friends." See also Nussbaum, "Memoirs," 9–10 (Best Friends), and Nussbaum to Polner, 20 November 1975, Nussbaum Papers, Ms. Coll. #430, AJA.

83. Nussbaum to Polner, 20 November 1975, Nussbaum Papers, Ms. Coll. #430, AJA.

84. Nussbaum, "Memoirs," 9–10 (Best Friends).

85. Ibid. Nussbaum to Eisendrath, 14 December 1967, Nussbaum Papers, Ms. Coll. #430, AJA. On Nussbaum's retirement, see Nussbaum to Polner, 20 November 1975, and Nussbaum's notes on his retirement negotiations ("My Retirement"), Nussbaum Papers, Ms. Coll. #430, AJA. Mrs. Arene Nussbaum still lives in San Diego. I wish to express my gratitude to Mrs. Nussbaum for permitting me to scrutinize the entire collection of Nussbaum Papers deposited in the AJA.

86. "Report of Dr. Perry E. Nussbaum, Rabbi of Beth Israel Congregation," 3 May 1964 and 2 May 1965, Nussbaum Papers, Ms. Coll. #430, AJA. Nussbaum, "And Then There Was One," 17–18.

87. Nussbaum, "And Then There Was One," 17, 19.

Jacob M. Rothschild: His Legacy Twenty Years After

1. Rabbi Rothschild died on 31 December 1973. The following is based on Janice Rothschild Blumberg, *One Voice: Rabbi Jacob M. Rothschild and the Troubled South* (Macon: Mercer University Press, 1985). All verifying

documents in Jacob M. Rothschild Manuscripts, Special Collections, Robert W. Woodruff Library, Emory University (hereafter JMR MSS).

2. Joseph P. Schultz, ed., *Mid-America's Promise: A Profile of Kansas City Jewry* (Kansas City, Mo.: Jewish Community Federation of Greater Kansas City and American Jewish Historical Society, 1982); Frank J. Adler, *Roots in a Moving Stream: The Centennial History of Congregation B'Nai Jehudah of Kansas City, 1870–1970* (Kansas City, Mo.: The Temple, Congregation B'Nai Jehudah, 1972); Samuel S. Mayerberg, *Chronicle of an American Crusader* (New York: Bloch, 1944); Jacob S. Feldman, *The Jewish Experience in Western Pennsylvania 1755–1945* (Pittsburgh: Historical Society of Western Pennsylvania, 1986).

3. Blumberg, *One Voice,* 4

4. On David Marx and The Temple see Janice Rothschild Blumberg, *As But a Day to a Hundred and Twenty, 1967–1987* (Atlanta: Hebrew Benevolent Congregation, 1987); Mark K. Bauman and Arnold Shankman, "The Rabbi as Ethnic Broker: The Case of David Marx," *Journal of American Ethnic History* 2 (Spring 1983): 51–68; Steven Hertzberg, *Strangers within the Gate City: The Jews of Atlanta, 1845–1915* (Philadelphia: Jewish Publication Society, 1978).

5. For earlier divisions see Mark K. Bauman, "Centripetal and Centrifugal Forces Facing the People of Many Communities: Atlanta Jewry from the Leo Frank Case to the Great Depression," *Atlanta Historical Journal* 23 (Fall 1979): 25–54.

6. Rosh Hashana sermon, September 1947.

7. Blumberg, *One Voice,* 31–33.

8. The literature on Leo Frank is extensive. The standard version remains Leonard Dinnerstein, *The Leo Frank Case* (New York: Columbia University Press, 1968).

9. Sermons and sermon notes, 1947–1954, JMR MSS.

10. Sermon, 13 October 1948, JMR MSS.

11. "Is Brotherhood Just a Dream?" (address to students at Morehouse College, 17 February 1952, JMR MSS).

12. "The Challenge of a Dream" (sermon, 7 October 1954, JMR MSS).

13. Sermon, September 1956, JMR MSS.

14. Blumberg, *One Voice,* 57.

15. Jacob M. Rothschild (hereafter JMR) to W. C. Henson, 10 April 1951, JMR MSS.

16. "Fires of Fear-Flame of Faith" (address at Central Synagogue, New York City, 4 January 1957, JMR MSS); "Rabbi Finds Curbs on Liberty in South," *New York Times,* 5 January 1957.

17. Blumberg, *One Voice*, 68.

18. "Judaism-A Living Faith" (address to B'nai B'rith, Jackson, Miss., 29 April 1956, JMR MSS).

19. Blumberg, *One Voice*, 68.

20. JMR to Rabbi Norman Goldburg, 27 March 1958, JMR MSS.

21. "Text of Ministers' Racial Statement," *Atlanta Journal and Constitution*, 3 November 1957.

22. *Atlanta Journal and Constitution*, 17 November 1957.

23. Sermon, "Can This Be America?" 9 May 1958, JMR MSS.

24. Atlanta newspapers, 16 October 1958–30 January 1959; Blumberg, *One Voice;* Arnold Shankman, "A Temple Is Bombed–Atlanta, 1958," *American Jewish Archives* 23 (November 1971): 125–53.

25. "And None Shall Make Them Afraid" (sermon, 17 October 1958, JMR MSS).

26. "Letters That Cross My Desk" (sermon, 23 January 1959, JMR MSS).

27. *Atlanta Constitution*, 13 October 1958.

28. Statement by President Dwight D. Eisenhower, *Atlanta Constitution*, 13 October 1958.

29. JMR to Eisenhower, 24 October 1958; Eisenhower to JMR, 30 October 1958, JMR MSS.

30. " 'Out of Conviction': A Second Statement on the South's Racial Crisis," 22 November 1958, pamphlet signed by 312 ministers of greater Atlanta (Atlanta: Georgia Council of Churches, 1958); "Light for the Lamp of Learning" (sermon, 19 December 1958, JMR MSS).

31. Rothschild, "The Atlanta Story," *American Judaism* 12 (Fall 1967) (original in JMR MSS).

32. "Guide to the Use of Jewish Communal Buildings if Public Schools are Closed" (confidential notice to members of Atlanta Jewish Community Council, Community Relations Committee, unsigned and undated JMR MSS).

33. Address to Youth Conclave, Human Rights Day, August 1960, JMR MSS.

34. "Man Calls—God Answers" (sermon, 1 October 1960, JMR MSS).

35. Rothschild, "Atlanta Story."

36. "Isaac Unbound" (sermon, 11 September 1961, JMR MSS).

37. Morris B. Abram, *The Day Is Short: An Autobiography* (New York: Harcourt, Brace, Jovanovich, 1982).

38. JMR to Richard R. Rich, 9 March 1961, JMR MSS.

39. "Yearning to Breathe Free" (sermon, 20 April 1962, JMR MSS).

40. "Restoring Souls in a Shaken Society" (address to Interdenominational Theological Center, 3 May 1962, JMR MSS).

41. "A Year of Happiness" (sermon, 28 September 1962, JMR MSS).

42. "Courageous Clergy in Mississippi" (sermon, 5 October 1962, JMR MSS).

43. Jo Anne Crawford, "Churches Only Partly Responsible in Moral Crisis, Leaders Say Here," *Atlanta Constitution*, 15 June 1963.

44. "Social Upheaval and Personal Crisis" (Joshua Loth Leibman Memorial Lecture, Temple Israel, Boston, 6 April 1962).

45. "No Place to Hide," *Southern Israelite*, August 1963.

46. JMR to Martin Luther King Jr., 10 June 1963, JMR MSS.

47. Irving Spiegel, "Clergymen in Many Cities Back Aim of Washington March," *New York Times*, 2 September 1963.

48. "The Journey through Time" (sermon, 18 September 1963, JMR MSS).

49. JMR to Rev. John H. Cross, 27 September 1963, JMR MSS.

50. Sermon notes, 20 September 1963, JMR MSS.

51. JMR to Meg and Sophie Mantler; JMR to Carol Zaban, 25 October 1963, JMR MSS.

52. Rothschild, "One Man's Meat—A Personal Chronicle," *CCAR Journal* 1965 (original in JMR MSS).

53. Sam A. Williams, Jr., to JMR, 15 December 1964; JMR to Sam A. Williams, Jr., 28 December 1964, JMR MSS.

54. Address notes, hotel and restaurant proprietors, 1964, JMR MSS.

55. "Using God's Gifts" (address to North DeKalb Rotary Club, Atlanta, 12 May 1964, JMR MSS).

56. "Crisis and Decision in Today's South" (address to United Church Women of Atlanta, 1 May 1964, JMR MSS).

57. JMR to Rabbi Charles Mantinband, 10 February 1964, JMR MSS.

58. Rothschild, "One Man's Meat."

59. Introduction of Martin Luther King, Jr. (Union of American Hebrew Congregations Biennial, Chicago, Ill., 20 November 1963, JMR MSS).

60. Opening remarks (dinner honoring Dr. Martin Luther King, Jr., Atlanta, Ga., 27 January 1965, JMR MSS).

61. Martin Luther King, Jr., to JMR, 8 March 1965, JMR MSS.

62. Archbishop Paul J. Hallinan to JMR, 9 February 1965, JMR MSS.

63. "A Love Affair with Life" (sermon, 6 September 1964, JMR MSS).

64. JMR to Martin Luther King, Jr., 7 September 1967; Martin Luther King, Jr., to JMR, 28 September 1967, JMR MSS.

65. "Martin Luther King, Jr.—A Memorial," 5 April 1968, JMR MSS.

66. "Promise Denied and Hope Fulfilled" (address to the Hungry Club, 13 November 1968, JMR MSS).

67. "We Agree with Rabbi Rothschild," *Atlanta Daily World*, 16 November 1968.

68. "A Rabbi in the South" (sermon delivered at Hebrew Union College-Jewish Institute of Religion, Cincinnati, Ohio, 9 January 1970, JMR MSS).

The Year They Closed the Schools: The Norfolk Story

Rabbi Malcolm H. Stern taught history at the New York campus of Hebrew Union College-Jewish Institute of Religion. On 27 February 1959, less than four weeks after Norfolk's schools became integrated, he delivered a lecture, "Living the Norfolk Story," at his native congregation, Rodeph Shalom of Philadelphia. The documentation used for that lecture disappeared when the lawyer for the Norfolk parents destroyed his files. Much of this essay derives from that lecture.

1. In 1948 the Virginia chapter of the Anti-Defamation League succeeded in getting the Virginia legislature to pass a bill prohibiting discriminatory advertising, and the billboards disappeared.

2. My predecessor at Ohef Sholom, Louis D. Mendoza, was dubbed "Doctor" long before he was granted an honorary degree at Elon College in North Carolina. The title was also conferred on me prior to my earned doctorate. Assimilated southerners seemed to prefer "doctor" to "rabbi." The Gentile community followed suit until my insistence on my distinctive title led Mabel Hecht, the temple secretary who came from one of the well-established families, to say, "Malcolm, you've made the title 'rabbi' honorable." I assured her that it was honorable centuries prior to my ordination.

3. The Moses Myers House with many of its original furnishings—including Gilbert Stuart portraits of Moses and his wife—is now the property of the city of Norfolk and one of its treasured sights as an annex to the city-owned Chrysler Museum.

4. Dr. Proctor became the eminent preacher of Harlem's Abyssinian Baptist Church.

5. Norfolk's two newspapers were owned and published by Frank Batten and his family. The papers deliberately adopted opposing views on the school issue. The morning *Virginian-Pilot* subsequently earned a Pulitzer Prize for its prointegrationist coverage. The evening *Ledger-Star* was so vehe-

mently segregationist that even some of its advocates accused the paper of inciting violence.

6. I subsequently learned that Joel Spingarn, a sometime professor at Columbia University and literary critic, had founded and led the NAACP from 1913 to 1918. Following his death in 1939 his brother Arthur became the organization's president. Neither of the Spingarns was active in Jewish affairs or belonged to a congregation. This led me to respond to those who tried to make a canard of their Jewish leadership that the Spingarns were motivated by humanitarianism.

7. Robert Stern, a native of Albany, New York, headed the department of political science at what was then the Norfolk Division of the College of William and Mary, now Old Dominion University. Although we were not kin, Bob and I became close friends. In 1958 and 1959 he also served as the temple's religious school principal.

8. Under Virginia law, municipalities are separate from surrounding counties and known as boroughs. South Norfolk, then a rural borough, became part of today's city of Chesapeake.

9. In the early 1950s Norfolk became one of the first southern cities to take advantage of federal grants to create the Norfolk Housing and Redevelopment Commission, headed by the city's leading Jewish attorney, a former temple president, Charles L. Kaufman. With some vision Kaufman and his commission razed hundreds of acres of deteriorated buildings in downtown Norfolk and nearby. This paved the way for large-scale redevelopment and new highways. Old neighborhoods like Ghent were gentrified, and what may have been the first planned housing for southern blacks rose as Roberts Park.

10. From 1907 to 1945 Ohef Sholom was served by Louis D. Mendoza, dubbed "the golden-voiced orator of the Reform rabbinate." A bachelor until just before his retirement, he had no interest in attending board meetings, thereby creating the tradition that rabbis did not attend. My activist tendencies finally convinced the board in 1959 that my presence added to the proper administration of the congregation.

11. The South attempted a number of ploys to inhibit blacks from voting. One was the poll tax, which by 1958 amounted to a dollar and a half per year. To vote, however, one had to have paid the tax for at least three years before exercising the right to vote. An exception was made for armed forces personnel who were exempted from the tax. Following the Supreme Court decision of 1954 Virginia attempted another ploy: blank-form registration. This strategy required that anyone who wished to register to vote was presented with a blank form to be filled out in the presence of the registrar with twelve rubrics in specific order. When the black churches began training their people to memorize the rubrics, and more whites than blacks were failing the test, the legislature abandoned this

test. Virginia had its share of apathetic voters as illustrated by the following experience. During the important elections of 1958 my wife and I attempted to secure every voter we could. We always required our black domestic help to keep current with their poll tax and to vote. Our polling place was nearly a mile from our house. On election day my wife offered a ride to a widowed neighbor, who responded, "Oh, Mrs. Stern, what a gracious idea! Can't we make it some other day?"

12. I am grateful to Forrest R. (Hap) White of Norfolk for supplying me with the name of the lawsuit, derived from *Race Relations Law Reporter* 4 (Spring 1959): 46–54.

13. The speed with which the effigy was removed kept it a secret from anyone we knew until I revealed it in a lecture at Ohef Sholom Temple in 1992.

A Personal Memoir

1. Myron Berman, *Richmond's Jewry, 1769–1976: Shabbat in Shokoe* (Charlottesville: University Press of Virginia for the Jewish Community Federation of Richmond, 1979).

"Then and Now": Southern Rabbis and Civil Rights

1. Robert St. John, *Jews, Justice and Judaism* (New York: Doubleday & Company, Inc., 1969), 293–308.

2. *Central Conference of American Rabbis Yearbook,* 71 (1961): 67.

3. Ibid., 74 (1964): 80.

4. Harry Golden, *Our Southern Landsman* (New York: G. P. Putnam's Sons, 1974), 74.

5. Rabbi Allan H. Schwartzman at Anshe Chesed Congregation in Vicksburg, Mississippi, makes the honest admission that "most of my predecessors steered clear of involvement for fear that it would endanger the Jewish community if not their own positions."

6. The conviction and courage of these pioneering rabbinic leaders are even more admirable in view of the fact that they acted decisively long before the development of any organized community support on behalf of civil rights. Rabbi Steven W. Engel at Temple Beth Israel in Jackson, Mississippi, explains, "Now there is an official organization in the state called 'Mississippi Religious Leadership Conference,' which deals with civil rights issues on a coalition basis. However, my predecessors were much more on their own and isolated."

7. St. John, *Jews, Justice and Judaism,* 298–301.

8. Rabbi Stephen L. Fuchs (Temple Ohabai Shalom, Nashville, Tennessee) to Rabbi Micah D. Greenstein, 20 August 1993.

9. These statistics were gleaned from the *Statistical Abstract of the United States* (Lanham, Md.: Bernan Press, 1992) and the *Digest of Educational Statistics* (Washington, D.C.: U.S. Government Printing Office, 1993).

10. Rabbi David E. Ostrich (Temple Beth El, Pensacola, Florida) to Rabbi Micah D. Greenstein, 24 August 1993.

11. Dr. Julius Lester, "Black-Jewish Relations" (paper presented at White Station Senior High School under the auspices of the Memphis Jewish Community Center, 25 October 1993).

12. Rabbi Edward P. Cohn of New Orleans, interview by Rabbi Micah D. Greenstein, Memphis, Tenn., 7 June 1994.

13. Ibid.

14. Rabbi Donald M. Kunstadt to Rabbi Micah D. Greenstein, 8 September 1993.

15. Rabbi Edward P. Cohn, interview by Rabbi Micah D. Greenstein, Memphis, Tenn., 7 June 1994.

16. Rabbi Arnold G. Fink (Beth El Hebrew Congregation, Alexandria, Virginia) to Rabbi Micah D. Greenstein, 30 August 1993.

17. Malcolm H. Stern, "The Role of the Rabbi in the South," in Nathan M. Kaganoff and Melvin Urofsky, eds., *Turn to the South: Essays on Southern Jewry* (Charlottesville: University Press of Virginia, 1979), 21–32.

Contributors

Terry Barr obtained his B.A. degree in English and political science from the University of Montevallo and his M.A. and Ph.D. degrees from the University of Tennessee, Knoxville, concentrating on twentieth-century literature and film studies. He is currently associate professor of English at Presbyterian College. His article, "Stars, Light, and Finding the Way Home: The Emergence of Jewish Characters in Contemporary Film and Television," appeared in the spring 1993 issue of *Studies in Popular Culture*. He is presently working on a longer study tracing the proliferation of contemporary Jewish American films.

Mark K. Bauman holds a B.A. degree from Wilkes University, M.A. degrees from Lehigh and the University of Chicago, and a Ph.D. from Emory University. A professor of history at Atlanta Metropolitan College, he has published biographies of conservative Southern Methodist Bishop Warren Candler (1981) and Rabbi Harry H. Epstein of Atlanta (1994) as well as more than two dozen articles in professional journals and anthologies. He served as guest editor of a special issue of *American Jewish History* (Autumn 1989) on the use of role theory to understand American Jewish history, and he edited the journal of the Georgia Association of Historians from 1991 to 1994. His most recent publication is an American Jewish Archives brochure titled "The Southerner as American: Jewish Style" (1996). Bauman's research concerns interaction between and within ethnic groups and identifying patterns to explicate behavior. He was president of the Georgia Association of Historians. (1996–97)

Myron Berman, adjunct professor at Virginia Commonwealth University, served as the rabbi of Richmond's Temple Beth El for twenty-eight years. He holds master's and doctorate degrees from Columbia University; M.H.L., B.H.L., and D.D. (honoris causa) degrees from Jewish Theological Seminary; and a B.S.S. from City College of New York (now CUNY). He is the author of a history of the Jews of Richmond (1979) and is currently working on "The Last of the Jews: The Century and One-half Social History of a Southern Jewish Family."

Janice Rothschild Blumberg, a graduate of the University of Georgia, is the author of *One Voice* (1985), a biography of her late husband, Rabbi Jacob Rothschild, that documents his role in the civil rights movement; *As But a Day* (1967; repr. 1987), a history of Atlanta's Hebrew Benevolent Congregation; articles in *Encyclopedia Judaica* (1971) and various professional journals; a docudrama; and musical parody. Her text and photography for the exhibit "Jerusalem: Roots of Stone" (1977) appeared at B'nai B'rith's Klutznick National Jewish Museum, an organization she currently serves as board chairperson. Active in the American Jewish Historical Society and the Jewish Historical Society of Greater Washington among numerous other associations, she is a past president of the Southern Jewish Historical Society. Janice R. Blumberg was a regular panelist with Coretta Scott King for the "Rearing Children of Good Will" program of the National Conference of Christians and Jews in the Atlanta area (1962–1964). Her most recent work is a historically based novel set in South Africa, written in collaboration with Israel and Zelda Heller.

Mark Cowett is presently chair of the history department and assistant director of academic affairs at the Isadore Newman School in New Orleans. His *Birmingham's Rabbi: Morris Newfield and Alabama, 1895–1940* appeared in 1986. He has also published other articles on Newfield. He is presently writing a biography of Jacob Billikopf, a Philadelphia Jewish social worker.

Marc Dollinger completed his B.A. degree at the University of California, Berkeley, and his M.A. and Ph.D. degrees at UCLA. The title of his dissertation is "The Politics of Acculturation: American Jewish Liberalism, 1933–1975." He was the Andrew W. Mellon Post-Doctoral Fellow in the Humanities at Bryn Mawr College and is currently teaching at Pomona City College. His article, "American Jews and Post-war Liberalism: Anti-Semitism, Racism, and the Politics of Acculturation," appeared in Jeffrey S. Gurock and Marc Lee Raphael, editors, *Rischin Festschrift*. He is currently studying American Jewish responses to the 1960s cultural rebellion.

Rabbi Howard R. Greenstein is senior rabbi of Congregation Ahavath Chesed in Jacksonville, Florida. He earned his undergraduate degree from Cornell University and a master's degree from the Hebrew Union College–Jewish Institute of Religion, where he was ordained. Rabbi Greenstein was also the first Ph.D. recipient in the Jewish studies program at Ohio State University. Rabbi Greenstein has held numerous leadership positions in local, regional, and national Jewish and civic organizations. He is the founding president of the Jacksonville Interfaith Council and was president of the Jacksonville Community Council. Rabbi Greenstein has served as adjunct professor of Jewish thought at the University of Florida since 1986. He has published articles in *The Reconstructionist* and *Reform Judaism* and has written two books, *Turning Point: Zionism and Reform Judaism* (Brown University) and *Judaism: An Eternal Covenant* (Fortress Press).

Rabbi Micah D. Greenstein is associate rabbi of Temple Israel in Memphis, Tennessee. He earned his undergraduate degree from Cornell University and received master's degrees from Harvard University and the Los Angeles campus of the Hebrew Union College-Jewish Institute of Religion. Rabbi Greenstein was ordained from the Cincinnati campus of HUC-JIR in 1991 and wrote his rabbinic thesis on Classical Reform Judaism under the advisorship of Dr. Jacob Rader Marcus. Rabbi Greenstein teaches Jewish thought at the Memphis Theological Seminary and served on the steering committee for the recently unveiled Memphis Race Relations and Diversity Institute. He has published articles in the *CCAR Journal* and *Religious Studies Review*. Micah and his father, Howard, are currently writing a book titled *The World of Judaism: Its Challenges and Changes* to be published by Trinity Press.

Berkley Kalin, a professor of history at the University of Memphis, earned his undergraduate degree from Washington University and graduate degrees from St. Louis University. His popular and scholarly publications deal with the history of women, the history of the arts, Tennessee history, and ethnic groups in the South. He served as editor of the *West Tennessee Historical Papers* for three years and is currently (1995-97) president of the Southern Jewish Historical Society.

Patricia M. LaPointe is the senior librarian/curator of the Memphis and Shelby County Room of the Memphis/Shelby County Public Library and Information Center. An adjunct faculty member at Christian Brothers University, she holds B.A. and M.A. degrees from the University of Memphis, where she has also completed course work toward her doctorate. She is the author of *From Saddlebags to Science: A Century of Health Care in Memphis, 1830–1930* and articles in the *Tennessee Historical Quarterly* and the *West Tennessee Historical Society Papers*.

Carolyn Gray LeMaster, a Little Rock native, has studied and lectured on Jewish history for more than thirty-five years. She holds B.A.

and M.A. degrees from the University of Arkansas at Little Rock in journalism and communications. Besides numerous newspaper, magazine, and journal articles, she is the author of *The Ottenheimers of Arkansas: A History* and *A Corner of the Tapestry: A History of the Jewish Experience in Arkansas, 1820s–1990s* (1994).

Bobbie S. Malone is a native Texan who resided in New Orleans for thirty years. She received a B.A. in art history from Newcomb College, an M.Ed. in elementary education, and M.A. and Ph.D. degrees in American history from Tulane University. Her dissertation, " 'Standing Unswayed in the Storm': Rabbi Max Heller, Reform and Zionism in the American South, 1860–1929," was published by the University of Alabama Press (1997). She is currently employed as the educational program specialist at the State Historical Society of Wisconsin. Besides her research, she and her husband, Professor Bill C. Malone, perform as the Texas Songbirds and sing old-fashioned country music accompanied by mandolin and guitar.

Karl Preuss received his doctorate in modern European history from the University of California at Santa Barbara. He served as a historian for the U.S. Air Force from 1984 until 1992 and won the Air Force History Program's Award (1992) for a study of the evolution of air base ground defense since World War II. He was the recipient of a German Exchange Service grant from the German government (1980) and was a Fulbright-Hayes Fellow at the University of Bonn (1983). Since leaving the air force in 1992, Preuss has worked as an independent historical consultant. His research interests include the history of twentieth-century Germany, Jewish history, and the history of anti-Semitism.

Leonard Rogoff holds a Ph.D. in English literature from the University of North Carolina at Chapel Hill. He has served as associate professor of English at North Carolina Central University and contributing staff writer to *The Spectator Magazine* of Raleigh. He has completed *Migrations: A History of the Durham–Chapel Hill Jewish Community* and has contributed entries to *Biographical Directory of Governors of the United States* and *Jewish-American History and Culture: An Encyclopedia*.

Rabbi Malcolm H. Stern was often called the "dean" or "father" of American Jewish genealogy. He compiled *American Families of Jewish Descent*, the premier genealogical survey of Jewish families who settled in America between 1654 and 1849, and wrote articles on the Jews of colonial Savannah, among other publications. Rabbi Stern established and led (1964–1980) the rabbinic placement office of the Central Conference of American Rabbis and on "retirement" served as adjunct professor of American Jewish history at Hebrew Union College-Jewish Institute of Religion, New York. A graduate of the University of Pennsylvania and Hebrew Union College, he became an air force chaplain during World War II. Stern, a founding member of the Southern Jewish Historical Society, presided over the American Society of Genealogists, the Jewish Genealogical Society, and the Jewish Historical Society of New York.

Clive Webb is completing his doctoral dissertation on black-Jewish relations in the South under Professor Anthony Badger at Cambridge University while serving as a lecturer at the University of Reading. He spent 1993–1994 traveling across the South conducting research under Professor Dan Carter of Emory University. Webb graduated from the University of Warwick with first-class honors and received his M.A. from the University of Sheffield with distinction. His main research interests are race relations and American culture.

Hollace Ava Weiner, a native of Washington, D.C., has lived in Texas since 1977. She obtained a B.A. degree from the University of Maryland and a Certificate of German Proficiency from the University of the Saar. A daily reporter covering regional news for the *Fort Worth Star-Telegram,* she has won awards for her coverage of the gay and lesbian community. A past president of the Association of Women Journalists and a member of the Journalism and Women's Forum, she is currently researching a book on the Lone Star state's pioneer rabbis and their wives.

Gary Phillip Zola is the national dean of Admissions, Student Affairs and Alumni Relations at Hebrew Union College-Jewish Institute of Religion. He is the author of *Isaac Harby of Charleston, 1788–1828: Jewish Reformer and Intellectual,* which was published by the University of Alabama Press in 1994. He is also editor of a forthcoming volume titled *Exploration and Celebration: Two Decades of Women in the Rabbinate.*

Index